of

Windows® Shell Programming

ISBN 0-13-025496-7

90000

80130 254962

PRENTICE HALL PTR MICROSOFT® TECHNOLOGIES SERIES

- Supporting Windows NT and 2000 Workstation and Server
  Mohr
- Zero Administration Kit for Windows
  McInerney
- Tuning and Sizing NT Server
  Aubley
- Windows NT 4.0 Server Security Guide
  Goncalves
- Windows NT Security
  McInerney
- Windows NT Device Driver Book
  Baker

CERTIFICATION

- Core MCSE: Windows 2000 Edition
  Dell
- Core MCSE
  Dell
- Core MCSE: Networking Essentials
  Keogh
- MCSE: Administering Microsoft SQL Server 7
  Byrne
- MCSE: Implementing and Supporting Microsoft Exchange Server 5.5
  Goncalves
- MCSE: Internetworking with Microsoft TCP/IP
  Ryvkin, Houde, Hoffman

- MCSE: Implementing and Supporting Microsoft Proxy Server 2.0
  Ryvkin, Hoffman
- MCSE: Implementing and Supporting Microsoft SNA Server 4.0
  Mariscal
- MCSE: Implementing and Supporting Microsoft Internet Information Server 4
  Dell
- MCSE: Implementing and Supporting Web Sites Using Microsoft Site Server 3
  Goncalves
- MCSE: Microsoft System Management Server 2
  Jewett
- MCSE: Implementing and Supporting Internet Explorer 5
  Dell
- Core MCSD: Designing and Implementing Desktop Applications with Microsoft Visual Basic 6
  Holzner
- Core MCSD: Designing and Implementing Distributed Applications with Microsoft Visual Basic 6
  Houlette, Klander
- MCSD: Planning and Implementing SQL Server 7
  Vacca
- MCSD: Designing and Implementing Web Sites with Microsoft FrontPage 98
  Karlins

PRENTICE HALL PTR MICROSOFT® TECHNOLOGIES SERIES

Windows® Shell Programming

Scott Seely

Prentice Hall PTR Upper Saddle River, New Jersey 07458

www.phptr.com

Library of Congress Cataloging-in-Publication Data

Seely, Scott, 1972-
  Windows shell programming / Scott Seely.
      p. cm. -- (Prentice Hall PTR Microsoft technologies series)
  ISBN 0-13-025496-7
    1. Microsoft Windows (Computer file) 2. Operating systems (Computers) 3. Microsoft
  Visual C++. I. Title. II. Series.

  QA76.76.O63 S467 2000
  005.4'469--dc21   00-039988

Editorial/production supervision: *Vincent Janoski*
Acquisitions editor: *Tim Moore*
Marketing Manager: *Bryan Gambrel*
Manufacturing manager: *Jerry Votta*
Series Design: *Gail Cocker-Bogusz*

© 2000 by Prentice Hall PTR
Prentice-Hall, Inc.
Upper Saddle River, New Jersey 07458

Prentice Hall books are widely used by corporations and government agencies
for training, marketing, and resale.

The publisher offers discounts on this book when ordered in bulk quantities.
For more information, contact Corporate Sales Department, Phone: 800-382-3419;
FAX: 201-236-7141; E-mail: corpsales@prenhall.com; or write: Prentice Hall PTR,
Corp. Sales Dept., One Lake Street, Upper Saddle River, NJ 07458.

All Products or services mentioned in this book are the trademariks or service marks of
their respective companies or organizations. Screen shots reprinted by permission from
Microsoft Corporation.

Printed in the United States of America
10 9 8 7 6 5 4 3 2 1

ISBN 0-13-025496-7

Prentice-Hall International (UK) Limited, *London*
Prentice-Hall of Australia Pty. Limited, *Sydney*
Prentice-Hall Canada Inc., *Toronto*
Prentice-Hall Hispanoamericana, S.A., *Mexico*
Prentice-Hall of India Private Limited, *New Delhi*
Prentice-Hall of Japan, Inc., *Tokyo*
Prentice-Hall Asia Pte. Ltd
Editora Prentice-Hall do Brasil, Ltda., *Rio de Janeiro*

To Jean & Vince

CONTENTS

- Add various types of toolbars to Windows and Internet Explorer
- Allow the shell to do work for you in your own applications, such as filename auto-completion

Looking at the list, it should be clear that the shell is no longer a simple windowing environment. We can customize Windows as we see fit and Microsoft gives us this ability at a price—they increase the chance of Windows' instability. This level of customization makes it such that no two installations of Windows ever remain the same for very long. As the user installs more applications on their machine, the shell gains new capabilities and features. A few applications will add items to the system tray (clock area) on the taskbar. Another may add items to a context menu in Explorer. If the machine suddenly (or worse, slowly) becomes unstable, the user will not blame the people at Foobar, Inc. for a bad shell extension. To the user, all of the right-click functionality, drag-and-drop capabilities, and Explorer enhancements are part of the operating system , so Microsoft will be blamed for shoddy workmanship. This means that we have a responsibility to create stable additions so that people continue to trust Microsoft operating systems with their corporate and personal data. Failing to do so may lead Microsoft to remove our ability to customize the shell.

1.1   Goals of this Book

It is my belief that a book on a specific technology should not just explain the technology; it should also make it easier to use that technology. For example, I have a few fairly popular C++ books:

- *Effective C++* by Scott Meyers
- *More Effective C++* by Scott Meyers
- *Large Scale C++ Software Design* by John Lakos
- *C++ FAQs* by Marshall Cline and Greg Lomow
- *The C++ Programming Language* by Bjarne Stroustrup

I have learned more from the first four books than from the fifth, which was written by the inventor of the language! Do not get me wrong, Stroustrup's text has helped me around syntactical errors, but the others have given me tools to write better code faster.[1] I will try to show how to write good code that uses and enhances the Windows shell. In order to accomplish this, I provide a lot of fully functional examples as well as what I hope are production-quality libraries and wizards to make your life easier.

---

1. Stroustrup has written many articles and USENET posts that will help you use the language better. However, *The C++ Programming Language* is just a language reference, not a "how to do it better" kind of book.

Windows Shell Programming

With each operating system release, service pack, and Internet Explorer upgrade, Microsoft adds more possibilities for vendors to extend and enhance the Windows user interface. This has been the case with earlier versions of Windows through its latest release, Windows 2000. The first version of Windows many of us did any serious development for was Windows 3.x. With the 3.x versions, you could add limited modifications to the shell:

- Control Panel applets
- Screen savers
- File manager extensions

The early file manager extensions allowed developers to only add menu items and toolbar buttons. On any given Windows installation, a computer could have up to five extensions installed. A lot of time has passed since then, and the developers at Microsoft have continued to enhance the extensibility of the shell. With Windows 2000, the shell still allows you to write your own Control Panel applets and screen savers, but you can also do more— much more. For example, you can:

- Customize the Windows taskbar
- Add extra menu options when right-clicking on a file
- Add advanced handling of folders, drives, and printers
- Handle new data formats when a file is copied and pasted
- Allow specialized actions when a file gets dropped on a file type
- Monitor copying of folders, drives, and printers
- Add your own views of data in Windows Explorer

ACKNOWLEDGMENTS

While writing this book I got a lot of help and encouragement from many people. This whole project started as a result of an interview I went on almost two years ago. While going through my technical evaluation, one interviewer asked me if I had ever done any interesting side projects. Of course I had. I explained an animated icon class I had written that allows an individual to easily put icons into the system tray (the area by the clock on the taskbar) and animate them. The person asked if I read Windows Developers Journal (WDJ) and mentioned that the whole idea might make a good article.

About four months later, I proposed the idea to Ron Burk at *WDJ*. He liked the idea, so I wrote the article. By November 1998, I had my first article published. I got a lot of positive feedback on it, which encouraged me to keep writing. Exhilarated by the first article, I wrote a second for *WDJ,* this time on screen savers. While waiting for the article to be published in the March 1999 *WDJ,* I got an e-mail from Tim Moore at Prentice Hall. He liked the style of the November 1998 article and wondered if I had a desire to write a book. We talked on the phone and I threw the idea of a book on the Windows shell at him. As a result of that conversation, I wrote up a proposal, sent it to Tim, and waited. By March 1999, I had a signed contract and started writing this book. Almost a year later, I finished the darn thing.

During the course of this project, I received help from a lot of people. First and foremost, my wife Jean and my son Vince have been unbelievably supportive and helpful throughout the whole project. If they had not taken up the slack in the household duties, this book would have been impossible to write. I also need to thank my parents and my in-laws for helping out when I needed some extra time to get a chapter done. My grandparents and my sister also helped motivate me when the job seemed to take forever.

I received a good deal of help from people outside of my family, as well. Thanks to Andy Skwierawski, Thad Phetteplace, Arjen deKlerk, and Hunter Hudson for reviewing the book. I also want to thank the Microsoft shell development team for answering my questions on the *msnews. microsoft.com* news server. If you ever need their help, they hang out in the *microsoft.public.platformsdk.ui_shell* group and will answer most questions quickly. Be careful about flaming the documentation or the product—the tech writers and developers read the group too, and they prefer constructive comments. Most of them do this on their own time, so be happy that they are willing to answer your questions without making you go through Microsoft support.

Finally, I want to thank the staff at Prentice Hall for all the effort that they put into developing this book, from the idea stage to the final product. If I did not have the support of this great company, I would not have been able to get this book out. This has been a lot of fun.

▼ APPENDIX B   Shell Functions, Structures, and Enumerations   473

In the following pages I want to accomplish a number of things:

1. **Explain how the shell works and what opportunities for enhancement are available.** The first thing the reader expects from this book is that it will explain the shell in detail. This means going over many of the interfaces, functions, and other items needed to understand the shell. There is a need to explain these things more clearly than the Microsoft Developer Network does.

2. **Show how to use MFC and ATL to enhance the shell.** The book targets a specific group of developers: those who use Visual C++ as their development tool of choice. Consequently, I have a responsibility to show the readers how to develop solutions that leverage what they already know. For example, if something displays a window, the reader wants to know how to use a CWnd to handle the message loop.

3. **Speed up development time.** This book targets programmers who have projects to complete as fast as possible. Many of them will not even read an entire chapter unless they have problems that they cannot figure out. For some readers, the most valuable part of the book will probably be the included CD. To them, the book is nothing more than a user manual for that CD.

Because I went the extra step to see how to create generic solutions, I forced myself to understand the technology outside the scope of my current sample project. Many of the libraries and wizards presented in the book take the unfamiliar Windows shell and mold it to the world of the MFC/ATL developer. C++ is an extremely pliant language and will let you do almost anything. Together, MFC, ATL and C++ allow you to do amazing things. Using them along with the libraries and wizards in this book, the reader will realize the benefits of learning the ins and outs of MFC.

1.2   What is the Windows Shell?

The Windows shell is nothing like the UNIX or the DOS shells. With UNIX shells and their command line interfaces (CLI),[2] users have to know that a feature exists before they can use it. Compare this to the Windows shell, which can advertise new features to the user. For example, let us look at how a user would go about opening a JPEG file. To view the picture with a command line interface, users have to know that they need a graphics viewer to

---

2. If you have no UNIX experience, think back to the days of MS-DOS. Now imagine a lot more expressiveness and power on the command line.

look at the file and how to start a viewer. Windows provides hooks that allow the viewer application to advertise its association with the JPEG files. When users select a file with the right mouse button, Windows will reveal a menu allowing them to view, move, or possibly even translate the file to another graphics format. They discover these capabilities simply by knowing that a right mouse click will tell them what they can do with the file. This circumvents the need to tell the users about all the different programs available for file manipulation.

The Windows shell provides the means to interact with the computer. The shell is composed of the following elements:

- **The Desktop.** When Windows starts up, this is the first thing a user sees.
- **The Taskbar.** The taskbar provides a clock, a way to start applications, and a place for applications to notify the user about program activity. With Active Desktop installed, the taskbar can contain toolbars beyond the standard task list.
- **The Control Panel.** The Control Panel provides a single location to configure devices and programs on the computer. Besides the ability to add applets to the Control Panel, some of the packaged Control Panel applets allow third parties to add extra property pages.[3]
- **Internet Explorer.** Like it or not, Microsoft has made the browser part of the shell. For some time now, we have been able to view drives across the network as if they were on the local machine. It is easy to see the benefits of viewing FTP sites the same way. The only stretch happens when looking at hyperlinks. Hyperlinks and HTML documents allow us to navigate to new directories and files by clicking on links in files. This navigational model seems as valid as the hierarchical file systems we use on a daily basis. Because of the spider web that HTML documents produce, browsers present the best-known way to navigate these documents. Integrating the browser allows Internet Explorer to be the ultimate in common file type navigation.
- **Windows Explorer.** Windows Explorer allows us to navigate whatever information is presented on our machines. It provides the ability to move files around, drop files on other files, and display information regarding files, among other things. If you want to add something that is not file related, you can do so by extending Explorer's capabilities.[4]
- **File Viewers.** The people at Microsoft will cringe when they see this because the feature has been removed from the operating sys-

---

3. Specifically, these are the display, keyboard, and mouse applets.
4. See Chapter 9 for how to customize Explorer.

tem as of Windows 98 SE. Still, Windows 95, 98, and Windows NT 4.0 all provide hooks that allow vendors to distribute DLLs which present a read-only view of a file. Typically users can distribute the viewer without risk of copyright or licensing violations.

- **Disk Cleanup.** Starting with Windows 98, the shell provides a janitor named CLEANMGR.EXE. Applications can provide the janitor with instructions on how to free up space on the local hard drives. This way, when users need more space, they do not have to start by deciding which files they should get rid of. Instead, the janitor gets rid of all the truly useless stuff first.
- **The Registry.** The entire registry is not a part of the shell, although two parts of the registry do a significant job of customizing the user's interaction with Windows: HKEY_CURRENT_USER (HKCU) and HKEY_LOCAL_MACHINE (HKLM). Because of this, the shell team has created a number of functions that make it easier for programs to interact with those two hives.

1.3   Chapter Summaries

My aim was to present each topic so that it stands on its own. You should be able to go to any one chapter and find all the information you need to get your job done. The only required reading in this book is this chapter and the chapter that covers your topic, unless your topic is namespace extensions. A namespace extension can be a fairly complex beast. As a result, that topic is split into three chapters: one to explain namespace extensions, one to document the library and wizard I wrote, and one to design and create an extension. Furthermore, in each chapter I reference the related material found in the appendices and other chapters as needed. For example, many of the shell customizations require you to implement the COM interface IcontextMenu, so whenever IContextMenu enters the discussion, I reference section 7.2.

Each of the following sections describes a chapter in the book and what extending the shell in that area can do.

1.3.1   Chapter 2: The Taskbar

This chapter explains how to manipulate the taskbar. It teaches how to do the following:

- Get information about the taskbar (location, size, auto-hide, always-on-top)
- Add and remove taskbar buttons, which can either increase or decrease the number of applications that appear to be running
- Add and remove links on the Start menu

- Add icons to the system tray.[5] It also shows how to animate an icon in the tray

1.3.2   Chapter 3: Application Desktop Toolbars

The best-known application desktop toolbar, or *appbar*, is the taskbar. The first runner up in popularity is the Microsoft Office Shortcut Bar. Appbars provide a nice way to present information without getting in the user's way. They usually dock to one of the edges of the desktop and sit there. The user can even make them automatically hide themselves so that they take up almost no space on the screen. Chapter 3 covers the following topics:

- Guidelines for creating appbars
- Explanation of how appbars work
- Explanation of AppBarLib and the MFC Application Desktop Toolbar AppWizard
- How to use the tools presented to build an appbar of your own

1.3.3   Chapter 4: Control Panel Applets

The Control Panel provides a place to put any utilities for configuring hardware or software. For example, you would place applets to configure a service or fax machine there. People expect to find the configuration utility for background processes and hardware in the Control Panel. Microsoft also has a new utility out: the Microsoft Management Console. If your configuration user interface works best in a dialog, write an applet. Otherwise, write an MMC snap-in.[6] Chapter 4 covers the following items:

- How to decide if the Control Panel is an appropriate place to put your applet
- Ways of packaging Control Panel applets
- Control Panel basics
- Motivation and design of a Control Panel applet wizard
- Building an applet using the wizard

1.3.4   Chapter 5: Screen Savers

Screen savers do so much more than entertain and delight bored workers. They also help extend the life of a monitor, "lock up" a computer when the user is away, and hide what one was working on when called away from the machine. This chapter presents a library that is feature-compatible with

---

5. This is the little window on the taskbar that the clock lives in.

6. MMC Snap-ins are not part of the shell. Thankfully, wizards and libraries are provided for them in Visual C++.

SCRNSAVE.LIB with an added benefit: you can use MFC to do all your work. Chapter 5 covers the following topics:

- Screen saver responsibilities
- Screen saver internals
- Benefits of SCRNSAVE.LIB over writing your own
- An MFC Screen Saver App wizard
- Writing a screen saver using the wizard

1.3.5   Chapter 6: File Viewers

A file viewer presents a read-only view of the file. You can look at and some-times even print the file, but you cannot do anything else to the file. Viewers exist for most Microsoft documents, including Word, Excel, and PowerPoint. You can also find them for viewing other file types, including bitmaps, text files, and executables (DLLs and EXEs). Chapter 6 covers these topics:

- File viewer basics—when to create a viewer, how to invoke one, etc.
- File viewer internals
- A File Viewer library/wizard
- A sample file viewer

1.3.6   Chapter 7: Shell Extensions

If you want to find out how to set what users will see and what they can do within Windows Explorer, check out this chapter. You can also do some in-teresting things to the folders, printers, and drives attached to the machine. Chapter 7 explains the following items:

Extensions registered by file type (a.k.a. class)

- **Context Menu Handler:** Adds items to the context menu (a.k.a. right-click menu) for a file object. You may add verbs and other ac-tions for a file type. (7.2)
- **Icon Handler:** Typically used to add icons specific to the file ob-ject. You can also use this to add icons for all files belonging to the same class. (7.3)
- **Data Handler:** Provides an IDataObject interface for a specific class type. The shell passes this interface to the OLE DoDragDrop func-tion. (7.4)
- **Drop Handler:** Provides drop behavior for files that can accept drag and drop objects. (7.5)
- **Property Sheet Handler:** Adds pages to the property sheet that the shell displays for a given file type. You can also extend items such as the Display Properties dialog using a property sheet handler. (7.6)

Extensions associated with file operations and directories (move, copy, rename, etc.)

- **Copy Hook Handler:** These get called whenever a folder object is about to be copied, moved, deleted, or renamed. The handler can allow or prevent the operation. (7.7)
- **Drag-and-Drop Handler:** A context menu handler that the shell calls when the user drops an object after dragging it to a new position. (7.8)

1.3.7   Chapter 8: Disk Cleanup Handlers

Today's large hard drives allow us to install many programs and store thousands of files. Because of all this space, most of us do not actively clean up anymore. If an application leaves temp files strewn about our machines, we will not notice the decline in space for months. Other programs, such as web browsers, cache web pages to speed up perceived download times. As a result, the task of maintaining one's hard drive has become very difficult. To address the problem, Microsoft introduced disk cleanup handlers with Windows 98. As a developer you have a responsibility to provide a handler for any application you create that leaves behind temporary or unnecessary files. A handler also comes in handy when an application that you think is well-behaved uses temporary files. Many applications will leave these behind if the computer loses power. A handler can clean up part of the resulting mess. Most sizable applications need a cleanup handler. On any non-trivial project, make sure you include development time for one of these.[7] Chapter 8 covers the following topics:

- The Disk Cleanup Utility and its relationship to disk cleanup handlers
- The various interfaces employed by disk cleanup handlers and how they work
- An example program

1.3.8   Chapter 9: Namespace Extensions

Starting with this chapter and continuing through Chapter 11, I departed from the rule of one topic per chapter. Developing a namespace extension can be as complex as developing a full-scale application. As a result, I chose to separate the subject matter into distinct chapters. When a namespace extension is activated, it assumes a lot of control over Explorer's menus, toolbars, and right-hand pane. You have to make a lot of design decisions and understand user expectations. This chapter goes into detail explaining the interaction between Explorer and an extension. It then explains what a user will expect from a full-featured namespace.

---

7. I would really appreciate a cleanup handler from the Visual Studio team that would delete all the PCH, SBR, OBJ, APS, PLG, and OPT files from the hard drive.

1.3.9 Chapter 10: Tools to Build a Namespace Extension

Once the interaction and design of a namespace extension has been explained (Chapter 9), we need to make the whole experience of building a namespace something easier to do. For example, I have no desire to build menus the way I would for context menu handlers. I would rather handle these by building them using the Visual Studio menu editor. This chapter explains a library and wizard that allow quick creation of a namespace extension. Along the way, I explain why I chose one design over another so that you have more insight as you debug your own namespaces.

1.3.10 Chapter 11: Namespace Extension Example: The Registry

This chapter covers the design and construction of a namespace extension that contains many of the capabilities found in REGEDIT.[8] It also covers all the decisions I had to make:

- What should I put into the Explorer menu?
- What buttons should show up in the toolbars?
- What should the context menus look like?
- What data should I display?

1.3.11 Chapter 12: Explorer Bars and Desktop Bands

Way back in Chapter 2, I explained how to manipulate the taskbar but avoided the topic of adding extra band objects. The topic really deserves separate treatment because of the breadth of things you can do. Using band objects, you can add the following types of toolbars:

- **Desk bands:** These augment the toolbars available in the taskbar. They are only available when Active Desktop has been installed. This feature is included with Windows 98, 2000, and courtesy of Internet Explorer, version 4.x and Active Desktop.[9]
- **Comm Bands:** These display information at the bottom of Internet Explorer and Windows Explorer. Only one comm band can display at any given time.
- **Explorer Bands:** These display on the left hand side of Internet Explorer and Windows Explorer. Only one explorer band can display at any given time.

---

8. This example has a few more capabilities than the SDK registry namespace extension example and takes nothing from the SDK version.

9. The desktop update did not ship with Internet Explorer 5.0 as an installable component.

- **Radio Bars:** You can add extra toolbars to the top of Internet Explorer and Windows Explorer to do whatever you want them to do.
- **HTML Based Bands:** Microsoft implemented an HTML-capable band object. This band object allows you to display HTML by simply writing a REG script and some HTML.

1.4 Versions of the Shell

In order to use the content in chapters 6 through 12 and the appendices effectively, you must be cognizant of the shell version your application works with. Your user will be able to use pretty much anything you write as long as they are running version 4.72 of the shell, distributed with Internet Explorer 4.01 and Internet Explorer 4.0, SP1. In the past, Microsoft has bundled interim shell updates with Internet Explorer, not as a separate package. The grid below shows the various versions of the shell and gives you an idea of how to upgrade your users to the correct version:

Version	DLL	Distribution Platform
4.00	All	Windows 95/NT 4.0
4.70	All	Internet Explorer 3.x
4.71	All	Internet Explorer 4.0
4.72	All	Internet Explorer 4.01 and Windows 98
5.00	Shlwapi.dll	Internet Explorer 5
5.00	Shell32.dll	Windows 2000
5.80	Comctl32.dll	Internet Explorer 5
5.81	Comctl32.dll	Windows 2000

Along with the preceding table, Microsoft delivers these clarifying notes:[10]

Note 1

The 4.00 versions of Shell32.dll and Comctl32.dll are found on the original versions of Windows 95 and Windows NT 4. New versions of Commctl.dll were shipped with all Internet Explorer releases. Shlwapi.dll first shipped with Internet Explorer 4.0, so its first version number is 4.71. The shell was not updated with the Internet Explorer 3.0 release, so Shell32.dll does not have a version 4.70. While Shell32.dll versions 4.71 and 4.72 were shipped with the corresponding Internet Explorer releases, they were not necessarily installed (see Note 2). For subsequent releases, the version numbers for the three DLLs are not identical. In general, you should assume that all three DLLs may have different version numbers, and test each one separately.

10. From MSDN. Article Title: *Shell and Common Controls Versions.*

Note 2

All systems with Internet Explorer 4.0 or 4.01 will have the associated version of Comctl32.dll and Shlwapi.dll (4.71 or 4.72, respectively). However, for systems prior to Windows 98, Internet Explorer 4.0 and 4.01 can be installed with or without the *integrated shell*. If they are installed with the integrated shell, the associated version of Shell32.dll will be installed. If they are installed without the integrated shell, Shell32.dll is not updated. In other words, the presence of version 4.71 or 4.72 of Comctl32.dll or Shlwapi.dll on a system does not guarantee that Shell32.dll has the same version number. All Windows 98 systems have version 4.72 of Shell32.dll.

Note 3

Version 5.80 of Comctl32.dll and version 5.0 of Shlwapi.dll are distributed with Internet Explorer 5. They will be found on all systems on which Internet Explorer 5 is installed, except Windows 2000. Internet Explorer 5 does not update the shell, so version 5.0 of Shell32.dll will not be found on Windows NT, Windows 95, or Windows 98 systems. Version 5.0 of Shell32.dll will be distributed with Windows 2000, along with version 5.0 of Shlwapi.dll, and version 5.81 of Comctl32.dll.

1.5 Summary

Chapter 1 outlines what the book is about and where to find information on the various extensions. I have tried to make each chapter independent of the others and I have cross-referenced other sections as needed. Chapters 9 through 11 break this rule because namespace extensions make for bigger projects than things like context menu extensions. Section 1.4 outlined the versions of the shell and how to get them to your users.

This book covers a lot of the shell, but you may discover that pieces are missing. Before you send me an e-mail, flaming me for incompetence, poor upbringing, or anything else, check out the Prentice Hall Web site at *www.phptr.com* or visit my site at *www.scottseely.com*. These sites are updated regularly, so if neither contains the new information you have uncovered, e-mail me to let me know what I've missed. The first person to name any missing feature will be named on the Web site and in the acknowledgements section of the next revision of this book. I will list your name (unless you ask me not to) and the item you caught to acknowledge your contribution. I apologize for not covering everything in the shell this first go around. Microsoft has updated the shell seven times in five years. I had to decide to leave out some minor features.

Now, go extend the shell!

The Taskbar

The taskbar, introduced with Windows 95, makes Windows a lot easier to use. It gives us a clear view of what applications are running and allows us to pull a program or two out of the Startup group. The taskbar has a little area called the system tray. The system tray displays the current time and serves as a location for applications to notify users when an application's status changes. Mail programs like Microsoft Outlook put a little envelope in the tray area when mail shows up. If your system has multiple monitors, the taskbar can be found on the one marked as the primary display.

The taskbar replaced PROGMAN.EXE with the Start button. It cleaned up the screen and made navigation easier. With the release of Internet Explorer 4.0 and Active Desktop, the taskbar received one more noticeable enhancement: extra toolbars.[1]

Unfortunately, a lot of developers use the taskbar without thinking about what benefits they provide the end user. Many applications use the system tray as a program launcher and install useless files in the Start menu (yet another part of the taskbar). The Windows 2000 logo requirements aim to curtail the abuse of the taskbar and the Start menu. The rules set forth by Microsoft are fairly succinct.

---

1. Creation of extra taskbar toolbars is covered in Chapter 13, "Explorer Bars and Desk Bands."

The Start Menu is designed to give users easy access to launch applications. Usability studies show that when the Start Menu becomes too cluttered, users can no longer do this.

- Do not place shortcuts to documents, such as readme files, in the Start Menu. If you have important information that the user should see, consider displaying that information during the install process.
- Do not put shortcuts to help files in the Start Menu. Users can access help once they launch the application.
- Do not place shortcuts to uninstall in the Start Menu. The Add/Remove Program control panel applet provides this functionality.

The following behaviors, though not required, are recommended:

- Place your icon to launch your application directly under Start → Programs. Avoid placing it in a folder under Programs. In particular, do not create a folder in the Start Menu in which you only put one item. Often, applications will create a folder based on company name and then put a single shortcut to launch the application inside that folder. Instead, consider renaming the shortcut to include the company name and dropping the use of the folder.
  Programs →   My Company →   My App   _____ (Avoid this)
  Programs →   My Company My App   (Recommended)
- Do not put anything in the top of the Start Menu, as users consider this their own personal space.
- If you have support applications, tools, or utilities associated with your application, and you wish to publish these in the Start Menu, create a single folder in the Start Menu as a peer of the icon to launch your application and place them there.[2]

You can discover the parts of the taskbar by using Spy++. Figure 2-1 gives a layout of the window classes used to put together the taskbar. It uses three custom window classes and three common controls to implement itself. The main area of the taskbar is a simple tab control with the TCS_BUTTONS style bit turned on.

In this chapter, I will cover the following items:

- How to get taskbar information
- How to add and remove buttons from the taskbar
- How to add items to the Start menu

---

2. Microsoft Windows 2000 Application Specification for client applications, available at *http://msdn.microsoft.com/winlogo/downloads.asp,* pp. 46–7

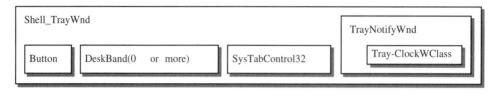

Figure 2.1
The windows that make up the taskbar.

- How to add icons to the system tray
- Creating an animated tray icon

Along the way, we will build an application that incorporates all of these pieces and a few classes as well.

2.1   How to Get Taskbar Information

With the taskbar, as with any application toolbar (a.k.a. *appbar*), it is fairly simple to find out where the toolbar is located as well as its state. In order to get the taskbar's location and state, we simply need to get the task-bar's HWND and then use the SHAppBarMessage() shell function. SHAppBarMessage() has the following prototype:

UINT SHAppBarMessage(DWORD dwMessage, PAPPBARDATA pData);

The APPBARDATA structure looks like this:

```
typedef struct _AppBarData {
      DWORD cbSize; // Always equal to sizeof( APPBARDATA )
      HWND hWnd;    // Appbar to get data from
      UINT uCallbackMessage;
      UINT uEdge;   // Specifies which side of the screen the
            // appbar is attached to.
      RECT rc;      // Gives the AppBar's bounding rectangle
      LPARAM lParam;// Message dependent value
} APPBARDATA, *PAPPBARDATA;
```

Only two of the ten available values for dwMessage are of interest to us: ABM_GETTASKBARPOS and ABM_GETSTATE. ABM_GETTASKBARPOS retrieves the bounding rectangle and edge that the appbar is attached to. The taskbar is always attached to an edge. It does not float like the Microsoft Office Short-cut Bar does. The ABM_GETSTATE message tells the caller if the appbar has the ABS_ALWAYSONTOP or ABS_AUTOHIDE attributes set. Using this information, we can begin to write a taskbar class that retrieves this information for us whenever we want it.

2.1.1 Getting the Taskbar's State and Position

Let's create a class called CTaskBar. This class will evolve throughout the chapter and will live in a DLL. At first, the class will give us the current side, size, and state of the taskbar. The class declaration looks like this:

```
class AFX_EXT_CLASS CTaskBar
{
public:
    CTaskBar();
    virtual ~CTaskBar();

    HWND GetHWND();
    CRect GetPosition();
    UINT GetSide();
    UINT GetState();
};
```

By using the class and its methods, we can easily interrogate the taskbar without having to remember how to use the APPBARDATA structure with the related function calls. We also do not need to remember how to grab the taskbar—the class encapsulates it all for us. All calls to SHAppBarMessage() require that the hWnd member of the APPBARDATA structure is filled in. By making CTaskBar::GetHWND() public, users of the class can interrogate the taskbar for other information or they can subclass parts of it. CTaskBar::GetHWND() has a fairly simple implementation:

```
HWND CTaskBar::GetHWND()
{
  HWND retval = NULL;
  CWnd* pWnd;
  // The taskbar does not have a window title.
  pWnd = CWnd::FindWindow( _T("Shell_TrayWnd"), NULL );
  if ( pWnd )
  {
      retval = pWnd->GetSafeHwnd();
  }
  return retval;
}
```

The remaining methods are also fairly simple. They all involve calling SHAppBarMessage() and then interpreting the results. Here is CTaskBar::GetSide():

```
UINT CTaskBar::GetSide()
{
  UINT retval = 0;
  APPBARDATA appBarData;
  HWND hwnd = GetHWND();
  if ( hwnd )
```

```
{
  ZeroMemory( &appBarData, sizeof( appBarData ) );
  appBarData.cbSize = sizeof( appBarData );
  appBarData.hWnd = hwnd;
  if ( SHAppBarMessage(ABM_GETTASKBARPOS, &appBarData) )
  {
     retval = appBarData.uEdge;
  }
}
return retval;
}
```

As you can see, the uEdge member of appBarData was set to the edge of the screen that the taskbar is attached to. The code for GetPosition() looks similar to GetSide(). Instead of returning uEdge, GetSide() returns the rc member of appBarData. I split these up into two separate methods to enhance usability. Most of the time, the users of the class will ask for one attribute instead of asking for everything at once.

2.1.2   Using CTaskBar

Let's develop a small application that uses CTaskBar. It will simply report the current edge, state, and size of the taskbar. The code for the sample is in the Examples\Chapter 2\Step 1 directory on the CD. Using the AppWizard, select MFC AppWizard (exe) and give the project the name *TaskBarApp*. Press OK and the on the Step 1 page, select the Dialog based radio button. Accept all the defaults.

Lay out the dialog so that it looks like the example in Figure 2-2. Map CStrings to IDC_CURRENT_SIDE, IDC_CURRENT_SIZE, and IDC_CURRENT_STATE. Lastly, add a BN_CLICKED message handler for the Refresh button.

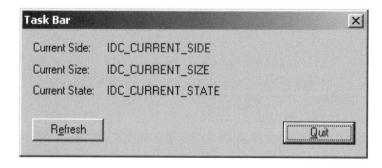

Figure 2.2   *Layout of dialog for the Chapter 2/Step 1 example.*

To initialize all the data, we will call the Refresh button's BN_CLICKED handler from OnInitDialog(). This keeps the code for updating the display in one location. The code to update the display, CTaskBarAppDlg::OnBtnRefresh(), winds up looking like this:

```
void CTaskBarAppDlg::OnBtnRefresh()
{
   CTaskBar taskbar;

   // Get the position of the taskbar
   CRect rect = taskbar.GetPosition();

   // Format the display string for the user
   m_szCurrentSize.Format( "Height: %d, Width: %d",
     rect.Height(), rect.Width() );

   // Using the ABE_XXX constants, figure out
   // which the the taskbar is attached to
   switch( taskbar.GetSide() )
   {
     case ABE_TOP:
        m_szCurrentSide = _T("Top");
        break;
     case ABE_BOTTOM:
        m_szCurrentSide = _T("Bottom");
        break;
     case ABE_LEFT:
        m_szCurrentSide = _T("Left");
        break;
     case ABE_RIGHT:
        m_szCurrentSide = _T("Right");
        break;
    }

   // Using the ABS_XXX constants, figure out
   // whether the taskbar is set to be always on top,
   // autohide, or both.
   switch( taskbar.GetState() )
   {
        case ABS_ALWAYSONTOP:
           m_szCurrentState = _T("Always on top");
           break;
        case ABS_AUTOHIDE:
           m_szCurrentState = _T("Autohide");
           break;
        case ABS_ALWAYSONTOP | ABS_AUTOHIDE:
           m_szCurrentState = _T("Always on top\n"
             "and autohide");
           break;
    }
```

```
    UpdateData( false );
}
```

2.2   How to Add and Remove Buttons From the Taskbar

The shell exports an interface named ITaskbarList. ITaskbarList derives from IUnknown and exports the following functions:

- **ActivateTab:** Activates an item on the taskbar but does not activate the window
- **AddTab:** Adds an item to the taskbar
- **DeleteTab:** Deletes an item from the taskbar
- **HrInit:** Initializes the taskbar list object This method does not need to be called by users of the interface
- **SetActiveAlt** marks a taskbar item as active but does not visually activate it

The documentation goes on to state that in order to use the interface, you must include SHLOBJ.H. The shipping version of Visual C++ that I am currently using[3] does not define what the ITaskbarList interface looks like. Fortunately, the latest platform SDK does define this interface. If you have got a good Internet connection, you can download the SDK for no charge from Microsoft.[4]

You can add and remove tabs from the taskbar with ITaskbarList. In fact, any window can be added to the taskbar. When a taskbar button is pressed, the taskbar activates and sets focus to the corresponding HWND. As a result, you could write a program that allows the user to go to any parent or child window in your application by using the taskbar. The only time the interface may be useful is when writing an application that you do not want to have show up in the taskbar. You can accomplish this with a tool window (a window that has the WS_EX_TOOLWINDOW style bit set). A tool window does not use an icon in its title bar, but you may need to have that icon, which would eliminate a tool window as an option.

Where would someone use this feature? In the case of an integrated application suite, it might make sense to have a unified front end for the system and several components that work together to complete the application. Often, these components are standalone executables with a full-blown user interface. Development along these lines allows a looser coupling between

---

3. I developed the code for this book using Visual C++ 6.0.

4. The SDK has changed URLs a few times in the past year. You should be able to find it somewhere on *http://msdn.microsoft.com*.

teams developing different pieces of functionality. To present a unified front, the applications may want to avoid placing buttons in the task bar. You have a few ways to accomplish this task. One way would be to remove the button from the Taskbar whenever it receives the WM_ACTIVATE or WM_SETFOCUS message.

Let's build a sample application that does just that. The application will add and remove its own button from the taskbar. To do this, we'll enhance the TaskBarApp application and the CTaskBar class. CTaskBar will get two new methods: AddTab(CWnd& wnd) and DeleteTab(CWnd& wnd). CTaskBar will also get a new private helper method that gets the ITaskbarList interface pointer, GetITaskbarList().

```
bool CTaskBar::AddTab( CWnd& wnd )
{
   bool retval = false;
   CComPtr<ITaskbarList> pList( GetITaskbarList() );

   if ( pList )
   {
      pList->AddTab( wnd.GetSafeHwnd() );
      retval = true;
   }

   return retval;
}
```

CTaskBar::DeleteTab() looks similar. The line

```
pList->AddTab( wnd.GetSafeHwnd() );
```

is replaced by

```
pList->DeleteTab( wnd.GetSafeHwnd() );
```

Within our application, we need to add the line CoInitialize(NULL) to the InitInstance() method. Failure to do so means that none of our COM calls will work. In particular, CTaskBar::GetITaskbarList() will not work without this line.

```
ITaskbarList* CTaskBar::GetITaskbarList()
{
   ITaskbarList* retval = NULL;
   HRESULT hr = CoCreateInstance(CLSID_TaskbarList, NULL,
      CLSCTX_SERVER, IID_ITaskbarList,
       reinterpret_cast<void**>(&retval));
   if ( !SUCCEEDED( hr ) )
   {
     retval = NULL;
   }
```

```
              return retval;
          }
```

We also need to add a mechanism to indicate whether or not we want our application to show up in the taskbar. I chose a checkbox, as shown in Figure 2-3. Controlling the display in the taskbar can then be done by adding the following methods to CTaskBarAppDlg:

```
void CTaskBarAppDlg::OnChkDisplayInTaskbar()
{
   CTaskBar taskbar;
   if ( m_chkDisplay.GetCheck() == 0 )
   {
      taskbar.DeleteTab( *this );
   }
   else
   {
      taskbar.AddTab( *this );
   }
}

void CTaskBarAppDlg::OnSetFocus(CWnd* pOldWnd)
{
   OnChkDisplayInTaskbar();
}

void CTaskBarAppDlg::OnActivate(UINT nState, CWnd* pWndOther,
   BOOL bMinimized)
{
   OnChkDisplayInTaskbar();
}
```

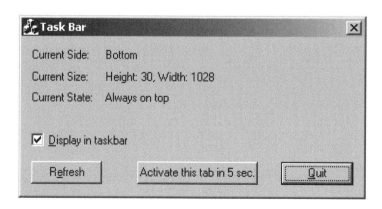

Figure 2.3   *Step 2 of the taskbar example.*

Pretty fancy, huh? If you need to hide any other top level window, code as succinct as CTaskBar().DeleteTab(theWindow) will cause the window to not show up in the taskbar.

2.3 How to Add Items to the Start Menu

Most of the time, the only type of application that touches the Start menu is an installation program. You may want to add items to the Start menu if you think it will help your users too. Many businesses buy a computer as a single-use device. Your company might sell medical record review stations, security monitoring software, or other applications that more or less define the computer's use. In this case, you might want to add some functionality to the Start menu similar to the Documents submenu. Instead of allowing the user to open up the most recently opened files, your application might allow the user to quickly review the last ten patient records. If you develop software similar to Microsoft Office, where the application will co-exist with applications from other vendors, you may want to decide if you want to be able to add and remove items from the Start menu. It may make sense. I would not mind if Visual C++ had an extra submenu that allowed me to pick one of the last ten projects I loaded. Yes, I can do this through the Most-Recently-Used (MRU) menus inside of the application. I usually have the application set up to automatically load the last project opened. I would like to see the MRU list available from within the application's part of the Start menu.

Now that I have covered when to use the Start menu (as well as a suggestion for a new standard practice), let's take a look at what the operating system sees the items as and what those items should be. The Start menu is not much more than a special view of a few special purpose directories. All the items in the Start menu should be links or directories. The shell builds the Start menu by reading the entries in the All Users\Start Menu and <User Name>\Start Menu directories. Any file that shows up in these directories automatically appears in the Start menu. You can place the actual file in these directories. Keep in mind that most users do not know that these directories exist or where to find them. Starting with Windows 2000, the user has to jump through a number of hoops to even see the contents of the Start Menu directories. Because of these problems,almost everyone follows the rule of "links only" in the Start menu directories. Adding entries to the Start menu involves knowing what actual directories items should be placed in. Unfortunately, the correct directory varies based on the Win32 version, the name of the installation directory, and the name of the user. The information presented in the start of this paragraph is accurate enough for demonstration purposes. We need some sort of API that tells us where the directories are so the current user doesn't have to jump through hoops. We need SHGetSpecial-

FolderPath(). This method has a new version with Windows 2000 called SHGetFolderPath(). The new version adds four new folders that can be retrieved. Otherwise, both methods do the same thing. For compatibility reasons, my code will use SHGetSpecialFolderPath(). This method has the following prototype:

```
BOOL SHGetSpecialFolderPath(
  HWND hwndOwner, //Handle to the owner window if a dialog
        //box needs to be displayed (ex.Creating
            // the folder if it is not found)
  LPTSTR lpszPath,// Buffer to receive path to folder
  int nFolder, // ID of folder
  BOOL fCreate      // Create folder if not found
);⁵
```

The value of nFolder can be any one of a litany of values found in SHLOBJ.H.⁶ The values all look like CSIDL_XXX. Using the SHGetSpecial-FolderPath() API is the easy part of the puzzle. Actually, the only hard part is learning how to properly add a link. To do this, we need to understand the IShellLink object.

IShellLink encapsulates everything about a link. The physical manifestation of an IShellLink is a .lnk file. In Windows parlance, think *shortcut.* IShellLink exposes interfaces that let you do everything from create the link and command line to resolve the link back to the actual item. From an active IShellLink object, you can call QueryInterface() to get an IPersistFile instance. This IPersistFile instance will allow you to save the link to disk. Of all the IShellLink methods, we are only interested in two: SetPath() and SetArguments(). If we want to link to things that are not files, such as printers, we would use SetIDList(). We will leave ID lists alone until we get into namespace extensions later in the book.

Windows composes the Start menu by merging the contents of the folders identified by the CSIDL values CSIDL_STARTMENU and CSIDL_COMMON_STARTMENU. These values respectively refer to the current user's Start menu and the Start menu shared by all users of the machine. Items in the base of either directory show up on the initial menu in the top section (Figure 2-4). Items in the Programs folder show up within the Programs group on the Start menu. Creating new folders and link items is fairly easy. To create a new folder, the following code does the trick:

```
mkdir( szNewDirectory );
```

---

5. See Appendix B for a full explanation of SHGetSpecialFolderPath() and SHGet-FolderPath().

6. The values are covered in Appendix B under the entry *CSIDL_XXX.*

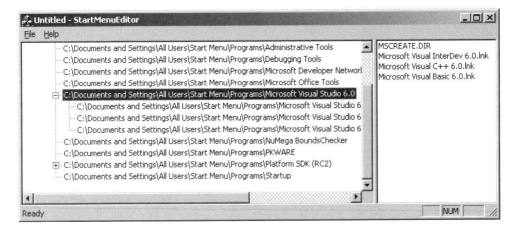

Figure 2.4   *The Start menu editor program in action.*

If the new directory is in the path of CSIDL_STARTMENU or CSIDL_COM-MON_STARTMENU, that new directory will show up in the Start menu. The hard part is creating a new link that will show up in the actual folder. Fortunately, it is not that hard. The following code will create a link based on a file chosen by the user. Similar code will work if you want to supply the filename differently.

```
void CStartMenuEditorView::OnAddlink()
{
    CFileDialog dlg( true );
    if ( dlg.DoModal() == IDOK )
    {
        CString szLinkName = dlg.GetFileName();

        // Make a link name that ends in ".lnk".
        CString szFileExtension = szLinkName.Right( 4 );

        // Make the comparison case-insensitive
        szFileExtension.MakeLower();
        if ( szFileExtension != _T(".lnk") )
        {
            if ( szFileExtension[0] == _T('.') )
            {
                szLinkName = szLinkName.Left(
                    szLinkName.GetLength() - 4 );
            }
            szLinkName += _T(".lnk");
        }
        GetListCtrl().InsertItem( 0, szLinkName, 0 );
        CString szTemp = szLinkName;
```

```
szLinkName.Format( "%s\\%s", m_szCurrentDirectory,
  szTemp );

HRESULT hres = NULL;
IShellLink* psl = NULL;

// Get a pointer to the IShellLink interface.
hres = CoCreateInstance(CLSID_ShellLink, NULL,
  CLSCTX_INPROC_SERVER, IID_IShellLink,
  reinterpret_cast<void**>(&psl));
if (SUCCEEDED(hres))
{
    IPersistFile* ppf = NULL;

    // Set the path to the shortcut target
    psl->SetPath(dlg.GetPathName());

    // Query IShellLink for the IPersistFile interface
    // for saving the shortcut in persistent storage.
    hres = psl->QueryInterface(IID_IPersistFile,
          reinterpret_cast<void**>(&ppf));

    if (SUCCEEDED(hres))
    {
      WCHAR wsz[MAX_PATH];

      // Ensure that the string is ANSI.
      MultiByteToWideChar(CP_ACP, 0, szLinkName, -1,
          wsz, MAX_PATH);

      // Save the link
      hres = ppf->Save(wsz, TRUE);
      ppf->Release();
    }
    psl->Release();
}
  }
}
```

The first few lines of the method simply convert the name to a plausible link name and insert the link into a CListCtrl. The rest of the code gets the IShellLink interface, sets it up to point to the selected file, and saves the link to the currently selected directory. Figure 2-4 shows the application this code came from. The left hand side shows a tree built of the names of the directories comprising the Start menu. The right hand side lists the names of all the links in each directory. The entire application and its source can be found in the Examples\Chapter 2\StartMenuEditor directory on the CD. The StartMenuEditor walks the directory tree and loads the left-hand side with information. It allows the user to add directories to the tree as well as links to each directory. Both actions are performed via the right mouse button.

When placing links into the user's Start menu, make sure that your code does not place these things in the Start menu for all users of a machine without asking for permission to do so. Please remember that—and let's hope that the authors of the Windows 2000 logo requirements learn that placing applications in the root of the Program menu is rude (Figure 2-5). The guidelines state: "Place your icon to launch your application directly under Start → Programs. Avoid placing it in a folder under [P]rograms." I believe that the folder under Programs is less obtrusive to your user. Look again at Figure 2-5.

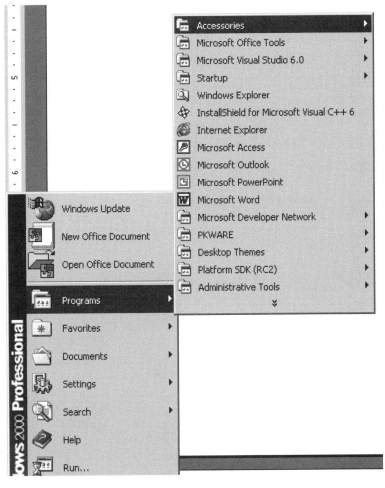

Figure 2.5   *Adding items to the Programs folder can make the menu bloat in size quickly.*

Do you see how much room that eats up? The rule contradicts another guide-line stated just a few sentences earlier: "The Start Menu is designed to give users easy access to launch applications. Usability studies show that when the Start Menu becomes too cluttered, users can no longer do this."[7]

2.4 How to Add Icons to the System Tray

As stated earlier in this chapter, the system tray is the area of the taskbar where the clock sits. Referring back to Figure 2-1, a TrayNotifyWnd implements the system tray. The tray allows programs to get the user's attention for various events. One example of a program using the tray properly is Microsoft Outlook. Outlook uses the tray to let the user know that new mail has arrived. When the user reads the mail, Outlook removes the icon. I have seen other applications put an icon in the system tray and leave it there. According to the *Microsoft Windows 2000 Application Specification,* applications that clutter the system tray are not serving their users. To quickly launch an application, there are other places that are less obtrusive.

- Allow the user to launch the application from the Start menu.
- Place a shortcut on the desktop.
- If the application runs as a service, create a GUI separate from the service. Then allow use of the Start menu to launch the GUI.

One technique I have used to make sure that the service and GUI stay in sync without having to restart the service is to use a configuration file. When the service starts up, it caches the time the configuration file was last modified. Running services usually have some piece of code that they execute at relatively frequent, fixed intervals. The interval may be minutes long, but at some point the service returns to what is essentially the starting point. At this point, check the timestamp of the configuration file. If the last modified time changed, reload the configuration. If time is a worry or the application is not sufficiently cyclic, you can use other mechanisms like mutexes or events to signal a change. Yes, capturing a mutex can be expensive, but it is cheaper than a disk access. The algorithm is simple: if the mutex has not been signaled, continue on your merry way. If you are thinking about using mutexes or other kernel objects (semaphores, threads, fibers, events, etc.), I recommend that you get a copy of Jeffrey Richter's *Advanced Windows* from Microsoft Press. Do not waste your money on any other books: Richter wrote the best one. That is enough about kernel objects. Let's get back to the topic at hand: adding icons to the system tray.

---

7. Microsoft Windows 2000 Application Specification for client applications, available at *http://msdn.microsoft.com/winlogo/downloads.asp,* p. 45.

The Windows API has a method, Shell_NotifyIcon(), that allows you to programmatically manipulate the system tray. The prototype for Shell_Notify-Icon() is

```
BOOL Shell_NotifyIcon(
    DWORD dwMessage,
    PNOTIFYICONDATA pnid
);
```

dwMessage can be any of the following values:

* NIM_ADD: Adds the icon specified in pnid to the system tray.
* NIM_MODIFY: Modifies the icon specified in pnid.
* NIM_DELETE: Removes the icon specified in pnid from the system tray.

This function also requires a pointer to a NOTIFYICONDATA structure. Each member gives specific information about the icon being added to the tray. Under pre-Windows 2000 versions of the Windows 95 style interface, NOTIFYICONDATA structure looked like this:

```
typedef struct _NOTIFYICONDATA {
    DWORD cbSize;
    HWND hWnd;
    UINT uID;
    UINT uFlags;
    UINT uCallbackMessage;
    HICON hIcon;
    TCHAR szTip[64];
    // The rest of the structure is specific to Version
    // 5.0 of the shell
    DWORD dwState;
    DWORD dwStateMask;
    TCHAR szInfo[256];
    union {
      UINT  uTimeout;
      UINT  uVersion;
    } DUMMYUNIONNAME;
    TCHAR szInfoTitle[64];
    DWORD dwInfoFlags;
} NOTIFYICONDATA, *PNOTIFYICONDATA;
```

Members:

cbSize: Set to sizeof(NOTIFYICONDATA). Always fill in this member.

hWnd: Set to the window that owns the icon. When this window disappears, the icon should be removed. If it isn't, Windows will remove the icon the next time the mouse passes over the system tray.

uID: Uniquely identifies the icon with respect to the HWND. You can have multiple icons associated with one window. In this case, the icons each need a different ID. Alternatively, you can use the same uID if the window to icon relationship is one to one.

uFlags: Identifies which other members contain valid data. You can have one or more of the following values:
- **NIF_ICON:** The hIcon member is valid.
- **NIF_MESSAGE:** The uCallbackMessage member is valid.
- **NIF_TIP:** The szTip member is valid.
- **NIF_STATE:** The dwState and dwStateMask members are valid.
- **NIF_INFO:** Use a balloon-style tooltip instead of a standard tooltip. The tooltip will display upon calling Shell_NotifyIcon. The szInfo, uTimeout, szInfoTitle, and dwInfoFlags members are valid.

uCallbackMessage: When an icon-related keyboard or mouse event occurs, the shell will post this message to the window identified by hWnd. wParam contains the value passed in for uID. This allows you to use one callback for all of your icons.

hIcon: Handle to the icon to add, modify, or delete.

szTip: Text to display when the mouse hovers over the icon in the system tray.

dwState: Can be set to one of these two values:
- **NIS_HIDDEN:** The icon is hidden.
- **NIS_SHARED:** The icon is shared.

dwStateMask: Identifies which bits of dwState will be retrieved or modified. Setting this to NIS_HIDDEN will only retrieve the value of NIS_HIDDEN in the dwState member.

szInfo: Think of the balloon help as a message box. This part represents the text of the message. If you want the balloon help to disappear before the 10-second minimum, set this value to a NULL string.

uTimeout: Tells windows how long to display the balloon help message. With Windows 2000, this value has to be between 10000 ms and 30000 ms (10 to 30 seconds). A value below 10000 will cause the balloon to display for 10 seconds. A value above 30000 will cause the balloon to display for 30 seconds.

uVersion: Tells Windows how to treat this icon. As of Windows 2000, you can use two values:
- **0:** Use pre-Windows 2000 behavior.
- **NOTIFYICON_VERSION:** Use Windows 2000 behavior.

szInfoTitle: If you think of balloon help as a message box, this part represents the title of the message box.

dwInfoFlags: If you think of balloon help as a message box, this part represents the icon to use in the message box. You can use one of the following values:
- **NIIF_WARNING:** Display the warning icon.
- **NIIF_ERROR:** Display the error icon.
- **NIIF_INFO:** Display the information icon.

2.4.1   A Class for Animating the Tray

You may have seen animated icons when using dial-up networking or when running a Visual Studio macro. By using the relationship between a tray icon and the owning window, you build a class that encapsulates the behavior of a tray icon. One example is a class I wrote called *CAnimTrayIcon*.

Programs use CAnimTrayIcon to manipulate an icon in the system tray. I tried to keep the class's interface simple. Whenever possible, the class does the hard part of the work. For example, CAnimTrayIcon derives from CWnd. A user of the class creates this window as a child window (the window is a 1 pixel x 1 pixel, invisible rectangle). When the parent window is destroyed, the child window is also destroyed. CAnimTrayIcon removes the icon from the tray at this point.

The class resides in a DLL and assumes that the icon IDs used for the tray will be known to the application prior to instantiation. Additionally, these icons must be accessible from the current resource handle.

To add this class to your application, you need to perform the following steps:

1. Create an icon for when the tray icon is not animated. (See Figure 2-6)
2. Create the sequence of icons for the animation. (See Figure 2-7)
3. Create a UINT array with the icon IDs using the following order: The non-animated icon first, the animated icons in the order they should be shown, and a 0 to terminate the list.
4. Add a CAnimTrayIcon member to the window that needs an animated tray icon.
5. Pass the UINT array and the version you want the icon to represent to the CAnimTrayIcon constructor. If you want features like bubble help and the ability to respond to WM_CONTEXTMENU for your icon instead of WM_RBUTTONDOWN, you will need to pass in NOTIFY-ICON_VERSION as the second argument to the constructor. Otherwise, you can take the default value, which will give you Win95 behavior.

 Figure 2.6   *Icon when tray icon is static (not-animated).*

Figure 2.7   *A sample seven-icon animation sequence.*

6. Pick the message ID you want to the tray icon to use.

7. Find where you want the icon to first show up and call CAnimTray-Icon::Init().

8. To get rid of the icon before the owning window closes, simply call yourIconInstance.PostMessage(WM_CLOSE).

When you need to set or change the icon's tooltip text, call SetTip(const CString&). To start the animation, call StartAnimation(). To stop the animation, call StopAnimation(). Last, if you want to respond to any system tray messages, add the following to your window implementation:

To your class: afx_msg LONG OnTrayMessage(WPARAM wparam, LPARAM lparam);

To the message map: ON_MESSAGE(ID_YOUR_MESSAGE, OnTray-Message)

There is one "gotcha" regarding tray icons. It looks like you should be using the small, 16x16 icons for the tray. After all, the tray icons are small. For some reason, you should use 32x32 icons instead. Windows will scale and draw the icons for you.

The class declaration looks like this:

```
class AFX_EXT_CLASS  CAnimTrayIcon : public CWnd
{
    friend CAnimIconHelper;
// Construction/Destruction
public:
    // unIconIDs: Pass a 0 terminated list of icons IDs.
    // The first icon is for when there is no animation.
    // The rest are for the animation.  The animation
    // moves from unIconIDs[1]—>unIconIDs[last], then
    // repeats.
    // unVersion: Can be 0 for pre-Win2K behavior or
    // for Win2K behavior NOTIFYICON_VERSION.
    CAnimTrayIcon( const UINT unIconIDs[],
      UINT unVersion = 0 );

    virtual ~CAnimTrayIcon();

    static const int INACTIVE_ICON;
    static const int FIRST_ANIMATED_ICON;

// Implementation
#if _WIN32_IE >= 0x0500
```

```
   // Displays a balloon in the taskbar for the icon.
   // szInfo: Text part of the balloon.
   // szTitle: Title for the balloon.
   // unType: NIIF_WARNING, NIIF_ERROR, or NIIF_INFO.
   // unDuration: Time to display balloon before it
   //   automatically disappears.  Windows sets this
   //   between 10000 ms and 30000 ms (10-30 seconds).
   void DisplayBalloon( const CString& szInfo,
      const CString& szTitle,
      UINT unType = NIIF_INFO,
      UINT unDuration = 10000 );
#endif // _WIN32_IE == 0x0500

   // If the tray icon is not moving, returns true.
   // Otherwise, it returns false.
   bool IsStopped();

   // Stops the tray icon animation
   void StopAnimation();

   // Starts the tray icon animation.
   void StartAnimation();

   // Sets the tooltip that is displayed when the
   // mouse cursor hovers over the tray icon
   void SetTip( const CString& szTip )
     throw( std::length_error );

   // Call this member only when the owner CWnd
   // has a valid HWND
   // unCallbackID: This message ID must be
   //   unique to the pParent window
   // pParent: Pointer to the owner of the
   //   CAnimTrayIcon
   void Init( UINT unCallbackID, CWnd* pParent );

protected:
   afx_msg void OnTimer(UINT nIDEvent);
   afx_msg void OnDestroy();
   DECLARE_MESSAGE_MAP()
// Attributes
private:
   // Set to the proper size depending on
   // the version the user sets the
   // shell to.
   const int m_KnNotifyIconDataSize;

   // Can be 0 for pre-Win2K behavior or
   //   for Win2K behavior NOTIFYICON_VERSION.
   UINT m_unVersion;
```

```
    // Indicates the "on-deck" icon.  This will be the
    // next icon that the class will display.
    UINT m_unCurrentIcon;

    // This value can be tweaked to speed up or slow
    // down the speed of the animation.
    UINT m_unTimerInterval;

    // Uniquely identifies the timer event.
    UINT m_unTimerID;

    // Used internally to check if Init has been called
    // yet. If Init hasn't been called, this is false.
    bool m_bInitialized;

    // Identifies the message to use when sending
    // messages back to the parent window from the tray.
    UINT m_unCallbackID;

    // Indicates the tip to display when the user hovers
    // over the tray icon.
    CString m_szTip;

    // Stores the IDs of the various icons to display
    // in the tray
    std::vector<UINT> m_vunIconIDs;

    // Points to the owner of the window.
    CWnd* m_pParent;

    // Points to top level window that helps me keep the
    // taskbar up to date.
    std::auto_ptr<CAnimIconHelper> m_pHelper;

    // Helper method that shows the specified icon at
    // the specified index
    void ShowIcon( UINT unIndex );

    // Call this member only when the icon needs to be
    // added to the taskbar and the object has already
    // been initialized.
    void AddIconToTray();
};
```

The first line within the class declaration declares the CAnimTrayIcon has a friend relationship with CAnimIconHelper.

What is *CAnimIconHelper?* Occasionally, EXPLORER.EXE (and the taskbar) crashes due to code that Microsoft or some other entity wrote. You can bring it back to life by running EXPLORER.EXE. I use the Microsoft Office Shortcut Bar for this very reason. The shortcut bar almost always survives an

EXPLORER.EXE crash and allows me to restart the taskbar.[8] When EX-PLORER.EXE restarts, it broadcasts a registered Window message named "TaskbarCreated" to all top-level windows.[9] To get the ID of this message, the following line creates a global constant that stores the ID:

```
const UINT g_KunTaskbarCreated = RegisterWindowMessage(
    _T("TaskbarCreated") );
```

As stated earlier, CAnimTrayIcon is a child window of the owner. Because child windows are not top-level windows, CAnimTrayIcon will not get the message. CAnimIconHelper gets created as a top-level window. This window's only purpose is to notify a related CAnimTrayIcon that the taskbar has restarted and that it should redisplay itself in the taskbar. CAnimIconHelper looks like this:

```
class CAnimIconHelper : public CWnd
{
// Construction
public:
    CAnimIconHelper(CAnimTrayIcon& animIcon);
    virtual ~CAnimIconHelper();

protected:
afx_msg LRESULT TaskbarCreated(WPARAM, LPARAM);
        DECLARE_MESSAGE_MAP()

private:
    CAnimTrayIcon& m_animIcon;
};
```

In CAnimIconHelper's constructor, it takes a reference to a CAnimTray-Icon. Later on, when EXPLORER.EXE redisplays the taskbar, the following code gets executed:

```
afx_msg LRESULT CAnimIconHelper::TaskbarCreated(WPARAM,
    LPARAM)
{
    m_animIcon.AddIconToTray();
    return 0;
}
```

---

8. Because not everyone has Microsoft Office, I have included an appbar (see Chapter 3) that allows you to restart the shell. You can find it on the CD in the Tools\ExplorerStarter folder.

9. This functionality was introduced with shell updates provided by Internet Explorer 4.0. Earlier versions of the shell do not broadcast this message.

AddIconToTray() simply adds the icon to the system tray. We'll get to the guts of CAnimTrayIcon in a bit. CAnimTrayIcon associates itself with the CAnim-IconHelper inside CAnimIconHelper's constructor. The two classes are tightly coupled. This tight coupling helps CAnimTrayIcon to clean up after itself. As I mentioned, CAnimIconHelper is a top-level window. The window gets created in CAnimTrayIcon's Init method with the following line:

```
m_pHelper->CreateEx( NULL, szClassName, "CAnimIconHelper",
   WS_POPUPWINDOW, CRect(0,0,1,1), NULL, 0);
```

The window gets removed from the screen with this line from CAnim-TrayIcon's OnDestroy() method:

```
m_pHelper->SendMessage( WM_CLOSE );
```

The CAnimTrayIcon constructor takes a const array of UINTs. The class stores the array as an STL vector. The constructor also initializes the member variables. CAnimTrayIcon::Init() makes sure all the machinery will be in place and will allow the class to work. When you call Init(UINT unCallbackID, CWnd* pParent), the class instantiates an invisible child window on the parent and puts an icon in the system tray. The child window allows the class to respond to Windows messages. The callback ID identifies the message to send to the parent when the system tray receives a message. Init() stores the parameters for use in other CAnimTrayIcon methods.

```
void CAnimTrayIcon::Init( UINT unCallbackID,
   CWnd* pParent )
{
   ASSERT_VALID( pParent );

   // You should initialize the list of IDs before
   // calling init
   ASSERT( m_vunIconIDs.size() > 0 );
   m_pParent = pParent;

   // Creates a small, invisible child window on the
   // parent. This allows us to receive WM_TIMER
   // messages. This also allows us to clean up after
   // ourselves.  We will receive a WM_DESTROY message
   // when our parent is destroyed.
   Create( NULL, "CAnimTrayIcon", WS_CHILD,
      CRect(0,0,1,1),m_pParent, 0 );
   CString szClassName = AfxRegisterWndClass(
      CS_HREDRAW|CS_VREDRAW
      |CS_SAVEBITS|CS_DBLCLKS, NULL);
   m_pHelper->CreateEx( NULL, szClassName,
      "CAnimIconHelper", WS_POPUPWINDOW,
      CRect(0,0,1,1), NULL, 0);
   m_bInitialized = true;
```

```
   m_unCallbackID = unCallbackID;
   AddIconToTray();
}

void CAnimTrayIcon::AddIconToTray()
{
   // We don't use ShowIcon here because
   // ShowIcon relies on the tray icon already
   // having been created. This creates the icon
   // in the tray.
   NOTIFYICONDATA strNIData;
   strNIData.cbSize = m_KnNotifyIconDataSize;
   strNIData.hWnd    = m_pParent->GetSafeHwnd();
   strNIData.uID     = m_unCallbackID;
   strNIData.uCallbackMessage = m_unCallbackID;
   _tcscpy( strNIData.szTip, m_szTip );
   strNIData.hIcon = ::LoadIcon( AfxGetResourceHandle(),
      MAKEINTRESOURCE(m_vunIconIDs[m_unCurrentIcon]));
   strNIData.uFlags = NIF_MESSAGE | NIF_TIP | NIF_ICON;
   Shell_NotifyIcon(NIM_ADD, &strNIData);
#if _WIN32_IE >= 0x0500
   // If this isn't compiled under the correct version
   // of the SDK and IE, this code will not compile.
   strNIData.uVersion = m_unVersion;
   Shell_NotifyIcon(NIM_SETVERSION, &strNIData);
#endif // _WIN32_IE >= 0x0500
}
```

When resting the mouse over an icon in the system tray, the icon will often display a tooltip. CAnimTrayIcon::SetTip(const CString&) allows the user to set and change the text of this tooltip as often as the user wants. The string can be no more than 64 characters long. If the string exceeds 64 characters, CAnimTrayIcon::SetTip() throws an exception. Assuming the icon has been displayed, CAnimTrayIcon::SetTip() sets the tooltip to the new string.

```
void CAnimTrayIcon::SetTip(const CString & szTip)
{
   const UINT KunTipLength = 64;

   // If your code asserts here, the string being
   // passed in is too long to go into the tooltip.
   ASSERT( szTip.GetLength() < KunTipLength );
   if ( szTip.GetLength() >= KunTipLength )
   {
      CString szError;
      szError.Format(
          _T("The maximum length of a tip string is %d"),
          KunTipLength );
      throw std::length_error( std::string( szError ) );
   }
```

```
// All is well, remember the new tip and set it if the
// user has initialized the tray icon.
m_szTip = szTip;
if ( m_bInitialized )
{
    NOTIFYICONDATA strNIData;
    strNIData.cbSize = m_KnNotifyIconDataSize;
    strNIData.hWnd   = m_pParent->GetSafeHwnd();
    strNIData.uID    = m_unCallbackID;
    _tcscpy( strNIData.szTip, m_szTip );
    strNIData.uFlags = NIF_TIP;
    Shell_NotifyIcon(NIM_MODIFY, &strNIData);
}
}
```

With Windows 2000 you can also display bubble-style tooltips (see Figure 2-8). If you use Windows 2000 and dial-up networking, you have likely seen one of these pop up when you establish a connection with an Internet Service Provider or another external network. The bubbles act like a hybrid between a message box and a tooltip. Like a message box, they are displayed due to a program request (as opposed to a user action) and they have a title, message, and an icon. They act like a tooltip by displaying for a short period of time, they have no buttons, and the bubble delivers information only. The bubbles display for 10 to 30 seconds depending on the value set in the NOTIFYICONDATA.uTimeout member. The user can dismiss the bubble before the timeout period by clicking on the bubble. To accommodate the bubbles CAnimTrayIcon has a DisplayBubble() method. The method is only available if _WIN32_IE (defines the version of Internet Explorer) is five or greater. The function will do nothing if you construct CAnimTrayIcon as an old-style icon.

```
void CAnimTrayIcon::DisplayBubble( const CString& szInfo,
    const CString& szTitle, UINT unType /*= NIIF_INFO*/,
    UINT unDuration /*= 10000*/ )
{
   if ( m_KnNotifyIconDataSize == NOTIFYICONDATA_V1_SIZE )
   {
       // The user of the class has access to this data,
       // but they chose to use a Win95 version
       // implementation of the shell.
       return;
   }
```

| Figure 2.8 | *Bubble-style tooltip in action.* |

```
NOTIFYICONDATA strNIData;

ZeroMemory( &strNIData, sizeof( strNIData ) );
if ( m_bInitialized )
{
    NOTIFYICONDATA strNIData;
    strNIData.cbSize = m_KnNotifyIconDataSize;
    strNIData.hWnd   = m_pParent->GetSafeHwnd();
    strNIData.uID    = m_unCallbackID;
    _tcscpy( strNIData.szInfo, szInfo );
    _tcscpy( strNIData.szInfoTitle, szTitle );
    strNIData.uFlags = NIF_INFO;
    strNIData.dwInfoFlags = unType;
    strNIData.uTimeout = unDuration;
    Shell_NotifyIcon(NIM_MODIFY, &strNIData);
}
}
```

Three methods, StartAnimation(), StopAnimation(), and OnTimer (UINT), help animate the icon. Both StartAnimation() and StopAnimation() are part of the public interface for CAnimTrayIcon. OnTimer(UINT), as you may have guessed, responds to WM_TIMER messages. StartAnimation() starts the timer and sets the current icon index to 1. Remember, the icon ID m_vunIconIDs[0] specifies the *inactive* icon. Icons m_vunIconIDs[1] through m_vunIconIDs [m_vunIconIDs.size()-1] specify the *animation* icons.

```
void CAnimTrayIcon::StartAnimation()
{
   // If you assert here, you are calling this method
   // before calling Init.
   ASSERT( m_bInitialized );

   // If you assert here, you are trying to animate an
   // icon that doesn't have enough icon ids to even work.
   ASSERT( m_vunIconIDs.size() > 1 );
   if ( m_bInitialized )
   {
      m_unCurrentIcon = FIRST_ANIMATED_ICON;
      m_unTimerID = SetTimer( m_unTimerID,
        m_unTimerInterval, NULL );
   }
}
```

StopAnimation() kills the timer, shows the inactive icon, and sets the current icon index to 0.

```
void CAnimTrayIcon::StopAnimation()
{
   // If you assert here, you are calling this method
   // before calling Init.
```

```
   ASSERT( m_bInitialized );
   if ( m_bInitialized )
   {
      KillTimer( m_unTimerID );
      m_unCurrentIcon = INACTIVE_ICON;
      ShowIcon( m_unCurrentIcon );
   }
}
```

OnTimer() handles animating the icon. This method shows the next icon in the animation, advances the index for the next iteration, and exits.

```
void CAnimTrayIcon::OnTimer(UINT nIDEvent)
{
   // There should only be one timer for this class.
   // An assertion here indicates that assumption
   // is no longer valid.
   ASSERT( m_unTimerID == nIDEvent );
   ShowIcon( m_unCurrentIcon );
   ++m_unCurrentIcon;
   if ( m_unCurrentIcon >= m_vunIconIDs.size() )
   {
      m_unCurrentIcon = FIRST_ANIMATED_ICON;
   }
   CWnd::OnTimer(nIDEvent);
}
```

OnTimer() updates the icon by calling ShowIcon(m_unCurrentIcon). ShowIcon() modifies the icon in the system tray.

```
void CAnimTrayIcon::ShowIcon(UINT unIndex)
{
   // if the user has initialized the tray icon,
   // show the icon at the specified index.
   if ( m_bInitialized )
   {
      NOTIFYICONDATA strNIData;
      strNIData.cbSize = m_KnNotifyIconDataSize;
      strNIData.hWnd   = m_pParent->GetSafeHwnd();
      strNIData.uID    = m_unCallbackID;
      strNIData.uFlags = NIF_ICON;
      strNIData.hIcon = ::LoadIcon(
            AfxGetResourceHandle(),
            MAKEINTRESOURCE(m_vunIconIDs[unIndex]));
      Shell_NotifyIcon(NIM_MODIFY, &strNIData);
   }
}
```

Because CAnimTrayIcon was created as a child window, it is able to receive and process the WM_DESTROY message. As a result, it can clean up after itself. For this class, "cleaning up" means killing the timer, removing the icon from the system tray, and destroying the CAnimIconHelper window. If cleanup was performed in the CAnimTrayIcon destructor, the system tray may try to send messages to the parent window when the parent window no longer existed. I believe this decision helps prevent a lot of potential programming headaches for users of this class. For example, if the tray icon is not explicitly removed in code, that icon will remain in the tray after the window that owned it no longer exists. The icon does not disappear until the mouse goes over the icon and the system tray discovers that the owner of the icon no longer exists. This responsibility belongs to the CAnimTrayIcon, not the user of the class.

```
void CAnimTrayIcon::OnDestroy()
{
    if ( !IsStopped() )
    {
     KillTimer( m_unTimerID );
    }
    NOTIFYICONDATA strNIData;
     strNIData.cbSize = m_KnNotifyIconDataSize;
     strNIData.hWnd   = m_pParent->GetSafeHwnd();
     strNIData.uID    = m_unCallbackID;
     Shell_NotifyIcon(NIM_DELETE, &strNIData);
     m_pHelper->SendMessage( WM_CLOSE );
     CWnd::OnDestroy();
}
```

To demonstrate using the class, I wrote the application in Examples\Chapter 2\Animtray directory. Figure 2-9 shows the application in when running without the animation. Figure 2-10 shows the icon when it is animated. You may have noticed that this same class can display a single icon. To do so, supply the ID of one icon and never, ever call CAnimTray-Icon::StartAnimation().

Figure 2.9   *Application with the static icon displayed.*

Figure 2.10 *Application with the animation in motion.*

2.5 Summary

With the information presented in this chapter, you can add and remove buttons, manipulate the Start menu, and place icons into the system tray. The coverage skipped over how to flash the button in the taskbar. There are two functions, CWnd::FlashWindow() and the SDK function, FlashWindowEx(). When using CWnd::FlashWindow(), your window controls how frequently the taskbar button inverts its colors. FlashWindowEx() contains facilities to do this for you. Unfortunately, FlashWindowEx() is only available in the 5.0 version of the shell (Windows 2000 only). For more information, see Appendix B.

The two classes presented in this chapter, CTaskBar and CAnimTray-Icon, are contained in the TaskBar project on the CD. To use the classes in your own applications, simply link in TASKBAR.LIB to your application and remember to distribute TASKBAR.DLL.

Information about adding new Desk Bands to the taskbar is covered in detail in Chapter 13, "Explorer Bars and Desk Bands."

Application Desktop Toolbars

*F*or developers there are many ways to customize the Windows shell. The taskbar, covered in Chapter 2, is one example of an Application Desktop Toolbar, or appbar. Another well-known example is the Microsoft Office Shortcut Bar. An appbar can do anything you think might be useful. It can provide a way to quickly launch applications, display machine statistics, provide a menu, or anything else you can come up with.

Normally, you find little more than the taskbar and the Microsoft Office Shortcut Bar on the desktop. Why? I would guess that because the average user has only one monitor and only four edges to attach a taskbar to, there is no perceived payback in adding another appbar. With the multiple monitor operation now becoming a standard part of the operating system, look for the edge count to increase. Monitor prices are decreasing everyday. Eventually, users will start getting extra monitors instead of bigger monitors. This means that you should start to look at appbars and how they might enhance the applications you develop and maintain.

In this chapter, I will cover the following topics:

- Guidelines for creating appbars
- Explanation of how appbars work
- Explanation of AppBarLib and the MFC Application Desktop Toolbar AppWizard
- How to use the tools presented to build an appbar of your own

3.1   Guidelines for Creating Application Desktop Toolbars

Appbars provide a way to make a lot of functionality available directly from the user's desktop without requiring the application to leave icons everywhere. Just because an appbar brings a lot to the table, it is not always a good solution. For instance, an appbar would make a poor Internet browser or word processor. To help decide when an appbar makes sense, I have developed a set of questions to help me figure out when to use an appbar.

1. Does it make sense for the user to begin their interaction with the application with an appbar? The taskbar and Microsoft Office Shortcut Bar answer this question with a resounding *yes*. The taskbar provides value by allowing the user to switch from one task to another. The Office Shortcut Bar allows you to launch a number of applications without having to navigate the Start menu and without having to see your desktop.

2. Would a toolbar or dialog bar be a good way for your user to interact with your application(s)? Here, you need to analyze how you intend to display the information to the user. It should be able to be expressed well in a vertical and/or horizontal column. If your design looks bad when doing this, just forget it. The shell does not prohibit you from making an appbar the same size as the screen. However, doing this will give you far fewer users.

3. Will your target user have a large number of appbars in use, prohibiting the addition of "just one more"? Your company may already supply appbars with some of its other products. Maybe some of your company's partners believe appbars are the best way to enhance the UI. I expect that most of the time you will find that the target user has a couple of free edges for appbars. But if they do not, then they probably will not want to sacrifice more screen real estate for you. If you give the appbar the ability to autohide, you will not need to worry about users with smaller monitors.

4. Does an appbar "feel" like the right thing to create? To answer this question, you may actually have to prototype something just to test it out. I rely on my own instincts to identify good and bad ideas. If something no longer seems like a good idea, I try again. Because user interface design is still more art than science, you have the benefit of being able to use your instincts as your guide. Add to your own instinct some quality peer review and you can harness the instincts of others. If nothing else, you will feel more confident that you are doing the right thing.

Once you have answered all these questions, you must understand what appbar features the user will expect.

- The ability to drag the appbar from one edge to another. Depending on the bar's layout, it may make sense to limit the edges to top/bottom or left/right.

- The appbar should be able to float. The taskbar has an excuse for not floating—its relatively constant location means less confusion for one of the most important windows on the desktop. If a floating appbar would make life difficult for your users, do not let it float.
- The appbar will support auto-hide. Users prize their screen real estate. Do not make your users mad by taking that space away from them.
- The user should be able to get a menu by right clicking on the appbar. At a minimum, this menu should allow the user to close the appbar window.

3.2 How Appbars Work

Now that you understand what an appbar does, it is time to understand how to implement one. On MSDN, there is only one article that attempts to explain appbars in their entirety: "Extend the Windows 95 Shell with Application Desktop Toolbars" by Jeffrey Richter. As a result, a lot of my information comes from Mr. Richter as well as from tinkering, and learning what works. In order to understand appbars, you need to understand the SHAppBarMessage() API and how and when to position the appbar.

3.2.1 The SHAppBarMessage() API

SHAppBarMessage() has the following prototype:

```
UINT SHAppBarMessage( DWORD dwMessage, PAPPBARDATA pData );
```

The pointer parameter, pData, is a pointer to an APPBARDATA structure. The structure looks like this:

```
typedef struct _AppBarData
{
    DWORD cbSize; // always set to sizeof( APPBARDATA )
    HWND hWnd;     // HWND of the appbar in question
    UINT uCallbackMessage; // Message sent to the appbar
         // for the to ABN_XXX messages
    UINT uEdge;    // Identifies the edge the bar is
         // attaching to: ABE_TOP, ABE_BOTTOM, ABE_LEFT,
         // or ABE_RIGHT
    RECT rc;       // Identifies the appbar's rectangle
    LPARAM lParam;// Depends on the value of dwMessage
         // in the call to SHAppBarMessage()
} APPBARDATA, *PAPPBARDATA;
```

The interpretation of the parameters and return value depends on the value of dwMessage. dwMessage can take on any one of ten values.

Message	**ABM_ACTIVATE**
Usage	Notifies the system that an appbar has been activated
hWnd	Required. Because the appbar itself sends this message, it should know the value of hWnd.
uCallBackMessage	Ignored
uEdge	Ignored
rc	Ignored
lParam	Ignored
return value	Ignored

Message	**ABM_GETAUTOHIDEBAR**
Usage	Retrieves the handle of an autohide appbar associated with an edge of the screen
hWnd	Required. Currently, this parameter is ignored, but it should be set. Supposedly, future versions of the shell will require this member to be set. Set it to the value of your appbar's HWND for now. If you are querying the shell for a list of autohide appbars and do not have a valid HWND to use, you should be safe. Just make sure to add a comment stating that the code may start to break if Windows starts requiring the member to be set.
uCallBackMessage	Ignored
uEdge	Edge that you want to know about
rc	Ignored
lParam	Ignored
return value	HWND of the autohide appbar attached to the specified edge. If no autohide appbars are attached to that edge, SPAppBarMessage() will return NULL.

Message	**ABM_GETSTATE**
Usage	Retrieves the autohide and alwaysontop states of the taskbar
hWnd	Same information as in ABM_GETAUTOHIDEBAR
uCallBackMessage	Ignored
uEdge	Ignored
rc	Ignored

lParam	Ignored
return value	Returns the states in a bit mask.
	To see if the taskbar is autohide, bitwise and the return value with ABS_AUTOHIDE.
	To see if the taskbar is always on top, bitwise and the return value with ABS_ALWAYSONTOP.
	The taskbar may be both autohide and always on top. As a result, once you have the return value, you should evaluate these values independently.

Message	**ABM_GETTASKBARPOS**
Usage	Retrieves the bounding rectangle of the taskbar
hWnd	Same information as in ABM_GETAUTOHIDEBAR
uCallBackMessage	Ignored
uEdge	Ignored
rc	Ignored
lParam	Ignored
return value	Returns TRUE if successful, FALSE otherwise. If SHAppBarMessage() returned TRUE, then the rc member of the APPBARDATA structure will be populated with the taskbar's bounding rectangle.

Message	**ABM_NEW**
Usage	Registers a new appbar and specifies the message identifier that the system should use to send it notification messages. An appbar must send this message before sending any other appbar messages. If you don't do this, the shell will not even pretend to recognize your appbar as anything other than a plain-old window.
hWnd	Required. Because the appbar itself sends this message, it should know the value of hWnd. This message should get called immediately after successfully creating the window.
uCallBackMessage	Names the message that the system will use to pass along ABN_XXX notifications
uEdge	Ignored
rc	Ignored

(continued)

Message	ABM_NEW
lParam	Ignored
return value	Returns TRUE if the appbar is successfully registered. If the SHAppBarMessage() returns FALSE, you are missing a required parameter or you have already registered the appbar. Registering the appbar many times should do no harm. However, I wouldn't recommend doing it; there may be unanticipated side effects.

Message	ABM_QUERYPOS
Usage	Requests a size and screen position for an appbar. When the request is made, the message proposes a screen edge and a bounding rectangle for the appbar. The system adjusts the bounding rectangle so that the appbar does not interfere with the Windows taskbar or any other appbars. As of this writing, it is not readily apparent how this relates to multiple monitor systems. This message should be sent before positioning the appbar.
hWnd	Required. Because the appbar itself sends this message, it should know the value of hWnd.
uCallBackMessage	Ignored
uEdge	Specifies the proposed edge for the appbar
rc	Specifies the proposed size of the appbar. You can also specify the monitor's rectangle and then let the shell reduce the rectangle down to the area available to your appbar. This comes in handy when an appbar is already attached to the edge you are interested in.
lParam	Ignored
return value	Always returns TRUE

Message	ABM_REMOVE
Usage	Unregisters an appbar by removing it from the system's internal list. The system no longer sends notification messages to the appbar or prevents other applications from using the screen area occupied by the appbar. Call this method in the appbar's WM_DESTROY message handler.
hWnd	Required. Because the appbar itself sends this message, it should know the value of hWnd.

uCallBackMessage	Ignored
uEdge	Ignored
rc	Ignored
lParam	Ignored
return value	Always returns TRUE

Message	**ABM_SETAUTOHIDEBAR**
Usage	Registers or unregisters an autohide appbar for an edge of the screen. The shell does not slide the appbar on and off the screen. The appbar has to provide these effects. The appbar also has to guess how big an area it will occupy on the edge of the screen. I recommend keeping at least a two pixel width or height, depending on the edge the appbar is attached to.
hWnd	Required. Because the appbar itself sends this message, it should know the value of hWnd.
uCallBackMessage	Ignored
uEdge	Specifies the screen edge related to the autohide bar
rc	Ignored
lParam	TRUE to register the window as an autohide appbar, FALSE to unregister it. The shell makes the appbar keep these values up to date. As a result, if your appbar moves from one edge to another, it must remove itself from the original edge and register itself on the other one. Failure to do so will result in the shell thinking that a given window is autohide on multiple edges.
return value	TRUE if successful, FALSE otherwise. If invoking SHAppBarMessage() with this message generates a FALSE return value, make sure that you update the appbar's position and assumptions about autohide. FALSE means that an autohide appbar has already docked to that edge.

Message	**ABM_SETPOS**
Usage	Sets the size and screen position of an appbar. The message specifies a screen edge and the

(continued)

Message	ABM_SETPOS
	bounding rectangle for the appbar. The system may adjust the bounding rectangle so that the appbar does not interfere with the Windows taskbar or any other appbars. If you have an auto-hide appbar, use this message to tell the shell that your window only occupies a two pixel deep part of the edge it is attached to. If the user just floated the appbar, simply adjust the related rectangle to zero size. This way, you do not have to re-register the appbar down the road.
hWnd	Required. Because the appbar itself sends this message, it should know the value of hWnd.
uCallBackMessage	Ignored
uEdge	Specifies the edge the appbar is getting attached to
rc	Specifies the rectangle that the appbar would like to occupy
lParam	Ignored
return value	Always returns TRUE

Message	ABM_WINDOWPOSCHANGED
Usage	Notifies the system when an appbar's position has changed. An appbar should call SHAppBarMessage() using this message in response to the WM_WINDOWPOSCHANGED message.
hWnd	Required. Because the appbar itself sends this message, it should know the value of hWnd.
uCallBackMessage	Ignored
uEdge	Ignored
rc	Ignored
lParam	Ignored
return value	Always returns TRUE

Overall, the shell provides a reasonably clean way for appbars and the shell to communicate. The shell appears to contain two lists for appbar information. I have not found anything documenting that the shell uses two lists. Instead, I found this through experimentation. One list contains information regarding what windows are appbar windows. The other list remembers which appbars have the autohide attribute set. One of the first bugs I had to tackle with respect to autohide appbars involved keeping these lists in sync. I discovered that if I made the taskbar autohide and my appbar autohide, I could produce some strange behavior. By moving my taskbar to the three edges not occupied by the taskbar on the primary monitor, I made those edges unavailable to an autohide taskbar. In order to keep this from happening, an autohide appbar must tell the shell that it no longer wants to be autohide on the edge it just left. I hesitate to call this annoyance a bug. Nevertheless, I do not care for this part of the shell's design. It does not make sense that the shell cannot figure out that the appbar has moved and update its internal information accordingly. Even on a system with 100 monitors, the shell would only have to check 400 edges to determine if the HWND had movedI doubt that anyone will ever attach 100 monitors to a Windows box.

Let's continue our look at SHAppBarMessage(). Of the messages for SHAppBarMessage(), only one, ABM_NEW, requires uCallbackMessage to be set. Perhaps the shell team has their reasons, but they could have eliminated this struct member by using the general-purpose lParam instead. Upon further examination, you will see that only one message uses lParam, ABM_SET-AUTOHIDEBAR. So much for a general-purpose parameter! (Sorry for stepping onto the soapbox, but I believe that pointing these things out will help all of us do a better job in the future.) Anyhow, back to uCallbackMessage. uCallbackMessage specifies the message the shell will call with any one of four notification messages. The handler for uCallbackMessage will have the following message map entry and function prototype:

```
ON_MESSAGE( g_KnCallBack, OnAppBarMessage )
afx_msg LRESULT OnAppBarMessage(WPARAM wparam, LPARAM lparam);
```

The wparam specifies the ABN_XXX message coming in. The message handler interprets the lparam argument with respect to the message. wparam can have four possible values: ABN_FULLSCREENAPP, ABN_POSCHANGED, ABN_STATECHANGE, or ABN_WINDOWARRANGE. Of these four messages, ABN_FULLSCREENAPP and ABN_WINDOWARRANGE interpret lparam. The messages have the following meanings:

- ABN_FULLSCREENAPP: This message notifies the appbar that a full screen application is opening or closing. For opening full screen applications, the shell sets lparam to TRUE. For closing full screen applications, lparam is FALSE.
- ABN_POSCHANGED: The shell sends this message when changes to the shell have the potential to affect an appbar. The shell triggers this message in response to changes in the taskbar's size, position, and visibility state, as well as the addition, removal, or resizing of another appbar on the same side of the screen. An appbar should respond to this message by verifying its size and position, resizing itself if needed.

- ABN_STATECHANGE: The shell fires this message whenever the taskbar's autohide or always on top state changes. If the appbar wants to mimic the state of the taskbar, it can use this message to do so.
- ABN_WINDOWARRANGE: The shell sends this message to notify the appbar that the user has selected the Cascade, Tile Horizontally, or Tile Vertically command from the taskbar's context menu. The shell sends the message twice. Before arranging the windows, lparam is set to TRUE. After the shell finishes arranging the windows, lparam is set to FALSE. The appbar should hide itself when lparam is TRUE. Upon receiving FALSE, the appbar should show itself again. The documentation states that this mechanism was put in to help the appbar avoid being arranged by the shell. I did not add this functionality until I reviewed the documentation for information I may have missed. (Not having this functionality did no harm; having the functionality has not changed things.)

Now you should have a good understanding of SHAppBarMessage() and how it establishes a means of communication between an appbar and the shell. The next big trick is figuring out where and when to move an appbar.

3.2.2   Positioning the Appbar

Depending on the decisions you make about your appbar, the user will be able to place it on

1. Only the vertical edges of the monitor
2. Only the horizontal edges of the monitor
3. All edges of the monitor

Additionally, you may want to allow the user to float the appbar à la the Microsoft Office Shortcut Bar. By understanding how the taskbar and Microsoft Office Shortcut Bar handle these situations, you can figure out how Microsoft wants you to use appbars. This involves understanding how to divide the monitor. In the case of floating appbars, you must also know where the line is drawn that tells when an appbar should be docked or floating. The appbar moves whenever the user drags the appbar to a new location using the mouse. The visual manifestation of the movement depends on the edges the appbar docks on and whether or not the appbar can float. If the appbar cannot float, it will appear to jump from edge to edge. If the appbar can float, it will jump from the edge to its floating position, and back to an edge again (if the user keeps dragging it).

The monitor is divided based on what edges the appbar can dock on. If the appbar can dock on the top or bottom, you can divide the screen horizontally. If the appbar can dock on the left or right, you can divide the screen vertically. Lastly, if the appbar can dock on any edge, an 'X' divides the screen. See Figure 3-1 for a visual description. As a programmer, this means you need to come up with some mechanism to figure out where the appbar should go and how it should look as the user drags it from one location to another. With the addition of multiple monitor support in Windows, applications need to be able to handle new situations. For example, application windows can now have valid negative coordinates with the default coordinate-mapping mode. Guess what. Appbars must be able to dock on any edge of any monitor. This may seem obvious to many of you. Keep in mind that many appbars were written using Jeffrey Richter's MSDN article.[1] This article suggested using the GetSystemMetrics() API with SM_CXSCREEN, and SM_CYSCREEN to figure out the area of the screen that is available for an

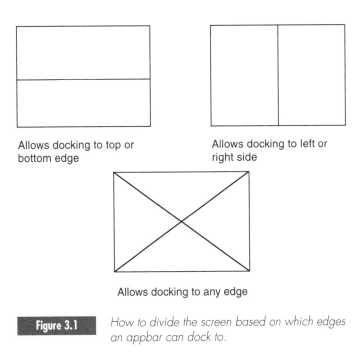

Allows docking to top or
bottom edge

Allows docking to left or
right side

Allows docking to any edge

Figure 3.1   *How to divide the screen based on which edges an appbar can dock to.*

1. Richter, Jeffrey. "Extend the Windows Shell with Application Desktop Toolbars," MSDN

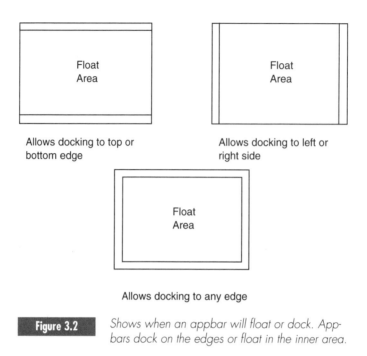

Allows docking to top or
bottom edge

Allows docking to left or
right side

Allows docking to any edge

Figure 3.2   *Shows when an appbar will float or dock. Appbars dock on the edges or float in the inner area.*

appbar. To summarize this part of his article, Mr. Richter suggests using the
total screen area combined with a call to SHAppBarMessage(ABM_QUERY-
POS, &appbardata) to find the area of the screen not in use by appbars. The
documentation for the GetSystemMetrics() values reveals that they return the
width and height of the primary display monitor. Not very useful for appbars
that want to reside on other monitors, is it? When the article was written, the
assumptions about the monitor were valid. MULTIMON.H did not even exist
at the time. So, if you have an appbar and want to enable it to move off the
primary monitor, you have some work to do.

    With floating appbars, the above information still applies. However, you
now have a region within the edges that allows the appbar to float. Because
the taskbar does not float, I relied on the Microsoft Office Shortcut Bar to figure this out. The floating region appears to exist within a vertical scrollbar's
width of the monitor area not occupied by appbars. Figure 3-2 shows this a
little better. Within your application, you use this information to decide when
to dock the appbar and when to float the appbar.

    From my experience, I found that understanding what the shell expects
of an appbar and what the appbar needs to do in order to fulfill those expectations is the easy part. ***The devil is in the details*** went through my mind time
and again while trying to get those details correct.

3.3   An Application Desktop Toolbar Library

While designing the library, I spent about two days pacing in front of a white board and walking the streets of Hartford, Wisconsin, trying to decide what should be done for users of the library and what the users themselves should be responsible for. In the end, I made the user responsible for almost nothing related to appbars. They only have to draw the appbar in the resource editor and set the tab order to the order in which they want to see things displayed. However, I put in lots of virtual functions to allow them to change behavior on a whim.

Figure 3-3 shows the class design of the appbar library. CAppBarMonitor and AppBarRegion help with maintaining monitor geometry and determining appbar positioning. CAppBarLayout has the thankless job of maintaining the appbar's layout as it moves from side to side and when it floats. CAppBarLayout works best for the average, simple appbar. If you want to get into the functionality and features of the Microsoft Office Shortcut Bar, the architecture leaves an opportunity for you as well. That's right, you can derive a class from CAppBarLayout and do the layout manipulations yourself.

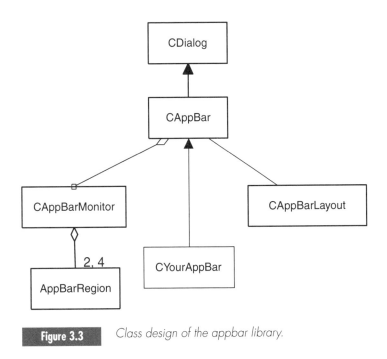

Figure 3.3   *Class design of the appbar library.*

Finally, we have CAppBar. CAppBar implements all the code you could ever want to make a simple appbar work. It handles floating, discovering the monitor layout, and coordinating the jobs of CAppBarMonitor and CAppBarLayout (or derived versions of CAppBarLayout).

Let's start out with a description of the various classes and their jobs. AppBarRegion and CAppBarMonitor work together to remember the desktop's layout. AppBarRegion has the following declaration:

```
// Class AppBarRegion:
//  Depending on the sides an appbar can dock to
//  this structure defines the areas that correspond
//  to a given edge of the monitor.  ie if the
//  appbar's top-left corner is in the CRgn m_region
//  it docks to the edge defined in m_unEdge.
struct AppBarRegion
{
    AppBarRegion();
    AppBarRegion( const AppBarRegion& rhs );
    AppBarRegion& operator =( const AppBarRegion& rhs );
    CRgn m_region;
    UINT m_unEdge;
};
```

CAppBarMonitor has this declaration:

```
class CAppBarMonitor
{
public:
    // Copy constructor
    CAppBarMonitor( const CAppBarMonitor& rhs );

    // rect: Rectangle that this monitor represents
    // bLeftRight: Does appbar support vertical docking?
    // bTopBottom: Does appbar support horizontal docking?
    CAppBarMonitor(const CRect& rect,
                  bool bLeftRight,
                  bool bTopBottom);
    virtual ~CAppBarMonitor();
    CAppBarMonitor& operator=(const CAppBarMonitor& rhs );

    // Tells the object to fill in its data members with
    // useful info.  Call this before any other data members.
    void Init();

    // Tells you if the appbar should float or dock and if it
    // should dock, tells you the edge.  This returns:
    // ABE_TOP, ABE_BOTTOM, ABE_LEFT, ABE_RIGHT, or ABE_FLOAT.
    UINT GetEdge( const CPoint& point, HWND hWnd,
        bool bFloat = false );
```

```
    // Returns the screen rect that represents this monitor.
    CRect GetRect();

private:
    std::list<AppBarRegion> m_rgnList;
    CRect m_rect;
    bool m_bLeftRight;
    bool m_bTopBottom;
};
```

CAppBarMonitor has a list of AppBarRegions. An AppBarRegion represents a portion of the screen. Referring back to Figures 3-1 and 3-2, you see that an appbar must have a way of knowing what it should be doing when it is dragged to a given position on the screen. In the hierarchy presented in Figure 3-3, CAppBarMonitor contains the smarts about when the appbar should dock or float at any given point within a specific monitor. Note that CAppBar must figure out which CAppBarMonitor to use. CAppBar figures this out by seeing if the point in question lies within the monitor's rectangle via CAppBarMonitor::GetRect(). AppBarRegion represents the shapes shown in Figure 3-1. Given that we have no guarantee that the shape will be rectangular, AppBarRegion uses a CRgn to record the area.

CRgn, AppBarRegion::m_region's type, does not define a const operator=. In order to copy a region, one must invoke the non-const CRgn::CopyRgn(). With much of my code, I usually define an operator= and the copy constructor to take const references to the item being copied. When possible, I perform an additional maintenance enhancement by using operator= to do the work in the copy constructor. With respect to the CRgn member, m_region, this means that I had to either write the copy constructor and operator= using non-const arguments or that I had to come up with something else. When you need to remove the const-ness of anything, remove it using const_cast. Doing this with the pointer to the CRgn results in fairly straightforward code.

```
AppBarRegion::AppBarRegion( const AppBarRegion& rhs )
{
    // This allows the copying code to be maintained
    // in one place.  This sacrifices constructor speed
    // for maintainability and minimizing the
    // potential for bugs.
    *this = rhs;
}

AppBarRegion& AppBarRegion::operator =( const AppBarRegion&
    rhs )
{
    // Create a region just so that the CRgn::m_hObject
    // member will be valid.  Basically, I am working
    // around some parts of MFC.
    m_region.CreateRectRgn( 0, 0, 1, 1 );
```

```
    m_region.CopyRgn( const_cast<CRgn*>(&(rhs.m_region)) );
    m_unEdge = rhs.m_unEdge;
    return *this;
}
```

CAppBar contains a list of CAppBarMonitors. CAppBar creates the list in CAppBar::OnInitDialog(). It uses the EnumDisplayMonitors() API to get all the monitors. EnumDisplayMonitors() has the following prototype:

```
BOOL EnumDisplayMonitors (
    HDC hdc, // handle to a display device context
    LPCRECT lprcClip, // specifies a clipping rectangle
    MONITORENUMPROC lpfnEnum, // pointer to a callback
        // function
    LPARAM lparam // data passed to the callback function
);
```

The MONITORENUMPROC callback function has this signature:

```
BOOL CALLBACK MonitorEnumProc(
    HMONITOR hMonitor,    // handle to display monitor
    HDC hdcMonitor,       // handle to monitor-appropriate
                          // device context
    LPRECT lprcMonitor,   // pointer to monitor intersection
                          // rectangle
    LPARAM dwData         // data passed from
                          // EnumDisplayMonitors
);
```

CAppBar creates the list of CAppBarMonitor objects by enumerating the monitors attached to the system. In order to make monitor enumeration backwards compatible, the file MULTIMON.H links to the multiple monitor functions at run-time. If the implementations of multiple monitor functions cannot be found in the Windows DLLs, the functions in MULTIMON.H return data for a single monitor system. The multiple monitor functions cannot be found when the user is running Windows 95 or any version of Windows NT before Windows 2000. These earlier versions of Windows do not ship with the multiple monitor DLLs. When the function definitions in MULTIMON.H try to locate the real multiple monitor functions via Load Library() and GetProcAddress(), the functions that the MULTIMON.H headers expect to exist cannot be found. To allow the magic to happen, define COMPILE_MULTIMON_STUBS before including MULTIMON.H.

```
#ifndef COMPILE_MULTIMON_STUBS
    #define COMPILE_MULTIMON_STUBS
#endif // COMPILE_MULTIMON_STUBS

#include <multimon.h>
```

The collaboration between CAppBar and CAppBarMonitor works something like this:

1. In CAppBar::OnInitDialog(), CAppBar calls EnumDisplayMonitors().

2. For each monitor that is enumerated, the callback function tells CAppBar to add a CAppBarMonitor to the list by calling CAppBar::AddMonitor().

3. In CAppBar::AddMonitor(), a new CAppBarMonitor gets created. CAppBarMonitor takes some configuration information in its constructor, the rectangle that represents the monitor as well as the edges supported by the CAppBar.

4. CAppBar calls CAppBarMonitor::Init() here. CAppBarMonitor stores the various regions that correspond to the edges supported by the CAppBar.

5. Later, when CAppBar needs to know what monitor a given point lies in, CAppBar iterates through its list of CAppBarMonitors, calling CAppBarMonitor::GetRect().PtInRect(point) to determine the monitor of interest. Then, CAppBar may simply store the CAppBarMonitor's rectangle or call CAppBarMonitor::GetEdge().

Here's the code that implements steps one and two:

```
BOOL CAppBar::OnInitDialog()
{
    CDialog::OnInitDialog();

    // Set the icon for this dialog.  The framework does this
    // automatically when the application's main window is not
    // a dialog
    SetIcon(m_hIcon, TRUE);   // Set big icon:bBigIcon=TRUE
    SetIcon(m_hIcon, FALSE); // Set small icon:bBigIcon=FALSE

    EnumDisplayMonitors( NULL,
                         NULL,
                         MonitorEnumProc,
                         reinterpret_cast<LPARAM>(this) );

    // For some reason, the code works best when
    // initialization happens after OnInitDialog finishes.
    PostMessage( g_KnCallBack, ABN_INIT );

    // Setup the timer so that we can make the autohide
    // feature work.
    SetTimer( g_KnAutoHideEvent, g_KnAutoHideInterval, NULL );

    return TRUE;
}
```

```
BOOL CALLBACK MonitorEnumProc(
    HMONITOR hMonitor,
    HDC hdcMonitor,
    LPRECT lprcMonitor,
    LPARAM dwData
)
{
    // Cast the dwData (essentially a void*) to a CAppBar*.
    CAppBar* pDlg = reinterpret_cast<CAppBar*>(dwData);
    bool bRetVal = false;
    if ( pDlg )
    {
        // Add the monitor to the list
        pDlg->AddMonitor( CRect( lprcMonitor ) );
        bRetVal = true;
    }
    return bRetVal;
}
```

Notice that the call to EnumDisplayMonitors() passes a pointer to the appbar so that the MonitorEnumProc() can then tell the appbar to add the newly discovered monitor to the list. The callback could have been a static member function. As you know, static member functions cannot call non-static member functions. As a result, I still would have had to pass the pointer to the instantiation of CAppBar to the callback function. The only real benefit is that I could have made AddMonitor() a private or protected member function. In the end, this became a "flip a coin" decision.

Steps three and four get implemented with this code:

```
bool CAppBar::SupportsTopBottom()
{
    return true;
}

bool CAppBar::SupportsLeftRight()
{
    return true;
}
```

CAppBar::SupportsTopBottom() and CAppBar::SupportsLeftRight() are virtual functions. Override these to change the behavior of your derived class. If you want to disallow docking on the top or bottom, override SupportsTop-Bottom() to return false. You can do the same thing with SupportsLeftRight() to disable docking on the vertical edges of the monitor. The code for steps three and four continue:

```
void CAppBar::AddMonitor(const CRect& rect)
{
    // Create a new monitor object.
```

```
    CAppBarMonitor appBarMonitor( rect, SupportsLeftRight(),
        SupportsTopBottom() );

    // Have the monitor examine itself and discover how
    // to set up its regions.
    appBarMonitor.Init();

    // Add the monitor to the list.
    m_monitorList.push_back( appBarMonitor );
}

CAppBarMonitor::CAppBarMonitor( const CRect& rect,
    bool bLeftRight, bool bTopBottom):
    m_rect( rect ),
    m_bLeftRight( bLeftRight ),
    m_bTopBottom( bTopBottom )
{
    // If this asserts, you have an appbar that perpetually
    // floats. I like to call those dialog boxes.
    ASSERT( m_bLeftRight || m_bTopBottom );
}

void CAppBarMonitor::Init()
{
    // Allow the monitor to re-initialize when needed.
    m_rgnList.clear();

    if ( m_bLeftRight && m_bTopBottom )
    {
        // Allow docking on all four edges.  This
        // Means we divide the monitor into four triangles,
        // Base on the sides, points meet in the middle.
        AppBarRegion leftTriangle;
        AppBarRegion rightTriangle;
        AppBarRegion topTriangle;
        AppBarRegion bottomTriangle;

        // Assign the edges.
        leftTriangle.m_unEdge = ABE_LEFT;
        rightTriangle.m_unEdge = ABE_RIGHT;
        topTriangle.m_unEdge = ABE_TOP;
        bottomTriangle.m_unEdge = ABE_BOTTOM;

        // Calculate the five points used in the four
        // triangles
        CPoint middlePoint( m_rect.left + m_rect.Width() / 2,
                        m_rect.top + m_rect.Height() / 2 );
        CPoint upperLeftCorner( m_rect.TopLeft() );
        CPoint lowerLeftCorner( m_rect.left, m_rect.bottom );
        CPoint upperRightCorner( m_rect.right, m_rect.top );
```

```
    CPoint lowerRightCorner( m_rect.BottomRight() );

    // Create the list of points that make up
    // the four triangles.
    CPoint leftArray[] = {upperLeftCorner,
                          middlePoint,
                          lowerLeftCorner};
    CPoint rightArray[] = {upperRightCorner,
                           middlePoint,
                           lowerRightCorner};
    CPoint topArray[] = {upperLeftCorner,
                         middlePoint,
                         upperRightCorner};
    CPoint bottomArray[] = {lowerLeftCorner,
                            middlePoint,
                            lowerRightCorner};

    // Create the actual regions
    leftTriangle.m_region.CreatePolygonRgn(
        leftArray, 3, ALTERNATE );
    rightTriangle.m_region.CreatePolygonRgn(
        rightArray, 3, ALTERNATE );
    topTriangle.m_region.CreatePolygonRgn(
        topArray, 3, ALTERNATE );
    bottomTriangle.m_region.CreatePolygonRgn(
        bottomArray, 3, ALTERNATE );

    // Add the regions to the list of regions
    // for the monitor object.
    m_rgnList.push_back( leftTriangle );
    m_rgnList.push_back( rightTriangle );
    m_rgnList.push_back( topTriangle );
    m_rgnList.push_back( bottomTriangle );
}
else if ( m_bLeftRight && !m_bTopBottom )
{
    // Only docks on the left or right sides.
    AppBarRegion leftRgn;
    AppBarRegion rightRgn;

    // Indicate the edges the regions correspond to.
    leftRgn.m_unEdge = ABE_LEFT;
    rightRgn.m_unEdge = ABE_RIGHT;

    // Find the middle of the monitor (between left
    // and right)
    int nMidPoint = m_rect.top + (m_rect.Width() / 2);

    // Create two rectangles and add them to
```

```
        // the monitor's list of regions.
        leftRgn.m_region.CreateRectRgn( m_rect.left,
            m_rect.top, nMidPoint, m_rect.bottom );
        rightRgn.m_region.CreateRectRgn( nMidPoint,
            m_rect.top, m_rect.right, m_rect.bottom );
        m_rgnList.push_back( leftRgn );
        m_rgnList.push_back( rightRgn );
    }
    else if ( !m_bLeftRight && m_bTopBottom )
    {
        // The appbar can only dock to the top or bottom
        // edge of the monitor
        AppBarRegion topRgn;
        AppBarRegion bottomRgn;

        // Indicate the edges the regions correspond to.
        topRgn.m_unEdge = ABE_TOP;
        bottomRgn.m_unEdge = ABE_BOTTOM;

        // Find the middle of the monitor (between top
        // and bottom)
        int nMidPoint = m_rect.top + (m_rect.Height() / 2);
        // Create two rectangles and add them to
        // the monitor's list of regions.
        topRgn.m_region.CreateRectRgn( m_rect.left,
            m_rect.top, m_rect.right, nMidPoint );
        bottomRgn.m_region.CreateRectRgn( m_rect.left,
            nMidPoint, m_rect.right, m_rect.bottom );
        m_rgnList.push_back( topRgn );
        m_rgnList.push_back( bottomRgn );
    }
    else
    {
        // If this asserts, you have an appbar that
        // perpetually floats. I like to call those dialog
        // boxes.
        ASSERT( false );
    }
}
```

Looking at CAppBarMonitor::Init(), you may begin to wonder why I have so many variables in use. After all, couldn't most of the information be stored in arrays? I had a real bear of a time getting the logic correct in my head. My white board was loaded with drawings as I tried to figure out how to tell the program to get the geometry correct. Once I had the ideas straight, I found that I could keep everything consistent by expressing the information the way that I saw the problem. As depicted in Figure 3-1, the regions that change the side the appbar docks to can be expressed in one of three ways:

1. The appbar docks to any edge.
2. The appbar docks to the horizontal edges.
3. The appbar docks to the vertical edges.

As a result, I broke CAppBarMonitor::Init() into three sections, each with its own variables. I wound up with code that correctly and efficiently expresses the various regions that an appbar would need to know about.

Implementing step 5 became very easy. Because the code heavily relies on existing classes, I was able to keep the math requirements to a minimum. CAppBarMonitor::GetEdge (const CPoint &point, HWND hWnd, bool bFloat) tries to figure out what the appbar should look like (docked or floating) if it is at a specific point. The hWnd parameter allows CAppBarMonitor to reduce the known size of the monitor to a rectangle representing the available workspace. Once CAppBarMonitor knows the size of the workspace, it can go on its way.

Next, CAppBarMonitor must determine whether or not the appbar should float. If the caller sets bFloat to false, this becomes a moot point. Assuming that GetEdge() determined that the appbar can be docked, GetEdge() then checks to see which AppBarRegion contains the passed in point. Once a region is found, GetEdge() returns the m_unEdge member corresponding to the AppBarRegion that contained the point. The magic looks like this:

```
UINT CAppBarMonitor::GetEdge(const CPoint &point,
                              HWND hWnd, bool bFloat)
{
    // At the start, we don't know which edge.
    UINT retval = ABE_UNKNOWN;

    // Let the caller know we cannot get the edge
    // for a point that is not on this monitor
    ASSERT( GetRect().PtInRect( point ) );
    if ( !GetRect().PtInRect( point ) )
    {
        // We assert, but we play nice if the user
        // just did not care in debug code.
        return retval;
    }
    CRect rect = m_rect;

    APPBARDATA appBarData;
    ZeroMemory( &appBarData, sizeof( appBarData ) );

    // The user has picked the correct monitor.  Now we
    // should check the amount of space available on the
    // monitor.
    appBarData.cbSize = sizeof( appBarData );
```

```
appBarData.hWnd = hWnd;

// Some edge must be filled in and ABE_LEFT works as
// well as the others.
appBarData.uEdge = ABE_LEFT;
appBarData.rc = rect;
SHAppBarMessage( ABM_QUERYPOS, &appBarData );

// We originally assumed the whole monitor was
// available.  Refine the assumption to how much
// space we know is available.
rect = appBarData.rc;

if ( bFloat )
{
    // Get the width of a scroll bar
    // Use this width to see if we are close enough to
    // dock (since the appbar allows floating).
    int nOffset = GetSystemMetrics( SM_CXVSCROLL );

    // Next, what we really want to do is see if
    // we are floating.  If we aren't floating,
    // then we can use the rest of the code to
    // pick the correct triangle.
    retval = ABE_FLOAT;

    // If the monitor is setup for docking on
    // the top or bottom edges, see if we
    // are close enough to dock.
    if ( m_bTopBottom )
    {
        if ( ( rect.top + nOffset ) >= point.y )
        {
            retval = ABE_UNKNOWN;
        }
        else if ( ( rect.bottom - nOffset ) <= point.y )
        {
            retval = ABE_UNKNOWN;
        }
    }

    // If the monitor is setup for docking on
    // the left or right edges, see if we
    // are close enough to dock.
    if ( m_bLeftRight )
    {
        // If we already decided that we will dock to
        // an edge, skip this.  Otherwise, keep going.
        // We may be sufficiently close to the left
```

```
            // and right edge to not know what side of the
            // diagonal we are on.  That's why ABE_UNKNOWN
            // is used.
            if ( ABE_FLOAT == retval )
            {
                // We aren't within the top or bottom band.
                // Let's see if we are in the left or right
                // band.
                if ( ( rect.left + nOffset ) >= point.x )
                {
                    retval = ABE_UNKNOWN;
                }
                else if ( ( rect.right - nOffset ) <=
                    point.x )
                {
                    retval = ABE_UNKNOWN;
                }
            }
        }
    }

    if ( ABE_UNKNOWN == retval )
    {
        // We know that we are close enough to one edge to
        // dock.  Let's see what region we are in (and
        // what edge we dock to).
        for ( std::list<AppBarRegion>::iterator it =
            m_rgnList.begin(); it != m_rgnList.end(); ++it )
        {
            if ( it->m_region.PtInRegion( point ) )
            {
                // Each region corresponds to one edge.
                // We found the edge, so we are done.
                retval = it->m_unEdge;
                break;
            }
        }
    }
    return retval;
}
```

By now, we have seen a lot of the functionality that CAppBar provides, yet we have no idea what it really looks like. CAppBar contains no data or functions that a derived class cannot access. I thought about this design decision for quite some time. In the end, I decided that derived classes should have access to everything. On the flip side, I did not want the user having to do too much work. So, use what you like, avoid what you do not like. I may have over-engineered some other pieces. For example, instead of passing in a litany of constructor arguments that modify the ability to dock and float, I added virtual functions to answer those questions. The code also avoids use of pure virtual functions. For every virtual function, I had a good guess as to what the normal implementation would look like. If I guessed wrong, please send me e-mail. That said, here is CAppBar in all its glory:

```
class CAppBar : public CDialog
{
// Construction
public:
    CAppBar(CAppBarLayout* pLayout, UINT unID, CWnd* pParent
        = NULL);
    virtual ~CAppBar();

    // Primarily used by CAppBarLayout
    void SetCalculatedSize( const CRect& rect );

    // By default, CAppBar returns true for all
    // of these
    virtual bool SupportsLeftRight();
    virtual bool SupportsTopBottom();
    virtual bool CanFloat();

    // By default, grabs a value from the registry
    // which was set when the appbar was last closed
    // Override if you want different behavior
    virtual UINT GetStartEdge();

    // Used to initially position the appbar.  Again,
    // by default the data is saved when the appbar closes.
    virtual CPoint GetStartTopLeftCorner();

    // Used to decide what monitor to start in.
    // Restored from data saved when the appbar closed.
    virtual CRect GetStartMonitorRect();

    // Adds a monitor to the list of available monitors.
    void AddMonitor(const CRect& rect);

    // Sets the appbar to autohide on its current edge.
    // Returns false if an auto-hide appbar is already
    // docked on the appbar's edge
    bool SetAutoHide();
    bool IsAutoHide();

    // Registry Section/Keys for everyone to know about
    static const CString m_KszFlags;
    static const CString m_KszAutoHide;
    static const CString m_KszAlwaysOnTop;
```

```
        static const CString m_KszPosition;
        static const CString m_KszEdge;
        static const CString m_KszTop;
        static const CString m_KszLeft;
        static const CString m_KszBottom;
        static const CString m_KszRight;

// Dialog Data
    //{{AFX_DATA(CAppBar)
    // NOTE: the ClassWizard will add data members here
    //}}AFX_DATA

    // ClassWizard generated virtual function overrides
    //{{AFX_VIRTUAL(CAppBar)
    protected:
    virtual void DoDataExchange(CDataExchange* pDX);
    //}}AFX_VIRTUAL


    // Implementation
protected:
// Generated message map functions
    //{{AFX_MSG(CAppBar)
    virtual BOOL OnInitDialog();
    afx_msg void OnPaint();
    afx_msg HCURSOR OnQueryDragIcon();
    afx_msg void OnDestroy();
    afx_msg int OnCreate(LPCREATESTRUCT lpCreateStruct);
    afx_msg void OnLButtonDown(UINT nFlags, CPoint point);
    afx_msg void OnLButtonUp(UINT nFlags, CPoint point);
    afx_msg void OnMouseMove(UINT nFlags, CPoint point);
    afx_msg void OnMove(int x, int y);
    afx_msg void OnMoving(UINT fwSide, LPRECT pRect);
    afx_msg void OnNcMouseMove(UINT nHitTest, CPoint point);
    afx_msg void OnContextMenu(CWnd* pWnd, CPoint point);
    afx_msg void OnActivate(UINT nState, CWnd* pWndOther, BOOL
        bMinimized);
    afx_msg void OnTimer(UINT nIDEvent);
    afx_msg void OnWindowPosChanged( WINDOWPOS* lpwndpos );
    afx_msg void OnNcLButtonDown(UINT nHitTest, CPoint point);
    afx_msg void OnNcLButtonUp( UINT nHitTest, CPoint point );
    //}}AFX_MSG
    afx_msg LRESULT OnAppBarMessage( WPARAM wparam, LPARAM
        lparam );
    afx_msg void OnAlwaysOnTop();
    afx_msg void OnAutoHide();
    afx_msg void OnAppBarExit();
    DECLARE_MESSAGE_MAP()

    // The ABN_XXX handlers
    virtual void OnPosChanged();
```

```
virtual void OnInit();
virtual void OnFullScreenApp( bool bFullScreen );
virtual void OnWindowArrange( bool bArrange );
virtual void OnStateChange();

// Called whenever an attempt to autohide fails.
// Default does nothing.  Should display some sort
// of informational message if you want the user
// to know why the appbar no longer slinks away.
virtual void OnAutoHideFail();

// Called whenever the appbar's state might have
// changed (doesn't mean it really did).
virtual void UpdateAppBar( CPoint point );
bool IsAlwaysOnTop();
void SetAlwaysOnTop();

// Call this from OnStateChange() or OnInit()
// if you want your appbar to mimic the taskbar's
// state
void MimicTaskBar();

// Returns the current edge.
UINT GetEdge();

HICON m_hIcon;
std::list<CAppBarMonitor> m_monitorList;
CAppBarLayout* m_pAppBarLayout;
UINT m_unEdge;
bool m_bFloating;
bool m_bInitialized;
bool m_bAutoHide;
bool m_bAlwaysOnTop;
bool m_bFullScreenApp;
CRect m_calculatedRect;
};
```

By now you should understand how CAppBar and CAppBarMonitor work together to figure out where the appbar should be. But knowing where one should be and its actually being there are two separate issues. To tackle the issue of "being there," I introduced the class CAppBarLayout. CAppBar-Layout has the following responsibilities:

1. Properly dock an appbar to a given edge on any monitor.
2. Properly float an appbar.
3. Keep the appbar informed about the rectangle that it should want to occupy.

CAppBarLayout accomplishes the first two goals by acquiring an intimate knowledge of how the dialog is laid out. The version of CAppBarLayout that the library provides assumes that your appbar does not do anything interesting with regards to control placement or creation. It only handles the simplest of layouts. If any of the controls contain other controls or windows, you may find CAppBarLayout's behavior unsettling. CAppBarLayout takes each child window and lays the child windows out from top to bottom or side by side. As a result, it may dismantle your control and lay it out in ways you did not envision. Never fear. I have added a few ways to make it all work. First, you can explicitly set the control order. This stops CAppBarLayout from laying out the controls in its own way. If you use something like a tab control, you will probably end up writing your own version of CAppBarLayout and throw away much of what CAppBarLayout gives you. At this point, you may be wondering why I did not just make an abstract base class and provide an implementation that users could put to use if so desired. To answer that, let's take a look at CAppBarLayout's declaration:

```
class CAppBarLayout
{
public:
    CAppBarLayout( CAppBar& appBar );
    virtual ~CAppBarLayout();

    // Positions the appbar on the given edge.
    // The rect should occupy the entire monitor
    virtual bool PositionEdge(UINT unEdge, const CRect& rect);

    // Initializes CAppBarLayout.  Normally,
    // this can't be done until after the CAppBar
    // member shows itself on the screen.
    virtual bool Init();

    // Defines the order that the controls should display
    // in.  Uses the control IDs.
    virtual bool SetControlDisplayOrder(
        const std::vector<UINT>& order );

    // Undocks the appbar and floats it on the screen.
    virtual bool FloatWindow( const CPoint& topLeft );

    // Used by the enumeration proc to add a window
    // to the list of appbar child windows.
    // Can also use it for your own purposes.
    virtual void AddWindowToList(HWND hWnd);

protected:

    // Called when positioning the appbar on the left
```

```
      // or right edges
      virtual void PositionChildrenVertically();

      // Called when positioning the appbar on the top
      // or bottom edges
      virtual void PositionChildrenHorizontally();

      typedef std::pair<HWND, CRect> WND_RECT_PAIR;
      CRect m_rectMain;
      std::list<WND_RECT_PAIR> m_wndList;
      CAppBar& m_theAppBar;

      // Only used for appbars docked on the
      // ABE_TOP or ABE_BOTTOM
      int m_nVerticalHeight;

      // Only used for appbars docked on the
      // ABE_LEFT or ABE_RIGHT
      int m_nHorizontalWidth;

      // Store the style for when this baby floats
      DWORD m_dwStyle;
};
```

You should notice that all of CAppBarLayout's methods are virtual. If your appbar needs to do anything different, just provide a new implementation, then, pass that new implementation in your call to CAppBar's constructor. CAppBar-Layout contains a full implementation because while I was going over the designs, I came up with situations where I only wanted to override a subset of the methods provided in CAppBarLayout. For example, suppose you were to use the class to handle the layout of the Microsoft Office Shortcut Bar. The window contains the Office toolbar as well as other toolbars (desktop, favorites, etc.). Only one toolbar is on top at a time. Laying out a toolbar depends on which toolbar is on top and which ones are underneath. This would most likely mean that CAppBarLayout::PositionChildrenVertically and CAppBarLayout::Position-ChildrenHorizontally would need to be overridden.

So, how does CAppBarLayout find out about the appbar's layout in the first place? It enumerates all the child windows of the appbar and records the size and position of each within the appbar. This way, when the appbar needs to float it, does not need to remember how to return to its original state. Also, when the appbar needs to be docked, it does not need to know its minimum height for horizontal docking or its minimum width for vertical docking. CApp-Bar instructs CAppBarLayout to discover this information by calling CAppBar-Layout::Init(). CAppBarLayout::Init() enumerates the child windows and adds each child window's HWND and position to a list. CAppBar has a method called OnInit(). OnInit() is a response to an ABN_XXX message that I added: ABN_INIT. This message gets sent from CAppBar::OnInitDialog().

```
void CAppBar::OnInit()
{
    // Record out the initial layout of the appbar.
    m_pAppBarLayout->Init();
    // Find out what edge the appbar should dock to.
    // This might be ABE_FLOAT
    m_unEdge = GetStartEdge();
    if ( ABE_FLOAT == m_unEdge )
    {
        // Put the appbar back in the same location
        // the user left it in last time.
        CPoint point = GetStartTopLeftCorner();
        CRect rect;
        GetWindowRect( rect );
        MoveWindow( point.x, point.y, rect.Width(),
            rect.Height() );
        m_bFloating = true;
    }
    else
    {
        // Dock the window to the start edge.
        m_pAppBarLayout->PositionEdge( m_unEdge,
            GetStartMonitorRect() );
        m_bFloating = false;
    }
    m_bInitialized = true;
}
```

The call to EnumChildWindows() in CAppBarLayout::Init() enumerates all the child windows of the passed in hWnd. For each child, the EnumChild-Proc() gets called with the HWND of a child window and the lParam value passed into EnumChildWindows(). EnumChildProc() takes the lParam, converts it into a pointer to a CAppBarLayout(), and adds the window to the list. EnumChildWindows() enumerates the windows according to their z-order. As a result, the method used by CAppBarLayout to record positions will lay out the controls according to their tab order, not their right to left, top to bottom order.

```
BOOL CALLBACK EnumChildProc( HWND hWnd, LPARAM lParam )
{
    BOOL retval = FALSE;
    // The lParam is used as a void* to get the
    // pointer to the layout class.
    CAppBarLayout* pLayout =
        reinterpret_cast<CAppBarLayout*>(lParam);
    if ( pLayout )
    {
        // Add the window to the list so that the
        // appbar can be re-shaped when the user
        // makes it float and so that the controls
```

```
        // get laid out properly.
        pLayout->AddWindowToList( hWnd );
        retval = TRUE;
    }
    return retval;
}

bool CAppBarLayout::Init()
{
    bool retval = true;

    // Record the size of the window when it is
    // floating.
    m_theAppBar.GetWindowRect( m_rectMain );

    // Store the starting style so it can be restored
    // when the appbar is floating (different style
    // is required when it is docked).
    m_dwStyle = m_theAppBar.GetStyle();

    // Find and record all the appbar controls.
    EnumChildWindows( m_theAppBar.GetSafeHwnd(),
        EnumChildProc,
        reinterpret_cast<LPARAM>(this) );
    return retval;
}

void CAppBarLayout::AddWindowToList(HWND hWnd)
{
    CRect rect;
    // The enum function just gets HWNDs.  No real
    // payback in translating the HWND into a CWnd.
    if ( ::GetWindowRect( hWnd, &rect ) )
    {
        // Store the rectangle in client co-ordinates
        // so that we can easily restore the window to its
        // position when it floats.
        m_theAppBar.ScreenToClient( rect );
        WND_RECT_PAIR thePair;
        thePair.first = hWnd;
        thePair.second = rect;
        m_wndList.push_back( thePair );

        // Used to figure out how wide the bar should be
        // when docked to the left or right side of the
        // monitor.
        if( rect.Width() > m_nHorizontalWidth )
        {
            m_nHorizontalWidth = rect.Width();
        }
```

```
        // Used to figure out how tall the bar should be
        // when docked to the top or bottom side of the
        // monitor.
        if ( rect.Height() > m_nVerticalHeight )
        {
            m_nVerticalHeight = rect.Height();
        }
    }
}
```

In CAppBar::OnInit(), we saw a call to CAppBarLayout::PositionEdge().
PositionEdge() gets called at startup and when the user moves the appbar to
a new edge. CAppBar::UpdateAppBar() and CAppBar::OnPosChanged() also
call PositionEdge(). UpdateAppBar() handles any changes and will move the
appbar to a new edge of the screen or float the appbar as indicated by the
new location. OnPosChanged() handles any changes in the available workspace due to changes with other appbars. First, let's take a look at how Posi-
tionEdge() gets called:

```
void CAppBar::OnPosChanged()
{
    // If the appbar is floating, a change in
    // position does not mean a change in layout.
    if ( m_bFloating )
    {
        return;
    }
    CPoint point;
    CRect rect;
    GetWindowRect( rect );
    // Pick a point in the middle of our window.
    point.x = ( rect.left + rect.right ) / 2;
    point.y = ( rect.top + rect.bottom ) / 2;
    // Which monitor is the middle of our window located
    // on?
    for ( std::list<CAppBarMonitor>::iterator it =
            m_monitorList.begin();
        it != m_monitorList.end(); ++it )
    {
        if ( it->GetRect().PtInRect( point ) )
        {
            // We found out the correct monitor.  Where
            // should we dock?
            m_unEdge = it->GetEdge( point, GetSafeHwnd() );

            // Move the window to the new location.
            m_pAppBarLayout->PositionEdge( m_unEdge,
                it->GetRect() );
        }
```

```
        }
}

void CAppBar::UpdateAppBar( CPoint point )
{
    if ( !m_bInitialized )
    {
        return;
    }
    // Get the window rect and see if the point is in the
    // current window.  If it is, we do not want to initiate
    // any movement of the window
    CRect rect;
    GetWindowRect( rect );
    ClientToScreen( &point );
    if ( ( !(rect.PtInRect( point ))) || ( point ==
            rect.TopLeft() ) ||
        ( point == rect.BottomRight() ) ||
        (rect.PtInRect( point ) && m_bFloating ) )
    {
        for ( std::list<CAppBarMonitor>::iterator it =
                m_monitorList.begin();
            it != m_monitorList.end(); ++it )
        {
            if ( it->GetRect().PtInRect( point ) )
            {
                UINT unOldEdge = m_unEdge;
                m_unEdge = it->GetEdge( point, GetSafeHwnd(),
                    CanFloat() );
                if ( IsAutoHide() )
                {
                    // If the appbar is autohide,
                    // we need to tell the shell that
                    // the current edge is free again.
                    // The shell keeps two lists, one of
                    // autohide appbars, one of appbars.
                    APPBARDATA appBarData;
                    ZeroMemory( &appBarData, sizeof(
                        appBarData ) );
                    appBarData.cbSize = sizeof( appBarData );
                    appBarData.hWnd = GetSafeHwnd();
                    appBarData.uEdge = unOldEdge;
                    appBarData.lParam = FALSE;
                    CRect rect = m_calculatedRect;
                    SHAppBarMessage( ABM_SETAUTOHIDEBAR,
                        &appBarData );
                }
                if ( ABE_FLOAT == m_unEdge )
                {
                    if ( !m_bFloating )
```

```
                     {
                         m_pAppBarLayout->FloatWindow( point );
                         m_bFloating = true;
                     }
                 }
                 else
                 {
                     m_pAppBarLayout->PositionEdge( m_unEdge,
                         it->GetRect() );
                     m_bFloating = false;
                     if ( IsAutoHide() )
                     {
                         SetAutoHide();
                     }
                 }

                 break;
             }
         }
     }
 }
```

CAppBarLayout::PositionEdge() is a fairly simple function. It relies on a couple of helpers to get the work done: PositionChildrenVertically() and PositionChildrenHorizontally().

```
bool CAppBarLayout::PositionEdge( UINT unEdge, const CRect&
    rect )
{
    bool retval = true;

    // Set the style to something appropriate
    m_theAppBar.ModifyStyle( WS_CAPTION, 0 );

    // Figure out the target rectangle
    CRect targetRect = rect;
    APPBARDATA appBarData;
    ZeroMemory( &appBarData, sizeof( appBarData ) );
    // Step 1, reduce the monitor down to its piece of the
    // work area. This appbar is not included in the
    // excluded area.
    if ( !m_theAppBar.IsAutoHide() )
    {
        appBarData.cbSize = sizeof( appBarData );
        appBarData.hWnd = m_theAppBar.GetSafeHwnd();
        appBarData.uEdge = unEdge;
        appBarData.rc = targetRect;
        SHAppBarMessage( ABM_QUERYPOS, &appBarData );
        targetRect = appBarData.rc;
```

```
    }

    // Based on the edge, calculate the
    // correct size for the monitor.
    switch( unEdge )
    {
        case ABE_TOP:
            targetRect.bottom = targetRect.top +
                m_nVerticalHeight + g_KnOffset;
            break;
        case ABE_BOTTOM:
            targetRect.top = targetRect.bottom -
                m_nVerticalHeight - g_KnOffset;
            break;
        case ABE_LEFT:
            targetRect.right = targetRect.left +
                m_nHorizontalWidth + g_KnOffset;
            break;
        case ABE_RIGHT:
            targetRect.left = targetRect.right -
                m_nHorizontalWidth - g_KnOffset;
            break;
    }

    // The WM_MOVING message can mess with the size.
    // Make sure that the appbar can handle the message
    // by telling Windows just what size the window should be.
    m_theAppBar.SetCalculatedSize( targetRect );
    appBarData.rc = targetRect;

    // Tell Windows how much space we are taking and where
    // we are taking it.
    SHAppBarMessage( ABM_SETPOS, &appBarData );

    // Move the window to the new location.
    m_theAppBar.MoveWindow( targetRect );

    // Position the child windows appropriately.
    switch( unEdge )
    {
        case ABE_TOP:
        case ABE_BOTTOM:
            PositionChildrenHorizontally();
            break;
        case ABE_LEFT:
        case ABE_RIGHT:
            PositionChildrenVertically();
            break;
    }
    return retval;
}
```

Close to the end, you will see the line

```
m_theAppBar.SetCalculatedSize( targetRect );
```

The appbar requires this line in order to properly respond to a WM_MOVING message. This message will attempt to set the dialog to the size specified in the dialog template. We don't want that to happen. Instead, we want it to be the size that we specified in PositionEdge(). To do this, we tell the appbar what size it should want to be. Then, in response to the WM_MOVING message, the appbar relays that rectangle to Windows.

```
void CAppBar::OnMoving(UINT fwSide, LPRECT pRect)
{
    if ( !m_bFloating )
    {
        *pRect = m_calculatedRect;
    }
}
```

PositionChildrenHorizontally() and PositionChildrenVeritically() position the child windows in their respective z-order on the new window. Note: for the code below, CAppBarLayout defines g_KnControlSpacing as 3 pixels.

```
void CAppBarLayout::PositionChildrenVertically()
{
    // Start 2 pixels from the right.
    const int xCoordinate = 2;
    int yCoordinate = g_KnControlSpacing;

    for ( std::list<WND_RECT_PAIR>::iterator it =
            m_wndList.begin();
        it != m_wndList.end(); ++it )
    {
        // Move the child window to the new position.
        MoveWindow( it->first, xCoordinate, yCoordinate,
            it->second.Width(), it->second.Height(), true );
        // Figure out where to place the next child window.
        yCoordinate += it->second.Height() +
            g_KnControlSpacing;
    }
}

void CAppBarLayout::PositionChildrenHorizontally()
{
    int xCoordinate = g_KnControlSpacing;
    const int yCoordinate = 2;

    for ( std::list<WND_RECT_PAIR>::iterator it =
            m_wndList.begin();
        it != m_wndList.end(); ++it )
```

```
    {
        // Move the child window to the new position.
        MoveWindow( it->first, xCoordinate, yCoordinate,
            it->second.Width(), it->second.Height(), true
);
        // Figure out where to place the next child window.
        xCoordinate += it->second.Width() +
            g_KnControlSpacing;
    }
}
```

Using the above code, CAppBarLayout can position the appbar on any edge of any screen. The last task we need to go over relates to floating the appbar. First off, the appbar has to allow floating. By default, all CAppBar derived classes will float. To change this behavior, override CAppBar::CanFloat() and have it return FALSE.. Assuming that the appbar was allowed to float, CAppBar::UpdateAppBar() will call CAppBarLayout::FloatWindow(). FloatWindow() should only get called once to begin the floating behavior. FloatWindow(const CPoint& topLeft) centers the top edge of the appbar on the topLeft point. Next, it restores the appbar to its original style settings and size. It then moves all the child windows to their original positions, completing the reconstruction of the appbar.

In order for all this magic to work, the dialog must have the Tool Window style turned on (WS_EX_TOOLWINDOW) and the application window style turned off (WS_EX_APPWINDOW). If you use the supplied wizard, MFC Application Desktop Toolbar, you should have nothing to worry about. However, you will have to edit the resource file by hand if you are adding an application desktop toolbar to your application. As of VC++ 6.0, you are unable to turn off the WS_EX_APPWINDOW style using the resource editor. Fortunately, you can use the resource editor to add the Tool Window style (Figure 3-4). Here is FloatWindow():

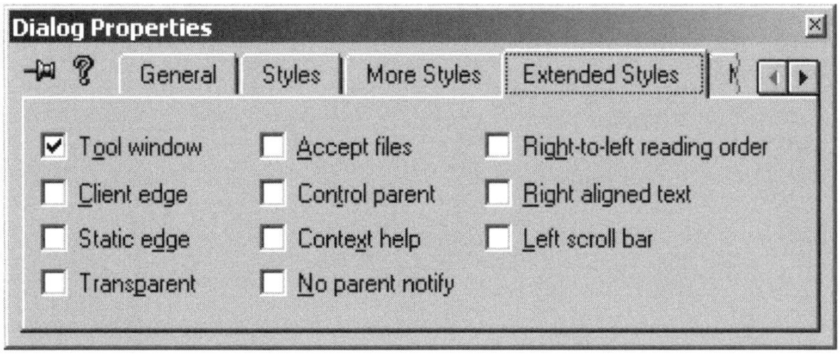

Figure 3.4   *Where to set the Tool window style for the dialog.*

```
bool CAppBarLayout::FloatWindow( const CPoint& topLeft )
{
    bool retval = true;

    // Reduce the window size to nothing
    // so that the window remains in the list of
    // appbars but the space it occupies is nothing.
    APPBARDATA appBarData;
    ZeroMemory( &appBarData, sizeof( appBarData ) );
    appBarData.cbSize = sizeof( appBarData );
    appBarData.hWnd = m_theAppBar.GetSafeHwnd();
    appBarData.rc = CRect( 0, 0, 0, 0 );
    SHAppBarMessage( ABM_SETPOS, &appBarData );

    // Set the appbar back to its original style.
    m_theAppBar.ModifyStyle( 0, m_dwStyle );
    // Get the location of the mouse pointer.
    CPoint point(::GetMessagePos());

    // Figure out where the floating appbar should go.
    CRect rect = m_rectMain;
    int left = point.x - (m_rectMain.Width() / 2);
    rect.SetRect( left,
                  point.y,
                  left + m_rectMain.Width(),
                  topLeft.y + m_rectMain.Height() );

    // Move the appbar to its new spot.
    m_theAppBar.MoveWindow( rect );

    // Restore the child windows to their original
    // locations within the floating appbar.
    for ( std::list<WND_RECT_PAIR>::iterator it =
              m_wndList.begin();
          it != m_wndList.end(); ++it )
    {
        MoveWindow( it->first,
            it->second.left,
            it->second.top,
            it->second.Width(),
            it->second.Height(),
            true );
    }
    // Redraw the appbar.
    m_theAppBar.Invalidate();
    return retval;
}
```

Two items of interest remain in the library: the implementations of auto-hide and always on top. In response to a right mouse click, CAppBar will dis-

play a popup menu with the options *Autohide, Always on top,* and *Exit.* If
the appbar is floating, only *Exit* will be available. If you don't like this behavior, all you have to do is override OnContextMenu(). When the user sets autohide mode for the appbar, the appbar has to make sure that it gives the
user as much screen real estate as possible. Also, an autohide appbar must
move to the outermost edge of the screen. If you have two appbars docked
to the same edge and the innermost appbar gets set to autohide, the innermost appbar becomes the outermost appbar.

So that the user can reactivate the appbar, the appbar needs to maintain
some width. If it did not do this, where would one take the mouse in order
to activate the appbar? CAppBar maintains a minimum width/height of two
pixels. This way, it still can detect mouse movement within the appbar. In
order to accomplish this, CAppBar starts a timer in OnInitDialog(). Every mil-
lisecond, OnTimer() checks to see if the appbar has autohide turned on.
When autohide is turned on, OnTimer() checks the position of the mouse. If
the mouse is within the appbar's rectangle, it grows the appbar to its maximum width/height. Otherwise, it shrinks the appbar to that two pixel minimum width/height. As long as autohide is turned on, this method calculates
the ideal rectangle and then tries to resize the window. Fortunately, the call
to MoveWindow() has been optimized to not move windows that are already
where you want them to be. Because I kept the math in OnTimer() relatively
simple, the code wastes little processor time.

```
void CAppBar::OnTimer(UINT nIDEvent)
{
    if ( g_KnAutoHideEvent == nIDEvent )
    {
        // Stop timer events from piling up.
        KillTimer( g_KnAutoHideEvent );
        // Is this an autohide appbar?
        if( IsAutoHide() )
        {
            // It is an autohide appbar.  Where is
            // the mouse?  This determines how to show the
            // appbar: stay open, close, or opening.
            CPoint point(::GetMessagePos());
            CRect rect;
            bool bMove = false;
            GetWindowRect( rect );
            if ( rect.PtInRect( point ) )
            {
                // The mouse is within the appbar window.
                // Are we at the correct size?  Note: we leave
                // a narrow lip for the user to position the
                // mouse over the appbar.  An autohide appbar
                // still occupies some of the screen, just not
                // very much of it.
```

```
if ( rect != m_calculatedRect )
{
    // We are not the right size.  Because
    // we only grow to m_calculatedRect,
    // we must be too small.  Grow!
    // Depending on our edge we need to grow
    // wider or taller.
    switch ( GetEdge() )
    {
        case ABE_LEFT:
            rect.right += g_KnShrinkVal;
            if ( rect.right >
                m_calculatedRect.right )
            {
                rect.right =
                m_calculatedRect.right;
            }
            break;
        case ABE_RIGHT:
            rect.left -= g_KnShrinkVal;
            if ( rect.left <
                m_calculatedRect.left )
            {
                rect.left =
                m_calculatedRect.left;
            }
            break;
        case ABE_TOP:
            rect.bottom += g_KnShrinkVal;
            if ( rect.bottom >
                m_calculatedRect.bottom )
            {
                rect.bottom =
                m_calculatedRect.bottom;
            }
            break;
        case ABE_BOTTOM:
            rect.top -= g_KnShrinkVal;
            if ( rect.top <
                m_calculatedRect.top )
            {
                rect.top =
                m_calculatedRect.top;
            }
            break;
    }
    bMove = true;
}
}
else
```

```
{
    // The mouse is not in our window.  What
    // should we be doing?  If we are the
    // active window (user clicked on us), we
    // do not want to shrink.  We want
    // to stay at full size.
    if ( CWnd::GetActiveWindow() != this )
    {
        // We want to start shrinking.
        // What edge are we docked to?
        switch ( GetEdge() )
        {
            case ABE_LEFT:
                // Same pattern for all.
                // if we are not too small
                // keep shrinking.
                if ( rect.Width() >
                        g_KnMinDimension )
                {
                    rect.right -= g_KnShrinkVal;
                }
                else
                {
                    // We got too small, fix the
                    // size.
                    rect.right = rect.left +
                      g_KnMinDimension;
                }
                break;
            case ABE_RIGHT:
                // See ABE_LEFT for pattern
                if ( rect.Width() >
                        g_KnMinDimension )
                {
                    rect.left += g_KnShrinkVal;
                }
                else
                {
                    rect.left = rect.right -
                      g_KnMinDimension;
                }
                break;
            case ABE_TOP:
                // See ABE_LEFT for pattern
                if ( rect.Height() >
                        g_KnMinDimension )
                {
                    rect.bottom -= g_KnShrinkVal;;
                }
                else
```

```
                        {
                            rect.bottom = rect.top +
                                g_KnMinDimension;
                        }
                        break;
                    case ABE_BOTTOM:
                        // See ABE_LEFT for pattern
                        if ( rect.Height() >
                                g_KnMinDimension )
                        {
                            rect.top += g_KnShrinkVal;
                        }
                        else
                        {
                            rect.top = rect.bottom -
                                g_KnMinDimension;
                        }

                        break;
                }
                bMove = true;
            }
        }
        if ( bMove )
        {
            MoveWindow( rect );
        }
    }

    // Start the timer back up.
    SetTimer( g_KnAutoHideEvent, g_KnAutoHideInterval,
            NULL );
    }
    CDialog::OnTimer(nIDEvent);
}
```

Handling always on top uses a lot less code. Unless a full-screen app is open, just set the appbar to the top of the z-order.

```
void CAppBar::SetAlwaysOnTop()
{
    // Assume normal Z-Order
    const CWnd* pWnd = &wndNoTopMost;
    if (IsAlwaysOnTop())
    {
        // If we are supposed to be always-on-top, put us
        // there.
        pWnd = &wndTopMost;

        if (m_bFullScreenApp)
        {
```

```
        // But, if a full-screen window is opened, put
        // ourself at the bottom of the z-order so that we
        // don't cover the full-screen window
        pWnd = &wndBottom;
    }
}
SetWindowPos(pWnd, 0, 0, 0, 0, SWP_NOMOVE | SWP_NOSIZE |
    SWP_NOACTIVATE);
}
```

Depending on where you are in the life of the appbar, you need to call SetAlwaysOnTop(). It gets called in each of these four situations:

1. When a full screen app opens
2. When the appbar is mimicking the taskbar[2]
3. When the appbar gets created
4. When the user toggles the always on top style

The rest of the code in the library holds very little, if any, interest. When the user clicks on the appbar, we grab the mouse cursor. As soon as they let go, we release the mouse. This allows us to track the movement of the mouse even when the mouse isn't on top of our window.

While constructing the library, I had the biggest problems with making everything work as expected. The library presented in this chapter is a direct result of my attempt at making this whole process easy. If you want to do fancy things like the Microsoft Office Shortcut Bar, you have more work to do. By reducing the problem to writing a layout manager, I tried to make your life a little easier. Beyond the library, I also wrote an AppWizard to do most of the setup. If you want to use an appbar as part of a larger application, I recommend using the wizard anyhow, and then copying the generated files into your project. Be sure that you link in the appropriate library. All the libraries I provide differentiate themselves by having the debug version tack a *d* onto the end of the filename prefix. For this library, link in AppBarLibd.LIB for debug mode and AppBarLib.LIB for release mode.

3.4   An Application Desktop Toolbar Application

All the information in this chapter should help you build an appbar with ease. The time has come to build an actual, useful application with the tools presented. We will build a calculator. It will have a somewhat minimal imple-

---

2. If the taskbar is autohide, the appbar will be autohide. If the taskbar is always on top, the appbar is always on top. Windows provides all appbars with the ability to do the same things the taskbar does. The idea is that if the user wants to save screen real estate with the taskbar, they will want to do the same thing with all appbars.

mentation. I have provided the source code in the \Examples\Chapter 3\Calculator directory. This calculator will allow the user to add, subtract, multiply, and divide. To keep things real simple, all operators will have the same precedence. This mimics the behavior of the calculator that ships with Windows. If you have not installed the libraries, classes, and wizards from the CD, you should stop and run the installation program now.

To start, go into Visual Studio and create a new project. Select the MFC Application Desktop Toolbar as the project type and name the project *Calculator.* Press OK and let the wizard create all of its files. Once the wizard is done, you should have the following items:

Classes:
- CCalculatorApp
- CCalculatorBar

Resources:
- A default dialog: IDD_CALCULATOR_DIALOG
- A default icon: IDR_MAINFRAME
- A string table with a default warning string,
  IDS_AUTOHIDE_ERROR, for when the user tries to dock to an
  edge that already has an autohide toolbar:
  "A toolbar is already hidden on this side of your screen.
  You can only have one autohide toolbar per side."

CCalculatorApp does nothing special. The code the wizard produced should look exactly like the code the wizard produces for a dialog-based applicationæit is the same code. CCalculatorBar has all the code needed to get the default appbar up and running, and nothing else. Even the overridden OnAutoHideFail() has no surprising code:

```
void CCalculatorBar::OnAutoHideFail()
{
    AfxMessageBox( IDS_AUTOHIDE_ERROR,
        MB_OK | MB_ICONINFORMATION );
}
```

The next task involves laying out the dialog itself. Figure 3-5 shows the dialog as it looks in the development environment with and without the tab order. Please note that I manufactured this figure. As far as I can tell, you cannot open up the same dialog twice for editing. The calculator uses an odd tab order, but it does accurately show the order that I want things to appear when the appbar is docked to an edge. I fully expect the user to use the number pad instead of tab key navigation. As a result, I am not concerned about the odd tab order.

Looking at the dialog, I became convinced that the calculator should not allow docking on the left or right. The appbar would be too wide due to

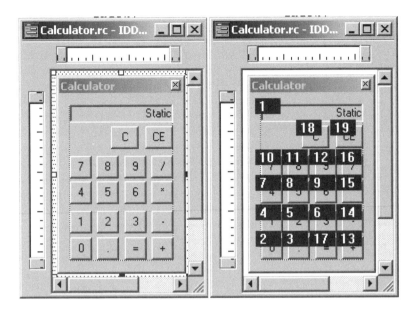

Figure 3.5   *Tab order for the calculator appbar.*

the static text field that displays the answer. This decision represents the last bit of appbar-specific code that I had to write for the calculator appbar.

```
bool CCalculatorBar::SupportsLeftRight()
{
    return false;
}
```

The next task is to actually implement the calculator. The calculator will accept expressions similar to *34 + 93 / 7 =* and know to display the answer *18.1429*. The calculator will allow keyboard and mouse data entry. As on other calculators, *C* clears everything and *CE* clears the entry on the display.

Obviously, the calculator needs to know what operation it should be performing. That information needs to be stored in a member variable. I could use a number, a string, an enum, or some other choice. I chose to use an enumeration. Enums offer a lot to C++ programmers. Because an enum can be declared as a type, you get the benefits of type safety along with easily read code. Looking at my solution will show the benefits quite quickly. I declared the enum within the CCalculatorBar class declaration.

```
enum Operator{ UNKNOWN, ADD, SUBTRACT, MULTIPLY, DIVIDE };
```

To access Operator at file scope, use the type CCalculatorBar::Operator. SetOperator(Operator op) realizes the benefits of the enumeration immedi-

ately. If the method took an int, I could pass invalid values to SetOperator().
This would then have the code performing range checking to make sure the
value was valid. Instead, by using the named type, I get the compiler to do
validation work for me. A programmer could still subvert my good intentions
by using a typecast. I like to use enums in public interfaces as well. It allows
me to declare a type that I know is unique and it makes the interface more
self-documenting. I know that the compiler internally represents UNKNOWN,
ADD, and SUBTRACT as the values 0, 1, and 2. To me, these are programmer-
defined symbols that map to the concepts of *I don't know* (UNKNOWN), *Add
two numbers* (ADD), and *Subtract two numbers* (SUBTRACT).

```
void CCalculatorBar::SetOperator(CCalculatorBar::Operator op)
{
    // Capture any information from the display.
    UpdateData();

    // Convert the string to a number.
    double value = atof( m_szDisplay );

    // The user pressed a new operator. Do the math using the
    // old operator first.  Ex.: User presses '4', then
    // '+' then '5', and now pressed '-'.  We need to
    // evaluate 4 + 5.
    switch ( m_currentOperator )
    {
        case ADD:
            m_dRunningTotal = m_dRunningTotal + value;
            break;
        case SUBTRACT:
            m_dRunningTotal = m_dRunningTotal - value;
            break;
        case MULTIPLY:
            m_dRunningTotal = m_dRunningTotal * value;
            break;
        case DIVIDE:
            m_dRunningTotal = m_dRunningTotal / value;
            break;
        case UNKNOWN:
            m_dRunningTotal = value;
            break;
    }
    m_szDisplay = g_KszZero;
    UpdateData( false );
    m_bDecimalPressed = false;
    m_currentOperator = op;
}
```

All operations are based off the previous operator, not the one just
pressed. The class keeps a running total, m_dRunningTotal, and tracks when
the decimal key gets pressed.

In order to handle the display, I wrote a method called CCalculator-Bar::AddNumToDisplay(CString szNumber). The method simply tacks the new number onto the end of the display string. The method formats the number differently based on whether or not the user has hit the decimal point yet. If the user has not used the decimal point, numbers get inserted before the decimal on the display. Otherwise, the numbers get tacked onto the end of the string.

```
void CCalculatorBar::AddNumToDisplay(CString szNumber)
{
    // If the decimal button was pressed,
    // just tack the number onto the end.
    if ( m_bDecimalPressed )
    {
        m_szDisplay += szNumber;
    }
    else
    {
        // If the text in the display is set to zero,
        // clear it.
        if ( m_szDisplay == g_KszZero )
        {
            m_szDisplay.Empty();
        }
        else if ( m_bClearIfNumber )
        {
            // The user pressed the '=' button before
            // pressing this key.  Clear the text in
            // the display.
            m_bClearIfNumber = false;
            m_szDisplay.Empty();
        }
        CString szTemp;
        // Get all the charaters except for the '.'
        szTemp = m_szDisplay.Left(m_szDisplay.GetLength()- 1);
        // Tack the new number onto the end.
        szTemp += szNumber;
        szTemp += _T(".");
        m_szDisplay = szTemp;
    }
    // Update the display
    UpdateData( false );
}
```

A typical caller looks like this:

```
void CCalculatorBar::OnEight()
{
    AddNumToDisplay( _T("8") );
}
```

You will find similar code for all the other digits as well. While implementing the code for the key presses, I saw that the buttons ate all the WM_KEYDOWN and WM_KEYUP messages. I wanted the dialog to process these messages. To do this, I had a few choices:

1. Override OnCmdMessage() in CCalculatorBar.

2. Derive a class from CButton and override WM_KEYDOWN and WM_KEYUP processing to forward the message to the parent.

3. Remove the requirement to handle the keyboard.

Unless absolutely necessary, I never touch OnCmdMessage(). OnCmdMessage() will let you do amazing things. It will also let you shoot yourself in the foot. Many times, I have seen MFC developers who "know enough to be dangerous" use OnCmdMessage() as the solution to their problem. They overlook a big part of MFC—message maps. Understanding message maps and what messages get sent when will make your productivity as an MFC developer skyrocket. If you are ever tempted by OnCmdMessage(), I urge you to pull out Spy++ and analyze the messages the window or child window in question receives. In particular, identify the messages that it receives when you perform the actions that should invoke your code. More often than not, this will provide you with a better way than OnCmdMessage(). I have the same opinion about overriding CWnd::PreTranslateMessage().

The third option, remove the requirement to handle the keyboard, looks tempting. However, I rarely use the mouse to operate the calculator that ships with Windows. As a result, I doubt that this calculator would be useful if I removed the requirement. This leaves us with option two, derive a new class from CButton.

Why would I forward the WM_KEYDOWN and WM_KEYUP messages to the parent? Because doing this allows me to use the message map to handle everything. As an alternative, I could have the button directly call into the CWnd derived class. This would make the coupling far too tight for my liking. Instead, we can use the message map as a sort of Windows-based v-table.[3] In general, if the receiver of the message actually has the message in its message map, then the sender can invoke various methods in the receiver. This method works really well to allow new classes to interact with old ones without having to teach the old class anything about the new one.

To implement the keyboard message passing, I derived a class from CButton and named it CKeyStrokeButton. This class has one responsibility—

---

3. For more on message maps, check out Chapter 3 of *MFC Internals* by George Shepherd and Scot Wingo. Published in 1996, it still ranks as the best book to explain the guts of MFC. On a side note, after David Kruglinski's death this duo has also taken over *Inside Visual C++*.

pass all keystrokes to the parent. Not surprisingly, CKeyStrokeButton is relatively compact.

```
class CKeyStrokeButton : public CButton
{
// Construction
public:
     CKeyStrokeButton();
     virtual ~CKeyStrokeButton();
// Overrides
     // ClassWizard generated virtual function overrides
     //{{AFX_VIRTUAL(CKeyStrokeButton)
     public:
     virtual BOOL PreTranslateMessage(MSG* pMsg);
     //}}AFX_VIRTUAL

     // Generated message map functions
protected:
     //{{AFX_MSG(CKeyStrokeButton)
     afx_msg void OnKeyDown(UINT nChar, UINT nRepCnt, UINT
         nFlags);
     afx_msg void OnKeyUp(UINT nChar, UINT nRepCnt, UINT
         nFlags);
     //}}AFX_MSG

     DECLARE_MESSAGE_MAP()
};
```

CKeyStrokeButton implements OnKeyDown() and OnKeyUp(). Both implementations take the message and then forward it to the parent window via a PostMessage() call.

```
void CKeyStrokeButton::OnKeyDown(UINT nChar, UINT nRepCnt,
                                 UINT nFlags)
{
     GetParent()->PostMessage( WM_KEYDOWN, nChar,
       MAKELPARAM( nRepCnt, nFlags ) );
     CButton::OnKeyDown(nChar, nRepCnt, nFlags);
}

void CKeyStrokeButton::OnKeyUp(UINT nChar, UINT nRepCnt,
                               UINT nFlags)
{
    GetParent()->PostMessage( WM_KEYUP, nChar,
        MAKELPARAM( nRepCnt, nFlags ) );
    CButton::OnKeyUp(nChar, nRepCnt, nFlags);
}
```

I also did something that I stated you should not do unless you have a good reason. I provided an override of PreTranslateMessage(). Why would I do that? When using CALC.EXE, you can use the [Enter/Return] key to mean the same as if you pressed the "=" button. With CButton, pressing [Enter] is the same as clicking the button. When the "=" button has focus, this works fine. When the "4" button has focus, you get an extra "4" in the display. By overriding PreTranslateMessage(), I was able to see the message for what it was, a WM_KEYDOWN with the key VK_RETURN pressed. At this point, I could forward the true message to the parent window and not allow CKeyStrokeButton or its parent classes to mess with the message.

```
BOOL CKeyStrokeButton::PreTranslateMessage(MSG* pMsg)
{
    if ( pMsg->message == WM_KEYDOWN )
    {
        if ( pMsg->wParam == VK_RETURN )
        {
            // If the user pressed the return key,
            // don't fire off a BN_CLICKED.
            // Instead, send the message to the parent.
            // A PostMessage will not work here.
            // The message needs to be handled before
            // we return.
            GetParent()->SendMessage( pMsg->message,
                pMsg->wParam, pMsg->lParam );
            return TRUE;
        }
    }
    return CButton::PreTranslateMessage(pMsg);
}
```

CCalculatorBar has OnKeyDown() in its message map. Upon receiving a key press, it processes the key and then invokes the appropriate response.

```
void CCalculatorBar::OnKeyDown(UINT nChar, UINT nRepCnt,
    UINT nFlags)
{
    SHORT keystate = GetKeyState(VK_SHIFT);
    if ( GetKeyState(VK_SHIFT) < 0 )
    {
        // The user has the shift key pressed.
        // See if the user is entering an aritmetic
        // operator.
        switch ( nChar )
        {
            case '8':
                nChar = '*';
                break;
            case '=':
                nChar = '+';
                break;
            default:
```

```
                return;
        }
}


// Interpret the character.
switch( nChar )
{
    case '0':
    case VK_NUMPAD0:
        OnZero();
        break;
    case '1':
    case VK_NUMPAD1:
        OnOne();
        break;
    case '2':
    case VK_NUMPAD2:
        OnTwo();
        break;
    case '3':
    case VK_NUMPAD3:
        OnThree();
        break;
    case '4':
    case VK_NUMPAD4:
        OnFour();
        break;
    case '5':
    case VK_NUMPAD5:
        OnFive();
        break;
    case '6':
    case VK_NUMPAD6:
        OnSix();
        break;
    case '7':
    case VK_NUMPAD7:
        OnSeven();
        break;
    case '8':
    case VK_NUMPAD8:
        OnEight();
        break;
    case '9':
    case VK_NUMPAD9:
        OnNine();
        break;
    case '*':
    case VK_MULTIPLY:
        OnMultiply();
```

```
                        break;
                case '/':
                case VK_DIVIDE:
                    OnDivide();
                    break;
                case '+':
                case VK_ADD:
                    OnAdd();
                    break;
                case '-':
                case VK_SUBTRACT:
                    OnSubtract();
                    break;
                case '=':
                case VK_RETURN:
                    OnEquals();
                    break;
                case VK_ESCAPE:
                    OnClearentry();
                    break;
                case VK_BACK:
                    OnClear();
                    break;
                case VK_OEM_PERIOD:
                case VK_DECIMAL:
                    OnDecimalpoint();
                    break;
        }
        CAppBar::OnKeyDown(nChar, nRepCnt, nFlags);
}
```

To make the calculator different, I added some custom colors. If you run the calculator, you will see that the display area grabs the background color from what you set on your system for the default window and window text colors. The dialog has a slightly more customized color that just caught my eye as being nice.

```
HBRUSH CCalculatorBar::OnCtlColor(CDC* pDC, CWnd* pWnd,
                                  UINT nCtlColor)
{
    int nID = pWnd->GetDlgCtrlID();
    // Make a brush that has a nice shade of purple.
    static CBrush test( RGB( 128, 128, 190 ) );
    HBRUSH hbr = test;

    if ( ( CTLCOLOR_STATIC == nCtlColor ) &&
         ( IDC_DISPLAY == nID ) )
    {
        // If the display area was picked, paint it
        // white with black text (or whatever the user
```

```
        // usually has in this situation).
        static CBrush test( GetSysColor( COLOR_WINDOW ) );
        hbr = test;
        pDC->SetBkColor( GetSysColor( COLOR_WINDOW ) );
        pDC->SetTextColor( GetSysColor( COLOR_WINDOWTEXT ) );
    }
    return hbr;
}
```

The rest of the methods in CCalculatorBar have been left as an exercise for the reader. All the math is handled by calls to SetOperator() and all the numbers are handled by calls to AddNumToDisplay(). Once you finish off the details, you will have a fully functional calculator.

3.5 Summary

Application Desktop Toolbars allow you to enhance the usability of you application suite and to add some new functionality to the user's desktop. When deciding to add an appbar, make sure you are doing so because it makes sense. I actually use the calculator appbar instead of the Windows calculator for quick math. I find that I usually just let it float on my desktop. Occasionally I dock the calculator because I am using it enough to have it always available, but I want it out of the way. The calculator represents a situation where the appbar is useful because it allows easy access to the functionality you are after—in this case, basic math.

Appbars communicate with the shell through the SHAppBarMessage() API and a set of messages. They can be docked to any edge of any monitor attached to the computer. By using the library and wizard presented in this chapter, you can build appbars using the same techniques you would use to build a dialog. CAppBar and its related classes implement the appbar behavior; you add the rest. With the design of the class library, I have left the doors wide open for you to modify almost all of the appbar behavior.

Control Panel Applets

When a person begins using Windows, they must learn how to use a few different pieces of their system. They need to know how to start Windows Explorer so they can manipulate the files on their system and possibly navigate their network. They need to know how to use the taskbar so that they can launch any applications on their PC. Lastly, they need to know how to find the Control Panel so that they can adjust the myriad applications, peripherals, and services that make their computer useful.

All a user needs to know about the Control Panel is how to find it and how to use the Control Panel applets on an as-needed basis. However, as a developer there will come a point when you will want to put an applet into the Control Panel.

A Control Panel applet lives in a dynamically linked library file that has a .CPL extension. The .CPL file may contain one or more distinct applets. The .CPL file bears the responsibility of bringing up the correct applet when asked to do so.

In this chapter, we will go over the following items:

- How to decide if the Control Panel is an appropriate place to put your applet
- Ways of packaging Control Panel applets
- Control Panel basics
- Motivation and design of a Control Panel applet wizard
- Building an applet using the wizard

4.1   When to Use the Control Panel

When I first saw the Control Panel, I thought of it as a good place to put general-purpose configuration tools. After becoming accustomed to the Control Panel, I had no problem figuring out what I could expect to find there. Was new hardware generating IRQ conflicts? Go to the Control Panel and resolve the problem. Did my network card need to be changed to start using DHCP? Go to the Control Panel.

As more software packages became available for the Windows operating system, I saw that not everybody puts configuration utilities into the Control Panel. The tape drive on one of my machines has the configuration utility in the tape backup program, not in the Control Panel. To make matters worse, the drive came with a bunch of programs. Not all programs provide a way to configure the tape drive. I did not bring up this point to malign tape drive manufacturers. I configured my tape drive the day I bought it and have not had to use the utility since. This point highlights the fact that many developers do not know when they should use the Control Panel. That said, let's look at some guidelines that I came up with.

1. Configuring hardware: Of all the guidelines, this one has to be the most obvious. If you are a hardware manufacturer, you should create a Control Panel applet so that your customers can configure the hardware.

2. Updating System-wide settings: If a product can globally affect the behavior of the system, the user should be able to update any settings via the Control Panel. Examples include:
    *   The Display applet: Can change the appearance of title bars, fonts, menus, and other elements for all applications.
    *   The Date and Time applet: Affects the system time, how the computer reacts to daylight savings time adjustments, and the time that the system uses. Many applications rely on Universal Coordinated Time (UTC) to figure out what time it is. This applet defines the time zone for the computer so that these applications behave properly. Just think how often you use CTime, COleTime, or other time manipulation functions in your own code.

3. Setup and configuration of a "boxed" solution: If your product dictates how the computer will be configured and what applications will be on the system, you have a boxed solution. Examples include medical workstations, factory automation PCs, and other dedicated-use computers. If you have any utility that configures how the PC will be used, such as routing of printed output, consider using the Control Panel as the home for your utility.

4. "Integrationware": As the Windows operating system creates more and more ways of integrating our applications with other applications, the

Control Panel may be the best place to put our utilities. Using the canonical "what if you had a COM-based spell checker" example, imagine you have one. The user of your spell checker could use a Control Panel applet to set the default language for your engine. As the engine becomes more sophisticated, maybe by providing language detection, the applet could set the language order and heuristics. For example, the user could set the engine to switch to the next language in the list if ten misspelled words are found in a fifteen-word block.

As you can see, the Control Panel is a useful tool in your design arsenal. Keep in mind that the short list above is a list of *do's*. After you digest all the information in this chapter, you may come up with something that does not quite fit in the above list. That does not mean you should stay away from the Control Panel. Bounce the idea off of your peers. If you find it easy to convince them that you have a good candidate for the Control Panel, go for it.

4.2   Applet Expectations

An applet must provide a predefined set of functionality in order to make the Control Panel recognize and use it. The documentation for most of this lives in one of the SDK headers, CPL.H. The applet must export one function: CPlApplet(). The applet must also respond to a set of eight different messages. Once all this appears to be working, you have to integrate the applet with the Control Panel. This can be done by placing the applet into the Windows system directory. There is one more thing to keep in mind: Windows does not guarantee that the Control Panel will be the only user of your applet. The Desktop might use it, or another application might use it. Regardless of the user, if the applet works with the Control Panel, you should not worry about what else might use the applet.

4.2.1   CPlApplet()

As the only function the Control Panel really cares about, CPlApplet() makes Control Panel applets come to life. The Control Panel uses this function to access all of the functionality embedded in the .CPL file. CPlApplet has the following prototype:

```
LONG APIENTRY CPlApplet( HWND hwndCPl,
    UINT uMsg,
    LONG lParam1,
    LONG lParam2);
```

As a general purpose function, CPlApplet() must properly interpret the parameters based on the value of uMsg. The interpretation responsibility extends to the return value. In some instances, a return value of 0 means success. In other instances, 5 might indicate success. If the value of uMsg indicates that the caller wants a dialog to appear, hwndCPl will be non-NULL and can be used as a parent window. The two parameters, lParam1 and lParam2, get their meanings from of the value of uMsg. This method closely resembles the way message handlers behave when programming for Windows without a class library like MFC. The message handler must determine the meaning, if any, of wparam and lparam based on the incoming message.

4.2.2 Messages

Starting with Windows 95, a Control Panel applet has eight messages to deal with. If you look in the SDK documentation, you will see nine messages mentioned. One message, CPL_SELECT, is obsolete. These are the messages an applet must deal with:

1. CPL_INIT: Sent immediately after the applet is loaded. The applet should perform any global initialization in response to the message. The caller uses this message as a way of making sure that it found the function CPlApplet().

2. CPL_GETCOUNT: Sent to find out how many applets live in the .CPL file.

3. CPL_INQUIRE: Sent to get static display information. This message gets sent once for each applet in the .CPL file. Additionally, this message allows the Control Panel and any other controlling application to cache the information. It appears that the information gets cached across invocations of the Control Panel itself. If you are not sure what the final icon, label, or description should be, override CPL_NEWINQUIRE instead of CPL_INQUIRE. If these parts of your applet have not been decided, specify CPL_DYNAMIC_RES as the value for all CPLINFO struct members in response to this message.

4. CPL_NEWINQUIRE: Sent to get dynamic display information. This message gets sent once for each applet in the .CPL file. Typically, the applet will respond by telling the caller that it does not have any dynamic information.

5. CPL_DBLCLK: Sent to invoke one of the applets in the .CPL file. This message is called when the user double clicks on an icon in the Control Panel.

6. CPL_STARTWPARAMS: Sent to invoke one of the applets, possibly with some special information. In practice, this method is treated the same as CPL_DBLCLK.

7. CPL_STOP: Sent once to each applet in the .CPL file. This informs the applet that the controlling application is about to close.

8. CPL_EXIT: Sent just before the controlling application calls FreeLibrary() for the .CPL. The .CPL file should finish clean up in response to this message.

An applet will always receive CPL_INIT first, CPL_GETCOUNT second, CPL_STOP second to last, and CPL_EXIT last. The other four messages can be sent in any order in between CPL_GETCOUNT and CPL_STOP. Table 4.1 explains the meaning of the CPlApplet() parameters for each message. Assuming that CPlApplet() responds properly to all of these messages, the control panel and the CPL file should get along.

| Table 4.1 | *How to interpret and respond to Control Panel messages.* |

uMsg	hwndCPI	lparam1	lparam2	Return Value
CPL_INIT	No meaning	No meaning	No meaning	Failure: 0 Success: 1
CPL_GETCOUNT	No meaning	No meaning	No meaning	Failure 0: or lower Success: 1 or higher
CPL_INQUIRE	No meaning	Indicates the applet index (zero-based)	Pointer to a CPLINFO structure	Failure: 1 Success: 0
CPL_NEWINQUIRE	No meaning	Indicates the applet index (zero-based)	Pointer to a NEWCPLINFO	Failure: 1 Success: 0
CPL_DBLCLK	Calling HWND	Indicates the applet index (zero-based)	Applet specifc data. Set in CPL_INQUIRE or CPL_NEWINQUIRE	Failure: 1 Success: 0
CPL_STARTWPARAMS	Calling HWND	Indicates the applet index (zero-based)	Applet specific data. Set in CPL_INQUIRE CPL_NEWINQUIRE	Failure: 1 Success: 0
CPL_STOP	No meaning	Indicates the applet index (zero-based)	No meaning	Failure: 1 Success: 0
CPL_EXIT	No meaning	No meaning	No meaning	Failure: 1 Success: 0

4.3   A Control Panel Library and Wizard

When writing my first Control Panel applet, I wrote a lot of boilerplate code be-fore making the applet do the work that mattered to me. Writing one applet from scratch was fun. Doing that work again did not sound like more fun. So, I sat down to analyze the problem at hand. First, what set of functionality defined the bare minimum for a Control Panel applet? Second, how much of that func-tionality can be implemented before deciding what the applet will do?

The answer to the first question is simple: the applet and the CPL file must respond properly to all eight messages. What about the answer to question number two? All of that functionality can be implemented before you even know what the applet will do. This means that, with a little effort, we can make sure that we can get to the real problem, the applet's dialog box, a lot faster.

4.3.1   Design

To automate the building of Control Panel applets, I did a quick analysis of the problem. Looking at the messages, I noticed that some messages were meant to be answered by the CPL file as a whole. With other messages, only the individual applets know how to respond. As a result, we have a definite line of responsibility. After some thinking, I came up with the following divi-sion of responsibility:

- CPL File: CPL_INIT, CPL_GETCOUNT, CPL_EXIT, applet message delegation
- Applet(s): CPL_NEWINQUIRE, CPL_DBLCLK, CPL_STARTWPARAMS, CPL_STOP

In the CPL list, you will notice that I added something that is not quite a message. I gave the responsibility of applet message delegation to the CPL file as a whole because it must make sure that the correct entities respond to the messages. From our quick analysis, it looks like we have two entities: the CPL file and the applet. There is a one-to-many relationship between the CPL file (one) and the applet (many). Because there should only be one object handling the global responsibilities of the CPL file, we know we should make the object a Singleton.[1] Since the Singleton will be responsible for managing the applets, let's call the class ControlPanelAppletManager. To make things fairly efficient, we can define an interface that all applets must implement. This way, the Con-trolPanelAppletManager can hold a collection of applets and know how to call into each applet without knowing the final type of the applet's class. In the end, we will have to integrate all of this with CPlApplet().

ControlPanelAppletManager inherits from a template class named Sin-gleton<>. Singleton<> implements the Singleton design pattern by making

---

1. Gamma, Helm, Johnson, Vlissides, *Design Patterns,* Addison-Wesley, 1996

sure one and only one instance of the class exists in the current process. Users of the template privately inherit from Singleton like this:

```
class foo : private Singleton<foo>
{
private:
    friend Singleton<foo>;//so the parent can create the child
    foo();
    foo( const foo& );
    foo& operator=(const foo&); // These three so that you
        // can't create foo on the
        // stack and you can't copy foo around

public:
    virtual ~foo();
    static foo& Instance(); // hides the copy in Singleton<>
    // so that only one path is created to the instance.
...
};
```

The handling of the Instance() method relates to the fact that compiler writers still do not know how to make a static template argument unique beyond the compilation unit. Fortunately, they perfected this technique for normal classes. As a result, hiding the signature of Singleton<foo>::Instance() allows us to make the code work as intended. We privately inherit from Singleton for a few different reasons. Perhaps the most obvious is that the template class causes a class Singleton<derived> to be created. We do not have any use for the base class, Singleton<derived>, other than for it to be the parent of the derived class. I also have a less obvious reason. Inheritance allows us to treat objects polymorphically. From a design standpoint, it does not make sense to make Singleton the common behavior between a family of classes. For example, let's assume that your model defines an abstract base class Widget. In your model, there exist three Widget-derived classes that also happen to be Singletons. You will treat the Widget behavior polymorphically. The Widget behavior makes the class interesting. You may have other Singletons in the system that have nothing to do with Widget. I cannot think of a reason why it would be handy to use Singleton::Instance() polymorphically.

What does the ControlPanelAppletManager need to do? From the list above, it must be able to delegate or directly respond to all the messages a user might throw at it. The messages must be translated at some level and delegated at the next level. For the moment, let's assume that CPlApplet() will translate the messages for us and then call the appropriate method in ControlPanelApplet-Manager. That means that ControlPanelAppletManager needs to come up with a way to respond to all the messages. I named the class that implements the visible functionality of the applet *ControlPanelApplet*. The ControlPanelApplet class defines the functionality that the actual applet must implement.

The set of messages defines the requirements for the ControlPanel-AppletManager and ControlPanelApplet. ControlPanelAppletManager has the following requirements:

1. Has to allow user to add applets to the set of applets being managed

2. Must know how many applets it manages

3. Must know how to forward messages to the appropriate ControlPanelApplet

In order to satisfy the first requirement, ControlPanelAppletManager has a method named void AddApplet(ControlPanelApplet* pApplet). This method adds the applet to the collection of applets being managed by the class. I chose to use an std::vector<> to manage the collection.

```
void ControlPanelAppletManager::AddApplet( ControlPanelApplet*
    pApplet )
{
    AFX_MANAGE_STATE(AfxGetStaticModuleState( ));
    m_vControlPanelApplet.insert( m_vControlPanelApplet.end(),
      pApplet );
}
```

When CPlApplet receives an applet-bound message, the index of the applet is specified in one of the parameters. The user of the applet is responsible for keeping the indexes straight. This makes CPlApplet's job relatively easy. By putting all the ControlPanelApplets into a vector, we just have to pass the message to the ControlPanelApplet at the indicated index.

```
LONG ControlPanelAppletManager::DisplayDialogBox(
    HWND hwndCPl,
    UINT unDlgNumber,
    LONG lData )
{
    AFX_MANAGE_STATE(AfxGetStaticModuleState( ));
    LONG lRetVal = FAILURE;
    if ( unDlgNumber < m_vControlPanelApplet.size() )
    {
        if ( m_vControlPanelApplet[unDlgNumber]->Display(
            hwndCPl, lData ) )
        {
            lRetVal = SUCCESS;
        }
    }
    return lRetVal;
}

LONG ControlPanelAppletManager::Inquire( UINT unDlgNumber,
    LPCPLINFO pCPLInfo )
{
```

```cpp
    AFX_MANAGE_STATE(AfxGetStaticModuleState( ));
    LONG lRetVal = FAILURE;
    if ( unDlgNumber < m_vControlPanelApplet.size() )
    {
        if ( m_vControlPanelApplet[unDlgNumber]
            ->GetCPLInfo(*pCPLInfo) )
        {
            lRetVal = SUCCESS;
        }
    }
    return lRetVal;
}

LONG ControlPanelAppletManager::NewInquire( UINT unDlgNumber,
    LPNEWCPLINFO pNewCPLInfo )
{
    AFX_MANAGE_STATE(AfxGetStaticModuleState( ));
    LONG lRetVal = FAILURE;
    if ( unDlgNumber < m_vControlPanelApplet.size() )
    {
        if ( m_vControlPanelApplet[unDlgNumber]
            ->GetNewCPLInfo(*pNewCPLInfo) )
        {
            lRetVal = SUCCESS;
        }
    }
    return lRetVal;
}

LONG ControlPanelAppletManager::Stop( UINT unDlgNumber,
    LONG lData )
{
    AFX_MANAGE_STATE(AfxGetStaticModuleState( ));
    LONG lRetVal = FAILURE;
    if ( unDlgNumber < m_vControlPanelApplet.size() )
    {
        if ( m_vControlPanelApplet[unDlgNumber]->Stop(lData) )
        {
            lRetVal = SUCCESS;
        }
    }
    return lRetVal;
}
```

ControlPanelAppletManager has a simple interface because the Control Panel sends only eight different messages. After some experimentation and observation, I found that two of the messages, CPL_DBLCLK and CPL_STARTWPARAMS, invoke the same behavior. The documentation states that some differences do exist. In practical use, I found no differences. Feel free to e-mail me if you have a different experience.

```cpp
class ControlPanelAppletManager : private Singleton<ControlPanelAppletManager>
{
private:
    friend Singleton<ControlPanelAppletManager>;
    ControlPanelAppletManager();
    ControlPanelAppletManager( const
ControlPanelAppletManager& );
    ControlPanelAppletManager& operator=( const
ControlPanelAppletManager& );
public:
    virtual ~ControlPanelAppletManager();

    // Return the one and only instance
    static ControlPanelAppletManager& Instance();

    // Add an applet to the managed collection
    void AddApplet( ControlPanelApplet* pApplet );

    // Display the dialog box at the given index
    LONG DisplayDialogBox( HWND hwndCPl, UINT unDlgNumber,
      LONG lData );

    // Called just before the CPL file is removed from
    // memory
    LONG Exit();

    // Returns the number of applets being managed
    LONG GetCount();

    // Initializes the manager and attached applets
    BOOL Init();

    // Get static display information for the Control Panel
    // window
    LONG Inquire( UINT unDlgNumber, LPCPLINFO pCPLInfo );

    // Get dynamic display information for the Control Panel
    // window
    LONG NewInquire( UINT unDlgNumber, LPNEWCPLINFO
      pNewCPLInfo );

    // Inform the given dialog that it's time to shut down
    LONG Stop( UINT unDlgNumber, LONG lData );

    //data members for return values
    static const LONG SUCCESS;
    static const LONG FAILURE;
private:
    std::vector<ControlPanelApplet*> m_vControlPanelApplet;
};
```

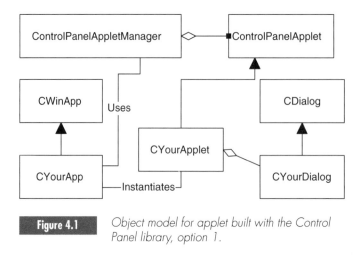

Figure 4.1 *Object model for applet built with the Control Panel library, option 1.*

ControlPanelApplet's relationship to the other classes can be found in Figure 4-1 and Figure 4-2. Because of design options for ControlPanelApplet, which we will discuss next, you may find the relationships in Figure 4-2 easier to use.

ControlPanelApplet defines an abstract base class. It implements three methods that you will override on an as needed basis. For example, most people will not want to implement ControlPanelApplet::GetNewCPLInfo() for efficiency reasons. By default, this method returns false to indicate that the applet will not dynamically update its information. ControlPanelApplet::Init() and ControlPanelApplet::Stop() both return true to indicate that they succeeded. Override these if your applet dynamically allocates resources or has

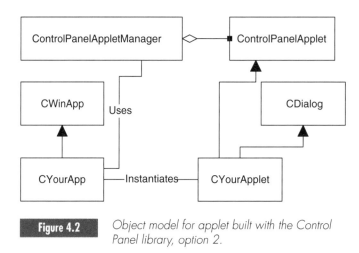

Figure 4.2 *Object model for applet built with the Control Panel library, option 2.*

other initialization or cleanup it may need to perform outside of the constructor/destructor.

Because ControlPanelApplet is an abstract base class, you must implement two methods to make the applet work. First, you must implement GetCPLInfo(CPLINFO&cplInfo). Look again at Table 4.1. The related message, CPL_INQUIRE, passes a pointer to a CPLINFO struct. GetCPLInfo() uses a reference. The library translates the pointer to a reference, guaranteeing that the structure pointed to is valid. I did this for CPL_INQUIRE, and CPL_NEWINQUIRE too, because I wanted to guarantee that the actual pointer did not get manipulated. As one of the best sets of C++ guidelines states "Pointers are a powerful and valuable part of any programmer's toolbox. However, you should use this heavy machinery only when necessary. Don't give a chain saw to a user who just wants a manicure."[2]

Classes derived from ControlPanelApplet must also implement Display(HWND hwndCPl, LONG lData). lData was set when GetCPLInfo() or GetNewCPLInfo() were called. As the entity that set the data, the class should know how to use the data. It might be a pointer; it might be a number; it might be nothing—you get the picture. When the ControlPanelApplet receives the Display() message, it has to bring its dialog to life.

```
class ControlPanelApplet
{
public:
    ControlPanelApplet(){}
    virtual ~ControlPanelApplet(){}
    virtual bool GetCPLInfo( CPLINFO& cplInfo ) = 0;

    // Fills in the NEWCPLINFO struct with the appropriate
      //information. Only provide an override of this if you
      //are using CPL_DYNAMIC_RES
    // as the IDs in GetCPLInfo's implementation.
    virtual bool GetNewCPLInfo( NEWCPLINFO& newCplInfo )
            { return false; }
    virtual bool Display(HWND hwndCPl, LONG lData) = 0;
    virtual bool Stop(LONG lData)
            { return true; }
    virtual bool Init()
            { return true; }
};
```

Look again at Figure 4-2. CYourApplet derives from both CDialog and ControlPanelApplet. For those of you who experience shortness of breath when you see multiple inheritance, I have some advice: get over it. From my viewpoint, a simple applet should not complicate itself by using single inheritance to

2. Marshal P. Cline, Greg A. Lomow, *C++ FAQs*, FAQ 297, page 300, 1995, Addison-Wesley

provide an implementation for two methods. If the Init() or Stop() methods are complex, then you might be better off modeling your applet like Figure 4-1. My experience tells me that I do not gain anything by getting ready for the applet to be invoked. After all, how often do you go into the Control Panel and invoke even two applets? If you are like me, as a user you rarely do this.

Regardless of how you choose to implement your applet within this framework, ControlPanelAppletManager relies on the ControlPanelApplet interface to provide the mechanism necessary to invoke the correct methods on your applet. Because of polymorphism, ControlPanelAppletManager knows how to use your applet without knowing the applet's final type.

By now, you should have a good understanding of the design issues I ran into and the decisions I made. Let's take a look at developing a Control Panel library.

4.3.2   The Control Panel Library

From the previous discussion, we saw that CPlApplet and ControlPanelAppletManager are partners. CPlApplet translates the incoming messages and parameters and then ControlPanelAppletManager carries out the work. These two entities comprise the lion's share of boilerplate code. Because of the relationship between ControlPanelAppletManager and any given ControlPanelApplet-derived class, the CPlApplet and ControlPanelAppletManager can be compiled ahead of time and placed into a library. Technically speaking, they could also be placed in a DLL as well. Because a DLL would add little value, I chose to use a library. The release version of the library is small, about 20KB. The bare-bones CPL file produced by the wizard is about 36KB.

In order to make CPlApplet() visible to the users of your CPL file, your CPL file must explicitly export CPlApplet in the .DEF file like this:

```
; sample.def : Declares the module parameters for the DLL.

LIBRARY      "sample"
DESCRIPTION  'sample Control Panel Application'

EXPORTS
    ; Explicit exports can go here
CPlApplet
```

The actual code for the library is fairly simple. The previous section showed much of it. CPlApplet uses ControlPanelAppletManager to do the work of being a CPL file.

```
LONG APIENTRY CPlApplet( HWND hwndCPl,  // window handle
    UINT uMsg,     // message
    LONG lParam1,  // first message parameter
    LONG lParam2   // second message parameter
)
```

```
{
    ControlPanelAppletManager& theAppletManager =
        ControlPanelAppletManager::Instance();
    LONG lRetVal = 0;
    switch ( uMsg )
    {
        case CPL_DBLCLK:
            lRetVal = theAppletManager.DisplayDialogBox(
                    hwndCPl, lParam1, lParam2 );
            break;
        case CPL_EXIT:
            lRetVal = theAppletManager.Exit();
            break;
        case CPL_GETCOUNT:
            lRetVal = theAppletManager.GetCount();
            break;
        case CPL_INIT:
            lRetVal = theAppletManager.Init();
            break;
        case CPL_INQUIRE:
            lRetVal = theAppletManager.Inquire( lParam1,
                    reinterpret_cast<LPCPLINFO>(lParam2) );
            break;
        case CPL_NEWINQUIRE:
            lRetVal = theAppletManager.NewInquire( lParam1,
                    reinterpret_cast<LPNEWCPLINFO>(lParam2) );
            break;
        case CPL_STOP:
            lRetVal = theAppletManager.Stop( lParam1,
                        lParam2 );
            break;
        case CPL_STARTWPARMS:
            lRetVal = ( ControlPanelAppletManager::SUCCESS ==
                    theAppletManager.DisplayDialogBox( hwndCPl,
                        lParam1, lParam2 ) );
            break;
        default:
            break;
    }
    return lRetVal;
}
```

4.3.3 The Control Panel AppWizard

By the time I was ready to create the AppWizard, I already had finished the library and a small CPL file. The CPL file had limited capabilities. Its end design looked much like Figure 4-2. It returned an icon, label, and description via the overridden GetCPLInfo() method. When it had to display itself, it displayed a dialog with nothing more than an OK and Cancel button. Making an effective

AppWizard means knowing the minimal amount of work required to get the job started. If you can create a project that resembles the output you would want from a wizard, then you are just a few short steps from making the wizard.

I fired up the VC++ AppWizard for AppWizards and told it to base the new project on my minimal implementation. This generated a wizard that made DLLs. The new wizard did not include the Control Panel library in the link settings. This problem was easily solved. I updated CControlPanel-WizardAppWiz::CustomizeProject() to change the output file name to end in *CPL*. In order to decide which version of ControlPanelLib to use, the method checks to see the different build names. For the Release build, Customize-Project tells the project to link with ControlPanelLib.Lib. For Debug versions, the projects links with ControlPanelLibd.lib.

```
void
CControlPanelWizardAppWiz::CustomizeProject(IBuildProject*
    pProject)
{
    using namespace DSProjectSystem;
    long lNumConfigs;
    IConfigurationsPtr pConfigs;
    IBuildProjectPtr pProj;
    // Needed to convert IBuildProject to the DSProjectSystem
    // namespace
    pProj.Attach((DSProjectSystem::IBuildProject*)pProject,
      true);
    pProj->get_Configurations(&pConfigs);
    pConfigs->get_Count(&lNumConfigs);
    //Get each individual configuration
    for (long j = 1 ; j < lNumConfigs+1 ; j++)
    {
        _bstr_t varTool;
        _bstr_t varSwitch;
        IConfigurationPtr pConfig;
        _variant_t varj = j;
        _variant_t reserved;
        pConfig = pConfigs->Item(varj);
        // Remove old output name (exe)
        varTool = "link.exe";
        varSwitch = "/out:";
        pConfig->RemoveToolSettings(varTool, varSwitch,
            reserved);

        // we only generate two configurations.  The first one
        // is debug, the second is release.  Should this ever
        // change, then update the logic.
        BSTR bstrName;
        pConfig->get_Name(&bstrName);
        CString szName = bstrName;
```

```
int nLoc = szName.Find( "Release" );
if ( nLoc == -1 )
{
    varSwitch = "controlpanellibd.lib /out:Debug\\";
}
else
{
    varSwitch = "controlpanellib.lib /out:Release\\";
}
varSwitch +=
    m_Dictionary[_T("safe_root")].AllocSysString();
varSwitch += ".cpl";
pConfig->AddToolSettings(varTool, varSwitch, varj);
    }
}
```

As for the rest of the customization, I customized the template files to make sure that the resources and classes got appropriate names. Likewise, the class names show that the class definitely belongs to the project. The wizard generates the following items for you:

Resources:
- Dialog
- Icon
- String table: one string for the applet name, another for the applet description
- Version

Classes:
- One class derived from CWinApp
- One class derived from CDialog and ControlPanelApplet

Other:
- <ProjectName>.DEF to export CPlApplet for the CPL file
- README.TXT explains what to do with the generated code

At this point, you should have a good understanding of how ControlPanelLib and the MFC Control Panel AppWizard work. Beyond that, you should understand how the Control Panel and an applet communicate with each other. Let's go ahead now and build an applet.

4.4 Using the Tools

The sample presented here does not do anything really worthwhile. It does not provide another way to set up your keyboard or manipulate the set of cursors you can use. While those types of examples can be interesting, even entertaining, they often detract from the task at hand—making a feature work. With the following example, I hope to accomplish these goals:

1. Demonstrate how to place multiple applets into one CPL file.
2. Show how to use GetNewCPLInfo().
3. Show a simple applet that writes and reads values from a file. Don't worry. The second applet can be used to remove the file from your machine.

Let's get started. You can work along with the book or review the finished code included on the CD-ROM. This example, like all others in the book, assumes that you ran the installation program on the CD-ROM. All the wizards and libraries were built using Visual C++ 6.0, Service Pack 3. If you have a different version of Visual C++, now would be a good time to build the library and wizard using your environment. The wizard will probably fail to build when it sees the #import statement in ControlPanelWizard\ControlPanelWizardAW.CPP. Locate DEVBLD.PKG on your machine and modify the import statement appropriately.

4.4.1   Create the Base Project

Create a new project and select MFC Control Panel AppWizard. Then type in an appropriate project name and press OK. You should also OK the New Project Information dialog. As of right now, you have all the code you need to display an applet in the Control Panel. Just to test things out, build the project, copy the CPL file into the C:\WINDOWS\SYSTEM32 directory and run Control Panel. You should see an applet with the name you chose in the Control Panel. If you double click on it, you get a dialog box with an OK and Cancel button (see Figure 4-3). This happens because the AppWizard wrote GetCPLInfo() and Display() for us already. The applet was registered with ControlPanelAppletManager in the ControlPanelAppletManager::InitInstance() method.

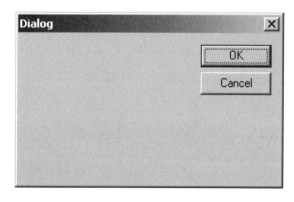

Figure 4.3   *Default dialog generated by the MFC Control Panel AppWizard.*

If you only wanted one applet in the CPL file, the wizard has already done the work required to get the applet to show up in the Control Panel. At this point, you could go ahead and write the code for your dialog. Before you go any further, please take a moment and look at the code the wizard generated for the ControlPanelApplet-derived class. The header has a section of code that looks like this:

```
#ifdef _DEBUG
virtual bool GetNewCPLInfo( NEWCPLINFO& newCplInfo );
#endif // _DEBUG
```

This section has a companion piece in the CPP file.

```
#ifdef _DEBUG
bool CDlgControlPanelApplet::GetNewCPLInfo(
    NEWCPLINFO& newCplInfo )
{
    CString szInfo;
    CString szName;
    szInfo.LoadString( IDD_DLG_CONTROLPANELAPPLET_INFO );
    szName.LoadString( CDlgControlPanelApplet::IDD );

    newCplInfo.dwSize = sizeof( newCplInfo );
    _tcscpy( newCplInfo.szInfo, szInfo );
    _tcscpy( newCplInfo.szName, szName );

    // The value has to transcend the lifespan of the
    // method call.
    m_hIcon = AfxGetApp()->LoadIcon(
        CDlgControlPanelApplet::IDD );
    newCplInfo.hIcon = m_hIcon;
    return true;
}

// If you start using the dynamic information, then delete
// the debug set of information.
bool CDlgControlPanelApplet::GetCPLInfo( CPLINFO& cplInfo )
{
    cplInfo.idIcon = CPL_DYNAMIC_RES;
    cplInfo.idName = CPL_DYNAMIC_RES;
    cplInfo.idInfo = CPL_DYNAMIC_RES;
    cplInfo.lData  = 0;
    return true;
}

#else // _DEBUG
bool CDlgControlPanelApplet::GetCPLInfo( CPLINFO& cplInfo )
{
    cplInfo.idIcon = CDlgControlPanelApplet::IDD;
    cplInfo.idName = CDlgControlPanelApplet::IDD;
```

```
        cplInfo.idInfo = IDD_DLG_CONTROLPANELAPPLET_INFO;
        cplInfo.lData  = 0;
        return true;
    }


#endif // _DEBUG
```

What's going on here? Earlier in the chapter, in section 4.2.2, I alluded to a set of difficulties involved in relying on GetCPLInfo() throughout development. The Control Panel uses the CPLINFO struct to cache information about the applet. The caching should decrease the amount of time required to load the applet into the Control Panel. Windows stores the icon and string information across invocations of the Control Panel and across reboots of the computer. As a result, you probably do not want to lock in the settings for this information on your machine until the code is put into production. To prevent this from happening, the generated application code uses the preprocessor to compile two sets of display instructions for the applet. When running a debug build of the applet, the Control Panel dynamically retrieves the information from the applet. When the release version gets built, the Control Panel can start using the optimized version of the applet. The system appears to permanently cache this information, tying the information to the applet name. If you want to change the icon or display strings after the fact, things can and do get difficult. You cannot delete the applet and then reinstall it. The settings stay across reboots, even without the applet on the machine. One approach does seem to work: run the dynamic version of the applet, then replace that with your new release version. This causes the icon and strings to update.

4.4.2   Implement the Applet

As I stated before, this example shows an applet in action. This applet will maintain some personal information about the user that we want to make accessible to a hypothetical application suite. The applet will allow the user to save their first name, last name, and e-mail address for use with the application suite. The dialog is presented in Figure 4-4. The applet stores the user information in a text file when the user presses OK.

```
void CDlgControlPanelApplet::OnOK()
{
    if ( UpdateData() )
    {
        CString szFileName;
        szFileName.LoadString( IDS_FILENAME );
        std::ofstream file;
        file.open( szFileName );
        if ( file.is_open() )
        {
```

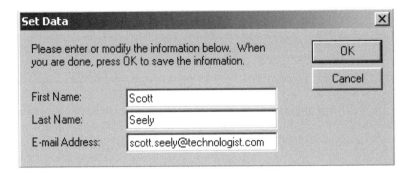

Please enter or modify the information below. When you are done, press OK to save the information.

First Name: Scott
Last Name: Seely
E-mail Address: scott.seely@technologist.com

Figure 4.4   *Example applet that sets user information.*

```
file << std::string(m_szEMailAddress) <<
    std::endl;
file << std::string(m_szFirstName) << std::endl;
file << std::string(m_szLastName) << std::endl;
        }
    }
    CDialog::OnOK();
}
```

When the applet displays the dialog, it checks for the file. If the file exists, the applet reads the contents and populates the fields with the matching data.

```
BOOL CDlgControlPanelApplet::OnInitDialog()
{
    CDialog::OnInitDialog();

    CString szFileName;
    szFileName.LoadString( IDS_FILENAME );
    std::ifstream file;
    file.open( szFileName );
    const int KnBufferSize = 100;
    char buffer[KnBufferSize];
    if ( file.is_open() )
    {
        file.getline( buffer, KnBufferSize );
        m_szEMailAddress = buffer;
        file.getline( buffer, KnBufferSize );
        m_szFirstName = buffer;
        file.getline( buffer, KnBufferSize );
        m_szLastName = buffer;
        UpdateData( false );
    }

    return TRUE;
}
```

4.4.3   Adding Another Applet

To complete the example, we are going to add another applet, CDlgRemove-File, to the CPL file. CDlgRemoveFile will take care of removing the information file. The applet demonstrates how to use GetNewCPLInfo() to change the display charactcristics of an applet at runtime. To do this, we need to add a method to detect the presence of the file the applet uses to store the user information.

```
bool CDlgRemoveFile::IsFilePresent()
{
    AFX_MANAGE_STATE(AfxGetStaticModuleState( ));
    bool bRetVal = false;
    CFileStatus status;
    CString szFileName;
    szFileName.LoadString( IDS_FILENAME );

    if ( CFile::GetStatus( szFileName, status )  )
    {
        bRetVal = true;
    }
    return bRetVal;
}
```

In order to allow the user to tell whether or not the file exists, we will change the icon and related text. If the file exists, the user will see a burning trash barrel along with some special text (Figure 4-5). If the file does not exist, the user will only see a trash barrel along with some descriptive text (Figure 4-6). All this magic is accomplished in CDlgRemoveFile::GetNewCPLInfo().

```
bool CDlgRemoveFile::GetNewCPLInfo( NEWCPLINFO& newCplInfo )
{
    AFX_MANAGE_STATE(AfxGetStaticModuleState( ));
    newCplInfo.dwSize = sizeof( newCplInfo );
    CDlgRemoveFile::IDD;
    IDD_DLG_CLEANUP_FILE_INFO;
    if ( IsFilePresent() )
    {
        m_szInfo.LoadString(IDD_DLG_CLEANUP_FILE_INFO);
        m_szName.LoadString(IDD_DLG_CLEANUP_FILE);
        newCplInfo.hIcon = m_hDirty;
    }
    else
    {
        m_szInfo.LoadString(IDS_FILE_CLEAN_INFO);
        m_szName.LoadString(IDS_FILE CLEAN);
        newCplInfo.hIcon = m_hClean;
    }

    _tcscpy( newCplInfo.szInfo, m_szInfo );
```

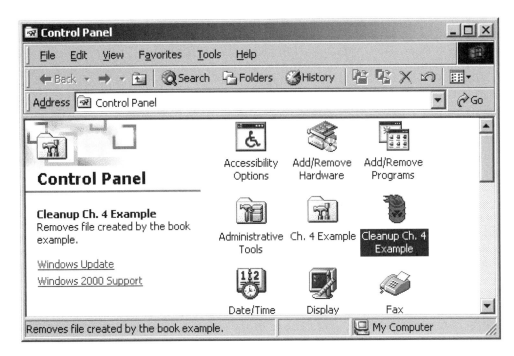

Figure 4.5   *Shows dynamic icon selection in action. Here, the user data can be removed from the machine.*

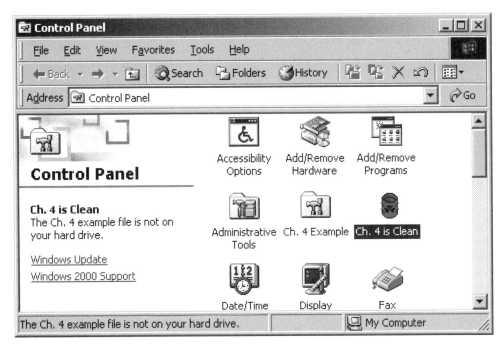

Figure 4.6   *Shows dynamic icon selection in action. Here, the user data is not present on the machine.*

115

```
_tcscpy( newCplInfo.szName, m_szName );
return true;
}
```

To test this out, first run the applet Ch.4 Example. Before any information has been entered, the icon for the applet controlled by CDlgRemoveFile does not have a fire burning and the label reads *Ch. 4 is Clean*. The description reads *The Ch. 4 example file is not on your hard drive.* Now, enter some information and press OK. Given the implementation CDlgRemoveFile, you probably expected that the trash barrel icon would be on fire now. Never fear. From the Control Panel, select *View→Refresh*. Ahh, fire.

4.4.4 Debugging Control Panel Applets

The tools provided in this chapter get a lot of the work done, but not all of it. The applet still has to be debugged. To debug, you will need to use RUNDLL32.EXE. RUNDLL32 lives in the system32 directory within your Windows installation. Within DevStudio and with your Control Panel applet project open, open up the project settings dialog (*Project→Settings*). On the debug tab, set the *Executable for debug session:* to RUNDLL32.EXE. In the *Program arguments:*, put the following text:

```
SHELL32.DLL,Control_RunDLL debug\[name of CPL file], @[applet index]
```

RUNDLL32.EXE uses SHELL32.DLL to run the Control Panel applet. The above command line runs the specified Control Panel applet using the applet specified at the zero-based index. To debug the CDlgRemoveFile, the line would read:

```
SHELL32.DLL, Control_RunDLL debug\ControlPanelApplet.CPL, @1
```

Because CDlgRemoveFile was added second, we use *@1* to indicate we want to debug the second applet in the CPL file.

4.5 Summary

The Control Panel provides a place for you to put tools to configure hardware and software. For software, make sure that it seems right to configure the software from the Control Panel and not from the application. For example, system services would benefit from a Control Panel applet. On the other hand, having the user configure applications like Microsoft Word from the Control Panel would only clutter the system. In the end, think about what you want to put into the Control Panel. If you have a hard time justifying the decision, think of a different way to configure your application.

This chapter presented a library, wizard and base class to help you build Control Panel applets more easily and quickly. The library implements the basic functionality of a CPL file: message translation and applet management. Using the wizard, you can get a basic CPL applet up and running in no time. This allows you to worry about the more important things—namely, getting the applet to do its job. The class, ControlPanelApplet, provides a base for your applet to build on. Using the interface defined by ControlPanelApplet, you can hook into the ControlPanelAppletManager and let it do the tedious job of communicating with the Control Panel.

Screen Savers

*M*ost items in the Windows shell can be used in one way or another to enhance an application's functionality. Few applications need to use everything the shell can provide. Even fewer need a screen saver. Just try to say this sentence aloud and keep a straight face: More people will want our financials package if we write a really cool screen saver.

Well? I think I made my point. It is fun to write screen savers—not necessary. When thinking of ways to customize your computer, few things come close to the personal touch of a screen saver that you wrote yourself. People see it and ask where you got it, and when you respond "I wrote it myself," they are impressed.

When I first started trying to figure out screen savers, I did it because it looked like fun. The attraction to write a screen saver is similar to the attraction to write games. Most of the people I know who are really into computers started in this field because of games. After spending hours with these machines, we got an itch to find out how they work. Years later, most of us are still fairly clueless when it comes to writing a decent game engine. Some of us know just enough to be dangerous when it comes to graphics. But with a little help, many of us know enough to create the graphics for a decent screen saver.

In this chapter, we will cover the following topics:

- Screen saver responsibilities
- Screen saver internals
- Benefits of SCRNSAVE.LIB over writing your own
- An MFC Screen Saver AppWizard
- Writing a screen saver using the wizard

5.1   Screen Saver Responsibilities

When screen savers first came on the scene, they had one purpose: to extend the lifetime of the monitor. If the images on a computer monitor do not change often enough, the monitor will eventually have an image burned into its screen. Someone proposed that the computer could draw different things on the screen so that the same image did not show up for hours or days on end. By changing the monitor's display often enough, a screen saver could extend the lifetime of a monitor. Most computers will display a screen saver after a period of time with no mouse or keyboard activity.

Over time, screen savers picked up another job: securing a computer from direct access. With a password protected screen saver, a user can block others from using their computer while the screen saver is active. Screen savers, coupled with password protection, have a side benefit: people cannot see what you are working on. We have all had the "quick question" turn into the one-hour discussion. While you are away, you do not want to leave personal e-mail or other information visible for passersby to see.

In the Windows world, a screen saver has a few more responsibilities. The extra responsibilities relate to how the user selects and sets up a screen saver. A Windows screen saver must provide a preview window of some sort for the Display Control Panel applet's Screen Saver tab. Additionally, a screen saver has to provide a way for the user to configure the screen saver. Even if the screen saver does not have any configurable options, it should display an "about" dialog. Starting with Windows 98 and continuing with Windows 2000, a screen saver needs to be able to protect more that just one monitor.

5.2   Screen Saver Internals

On the outside, a screen saver either saves the screen as a full-screen window, displays a configuration dialog, or demonstrates itself on the screen saver tab of the Display Properties Control Panel applet. Inside, it has to know which of these behaviors it should display when invoked by the user or the operating system. It learns this by examining the command line used to invoke the screen saver. Additionally, it should let Windows know when it gets activated or deactivated.

On Windows NT or 2000, the screen saver runs on a separate desktop named "screen-saver."[1] Windows 2000, and all versions of NT, monitor that

---

1. MSDN, "HOWTO: Detect If a Screen Saver Is Running on Windows NT", Article ID: Q150785

desktop. If the user has password protection turned on for the screen saver, the Winlogon process will display a dialog indicating that the workstation is locked. In order to unlock the workstation, the user has to follow the directions on the dialog. As you may be aware, the CTRL-ALT-DEL key sequence should not allow a reboot option when the screen saver is running and secured. Winlogon accomplishes this protection by registering the "three finger salute," or Secure Attention Sequence (SAS) with the system when Winlogon initializes. Making this the first process ensures that no other application has hooked that key sequence.[2]

On Windows NT and Windows 2000, the screen saver executes in the context of the currently logged in user. As a result, it can do anything the currently logged in user can do. This includes shutting down Windows, adding users, and modifying the registry. Because the screen saver executes on its own desktop, it cannot enumerate the windows of user-mode applications. This design prevents unauthorized users from seeing what you are doing.[3] On all other versions of Windows, the screen saver does have access to the user-mode applications and the desktop.

When a screen saver is invoked, it has to properly handle the information passed to it on the command line. Based on the command line parameters, it must perform a prescribed action. See Table 5.1 for more information.

Table 5.1	*Interpretation of the screen saver command line.*
Command	**Meaning**
/s, -s	Run in full screen mode.
/c, -c	Display configuration dialog.
/a, -a	Change screen saver password. This command is not invoked under Windows NT or Windows 2000 because the screen saver dialog does not have a Change Password button.
/p [HWND], -p [HWND]	Display in demonstration mode in indicated HWND.

---

2. MSDN, "Window Stations And Desktops", MSDN Library\Specifications\Platforms\Telephone Application Programming Interface(TAPI)\Windows NT Security: Replaceable Winlogon User Interface\Model Overview\Window Stations and Desktops

3. MSDN, "Security and Screen Savers", Article ID: Q96780

A screen saver is a full-fledged executable with an .SCR extension (instead of .EXE). The Windows 3.*x* documentation for screen savers states that you need to have a certain resource ID to use as the name of the screen saver in the display properties dialog. Since Windows 95, that requirement no longer exists. Now, the screen saver selection list on the Display Properties property sheet gets the list of screen savers by searching for all the .SCR files in the system32 directory. The filename preceding .SCR is used as the screen saver name. If a screen saver is named SS[screen saver name].SCR, only the [screen saver name] portion is used for display. If the file is named [screen saver name].SCR, then [screen saver name] appears in the selection list.

5.3   Writing A Screen Saver

When writing a screen saver, you have two choices: use SCRNSAVE.LIB or roll your own. If you enjoy writing straight C code and have little or no interest in using MFC, then you should be just fine with SCRNSAVE.LIB. If you choose to go down this path, check out MSDN. MSDN has an article detailing what you need to do to make the screen saver work at the following location on the CD: \MSDN Library\Platform SDK\User Interface Services\Shell and Common Controls\Shell Programmers Guide\Handling Screen Savers. SCRNSAVE.LIB does everything your heart could desire and more. However, the library and MFC do not play well together. I am certain that they can work together, but so far I have not found a solution that is easier than rolling my own. Most of the time, the old adage "Don't re-invent the wheel" rings true—just not with screen savers. I would love for someone to come up with a better solution than the one about to be presented. My solution does not leverage the work done to keep SCRNSAVE.LIB up to date. As a result, I will have to maintain my library so that it keeps up with SCRNSAVE.LIB.

The MFC-based screen saver library must implement all the functionality made available by SCRNSAVE.LIB. Because we do not want to exclude users of Windows 9x, we have some additional work to do. Namely, the screen saver will need to detect mouse movement and keyboard activity. In response, it will have to know whether or not the screen saver is password protected. If password protection was enabled, then the screen saver needs to ask for the password. The solution must be easy to apply for new applications. The screen saver must also be able to operate on multiple screens, but fail gracefully if the operating system does not support this feature.

The last requirement, multiple monitor operation, is the easiest to implement. MULTIMON.H, the header file for the multiple monitor support, uses GetProcAddress() to hook up to the correct monitor function depending on the operating system. If the function does not exist on the platform, MULTIMON.H will return information consistent with a single monitor system. For example, the MonitorFromWindow() function obtains a handle to the display monitor that has the largest area of intersection with the bounding rectangle of a specified window. In Windows 95 and NT, MonitorFromWindow() returns PRIMARY_MONITOR since the operating system does not support multiple monitors.

5.3.1 Implementing an MFC Screen Saver AppWizard and Library

When I first started implementing AppWizards, I wondered whether I was applying them too often. Before you create an AppWizard, you have to analyze your goals. With the screen saver, I want to make sure that at the click of a button I get a fully functional one. All screen savers share common code. While developing this AppWizard, I put a lot of the common functionality into a library and the rest into the AppWizard-generated code. The first design was just a library. This worked fine and allowed the user to build an MFC-based screen saver fairly easily. However, this had a major drawback: too many steps to get something working.

I also wanted to publish an article.[4] In order for the article to be useful, I could not force the reader to go through a bunch of contortions just to make my library work. This included making the reader put a library and header files into a location visible to Visual C++. As a result, I implemented 100 percent of the code in an AppWizard. This approach proved successful. I received a lot of good feedback from my article, "Writing Screen Savers Using MFC," which was published in the March 1999 *Windows Developer's Journal*.[5] As I used the wizard to generate different screen savers, I noticed that I never did much to the code that made the program a screen saver. I never modified the CWinApp-based class and did not touch the window code beyond Create() and OnPaint()—essentially, the code that belonged in a library. So, what was I to do?

Well, I restructured everything. The restructuring became possible because of this book. The book's CD comes with an installation program that installs all of the libraries and header files into appropriate locations. The installer also modifies the Visual C++ development environment to see the headers and libraries wherever you, the reader, installed them. As a result, I did not need to worry about the setup issues you might face. As long as you ran the installation program, everything would be OK.

---

4. I had to start writing somewhere and it's a lot easier to get articles published than books.

5. Article lead times can be pretty large. The article was submitted in September 1998 and I started on the book in February 1999, before *Windows Developer's Journal* hit the streets.

As you will soon see, the choice to implement all the screen saver functionality in a library has a lot of benefits. The original idea had one major drawback: it mixed all the boilerplate screen saver functionality in with the code specific to a given screen saver. When Microsoft updates the requirements, you have to update the code for every screen saver you have ever written. Yuck!

Putting all the functionality into a library has a big benefit. When the changes come, just update the library to handle the new requirements. Then, relink your screen savers. That is the way screen saver programming is supposed to work when you use SCRNSAVE.LIB.

5.3.2   CScreenSaverApp

As I mentioned earlier, a screen saver is an executable file. When the screen saver starts up, it interprets the command line and invokes the requested behavior. To implement the application behavior, I created a class named CScreenSaverApp. CScreenSaverApp acts as a base class for all screen saver applications.

```
class CScreenSaverApp : public CWinApp
{
public:
    CScreenSaverApp();

    // Add a screen saver window using the specified HWND
    // inside the specified CRect.
    bool AddScreenSaverWindow( HWND hWnd, CRect oRect =
        CRect() );

    // Helps decode how the screen saver was started.
    enum StartType { ScreenSaver, ConfigureSaver,
        DemoScreenSaver, ChangePassword, NothingSpecified };

    virtual BOOL InitInstance();

    DECLARE_MESSAGE_MAP()

protected:
    // Examines the command line and figures out the start
    // type.If the start type is DemoScreenSaver, then the
    // hWnd value will be set to the preview window's hWnd.
    // Otherwise, it will be NULL.
    StartType GetStartType(HWND& hWnd);

    // Must override this to provide a pointer to the
    // configuration dialog created by your application.
    virtual CDialog* GetNewConfigurationDialog(CWnd* pParent)
        = 0;
```

```
// This method provides a pointer to the screen saver
// window used by your application.
virtual CScreenSaverWnd* GetNewScreenSaverWnd() = 0;

private:
    // Enumerates all the monitors and invokes the screen
    // saver for each one.
    bool SaveAllMonitors();
};
```

InitInstance() gets invoked after all the application initialization is complete and before the application begins its work. CScreenSaverApp overrides InitInstance() and performs all the necessary screen saver tasks. A separate instance of the screen saver handles each task in Table 5.1. One instance will display the preview version of the screen saver and another instance handles setup. Yet another instance displays the screen saver in full screen mode. Windows handles synchronizing all of this. For example, between the time that you modify the settings of the screen saver and the time that you return to the Display Settings property sheet, the preview version of the screen saver will be stopped and restarted.

Upon exiting CScreenSaverApp::InitInstance(), the application will either be in full screen saver mode or will simply exit and terminate the program like a dialog based application. Let's go through CScreenSaverApp::InitInstance(). Along the way, we will see how a screen saver starts up.

```
BOOL CScreenSaverApp::InitInstance()
{
    BOOL bRetVal = FALSE;

    // Note: only allows linking to MFC dynamically
    Enable3dControls();

    HWND hWnd = NULL;
    switch (GetStartType(hWnd))
    {
        case ScreenSaver:
            bRetVal = SaveAllMonitors();
            break;
        case DemoScreenSaver:
            bRetVal = AddScreenSaverWindow( hWnd );
            break;
        case ConfigureSaver:
            {
                std::auto_ptr<CDialog> pDlg(
                    GetNewConfigurationDialog(
                        CWnd::GetActiveWindow()));
                pDlg->DoModal();
            }
            break;
```

```
    case ChangePassword:
        {
            HINSTANCE mpr = LoadLibrary(g_KszMprDll);
            if(NULL != mpr)
            {
                PWCHGPROC pwd = (PWCHGPROC)GetProcAddress(
                    mpr,
                    g_KszPwdChangePW);
                if(NULL != pwd)
                {
                    pwd(g_KszProviderName,
                        CWnd::GetActiveWindow()
                        ->GetSafeHwnd(),
                        0, NULL);
                }
            }
            FreeLibrary(mpr);
        }
        break;
    }
    return bRetVal;
}
```

By reading InitInstance(), you see how the screen saver handles each of its four responsibilities. If told to go into full screen mode, it invokes SaveAll-Monitors(). SaveAllMonitors() invokes one screen saver window per monitor. If the user has the Display Properties dialog open, then the application invokes a demonstration version of the screen saver. All classes deriving from CScreenSaverApp must implement a method called GetNewConfiguration-Dialog(). This method returns a pointer to the dialog to be used to configure the screen saver. CScreenSaverApp assumes the responsibility for maintaining the pointer to the dialog.

Under Windows 9x, the user has the option to change the screen saver password. The screen saver can either provide its own password setup facilities or use the facilities provided by the operating system. CScreenSaverApp lets the operating system handle this piece of work. It loads MPR.DLL and gets the address of PwdChangePasswordA. The code then invokes the PwdChangePassword function, passing in *SCRSAVE* as the name of the password provider to change.

In order to handle multiple monitors, CScreenSaverApp relies on two functions, CScreenSaverApp::SaveAllMonitors() and MonitorEnumProc(). Save-AllMonitors() calls EnumDisplayMonitors() to get all the available monitors. For each one, MonitorEnumProc() gets called. MonitorEnumProc() receives the window coordinates for the monitor and, in my implementation, a pointer to the calling CScreenSaverApp. This pointer allows MonitorEnumProc to call back into CScreenSaverApp and ask CScreenSaverApp to add a screen saver window for a given monitor. The code to implement this is found in CScreen-

SaverApp::AddScreenSaverWindow(). AddScreenSaverWindow() relies on the other pure virtual function declared in CScreenSaverApp, GetNewScreen-SaverWnd(). GetNewScreenSaverWnd() creates a new instance of the CScreenSaverWnd derived class in your screen saver application and returns it. CScreenSaverApp and CScreenSaverWnd will work together to make sure that there are no memory leaks. The code looks like this:

```
BOOL CALLBACK MonitorEnumProc(
    HMONITOR hMonitor    // handle to display monitor
    HDC hdcMonitor,      // handle to monitor-appropriate device
                         //     context
    LPRECT lprcMonitor,  // pointer to monitor intersection
                         //     rectangle
    LPARAM dwData        // data passed from EnumDisplayMonitors
)
{
    CScreenSaverApp* pApp =
        reinterpret_cast<CScreenSaverApp*>(dwData);
    bool bRetVal = false;
    if ( pApp )
    {
        bRetVal = pApp->AddScreenSaverWindow( NULL, CRect(
            lprcMonitor ) );
    }
    return bRetVal;
}


bool CScreenSaverApp::SaveAllMonitors()
{
    EnumDisplayMonitors( NULL,
                         NULL,
                         MonitorEnumProc,
                         reinterpret_cast<LPARAM>(this) );
    return true;
}

bool CScreenSaverApp::AddScreenSaverWindow( HWND hWnd, CRect
   oRect /*= CRect()*/)
{
    bool bRetVal = false;
    CScreenSaverWnd* pWnd = GetNewScreenSaverWnd();
    if ( pWnd->Create( hWnd, oRect ) )
    {
        bRetVal = true;
        if ( NULL == m_pMainWnd )
        {
            m_pMainWnd = pWnd;
        }
```

```
    }

    return bRetVal;
}
```

That's pretty much all there is to implementing the CScreenSaverApp. The required overrides, GetNewConfigurationDialog() and GetNewScreen-SaverWnd(), are fairly simple. If you create a project called MyScreenSaver with the MFC Screen Saver AppWizard, these methods will look like this:

```
CDialog* CMyScreenSaverApp::GetNewConfigurationDialog( CWnd*
    pParent )
{
    return new CMyScreenSaverDlg( pParent );
}

CScreenSaverWnd* CMyScreenSaverApp::GetNewScreenSaverWnd()
{
    return new CMyScreenSaverWnd();
}
```

5.3.3   CScreenSaverWnd

CScreenSaverWnd is the part of the screen saver that you really care about. First and foremost, it owns the responsibility of changing the screen often enough so that no images are burned into the screen. Second, it keeps your computer secure when you are away for extended periods of time. CScreen-SaverWnd takes care of the security piece of the puzzle. Your derived class does the fun part: saving the screen. The security piece is fairly simple. If the screen saver window detects any user activity, it checks to see if password protection is turned on. The application then asks the user for their password if needed.

At startup, the screen saver registers the message MFCScreenSaverClosing. This message gets sent to all top level windows when the screen saver needs to shut down. In a multi-monitor system, all the screen saver windows will be running as top level windows. Upon receiving this message, the window closes itself. The action of closing the window destroys the window and its associated memory.

When the CScreenSaverWnd instance first displays itself, it also performs some initialization. The CScreenSaverWnd provides a version of Create() that takes an HWND and a CRect as parameters.

```
BOOL CScreenSaverWnd::Create(HWND hParentWnd/*= NULL*/,
    CRect oRect/*= CRect()*/)
{
    DWORD dwStyle = 0;
    DWORD dwExStyle = 0;
```

```
if (NULL == hParentWnd)
{ // Setup options for screensaver mode
    dwStyle = WS_POPUP | WS_VISIBLE;
    dwExStyle = WS_EX_TOPMOST;
    SystemParametersInfo( SPI_SETSCREENSAVEACTIVE, TRUE,
        &m_nPrev, 0);
}
else
{ // Setup options for preview mode
    dwStyle = WS_VISIBLE | WS_CHILD;
    CWnd* pParent = CWnd::FromHandle(hParentWnd);
    // If the window is invalid, leave.
    if ((NULL == pParent) || (!::IsWindow(hParentWnd)))
    {
        return FALSE;
    }
    pParent->GetClientRect(&oRect);
}
CString szClassName = AfxRegisterWndClass(
        CS_HREDRAW|CS_VREDRAW|CS_SAVEBITS|CS_DBLCLKS,NULL);


// look in registry to see if password protection is
// turned on, otherwise don't bother to load the password
// handler DLL
HKEY hKey;
if (NULL == hParentWnd)
{ // Don't do this unless we are in screen saver mode
    if (ERROR_SUCCESS == RegOpenKey(HKEY_CURRENT_USER,
        REGSTR_PATH_SCREENSAVE,&hKey))
    {
        DWORD dwVal = 0;
        DWORD dwSize=sizeof(dwVal);
        if ((RegQueryValueEx( hKey,
                REGSTR_VALUE_USESCRPASSWORD, NULL,
                NULL,(BYTE *) &dwVal,&dwSize) ==
                    ERROR_SUCCESS) && dwVal)
        {
            // try to load the DLL that contains password
            // proc.
            m_hPWDDLL = LoadLibrary(g_KszPwdDLL);
            if (m_hPWDDLL)
            { // Get the address of the procedure
                VerifyPasswordProc = (VERIFYPWDPROC)
                    GetProcAddress(m_hPWDDLL,g_KszFnName);
                if( !VerifyPasswordProc)
                {
                    FreeLibrary(m_hPWDDLL);
                    m_hPWDDLL = NULL;
                }
            }
        }
```

```
        }
        RegCloseKey(hKey);
    }
}
// Lastly, create the screen saver window.
return CreateEx(dwExStyle, szClassName, _T(""), dwStyle,
    oRect.left, oRect.top, oRect.Width(),
    oRect.Height(), hParentWnd, NULL, NULL);
}
```

When Create() first starts off, it checks to see if it will be taking over the entire screen or displaying itself in another window. When Windows wants the screen saver to run in demonstration mode, it passes it an HWND value. A NULL HWND indicates that the screen saver should run in full-screen mode. In your own screen saver, you can use a call to GetParentWnd() to see if you are running as a child window or as a full-screen screen saver. A NULL return value means that the screen saver is protecting the screen. A valid pointer indicates that the demonstration version is running. CScreenSaverApp passes this value to CScreenSaverWnd::Create(). When running in full screen mode, Create() makes the window a visible popup window. Additionally, it places the window at the top of the z-order and sets the SPI_SETSCREEN-SAVEACTIVE flag to TRUE. Because the window may need to protect a monitor other that the primary monitor, Create() also receives a CRect. The CRect indicates the coordinates of the monitor. CScreenSaverApp enumerates the monitors in its InitInstance() method. If the window needs to run in demonstration mode, Create() makes a visible child window. Create() also grabs the rectangle of hParentWnd. The window will be displayed in that rectangle. As a child window, it moves with the parent window.

Next, Create() registers the window class. CScreenSaverWnd requires the generated string as a parameter for the call to CreateEx() at the end of the Create(). After registering the class, Create() sets up the information needed for password authentication. If password protection is turned on, Create() loads PASSWORD.CPL and looks for the password authentication method, VerifyScreenSavePwd(). Under Windows NT and Windows 2000, this section of code never executes. These versions of Windows rely on Winlogon to do the security work. Finally, Create() actually creates and displays the screen-saver window.

In order to close the screen saver, two methods, CheckClosing() and VerifyPassword(), get invoked.. CheckClosing() makes sure that the system is not bombarding us with messages. Every mouse movement, key press, or button click generates another message and stuffs it into the message queue. During CheckClosing(), the code blocks the queue, allowing it to fill up. Once the function exits, it uses a one-second delay to allow the queue to clear itself. This behavior does not exactly mimic the behavior one can obtain by using SCRNSAVE.LIB. Because I can use MFC to build a screen saver, I have learned to live with this minor inconsistency. CheckClosing() calls VerifyPassword(), which in turn calls VerifyScreenSavePwd() if it is available. If the password is verified, CheckClosing() will set the SPI_SETSCREENSAVE-ACTIVE flag to FALSE and then broadcast the MFCScreenSaverClosing message to all other windows.

```
bool CScreenSaverWnd::VerifyPassword()
{
    bool bRetVal = false;
    m_bVerifyingPassword = true;
    if (NULL != VerifyPasswordProc)
    {
        bRetVal = (VerifyPasswordProc(GetSafeHwnd()) != 0);
    }
    else if ( NULL == GetParent() )
    {
        bRetVal = true;
    }
    m_bVerifyingPassword = false;
    return bRetVal;
}


void CScreenSaverWnd::CheckClosing()
{
    // Don't verify less than 1s after the last check
    CTime oNow = CTime::GetCurrentTime();
    static const CTimeSpan SKoTimeSpan(0, 0, 0, 1);
    if ((oNow - m_oLastCheckTime) > SKoTimeSpan)
    {
        if (VerifyPassword())
        {
            SystemParametersInfo(SPI_SETSCREENSAVEACTIVE,
                FALSE, &m_nPrev,0);
            ::PostMessage(HWND_BROADCAST, g_unCloseAll, 0, 0);
        }
        m_oLastCheckTime = CTime::GetCurrentTime();
    }
}
```

In the end, to make a screen saver window, you just need to write an OnPaint() method and set up any needed timers in an override of Create(). The AppWizard's minimal implementation writes the methods like this:

```
BOOL CMyScreenSaverWnd::Create(HWND hParentWnd/*= NULL*/,
    CRect oRect/*= CRect()*/)
{
    BOOL bRetVal = CScreenSaverWnd::Create(hParentWnd, oRect);

    // TODO: Add any timers or other initialization code here.
    return bRetVal;
```

```
}

void CMyScreenSaverWnd::OnPaint()
{
    CPaintDC dc(this); // device context for painting
    CRect oRect;
    CBrush oBrush(RGB(0,0,0));
    GetClientRect(oRect);
    dc.FillRect(oRect, &oBrush);
}
```

Implementing the CDialog derived class is fairly simple. Just decide what you want the configuration dialog to look like and what you want it to do. It will either edit some screen saver specific values from the registry or display information about the screen saver. Either way, you are just writing a regular dialog class.

5.4 Example: The Bouncing Ball

Up to this point, we have seen how a screen saver works and learned how to make this functionality work using MFC. An MFC-based library was created to mimic the functionality provided by SCRNSAVE.LIB. I created a wizard that integrates the library with the basic code needed to make a screen saver. The generated screen saver creates an OnPaint() method similar to the one at the end of the last section. Now, let's build a screen saver that has a little ball that bounces around the screen. The user will be able to select the color of the ball. The screen saver will scale the ball to the size of the window.

Fire up Visual Studio and create a new project. Select the MFC Screen Saver AppWizard as the project type, fill in the name *Bouncing Ball*, and press OK. One more press of OK and the wizard will generate all the needed starter code. If you compile the code and copy it with your other screen savers, you should have a screen saver that exactly mimics the Blank Screen screen saver.

We want the screen saver to be able to store the color of the ball. To make our lives easy, let's store the information in the registry. As you know, CWinApp allows the user to store things in the registry using the old WriteProfileXXX and GetProfileXXX functions that used to be for INI file manipulation. The user specifies the company name (in my case, *Prentice Hall*), and CWinApp takes care of saving the files under the application name. In order to do this, we need to enhance CBouncingBallApp::InitInstance() to know what registry key to look at.

```
BOOL CBouncingBallApp::InitInstance()
{
    this->SetRegistryKey( _T("Prentice Hall") );
```

```
        return CScreenSaverApp::InitInstance();
}
```

Later on, when we write the code to save the user selected color, we can go use the WriteProfileInt() and GetProfileInt methods to write and read the registry. The application data for the Bouncing Ball screen saver gets saved under \HKEY_CURRENT_USER\Software\Prentice Hall\Bouncing Ball. Our application object is now complete. Let us begin working on the screen saver window.

I developed this screen saver over a series of iterations. With each iteration, I figured out what I needed to do and how to get it done. So far, we decided that we would store the application data in the registry. Deciding where to store the data and implementing that decision took no time. Two pieces must be written in order to make this screen saver work: the CBouncingBallWnd class and the CBouncingBallDlg class. CBouncingBallWnd saves the screen. CBouncingBallDlg configures the behavior of CBouncingBallWnd. Because of this, we are going to design and implement CBouncingBallWnd first. After designing and implementing the window class, we will have a good idea of what parts we want to allow the user to configure. By giving default return values for the registry queries, we can get CBouncingBallWnd ready to play with CBouncingBallDlg before we save any information to the registry.

CBouncingBallWnd needs a way to track where it last drew the ball, a way to figure out the ball's starting size, and a place to start the timer. All of this can be done by providing a custom version of Create(). So that the ball will scale well, the window will determine how big it is. Based on this information, it will make the ball's height and width equal to one-tenth the height of the window. To initialize the ball's color, a COLORREF member variable, m_color, also needs to be initialized in Create().

```
BOOL CBouncingBallWnd::Create(HWND hParentWnd, CRect oRect)
{
    BOOL bRetVal = CScreenSaverWnd::Create(hParentWnd, oRect);

    m_bHasParent = ( hParentWnd != NULL );

    if ( bRetVal )
    {
        m_color = AfxGetApp()->GetProfileInt(
            RegistryData::m_szSection,
            RegistryData::m_szKey,
            RGB( 255, 0, 0 ) );
        m_unEventID = SetTimer(m_unEventID,
            m_nDuration, NULL);

        CRect oThisRect;
        GetClientRect( oThisRect );
        int nSize = oThisRect.Height() / 10;
```

```
    m_oLastFilledRect = CRect( oThisRect.TopLeft(),
                               CSize( nSize, nSize ) );
}
return bRetVal;
}
```

The bouncing ball should have a black background because this helps us accomplish our primary goal: saving the screen. A black background guarantees that the screen has been wiped clean. We could also have the ball erase the screen as it moves. Unfortunately, it may take a while to remove all the information that was on the screen and the screen saver would not conceal any information. The background painting can be handled by handling the WM_ERASEBKGND message.

```
BOOL CBouncingBallWnd::OnEraseBkgnd(CDC* pDC)
{
    CRect oRect;
    CBrush oBrush( RGB( 0, 0, 0 ) );

    GetClientRect( oRect );
    pDC->FillRect( oRect, &oBrush );
      return CScreenSaverWnd::OnEraseBkgnd(pDC);
}
```

The ball will get painted by adding a handler for the WM_PAINT message. This message will not be fired if the window does not have an area in need of painting. The timer created in the Create() method makes sure that WM_PAINT gets called at regular intervals. Every time a CBouncingBallWnd receives a WM_TIMER message, it invalidates the m_oLastFilledRect. This sets off the chain of events that lead to the ball being repainted at its new location.

```
void CBouncingBallWnd::OnTimer(UINT nIDEvent)
{
    if ( nIDEvent == m_unEventID )
    {
        KillTimer( m_unEventID );
        InvalidateRect( m_oLastFilledRect );
        m_unEventID = SetTimer( m_unEventID,
                                m_nDuration,
                                NULL);
    }

    CScreenSaverWnd::OnTimer(nIDEvent);
}
```

Last, we add the code to draw a bouncing ball. The ball bounces by knowing if it is moving up or down and left or right. Whenever the ball hits a window edge, it changes its direction with respect to that edge. For example, if the ball currently moves left and up, then hits the top of the window, it will change its direction to left and down. The OnPaint method also contains one bit of frivolous code. The same window can also be used to just draw a bouncing ball. When the window is not running as a screen saver, it checks the registry every time through to see if the ball's color has changed. This functionality is used by the configuration dialog to display a sample of the changes on the dialog. OnPaint() looks like this:

```
void CBouncingBallWnd::OnPaint()
{
    CPaintDC dc( this );
    CRect oRect;
    GetClientRect(oRect);

    if ( m_bHasParent )
    {
        m_color = AfxGetApp()->GetProfileInt(
            RegistryData::m_szSection,
            RegistryData::m_szKey, RGB( 255, 0, 0 ) );
    }

    CBrush oBrush( m_color );
    dc.SelectObject( &oBrush );

    int nXOffset = ( m_bMoveRight ? 1 : -1 );
    int nYOffset = ( m_bMoveDown ? 1 : -1 );
    m_oLastFilledRect.OffsetRect( nXOffset, nYOffset );
    dc.Ellipse( &m_oLastFilledRect );

    if ( oRect.TopLeft().x > m_oLastFilledRect.TopLeft().x )
    {
        m_bMoveRight = true;
    }
    else if ( oRect.BottomRight().x <
            m_oLastFilledRect.BottomRight().x )
    {
        m_bMoveRight = false;
    }
    if ( oRect.TopLeft().y > m_oLastFilledRect.TopLeft().y )
    {
        m_bMoveDown = true;
    }
    else if ( oRect.BottomRight().y <
            m_oLastFilledRect.BottomRight().y )
    {
        m_bMoveDown = false;
    }
}
```

The configuration dialog does not do much. The user can change the color by pressing the Change Color button and then the demonstration running in the dialog changes its color. The CBouncingBallWnd in the dialog uses the client area of a static control as its drawing surface. To make this happen, I mapped the static control to a CStatic member variable, m_lblDemo. Then I added these lines to CBouncingBallDlg::OnInit-Dialog():

```
CBouncingBallApp* pApp =
     dynamic_cast<CBouncingBallApp*>(AfxGetApp());
if ( pApp )
{
    pApp->AddScreenSaverWindow( m_lblDemo.GetSafeHwnd() );
}
```

When the configuration dialog runs, it looks like the screen shot in Figure 5-1. With the dialog completed, our screen saver is done. To use it, either copy it to the Windows\System (Win 9x) or WinNT\System32 (WinNT, Windows 2000) directory or right-click on the screen saver file and select *Install*. You should now be able to see the ball bouncing on your screen.

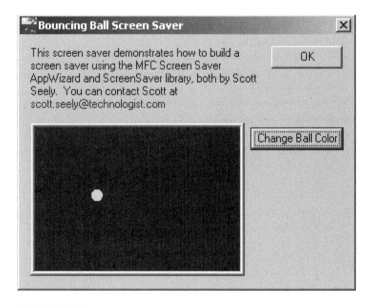

Figure 5.1   *Example screen saver configuration dialog.*

5.5 Summary

Screen savers stop the computer from burning images into the monitor. Additionally, they provide security by locking the computer down after a preset number of minutes and by removing potentially sensitive information from the screen. Visual C++ puts the programmer in an awkward position by making it difficult for the programmer to access this functionality using MFC. I believe that this is the unfortunate side effect of a decision made early on in the development of SCRNSAVE.LIB and Windows. ScreenSaverLib.LIB allows the MFC programmer to write a few pieces of code and magically see a screen saver appear. With the MFC Screen Saver AppWizard, the programmer can easily generate the most minimal of the screen savers, the blank screen screen saver.

When writing a screen saver, always provide something for the configuration dialog box. Even if the dialog says *This screen saver generated by I. M. Cool,* make sure that the user sees something. If the dialog does not show up, the user may think that the screen saver is defective or that it does not run on their platform. If any one of you generates a really cool screen saver, I would love to see it. My graphics abilities are somewhat lacking so I am curious to see what a graphics guru could do with the help of the library and wizard presented in this chapter.

File Viewers

*W*hen *Windows 95 came out, Microsoft introduced their answer to the common problem of file distribution. This solution did not provide a better way to get a file from A to B. Instead, it addressed a more human problem. We often send files without thinking about whether or not the recipient can view the data. Prior to Windows 95, two archaic solutions existed. We could install an application on the recipient's machine or we could send a paper copy.*

We got a better option with the arrival of Windows 95: Quick View. Microsoft distributed this as an application named QUIKVIEW.EXE. Quick View allows the user to open any file for which they have a file viewer. A viewer presents a read only view of the file. In a very real sense, file viewers represent the ultimate in "cripple-ware." You can look at and sometimes even print the file, but you cannot do else anything to the file. Viewers exist for most Microsoft documents, including Word, Excel, and PowerPoint. Viewers also exist for bitmaps, text files, executables (DLLs and EXEs), and other file types. You can usually get the file viewers from the application vendor's Web site. Vendors also distribute file viewers with their licensed software.

One of the facts of a developer's life is that they do not always create applications that center around a custom file format. Instead, many of our applications focus on a database. If we take on a hardware project, then we concentrate on configuration files that are meaningful only to us and to the program. So, why would we need a file viewer? An application may generate log files that are fairly difficult to read. It could store information in some cryptic fashion that focuses on saving disk space. A file viewer could translate the file from "Applicationese" to a human readable language. ("Applicationese" allows developers to communicate errors with descriptions such as *34: 17*.) It could then expand the ones and zeros to something like *The database could not be accessed. All of the system tables have been deleted.*[1] Likewise, the hardware developer could develop a file viewer to aid people in reading a mostly binary configuration file. Instead of having to remember what the location was of a given configuration byte, the user could run Quick View for the file and see what the file meant. Often, a configuration utility would fill this role. If the file stores hints not normally shown to the user, you could implement a file viewer as a troubleshooting tool.

You may be wondering when you should create a file viewer. I have only one rule here: If you want a read-only view of a file, you can write a file viewer. Typically, a file viewer has a button and menu item that allows you to open up the file in an editor. Are you violating any rules if your viewer does not allow this to happen? Absolutely not! Just make sure that the file viewer does not enable the buttons that cannot be activated.

In this chapter, I will cover the following items:

- File viewer basics such as when to create a viewer and how to invoke one
- File viewer internals
- A file viewer library/wizard
- A sample file viewer

6.1   File Viewer Basics

In this section, I define what a file viewer is and its relationship with QUIKVIEW.EXE. It is very important to understand how things should appear to the user and how the QUIKVIEW.EXE application handles communicating when the user selects a new file to view. The better you understand how things work and how they need to look, the better you will understand why a file viewer works as it does.

As a user, you right-click on a file and select Quick View to bring up a copy of a file (see Figure 6-1). If you want to open another file, you can drag a file onto the viewer. The new file opens and it looks like you are in the same window with a new file.

Quick View itself has only a command line interface. The shell typically invokes QUIKVIEW.EXE with the filename as the sole argument. Quick View has the following options:

---

1. For the humor impaired, this is meant as an absurd example.

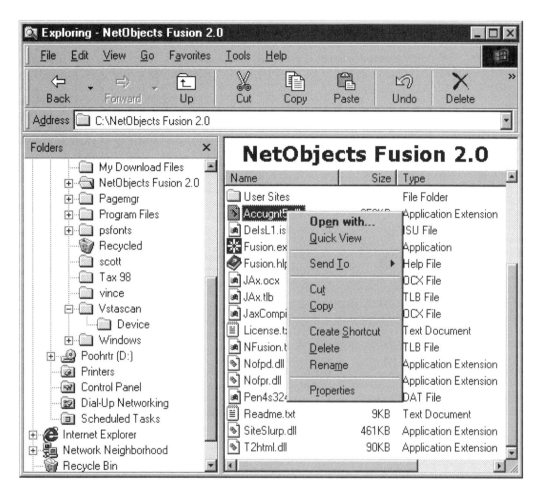

Figure 6.1   *Quick view in the context menu.*

- **-f:** *pathname*: Path of the file to view. Universal Naming Convention (UNC) names are allowed. If the command line does not specify a file-name, Quick View terminates without displaying any error messages.
- **-v**: Open the file using the file viewer. When the command line contains this parameter, Quick View ignores the **-d**, **-p**, and **-&:** *pathname* parameters.
- **-d**: Quick View and the file viewer will suppress all user interface elements if the command line also contains **-p**. Quick View suppresses any error messages and the file viewer should not display any dialog boxes for printing. Quick View ignores this option when the command line does not contain **-p**.

- **-p**: Print the file.
- **-&:***pathname*: Printer driver to use to print the file. Quick View ignores this option when **-p** is not specified. When **-p** is specified and **-&** is not, Quick View instructs the file viewer to print to the default printer driver.

The Quick View window can also be *pinned*. When the Quick View window is pinned, QUIKVIEW.EXE opens all other documents in the same window. For example, if you were to use the Quick View option to open three documents and you never pressed the Replace Window button to pin a window, you would have three windows open. With three windows open, you may choose to pin one of them and then use Quick View to open a fourth document. That fourth file will appear in the pinned window and you will still have three Quick View windows open. At any given time, only one window can have the Replace Window button selected. QUIKVIEW.EXE collaborates with the visible Quick View windows to help make this happen. This feature was implemented before the pushpin idea became popular. The term Quick View uses is *Replace Window*. You can see the item activated in Figure 6-2.

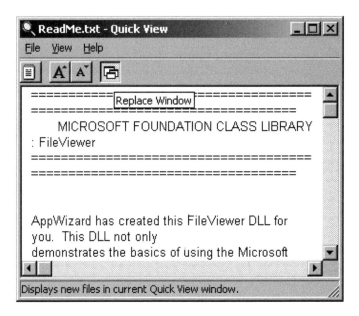

Figure 6.2   *The Replace Window button (i.e., the pinned window button) activated.*

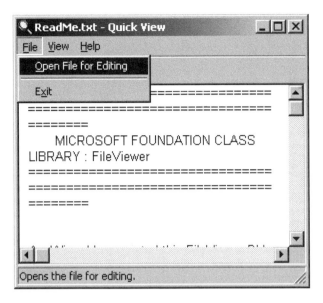

Figure 6.3 *Selecting* Open File for Editing *will bring up NOTEPAD.EXE.*

Every Quick View window has a minimum of four buttons in the tool-bar. Starting from the left, these buttons have the following purposes:

1. Open the file in its native editor. For the Quick View window presented in Figure 6-3, pressing this button would normally bring up Notepad (the only time it would not is if you changed the default file association).

2. Increase the size of the contained information. If the viewer displays text, increase the font size.[2] If the document displays an image, zoom-in. If this functionality does not make sense, present the button but disable it.

3. Decrease the size of the contained information. If the viewer displays text, decrease the font size. If the document displays an image, zoom-out. If this functionality does not make sense, present the button but disable it.

4. Pins the window so that all new files open in this location.

---

2. Yes, you actually should increase/decrease the size of the font, but change the size of all fonts proportionately.

A Quick View application also has a menu with File, View, and Help as the top-level elements. Within the File menu, there should be an *Open File for Editing* and an *Exit* item. The View menu has options to turn the toolbar and status bar on or off as well as to pin the Quick View window. Lastly, the Help menu offers an *About Quick View* option that displays an about dialog.

By now, you should be getting the idea that these various Quick View windows are only loosely related. Each viewer is implemented in a separate DLL and is responsible for creating, showing, and destroying the view of the file. Let's move on and see what makes a file viewer tick.

6.2   File Viewer Internals

In a very real way, QUIKVIEW.EXE is the ultimate in implementation of a universal document/view architecture. Every type of file can be opened and examined as long as a file viewer exists for that file type. The user experience is that of working with a single application. Section 6.1 dealt with the user's interaction with a file viewer. This section deals with the implementation of the file viewer.

Behind the scenes, we have an application named QUIKVIEW.EXE and a DLL for every file that can be viewed. If a file type does not have a corresponding file viewer DLL, QUIKVIEW.EXE gives the user the option of viewing the file as it is—a straight dump of the file as if it were text. Sometimes this is valuable. Each file viewer DLL implements two COM interfaces, IPersistFile[3] and IFileViewer. We will cover IFileViewer shortly.

When a user uses Quick View to open a file, QUIKVIEW.EXE goes to the registry under the key HKCR\QuickView\<extension>\{<CLSID>} to get the CLSID of the implementer of IFileViewer. The file viewer then registers additional information under HKCR\CLSID\{<CLSID>} so that the object can be loaded by the COM infrastructure. Under HKCR\CLSID\{<CLSID>}, the file viewer registers \InprocServer32 = <full file viewer path>. All file viewers must use the single threaded apartments.[4] As an example, let's look at what the registry script would be for a file viewer for the .PBJ[5] extension, assuming it is implemented by PBJVIEW.DLL.

---

3. IPersistFile is covered in Appendix A.

4. For a discussion of the various COM apartments, take a look at the September 1997 "ActiveX/COM Q&A" article in *Microsoft Systems Journal* by Don Box. This article is in the MSDN archive.

5. Yes, a peanut butter and jelly file.

```
HKCR
{
 NoRemove CLSID
 {
  ForceRemove {77CA26EA-41F5-11D3-A579-0000B49D5993} =
    s 'PBJ File Viewer'
   {
    InprocServer32 = s '%MODULE%'
     {
      val ThreadingModel = s 'Apartment'
     }
       'TypeLib' =
         s '{531F9CD1-41F5-11D3-A579-0000B49D5993}'
     }
    }
    QuickView
    {
     .pbj
     {
       {77CA26EA-41F5-11D3-A579-0000B49D5993} =
         s 'PBJ File Viewer'
     }
    }
   }
}
```

Multiple DLLs may implement a viewer for one extension. QUIKVIEW.EXE resolves any problems by loading the last registered CLSID in the list under a given extension. If a particular implementer fails to load a file, the next to last CLSID is given a shot. This continues until a DLL successfully loads the file or until QUIKVIEW.EXE exhausts the list. At this point, QUIKVIEW.EXE throws up its hands and asks if the user would like to try a default viewer. As mentioned earlier in this section, the default viewer provides a straight dump of the file. Of course, if the file does not store its information as straight text, the file may not make much sense to the user.

Quick View and the related file viewers communicate with each other through a pair of interfaces: IFileViewerSite (implemented by QUIK-VIEW.EXE) and IFileViewer (implemented by the file viewer). The file viewer implements one additional interface, IPersistFile. Because a file viewer implements a read only view of an application, file viewers only need to implement the IPersistFile::Load method. Technically speaking, you must implement all of the methods in IPersistFile. How much work is it to copy the method signature and have it return E_NOTIMPL? If you answered, "Almost none," give yourself a gold star. Next, we will see what the IFileViewerSite and IFileViewer interfaces look like.

6.2.1   IFileViewerSite

The IFileViewerSite interface allows a file viewer to retrieve a handle to the currently pinned window. If the user presses the Replace Window button, this interface can clear the currently pinned window and set the window the user selected as the next pinned window. IFileViewerSite has two methods: GetPinnedWindow and SetPinnedWindow.

```
HRESULT GetPinnedWindow(
    HWND* phwnd
);
```

Parameters:

phswnd: On return, this points to the HWND of the currently pinned window.

Returns:

Returns NOERROR if successful or an OLE-defined error value if the call fails.

```
HRESULT SetPinnedWindow(
    HWND hwnd
);
```

Parameters:

hwnd: The HWND of the new pinned window.

Returns:

Returns NOERROR if successful or an OLE-defined error value if the call fails.

Remarks:

To change the pinned window, you must call this method twice. The first call clears the currently pinned window by calling SetPinnedWindow(NULL). Call the method one more time with the HWND of your window to pin the window. To unpin the window, just call SetPinnedWindow(NULL).

6.2.2   IFileViewer

You implement IFileViewer, . an interface that allows Quick View to either show or print a file. This interface also provides the mechanism to tell the file viewer about quick view.

```
HRESULT PrintTo(
    LPSTR pszDriver,
    BOOL fSuppressUI
);
```

Parameters:

pszDriver: This string contains the name of the printer driver to be used to print the file. If the parameter is NULL, the file viewer determines which device driver to use.

fSuppressUI: If this parameter is TRUE, the file viewer should display no user interface—no error messages, no dialogs, nothing. If this parameter is FALSE, the file viewer can show dialog boxes as needed.

Returns:

Returns NOERROR if successful or an OLE-defined error value if the call fails.

Remarks:

While you should implement this method, in some cases it may be acceptable to not do this. However, if you built the file viewer as a debugging tool, it may not hurt to be able to generate paper copies of any information.

```
HRESULT ShowInitialize(
    LPFILEVIEWSITE lpfsi
);
```

Parameters:

lpfsi: Address of an IFileViewerSite interface. Store this pointer for later use. This interface allows you to get and change the currently pinned Quick View window.

Returns:

Returns NOERROR if successful or an OLE-defined error value if the call fails.

Remarks:

Within this method, the file viewer should determine if it can display the file that was passed in. The viewer may not be able to display the file for a number of reasons: embedded OLE objects cannot be shown,[6] a particular library, like OpenGL, needs to be installed first, or for some other reason. This method should perform any initializations that are prone to failure so that if this method succeeds, IFileViewer::Show will also succeed.

---

6. A file viewer can ordinarily show embedded OLE objects; however, the COM object implementing the class may not have been installed on the user's machine. If this is the case, you will not be able to display the embedded OLE objects.

```
HRESULT Show ( LPFVSHOWINFO pvsi )
```

Parameters:

> **pvsi:** Address of an FVSHOWINFO structure. This structure contains information to display the file loaded when Quick View calls IPersist-File::Load. This structure is discussed in Section 6.2.3.

Returns:

> Returns NOERROR if successful or E_UNEXPECTED if IFileViewer:: ShowInitialize was not called before IFileViewer::Show.

Remarks:

The SDK makes no mention of this, but if you successfully show your Quick View window in this method, you cannot return until after the user closes the window or displays another file within the view. This means that your message loop must be contained within the scope of this function. Assuming no more files are viewed via Quick View, QUIKVIEW.EXE shuts down sixty seconds after the last viewer exits its Show method.

Depending on what happens while executing one of the methods defined by IPersistFile or IFileViewer, the methods may return one of the following return codes in addition to the codes listed above:

- **FV_E_BADFILE:** Return this method as soon as you detect that the file cannot be opened. This could happen in IPersistFile::Load, IFile-Viewer::ShowInitialize, or IFileViewer::PrintTo.
- **FV_E_EMPTYFILE:** IPersistFile::Load should be able to detect when the file is empty and cannot be shown. Sometimes, it may be okay to display an empty file. The filename alone may contain interesting, non-intuitive information.
- **FV_E_FILEOPENFAILED:** If IPersistFile::Load fails, it may fail because the file cannot be opened.
- **FV_E_INVALIDID:** Probably useful for displaying a quick view of a compound document. If an embedded item cannot be shown, this return value may provide more information than FV_E_FILEOPEN-FAILED.
- **FV_E_MISSINGFILES:** Return this value when the file passed to the file viewer does not exist.
- **FV_E_NOFILTER:** This looks like an internal error. Quick View probably uses this when viewers exist but none of them successfully load a given file.
- **FV_E_NONSUPPORTEDTYPE:** The viewer loaded just fine. Unfortunately, the viewer does not have the machinery to view this file.

- **FV_E_NOVIEWER:** This is an internal error. When Quick View cannot find the file extension in its part of the registry, this is how it tells itself what happened.
- **FV_E_OUTOFMEMORY:** It means what it says—not enough memory is available to open the viewer.
- **FV_E_PROTECTEDFILE:** The file could not be opened because it was protected. For example, if a Microsoft Word file was protected by a password and the viewer had no method of decrypting using the password, the file viewer could return this value.
- **FV_E_UNEXPECTED:** Use this value when something bad happens. Usually, you know exactly what happened and why. The main problem is that no error value describes the problem well.

6.2.3   FVSHOWINFO

Quick View uses FVSHOWINFO to communicate information related to how the file viewer should be shown. The only method that uses this structure is IFileViewer::Show. In IFileViewer::Show, the pvsi argument is an in/out argument. As a result, the file viewer can use this structure to pass information back to Quick View. FVSHOWINFO has the following definition:

```
typedef struct {
  DWORD cbSize;
  HWND hwndOwner;
  int iShow;
  DWORD dwFlags;
  RECT rect;
  LPUNKNOWN punkRel;
  OLECHAR strNewFile[MAX_PATH];
} FVSHOWINFO, *LPFVSHOWINFO;
```

Members:

cbSize: This is the size of the structure, in bytes. Always set this member to `sizeof( FVSHOWINFO )`.

hwndOwner: Window handle to the owner of the window in which the file will be displayed.

iShow: The show command for the window. It will be one of the SW_XXXX values listed in MSDN for ShowWindow.

dwFlags: These flags determine what the file viewer will display. They also communicate any changes that should happen as a result of a failure to open a file. The user can drag a file that is incompatible with the current viewer onto the file viewer. The viewer passes this information on to Quick View via some of the flags. The flags can have any combination of the following values:

- **FVSIF_CANVIEWIT:** The file viewer can display the file. The viewer sets this flag.
- **FVSIF_NEWFAILED:** The file viewer specified a new file to display, but no viewer could do this. The file viewer should either continue to display the previous file or terminate. Quick View sets this flag.
- **FVSIF_NEWFILE:** A drag-and-drop operation dropped a file on the file viewer window. The viewer is responsible for setting the name of the strNewFile member. Quick View then tries to find a file viewer that can display a new file. Note: if the current viewer is pinned, then opening a file from Explorer using Quick View will mimic a drag-and-drop operation from the file viewer's perspective (i.e. it will not be able to tell the difference). The viewer sets this flag.
- **FVSIF_PINNED:** A pinned window exists. A file viewer should either use the pinned window to display the file or set a new pinned window and display the file in it. In practice, this means that a pinned window exists. The new file viewer should set itself as the pinned window. The old one will be going away as soon as you call punkRel→Release().
- **FVSIF_RECT:** The rect member contains valid data. Use this rectangle as the coordinates for your window. If the RECT is too big or too small, you must make the top left corner of your frame window match the top left corner of rect. Quick View sets this flag to tell a viewer where to display. This flag indicates that Quick View is sending display coordinates over. A file viewer must send its coordinates when it is the pinned window or when the user drops a file onto the file viewer.

rect: Specifies the size and position of the file viewer's window. This member becomes meaningful when dwFlags has the FVSIF_RECT flag set.

punkRel: Address of an IUnknown interface that must have its Release method called by the new file viewer to release the previous file viewer. This method is used whenever a drag-and-drop operation drops a file on the file viewer's window. Remember, if a window is pinned, it thinks that any files the user chooses to Quick View were dropped. In the pinned window case, Windows performs the drag-and-drop operation.

strNewFile: Address of a string that specifies the name of a new file to display. A viewer should not bother passing on this information and exiting its Show method if the viewer knows how to open this file. Quick View does not use this member. When Quick View gets a FVSHOWINFO struct with FVSIF_NEWFILE set, it examines strNew-

File. strNewFile is used to locate the new file viewer. Assuming a viewer could be located, its IPersistFile::Load method is invoked, passing along strNewFile. The new file viewer may fail, in which case we will get an invocation of Show with the FVSIF_NEWFAILED flag set.

6.2.4 File Viewer User Interface Expectations

When setting up the menu structure for your application, keep in mind that the user expects a certain, minimal set of menu items. You can expand on the menu items as far as you see fit. Microsoft has specified the contents for the top-level File, View, and Help menus. Tables 6.1, 6.2, and 6.3 list the standard menu items, actions for the items, status window text, and tool-tip text.

Table 6.1 _File Viewer File Menu Items_

Menu Item	Action	Status Bar Text	Tool-tip Text
Open File for Editing	Opens the file using the full application that created the file. After successfully opening the application, the file viewer should exit. If the application does not start, display the following message: "There is no application available that can open this file."	Opens the file for editing.	Open File for Editing
Separator			
Page Setup (optional)	Activates the standard Page Setup dialog box. The result affects the current file while it is in the viewer. This menu item should only appear when the application supports printing via the Print menu item.	Changes the page setup for printing.	N/A
Print Ctrl+P (optional)	Prints the file by invoking the standard Print/Printer Setup property sheet. Only add this item if you can support printing without the full application.	Prints the file contents.	N/A
Separator			
Exit	Closes the main window and exits the file viewer.	Quits Quick View	N/A

Table 6.2   *File Viewer View Menu Items*

Menu Item	Action	Status Bar Text	Tool-tip Text
Toolbar	Toggles between hiding and showing the toolbar.	Shows or hides the toolbar.	N/A
Status Bar	Toggles between hiding and showing the status bar	Shows or hides the status bar.	N/A
Page View (optional)	Used to switch between a full-sized view and a single-page view.	Switches between the document and page views.	N/A
Replace Window	Used to switch between using the current window to view a file and creating a new window to view a file.	Displays new files in current Quick View window.	Replace Window
Separator			
Landscape (optional)	Used to switch between landscape and portrait views when in page view.	Switches between portrait and landscape.	Toggle portrait/landscape
Rotate (optional)	Rotates a raster graphic image 90 degrees every time the option is selected	Rotates the image by 90 degrees	Rotate image 90 degrees
Separator			
Font (optional)	Displays a dialog that allows the user to select a font and point size for viewing text in the document.	Changes the display font	N/A

Table 6.3   *File Viewer Help Menu Items*

Menu Item	Action	Status Bar Text	Tool-tip Text
Help Topics	Activates help with the file viewer's help file.	Displays the Help Contents and Index.	N/A
About *file viewer name*	Displays an About dialog box for the file viewer. The About dialog identifies the creator of the file viewer.	Displays program information, version number, and copyright.	N/A

6.2.5 Testing File Viewers

Testing a file viewer is fairly easy once you get it running. To get the file viewer running, just make sure that all the registry entries are in their correct places as shown in the beginning of Section 6.2. Once you have that done, I recommend building a minimal file viewer and then trying to use Quick View on a file that you will support. If you do not have a valid file available, just take a file, copy it, and give it the extension you want to support. In Visual Studio, set the *Executable for debug session* to QUIKVIEW.EXE. You can find this file in the System32\Viewers directory. Set the *Program arguments* option to the path of the file you created. By running the file like this once, you can check to make sure that everything is plugged in correctly. If your basic view does not show up, I have a checklist to help debug your viewer. Run the tests in the prescribed order. Eventually your viewer will start showing up and you can stop debugging.

1. Set a breakpoint in DllGetClassObject to see if the method is getting called. If the file is not getting called, your registry entries are wrong and the viewer cannot locate your DLL.

2. If DllGetClassObject gets called but does not return S_OK (zero) then the CLSID registered under Quick View\<file extension\<CLSID> is not the same CLSID as the one used by the implementer of IFileViewer. You need to update the CLSID.

3. Place a breakpoint in your implementation of IPeristFile::Load. It should be getting called. Make sure that you are not returning failure.

4. Set a breakpoint in your implementation of IFileViewer::ShowInitialize. Make sure that you are returning S_OK.

5. Set a breakpoint in your implementation of IFileViewer::Show. This method should be creating a new window and displaying it. The viewer should stay in this method until the user quits. Section 6.3 describes how CFileViewerApp, a class I created, handles this.

This checklist should help you debug most of the problems you will encounter. When you create a file viewer, try invoking it right away. Doing so will save you hours of debugging time later down the road. Once you make sure that the file viewer is plugged in, you can spend the rest of your development time debugging real problems.

6.3 Building a File Viewer

Figure 6-4 depicts the typical interaction between the various interfaces involved in displaying a Quick View of a file. Keep in mind that this diagram shows what happens when things go well. If any method fails, the file is not

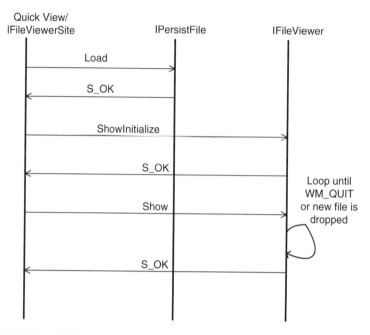

Figure 6.4   *"High-level" event sequence diagram for a file viewer.*

shown and the sequence halts. If the failed file was opened via a previously opened file viewer, that file viewer will see that FVSHOWINFO.dwFlags has FVSIF_NEWFAILED set when Show gets called again. At this point, the file viewer has an option of either re-showing its currently open file or exiting. The SDK says you have this choice. I would advise you to ignore the SDK on this point. Your users will expect the previous file to remain open when opening another file fails. Most file viewers work this way, and yours should, too.

Within the IFileViewer::Show method, Quick View expects the file viewer to display a document within a view that is housed by a frame window. Any seasoned MFC programmer knows that this is a job for the document/view architecture. There are a few subtle differences between how document/view works and how a file viewer should work. In traditional document/view applications, we open a file, verify it for correctness, and display the file within the context of one function call. A file viewer splits this sequence into three distinct steps. Referencing Figure 6-4 again, we see that the file viewer

1. Loads the file in IPersistFile::Load
2. Verifies that the file can be displayed in IFileViewer::ShowInitialize
3. Displays the file in IFileViewer::Show

Within document/view, this corresponds to calling the following methods:

1. Open the document by calling CWinApp::OpenDocumentFile().
2. Get the document template the open document is based off of and call pDocTemplate→CreateNewFrame(pOpenDoc, NULL)
3. For the window created in step 2, call pWnd→ShowWindow(pvsi->iShow) .

Of course, I wrote a library to handle the bulk of this stuff and a wizard to handle the repetitive, semi-customized parts. I used code written by Paul DiLascia in the June 1997 *Microsoft Systems Journal*[7] as a reference when I got stuck with my code. My implementation borrows from his, but I took the implementation in a different direction. Instead of implementing an all MFC version, I implemented a mixture of ATL and MFC. ATL handles the COM specific stuff; MFC handles the display specific stuff. I state this elsewhere in the book, but it bears repeating: ATL makes COM programming a breeze, but I still find it does a poor job with user interface issues. Likewise, MFC does an excellent job doing user interface development but makes writing COM interfaces difficult. As a rule, I combine the two and let each object model shine with its strengths. When you do your development, do not be afraid to mix and match the class libraries. They play very well with each other.

I do not maintain the state machine that Mr. DiLascia wrote. I did not see a need to maintain my current state as I moved along. My improvements over the original implementation were possible only because I was able to stand on the shoulders of a giant. Now that I have given credit where credit is due, it is time to see what it is that I did.

6.3.1 File Viewer Library

If you have already read a chapter that introduced a library, feel free to skip this paragraph. I am only rehashing some design decisions regarding libraries over DLLs. I chose a statically linked library to house the two classes that handle much of the task related to being a file viewer. The book contains a number of these libraries, which I could have put into one big DLL. However, it is highly unlikely that anyone would ever create an application that uses every shell extension and library enhancement that I could come up with. Creating a library for a third party extension does two things a DLL does not do. It reduces the number of files you need to distribute and it reduces the amount of space your application occupies on a customer's machine. Yet another reason is that many

---

7. DiLascia, Paul. "More Fun with MFC: DIBs, Palettes, Subclassing, and a Gamut of Goodies, Part III." *Microsoft Systems Journal*, June, 1997.

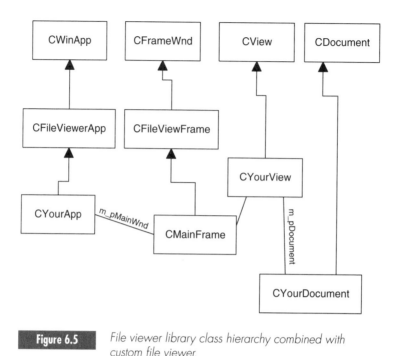

Figure 6.5   *File viewer library class hierarchy combined with custom file viewer.*

people will buy this book and use the libraries.[8] Because the source code has been provided, many of them will alter the code for their own purposes. As a result, there may be many versions of the shared DLL in existence. Do you want to worry about version inconsistencies? I did not think so.

The library FileViewer.LIB houses the classes CFileViewFrame and CFileViewerApp. In a typical document/view application, you have classes descended from CWinApp, CFrameWnd, CView, and CDocument. File viewers have a few requirements beyond the regular MFC document/view architecture. CFileViewFrame handles the extra requirements of the CFrameWnd derived class and CFileViewerApp extends the capabilities of CWinApp. You can see this in Figure 6-5. The two classes have the following responsibilities:

CFileViewFrame:
- Accept dropped files and pass the name of the new file to CFile-ViewerApp.
- Properly close the window, including sending an application terminate message if needed.

---

8. I can dream, can't I?

CFileViewerApp:

* Handle pinning and unpinning the main window as needed.
* Read files that the viewer knows how to handle.
* Tell Quick View about files the viewer does not know how to handle.
* Perform any initialization tasks.
* Handle the message dispatcher.
* Implement the functionality required of the IFileViewer interface.

These classes allow you, the programmer, to worry more about presenting your file and less about plugging everything in correctly. CFileViewFrame and the wizard-generated ATL class rely on a global function that returns a pointer to a CFileViewerApp object. I had two choices: writing two lines to get and cast the application object to a CFileViewerApp pointer or writing a quick method that did the work for me. I chose the latter. The function is:

```
CFileViewerApp* FVGetApp()
{
  AFX_MANAGE_STATE(AfxGetStaticModuleState());
  CFileViewerApp* retval =
    dynamic_cast<CFileViewerApp*>(AfxGetApp());
  return retval;
}
```

FileViewerApp.h declares the function and FileViewerApp.cpp defines it. The call to AFX_MANAGE_STATE(AfxGetStaticModuleState()) brings the current CWinApp-derived object into view. While we are reviewing short methods, we should look at how CFileViewFrame handles a dropped file and the close of the main window. When the user drops a file onto the view, CFileViewFrame leaps into action by grabbing the name of the file and telling CFileViewerApp to open it. CFileViewFrame::OnDropFiles also gets invoked if the window was pinned and the user opened the file from some other location using Quick View.

```
void CFileViewFrame::OnDropFiles(HDROP hDropInfo)
{
  TCHAR szFileName[MAX_PATH];
  ::DragQueryFile(hDropInfo, 0, szFileName, MAX_PATH);
  FVGetApp()->OpenDocumentFile(CString(szFileName));
  ::DragFinish(hDropInfo);
}
```

The frame window may close for one of two reasons. Either the user closed the window or a new file is opening. If the user closed the window, we need to post a quit message to terminate the message loop. If the user opened a new file within the current Quick View window, the application has already dropped out of the message loop and posted a quit message. If we posted another quit message while the new viewer started, that message would go to the window that just popped up. The new window would think it was time to quit when it was not supposed to quit. CFileViewFrame handles this requirement with the following instructions:

```
void CFileViewFrame::OnClose()
{
  if ( FVGetApp()->m_pMainWnd->GetSafeHwnd() )
  {
      FVGetApp()->CloseAllDocuments(FALSE);
      if ( !FVGetApp()->IsNewFileOpening() )
      {
          AfxPostQuitMessage(0);
      }
  }
}
```

I may have exaggerated when I said that the application object does not keep track of state information. The object does know whether or not it is opening up a new file. CFileViewerApp keeps an FVSHOWINFO pointer that keeps track of information for transfer between the methods that open, initialize, and show a file. By the time a new file has been opened, FVSHOWINFO.dwFlags has the FVSIF_NEWFILE flag set. CFileViewerApp::IsNewFileOpening() tests for this condition and returns true when the flag has been set.

```
bool CFileViewerApp::IsNewFileOpening()
{
    unsigned int val = m_pfvsi->dwFlags & FVSIF_NEWFILE;
    return val != 0;
}
```

CFileViewerApp has this class declaration:

```
class CFileViewerApp : public CWinApp
{
public:
  bool IsNewFileOpening();
  CFileViewerApp();

  virtual void ShutDown();
  virtual CString GetOpenFile();

  // File Viewer handlers
  // ShowInitialize:
  // Initializes the file.  Makes sure that it is
  // "load-able".  If the file can not be read,
  // it should fail here.
  virtual HRESULT ShowInitialize(LPFILEVIEWERSITE lpfsi);

  // Actually shows the file.  If the file
```

```
// can not be read by this viewer,
// then Quick View will try to locate a new
// viewer.
virtual HRESULT Show(LPFVSHOWINFO pvsi);

// Used to communicate the Quick View interface
// pointer.
virtual void SetViewer( IFileViewer* pViewer );

// Implements the message loop needed by the Show
// method.
virtual int DispatchMessages ();

// Overrides
// ClassWizard generated virtual function overrides
//{{AFX_VIRTUAL(CFileViewerApp)
public:
virtual BOOL InitInstance();
virtual int ExitInstance();
virtual CDocument* OpenDocumentFile(LPCTSTR lpszFileName);
//}}AFX_VIRTUAL

//{{AFX_MSG(CFileViewerApp)
afx_msg void OnUpdateViewReplacewindow(CCmdUI* pCmdUI);
afx_msg void OnViewReplacewindow();
afx_msg void OnFileOpen();
//}}AFX_MSG
virtual afx_msg void OnAppAbout() = 0;
DECLARE_MESSAGE_MAP()
protected:
// Used to check if this file viewer is pinned.
bool IsPinned();

// Helper methods
// Gets the correct template for a given
// file name.  The file viewer can support
// more than one document type.
virtual CDocTemplate* GetTemplate(CString szPath);

BOOL InitATL();

// Pointer to the active IFileViewer interface.
IFileViewer* m_pViewer;

// Pointer to the IFileViewerSite object
// hosting this quick viewer.
  LPFILEVIEWERSITE m_lpfsi;

// The current active document.
CDocument* m_pDoc;
```

```
// The current, active Document Template.
CDocTemplate* m_pDocTemplate;

// FVSHOWINFO pointer used to communicate
// any needed changes across OpenDocumentFile,
// ShowInitialize, and Show.
LPFVSHOWINFO m_pfvsi;
};
```

I will start with the four most important methods within CFileViewer-App: DispatchMessages, OpenDocumentFile, ShowInitialize, and Show. CFile-ViewerApp:: DispatchMessages gives the file viewer app the ability to dispatch messages without dropping out of the scope of the Show method. CFileViewerApp::DispatchMessages is a copy of CWinThread::Run with one notable deletion: no call to ExitInstance. In most applications, calling ExitInstance causes no problems. File viewers are different. CFileViewerApp::Show calls CFileViewerApp::DispatchMessages. CFileViewerApp::Show implements the functionality required of the IFileViewer::Show method. This means that CFileViewerApp::Show can not exit until the user either opens a file type not supported by the current viewer in the current Quick View session, or the user closes the current window. CFileViewerApp::DispatchMessages fulfills this requirement by dispatching messages until one of these stop conditions occurs.

```
int CFileViewerApp::DispatchMessages()
{
    ASSERT_VALID(this);

    // for tracking the idle time state
    BOOL bIdle = TRUE;
    LONG lIdleCount = 0;

#ifdef _DEBUG
    // In debug mode, MFC uses the following counter
    // to prevent you from calling Run twice; i.e.,
    // reentering the message loop. But we want to
    // do just that whenever creating a new file fails.
    // Solution: lie to MFC.
        m_nDisablePumpCount = 0;
#endif

    // acquire and dispatch messages until a
    // WM_QUIT message is received.
    for (;;)
    {
        // phase1: check to see if we can do idle work
        while (bIdle &&
          !::PeekMessage(&m_msgCur, NULL, NULL, NULL,
            PM_NOREMOVE))
```

```
          {
            // call OnIdle while in bIdle state
            if (!OnIdle(lIdleCount++))
               bIdle = FALSE; // assume "no idle" state
          }

          // phase2: pump messages while available
          do
          {
            // pump message, but quit on WM_QUIT
            if (!PumpMessage())
             {
               m_lpfsi->Release();
               return 0; // DON'T CALL ExitInstance!
             }

            // reset "no idle" state after pumping "normal"
            // message
            if (IsIdleMessage(&m_msgCur))
             {
             bIdle = TRUE;
             lIdleCount = 0;
            }

          }
          while (::PeekMessage(&m_msgCur, NULL, NULL, NULL,
              PM_NOREMOVE));
          }

       ASSERT(FALSE);   // not reachable
       return FALSE;
     }
```

CFileViewerApp::OpenDocumentFile implements the IPersistFile:: Load functionality. It checks to make sure that the viewer can open the file and that the file is not already open. If the viewer already has the file open, it just returns a pointer to the current document. When the method opens the document, it calls on all the usual document/view architecture to open the file. The investment in sticking with the document view architecture starts paying off here. When CFileViewerApp::OpenDocumentFile cannot open the file, it copies the name of the file into the FVSHOWINFO pointer, m_pfvsi. Additionally, it sets the FVSIF_NEWFILE flag and sets an IUnknown pointer. The new file viewer will release this pointer if it successfully loads the new file.

```
CDocument* CFileViewerApp::OpenDocumentFile(LPCTSTR
 lpszFileName)
{
 // Loading a document via a file viewer is a three step
```

```
// process.  Load the document, create the window, show
// the window.  Welcome to step one, load the document
m_pDocTemplate = GetTemplate(lpszFileName);
CDocument* pDoc = NULL;
if ( NULL != m_pDocTemplate )
{   // if can open:
    if (GetOpenFile() == CString(lpszFileName))
    {   // if already open:
        pDoc = ((CFrameWnd*)m_pMainWnd)
            ->GetActiveDocument();
    }
    else
    {   // open it
        pDoc = CWinApp::OpenDocumentFile(lpszFileName);
        // Prevent Windows confusion
        m_pMainWnd->SetForegroundWindow();
    }
}
else
  {
    // I can't open this doc, so quit message loop and
    // pass filename back to QuickView as new file to
    // view.
    if ( m_pfvsi == NULL )
    {
      m_pfvsi = new FVSHOWINFO;
    }
    mbstowcs(m_pfvsi->strNewFile, lpszFileName,
      strlen(lpszFileName)+1);
    m_pfvsi->dwFlags |= FVSIF_NEWFILE;
    m_pViewer->QueryInterface(IID_IUnknown,
      (LPVOID*)&m_pfvsi->punkRel);
    if ( m_pMainWnd )
    {
      m_pMainWnd->GetWindowRect( &(m_pfvsi->rect) );
      m_pfvsi->dwFlags |= FVSIF_RECT;
    }
   if ( m_pMainWnd->GetSafeHwnd() )
   {
     AfxPostQuitMessage(0);
   }
  }
  m_pDoc = pDoc;
  if (!pDoc)
  {
      TRACE("***CFileViewerApp::OpenDocumentFile returning "
        "NULL\n");
  }
  return pDoc;
}
```

CFileViewerApp::ShowInitialize just creates the frame window and shows it. This implements functionality required by the IFileViewer::ShowInitialize method.

```
HRESULT CFileViewerApp::ShowInitialize(LPFILEVIEWERSITE lpfsi)
{
    m_lpfsi = lpfsi;
    m_lpfsi->AddRef();
    if (m_pMainWnd==NULL)
    {
        m_nCmdShow = SW_HIDE;     // don't show window yet
        // Manually create the frame/view and attach to our
        // loaded doc
        CDocTemplate *pDocTemplate = m_pDoc->GetDocTemplate();
        m_pMainWnd = pDocTemplate->CreateNewFrame(m_pDoc,
            NULL);
    }

    return S_OK;
}
```

Finally, let's take a look at CFileViewerApp::Show. Show takes one parameter: a pointer to an FVSHOWINFO structure. This structure contains information on where to place the view, tells if the window should be pinned, and contains a pointer to the previous file viewer. The pointer to the previous file viewer allows the new viewer to let the old viewer stop displaying itself and remove itself from memory. This mechanism allows Quick View to appear to handle a file display failure in a user-friendly fashion. It also removes the perception that trying to open a file with no viewer caused the application to crash. Instead, Quick View looks like a robust application. To help maintain this perception, we must write robust file viewer DLLs. For more on CFileViewerApp::Show, please read the method. I believe that the comments do a good job of guiding you through what the method does.

```
HRESULT CFileViewerApp::Show(LPFVSHOWINFO pvsi)
{
    ASSERT_VALID(m_pMainWnd);

    CFrameWnd* pFrame = dynamic_cast<CFrameWnd*>(m_pMainWnd);
    if ( m_pfvsi == NULL )
    {
        m_pfvsi = new FVSHOWINFO;
    }
    *m_pfvsi = *pvsi;
    // If QuickView specified a rectangle, use it
    if (pvsi->dwFlags & FVSIF_RECT)
    {
        m_pMainWnd->MoveWindow( CRect( pvsi->rect ) );
    }
```

```
// Show window. Unless this is a failed NEWFILE, the
// window should be empty since I haven't called
// InitialUpdateFrame yet
//
m_pMainWnd->ShowWindow(pvsi->iShow);

// If there was a previous viewer, Release it.
if (pvsi->punkRel)
{
    pvsi->punkRel->Release();
    pvsi->punkRel = NULL;
}

// Check for pinned state
if (pvsi->dwFlags & FVSIF_PINNED)
{
  OnViewReplacewindow();
}

if (pvsi->dwFlags & FVSIF_NEWFAILED)
 {
    // In the case of FVSIF_NEWFAILED, everything is
    // fine: The window is still here and I just drop
    // into a new message loop. Some implementations
    // destroy the window and recreate it again here,
    // but there's no need—that's the whole point of
    // pvsi->punkRel and the deferred final Release.
    m_lpfsi->AddRef();
 }
else
{
    // Not FVSIF_NEWFAILED: I have a new loaded doc
    // whose frame I need to initialize.
    ASSERT(m_pDoc);

    // Must move to foreground so palette stuff all
    // works fine
    m_pMainWnd->SetForegroundWindow();

    // Now call InitialUpdateFrame. This is part of
    // what normally happens in OpenDocumentFile
    // that now got split off as part of Show. This
    // will send OnInitialUpdate to the view.
    m_nCmdShow = pvsi->iShow;
    m_pDoc->GetDocTemplate()->
     InitialUpdateFrame(pFrame, m_pDoc, TRUE);
    m_pDoc = NULL;   // doc belongs to frame now
    m_pMainWnd->UpdateWindow();     // paint it
}
```

```
        pvsi->dwFlags = 0; // clear flags

        // Enter message loop until user quits or I get
        // a WM_DROPFILES from somewhere (shell or QuickView).
        DispatchMessages();

        // There are only two ways we could have exited
        // the message loop:
        // * the user closed, in which case the main
        //   window should be gone; or
        // * I got a WM_DROPFILES to view a new file,
        //   in which case, the main window should still
        //   be here. I must give QuickView an IUnknown to
        //   release, and when it does (after the new
        //   viewer has displayed itself over my window),
        //   I'll destroy my main window, in OnFinalRelease
        if (pvsi->dwFlags & FVSIF_NEWFILE)
        {
            // main window should still be here
            ASSERT_VALID(m_pMainWnd);

            // Return my pinned state to QuickView/new viewer.
            if (IsPinned())
            {
                pvsi->dwFlags |= FVSIF_PINNED;
            }

            // Return my main window coordinates to
            // QuickView/new viewer.
            m_pMainWnd->GetWindowRect(&pvsi->rect);
            pvsi->dwFlags |= FVSIF_RECT;

            // Give QuickView an IUnknown to release me.
            // (That's when I'll destroy the main window)
            m_pViewer->QueryInterface(IID_IUnknown,
                (LPVOID*)&pvsi->punkRel);
        }
        else
        {
            *pvsi = *m_pfvsi;
        }

        return S_OK;
}
```

A wizard accompanies this library so that you do not need to put all these pieces together yourself. I will present the output of the wizard along with some other code in the next section. The wizard and the library do not do anything with the IFileViewer::PrintTo method. As noted in section 6.1, in order to print using the interface, one has to use the command line. Quick View does not implement anything to handle printing from Windows Explorer. When the Print option does appear in the context menu for a given file, the actual application provides that functionality. Unless you have a need for IFileViewer::PrintTo, you can probably get away with not implementing it. On the flip side, if you provide print support from the Quick View, then you may as well support the method. The following address book example does not support printing in any way.

6.4   Address Book Example

By now you should have a good idea of what a file viewer is and how FileViewer.LIB implements most of the functionality. In my search for a good example, I wanted something simple and easy to understand. I may be going out on a limb here, but I think everyone reading this understands the basic concepts behind an address book. The address book presented here could not be more basic. The main application, included on the CD, allows the user to add an individual's name, address, phone number, and e-mail address. The application does not provide any sorting or searching capabilities. It would take a few more hours of effort to carry the example past the toy stage. Unfortunately, that would lead us into discussions about address book design that would take us far off the topic of this chapter.

The main application took very little time to actually write, maybe four hours. I did not want a sophisticated application, just a toy. Figure 6-6[9] shows a screen shot of AddressBook.EXE. You can move between the various addresses. The address class, used to store, retrieve, and display addresses, derives from CObject and it supports serialization. The object has the following declaration:

```
class Address : public CObject
{
public:
  DECLARE_SERIAL(Address);
      Address();
  Address(const Address& rhs);
  Address& operator=(const Address& rhs);
      virtual ~Address();
```

9. In case you are curious, only the e-mail address is real. If you feel the need to send something to me, please verify my mailing address via the e-mail address. Offers for telecommuting contracts are always welcome (really).

Figure 6.6   *AddressBook.EXE interface.*

```
// This can be used by the document to determine if a save
// is necessary or not
    bool HasChanged();
virtual void Serialize(CArchive& ar);

// Raft of getters and setters.  Should
// be self-documenting.
CString GetName();
CString GetAddress1();
CString GetAddress2();
CString GetCity();
CString GetState();
CString GetZip();
CString GetPhoneNumber();
CString GetEMail();

void SetName( const CString& value );
void SetAddress1( const CString& value );
void SetAddress2( const CString& value );
void SetCity( const CString& value );
void SetState( const CString& value );
void SetZip( const CString& value );
void SetPhoneNumber( const CString& value );
```

```
   void SetEMail( const CString& value );

private:
   // Helper method that updates m_bChanged if old value
   // != new value. The method is templatized in case
   // a non CString member comes along.  The code
   // will not change except for the types.
   template <class T>
   void UpdateValue( const T& newValue, T& memberVariable )
   {
      if ( newValue != memberVariable )
      {
         memberVariable = newValue;
         m_bChanged = true;
      }
   }

   CString m_szName;
   CString m_szAddress1;
   CString m_szAddress2;
   CString m_szCity;
   CString m_szState;
   CString m_szZip;
   CString m_szPhoneNumber;
   CString m_szEMail;
   bool m_bChanged;
};
```

The template member function Address::UpdateValue took as much time to write as one that would take only CString objects. Address::Update-Value allows me to write the *set* methods like this:

```
void Address::SetName( const CString& value )
{
   UpdateValue( value, m_szName );
}
```

Pretty neat, huh? This beats the pants off a repetitive cut and paste operation and even makes the toy easy to grow into something bigger. The method Address::Serial simply streams the CString members to the CArchive object.

Once the application was built, I built a file viewer using the File Viewer AppWizard. AddressBook files use the file extension *.abk*. For step one of the wizard, tell it that you want to handle the .abk extension (Figure 6-7) and press Finish. Once you build the project, you will have a file viewer that will come up for all .abk files. Unfortunately, the file viewer will not do anything useful.

Next, I took the files for the Address class and put them into a library named Ch6Shared.LIB. I modified the include path and library path for the

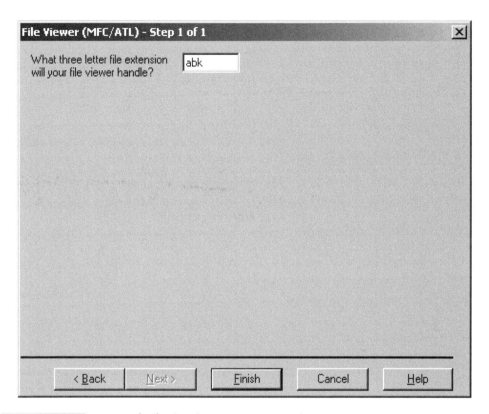

Figure 6.7 *Step 1 of 1 for the File viewer AppWizard.*

main application and rebuilt. Doing this allows me to use the same code for the application data in the file viewer and the main application. This reduces maintenance headaches by keeping a common code base for the basic data.

Now that we have a way of enforcing a common data format, we should design the file viewer interface. To present a read-only view of the data, we can just take the old layout and apply it to our new view. To create the new view and tie it into the file viewer, follow these steps:

1. Create a dialog template suitable for a CFormView.

2. Copy all the old labels and replace the text boxes with static text controls.

3. Tie the dialog template to a new CFormView-derived class, CAddress-Form.

4. In CAddressBookFVApp::InitInstance, replace the view class in the CSingleDocTemplate constructor with CAddressForm:

```
CDocTemplate* pDoc = new CSingleDocTemplate(
IDR_MAINFRAME,
RUNTIME_CLASS(CAddressBookFVDocument),
RUNTIME_CLASS(CMainFrame),
RUNTIME_CLASS(CAddressForm) );
```

5. Delete the old view class from your hard drive and remove it from the project.

6. Remove the #include for the old view class and replace it with "AddressForm.h".

7. Build and test (see section 6.2.5).

Now that we know we have something that can talk to Quick View, we need to provide a way to load the document. CAddressBookFVDocument needs a few enhancements. It needs to:

1. Hold all the addresses: add `std::vector<Address> m_address-Book` to the private section of CAddressBookFVDocument.

2. Provide a way to tell external sources the document's address count:

```
int CAddressBookFVDocument::GetSize()
{
    return m_addressBook.size();
}
```

3. Provide a way to get at addresses in the document:

```
Address& CAddressBookFVDocument::GetAddress(int index)
{
    if ( m_addressBook.size() <= index )
    {
        // Use os to fill in the string returned by
        // exception.what()
        std::ostringstream os;
        os << std::string("The submitted value is too large")
            << std::endl
            << std::string( "Value: " ) << index << std::ends;
        throw std::out_of_range( os.str() );
    }
    else if ( index < 0 )
    {
        // Use os to fill in the string returned by
        // exception.what()
        std::ostringstream os;
        os << std::string("The submitted value is too small")
            << std::endl
            << std::string( "Value: " ) << index << std::ends;
        throw std::out_of_range( os.str() );
    }
```

```
// This is OK. If we didn't throw by now, we should have
// no worries.
return m_addressBook[index];
}
```

For number three above, most of the code involves range checking. The line that does what the code claims it will do is on the last line. I personally believe that most C++ programmers know too little about what the C++ library can do for them. I see printf and custom exception types used far too often in what some people call C++ code. I can either gripe about it or I can demonstrate the power of the library. For example, the above code demonstrates the power of the library and this paragraph contains a gripe.

CAddressForm handles the task of displaying data. It handles displaying data through a private helper method called CAddressForm::DisplayRecord. Given the index of the address to display, CAddressForm::DisplayRecord grabs that address from the document and updates the view. As the user presses the Next and Previous buttons (see Figure 6-8), the interface increments or decrements the member variable m_nCurrent and then displays the current record.

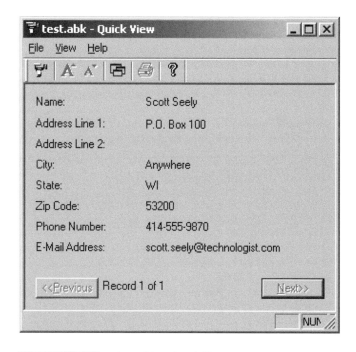

Figure 6.8   *The address book file viewer.*

```
void CAddressForm::OnNext()
{
    ++m_nCurrentRecord;
    if ( GetDocument()->GetSize() <= m_nCurrentRecord )
    {
        m_nCurrentRecord = GetDocument()->GetSize() - 1;
    }

    // Note that this will disable the button if only
    // one record exists.  There is no second record
    // to go to.
    m_btnNext.EnableWindow( m_nCurrentRecord !=
      ( GetDocument()->GetSize() - 1 ) );
    m_btnPrevious.EnableWindow( true );
    DisplayRecord( m_nCurrentRecord );
}

void CAddressForm::OnPrevious()
{
    --m_nCurrentRecord;
    if ( 0 >= m_nCurrentRecord )
    {
      m_nCurrentRecord = 0;
      m_btnPrevious.EnableWindow( false );
    }
    m_btnPrevious.EnableWindow( m_nCurrentRecord != 0 );
    m_btnNext.EnableWindow( true );
    DisplayRecord( m_nCurrentRecord );
}

void CAddressForm::DisplayRecord(int index)
{
    Address& address = GetDocument()->GetAddress( index );
    m_szAddress1 = address.GetAddress1();
    m_szAddress2 = address.GetAddress2();
    m_szCity = address.GetCity();
    m_szEMail = address.GetEMail();
    m_szName = address.GetName();
    m_szPhoneNumber = address.GetPhoneNumber();
    m_szState = address.GetState();
    m_szZip = address.GetZip();

    m_szStatus.Format( "Record %d of %d",
      m_nCurrentRecord + 1,
      GetDocument()->GetSize() );
    UpdateData( false );
}
```

Outside of a few other user interface tweaks, I did not have to worry about the file viewer. The AppWizard took care of this work when it generated CAddressBookFVViewer, the DLL's implementation of the IFileViewer and IPersistFile interfaces. Unless something goes wrong, you should never even need to look at this code. The following code has been modified to include a lot more comments than the wizard generates. Please read the comments and the code to get a feel for what the wizard does for you.

```
// All file viewers must implement the IFileViewer and
// IPersistFile interfaces.
class ATL_NO_VTABLE CAddressBookFVViewer :
   public CComObjectRootEx<CComSingleThreadModel>,
   public CComCoClass<CAddressBookFVViewer,
     &CLSID_AddressBookFVViewer>,
   public IPersistFile,
   public IFileViewer,
   public IAddressBookFVViewer
{
public:
   CAddressBookFVViewer();

   // IPeristFile methods
   // On the IPersistFile interface,
   // only Load is needed.  The rest can return
   // E_NOTIMPL.  The wizard implements GetClassID
   // and GetCurFile: these are no brainers and
   // may be useful in the future.
   STDMETHOD (GetClassID)(CLSID *pClassID);
   STDMETHOD (IsDirty)();
   STDMETHOD (Load)(LPCOLESTR pszFileName, DWORD dwMode);
   STDMETHOD (Save)(LPCOLESTR pszFileName, BOOL fRemember);
   STDMETHOD (SaveCompleted)(LPCOLESTR pszFileName);
   STDMETHOD (GetCurFile)(LPOLESTR *ppszFileName);

   // IFileViewer methods
   // Nothting ever calls PrintTo, unless
   // Quick View (QUIKVIEW.EXE) is run from the
   // command line.  You shoul implement
   // PrintTo if you support printing.
   STDMETHOD (PrintTo)(LPSTR pszDriver, BOOL fSuppressUI);
   STDMETHOD (Show)(LPFVSHOWINFO pvsi);
   STDMETHOD (ShowInitialize)(LPFILEVIEWERSITE lpfsi);

DECLARE_REGISTRY_RESOURCEID(IDR_ADDRESSBOOKFVVIEWER)

DECLARE_PROTECT_FINAL_CONSTRUCT()

BEGIN_COM_MAP(CAddressBookFVViewer)
  COM_INTERFACE_ENTRY(IAddressBookFVViewer)
  COM_INTERFACE_ENTRY_IID(IID_IPersistFile, IPersistFile)
  COM_INTERFACE_ENTRY_IID(IID_IFileViewer, IFileViewer)
```

```
END_COM_MAP()

  // Destroys the main window when the last
  // interface to the DLL is released.
  // This is used only for drag and drop operations.
  void FinalRelease( );

private:
  // The name of the file being viewed quickly.
  CComBSTR m_szCurrentFile;
};

CAddressBookFVViewer::CAddressBookFVViewer()
{
  // Informs the application who the viewer is.
  // Later, this pointer will be used if the
  // viewer opens a new file within the
  // "current" window.  The application
  // will get an IUnknown pointer for the
  // other File Viewer to release in its Show
  // method.  At this time, we hide our window
  // and go away.
  FVGetApp()->SetViewer( this );
}

STDMETHODIMP CAddressBookFVViewer::GetClassID(CLSID *pClassID)
{
  *pClassID = GetObjectCLSID();
  return S_OK;
}

STDMETHODIMP CAddressBookFVViewer::IsDirty()
{
  // Viewers are not editors.  The file is never "dirty".
  return S_FALSE;
}

STDMETHODIMP CAddressBookFVViewer::Load(
  LPCOLESTR pszFileName, DWORD dwMode)
{
  AFX_MANAGE_STATE(AfxGetStaticModuleState());
  // Start out by assuming the worst.
  HRESULT hr = E_FAIL;

  // Remember the name of the file being loaded.
  m_szCurrentFile = pszFileName;

  // Tell the application to open the document.
  if ( FVGetApp()->OpenDocumentFile(
       CString(m_szCurrentFile) ) )
```

```
  {
      // We opened the file, so we can go on.
      hr = S_OK;
  }
  return hr;
}

STDMETHODIMP CAddressBookFVViewer::Save(
  LPCOLESTR pszFileName, BOOL fRemember)
{
  // Viewers are not editors.
  // This should not be implemented
  return E_NOTIMPL;
}

STDMETHODIMP CAddressBookFVViewer::SaveCompleted(
  LPCOLESTR pszFileName)
{
  // Viewers are not editors.
  // This should not be implemented
  return E_NOTIMPL;
}

STDMETHODIMP CAddressBookFVViewer::GetCurFile(
  LPOLESTR *ppszFileName)
{
  HRESULT hr = S_OK;

  // Make sure that a file has been loaded.
  if ( m_szCurrentFile.Length() == 0 )
  {
     hr = S_FALSE;
  }
  else
  {
     // Copy the file name into the pointer.
     *ppszFileName = m_szCurrentFile.Copy();
  }
  return hr;
}

STDMETHODIMP CAddressBookFVViewer::PrintTo(
  LPSTR pszDriver, BOOL fSuppressUI)
{
  // As far as I can tell, this function only
  // gets invoked via the command line.  Still,
  // if you offer printing support in
  // your application, then you might as well
  // hook this one up.
  return E_NOTIMPL;
```

```
}

STDMETHODIMP CAddressBookFVViewer::Show(
  LPFVSHOWINFO pvsi)
{
  AFX_MANAGE_STATE(AfxGetStaticModuleState());

  // Defer the command to the application object.
  return FVGetApp()->Show( pvsi );
}

STDMETHODIMP CAddressBookFVViewer::ShowInitialize(
  LPFILEVIEWERSITE lpfsi)
{
  AFX_MANAGE_STATE(AfxGetStaticModuleState());

  // Defer the command to the application object.
  return FVGetApp()->ShowInitialize( lpfsi );
}

void CAddressBookFVViewer::FinalRelease( )
{
  // We are no longer needed.   Tell the application
  // object to close up shop.
  FVGetApp()->ShutDown();
}
```

I might have been able to add a lot of this functionality to the library as well. I do not feel comfortable doing so because a lot of the information here depends on what class you have at the bottom of the derivation. With template based programming, the most derived class defines the behavior of its ancestors. In more traditional C++, the ancestors define the behavior of the children. As a result, I felt more comfortable letting the wizard generate this child in its entirety. At some future date, I may mold this class into yet another template class. In the end, you would have a header file that forced the compiler to generate the final class. At this point I am content to let the wizard do this job.

6.5 Summary

File viewers allow you to provide a read-only view of files generated by your applications. They benefit your users by allowing them to distribute files generated by your application. If the recipient of the file does not own your application, they can view the file with a file viewer. File viewers can also be useful for reading files that should not be edited by people, but that may need to be viewed by people.

This chapter presented a library and wizard to help make development of Quick View objects easy to do. These tools allow you to worry about presentation of data and forget about the trivia related to Quick View objects.

As of Windows 2000 and Windows 98 SE, Microsoft has chosen to drop support of Quick View from the operating system distribution. Jasc Software, the developer of Quick View, still sells the Quick View application from their Web site at *www.jasc.com*. If you do not want to shell out the money for Jasc's enhanced application, I intend to make a home-brewed version of Quick View available from my Web site, *www.scottseely.com*. Quick View will still be valuable to your customers who are running Windows 95, 98, and NT 4.0.

Shell Extensions

*H*ave *you ever wondered how installing the drivers for a new video card can alter the way your Display Properties dialog works? Maybe you want to add special handling for icons within Windows Explorer. Other people do it. They customize the shell, tweaking it here and there. I used to wonder how, and at one point, I had convinced myself that the code to enhance the Display Properties dialog was part of the Control Panel applet binary. As I later found out, the code that enhances Control Panel applets, the desktop, and Windows Explorer belongs to a group of COM objects collectively known as shell extensions.*

Most of the topics in this book discuss ways of extending the capabilities of the shell. This chapter specifically discusses shell extensions. Microsoft defines the following handlers as shell extensions:

Extensions registered by file type (or class)
- Context Menu Handler: Adds items to the context menu (the right-click menu) for a file object. You may add verbs and other actions for a file type.
- Icon Handler: Typically used to add icons specific to the file object. You can also use this to add icons for all files belonging to the same class.
- Data Handler: Provides an IDataObject interface for a specific class type. The shell passes this interface to the OLE DoDragDrop function.

- Drop Handler: Provides drop behavior for files that can accept drag-and-drop objects.
- Property Sheet Handler: Adds pages to the property sheet that the shell displays for a given file type. You can also extend items such as the Display Properties dialog using a property sheet handler.

Extensions associated with file operations and directories (move, copy, rename, etc.)

- Copy Hook Handler: These get called whenever a folder object is about to be copied, moved, deleted, or renamed. The handler can allow or prevent the operation.
- Drag-and-Drop Handler: A context menu handler that the shell calls when the user drops an object after dragging it to a new position.

In this chapter, I will cover all of these handlers. You can apply the information in this chapter to other extensible parts of the shell and use these ideas to build your own extensible applications. In each section, I will lay out the rules for when to add a given feature and then explain how to go about adding the feature. In Chapter 6, "File Viewers," I created a simple program for handling addresses. I have every intention of milking that example until the cow is dry. Section 7.5 has an example of a shell extension that can be applied outside of Windows Explorer. Before examining the extensions in depth, we will look at what these extensions have in common.

7.1 Common Features of Shell Extensions

The set of shell extensions that operate on specific file types (context menu, icon, data, drop, and property sheet handlers) have a few things in common. Sections 7.2 through 7.6 explain how you go about adding the extension-specific functionality. A lot of the functionality depends on the interfaces you implement.

Under the HKCR[1] (HKEY_CLASSES_ROOT) registry hive, there is a way to implement handlers for all objects in the file system. The ContextMenuHandlers and PropertySheetHandlers keys, parents of the keys to the extensions, can also be placed under HKCR*. The * means what you think it means: invoke the extension for all files. Other keys exist to extend

---

1. To get a good overview of the registry and how it is built, read "Accessing the Windows Registry Using Visual J++" by Al Saganich. This article appeared in the December 1998 *Visual J++ Developer's Journal.* The first few pages give a good summary of the registry. The Java registry information is the same as the Visual Basic and Visual C++ information.

file system objects globally. These keys all exist immediately under HKCR. The * key only applies to file objects. These other keys also apply:

- **Folder**: This key allows you to register a shell extension for all folder objects in the system. The drag-and-drop handler key:DragDropHandlers only applies to the Folder, Printers, Drive, Directory, and AllFileSystemObjects keys.

- **Printers**: This allows for the same registrations as the **Folder** key. It uses additional handlers for deletion or removal of printers via the copy hook handler. It also allows changes to the printer properties using property sheet handlers and context menu handlers.
- **Drive**: The Drive key acts as a more focused Folder key. Items in the **Folder** also apply to drive paths. Items in the **Drive** area only apply to root paths like c:\.
- **Directory**: This key only applies to extensions to file system folders. This does not apply to folders displayed by other namespace extensions.
- **Directory\Background**: This key affects actions that occur on the background of a file system folder view. For example, you could handle right mouse clicks by adding a shellex\ContextMenuHandlers\<CLSID> entry under this key.
- **AudioCD**: This affects items that represent an audio CD in the system's CD drive.
- **DVD** (Windows 2000) or **DVDFile** (Windows 98): This affects items that represent a DVD within the system's DVD drive.
- **AllFileSystemObjects**: You can use this key for the same registrations as the **Folder** key. This key affects all objects in the file system.

This specific set of handlers runs in the shell process, which is a system process. Windows NT/2000 administrators need to have control over what system level items get installed on the user's PC. On these machines, the shell extensions also need to be registered as approved extensions. Shell extensions must also add a registry entry in this location:

```
HKLM\Software\Microsoft\Windows\CurrentVersion\Shell Extensions\Approved
```

The shell extension adds a named string value under this key. The value's name must be the string form of the CLSID. The actual value does not have to be anything, but should be set to the value of the ProgID so that people can easily match up the extension to its other pieces within the registry. Ordinary users do not have permission to write to this key. Before installing a shell extension, your installation program should try to open the HKLM\ . . . \ Approved key requesting KEY_SET_VALUE permission. If the call succeeds, than the shell extension can be installed without any problems. If the call fails, a regular user is trying to install the extension. The install program has two choices at this point:

1. If the extension is not critical to the correct behavior of the application, the installation program can warn the user that some application features will be unavailable.

2. If the extension is critical, the installation program should cause the whole installation to fail completely. Notify the user that an administrator must install the program.

An extension does not have to be registered under this key to function properly under Windows 9x, although writing to this key under Windows 9x will not cause any harm. Be warned that under Windows 9x, you can get false failures. The previously mentioned test fails when the HKLM\…\Approved key does not exist. When the test fails, the installation code will need to check the version of the operating system using the GetVersionEx function:

```
bool bIsNT = false;
if ( testFailed )
{
    OSVERSIONINFO osversionInfo;
    ZeroMemory( &osversionInfo, sizeof( osversionInfo ) );
    osversionInfo.dwOSVersionInfoSize = sizeof(osversionInfo);
    if ( GetVersionEx( &osversionInfo ) )
    {
        if ( osversionInfo.dwPlatformId ==
            VER_PLATFORM_WIN32_NT )
        {
            bIsNT = true;
        }
    }
}
```

The above code fragment checks version of the platform. By the end of the fragment, you will know with 100 percent certainty why the test failed.

The shell initializes the shell extension handlers through the IShellExtInit or the IPersistFile interfaces. It uses IShellExtInit to initialize context menu handlers, drag-and-drop handlers, and property sheet handlers. For icon handlers, data handlers, and drop handlers, it uses IPersistFile. You can learn all about the IPersistFile interface in Appendix A. We will close out this section with a look at IShellExtInit.

IShellExtInit has a single method, Initialize, which the shell calls to initialize the shell extension. Initialize has the prototype:

```
HRESULT Initialize(
    LPCITEMIDLIST pidlFolder,
    LDATAOBJECT lpdobj,
    HKEY hkeyProgID
);
```

Parameters:

pidlFolder: Address of an ITEMIDLIST structure that uniquely identifies a folder. This value should always be NULL for property sheet extensions. Context menu extensions receive the item identifier list for the folder whose context menu the shell is about to display. Non-default drag-and-drop extensions receive the target folder in this parameter.

lpdobj: Address of an IDataObject that can retrieve the objects the user/shell is acting on.

hkeyProgID: Registry key for the file object or folder type.

Returns: On success this method returns S_OK/NOERROR.

Remarks:

The meaning of the pidlFolder parameter depends on the extension type. You will want to review the meaning of pidlFolder when implementing an extension to make sure that you do not make any mistakes. The shell calls this function right after it instantiates the extension.

This covers all the items common to shell extensions. The sample extensions will show different ways to integrate your application with the shell. Most of the extensions work well as an example of how to build the particular shell extension type. If you find yourself wondering why would you want to do that for an address book, I have an answer for you. I want to teach you how to build the extension. Small, simple examples work best to teach. As a rule, I use ATL for all the COM-based code, MFC for all the User Interface-based code, and the SDK when I must. This mixture works well for things that the user will not download more than once per release.[2] All the DLLs in this chapter will start out as MFC DLLs. When the ATL object gets added, Visual Studio adds the code to support ATL. These DLLs also employ the use of a library named ShellExtension.LIB. This library shows up in four versions:

1. ShellExtension.LIB: Compatible with the default release configuration generated by Visual Studio's DLL wizard

2. ShellExtensionD.LIB: Compatible with the default debug configuration generated by Visual Studio's DLL wizard

3. ShellExtensionU.LIB: Unicode version that is compatible with the default release configuration with UNICODE defined for the project in the C++ preprocessor settings

4. ShellExtensionUD.LIB: Unicode version that is compatible with the de-

---

2. This is a stark contrast to the marketed use of ATL: lightweight Web components. It just so happens that the ATL team made COM development easier, too.

fault debug configuration with UNICODE defined for the project in the C++ preprocessor settings

The library contains a number of *impl* classes—so called because they provide a bare bones *impl*ementation of an abstract base class. These help speed up development because you can construct your shell extension and have ready-to-use implementations of the various interfaces. You can then conduct a fairly simple test and build cycle because you already have the interface signatures typed in correctly. As you debug, you will see TRACE lines in the debugger indicating that a function was called but that it is not implemented. This provides a roadmap of which functions you need to write and the order in which you need to write them. As you finish up development, you should have no "Class::method not implemented" lines showing up in your debugger. In some instances, I have implemented the needed functions. For example, I always write my implementation of the IPersistFile interface the same way: everything returns E_NOTIMPL except for IPersistFile::Load. That function stores the name of the file in a CString and returns S_OK. The classes all follow the same naming pattern. If the class provides a do-nothing implementation of IContextMenu, it is called CContextMenuImpl. The previously mentioned IPeristFile class is called CPersistFileImpl. Does this sound simple enough?

During the rest of this chapter, I will include a note next to the COM interface indicating what class and header file implement that interface. This section introduced IShellExtInit and IPersistFile. Here is their information:

IPersistFile
- **Implemented by:** CPersistFileImpl
- **Header:** PersistFileImpl.h

IShellExtInit
- **Implemented by:** CShellExtInitImpl
- **Header:** ShellExtInitImpl.h

Because I did not provide wizards for this section, I need to at least help prevent you from banging your head against the wall. First tip: always add these lines to your .def file. They will help your DLL work with regsvr32.

```
EXPORTS
    ; Explicit exports can go here
    DllCanUnloadNow PRIVATE
    DllGetClassObject PRIVATE
    DllRegisterServer PRIVATE
    DllUnregisterServer PRIVATE
```

Second, make sure that your project settings dialog will register your extension when it successfully compiles. To achieve this, make the Custom Build tab look like Figure 7-1. The important information is in the two bottom text boxes. Now, let's write some shell extensions.

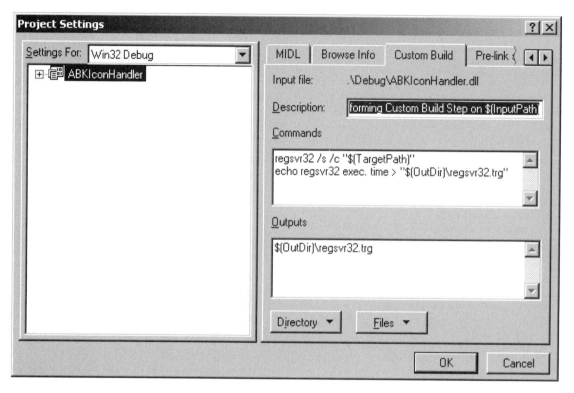

Figure 7–1 *Setting up the project to automatically register your COM object after a successful compile and link.*

7.2 Context Menu Handlers

ShellExtension library information:

- **Implemented by:** CContextMenuImpl
- **Header:** ContextMenuImpl.h

When the user right-clicks on an object displayed by the shell, or on nothing in the shell, a context menu appears. Typical menu items include *Open, Cut, Paste,* and *Rename.* A context menu handler can add new items to this menu.

The shell invokes context menu handlers in response to the user right-clicking an object or to the user dragging an object using the right mouse button. In the former case, the shell invokes context menu extensions. In the latter case, the shell looks at the drag-and-drop handlers. Shell extensions extend the context menu in the same way regardless of how the shell found and invoked the extension.

Many parts of the system use context menus. Band objects, shell extensions, Microsoft Management Console Snap-ins, and other applications all use IContextMenu.[3] When an IContextMenu represents a context menu handler, it must register itself under the shellex\ContextMenuHandlers key. Besides extending IContextMenu, the handler must also extend IShellExtInit. The actual root depends on what the interface extends, such as a file type, all files, a directory object, etc. By registering your extension in the correct place, you can extend the handlers for all files, for directories, or for other document types.

A context menu handler has very few responsibilities. It must perform the following tasks:

1. Add menu items to a context menu as needed.

2. Provide help text for the Windows Explorer status bar.

3. Respond to the user selecting a menu item.

The shell will call the following methods in this order:

1. IShellExtInit::Initialize

2. IContextMenu::QueryContextMenu

3. IContextMenu::GetCommandString ← may be called several times before calling IContextMenu::InvokeCommand.

4. IContextMenu::InvokeCommand ← may never be called. The user cannot choose all the menu items.

Because of all this, the only hard part is making the correct entries in the registry. For the registry script, add these lines to the HKCR section of the script:

```
HKCR
{
    inserted below the script generated by Visual Studio
    '<object name>'
    {
        'shellex'
        {
            'ContextMenuHandlers'
            {
                '{<CLSID>}'
            }
        }
    }
}
```

For the AddressBook.Document context menu handler, I created a class named CABKContextMenu. This class has a simple definition—nothing fancy

---

3. See Appendix A for details on IContextMenu.

is going on. Our handler will do two things: show the number of addresses in a file and display the first address in the file.

```
class ATL_NO_VTABLE CABKContextMenu :
    public CComObjectRootEx<CComSingleThreadModel>,
    public CComCoClass<CABKContextMenu,
        &CLSID_ABKContextMenu>,
    public IABKContextMenu,
    public CShellExtInitImpl,
    public CContextMenuImpl
{
public:
    CABKContextMenu(){}

    // IShellExtInit methods
    STDMETHOD (Initialize)(LPCITEMIDLIST pidlFolder,
        LPDATAOBJECT lpdobj,
        HKEY hkeyProgID);

    // IContextMenu methods
    STDMETHOD(QueryContextMenu)(HMENU hMenu,
        UINT indexMenu, UINT idCmdFirst,
        UINT idCmdLast, UINT uFlags);
    STDMETHOD(InvokeCommand)(LPCMINVOKECOMMANDINFO lpcmi);
    STDMETHOD(GetCommandString)(UINT idCmd, UINT uFlags,
        UINT* pwReserved, LPSTR pszName, UINT cchMax);

DECLARE_REGISTRY_RESOURCEID(IDR_ABKCONTEXTMENU)

DECLARE_PROTECT_FINAL_CONSTRUCT()

BEGIN_COM_MAP(CABKContextMenu)
    COM_INTERFACE_ENTRY(IABKContextMenu)
    COM_INTERFACE_ENTRY_IID(IID_IContextMenu, IContextMenu)
    COM_INTERFACE_ENTRY_IID(IID_IShellExtInit,
        IShellExtInit)
END_COM_MAP()

// IABKContextMenu
private:
    // Grabs the first address from each file in
    // m_fileList and displays it to the user
    void ShowAddresses();

    // Does the actual work of opening the file,
    // getting the address, and formatting it.
    CString GetFirstAddress( const CString& szFileName );

    // Opens the file, reads the number of addresses in the
    // file, and returns the number.
```

```
    int GetAddressCount( const CString& szFileName );

    // For each file in m_fileList, displays the
    // number of addresses in the file.
    void ShowAddressCounts();

    // Holds all the file names the user selects.
    std::vector<CString> m_fileList;
};
```

The implementation of IShellExtInit::Initialize gets the names of all the files that the user selected and places these names into the m_fileList vector.

```
STDMETHODIMP CABKContextMenu::Initialize(
    LPCITEMIDLIST pidlFolder,
    LPDATAOBJECT lpdobj,
    HKEY hkeyProgID)
{
    // Lets grab the data out of the
    // IDataObject pointer.
    STGMEDIUM stgMedium;
    FORMATETC formatetc = { CF_HDROP, NULL, DVASPECT_CONTENT,
        -1, TYMED_HGLOBAL };
    HRESULT hr = lpdobj->GetData(&formatetc, &stgMedium);
    HDROP hDrop = static_cast<HDROP>(stgMedium.hGlobal);
    TCHAR buffer[MAX_PATH];

    int nNumFiles = DragQueryFile( hDrop, -1, NULL, 0 );
    CString szTemp;

    for ( int i = 0; i < nNumFiles; ++i )
    {
        DragQueryFile( hDrop, i, buffer, MAX_PATH );
        szTemp = buffer;

        // Make sure that we only deal with
        // .abk files.
        szTemp = szTemp.Right(4);
        szTemp.MakeUpper();
        if ( szTemp == _T(".ABK") )
        {
            m_fileList.push_back(CString( buffer ));
        }
    }

    return S_OK;
}
```

When the user selects multiple files, the first file retrieved corresponds to the file with focus. The rest of the files may not belong to the same file class. For this reason, we filter out all files not ending in .ABK. To save some duplication of effort, the context menu handler links in Ch6Shared.LIB to get access to the Address class. Once the shell initializes the handler, the shell asks the handler to place its items into the context menu.

```
STDMETHODIMP CABKContextMenu::QueryContextMenu(
    HMENU hMenu,
    UINT indexMenu, UINT idCmdFirst,
    UINT idCmdLast, UINT uFlags)
{
    if(!(CMF_DEFAULTONLY & uFlags))
    {
        InsertMenu( hMenu,
            indexMenu,
            MF_STRING | MF_BYPOSITION,
            idCmdFirst + SHOW_ADDRESS_COUNT,
            L"Show Address Count");

        InsertMenu( hMenu,
            indexMenu,
            MF_STRING | MF_BYPOSITION,
            idCmdFirst + SHOW_FIRST_ADDRESS,
            L"Show First Address");
        return MAKE_HRESULT(SEVERITY_SUCCESS, 0,
            COMMAND_COUNT );
    }

    return E_FAIL;
}
```

Now that the handler loaded the items into the context menu, the shell will display the menu. When our menu items receive focus, the shell will call into our handler to retrieve the help text. The help text string must be less than forty characters in length. Our handler implements this in its implementation of IContextMenu::GetCommandString. The shell calls this method to get the help text, to validate a menu ID, and to get the verb corresponding to a given menu ID. Verbs allow the shell to invoke commands by a human readable name instead of by number.

```
STDMETHODIMP CABKContextMenu::GetCommandString(
    UINT idCmd, UINT uFlags,
    UINT* pwReserved, LPSTR pszName, UINT cchMax)
{
    // Validate the command.
    if ( ( idCmd < SHOW_ADDRESS_COUNT ) ||
        ( idCmd > SHOW_ADDRESS_COUNT + COMMAND_COUNT ) )
    {
        return E_INVALIDARG;
    }
```

```
_bstr_t theText;

// If the command is not doing validation,
// then we just need to lookup the string in
// the correct table.  This implementation
// may not be the easiest thing to internationalize.
// Still, it shouldn't be hard either.
switch( uFlags )
{
case GCS_HELPTEXT:
    theText = HELP_TEXT[idCmd];
    break;
case GCS_VALIDATE:
    return S_OK;
    break;
case GCS_VERB:
    theText = VERB_TEXT[idCmd];
    break;
default:
    return E_INVALIDARG;
}

if ( theText.length() <= cchMax )
{
    // Even building with UNICODE defined,
    // the compiler thinks LPSTR is a
    // typedef for char*.  COM expects
    // unicode.  It gets unicode.
    unsigned short* pName =
        reinterpret_cast<unsigned short*>( pszName );
    wcscpy(pName, theText);
}
else
{
    // The storage handed to me was far too small.
    // I can't tell the caller how much to send.
    // Technically, pszName points to a bit of memory
    // that is too small.
    return E_POINTER;
}
    return S_OK;
}
```

Some of the magic in this method was handled by a few global constants at the top of the CPP file:

```
// Identifies the show address menu item.
const UINT SHOW_ADDRESS_COUNT = 0;

// Identifies the show first address menu item.
const UINT SHOW_FIRST_ADDRESS = 1;
```

```
// Indicates the number of commands.
const USHORT COMMAND_COUNT = 2;

// Help strings which get displayed in the explorer
// status bar.
const _bstr_t HELP_TEXT[] = {
    _T("Show the number of addresses in the file."),
    _T("Displays the first address in the file.")
};

// If the commands are executed by verb, these
// are the verbs the handler understands.
const _bstr_t VERB_TEXT[] = {
    _T("ShowAddressCount"),
    _T("ShowFirstAddress")
};
```

Last, we need to add code to do something when the user selects one of the menu items we added.

```
STDMETHODIMP CABKContextMenu::InvokeCommand(
    LPCMINVOKECOMMANDINFO lpcmi)
{
    // We will allow the structure to grow, but we will
    // not accept versions smaller that the one we
    // are built for.
    if ( lpcmi->cbSize < sizeof( CMINVOKECOMMANDINFO ) )
    {
        return E_INVALIDARG;
    }

    // Set the command to an impossibly high value.
    // If this was actually a valid number, we added
    // far too many items to the menu.
    UINT unCommand = std::numeric_limits<UINT>::max();
    if ( HIWORD(lpcmi->lpVerb) != 0 )
    {
        for ( UINT i = 0; i < COMMAND_COUNT; ++i )
        {
            if ( VERB_TEXT[i] == _bstr_t(lpcmi->lpVerb) )
            {
                unCommand = i;
                break;
            }
        }
    }
    else
    {
        unCommand = LOWORD(lpcmi->lpVerb);
```

```
    }

    // In case the command was not found, tell the
    // caller that the argument is invalid.
    if ( unCommand == std::numeric_limits<UINT>::max() )
    {
        return E_INVALIDARG;
    }

    // We have what we think is a valid command.
    // Invoke it.
    switch (unCommand)
    {
    case SHOW_ADDRESS_COUNT:
        ShowAddressCounts();
        break;
    case SHOW_FIRST_ADDRESS:
        ShowAddresses();
        break;
    default:
        // I include default for completeness.
        // I catch more bugs by always adding this
        // to a switch that I care to count.
        return E_INVALIDARG;
    }

    return NOERROR;
}

void CABKContextMenu::ShowAddressCounts()
{
    CString szMessage;
    int count = m_fileList.size();
    for ( int i = 0; i < count; ++i )
    {
        CString szTemp;
        szTemp.Format( _T("%s has %d addresses.\n"),
            m_fileList[i],
            GetAddressCount( m_fileList[i] ) );
        szMessage += szTemp;
    }
    MessageBox( NULL, szMessage,
        _T("Address Count"), MB_OK );
}

int CABKContextMenu::GetAddressCount(
    const CString &szFileName)
{
    int retval = 0;
```

```
        CFile theFile( szFileName, CFile::modeRead );
        CArchive ar( &theFile, CArchive::load );
        ar >> retval;
        return retval;
    }

void CABKContextMenu::ShowAddresses()
{
    CString szMessage;
    int count = m_fileList.size();
    for ( int i = 0; i < count; ++i )
    {
        CString szTemp;
        szTemp.Format(
            _T("%s has the first address:\n%s.\n\n"),
            m_fileList[i],
            GetFirstAddress( m_fileList[i] ) );
        szMessage += szTemp;
    }
    MessageBox( NULL, szMessage,
        _T("First Address(es)"), MB_OK );
}

CString CABKContextMenu::GetFirstAddress(
    const CString &szFileName)
{
    CString retval;
    int nRecordCount = 0;
```

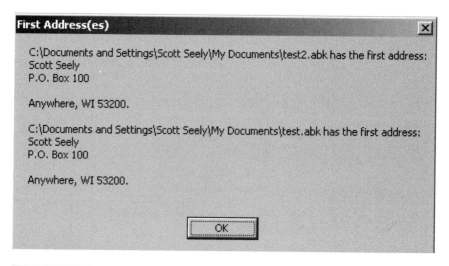

Figure 7–2   *First address context menu handler invoked with two files selected: TEST.ABK and TEST2.ABK.*

| **Figure 7–3** | *Address count context menu handler invoked with two files selected: TEST.ABK and TEST2.ABK* |

```
CFile theFile( szFileName, CFile::modeRead );
CArchive ar( &theFile, CArchive::load );

// The number is always first in the file.
ar >> nRecordCount;
Address address;

// Automagically reads one address, perfectly.
address.Serialize( ar );
retval.Format( _T("%s\n%s\n%s\n%s, %s %s"),
    address.GetName(), address.GetAddress1(),
    address.GetAddress2(), address.GetCity(),
    address.GetState(), address.GetZip() );
return retval;
}
```

You can create more sophisticated handlers if you want to. For example, PKWare's PKZip program[4] adds the menu item *Extract to* to the context menu. Selecting this command starts up PKZip and presents the *Extract to* dialog. The handlers presented here have much less interesting behavior. You can see the two message boxes in Figure 7-2 and Figure 7-3. Let's move on to an equally easy handler type, icon handlers.

7.3   Icon Handlers

ShellExtension library information:

- **Implemented by:** CExtractIconImpl
- **Header:** ExtractIconImpl.h

---

4. This example refers to PKZip 2.70 for Windows. For more details, go to *www.pkware.com.*

Within the shell you have two ways of telling the shell what icon to display for a given file object. You can set the HKCR\<File Object>\DefaultIcon key or you can write an icon handler. If you plan to represent all files of a given type with one icon, you only need to put information into the DefaultIcon key. The default value for the key should be formatted like this:

<full path to binary containing the icon>, <icon's resource id>

Example: If you have an application named MYAPP.EXE and you want to use the icon whose resource ID evaluates to the integer 129, the text in the DefaultIcon key would look like this:

```
C:\Program Files\My Apps\MYAPP.EXE, 129
```

If you want the icon to change based on various parameters, you will need to write an icon handler. It implements the IPersistFile and IExtractIcon interfaces. An icon handler only needs IPersistFile to get the filename with which to associate an icon. The shell passes the filename through IPersistFile::Load. An icon handler can return E_NOTIMPL for all the other IPersistFile methods. Within the IPersistFile::Load method, you should perform any initialization needed to get the correct icon to the shell.

Once you have the IPersistFile interface implemented, you need to implement IExtractIcon. IExtractIcon has the following methods:

```
HRESULT Extract(
    LPCSTR pszFile,
    UINT nIconIndex,
    HICON *phiconLarge,
    HICON *phiconSmall,
    UINT nIconSize
);
```

Parameters:

pszFile: If you passed a filename inside of IExtractIcon::GetIconLocation and returned S_FALSE from that function, pszFile should contain that same string.

nIconIndex: If you passed an icon index inside of IExtractIcon:: GetIconLocation and returned S_FALSE from IExtactIcon::GetIcon-Loaction, you get that string back here.

phiconLarge: This return value points to a handle to the icon to be used when the user instructs the shell to display large icons.

phiconSmall: This return value points to a handle to the icon to be used when the user instructs the shell to display small icons or the details view.

nIconSize: The low word contains the desired size of the large icon and the high word contains the size of the small icon. The shell requires all icons to be square. The value extracted from nIconSize is the requested width and height of the icon.

Returns: If the handler fills in the icon values, this method should return S_OK. If IExtractIcon::GetIconLocation specified an icon file and wants the shell to handle any needed extraction, then this method returns S_FALSE. Any other conditions should return an OLE defined error code.

```
HRESULT GetIconLocation(
    UINT uFlags,
    LPSTR szIconFile,
    INT cchMax,
    LPINT piIndex,
    UINT *pwFlags
);
```

Parameters:

uFlags: This parameter can be any combination of the following values:
- **GIL_ASYNC:** The calling application supports asynchronous icon retrieval. If the handler has cached the icon, then the handler should supply the icon and return S_OK. If the icon is not cached, the handler should start retrieving the icon. The handler should supply a default icon and return E_PENDING while it retrieves the correct icon. GetIconLocation will get called later to attempt to retrieve the icon again.
- **GIL_FORSHELL:** The caller wants an icon for display in a shell folder.
- **GIL_OPENICON:** The icon needs to be in the open state if open and closed images are available. Return the normal or closed state when the caller does not specify this flag. Typically, you only see this flag for folder objects.

szIconFile: Address of a buffer that receives the icon location. Specifically, this string identifies the file that contains the icon. When copying a string into this buffer, make sure that you use _mbscpy to move your string into the buffer. Failure to do this will cause you to create a forehead-shaped dent in your desk.

cchMax: Indicates the size of the buffer pointed to by szIconFile.

piIndex: Address of an INT so that the handler can specify the icon's index within szIconFile.

pwFlags: Address of a UINT that the handler can set to zero or a combination of the following values:
- **GIL_DONTCACHE:** The caller should not cache the actual bits for the returned icon. Windows may introduce a new flag,

GIL_DONTCACHELOCATION, to turn off caching of the file
name and icon location.

- **GIL_NOTFILENAME:** Callers that want to extract the icon from
  the file in szIconFile need to call IExtractIcon::Extract to get the
  correct icons.

- **GIL_PERCLASS:** All objects of this class use the same icon. The
  shell uses this flag internally. If you want all objects to use the
  same icon, consider setting the DefaultIcon key instead of creating a handler.

- **GIL_PERINSTANCE:** Each object of this class has its own icon.
  The shell uses this flag internally to handle cases like
  Setup.EXE where applications with the same name have differ-
  ent icons. Typically, you do not need to specify this flag.

- **GIL_SIMULATEDOC:** The caller should create a document icon
  using the specified icon. I have tried this flag and I am not certain what it is really supposed to do. As far as I can tell, it does
  nothing.

Returns: Returns S_OK if the function succeeded. It returns S_FALSE if
the shell should use a default icon.

So, what does this look like when implemented? In a normal case, you
should wind up with fairly little code. An icon handler has to be able to execute quickly. If you need to write a loop, invoke a database call, execute a
remote procedure call, or invoke a DCOM object, you should stop dead in
your tracks and not write another line. Your code will take too long to execute. The idea behind the icon may be a good one, but your users will not
want the information provided by the icon enough to wait for your code to
execute. Icon handlers should be small, fast objects. The icon handler I wrote
for this section, ABKIconHandler, does not take long to execute. Unfortunately, it does not provide any useful information. The toy application displays one icon if the file path has an even number of letters and a different
icon when the file path has an odd number of letters.

As with all my projects in this chapter, I created an MFC-based DLL. I
then added an ATL object using the object wizard. Besides the usual lines for
making the extension approved under Windows NT/2000, I added these lines
to the HKCR section:

```
'AddressBook.Document'
{
    'ShellEx'
    {
        'IconHandler' =
            s '{82571792-58D1-11D3-A593-0000B49D5993}'
```

```
    }
}
```

Do you notice anything odd about this? Many other shell extensions create a key beneath the name of the handler that indicates the names of associated handlers. An object can only have one icon handler. To enforce this rule, the default value of the IconHandler key must equal the CLSID implementing the one icon handler.[5]

Once you complete your RGS script, you should be ready to get rolling. Here is the header file for the icon handler object, CIABKIcon:

```
class ATL_NO_VTABLE CIABKIcon :
    public CComObjectRootEx<CComSingleThreadModel>,
    public CComCoClass<CIABKIcon, &CLSID_IABKIcon>,
    public CPersistFileImpl<CIABKIcon>,
    public CExtractIconImpl,
    public IIABKIcon
{
public:
    CIABKIcon();

    // IExtractIcon methods
    STDMETHOD (Extract)(LPCSTR pszFile, UINT nIconIndex,
        HICON *phiconLarge, HICON *phiconSmall,
        UINT nIconSize);

    STDMETHOD(GetIconLocation)(
        UINT    uFlags, LPSTR    szIconFile,
        UINT    cchMax, int    * piIndex,
        UINT    * pwFlags);

DECLARE_REGISTRY_RESOURCEID(IDR_IABKICON)

DECLARE_PROTECT_FINAL_CONSTRUCT()

BEGIN_COM_MAP(CIABKIcon)
    COM_INTERFACE_ENTRY(IIABKIcon)
    COM_INTERFACE_ENTRY_IID(IID_IPersistFile,
        IPersistFile)
    COM_INTERFACE_ENTRY_IID(IID_IExtractIcon,
        IExtractIcon)
END_COM_MAP()

        // IIABKIcon
};
```

---

5. I just saved you two hours. The SDK documentation does not highlight this oddity. It's something I picked up after examining the registry. REGEDIT's search feature is one of your best friends when messing with COM.

The extension returns the icons by itself. Because of this, the implementation of IExtractIcon::GetIconLocation does not do much.

```
STDMETHODIMP CIABKIcon::GetIconLocation(UINT uFlags,
    LPSTR  szIconFile, UINT   cchMax,
    int* piIndex, UINT * pwFlags)
{
    // Tell the caller that they shouldn't
    // cache the icon.
    *pwFlags |= GIL_DONTCACHE | GIL_NOTFILENAME;
    return S_OK;
}
```

All the work happens inside of CIABKIcon::Extract. *All the work* means that the method extracts the appropriate icon and places it into the correct pointer.

```
STDMETHODIMP CIABKIcon::Extract(LPCSTR pszFile,
    UINT nIconIndex, HICON *phiconLarge,
    HICON *phiconSmall, UINT nIconSize)
{
    // Base the icon on the # of characters
    // in the file's name— demonstrates
    // the dynamic nature of the extension
    UINT unResource = ( m_szFileName.GetLength() % 2 )
        ? IDI_HANDSHAKE : IDI_PHONE;

    // Load the large version
    *phiconLarge = reinterpret_cast<HICON>
        (LoadImage( _Module.GetModuleInstance(),
        MAKEINTRESOURCE(unResource), IMAGE_ICON,
        LOWORD(nIconSize), LOWORD(nIconSize), 0 ));

    // Load the small version
    *phiconSmall = reinterpret_cast<HICON>
        (LoadImage( _Module.GetModuleInstance(),
        MAKEINTRESOURCE(unResource), IMAGE_ICON,
        HIWORD(nIconSize), HIWORD(nIconSize), 0 ));
    return S_OK;
}
```

You could have implemented similar functionality by placing the icon into a file. CIABKIcon::Extract would reduce to return S_FALSE and CIABKIcon::GetIconLocation would grow to this:

```
STDMETHODIMP CIABKIcon::GetIconLocation(UINT    uFlags,
    LPSTR  szIconFile, UINT   cchMax,
    int    * piIndex, UINT * pwFlags)
{
    CString resource = ( m_szFileName.GetLength() % 2 )
        ? "HANDSHAKE.ICO" : "PHONE.ICO";
```

```
char buffer[MAX_PATH];
::GetModuleFileNameA( _Module.GetModuleInstance(),
    buffer, MAX_PATH );
char drive[MAX_PATH];
char dir[MAX_PATH];
_splitpath(buffer, drive, dir, NULL, NULL );
CString szFileName;
szFileName.Format( "%s%s%s", drive, dir, resource );
resource = szFileName;
_mbscpy( reinterpret_cast<unsigned char*>(szIconFile),
    reinterpret_cast<const unsigned char*>
    (resource.operator LPCTSTR()) );

// Tell the caller that they shouldn't
// cache the icon.
*pwFlags |= GIL_DONTCACHE;
*piIndex = 0;
// Returning false so that the caller calls
// IExtractIcon::Extract next.
return S_OK;
}
```

The above code implements the same rules as the original example, but the new version uses external icon files. I have left this code on the source disk in a comment block.

An icon handler provides nothing more than icons. Outside of the High-lander-esque "There can be only one"[6] rule in the registry that killed an after-noon for me, I have found icon handlers easy to write. Let's move on to the next extension type: data handlers.

7.4   Data Handlers

ShellExtension library information:

- **Implemented by:** CDataObjectImpl, CEnumFORMATETCImpl
- **Header:** DataObjectImpl.h, EnumFORMATETCImpl.h

A data handler allows you to specify the actual data passed to an application when the user copies a file and tries to paste the data into another file. Imagine that you wrote a graphics application. You discover that a number of your users try to paste images generated by your application into other image files by opening up Windows Explorer, selecting *copy* on the image file, and then pasting the information into another application. If you do not have a data

---

6. Maybe it's the geek in me, but whenever I hear anything described with the "there can be only one" rule I picture immortals being decapitated. If you don't get it, go rent the first *Highlander* movie.

handler present, the users will see an icon as a result of their paste into the file. In order to paste a bitmap, text, or some other object, you will have to write a data handler for your file object.

You can only have one data handler per file object. This means that if you want to be able to export the data to more than one format, then one handler must be able to handle all formats. I don't think that this rule makes a lot of sense. Many well-known file formats exist: bitmap, JPEG, GIF, MPEG, WAV, AVI, text, HTML, etc. I can easily imagine a scenario where one might want to write multiple data handlers for a file type. If multiple handlers were installed to a machine, we have the problem of "last write rules."[7] Here is just one scenario: one user wants to be able to paste C++ header and implementation files into other text documents by selecting the file and pasting it into the text file. Another user wants to be able to automatically generate an RTF or HTML version of the file that color-codes all the text when it is dropped into an appropriate document. (This scenario assumes that the appropriate clipboard formats exist and are well known.) The data handlers for all this activity must be coordinated and placed into one DLL. It would make more sense if each clipboard format had only one handler. This does complicate the registry somewhat, but it allows for a more flexible setup. Regardless of how sound my argument is, the fact remains that you can only have one data handler.

A data handler must implement two interfaces: IDataObject and IPersist-File.[8] IDataObject has a fairly large interface. Before covering the IDataObject interface, we need to review two structures that the interface uses heavily: FORMATETC and STGMEDIUM.

```
typedef struct tagFORMATETC
{
    CLIPFORMAT cfFormat;
    DVTARGETDEVICE *ptd;
    DWORD dwAspect;
    LONG lindex;
    DWORD tymed;
} FORMATETC, *LPFORMATETC;
```

Data members:

cfFormat: Specifies the clipboard format the caller wants. OLE recognizes three types of formats:
- Standard interchange formats such as CF_TEXT. Refer to WINUSER.H to get all the valid standard formats. Just open up the header file and search for CF_TEXT. You will find yourself in the midst of all the predefined clipboard formats.

---

7. This is also known as the problem of "all the previous writes didn't matter."
8. See Appendix A for information on IPersistFile.

- Private application formats that only the application and others like it understand.
- OLE formats used to create linked or embedded objects.

ptd: Points to a DVTARGETDEVICE structure that contains enough information to create device context for the target device. A NULL value means that the data format is independent of the target device or when the caller does not care what device is used.

dwAspect: One of the DVASPECT enumeration constants that tells how much detail should be contained in the rendering of the data. For example, a caller might request an object's iconic picture and use the metafile clipboard format to get the picture. Only one DVASPECT value can be used at a time.

- **DVASPECT_CONTENT:** Provides a representation of an object so that it can be displayed as an embedded object inside of a container.
- **DVASPECT_THUMBNAIL:** Provides a thumbnail representation of an object so it can be displayed in a browsing tool. Microsoft recommends using a 120 x 120 pixel, 16-color device-independent bitmap. You may also use a metafile that corresponds to the same requirements.
- **DVASPECT_ICON:** Provides an icon to represent the object.
- **DVASPECT_DOCPRINT:** Provides a representation of the object on the screen as if it was printed to a printer using the Print command from the File menu. The data may represent a sequence of pages.

lindex: Part of the aspect when the data must be split across page boundaries. A value of –1 means all data should be displayed. When dwAspect equals DVASPECT_THUMBNAIL or DVASPECT_ICON, the implementation can ignore lindex.

tymed: One of the TYMED enumeration constants used to indicate the storage medium to transfer an object's data. This member helps decide how a STGMEDIUM structure will get filled in by IDataObject::GetData or IDataObject::GetDataHere. Each value contains a description of what must be done to free any data sent to the caller. ReleaseStgMedium knows how to handle all of these cases for the actual STGMEDIUM in the IDataObject::GetData and IDataObject::GetDataHere calls. This value can be a combination of one or more of the following values:

- **TYMED_GLOBAL:** The storage medium is a global memory handle (HGLOBAL). If STGMEDIUM.punkForRelease is NULL, the caller must call GlobalFree to release the memory.
- **TYMED_FILE:** The storage medium is a disk file identified by a path. When STGMEDIUM.punkForRelease is NULL, the caller

should use OpenFile to delete the file—use OF_DELETE for the OpenFile uStyle parameter.

- **TYMED_ISTREAM:** The storage medium is a stream object identified by an IStream pointer. The caller can use ISequential-Stream::Read to read the data. If STGMEDIUM.punkForRelease is NULL, the caller should use IStream::Release to release the IStream interface.
- **TYMED_ISTORAGE:** The storage medium is a storage compo-nent pointed to by an IStorage pointer. The data lives in the streams and storages contained by the IStorage instance. If STGMEDIUM.punkForRelease is NULL, the caller should use IS-torage::Release to release the IStorage interface.
- **TYMED_GDI:** The storage medium is a GDI component, an HBITMAP. If STGMEDIUM.punkForRelease is NULL, the caller should use DeleteObject to delete the bitmap.
- **TYMED_MFPICT:** The storage medium is a metafile, HMETAFILE. If STGMEDIUM.punkForRelease is NULL, the caller should use DeleteMetaFile to delete the metafile.
- **TYMED_ENHMF:** The storage medium is an enhanced metafile. If STGMEDIUM.punkForRelease is NULL, the caller should use DeleteEnhMetaFile to delete the enhanced metafile.
- **TYMED_NULL:** No data is being passed. This value equals zero, 0.

Next we need to take a look at how the data actually gets passed from the data handler to the user of the data handler. Think of FORMATETC as the product description and STGMEDIUM as the product.

```
typedef struct tagSTGMEDIUM
{
    DWORD tymed;
    union {
        HBITMAP hBitmap;
        HMETAFILEPICT hMetaFilePict;
        HENHMETAFILE hEngMetaFile;
        HGLOBAL hGlobal;
        LPWSTR lpszFileName;
        IStream *pstm;
        IStorage *pstg;
    };
    IUnknown *pUnkForRelease;
} FORMATETC, *LPFORMATETC;
```

Data members:

tymed: One of the TYMED enumeration constants used to indicate the storage medium to transfer an object's data. While the FORMATETC structure allows this value to be a Boolean "or", the STGMEDIUM structure must only have one of the TYMED values. The internal union cannot take on more than one value or meaning at any given moment. You can interpret the union based on the tymed value.

- **TYMED_GDI:** Use the hBitmap union member.
- **TYMED_MFPICT:** Use the hMetaFilePict union member.
- **TYMED_ENHMF:** Use the hEnhMetaFile union member.
- **TYMED_GLOBAL:** Use the hGlobal union member.
- **TYMED_FILE:** Use the lpszFileName union member.
- **TYMED_ISTREAM:** Use the pstm union member.
- **TYMED_ISTORAGE:** Use the pstg union member.

pUnkForRelease: Pointer to an interface instance that allows the creator of the STGMEDIUM to control the way storage is released when the receiving process calls the ReleaseStgMedium function. When pUnkForRelease is set to NULL, the ReleaseStgMedium function uses the default procedures to release the storage. When the pUnkForRelease member points to a valid IUnknown instance, ReleaseStgMedium uses the IUnknown interface.

Now that we have covered the two structures used by IDataObject, we can delve into the methods that IDataObject has and that an IDataObject implementation can implement. To build a minimal implementation of IDataObject, read the remarks section of each of the methods. The first sentence will tell you whether or not the method is required for a bare minimum implementation.

```
HRESULT DAdvise(
    FORMATETC *pFormatetc,
    DWORD advf,
    IAdviseSink *pAdvSink,
    DWORD *pdwConnection
);
```

Parameters:

pFormatetc: Provided by the caller, this pointer defines the format, target device, aspect, and medium used for future notifications. For example, one sink may want to know about changes to the text representation of the object and another sink will want to know about changes to the bitmap representation of the object. This data gets passed to the advise sink after the sink gets notified about the changes.

advf: Specifies a group of flags for controlling the advisory connection. The valid values come from the ADVF enumeration. The valid values are:

- **ADVF_NODATA:** Asks the data object to avoid sending data with the notifications. Typically, the data object sends data with the notification. This flag overrides that default behavior. The caller takes responsibility for retrieving the data through a call to IDataObject::GetData.

- **ADVF_ONLYONCE:** Causes the advisory connection to be destroyed after sending the first change notification. The data object should call its implementation of IDataObject::DUnadvise on behalf of the caller to remove the connection after that first notification.
- **ADVF_PRIMEFIRST:** This asks for an additional initial notification. Combining this flag with ADVF_ONLYONCE works the same as an asynchronous IDataObject::GetData call.
- **ADVF_DATAONSTOP:** Before you destroy the IDataObject, send a notification with data. This overrides the ADVF_NO-DATA flag and sends data in spite of the flag. This makes sense to me since the object will not be around to respond to a IDataObject::GetData call.

pAdvSink: Points to the IAdviseSink interface that receives the change notification.

pdwConnection: This is the only output parameter for the method. This DWORD identifies the connection. IDataObject::DUnadvise later uses this token to delete the advisory connection. Return zero in this parameter to indicate that the object could not establish the connection.

Returns: This method can return the standard values E_INVALIDARG, E_UNEXPECTED, and E_OUTOFMEMORY, as well as the following:
- **S_OK:** The object created the advisory connection.
- **DV_E_LINDEX:** Invalid value for FORMATETC.lindex. Right now, the object only supports –1.
- **DV_E_FORMATETC:** Invalid value for pFormatetc or in the object besides the value of FORMATETC.lindex.
- **OLE_E_ADVISENOTSUPPORTED:** The data object does not support change notification. This return value is superior to E_NOTIMPL in that it makes it clear that this object is not a work in progress.

Remarks: You do not need this method for a minimal implementation of IDataObject.

```
HRESULT DUnadvise(
    DWORD dwConnection
);
```

Parameters:

dwConnection: This DWORD identifies the advisory connection to remove. IDataObject::DAdvise sent this same value to the caller in an earlier call.

Returns:
- **S_OK:** The object destroyed the advisory connection.
- **OLE_E_NOCONNECTION:** The specified dwConnection is not a valid connection.

- **OLE_E_ADVISENOTSUPPORTED:** The data object does not support change notification. Returning this value just means that you have thought about it and you will not be supporting change notifications.

Remarks: You do not need this method for a minimal implementation of IDataObject.

```
HRESULT EnumDAdvise(
    IEnumSTATDATA **ppEnumAdvise
);
```

Parameters:

ppEnumAdvise: Address of an IEnumSTATDATA* pointer that receives the pointer to the new enumerator object. Set this value to NULL if no connections to advise sinks exist.

Returns:
- **S_OK:** The enumerator object was instantiated or no connections exist.
- **OLE_E_ADVISENOTSUPPORTED:** The data object does not support change notification.

Remarks: You do not need this method for a minimal implementation of IDataObject.

```
HRESULT EnumFormatEtc(
    DWORD dwDirection,
    IEnumFORMATETC **ppEnumFormatetc
);
```

Parameters:

dwDirection: Indicates what formats the user wants. The value comes from the DATADIR enumeration.
- **DATADIR_GET:** Return an enumerator specifying the FORMATETC structures that are valid for a call to IDataObject::GetData. For our uses, we only need to support DATADIR_GET.
- **DATADIR_SET:** Return an enumerator specifying the FORMATETC structures that are valid for a call to IDataObject::SetData.

ppEnumFormatetc: Address of an IEnumFORMATETC* pointer that receives the pointer to the new enumerator object.

Returns:
- **S_OK:** The enumerator object was instantiated.
- **E_NOTIMPL:** The direction specified by dwDirection is not supported.
- **OLE_S_USEREG:** Requests that OLE enumerate the formats from the registry.

Remarks: You do not need this method for a minimal implementation of IDataObject. You could force the caller to enumerate values from the registry instead. Enumerating from the registry seems an awful lot like telling the caller to play twenty questions. I recommend implementing this method. It will not take much time and it makes life easier for your caller.

```
HRESULT GetCanonicalFormatEtc(
    FORMATETC *pFormatetcIn,
    FORMATETC *pFormatetcOut
);
```

Parameters:

pFormatetcIn: Indicates what format the user wants to use in a call to IDataObject::GetData. Your code should ignore the FORMATETC. tymed member.

pFormatetcOut: Used to return the most general information possible for a specific rendering of the data. This FORMATETC represents the IDataObject's best try at representing the data. Return NULL in this parameter if you support the exact FORMATETC specified in pFormatetcIn.

Returns:

- **S_OK:** An equivalent but different FORMATETC structure was returned.
- **DATA_S_SAMEFORMATETC:** The IDataObject supports the FORMATETC passed in via pFormatetcIn. pFormatetcOut should be set to NULL.
- **DV_E_LINDEX:** Invalid value for FORMATETC.lindex, which has to be set to −1.
- **DV_E_FORMATETC:** Invalid value within pFormatetcIn.

Remarks: You do not need this method for a minimal implementation of IDataObject.

```
HRESULT GetData(
    FORMATETC *pFormatetc,
    STGMEDIUM *pMedium
);
```

Parameters:

pFormatetc: Indicates what format the user wants to receive data in. The user can pass one or more values for FORMATETC.tymed to indicate multiple acceptable medium formats.

pMedium: Points to the storage medium that has the returned data. The IDataObject implementation indicates who has the responsibility for releasing the medium through the STGMEDIUM.punkForRelease member. A NULL value indicates that the caller must release the data. All other values indicate that the IDataObject will release the data.

Returns:

- **S_OK:** The storage medium has data in it.
- **DV_E_LINDEX:** Invalid value for FORMATETC.lindex, which has to be set to −1.
- **DV_E_FORMATETC:** Invalid value within pFormatetcIn.
- **DV_E_TYMED:** Invalid FORMATETC.tymed value.
- **DV_E_ASPECT:** Invalid FORMATETC.dwAspect value.
- **OLE_E_NOTRUNNING:** Object application not running.
- **STG_E_MEDIUMFULL:** An error occurred allocating space for the medium.

Remarks: You do need this method for a minimal implementation of IDataObject.

```
HRESULT GetDataHere(
    FORMATETC *pFormatetc,
    STGMEDIUM *pMedium
);
```

Parameters:

pFormatetc: Indicates what format the user wants receive data in. The user can pass only one value for FORMATETC.tymed and that value must be TYMED_STORAGE, TYMED_STREAM, TYMED_GLOBAL, or TYMED_FILE.

pMedium: Points to the storage medium that has the returned data. The caller must free the medium. The implementation must always supply a value of NULL on the STGMEDIUM.punkForRelease member.

Returns:

- **S_OK:** The storage medium has data in it.
- **DV_E_LINDEX:** Invalid value for FORMATETC.lindex, which has to be set to −1.
- **DV_E_FORMATETC:** Invalid value within pFormatetcIn.
- **DV_E_TYMED:** Invalid FORMATETC.tymed value.
- **DV_E_ASPECT:** Invalid FORMATETC.dwAspect value.
- **OLE_E_NOTRUNNING:** Object application not running.
- **STG_E_MEDIUMFULL:** An error occurred allocating space for the medium.

Remarks: You do not need this method for a minimal implementation of IDataObject.

```
HRESULT QueryGetData (
    FORMATETC *pFormatetc
);
```

Parameters:

pFormatetc: Indicates what format the user wants to receive data in if it calls IDataObject::GetData.

Returns:

- **S_OK:** A call to IDataObject::GetData would probably succeed.
- **DV_E_LINDEX:** Invalid value for FORMATETC.lindex, which has to be set to −1.
- **DV_E_FORMATETC:** Invalid value within pFormatetcIn.
- **DV_E_TYMED:** Invalid FORMATETC.tymed value.
- **DV_E_ASPECT:** Invalid FORMATETC.dwAspect value.
- **OLE_E_NOTRUNNING:** Object application not running.

Remarks: You do need this method for a minimal implementation of IDataObject.

```
HRESULT SetData (
    FORMATETC *pFormatetc,
    STGMEDIUM *pMedium,
    BOOL fRelease
);
```

Parameters:

pFormatetc: Tells the IDataObject about the format to use when interpreting the data in the storage medium.

pMedium: Points to the storage medium that contains the data.

fRelease: If this is FALSE, the caller owns the storage medium and the IDataObject uses the storage medium for the duration of the call. When this value is TRUE, the IDataObject owns the storage medium. When the IDataObject finishes with the storage medium, the object must release the storage using the ReleaseStgMedium function.

Returns:

- **S_OK:** Data was successfully transferred.
- **DV_E_LINDEX:** Invalid value for FORMATETC.lindex, which has to be set to −1.
- **DV_E_FORMATETC:** Invalid value within pFormatetcIn.
- **DV_E_TYMED:** Invalid FORMATETC.tymed value.
- **DV_E_ASPECT:** Invalid FORMATETC.dwAspect value.
- **OLE_E_NOTRUNNING:** Object application not running.

Remarks: You do not need this method for a minimal implementation of IDataObject.

We have one more interface to cover before going on to the example. In the description for IDataObject::EnumFormatEtc, I mention that you do not have to implement IEnumFORMATETC but that it is a good idea to do so. The IEnumXXX interfaces do not share any common parentage. Instead, they share a definite pattern. The XXX part always specifies what the interface enumerates. If you are familiar with the basic format, you can skip the text on IEnumFORMATETC and miss nothing. For everyone else, this will serve as a little lesson in how the IEnumXXX interfaces typically present themselves. IEnumFORMATETC contains four methods:

```
HRESULT Clone(
    IEnumFORMATETC **pEnum
);
```

Parameters:

pEnum: Pointer to an exact clone of the current IEnumFORMATETC instance.

Returns:

- **S_OK:** The storage medium has data in it.
- **DV_E_LINDEX:** Invalid value for FORMATETC.lindex, which has to be set to −1.

Remarks: You do not need this method for a minimal implementation of IEnumFORMATETC.

```
HRESULT Next(
    ULONG celt,
    FORMATETC *rgelt,
    ULONG* pceltFetched
);
```

Parameters:

celt: Indicates the number of FORMATETC elements being requested.

rgelt: Array of size celt or more FORMATETC structures.

pceltFetched: Pointer to the number of elements actually supplied in rgelt. The caller can set this pointer to NULL if it only needs one element.

Returns:

- **S_OK:** The number of elements supplied is equal to celt.
- **S_FALSE:** Unable to retrieve celt elements.

Remarks: You need this method for a minimal implementation of IEnumFORMATETC.

```
HRESULT Reset();
```

Returns:

- **S_OK:** The object successfully returned to the beginning of the enumeration sequence.
- **Any other error:** Something bad happened.

Remarks: You need this method for a minimal implementation of IEnumFORMATETC (even if you only have one element).

```
HRESULT Skip(
    ULONG celt
);
```

Parameters:

celt: The number of items in the enumeration to skip.

Returns:

- **S_OK:** Successfully skipped the number of items.
- **Any other value:** Could not skip that number of items.

Remarks: You do not need this method for a minimal implementation of IEnumFORMATETC.

The IEnumFORMATETC object allows the consumer of your data to discover what formats the object produces and then picks the one it likes best. It can also copy the enumerator using the Clone method. A client will clone the enumerator to store its position within the enumeration. The other methods allow the client to got to the start of the enumeration, read data, or skip elements as needed.

That was an awful lot of information to throw at you. I believe we now have gone through all the background information needed before writing a data handler. When you create that data handler using the ATL object wizard, you need to make the following modification to the registry script:

```
HKCR
{
    '<File Object Type>'
    {
        'ShellEx'
        {
            'DataHandler' = s '{<CLSID>}'
        }
    }
}
```

You will also have to add the code to add the handler to the approved list of shell extensions in the HKLM registry hive. I like to set up the registry information first. It is one part of the code that I usually can get right the first time and then I never have to look at that section again. From here, I will rely on code specific to the extension written for the AddressBook.Document file object. I wrote a data object that allows the user to copy an AddressBook.Document file object and paste it as a bitmap. I know, this is an odd thing to do. I chose this example to demonstrate how powerful an IDataObject can be. You can make a file object do whatever you want, no matter how odd it may be. The CABKData class in the ABKDataHandler project implements the IDataObject, IPersistFile, and IEnumFORMATETC interfaces. It has the following declaration:

```
class ATL_NO_VTABLE CABKData :
    public CComObjectRootEx<CComSingleThreadModel>,
    public CComCoClass<CABKData, &CLSID_ABKData>,
    public CDataObjectImpl,
    public IABKData,
    public CPersistFileImpl<CABKData>,
    public CEnumFORMATETCImpl
```

```
{
public:
    CABKData();

    // IDataObject methods
    STDMETHOD (GetData)( FORMATETC* pFormatetc,
        STGMEDIUM* pMedium );
    STDMETHOD (QueryGetData)( FORMATETC* pFormatetc );
    STDMETHOD (EnumFormatEtc)( DWORD dwDirection,
        IEnumFORMATETC** ppenumFormatEtc );

    // IEnumFORMATETC methods
    STDMETHOD (Next)(ULONG celt, FORMATETC* rgelt,
        ULONG* pceltFetched );
    STDMETHOD (Skip)(ULONG celt);
    STDMETHOD (Reset)();

DECLARE_REGISTRY_RESOURCEID(IDR_ABKDATA)

DECLARE_PROTECT_FINAL_CONSTRUCT()

BEGIN_COM_MAP(CABKData)
    COM_INTERFACE_ENTRY(IABKData)
    COM_INTERFACE_ENTRY_IID(IID_IPersistFile,
        IPersistFile)
    COM_INTERFACE_ENTRY_IID(IID_IDataObject,
        IDataObject)
    COM_INTERFACE_ENTRY_IID(IID_IEnumFORMATETC,
        IEnumFORMATETC)
END_COM_MAP()

// IABKData
private:
    ULONG m_formatIndex;

    // The class holds the responsibility for
    // destroying the GDI object.  It uses
    // CBitmap to encapsulate the GDI object for
    // GetData.
    CBitmap m_bitmap;
    static FORMATETC m_formatETC[];

    static const int m_KnNumFORMATETCElements;
};
```

The class does not use ATL's IDataObjectImpl class to handle the IDataObject implementation because IDataObjectImpl adds the ability to handle data changes. When implemented as a shell extension, an IDataObject object does not live long enough to ever show a data change. The shell never calls the DAdvise or other advise methods, making the ability to handle advise connections unnecessary. IDataObjectImpl also requires the derived class to implement some functionality that you may or may not want to implement. In its place, I implemented the CDataObjectImpl class.[9] To handle IEnumFORMATETC, I created an array of FORMATETC structures. The array on the CD has only one element, allowing you to experiment with the example. Once you are done with this section, you might want to figure out how to handle CF_TEXT and add it to the things the extension can do. The array on the CD looks like this:

```
FORMATETC CABKData::m_formatETC[] =
{ { CF_BITMAP, NULL, 0, -1, TYMED_GDI } };

const int CABKData::m_KnNumFORMATETCElements = 1;
```

The constant CABKData::m_KnNumFORMATETCElements should be updated when you add CF_TEXT to the array. With the above data, you should be able to handle any of the IEnumFORMATETC requests with the following implementation:

```
STDMETHODIMP CABKData::Next(ULONG celt, FORMATETC* rgelt,
    ULONG* pceltFetched )
{
    if ( m_formatIndex >= m_KnNumFORMATETCElements )
    {
        return E_INVALIDARG;
    }

    *pceltFetched = 1;
    memcpy ( rgelt, &m_formatETC[m_formatIndex],
        sizeof( FORMATETC ) );
    m_formatIndex++;
    return S_OK;
}

STDMETHODIMP CABKData::Skip(ULONG celt)
{
    if ( m_formatIndex + celt >= m_KnNumFORMATETCElements )
    {
        return E_INVALIDARG;
    }
    return S_OK;
}

STDMETHODIMP CABKData::Reset()
{
    m_formatIndex = 0;
    return S_OK;
}
```

To serve the IEnumFORMATETC interface to the caller, I implemented the IDataObject::EnumFormatEtc method.

---

9. Check out Section 7.1 and the ShellExtension library.

```
STDMETHODIMP CABKData::EnumFormatEtc( DWORD dwDirection,
    IEnumFORMATETC** ppenumFormatEtc )
{
    if ( DATADIR_GET == dwDirection )
    {
        QueryInterface(IID_IEnumFORMATETC,
            (void**)ppenumFormatEtc );
    }
    return S_OK;
}
```

To make experimentation as easy as possible, I have CABKData::
QueryGetData loop through all the entries in CABKData::m_formatETC. The
function performs a bitwise *and(&)* with the array's FORMATETC.tymed
value and the FORMATETC.tymed value that got passed in. If any of the bits
match, we some probability that the data can be copied from the file and
pasted using the requested format.

```
STDMETHODIMP CABKData::QueryGetData( FORMATETC* pFormatetc )
{
    HRESULT hr = DV_E_FORMATETC;
    for ( int i = 0; i < m_KnNumFORMATETCElements; ++i )
    {
        // The formats must be compatible and the
        // tymed formats must have something in common.
        // (The tymed values can be OR'd together.
        if (( pFormatetc->cfFormat == m_formatETC[i].cfFormat)
            && !( pFormatetc->tymed & m_formatETC[i].tymed ) )
        {
            // Update the error to one
            hr = DV_E_TYMED;
        }
        else if ( ( pFormatetc->cfFormat ==
                    m_formatETC[i].cfFormat )
            && ( pFormatetc->tymed & m_formatETC[i].tymed ) )
        {
            hr = S_OK;
            break;
        }
    }
    return hr;
}
```

Last, we need to export the data. This gets handled by the
CABKData::GetData. Here we create a bitmap and send its handle out. Because we own the bitmap, we take care of its destruction.

```
STDMETHODIMP CABKData::GetData( FORMATETC* pFormatetc,
    STGMEDIUM* pMedium )
{

    AFX_MANAGE_STATE(AfxGetStaticModuleState());
```

```cpp
// Make sure that the request is for a bitmap.
if ( ( CF_BITMAP == pFormatetc->cfFormat )
   && ( TYMED_GDI & pFormatetc->tymed ) )
{
    // Let the caller know that we will handle
    // any necessary cleanup.
    QueryInterface(IID_IUnknown,
        (void**)&(pMedium->pUnkForRelease) );

    // Set the storage up for a bitmap.
    pMedium->tymed = TYMED_GDI;

    // Read the number of addresses contained in
    // the file be copied.
    CFile theFile( m_szFileName, CFile::modeRead );
    CArchive ar( &theFile, CArchive::load );
    CString szText;
    int numAddresses;
    ar >> numAddresses;
    szText.Format( "%d addresses in %s", numAddresses,
        m_szFileName );

    // Create the drawing objects needed to do the job.
    CBrush brush( RGB(255,255,255) );
    CDC dcScreen;

    // We want a DC compatible with the current display
    // device.
    dcScreen.CreateDC(_T("DISPLAY"), NULL, NULL, NULL);
    CDC dc;
    dc.CreateCompatibleDC( &dcScreen );
    CSize size = dc.GetTextExtent(szText);
    CRect rect( CPoint(0, 0), size );

    // If the object has been around for a while, get rid
    // of the last version.
    m_bitmap.DeleteObject();
    m_bitmap.CreateCompatibleBitmap( &dc, rect.Width(),
        rect.Height() );

    // Select the bitmap into the DC so that we can
    // draw on it.
    CBitmap* pOldBMP = dc.SelectObject( &m_bitmap );
    dc.FillRect( rect, &brush );
    dc.DrawText( szText, rect, DT_LEFT );

    // Select the old object back into the DC
    dc.SelectObject( pOldBMP );

    // Set the handle to the bitmap.
    pMedium->hBitmap = m_bitmap;
```

```
        return S_OK;
    }
    // Add any new handler code here
    // else {...}

    return E_NOTIMPL;
}
```

To test the code for yourself, you need to create an ABK file using the Address Book application and to save that file to disk. Then, right-click on the file within Windows Explorer and select *Copy*. The file is on the clipboard. You need to open up Paint and paste the file into the new drawing. Copying C:\TEST.ABK generated the picture in Figure 7-4.

If you ever need to allow a user to copy a file directly into another application by copying the file from Windows Explorer and pasting it into another document, you will want to consider creating a data handler.

Figure 7–4   *The result of creating a bitmap using a data object handler.*

7.5   Drop Handlers

ShellExtension library information:

- **Implemented by:** CDropTargetImpl
- **Header:** DropTargetImpl.h

By adding a drop handler for a file object, you can make it into a drop target. Drop targets also fall under the "one and only one" rule. If a drop handler already exists for a given file type, you cannot add another drop handler. These handlers can expose a user interface or they can be completely silent based only on your requirements. The idea of being able to drop objects onto files seems very neat. It is one thing to appreciate the ability to do something and quite another thing to see whether one might want that capability. To help you see where drop handlers might come in handy, I have listed some ideas (not a complete list) of when to employ them:

- Your application is document-centric and you want to add the capability to merge documents without invoking a special user interface. You can provide message boxes and dialogs to facilitate the merge.
- Certain objects within the file system may represent real world objects such as modems, fax machines, or other information appliances. You may want to allow the user to transmit files or other data by dragging and dropping a file onto the file object that represents your device.
- Your application uses files to represent various computers the user has access to. The files themselves contain data on how to connect to the machines: x-modem, serial link, network, dial-up, etc. Again, the user sends data to the machines by dropping files the machine understands onto the device.

All the scenarios mentioned assume that the data handler would make sure that the file was valid and could display a user interface if needed. The above scenarios may give abilities to your users that you may not want them to have. For example, you may want to write a data handler to help with testing hardware. One project I worked on involved writing the user interface for a large factory automation system. Programmable logic controllers (PLCs) handled the automation and the Windows GUI provided a view of the system to the user. I would have loved to be able to change the program in the PLC by dragging ladder logic code onto something representing the controller. Drop handlers could be really helpful for your more advanced users by providing a great deal of automation for you and your team.

A drop handler must implement and expose an IPersistFile[10] interface and an IDroptarget interface. The IDropTarget interface exposes the following methods:

```
HRESULT DragEnter(
    IDataObject * pDataObject,
    DWORD grfKeyState,
    POINTL pt,
    DWORD * pdwEffect
);
```

Parameters:

pDataObject: Pointer to the IDataObject interface on the object being dragged. If the drop works, the data within the IDataObject will be incorporated into the target.

grfKeyState: Contains the state of the [Ctrl], [Shift], and [Alt] keys and mouse buttons. Value can be any one of the following flags:
- **MK_CONTROL**
- **MK_SHIFT**
- **MK_ALT**
- **MK_BUTTON**
- **MK_LBUTTON**
- **MK_MBUTTON**
- **MK_RBUTTON**

pt: A POINTL structure containing the current cursor coordinates. These coordinates are expressed using the coordinate space of the drop target window. A POINTL structure and a POINT structure are the same thing. POINTL was created to avoid a name collision with the Point function in Visual Basic.

pdwEffect: On entry, this member points to the value of the pdwEffect parameter of the DoDragDrop function. On return, it must contain one of the effect flags from the DROPEFFECT enumeration to indicate what the effects of a drop operation would be. The enumeration has the following values:
- **DROPEFFECT_NONE:** The drop target cannot accept the data.

- **DROPEFFECT_COPY:** The drop results in a copy. The drag source does not change the original data.

- **DROPEFFECT_MOVE:** The drag source should remove the data.

- **DROPEFFECT_LINK:** The drag source should create a link to the original data.

---

10. See Appendix A for information on IPersistFile.

- **DROPEFFECT_SCROLL:** Scrolling will start or has started in the target. This value can be used in combination with the other values.

Returns: On success, this method returns S_OK. If the method fails, you can return an OLE-defined error code.

Remarks:

To be friendly to your users, you should implement this method to at least tell the user whether or not the drop operation would succeed.

```
HRESULT DragOver(
    DWORD grfKeyState,
    POINTL pt,
    DWORD * pdwEffect
);
```

Parameters:

grfKeyState: Contains the state of the [Ctrl], [Shift], and [Alt] keys and mouse buttons. See IDragTarget::DragEnter for valid values.

pt: A POINTL structure containing the current cursor coordinates. These coordinates are expressed using the coordinate space of the drop target window. A POINTL structure and a POINT structure are the same thing. POINTL was created to avoid a name collision with the Point function in Visual Basic.

pdwEffect: On entry, this points to the value of the pdwEffect parameter of the DoDragDrop function. On return, it must contain one of the effect flags from the DROPEFFECT enumeration to indicate what the effects of a drop operation would be. See IDragTarget::DragEnter for valid values.

Returns: On success, this method returns S_OK. If the method fails, you can return an OLE-defined error code.

Remarks:

To be friendly to your users, you should implement this method to at least tell the user whether or not the drop operation would succeed. This function gets called a lot during the DoDragDrop loop. As a result, this method should be optimized as much as possible. I advise remembering to ask yourself whether or not the drop operation would work. If the operation works, you only need to interpret the key combinations. If not, then your job is already done.

```
HRESULT DragLeave();
```

Returns: On success, this method returns S_OK. If the method fails, you can return an OLE-defined error code.

Remarks:

This method gets called when the file object moves off the potential drop target. At this point in time, you should release any references to the IDataObject, remove any target feedback, and perform any other needed cleanup.

```
HRESULT Drop(
    IDataObject * pDataObject,
    DWORD grfKeyState,
    POINTL pt,
    DWORD * pdwEffect
);
```

Parameters:

pDataObject: Pointer to the IDataObject interface on the object being dragged. If the drop works, the data within the IDataObject will be incorporated into the target.

grfKeyState: Contains the state of the [Ctrl], [Shift], and [Alt] keys and mouse buttons. See IDragTarget::DragEnter for valid values.

pt: A POINTL structure containing the current cursor coordinates. These coordinates are expressed using the coordinate space of the drop target window. A POINTL structure and a POINT structure are the same thing. POINTL was created to avoid a name collision with the Point function in Visual Basic.

pdwEffect: On entry, this points to the value of the pdwEffect parameter of the DoDragDrop[11] function. On return, it must contain one of the effect flags from the DROPEFFECT enumeration to indicate what the effects of a drop operation would be. See IDragTarget:: DragEnter for valid values.

Returns: On success, this method returns S_OK. If the method fails, you can return an OLE-defined error code.

Remarks:

You must implement this method to actually make a drop work.

A drop handler registers itself under the shellex\DropHandler key. If you use ATL and a registry script, the registry script should contain the following lines:

```
HKCR
{
    '<File Object Type>'
    {
        'ShellEx'
```

---

11. See MSDN and look up the DoDragDrop SDK function.

```
                {
                      'DropHandler' = s '{<CLSID>}'
                }
            }
        }
```

You also need to add the lines to register the extension as an approved NT extension. See Section 7.1 for instructions on how to do this.

We are now ready to continue the overkill integration of the Address Book application. See Chapter 6, Section 6.4 for an overview of the application if you have not seen it yet. The drop handler will allow the user to concatenate two address files together. The drop target will tack the drop source data onto the end of the address list. The drop handler will not check for duplicate addresses.

As with the other examples, I used an MFC DLL and implemented the COM objects using ATL. I named the data handler CABKDrop. CABKDrop has the following declaration:

```
class ATL_NO_VTABLE CABKDrop :
    public CComObjectRootEx<CComSingleThreadModel>,
    public CComCoClass<CABKDrop, &CLSID_ABKDrop>,
    public IABKDrop,
    public CPersistFileImpl<CABKDrop>,
    public CDropTargetImpl
{
public:
      CABKDrop();

    // IDropTarget methods
    STDMETHOD (DragEnter)( IDataObject *pDataObject,
        DWORD grfKeyState, POINTL pt, DWORD* pdwEffect );
    STDMETHOD (DragOver)( DWORD grfKeyState, POINTL pt,
        DWORD* pdwEffect );
    STDMETHOD (DragLeave)();
    STDMETHOD (Drop)( IDataObject *pDataObject,
        DWORD grfKeyState, POINTL pt, DWORD* pdwEffect );

DECLARE_REGISTRY_RESOURCEID(IDR_ABKDROP)

DECLARE_PROTECT_FINAL_CONSTRUCT()

BEGIN_COM_MAP(CABKDrop)
     COM_INTERFACE_ENTRY(IABKDrop)
    COM_INTERFACE_ENTRY_IID(IID_IPersistFile,
        IPersistFile)
    COM_INTERFACE_ENTRY_IID(IID_IDropTarget,
        IDropTarget)
END_COM_MAP()

// IABKDrop
```

```
private:
    DWORD m_dwEffect;

    // Indicates if the file can be dropped on.
        bool IsUsableFile( const CString& szFileName );

    // Extracts the name of the file being
    // dropped onto us.
        CString GetDraggedFileName( IDataObject* pDataObject );

    // Reads the dragged file.
        void ReadFile( const CString& szFileName,
        std::vector<Address> &addresses );

    // Takes two files and meakes them into one file.
        void ConcatenateFiles( const CString& szConcatFromFile,
        const CString& szConcatToFile );
};
```

My first task was to work on the IDropTarget interface. The implementation of IDropTarget::DragEnter did not have to check out what keys or mouse buttons were pressed. The decision to only copy the contents to the end of the target file means that only two drop effects are possible: DROPEFFECT_COPY or DROPEFFECT_NONE. Dragging an Address Book document results in DROPEFFECT_COPY and all other file types result in DROPEFFECT_NONE. The code stores the drop effect for later use in the IDropTarget::DragOver implementation.

```
STDMETHODIMP CABKDrop::DragEnter( IDataObject *pDataObject,
    DWORD grfKeyState, POINTL pt, DWORD* pdwEffect )
{
    // Cache the effect for the file being dragged
    m_dwEffect =
        IsUsableFile( GetDraggedFileName( pDataObject ) ) ?
            DROPEFFECT_COPY : DROPEFFECT_NONE;
    *pdwEffect = m_dwEffect;
    return S_OK;
}

STDMETHODIMP CABKDrop::DragOver( DWORD grfKeyState, POINTL pt,
    DWORD* pdwEffect )
{
    // Return the cached effect
    *pdwEffect = m_dwEffect;
    return S_OK;
}

STDMETHODIMP CABKDrop::DragLeave()
{
    return S_OK;
}
```

CABKDrop::DragEnter gets the name of the file through the IDataObject passed into the method. The IDataObject is not the same one registered for the file type. Instead, it is the IDataObject created by the host application. The method CABKDrop::GetDraggedName then asks for the HDROP from the IDataObject and uses the HDROP to derive the name of the file.

```
CString CABKDrop::GetDraggedFileName(IDataObject *pDataObject)
{
    CString retval;
    // Get the HDROP from the data object
    STGMEDIUM stgMedium;
    FORMATETC formatEtc;
    ZeroMemory( &stgMedium, sizeof( stgMedium ) );
    ZeroMemory( &formatEtc, sizeof( formatEtc ) );
    formatEtc.tymed = TYMED_HGLOBAL;
    formatEtc.lindex = -1;
    formatEtc.dwAspect = DVASPECT_CONTENT;

    // Note that we can get an HDROP even though
    // the shellex\DataHandler does not support CF_HDROP
    formatEtc.cfFormat = CF_HDROP;
    if ( SUCCEEDED(pDataObject->GetData( &formatEtc,
        &stgMedium ) ) )
    {
        // Get the name of the file
        HDROP hDrop = static_cast<HDROP>(stgMedium.hGlobal);
        if ( hDrop )
        {
            TCHAR szDropFile[MAX_PATH];
            DragQueryFile( hDrop, 0, szDropFile, MAX_PATH );
            retval = szDropFile;
        }
    }
    return retval;
}
```

CABKDrop::IsUsableFile takes a filename and verifies that the extension looks like an Address Book extension. The function does not actually make sure that the file is valid.

```
bool CABKDrop::IsUsableFile(const CString &szFileName)
{
    bool retval = false;
    char ext[MAX_PATH];
    _splitpath(szFileName, NULL, NULL, NULL, ext );
    CString szExt = ext;
    szExt.MakeLower();

    // We can only use files that end in .abk.
    if ( CString(ext) == CString( _T(".abk") ) )
```

```
            {
                retval = true;
            }
            return retval;
    }
```

The implementation of IDropTarget::Drop concatenates two files together when the drop source looks like an Address Book file. If the files are
compatible, CABKDrop::Drop asks the user if they want to merge the two
files. If the user decides to go ahead, CABKDrop::Drop reads the two files
into one vector and then writes the vector out to the drop target.

```
STDMETHODIMP CABKDrop::Drop( IDataObject *pDataObject,
    DWORD grfKeyState, POINTL pt, DWORD* pdwEffect )
{
    // Get the name of the file that the user
    // dragged and check if we can use it.
    CString szDropFile = GetDraggedFileName( pDataObject );
    if ( IsUsableFile( szDropFile ) )
    {
        // We can copy the file.  Confirm the user's
        // intentions.  It's far too easy to make a
        // mistake when moving files.
        CString szMessage;
        szMessage.Format( _T("Do you want to add %s to the"
            " end of %s?"), szDropFile, m_szFileName );
        int nResult = MessageBox(NULL, szMessage,
            _T("Confirm Concatentation"), MB_YESNO );
        if ( IDYES == nResult )
        {
            // Concatenate the dragged file onto the
            // drop target.
            ConcatenateFiles( szDropFile, m_szFileName );
        }
    }
    else
    {
        return E_INVALIDARG;
    }
    return S_OK;
}


void CABKDrop::ConcatenateFiles(const CString &szConcatFromFile,
    const CString &szConcatToFile)
{
    std::vector<Address> addresses;

    // Read both files into memory.
    ReadFile( szConcatToFile, addresses );
```

```
    ReadFile( szConcatFromFile, addresses );

    // Open the target file for writing.
    // Make sure all the old data is nuked.
    // This is a bad idea: a temp file would
    // be smarter for non-toy applications.
    CFile theFile( szConcatToFile,
        CFile::modeWrite | CFile::modeCreate );
    CArchive ar( &theFile, CArchive::store );
    int count = addresses.size();

    // Write the file.
    ar << count;
    for ( std::vector<Address>::iterator it =
        addresses.begin();
        it != addresses.end(); ++it )
    {
        it->Serialize(ar);
    }
}

void CABKDrop::ReadFile(const CString &szFileName,
    std::vector<Address> &addresses)
{
    CFile theFile( szFileName, CFile::modeRead );
    CArchive ar( &theFile, CArchive::load );
    int count = 0;
    ar >> count;
    for ( int i = 0; i < count; ++i )
    {
        Address address;
        address.Serialize( ar );
        addresses.insert( addresses.end(), address );
    }
}
```

Like many of the examples, CABKDrop does not represent a truly useful class. It demonstrates how to implement a drop handler and nothing more. Hopefully, I have not cluttered up the example too badly. Using drop handlers, you can add some interesting functionality to your applications.

7.6   Property Sheet Handlers

ShellExtension library information:

- **Implemented by:** CShellPropSheetExtImpl
- **Header:** ShellPropSheetExtImpl.h

With a property sheet handler, you can add, remove, and replace pages within a property sheet. A property sheet handler must implement the IShellExtInit and IShellPropSheetExt interfaces. IShellPropSheetExt contains two methods: AddPages and ReplacePage. Only Control Panel extensions call the ReplacePage method. The methods have the following prototypes:

```
HRESULT AddPages(
    LPFNADDPROPSHEETPAGE lpfnAddPage,
    LPARAM lparam
);
```

Parameters:

lpfnAddPage: The shell uses this parameter to specify the address of the function that can add one or more pages to the property sheet. This function takes an HPROPSHEETPAGE and the value of lparam as arguments. CreatePropertySheet, an SDK function, returns a valid HPROPSHEETPAGE handle.

lparam: Value to pass as the second parameter to the function specified by lpfnAddPage.

Returns: On success, this method returns S_OK. If the method fails, you can return an OLE-defined error code.

Remarks:

When creating an extension for the shell, you have to do the setup of the PropSheetPage structure and call CreatePropertyPage yourself. I discuss the reasons why later in the chapter. When the extension extends a Control Panel applet, you can derive your ATL class from CSnapInPropertyPageImpl<*yourclass*, false>. You must set the second parameter of the template to false because you do not want the property page to automatically destroy itself.

```
HRESULT ReplacePage(
    UINT uPageID,
    LPFNADDPROPSHEETPAGE lpfnReplacePage,
    LPARAM lparam
);
```

Parameters:

uPageID: Identifies the page to replace. CPLEXT.H contains the values for this parameter.

lpfnReplacePage: This is the same as the lpfnAddPage parameter in IShellPropSheetExt::AddPage.

lparam: Value to pass as the second parameter to the function specified by lpfnReplacePage.

Returns: On success, this method returns S_OK. If the method fails, you can return an OLE-defined error code.

Remarks:

Take a look at the uPageID information. The shell sets this parameter, not you. In order to replace a page, your code must wait for the proper ID to come through before you replace anything. While CPLEXT.H does contain the values for this parameter, it does not contain all the values for all the different control panel applets. Just because CPLEXT.H only defines values for the keyboard and mouse applets does not mean that you cannot extend other applets. (It also does not mean that you can extend all applets.) This section demonstrates an extension of the Display Properties applet. Also, the shell does not make all property sheet pages available for replacement.

In order to actually implement this extension, you need a little bit of know-how and a lot of patience. My biggest hurdle came when I realized that the people who designed the shell did not think the way I did. I thought that when the shell instantiated my property page extension, the object's lifetime equaled the lifetime of the property page. It does not. The actual object that implements the interface may be dead and gone by the time the property page actually appears on the user's screen. This caused a number of headaches. Once I figured out what was going on, everything got easier. The method IShellPropSheetExt::AddPages passes in a method, lpfnAddPage, that expects the HPROPSHEETPAGE returned by a call to CreatePropertySheet-Page. CreatePropertySheetPage has the following prototype:

```
CreatePropertySheetPage( LPCPROPSHEETPAGE lppsp )
```

where lppsp is a pointer to a PROPSHEETPAGE structure. This structure held the reasons for all my problems and showed me their solutions. Among other things, this structure indicates the dialog procedure and the callback function. The dialog procedure handles the general message loop: initializing the dialog, sending focus messages, etc. The callback function gets called when the property sheet creates the property page and when the sheet destroys the page. Figuring out how to use these two pieces of information with MFC drove me nuts! I knew it had to be possible. I just had to figure out where to wire in the MFC machinery.

MFC's CPropertyPage uses an older version of the PROPSHEETPAGE structure named AFX_OLDPROPSHEETPAGE. A newer version of the class, CPropertyPageEx, claims to have an update to the new version. The header files disagree with MSDN—for now. Fortunately, you can copy data from the old version to the new version and then call CreatePropertySheetPage. In order to make CPropertyPage-derived classes work with the shell, you must call CreatePropertySheetPage with a proper PROPSHEETPAGE structure, and you must implement a callback function that performs similarly to MFC's callback. In order to work this magic, I had a few choices:

- Write a wizard that does the work for the user.
- Write a template class that extends the behavior via multiple inheritance.

Typically, the property page wants to know something about what it is supposed to display. The PROPSHEETPAGE structure contains a variable, lParam, to communicate information between the creator of the property page and the property page itself. The creator allocates the memory and the callback function deletes the data when the property page is deleted. Allowing this behavior in a simple manner looked difficult at best.

Although a wizard would solve all the problems fairly easily, this solution looked like overkill for something that the programmer would probably bundle with other shell extensions in one DLL. I rejected this idea as well.

A template class allows me to solve a few problems rather easily. First, it allows me to declare a member variable of the type being passed from the creator to the actual instance. Second, it allows me to avoid creating a library. And third, I really like writing templates. When writing the template I had to make some assumptions about the clients of the class.

- The client had to derive from CPropertyPage and the template class.
- The client had to have a way of setting the data it wanted transferred.
- The data transferred by the client had to implement operator= or a copy constructor.

TModPropertyPage represents the culmination of these assumptions.

```
// T is the class derived from TModPropertyPage,
// U is the data type.
template <class T, class U>
class TModPropertyPage
{
protected:
    U m_data;
    PROPSHEETPAGE m_psPage;

public:

    // CreatePage must be a instance method.
    // We want access to the m_data and
    // m_psPage for one instance, which will
    // soon go away.
    HPROPSHEETPAGE CreatePage()
    {
        // T must derive from CPropertyPage.
        // It needs to be able to load its template
```

```
    // properly.
    AFX_MANAGE_STATE(AfxGetStaticModuleState());

    T t;
    ZeroMemory( &m_psPage, sizeof( m_psPage ) );
    m_psPage.dwSize = sizeof( m_psPage );
    m_psPage.dwFlags = PSP_USEREFPARENT |
        PSP_USETITLE | PSP_USECALLBACK;

    // Assumption alert!  I assume that this is for
    // a IShellPropSheetExt and that you did the
    // sensible thing by using ATL for the COM part.
    m_psPage.hInstance = _Module.GetModuleInstance();
    m_psPage.pszTemplate = MAKEINTRESOURCE( T::IDD );
    m_psPage.pszTitle = t.m_psp.pszTitle;
    m_psPage.pfnDlgProc = t.m_psp.pfnDlgProc;

    // Make sure that the right static function
    // gets mapped.
    m_psPage.pfnCallback =
        TModPropertyPage<T,U>::CallBack;

    // Here's that ATL assumption again.
    m_psPage.pcRefParent =
        reinterpret_cast<UINT*>(&_Module.m_nLockCnt);

    // U must implement a copy constructor.
    U* pData = new U( m_data );

    // This particular instance of the
    // class will go away.  Pass the information
    // on to the descendent.
    m_psPage.lParam = reinterpret_cast<LPARAM>(pData);
    return ::CreatePropertySheetPage( &m_psPage );
}

static UINT CALLBACK CallBack(
    HWND hwnd, UINT uMsg,
    PROPSHEETPAGE *ppsp)
{
    AFX_MANAGE_STATE(AfxGetStaticModuleState());
    UINT retval = 0;
    switch (uMsg)
    {
    case PSPCB_CREATE:
        {
            // The page is being created.
            // Create the MFC class so
            // that we can hook it.
            T* pPage = new T;
```

```
            // We passed the data in the lParam.
            // Let's recover the info.
            U* pData = reinterpret_cast<U*>(ppsp->lParam);

            // The U class must work with
            // operator =
            pPage->m_data = *pData;

            // Clean up after ourselves.
            delete pData;

            // The ppsp stays with
            // this window throughout its life.
            // Make it possible to clean up
            // when the window is destroyed.
            ppsp->lParam =
                reinterpret_cast<LPARAM>(pPage);

            // Liberal stealing from MFC source
            TRY
            {
                // Map ourselves (and MFC) onto the
                // window
                AfxHookWindowCreate(pPage);
            }
            CATCH_ALL(e)
            {
                // Note: DELETE_EXCEPTION(e) not necessary
                return FALSE;
            }
            END_CATCH_ALL
        }
        retval = TRUE;
        break;
    case PSPCB_RELEASE:
        // The system is getting rid of the instance.
        // Unhook the message loop.
        AfxUnhookWindowCreate();
        try
        {
            T* pPage = reinterpret_cast<T*>(ppsp->lParam);
            delete pPage;
        }
        catch(...)
        {
            // If an exception gets thrown, the
            // page never showed itself.  The
            // pointer is to a U*.
            U* pData = reinterpret_cast<U*>(ppsp->lParam);
            delete pData;
```

```
            }
        break;
    }
    return retval;
    }
};
```

To demonstrate this class, I implemented a property sheet for the Address Book program from Chapter 6. If you have not read the chapter, you may find Section 6.4 helpful. The extension I implemented displays the number of addresses in the one selected file. It only displays itself if the user selected one file. This property sheet extension just shows the basics. I named the extension ABKPropertySheetHandler. The COM class has the following declaration:

```
class ATL_NO_VTABLE CPPgABK :
    public CComObjectRootEx<CComSingleThreadModel>,
    public CComCoClass<CPPgABK, &CLSID_PPgABK>,
    public IPPgABK,
    public CShellPropSheetExtImpl,
    public CShellExtInitImpl
{
public:
    CPPgABK();
    ~CPPgABK();
    // IShellPropSheetExt methods
    STDMETHOD (AddPages)(LPFNADDPROPSHEETPAGE lpfnAddPage,
        LPARAM lParam);

    // IShellExtInit methods
    STDMETHOD (Initialize)(LPCITEMIDLIST pidlFolder,
        LPDATAOBJECT lpdobj,
        HKEY hkeyProgID);

DECLARE_REGISTRY_RESOURCEID(IDR_PPGABK)

DECLARE_PROTECT_FINAL_CONSTRUCT()

BEGIN_COM_MAP(CPPgABK)
    COM_INTERFACE_ENTRY(IPPgABK)
    COM_INTERFACE_ENTRY_IID(IID_IShellPropSheetExt,
        IShellPropSheetExt)
    COM_INTERFACE_ENTRY_IID(IID_IShellExtInit,
        IShellExtInit)
END_COM_MAP()

// IPPgABK
private:
    CString m_szFile;
};
```

When the shell first calls into our code, it calls IShellExtInit::Initialize.

```
STDMETHODIMP CPPgABK::Initialize(LPCITEMIDLIST pidlFolder,
    LPDATAOBJECT lpdobj,
    HKEY hkeyProgID)
{
    // The data object ought to be null
    // and the method must be invoked with some file
    // in mind.
    if ( ( NULL == lpdobj ) || ( pidlFolder != NULL ) )
    {
        return E_INVALIDARG;
    }

    // Store these values in case we need them
    // before the page gets shown.

    // Lets grab the data out of the
    // IDataObject pointer.
    STGMEDIUM stgMedium;
    FORMATETC formatetc = { CF_HDROP, NULL, DVASPECT_CONTENT,
        -1, TYMED_HGLOBAL };
    HRESULT hr = lpdobj->GetData(&formatetc, &stgMedium);
    HDROP hDrop = static_cast<HDROP>(stgMedium.hGlobal);
    TCHAR buffer[MAX_PATH];

    // We want to limit ourselves to only one file.
    // If we have more, we leave.
    if ( DragQueryFile( hDrop, -1, NULL, 0 ) == 1 )
    {
        DragQueryFile( hDrop, 0, buffer, MAX_PATH );
        m_szFile = buffer;
        hr = NOERROR;
    }
    else
    {
        // The argument, technically, is invalid
        // because we don't handle that many files.
        hr = E_INVALIDARG;
    }

    // We have to return the memory
    ReleaseStgMedium( &stgMedium );

    return hr;
}
```

Next, the shell calls IShellPropSheetExt::AddPages. It never calls IShell-PropSheetExt::ReplacePage.

```
STDMETHODIMP CPPgABK::AddPages(LPFNADDPROPSHEETPAGE
    lpfnAddPage, LPARAM lParam)
{
    AFX_MANAGE_STATE(AfxGetStaticModuleState());
    // Note that the scope of ppgAddressBook
    // is only for the duration of the function.
    // The CallBack in the TModPropertyPage<T,U>
    // parent will instantiate the window when it comes
    // to show time.
    CPPgAddressBook ppgAddressBook;
    ppgAddressBook.SetFile( m_szFile );
    HPROPSHEETPAGE hPage = ppgAddressBook.CreatePage();
    if ( !lpfnAddPage( hPage, lParam ) )
    {
        ::DestroyPropertySheetPage(hPage);
    }
    return S_OK;
}
```

Because of TModPropertyPage and MFC, you implement your property sheet as if you were writing a vanilla MFC application. The property page that displays the address file information only needs to know the name of the file being opened. The page can share this information via a CString. This means that for the property page class, CPPgAddressBook, the type of TModProperty-Page<CPPgAddressBook, CString>::m_data will be CString. With the exception of multiple inheritance, the declaration of CPPgAddressBook looks fairly normal:

```
class CPPgAddressBook :
    public TModPropertyPage<CPPgAddressBook, CString>,
    public CPropertyPage
{
    DECLARE_DYNCREATE(CPPgAddressBook)

        // Construction
public:
    CPPgAddressBook();
    ~CPPgAddressBook();

    void SetFile( const CString& szFile );


    // Dialog Data
    //{{AFX_DATA(CPPgAddressBook)
    enum { IDD = IDD_PROPPAGE };
    CString m_szRecordCount;
    //}}AFX_DATA


    // Overrides
    // ClassWizard generate virtual function overrides
```

```
    //{{AFX_VIRTUAL(CPPgAddressBook)
protected:
    virtual void DoDataExchange(CDataExchange* pDX);     //}}AFX_VIRTUAL

    // Implementation
protected:
    // Generated message map functions
    //{{AFX_MSG(CPPgAddressBook)
    virtual BOOL OnInitDialog();
    //}}AFX_MSG
    DECLARE_MESSAGE_MAP()
};
```

> The weirdest concept in this design has to be the idea that any member data we need to have transferred between our COM object and our property page gets handled by the ambiguous TModPropertyPage::m_data member variable. Just to repeat: under the shell, the COM object that initialized the property page will be dead and gone by the time the property page must show itself. We needed some mechanism to handle this. A Singleton[12] could have been designed to survive from one instantiation to the other. This solution would still present the problem of mapping the property page data to a given property page. (IShellPropSheetExt::AddPages can add more than one property page.) We could write the data to a well-known location in the registry or on the hard drive. This solution would also have to later clean up any crumbs the code left behind. The main advantage of the solution with TMod-PropertyPage lies in the fact that the programmer does not have to decide how to pass the information. They only need to know what information they need to pass and how to bundle it. The solution also allows the programmer to write the following code without really thinking about what is happening:

```
// If our AddPages implementation handled multiple files
STDMETHODIMP CPPgABK::AddPages(LPFNADDPROPSHEETPAGE
    lpfnAddPage, LPARAM lParam)
{
    AFX_MANAGE_STATE(AfxGetStaticModuleState());
    int count = m_fileList.size(); //m_fileList is a vector
    for ( int i = 0; i < count; ++i )
    {
        CPPgAddressBook ppgAddressBook;
        ppgAddressBook.SetFile( m_fileList[i] );
        HPROPSHEETPAGE hPage = ppgAddressBook.CreatePage();
        if ( !lpfnAddPage( hPage, lParam ) )
        {
            ::DestroyPropertySheetPage(hPage);
```

---

12. For this and other design patterns, pick up a copy of *Design Patterns* by Gamma, Helm, Johnson, and Vlissides. Reading this book will help you design better objects and write better object-based code.

```
    }
  }
  return S_OK;
}
```

If you did not see anything weird with the above code, read it again. CPPgABK::AddPages creates the CPPgAddressBook objects on the stack. The object lives between the curly braces of the *for* loop. Thanks to TModPropertyPage, the information gets passed between the instances. The callback function in TModPropertyPage always gets called to release the property page so that any data allocated for the property page can be freed. This machinery allows the property page to behave as if it were alive since its instantiation in IShellPropPageExt::AddPages.

```
BOOL CPPgAddressBook::OnInitDialog()
{
    CPropertyPage::OnInitDialog();
    int nRecordCount = 0;
    CFile theFile( m_data, CFile::modeRead );
    CArchive ar( &theFile, CArchive::load );
    ar >> nRecordCount;
    m_szRecordCount.Format(
        _T("You have %d entries in the address book."),
        nRecordCount );
    UpdateData( false );
    return TRUE;
}


void CPPgAddressBook::SetFile(const CString &szFile)
{
    m_data = szFile;
}
```

When all is said and done, we get the dialog shown in Figure 7-5. Before moving on to the next topic, I would like to cover one other way to apply property sheet extensions. Some of the Control Panel applets allow themselves to be extended; I know for certain that the Display Properties, Keyboard, and Mouse applets do. I decided to extend the Display Properties applet. My project adds a BSOD tab to the Display Properties applet. BSOD stands for **B**lue **S**creen **O**f **D**eath. One can customize the colors of this screen by setting a couple of variables in the 386Enh section of SYSTEM.INI: MessageTextColor and MessageBackColor.[13] The user can only customize the

---

13. I received help for this from Nathan Lineback. He wrote a small utility for this under Windows 3.1. After he made a comment about seeing this on the Display Properties applet, I decided to do it. He helped me with the details about what to set and how to set it. Visit his Web site at *http://pla-netx.com/linebackn*. He also has some good information about how to remove Internet Explorer from Windows.

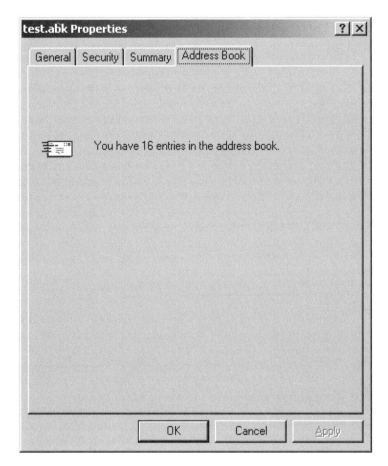

A property sheet extension for a file type.

BSOD under Windows 3.1, 95, and 98. These changes do not work under the Windows NT variants.

In order to have the operating system find the shell extension it must be registered   under   HKLM\SOFTWARE\Microsoft\Windows\CurrentVersion\ Controls Folder\<CPL File Prefix>\Shellex\PropertySheetHandlers. To add a Display Properties extension visible to all the Windows 32-bit desktop variants, you must register for both Desk.CPL and Display.CPL. I do not know why the same applet has two names. I just know that it's true. The extension still needs to register as an approved shell extension if the user installs it on Windows NT/2000. Control Panel extensions do not get much in the way of interesting data from the IShellExtInit::Initialize function, resulting in a transfer of no data between initialization and the time that the page shows up on the screen. Still, the TModPropertyPage extension comes in handy. I used an int as the type for the second template parameter so as to waste only a few bytes of memory. This makes our class slightly bigger than it has to be and avoids creating a new class just to save four bytes of memory and some unnecessary copies of unused memory. This makes the code easier to maintain and keep bug free, a tradeoff that most people are more than happy to make.

The source does not differ much from that for the Address Book property page extension. I include the Blue Screen of Death extension on the CD to show how you can extend the Control Panel Applets. You test applet extensions as if you were testing the applet itself. In other words, follow the instructions in Chapter 4, "Control Panel Applets," Section 4.4.3, for using the applet (for BSOD, this is DESK.CPL or DISPLAY.CPL depending on the version of Windows) as the CPL file to debug. You will be able to debug your applet if all the registry settings are correct. You can see the BSOD extension at work in Figure 7-6. In order to make the change effective, you need to reboot your PC.

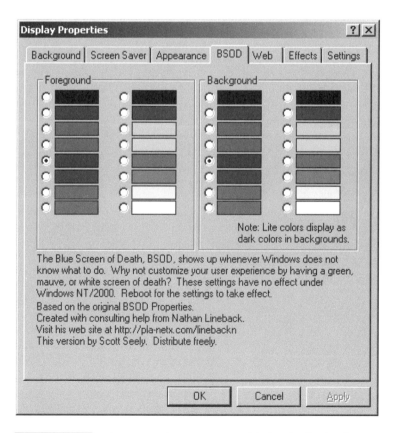

Figure 7–6   *A property sheet extension added to the Display Properties Control Panel applet.*

7.7   Copy Hook Handler

ShellExtension library information:

- **Implemented by:** CCopyHookImpll
- **Header:** CopyHookImpl.h

Copy hook handlers get called before the shell moves, copies, deletes, or renames a folder object. Folder objects include directories, drives, and printers. A copy hook handler can only approve or deny the operation. The shell does not inform a copy hook what happened after the operation has completed. When it comes time to call these handlers, the shell calls all of them for the object until either the operation is unanimously approved or one handler denies the operation. As a result you have no guarantes that all handlers will get called.

Only one shell extension does not have to implement IPersistFile or IShellExtInit: a copy hook handler. One question that comes to mind with this shell extension is, when would I want to implement it? If you have a need to monitor changes to folders that your application uses, you may need a copy hook handler. You may also need to write a handler if you write printer drivers. The only other time I see a need for writing a one is if you write a namespace extension. Namespace extensions are covered in detail later in the book. (If you really want to frustrate your co-workers and not allow them to move, copy, delete, or rename folders, you could use a copy hook handler to deny all operations.)

Copy hook handlers implement the ICopyHook interface. This interface has one method defined:

```
UINT CopyCallback(
    HWND hwnd,
    UINT wFunc,
    UINT wFlags,
    LPCSTR pszSrcFile,
    DWORD dwSrcAttribs,
    LPCSTR pszDestFile,
    DWORD dwDestAttribs
);
```

Parameters:

hwnd: If the copy hook handler needs a parent window, it can use this HWND. If FOF_SILENT is specified in the wFlags member, then the method should ignore this parameter.

wFunc: Operation to perform on the folder object. This parameter can be any of the self-explanatory values listed for the wFunc member of SHFILEOPSTRUCT:

- **FO_COPY**
- **FO_DELETE**

- **FO_MOVE**
- **FO_RENAME**

wFlags: Flags that control the operation. This parameter can be any combination of the values listed for the fFlags member of SHFILEOP-STRUCT. I have omitted values that you should not be seeing for the folders.

- **FOF_ALLOWUNDO:** Preserve undo information if possible.
- **FOF_NOCONFIRMATION:** Respond with *Yes to All* for any dialog boxes that might be displayed.
- **FOF_NOCOPYSECURITYATTRIBS:** Do not copy security attributes.
- **FOF_NOERRORUI:** Do not display any errors to the user.
- **FOF_NORECURSION:** Only operate on the local directory. Do not recursively operate on subdirectories.
- **FOF_RENAMEONCOLLISION:** Create a new name for the folder if one with the target name already exists.
- **FOF_SILENT:** Do not display a progress dialog box.
- **FOF_SIMPLEPROGRESS:** Display a progress dialog box but do not display file names.
- **FOF_WANTMAPPINGHANDLE:** If FOF_RENAMEONCOLLI-SION is specified the SHFILEOPSTRUCT will be updated with the correct information.
- **FOF_WANTNUKEWARNING:** Send a warning if a file will not go into the recycle bin during a delete operation. This flag overrides FOF_NOCONFIRMATION. The flag is valid for Windows 2000 and later.

pszSrcFile: The name of the folder before the operation started.

dwSrcAttribs: Attributes of the folder before the operation is approved. It may be any combination of the following self-explanatory values:

- **FILE_ATTRIBUTE_ARCHIVE**
- **FILE_ATTRIBUTE_COMPRESSED**
- **FILE_ATTRIBUTE_DIRECTORY**
- **FILE_ATTRIBUTE_DIRECTORY**
- **FILE_ATTRIBUTE_HIDDEN**
- **FILE_ATTRIBUTE_NORMAL**
- **FILE_ATTRIBUTE_READONLY**
- **FILE_ATTRIBUTE_SYSTEM**
- **FILE_ATTRIBUTE_TEMPORARY**

pszDestFile: The name of the folder if the operation is approved.

dwDestAttribs: Attributes of the folder if the operation is approved. Can be any combination of the values already explained in dwSrcAttribs.

Returns: Can return any one of the following values:
- **IDYES:** Allow the operation.
- **IDNO:** Prevent the operation on this folder but continue with any other approved operations (example: a batch copy operation).
- **IDCANCEL:** Prevents the current operation and cancels any pending operations.

To register a copy handler, you must register the handler as an approved shell extension. Section 7.1 explains how to do this. Then, you need to register the handler with the appropriate folder object. To register a copy handler for directories, the section of the script specific to the copy handler looks like this:

```
HKCR
{
    'Directory'
    {
        'ShellEx'
        {
            'CopyHookHandlers'
            {
                '<ProgID for your handler>' = s '<CLSID>'
            }
        }
    }
}
```

When you go to implement your handler, you will find that the interface ID name for ICopyHook is not IID_ICopyHook. For reasons unknown, the interface ID is named IID_IShellCopyHook. I mention this "gotcha" because the information is not mentioned on the MSDN CDs. I found the correct interface ID by searching for *CopyHook* in the Visual C++ header files. I later saw this fact mentioned by Dino Esposito in *Visual C++ Windows Shell Programming*. Apparently, Mr. Esposito had the same difficulties I had. When you get used to writing lots of COM code, you find yourself copying the interface name and tacking IID_ to the start of the name. Periodically, this habit will lash out and bite you.

Because copy handlers only get called for folder objects, I could not tack on more examples to the Chapter 6 Address Book example. To demonstrate a handler, I wrote a simple class that writes out the information handed to it in ICopyHook::CopyCallback. I registered the handler under the HKCR\Directory key. CCh7Copy implements the handler. It has the following class declaration:

```
class ATL_NO_VTABLE CCh7Copy :
    public CComObjectRootEx<CComSingleThreadModel>,
    public CComCoClass<CCh7Copy, &CLSID_Ch7Copy>,
    public ICh7Copy,
```

```
    public CCopyHookImpl
{
public:
    CCh7Copy();

    // ICopyHook methods
    UINT __stdcall CopyCallback( HWND hwnd,
        UINT wFunc, UINT wFlags, LPCSTR pszSrcFile,
        DWORD dwSrcAttribs, LPCSTR pszDestFile,
        DWORD dwDestAttribs );

DECLARE_REGISTRY_RESOURCEID(IDR_CH7COPY)

DECLARE_PROTECT_FINAL_CONSTRUCT()

BEGIN_COM_MAP(CCh7Copy)
    COM_INTERFACE_ENTRY(ICh7Copy)
    COM_INTERFACE_ENTRY_IID( IID_IShellCopyHook, ICopyHook)
END_COM_MAP()
};
```

The one method, CCh7Copy::CopyCallback, always returns IDYES since it has no real business disrupting the ordinary operations. I also had no urge to make my PC unusable. The function always appends data to the end of the file and never erases the file. If you do decide to test this project, make sure that you look at typing in regsvr32 –u ch7copyhandler.dll at some point in time. Otherwise, you will know about every directory change that was made on your machine. I did not include output of the file attributes. The function was getting a little long-winded for a simple example.

```
UINT __stdcall CCh7Copy::CopyCallback( HWND hwnd,
    UINT wFunc, UINT wFlags, LPCSTR pszSrcFile,
    DWORD dwSrcAttribs, LPCSTR pszDestFile,
    DWORD dwDestAttribs )
{
    // Global using directives are evil. Import
    // frequently used symbols into the scope you
    // want to use them.
    using std::endl;
    using std::string;
    // Monitor all directory operations
    std::ofstream ofs( "c:\\DirChange.log",
        std::ios::out | std::ios::app );

    ofs << "User attempted operation on directory on "
        << string( COleDateTime::GetCurrentTime()
        .Format( _T("%B %d, %Y at %I:%M:%S\n") ) );

    if ( NULL != pszSrcFile )
    {
```

```
    ofs << "\tSource directory name: " <<
        pszSrcFile << endl;
}
if ( NULL != pszDestFile )
{
    ofs << "\tDestination directory name: " <<
        pszDestFile << endl;
}
ofs << "\tAttempted operation: ";

switch ( wFunc )
{
case FO_COPY:
    ofs << "FO_COPY";
    break;
case FO_DELETE:
    ofs << "FO_DELETE";
    break;
case FO_MOVE:
    ofs << "FO_MOVE";
    break;
case FO_RENAME:
    ofs << "FO_RENAME";
    break;
default:
    ofs << "unknown operation: " << wFunc;
    break;
}

ofs << endl << "\tThe following flags were set:" << endl;
if ( wFlags & FOF_ALLOWUNDO )
{
    ofs << "\t\tFOF_ALLOWUNDO" << endl;
}
if ( wFlags & FOF_FILESONLY )
{
    ofs << "\t\tFOF_FILESONLY" << endl;
}
if ( wFlags & FOF_MULTIDESTFILES )
{
    ofs << "\t\tFOF_MULTIDESTFILES" << endl;
}
if ( wFlags & FOF_NOCONFIRMATION )
{
    ofs << "\t\tFOF_NOCONFIRMATION" << endl;
}
if ( wFlags & FOF_NOCONFIRMMKDIR )
{
    ofs << "\t\tFOF_NOCONFIRMMKDIR" << endl;
}
```

```
if ( wFlags & FOF_NO_CONNECTED_ELEMENTS )
{
    ofs << "\t\tFOF_NO_CONNECTED_ELEMENTS" << endl;
}
if ( wFlags & FOF_NOCOPYSECURITYATTRIBS )
{
    ofs << "\t\tFOF_NOCOPYSECURITYATTRIBS" << endl;
}
if ( wFlags & FOF_NOERRORUI )
{
    ofs << "\t\tFOF_NOERRORUI" << endl;
}
if ( wFlags & FOF_NORECURSION )
{
    ofs << "\t\tFOF_NORECURSION" << endl;
}
if ( wFlags & FOF_RENAMEONCOLLISION )
{
    ofs << "\t\tFOF_RENAMEONCOLLISION" << endl;
}
if ( wFlags & FOF_SILENT )
{
    ofs << "\t\tFOF_SILENT" << endl;
}
if ( wFlags & FOF_SIMPLEPROGRESS )
{
    ofs << "\t\tFOF_SIMPLEPROGRESS" << endl;
}
if ( wFlags & FOF_WANTMAPPINGHANDLE )
{
    ofs << "\t\tFOF_WANTMAPPINGHANDLE" << endl;
}
if ( wFlags & FOF_WANTNUKEWARNING )
{
    ofs << "\t\tFOF_WANTNUKEWARNING" << endl;
}

ofs << endl;

return IDYES;
}
```

A copy handler can be written rather quickly and easily. They would really come in handy for monitoring file copies, but the shell does not call a copy handler with respect to files. It would allow us to prevent users from deleting files that our programs need. Additionally, our code could move related files as a group. Copy handlers only get called for folder objects, though. Still, if you need a copy handler you have an easy task in front of you.

7.8 Drag-and-Drop Handler

Drag-and-drop handlers get called when the user drags and drops an item using the right mouse button. These handlers only work on folder objects. They add items to the context menu displayed when the user drops the object onto the folder. Like copy handlers in the previous section, they seem to be applicable to namespace extensions only. I have a real problem seeing when these would come in useful.

A drag-and-drop handler is the same as a context menu handler with one notable exception: it gets registered under the shellex\DragDropHandlers key. To register a drag-and-drop handler for all directory objects, the part of the script specific to the handler registration looks like this:

```
HKCR
{
    'Directory'
    {
        'shellex'
        {
            'DragDropHandlers'
            {
                <ProgID> = s '{<CLSID>}'
            }
        }
    }
}
```

I tested this by changing the applicable information under the address book context menu handler (Section 7.2). I replaced *AddressBook.Document* with *Directory* and *ContextMenuHandlers* with *DragDropHandlers*. The context menu shows up. You could register a context menu handler under a directory to get a similar effect. The only difference is that a right-click invokes one handler and a right mouse button drag-and-drop invokes the other.

7.9 Summary

The code presented in this chapter demonstrates how to build shell extensions. To keep things simple, I present each shell extension in a separate project. By putting each extension in a separate DLL, you can see what is needed to make that extension work without having to puzzle out any interdependencies I may inadvertently introduce. For a commercial product, you would probably bundle these extensions within one DLL. You can find the projects in the following directories:

- Context menu Handler: Examples\Chapter 7\ABKContextMenu-Handler
- Icon Handler: Examples\Chapter 7\ABKIconHandler
- Data Handler: Examples\Chapter 7\ABKDataHandler
- Drop Handler: Examples\Chapter 7\ABKDropHandler
- Property Sheet Handler: Examples\Chapter 7\ABKPropertySheetHandler
- Copy Hook Handler: Examples\Chapter 7\ABKCopyHookHandler

A drag-and-drop handler example was not presented. As explained in Section 7.8, drag-and-drop handlers differ from context menu handlers in the way the user invokes the handler and how the handler is registered. The differences stop then and there. Shell extensions enable you to expand the capabilities of the Windows interface. Tight platform integration does have its cost in limiting portability to new platforms. On the flip side, integration provides us with the opportunity to enhance the user's perception of our program. Smooth integration into Windows makes a program seem less complicated and more professional. If nothing else, some of these extensions might make your program easier to use and thus will make your clients happy.

Disk Cleanup Handlers

*H*ard disk capacity has increased at an incredible rate in recent years, and hard disk usage has grown with it. Many of today's newer applications assume that the user has a good-sized hard drive. The authors of Web browsers think nothing of using 100MB or more to cache Web pages and increase the performance of the browser. Other applications create non-critical files for performance and other reasons. All this optimization works great when the hard drive has plenty of free space available, but what happens when the user runs out of free space? How are they supposed to know what files can and cannot be deleted? If you document the non-critical files, how do you help them delete or compact only the right files?

Beginning with Windows 98, the Windows operating system ships with a facility to clean the user's hard drive: CLEANMGR.EXE. CLEANMGR.EXE is also known as the Disk Cleanup Utility. This utility answers all three of the questions in the first paragraph.

1. Windows detects when users are low on free disk space.

2. The Disk Cleanup Utility allows application vendors to provide mechanisms to free up disk space.

3. The user trusts that the operations performed by the Disk Cleanup Utility will not harm their computer.

The Disk Cleanup Utility cooperates with disk cleanup handlers to free up space on the computer's hard disk. Microsoft provides the *short of space* detection technology and application vendors provide the cleanup technology. This makes good sense. The creators of any application know better than anyone else what files can be removed. If your program uses files that can be removed without making your program unusable, you should provide your user with a disk cleanup utility. For example, Web browsers can function well without their file cache. If your program stores information in a temporary file for speedup reasons, it may have to rebuild tables for them. As we will see in the example, deleting data is not the only way to save space. You also can get more disk space by saving allocation units.

An allocation unit represents the minimum amount of space the operating system must reserve on disk for a file. If the allocation unit is 4096 bytes and you write out a file with one byte, the operating system will reserve 4096 bytes of space for the file. If my application usually writes short files that could be combined into a larger file, I can write a disk cleanup handler that will free up disk space without deleting data. To see the size of the allocation units on your hard drive, go to a command prompt and type *chkdsk* at the prompt. Among the various lines of output will be a line telling you the size of an allocation unit. On my machine I have two volumes with 512 byte allocation units and one volume with 4096 byte allocation units. Here is the output from running the chkdsk command on my C drive (the allocation unit size is stated in **bold** text):

```
4104575 KB total disk space.
2859054 KB in 27192 files.
   7488 KB in 1935 indexes.
      0 KB in bad sectors.
  38073 KB in use by the system.
   4096 KB occupied by the log file.
1199960 KB available on disk.

    512 bytes in each allocation unit.
8209151 total allocation units on disk.
2399920 allocation units available on disk.
```

In this chapter, I will to go over the following topics:

* The Disk Cleanup Utility and its relationship to disk cleanup handlers
* The various interfaces employed by disk cleanup handlers and how they work
* Developing a disk cleanup handler for address book files[1]

---

1. See Chapter 6, "File Viewers," Section 6.4 for an overview of the Address Book example program.

8.1   The Disk Cleanup Utility and Handlers

The Disk Cleanup Utility, CLEANMGR.EXE, provides a user interface to the cleanup handlers on the user's machine. Figure 8-1 and Figure 8-2 show the two primary screens the Disk Cleanup Handler provides.[2] When the Disk Cleanup Utility starts up, it displays the screen in Figure 8-1 to the user. They select the volume they want to free space on and then press OK. At this point, the utility looks under the HKLM\Software\Microsoft\Windows\-CurrentVersion\Explorer\VolumeCaches key and loads up any cleanup handlers it finds. The utility initializes each handler and then asks each handler how much space it thinks that it could save. Once each handler has made its estimates, the utility displays the screen shown in Figure 8-2. According to the utility, I could save 55MB if I pressed OK.

The cleanup utility and the cleanup handlers communicate with each other through three interfaces: IEmptyVolumeCacheCallBack, IEmptyVolume-Cache (Windows 98), and IEmptyVolumeCache2 (Windows 2000 and later). IEmptyVolumeCache2 derives from IEmptyVolumeCache and provides better support for localization. Later in the chapter, we will go over what you need to do to support both Windows 98 and Windows 2000 with one cleanup handler. The cleanup handler calls methods in IEmptyVolumeCacheCallBack to report how far along it is in scanning for space to free or how much space it has freed up after the user pressed OK on the dialog in Figure 8-2. The methods within IEmptyVolumeCache tell the handler when and where to start scanning as well as when to free up disk space.

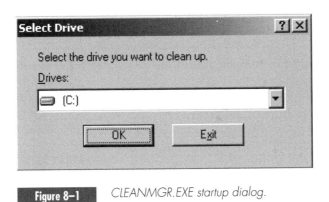

Figure 8–1   *CLEANMGR.EXE startup dialog.*

---

2. The second tab shown in Figure 8-2, More Options, allows the user to remove Windows components and other installed programs that Windows has not seen the user use.

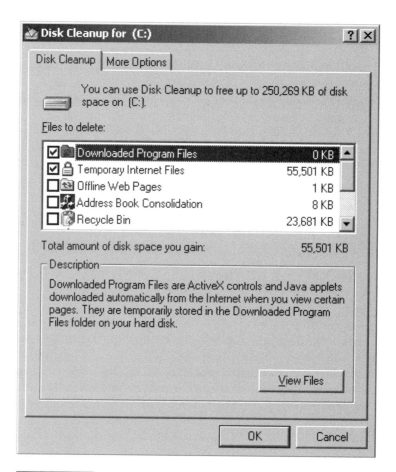

Figure 8–2   *After scanning the disk, this dialog shows the amount of space savings and how the savings were calculated.*

The cleanup utility implements IEmptyVolumeCacheCallBack. IEmpty VolumeCacheCallBack has these two methods:

```
HRESULT PurgeProgress(
    DWORDLONG dwSpaceFreed,
    DWORDLONG dwSpaceToFree,
    DWORD dwFlags,
    LPCWSTR pwszReserved
);
```

Parameters:

dwSpaceFreed: Communicates how many bytes have been freed in the purge.

dwSpaceToFree: Communicates how many bytes the cleanup handler has not freed yet.

dwFlags: The flag can either be zero or EVCCBF_LASTNOTIFICATION. EVCCBF_LASTNOTIFICATION lets the cleanup utility know that the handler has reached the point of no return and will not be updating its status any more.

pwszReserved: Set this to NULL. It is reserved.

Returns: On success, this method returns S_OK. If the user cancels the purge, it returns E_ABORT. At this point, stop what you are doing, restore things to the way they were before the purge started, and return E_ABORT.

Remarks: The only entity that should call this function is a cleanup handler. The cleanup handler calls this method from its IEmptyVolumeCache::Purge implementation.

```
HRESULT ScanProgress(
    DWORDLONG dwSpaceUsed,
    DWORD dwFlags,
    LPCWSTR pwszReserved
);
```

Parameters:

dwSpaceUsed: Communicates how many bytes have been freed in the purge.

dwFlags: The flag can either be zero or EVCCBF_LASTNOTIFICATION. EVCCBF_LASTNOTIFICATION lets the cleanup utility know that the handler is almost done scanning. If you never really know when that will be until you are done, you do not need to set the EVCCBF_LASTNOTIFICATION flag.

pwszReserved: Set this to NULL. It is reserved.

Returns: On success, this method returns S_OK. If the user cancels the scan, it returns E_ABORT. At this point, stop what you are doing.

Remarks: The only entity that should call this function is a cleanup handler. The cleanup handler calls this method from its IEmptyVolumeCache::GetSpaceUsed implementation.

A disk cleanup handler should expose two interfaces: IEmptyVolumeCache and IEmptyVolumeCache2. IEmptyVolumeCache2 derives from IEmptyVolumeCache and only adds one method: InitializeEx. As mentioned earlier, the cleanup handler informs the cleanup utility of its existence by registering itself under the HKLM\Software\Microsoft\Windows\CurrentVersion\Explorer\VolumeCaches key. Under this key, the handler adds a key, preferably named after the handler's ProgID. The default value of the ProgID must be the handler's CLSID. Windows 98 allows three additional values under the Handler Name key:

```
HKLM
    Software
        Microsoft
            Windows
                CurrentVersion
                    Explorer
                        VolumeCaches
                            <Handler ProgID>
                                (Default) = <CLSID>
                                Display
                                Description
                                AdvancedButtonText
```

The Display, Description, and AdvancedButtonText values are all string values. Display defines the text to place in the list box pictured in Figure 8-2. The cleanup utility displays the text in Description inside the group box when the handler is selected. AdvancedButtonText tells the handler what text to display on the button when the handler is selected. Of these three values, only one cannot be obtained through IEmptyVolumeCache: AdvancedButtonText. IEmptyVolumeCache contains the following methods:

```
HRESULT Deactivate(
    DWORD dwFlags
);
```

Parameters:

dwFlags: The flag can either be zero or EVCF_REMOVEFROMLIST. EVCF_REMOVEFROMLIST instructs the cleanup utility to delete the cleanup handler from the list of available handlers in the registry.

Returns: This method should always return S_OK.

Remarks: When I first saw this method I wondered why you would want to ever set EVCF_REMOVEFROMLIST. Then I wrote a handler. Looking for free space can mean scanning all the directories on the hard disk. This can take a long time and might yield nothing. If your application generates temporary files and, under normal conditions, cleans up those files when it is done with them, I can see a need for a removable handler. I imagine that a typical scenario would involve the application adding the handler under the VolumeCaches key, doing its thing, and then removing the entry under the VolumeCaches key. If the program cannot clean up because of programmer error (a.k.a. a crash) or because the user reboots the computer, the handler is still registered. The cleanup handler will be available to clean up any leftovers. When it is done, the cleanup utility will remove the handler from the list. Your program can and should beat the handler to the punch by checking for files to clean up on startup.

```
HRESULT GetSpaceUsed(
    DWORDLONG *pdwSpaceUsed,
    IEmptyVolumeCacheCallBack *picb
);
```

Parameters:

pdwSpaceUsed: Reports the number of bytes the handler thinks it can free up on the hard drive.

picb: Pointer to the cleanup utility interface.

Returns: This method should return S_OK if it completes the scan, and E_ABORT if a call to IEmptyVolumeCacheCallBack::ScanProgress returns E_ABORT.

Remarks: When the cleanup utility calls this method, start scanning for files. Do not worry about tying up the user interface—the cleanup utility has the smarts to call this method on a thread independent of the user interface. While the method runs, periodically call IEmptyVolume-CacheCallBack::ScanProgress to report how many bytes you think you will be able to free up. Be sure to report the final number via pdw-SpaceUsed. Eventually, the cleanup utility displays the value in pdw-SpaceUsed to the user.

```
HRESULT Initialize(
    HKEY hkRegKey,
    LPCWSTR pcwszVolume,
    LPWSTR *ppwszDisplayName,
    LPWSTR *ppwszDescription,
    DWORD *pdwFlags
);
```

Parameters:

hkRegKey: Handle to the registry key representing the handler object.

pcwszVolume: UNICODE string identifying the volume to free space on.

ppwszDisplayName: This is a pointer to a pointer to a string. The string returned in this value will be used in the list box of Figure 8-2. If you set the value to NULL, Windows 98 will use the value under VolumeCaches\<HandlerName>\Display.

ppwszDescription: This is a pointer to a pointer to a string. The string returned in this value will be used in the group box of Figure

8-2. If you set the value to NULL, Windows 98 will use the value under VolumeCaches\<HandlerName>\Description.

pdwFlags: On the way into the function, the flags may have one of the following values:

- **EVCF_OUTOFDISKSPACE:** The user has run out of space on the disk drive. Free up whatever you can, even if it means a loss in performance. Do not delete files that would make the application stop working or lose irreplaceable data.
- **EVCF_SETTINGSMODE:** The cleanup utility sets this flag when the operating system runs cleanup based on a schedule. The cleanup manager will not call GetSpaceUsed, Purge, or Show-Properties. Because Purge will not get called, this method must do any cleanup. The handler should ignore the pcwszVolume parameter and clean up any unneeded files on all volumes. No user interface will be present, so only remove files that can be deleted safely. The handler must set the ppwszDisplayName and ppwszDescription parameters.

The handler can pass these flags back to the disk cleanup utility:

- **EVCF_DONTSHOWIFZERO:** If the handler cannot find anything to free up, the utility should not display the handler in the handler list.
- **EVCF_ENABLEBYDEFAULT:** When the utility displays the screen shown in Figure 8-2, it should set the checkmark next to the handler's name. The user can still deselect the handler. This flag only matters the first time the handler is called.
- **EVCF_ENABLEBYDEFAULT_AUTO:** The handler should be run automatically during scheduled cleanup. Only set this flag when the deletion of files is low-risk. If the user deselects the item in the handler list, the utility will no longer automatically run the handler.
- **EVCF_HASSETTINGS:** Set this flag to let the cleanup utility display a user interface. When the handler sees that this flag is set, it displays a button on the screen, as in Figure 8-2. If your handler sets this flag, you should implement ShowProperties.
- **EVCF_REMOVEFROMLIST:** See Deactivate.

Returns:

- **S_OK:** Success.
- **S_FALSE:** No files were found to delete. This return value is only meaningful when the handler is run on a schedule.
- **E_FAIL:** The operation failed.

Remarks: IEmptyVolumeCache2::InitializeEx replaces this method in Windows 2000. Assuming that you need to support both operating systems, I recommend implementing the bulk of the required functionality in this function. See IEmptyVolumeCache2::InitializeEx for what to do.

Before continuing with the IEmptyVolumeCache methods, I think that now would be a good time to look at IEmtpyVolumeCache2::InitializeEx. This breaks the usual pattern in the book but it allows you to look at the method right away. (Windows 98 uses IEmptyVolumeCache and Windows 2000 uses the newer IEmptyVolumeCache2 interface and its InitializeEx method.) Initialize and InitializeEx look more or less the same. InitializeEx adds only one piece of useful information: ppwszBtnText. You can get the text for the handler's key easily and the rest of the members do not change in meaning or use.

```
HRESULT IEmptyVolumeCache2::InitializeEx(
    HKEY hkRegKey,
    LPCWSTR pcwszVolume,
    LPCWSTR pcwszKeyName,
    LPWSTR *ppwszDisplayName,
    LPWSTR *ppwszDescription,
    LPWSTR *ppwszBtnText,
    DWORD *pdwFlags
);
```

Parameters:

hkRegKey: Handle to the registry key representing the handler object.

pcwszVolume: UNICODE string identifying the volume to free space on.

pcwszKeyName: The handler's key as a UNICODE string.

ppwszDisplayName: This is a pointer to a pointer to a string. The string returned in this value will be used in the list box of Figure 8-2. You cannot use the registry instead of this value. Setting this to NULL causes the function to fail.

ppwszDescription: This is a pointer to a pointer to a string. The string returned in this value will be used in the group box of Figure 8-2. You cannot use the registry instead of this value. Setting this to NULL causes the function to fail.

ppwszBtnText: This is a pointer to a pointer to a string. The string returned in this value will be used as the button text for the button in the group box of Figure 8-2. You cannot use the registry instead of this value. Setting this to NULL causes the function to fail if the EVCF_HASSETTINGS flag is set in pdwFlags.

pdwFlags: Same meaning as in IEmptyVolumeCache::Initialize, as discussed above.

Returns:
- **S_OK:** Success.
- **S_FALSE:** No files were found to delete. This return value is only meaningful when the handler is run on a schedule.
- **E_FAIL:** The operation failed.

Remarks: If you need to support both Windows 98 and later versions of Windows, you should just set the ppwszBtnText and then return the results of the Initialize implementation. A typical implementation should look like this to help minimize code duplication:

```
STDMETHODIMP CleanupHandler::InitializeEx( HKEY hkRegKey,
    LPCWSTR pcwszVolume, LPCWSTR pcwszKeyName,
    LPWSTR *ppwszDisplayName,
    LPWSTR *ppwszDescription,
    LPWSTR *ppwszBtnText, DWORD *pdwFlags )
{
    HRESULT hr = Initialize( hkRegKey, pcwszVolume,
        ppwszDisplayName, ppwszDescription, pdwFlags );
    if ( SUCCEEDED(hr) )
    {
        // Note, SomeFuncToGetLocalizedText(); is a function
        // that the developer writes and names.  It could
        // have easily been named foo().
        *ppwszBtnText = SomeFuncToGetLocalizedText();
    }
    return hr;
}
```

Now, let's return to the IEmptyVolumeCache methods.

```
HRESULT Purge(
    DWORDLONG dwSpaceToFree,
    IEmptyVolumeCacheCallback *picb
);
```

Parameters:

dwSpaceToFree: Indicates how much space the handler should free. If this parameter is –1, the handler should clean up all its files. Under Windows 98, this is always set to the value returned in Get-SpaceUsed.

picb: Pointer to the interface to call to update progress.

Returns:

- **S_OK:** Success.

- **E_ABORT:** User pressed cancel.

Remarks: As a rule, the cleanup handler should clean up as much as possible. If the application will run faster by leaving some unnecessary files behind, the handler should implement ShowProperties so that the user can select what files to delete or how to delete files.

```
HRESULT ShowProperties(
    HWND hwnd
);
```

Parameters:

hwnd: Parent window to use for the user interface this method should display.

Returns:

- **S_OK:** The user changed one or more settings.
- **S_FALSE:** The user did nothing.

Remarks: In order to have this function get called, the Initialize method must set the EVCF_HASSETTINGS flag. Right now, returning S_FALSE from the method does not change the behavior of the cleanup utility, but it might in the future. If you do implement this method you should remember the user's choices in between invocations of this function and invocations of IEmptyVolumeCache::Purge. The user will assume that if they did set the handler for an aggressive removal of files before, they will not have to set this each and every time they run the handler.

You may have noticed that none of these functions tell the cleanup utility what icon to display next to the handler's display string. The cleanup utility finds this information in the registry. You can store the icon in the following locations:

- The cleanup handler DLL
- The icon from the application being cleaned up
- In an icon file
- You can borrow one from another application

This can all be accomplished by storing the icon's location in the registry at HKCR\CLSID\<CLSID>\DefaultIcon. The shell also uses the DefaultIcon key to get the icon for file types if an Icon Handler does not exist. Whenever DefaultIcon is used, the default value of this key has the following format: <file containing icon>, <icon ID>.

By now, we have a fairly complete picture of how the Disk Cleanup Utility interacts with disk cleanup handlers. The cleanup utility initializes each registered handler. It then tells each handler to see how much space it can free up. If the scheduler started the cleanup utility, the handler is responsible for performing a conservative cleanup. A conservative cleanup leaves performance related files alone. If the user started the cleanup utility, then the cleanup handler will wait for the user to invoke its user interface or start the purge process. While purging files, the handler should keep the cleanup utility informed about its progress. At some point in time, the handler will reach a point of no return where it must commit to deleting files. This commit may or may not be immediate. For example, the handler that cleans up after the Internet cache could stop at any time without any adverse effects. The example handler in this chapter consolidates address book entries. After it reads in all the addresses, it commits itself to performing a quick write followed by deleting the consolidated files. As long as the user does not reboot the machine, the consolidation should happen fairly quickly.

No library or base classes were developed for disk cleanup handlers. The most complex piece of the puzzle is pressing the *New ATL Object* menu item. Let's look at the example.

8.2 Address Book File Consolidation

When I first decided to create the address book application in Chapter 6, "File Viewers," I did not intend for it to be the catchall example application. For better or worse, I keep coming up with ways to reuse that little application. Address book files provide an opportunity to show how to free up disk space by consolidating information. This increases disk space by freeing up allocation units, the smallest amount of space the operating system allocates for a file. An address book provides a good opportunity to consolidate information. We will ignore the silliness of actually supporting the creation of multiple address books.[3] The disk cleanup handler for address books performs this consolidation by concatenating all address books on a volume into one location. Besides consolidating files, the handler will implement the IEmptyVolumeCache::ShowProperties method. This will not do anything other than show how to implement the method. The dialog displayed in IEmptyVolume-Cache::ShowProperties will show how the handler came up with the approximate space savings it will generate. Before getting into the example code, I want to explain how to debug a disk cleanup handler.

8.2.1 Debugging Disk Cleanup Handlers

The standard handlers that ship with Windows 98 and 2000 perform some fairly intense calculations. One of the handlers tries to figure out how much it can compress seldom used files. Needless to say, this takes a long time. On a volume with three gigabytes of information, it takes my computer about three minutes to bring up the main user interface for the Disk Cleanup Utility. Most programmers prefer to try little things and then test them. Frequent testing of a disk cleanup handler could result in spending lots of time waiting. To do cleanup handler development, you should have a partition that is more or less empty. If you do not have a volume available, you have the following options:

- Buy a new hard drive. Most people have a PC with room for another hard drive.

---

3. For example, Microsoft's Outlook allows the user to save addresses to an address book, but does not allow multiple address books.

- Use a product like Partition Magic from PowerQuest to reduce the size of one of your partitions. Then, create a new partition and use that for testing.
- Reformat your hard drive and set up the partitions to give yourself space for testing on one of the partitions.[4]

CLEANMGR.EXE is located in the WINDOWS directory on Windows 98 and in the WINNT\System32 directory on Windows 2000. Use this application as the *Executable for debug session* inside of Visual Studio. When you start debugging, do yourself a favor and set a breakpoint in the DllGetClassObject function. If the function does not get called you know that the disk cleanup handler was not properly registered. Most of the time this is caused by one of two things: you forgot to export the DllGetClassObject function or you never registered the handler. The .DEF file should have the following EXPORTS section:

```
EXPORTS
    ; Explicit exports can go here
    DllCanUnloadNow PRIVATE
    DllGetClassObject PRIVATE
    DllRegisterServer PRIVATE
    DllUnregisterServer PRIVATE
```

Your project should also have a Custom Build step:
Commands:

```
regsvr32 /s /c "$(TargetPath)"
echo regsvr32 exec. time > "$(OutDir)\regsvr32.trg"
```

Outputs:

```
$(OutDir)\regsvr32.trg
```

The registry script should register the handler under the VolumeCaches key as described in Section 8.1. Section 8.1 also explains how to set the icon for your handler. Now, if everything looks correct, your entries are in the right places in the registry, but things still do not work, you may have to restart the Windows shell. To do this, bring up the shutdown dialog by pressing the Start button on the taskbar and selecting the Shutdown menu item. Next, press [CTRL]+[ALT]+[SHIFT]+[ESC].[5] To restart the shell, start Windows Explorer. On startup, Explorer.exe performs a number of setup tasks. One of these tasks involves scanning the registry for new data. I usually have the Microsoft Office Shortcut Bar running for the purpose of restarting the shell. If you do not have Microsoft Office, I included in the Tools directory on the CD

---

4. Not exactly an appealing situation.

5. You can also press [CTRL]+[ALT]+[SHIFT] and click on the "Cancel" button.

an application desktop toolbar, ExplorerStarter, that has a button to start Windows Explorer.

Once you have the disk cleanup handler written and running well on your mostly clean partition, you should start testing on the partition that has the most data. Make sure you find all removable files on the drive. If you use CFileFind to look for directories and files, your code may have a common off-by-one error. I do not use this class a lot (once every four months at best) and when I do, I always forget that the function CFileFind::FindNextFile returns FALSE when it finds the last file. Code written like this will fail to find the last file:

```
CFileFind fileFind;
CString szFileFind;
szFileFind.Format( _T("%s*.abk"), szVolume );
// If FindFile returns true, at least one file exists
if ( fileFind.FindFile( szFileFind ) )
{
    // Need to call FindNextFile to get the first
    // and subsequent files.
    while ( !fileFind.FindNextFile() )
    {
        //Do something
    }
}
```

Instead, the code should be written like this:

```
CFileFind fileFind;
CString szFileFind;
szFileFind.Format( _T("%s*.abk"), szVolume );
// If FindFile returns true, at least one file exists
if ( fileFind.FindFile( szFileFind ) )
{
    // Need to call FindNextFile to get the first
    // and subsequent files.
    bool bDone = false;
    while ( !bDone )
    {
        bDone = fileFind.FindNextFile() == FALSE;
        //Do something
    }
}
```

In case you are curious, yes, I made this mistake while developing the example code. Because I make this mistake regularly, I can recognize the problem and solution immediately. Let's move on and build the disk cleanup handler.

8.2.2 Address Book Disk Cleanup Handler

A disk cleanup handler has to implement the IEmptyVolumeCache interface under Windows 98 and IEmptyVolumeCache2 under Windows 2000 and later. IEmptyVolumeCache2 derives from IEmptyVolumeCache. As a result, a class implementing the cleanup handler only has to derive from IEmptyVolume-Cache2. The class's COM map should have an entry for both interfaces. I named the class that implements the address book cleanup handler CAddr-BookCleanup. I also added a new class to the ShellExtension library:[6] CEmptyVolumeCache2Impl. You will find it in the EmptyVolumeCache2Impl.h header file. Remember, you do not need to explicitly link the library to your application: it will do so automatically.[7] CAddrBookCleanup has this class declaration:

```
class ATL_NO_VTABLE CAddrBookCleanup :
    public CComObjectRootEx<CComSingleThreadModel>,
    public CComCoClass<CAddrBookCleanup,
        &CLSID_AddrBookCleanup>,
    public IAddrBookCleanup,
    public CEmptyVolumeCache2Impl
{
public:
    CAddrBookCleanup();

    // IEmptyVolumeCache methods
    STDMETHOD (Deactivate)( DWORD *pdwFlags );
    STDMETHOD (GetSpaceUsed)( DWORDLONG *pdwSpaceUsed,
        IEmptyVolumeCacheCallBack *picb );
    STDMETHOD (Initialize)( HKEY hkRegKey,
        LPCWSTR pcwszVolume, LPWSTR *ppwszDisplayName,
        LPWSTR *ppwszDescription, DWORD *pdwFlags );
    STDMETHOD (Purge)( DWORDLONG dwSpaceToFree,
        IEmptyVolumeCacheCallBack *picb );
    STDMETHOD (ShowProperties)( HWND hwnd );

    // IEmptyVolumeCache2 methods
    STDMETHOD (InitializeEx)( HKEY hkRegKey,
        LPCWSTR pcwszVolume, LPCWSTR pcwszKeyName,
        LPWSTR *ppwszDisplayName,
        LPWSTR *ppwszDescription,
        LPWSTR *ppwszBtnText, DWORD *pdwFlags );

DECLARE_REGISTRY_RESOURCEID(IDR_ADDRBOOKCLEANUP)

DECLARE_PROTECT_FINAL_CONSTRUCT()
```

---

6. This library was introduced in Chapter 7, "Shell Extensions," Section 7.1.

7. Check out ShellExtensionLibrary.h on the CD to see how this is done.

```
BEGIN_COM_MAP(CAddrBookCleanup)
    COM_INTERFACE_ENTRY(IAddrBookCleanup)
    COM_INTERFACE_ENTRY_IID(IID_IEmptyVolumeCache,
        IEmptyVolumeCache)
    COM_INTERFACE_ENTRY_IID(IID_IEmptyVolumeCache2,
        IEmptyVolumeCache2)
END_COM_MAP()

// IAddrBookCleanup
private:
    HRESULT FindABKFiles( CString& szVolume );

    // Upon finding a file, adds the file size
    // to the total byte count.
    HRESULT AddBytesToTotal( int m_byteCount );

    // Adds the filename to the list of files.
    void AddFileName( const CString& szFileName );

    // Returns the volume being analyzed.
    CString GetVolume();

    // Stores the callback pointer.
    IEmptyVolumeCacheCallBack* GetCacheCallBack();

    CString m_szVolumeName;
    int m_nAllocationUnitSize;
    int m_nBytesInUse;
    int m_nAllocationUnitsInUse;
    int m_nBytesSaved;
    IEmptyVolumeCacheCallBack* m_pCallBack;
    std::list<CString> m_fileNames;
};
```

The first thing I did was put in bare bones implementations of the COM functions. They all returned E_NOTIMPL. Many of the helper functions used by the class, such as GetVolume(), did not exist until later. I implemented CAddrBookCleanup::Initialize and CAddrBookCleanup::InitializeEx first. These methods allow me to see if I have properly registered the cleanup handler. If all goes well, I should be able to select my handler. For the time being, CAddrBookCleanup::GetSpaceUsed will return S_OK and set the space savings to zero bytes. CAddrBookCleanup::GetSpaceUsed has to appear to work. In the example, I did not implement localization.

```
STDMETHODIMP CAddrBookCleanup::Initialize( HKEY hkRegKey,
    LPCWSTR pcwszVolume, LPWSTR *ppwszDisplayName,
    LPWSTR *ppwszDescription, DWORD *pdwFlags )
{
    if ( EVCF_SETTINGSMODE & *pdwFlags )
    {
```

```
        // This is a scheduled cleanup.
        // Leave the files alone.
        return S_OK;
    }
    m_szVolumeName = pcwszVolume;
    *ppwszDisplayName=L"Address Book Consolidation";
    *ppwszDescription=L"Concatenates address book files into "
        L"one file.  The resulting file will be placed in the "
        L"application directory and will be named UNIFIED.ABK."
        L"  All other files will be deleted.";
    *pdwFlags |= EVCF_HASSETTINGS;

    // Setup the cluster size.
    DWORD dwSectorsPerCluster = 0;
    DWORD dwBytesPerSector = 0;
    DWORD dwNumberOfFreeClusters = 0;
    DWORD dwTotalNumberOfClusters = 0;
    GetDiskFreeSpace( m_szVolumeName,
        &dwSectorsPerCluster, &dwBytesPerSector,
        &dwNumberOfFreeClusters,
        &dwTotalNumberOfClusters );
    m_nAllocationUnitSize = dwSectorsPerCluster
        * dwBytesPerSector;
    return S_OK;
}

STDMETHODIMP CAddrBookCleanup::InitializeEx( HKEY hkRegKey,
    LPCWSTR pcwszVolume, LPCWSTR pcwszKeyName,
    LPWSTR *ppwszDisplayName,
    LPWSTR *ppwszDescription,
    LPWSTR *ppwszBtnText, DWORD *pdwFlags )
{
    HRESULT hr = Initialize( hkRegKey, pcwszVolume,
        ppwszDisplayName, ppwszDescription, pdwFlags );
    if ( SUCCEEDED(hr) )
    {
        *ppwszBtnText = L"Space Savings";
    }
    return hr;
}
```

A quick build and test showed that the Disk Cleanup Utility found the address book handler. It appeared in the list as shown in Figure 8-3. Now that the utility shows up in the list, we are ready to implement the savings search functionality. CAddrBookCleanup::GetSpaceUsed does the easy part by placing the first call to the recursive FindABKFiles function.

```
STDMETHODIMP CAddrBookCleanup::GetSpaceUsed(
    DWORDLONG *pdwSpaceUsed,
    IEmptyVolumeCacheCallBack *picb )
{
```

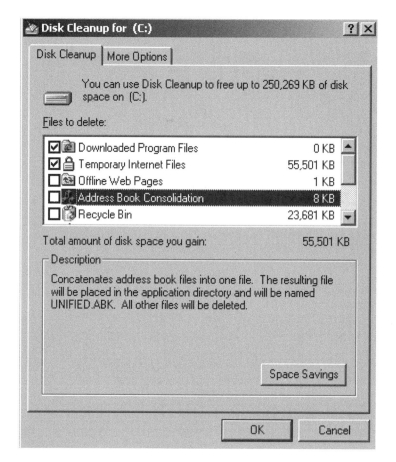

Figure 8–3   *The address book handler and its description. It sets the description text and the button text.*

```
    m_pCallBack = picb;
    HRESULT hr = FindABKFiles( *this, GetVolume() );
    *pdwSpaceUsed = m_nBytesSaved;
    m_pCallBack = NULL;
    return hr;
}
```

FindABKFiles calls the update functions AddFileName and AddBytes-ToTotal.

```
HRESULT CAddrBookCleanup::AddBytesToTotal( int m_byteCount )
{
    // Increment the savings information.
    m_nBytesInUse += m_byteCount;
    m_nAllocationUnitsInUse +=
```

```
        m_byteCount / m_nAllocationUnitSize;
    if ( m_byteCount % m_nAllocationUnitSize )
    {
        ++m_nAllocationUnitsInUse;
    }

    // Calculate the number of allocation
    // units we can free up.
    int nBytesUsed = m_nAllocationUnitsInUse *
        m_nAllocationUnitSize;
    int nClusterSavings = m_nAllocationUnitsInUse -
        ( m_nBytesInUse / m_nAllocationUnitSize );
    if ( m_nBytesInUse % m_nAllocationUnitSize )
    {
        —nClusterSavings;
    }
    m_nBytesSaved = m_nAllocationUnitSize *
        nClusterSavings;

    // Update the scanner.
    return m_pCallBack->ScanProgress(m_nBytesSaved, 0, NULL);
}

void CAddrBookCleanup::AddFileName(const CString& szFileName)
{
    m_fileNames.push_back( szFileName );
}

HRESULT CAddrBookCleanup::FindABKFiles( CString& szVolume )
{
    HRESULT hr = S_OK;
    // First, find all the abk files in this directory
    if ( szVolume[szVolume.GetLength() - 1] !=
        CString(_T("\\")) )
    {
        szVolume += CString(_T("\\"));
    }
    bool bDone = false;
    CFileFind fileFind;
    CString szFileFind;

    // Look for Address Book documents.
    szFileFind.Format( _T("%s*.abk"), szVolume );
    if ( fileFind.FindFile( szFileFind ) )
    {
        // At least one doc was found.
        while ( !bDone )
        {
            // Keep going until all the
            // docs in this directory are found.
            bDone = fileFind.FindNextFile() == FALSE;
```

```
        AddFileName( fileFind.GetFilePath() );
        hr = AddBytesToTotal(
            fileFind.GetLength() );
        if ( hr != S_OK )
        {
            return hr;
        }
    }
}


// Reset the flag.
bDone = false;
// Look at the rest of the files in the directory
szFileFind.Format( _T("%s*.*"), szVolume );
if ( fileFind.FindFile(szFileFind) )
{
    // Of course we found at least one file.
    // We always hit . and ..
    while ( !bDone )
    {
        bDone = fileFind.FindNextFile() == FALSE;
        // Only recurse on directories that are not
        // . or ..
        if ( fileFind.IsDirectory() &&
            !(fileFind.IsDots()) )
        {
            hr = FindABKFiles( fileFind.GetFilePath() );
            if ( FAILED( hr ) )
            {
                return hr;
            }
        }
    }
}
return hr;
}
```

By the time the cleanup handler is done with GetSpaceUsed, it has cached the files it will concatenate together. The code does not account for potential savings of moving the file onto a different volume. As indicated by the text in Figure 8-3, the handler moves the address book to UNIFIED.ABK. UNIFIED.ABK will be located in the same folder as the address book application. If the application lives on a different volume, then the savings will be greater than what the handler reports.

In CAddrBookCleanup::Initialize, we told the Disk Cleanup Utility that the handler has a user interface. This means that the handler must implement IEmptyVolumeCache::ShowProperties. The CAddrBookCleanup::ShowProperties brings up the dialog shown in Figure 8-4. CDlgCleanupMath implements this class. All the strings get formatted in the class's constructor.

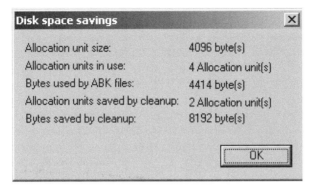

Figure 8–4 *The address book handler's space sav-ings dialog. Normally, a handler would display configuration options here.*

```
STDMETHODIMP CAddrBookCleanup::ShowProperties( HWND hwnd )
{
    AFX_MANAGE_STATE(AfxGetStaticModuleState());
    CWnd wnd;
    // Attach to the passed in window so we can start
    // using MFC.
    wnd.Attach( hwnd );
    // Display the properties dialog.
    CDlgCleanupMath dlg( m_nAllocationUnitSize,
        m_nAllocationUnitsInUse, m_nBytesInUse, &wnd );
    dlg.DoModal();
    // Detach from the window- we don't want the destructor
    // to destroy the window as the variable goes out of
    // scope.
    wnd.Detach();
    return S_FALSE;
}

CDlgCleanupMath::CDlgCleanupMath(int nAllocationUnitSize,
    int nAllocationUnitsInUse,
    int nBytesInUse, CWnd* pParent /*=NULL*/)
      : CDialog(CDlgCleanupMath::IDD, pParent)
{
    // Initialize the display string.
    m_szByteCount.Format( IDS_BYTE_INFO, nBytesInUse );
    m_szClustersInUse.Format( IDS_ALLOCATION_UNIT_INFO,
        nAllocationUnitsInUse );
    m_szClusterSize.Format( IDS_BYTE_INFO,
        nAllocationUnitSize );

    ASSERT( nAllocationUnitSize );
    // Figure out the bytes used and the
```

```
    // possible savings.
    int nBytesUsed = nAllocationUnitsInUse *
        nAllocationUnitSize;
    int nClusterSavings = nAllocationUnitsInUse -
        ( nBytesInUse / nAllocationUnitSize );
    if ( nBytesInUse % nAllocationUnitSize )
    {
        nClusterSavings--;
    }
    m_szByteSavings.Format( IDS_BYTE_INFO,
        nClusterSavings * nAllocationUnitSize );
    m_szClusterSavings.Format( IDS_ALLOCATION_UNIT_INFO,
        nClusterSavings );
}
```

The last thing the handler needs to do is consolidate the address book files. When the user selects the Address Book cleanup handler and presses OK, the disk cleanup handler calls IEmptyVolumeCache::Purge.

```
STDMETHODIMP CAddrBookCleanup::Purge(
    DWORDLONG dwSpaceToFree,
    IEmptyVolumeCacheCallBack *picb )
{
    // Where is the main application located?
    DWORD dwType = REG_SZ;
    TCHAR szData[MAX_PATH];
    DWORD dwDataSize = MAX_PATH;
    SHGetValue( HKEY_CLASSES_ROOT,
        _T("AddressBook.Document\\shell\\open\\command"),
        NULL, &dwType, szData, &dwDataSize );
    m_pCallBack = picb;
    TCHAR szDir[MAX_PATH];
    TCHAR szVolume[MAX_PATH];
    // We can ignore the %1 jive at the end of the string.
    // We only want the final directory, which _tsplitpath
    // will find quite nicely.
    _tsplitpath( szData, szVolume, szDir, NULL, NULL );
    CString newFileName;
    newFileName.Format( _T("%s%sUNIFIED.ABK"),
        szVolume, szDir );
    CFile newFile;
    std::list<Address> listAddresses;
    int nBytesFreed = 0;
    int nBytesToFree = m_nBytesSaved;

    // this number is not exact, but it is useful for the
    // purge progress.
    int nApproximateSavings = m_nBytesSaved /
        m_fileNames.size();
```

```
HRESULT hr = S_OK;
// If the unified file already exists, don't blow it
// away.  Just append to the end.  If
// we are consolidating the same volume do not
// read the unified file.  We already know about
// it and it will be handled.
if ( ( CString( szVolume ) + CString(_T("\\")) )
    != GetVolume() )
{
    ReadAddressFile( listAddresses, newFileName );
    nBytesFreed += nApproximateSavings;
    nBytesToFree -= nApproximateSavings;
    hr = m_pCallBack->PurgeProgress( nBytesFreed,
        nBytesToFree, 0, NULL );
    if ( FAILED( hr ) )
    {
        return hr;
    }
}

// We do not check the purge progress after this point.
// We're about to go too far and actually delete the
// files.  PurgeProgress will get called 2x with the only
// changed data being the fact that this is the last
// notification.
hr = m_pCallBack->PurgeProgress( nBytesFreed,
    nBytesToFree, EVCCBF_LASTNOTIFICATION, NULL );
if ( FAILED( hr ) )
{
    return hr;
}

std::list<CString>::iterator it;
for ( it = m_fileNames.begin();
    it != m_fileNames.end(); ++it )
{
    // Read the file into the list
    ReadAddressFile( listAddresses, *it );

    // Remove the file from the disk.
    // Risky, but we may be low on room.
    CFile::Remove( *it );
}

int count = listAddresses.size();
if ( count > 0 )
{
    CFile theFile( newFileName, CFile::modeCreate |
        CFile::modeWrite );
    CArchive ar( &theFile, CArchive::store );
```

```
    ar << count;
    for ( std::list<Address>::iterator it =
        listAddresses.begin();
        it != listAddresses.end(); ++it )
    {
        it->Serialize( ar );
    }
}

return hr;
}
```

The handler presented in this section does not do anything if users run it on a schedule. They may have chosen to spread their files out across the disk. The handler consolidates the files. I prefer that they do this intentionally because they do not need the surprise of seeing an address book disappear overnight. (The handler does not remove duplicates, either. This would be a handy addition.) To make the handler run unattended, you would need to add code to CAddrBookCleanup::Initialize to find all the logical hard drives on the machine. CAddrBookCleanup::GetSpaceUsed needs to be called for each volume and CAddrBookCleanup::Purge would need to be called once to consolidate all the files.

8.3 Summary

Disk cleanup handlers work to free up disk space on the user's hard drive. They might be started by an out of space error, automated maintenance, or manually by the user. A disk cleanup handler allows the user to remove unnecessary files without your having to know which files are safe to remove or where to find the files.

A handler should not take very long to write, but it will help your users and support department immensely. It can serve a secondary purpose by cleaning up files that your application leaves behind when it does not stop normally (user reboots the machine, application crashes, etc.). Also, it does not have to search the entire hard drive. If your application leaves all of its files in a small set of directories, your handler can both scan for files and clean up in less time than a handler that searches the hard drive.

Do not always look at deleting files when searching for ways to save disk space. You can produce big savings by freeing up allocation units. On a 2GB drive using FAT16, an allocation unit will take up 64KB. When I upgraded a machine from Windows 95 to NT4.0, I realized a substantial gain in disk space by using NTFS with 512 byte allocation units. (The biggest problem with small allocation units is that you increase the likelihood of file fragmentation. I'll bet you have plenty of files bigger than 512 bytes. My machine has 24,669 files bigger than 1KB and only 5,358 files bigger than 64KB. Almost 20,000 more files have the opportunity for fragmentation on my NTFS volume than if they were on a FAT16 volume.) Bigger files present an opportunity to utilize disk space better because they can use fewer allocation units for the same amount of information. Keep in mind that as the files grow, it will take more time to access data in them.

Namespace Extensions

From my reading of the newsgroups,[1] *it seems like everyone realizes that namespace extensions are really cool. However, I get the distinct impression that first-timers do not grasp what a namespace is until after going through some rather miserable failures.Let's begin this chapter by answering the question, "What is a namespace?"*

First off, do not confuse a C++ namespace with a shell namespace; they are two different concepts that share the same name. The Windows shell, implemented through EXPLORER.EXE and its related DLLs, uses namespaces to present almost everything the computer can do to the end user. *Everything* includes, but is not limited to, the following items:

- Local disk drives
- Networked computers
- Networked, shared drives
- The Control Panel
- The Internet
- The Recycle Bin
- The Desktop

---

1. If you have not done so already, point your newsreader (which is probably Outlook Express) to *msnews.microsoft.com*. You want to subscribe to the *microsoft.public.platformsdk.ui_shell* newsgroup. The shell development team monitors that newsgroup and can answer any questions you may have.

Handling all this information becomes complicated when you consider the differences between local storage, remote storage, various protocols, and all the other information Explorer presents. Instead of constructing a monolithic application that knows about everything, Microsoft created an extendable, hierarchical system. The Desktop functions as the base of the hierarchy, the system namespace. We can extend the system namespace by writing COM objects that implement a given set of interfaces (IShellFolder and IShellView, to name a few). These extensions to the system namespace add new names such as My Computer, Network Neighborhood, and Recycle Bin. These particular namespace extensions are considered non-rooted because you can navigate to them within the same Explorer window as the Desktop. You can add rooted namespace extensions as well.

A rooted namespace extension adds information to the system but does not include the Desktop in its hierarchy. Microsoft ships one well-known rooted namespace extension: CabView. CabView allows the user to view the files contained in a CAB file using a separate instance of Explorer. A little later on, we will get into the particulars of rooted and non-rooted namespaces.

By now you should be getting the idea of a namespace extension. Let's continue and make sure that you really understand it. Explorer navigates through the set of "spaces" on the computer, using unique names. Each name is represented by a GUID. That GUID maps to a namespace extension that specifies how to navigate through the space it controls. The data contained by that space could be anything and it is up to the extension to present that information to Explorer.

When you write your own namespace extension, you can choose to have it appear in a number of different ways:

- As a folder beneath the Desktop
- Under My Computer
- As a special view of a folder
- As a special view of a file
- Within the Control Panel
- Under a networked computer

Most of the existing namespace extensions focus on files, but a namespace extension can display any information that you see fit. Here are just a few namespace extensions I would like to see:

- **Digital camera**: This extension would allow a user to attach their digital camera to their machine and view any of the pictures on the camera. The extension should also allow the user to drag-and-drop the pictures from the camera to other places in Windows—Explorer, Paint, Word, etc.

- **Scanner**: Copies the image on the scanner to a directory. This extension may also contain the images scanned from this source over the past several days stored in folders based on date of scan, image subject matter, or whatever makes sense.
- **Archive viewer**: The actual implementation might be a database that keeps track of where a file really exists. You could then navigate through the archive and select the file you want. Once the file has been selected, the namespace might do something like prompt you to *Insert CD #45*.
- **Source control**: Not only could you navigate to files in source control, but you could also navigate into the files and view the file's revision history.
- **Device view**: (This one would probably go under Control Panel.) Imagine being able to view and configure all the routers and hubs on your network right from Explorer. This would also come in handy for devices hanging on the network. More and more manufacturers network their devices using TCP/IP so that customers can simply attach the equipment to the network. Imagine being able to navigate to the heart monitor in room 206 and see that the equipment is running normally, the patient's heart rate is normal, etc.
- **Television tuner**: These days, it does not cost much to hook up cable TV to your computer. If I had this, I would like to be able to find TV shows from Explorer. The navigation might work like this: Open up Explorer and navigate to my local Fox affiliate folder. The folder contains the following subfolders:

    1. Name of the show. Clicking on this folder brings up the broadcast in Explorer's right-hand pane.

    2. Program summary: Displays a synopsis of the show and its start/stop times.

    3. Later programming: Displays the shows and a little synopsis for each show over the next 4 to 24 hours.

    The extension would also allow me to search for a given show.

You cannot pick a more difficult shell customization than a namespace extension. You have many different COM interfaces to work with, a huge array of features you may or may not implement, and then you have to test all of it. Because of this difficulty, I split the topic across three chapters. This chapter, Chapter 9, goes over namespace extension basics. Chapter 10, "Tools to Build a Namespace Extension," explains the wizard and library classes I wrote to make the whole job a little bit easier. Finally, Chapter 11, "Namespace Extension Example: The Registry," goes over a namespace extension I built that explains the how and why of the extension's design as well as its implementation.

9.1   When to Build a Namespace Extension

Whenever you have hierarchical data, you can build a namespace extension to display that information. Sometimes, it may take some thinking and planning to properly display that data. If you just know that you need a namespace extension but you cannot decide how to look at the data you, should step back and figure out the point of view you want to display. Once you do this, you can hit the ground running and start designing.

The fact that you have hierarchical data does not mean you should create a namespace extension. For example, Chapter 11 provides a namespace extension that allows the user to navigate the registry as well as add, edit, and rename keys and values. I targeted this extension at developers and system administrators who have a frequent need to edit and peruse the registry. You, as a reader of this book, will have this need as soon as you start developing any shell-related COM objects. The extension also will come in handy for any other projects that use the registry in one way or another. On the other hand, I would not want to distribute this extension to users of a financials package. Make sure that the namespace extension will be useful to your users.

A namespace extension can display the contents of a folder or file using whatever view makes the most sense. Explorer displays the namespace as a hierarchy of folders in its left-hand pane. The right-hand pane displays the contents of any selected folder and can take on any appearance you desire. Users expect a list to show up somewhere within that view and probably expect that list to be the only element in there. If your namespace extension deviates from this, then the change should appear appropriate. As an example, look at the Television Tuner namespace extension suggested in the chapter's introduction. The television program is not a list view, but if I selected a program from Explorer, I would expect to see part of Explorer functioning as a television screen. Do not be afraid to experiment with a new look. If something seems like a good idea, try it. Experimentation allows good ideas to come forward and gives us an opportunity to learn.

9.2   Types of Namespace Extensions

All namespace extensions use the same COM objects. The namespaces may show up in different places and have different ways of identifying themselves to the system, but they all work the same. Namespace extensions are either rooted, non-rooted, or both. Explorer displays a non-rooted extension as a node reachable from the Desktop node, the root of the system namespace. Examples of non-rooted extensions include My Documents, My Computer, and the Control Panel. Non-rooted extensions show up without any special signals other than through registry settings or specially named folders. You can always navigate from a non-rooted extension up to the Desktop.

The other namespace extension type is a rooted extension. These require a separate instance of Explorer in order to be viewed. When viewing a rooted namespace extension, you can navigate from the root down to whatever leaf nodes may exist or up to the top of the space controlled by the extension. You cannot leave the space controlled by the namespace. You can open a non-rooted extension as a rooted extension by telling Explorer not to allow navigation outside of the namespace.

All namespace extensions must register themselves as *approved* extensions. The security model of Windows NT and Windows 2000 dictates that only Administrators can add a shell extension and Explorer enforces this by making sure that all shell extensions have their GUID registered under the approved key. Therefore, you tell Windows that it can load the extension by adding this bit of RGS script to your IShellFolder's RGS file:

```
HKLM
{
  Software
  {
    Microsoft
    {
      Windows
        {
          CurrentVersion
          {
            NoRemove 'Shell Extensions'
            {
              NoRemove 'Approved'
              {
                val
                  '{90ce2a9e-5335-4488-853c-df626168e96f}'=
                    s 'The Registry'
              }
            }
...[and so on, until the curly braces are all matched]
}²
```

Before moving into the differences between rooted and non-rooted namespace extensions, we need to define one more concept: *junction points.* Every extension to the system namespace defines a place that it shows up inside of Explorer. We call those locations junction points. If a namespace extension shows up on the Desktop, its junction point is specified in the registry and manifests itself as an icon on the Desktop. Other junction points

---

2. This part of the script can only be executed for members of the Administrators group.

may be directories or files. A junction point defines a spot within the system namespace where one extension loses control and another extension gains it.

9.2.1   Non-rooted Namespace Extensions

Once you have decided to try to write a namespace extension, you need to take a look and see if it belongs in any of the non-rooted "easy" locations. The non-rooted items must register themselves under

```
HKLM\SOFTWARE\Microsoft\Windows\CurrentVersion\Explorer\
    <someval>\Namespace\<CLSID of your IShellFolder>
```

where *<someval>* is equal to:

- **ControlPanel:** Makes the extension visible as a folder under Control Panel (Windows 2000 only).
- **Desktop:** Makes the extension visible as a folder on the Desktop.
- **MyComputer:** Makes the extension visible as a folder under My Computer (or whatever you rename My Computer).
- **NetworkNeighborhood:** Makes the extension visible as a folder under My Network Places (or whatever you rename My Network Places).
- **RemoteComputer:** Used to make the namespace extension appear when browsing computers other than your own. You actually use the string *RemoteComputer*. If you have 2 or 2000 machines on your network, this one entry will cause the namespace to appear under all the computers.

An extension designed to run under RemoteComputer has to implement one interface that no other extension needs to implement: IRemoteComputer. This interface has one method:

```
HRESULT Initialize(
    const WCHAR* pszMachine,
    BOOL bEnumerating
)
```

> **Parameters:**
>
> **pszMachine:** The UNC (Universal Naming Code) name for the machine. If connecting to a machine named Development, this argument will have the value `\\Development`.
>
> **bEnumerating:** Set to TRUE if Explorer is enumerating the extension, FALSE if Explorer is initializing the extension.
>
> **Return Values:**
> - **S_OK:** Successful.
> - **Other OLE-Defined value:** Something went wrong.

Remarks: Initialize gets called once for each and every folder with the machine name. Add this interface to your class that implements IShell-Folder.

You use the IRemoteComputer interface whenever you want the extension to run on the local machine but to provide a view of data located on another machine on the network. In other words, the computer you are looking at does not need to have the extension installed. The namespace only needs to be installed on the box doing the looking.

If your idea for a namespace extension does not fit into the above list, you have another option before making a rooted extension—specially named folders. Using only the CLSID and a read-only directory, you can make your namespace extension appear as a folder on the user's disk drive. The directory must be named [Display Name].[{CLSID}]. When you name your extension in this manner, you lose the ability to control the display name. When registered to appear under My Computer, Desktop, or one of the other options, Explorer will use the name attached to the CLSID of your IShell-Folder to display to the user. Using the special directory name option, the user can rename your extension on a whim. At this point, you only retain control of the icon used to display your extension.

Maybe, just maybe, you still do not have enough options for making a namespace extension show up. Here is your final option. Create a read-only directory wherever you like and name it whatever you like. Within that directory, place a file called DESKTOP.INI. The file needs to have the following lines in order to show an extension:

```
[.ShellClassInfo]
CLSID={CLSID of namespace extension}
```

Once you save the file, you will not be able to use Explorer to open the file. Instead, you will most likely find yourself opening up a command prompt and typing in

```
NOTEPAD.EXE [Path to file]\DESKTOP.INI
```

9.2.2   Rooted Namespace Extensions

You can only open a rooted namespace extension by opening EXPLORER.EXE using the /root switch on the command line. In order to open a rooted extension in Explorer, the file might need to have a pre-defined junction point. I hope a collective "Huh?" comes out right about here. Many methods of displaying a rooted namespace require the namespace to be viewable as a non-rooted namespace. A rooted namespace view provides a view of the folders and other items within the extension and does not allow the user to navigate to folders above the current one. For example, you could open up the MyComputer[3] namespace as a rooted namespace with the following command line:

```
explorer.exe /e,/root,::{20D04FE0-3AEA-1069-A2D8-08002B30309D}
```

That command generates the view seen in Figure 9-1. From here, you can access the ControlPanel namespace, but not the Desktop namespace that we know exists immediately above My Computer.

Explorer provides three ways to open up rooted extensions. If the junction point exists under the Desktop, the following command will open a rooted view:

```
explorer.exe /e,/root,::{CLSID}
```

Figure 9-1 used this technique to open the MyComputer namespace.

The second technique applies to namespaces contained by the Desktop. This applies to items registered under the ControlPanel, MyComputer, NetworkNeighborhood, or RemoteComputer namespaces. Execute this command to open up one of those items:

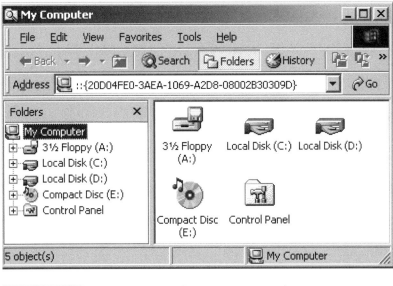

Figure 9–1   *Opening up My Computer as a rooted namespace.*

---

3. This is not a misspelling. While the display name of MyComputer defaults to "My Computer," you can rename it as "Scott's Machine," or anything else you desire.

```
explorer.exe/e,/root,::{Top Level CLSID}\::{CLSID of item}}
```

where {*Top Level CLSID*} has one of the following values:

- **MyComputer:** {20D04FE0-3AEA-1069-A2D8-08002B30309D}
- **NetworkNeighborHood:** {208D2C60-3AEA-1069-A2D7-08002B30309D}

For items registered under ControlPanel, you have a slightly more complicated task. The ControlPanel namespace extension hangs off of the MyComputer extension. To make it and the entities within it show up, you need to give the CLSID from MyComputer, ControlPanel, and your extension concatenated together as one, like this:

```
explorer.exe /e, /root,
   ::{20D04FE0-3AEA-1069-A2D8-08002B30309D}
   \::{21EC2020-3AEA-1069-A2DD-08002B30309D}
   \::{CLSID of item}
```

The first CLSID represents MyComputer, followed by ControlPanel, and ending with your CLSID. You build the path to your item similarly to the way that you would build a path to a file.

You cannot navigate straight to a namespace within the context of a remote computer. However, you can open up a remote computer as a root object with this command:

```
explorer.exe /e,/root,\\[Computer Name]
```

The above technique does let you navigate to the remote computer and you will be able to access any namespace extensions registered under the RemoteComputer key. On a side note, you can open up any folder using the fully qualified path as long as the command reads:

```
explorer.exe /e,/root,[full path]
```

This works on local paths, mapped drives, and UNC names.

Believe it or not, one option does exist that provides nothing but rooted namespace extensions. You can actually set up things so that a given file type (such as ZIP or CAB) is always opened using your extension. This is the only technique I was able to find that allows truly rooted extensions. All of the other techniques require a complementary non-rooted extension before allowing Explorer to display the rooted view of that extension. For the file type in question, you set the following value to point to your CLSID:

```
HKCR\[file extension]\(default) = CLSID\\[{Your CLSID}]
```

That double slash after CLSID refers to a real double slash, not the character literal you know and love from C/C++. Once you do this, you need to add a registry entry telling Windows how to open files with that extension. That entry looks like this:

```
HKCR\CLSID\[{Your CLSID}]\shell\open\command\(default) =
    "Explorer /root,[{Your CLSID}],%1"
```

The CabView utility that ships with PowerTools hooks all of its machinery up to the HKCR\.cab registry entry to allow users to browse CAB files. Explorer uses the default icon of the namespace extension when you make a file "browse-able." If you want to browse the file using a namespace extension but still have access to the shell extensions found in Chapter 7, you need to register all the extensions under the HKCR\CLSID\[{Your CLSID}] instead of the HKCR\[Something.Document] key. Alternatively, you can alter the key

```
HKCR\[Something.Document]\shell\open\command\(default) =
    "Explorer /root,[{Your CLSID}],%1"
```

As you can see, once you decide to write a namespace extension, you have a number of ways of making that extension available to the user. We had to cover how a namespace extension gets discovered and where it fits in to Explorer so that the following items have a chance of making sense.

9.3   What Is in a PIDL?

When writing a namespace extension, you wind up drowning in PIDLs. A PIDL (pronounced piddle) gets its nickname from a commonly used argument name seen in the MSDN documentation and in the literature. The shell lives and dies with properly formed ITEMIDLISTs[4] and these lists are passed as pointers between the various shell interfaces and functions. Pointer to ITEMIDLIST got shortened to *pidl,* and that is how things have been ever since. (I will interchange the names PIDL and ITEMIDLIST throughout the text. They mean the same thing.) Namespaces use ITEMIDLISTs to uniquely identify their contents. When Windows first opens a namespace, it assigns a PIDL to the namespace junction point. This PIDL means little to the namespace, but means everything to the operating system. Earlier, we called this root folder the junction point of the namespace. Once Explorer crosses over to our side of the junction point, we take over the responsibility for creating and maintaining meaningful PIDLs.

Windows only asks that the PIDLs within a given folder are unique. The namespace extension must know how to differentiate between different folders at the same level and how to chain PIDLs together. A namespace extension must place the chain into a contiguous block of memory. Why? All users

---

4. ITEMIDLIST owns a SHITEMID. These two structures are covered in Appendix B.

of the extension expect this setup. It also makes it easy to copy a PIDL from one COM apartment or process to another. The chain terminates on the first ITEMIDLIST entry whose mkid.cb member is zero, indicating that the particular item takes up zero bytes and contains no information.

What does the ITEMIDLIST structure look like? This structure contains one SHITEMID[5] structure. SHITEMID looks like this:

```
typedef struct _SHITEMID {
    USHORT cb;
    BYTE   abID[1];
} SHITEMID;
```

The cb member indicates the size of the array that starts at abID. As the developer of a namespace extension, you get to decide what the bytes starting at abID look like. How do you use SHITEMID? For an example, let's look at what structure we might define to present the files on the hard drive. A very simple structure would need to know if it represented a drive, directory, file, or link, and the name of the item. The code could look like this:

```
enum DiskEntityType { DRIVE, DIRECTORY, FILE, LINK };

struct DiskEntity {
    DiskEntityType m_type;
    char m_entityName[MAX_PATH];
};
```

Whenever we need to build an ITEMIDLIST for a single entity on the disk, we call SHGetMalloc()[6] to get a pointer to the shell's IMalloc interface. Using this pointer, you allocate and free memory used by your ITEMIDLIST. If you do not hand this memory allocated with the IMalloc pointer to another entity, you are responsible for freeing the memory using IMalloc::Free(). For our DiskEntity structure, we would write:

```
IMalloc * pMalloc = NULL;
LPITEMIDLIST pidl = NULL;

// Allocate one ITEMIDLIST for the start, one
// for the "null" ITEMIDLIST, and one DiskEntity
long newPidlSize = ( 2 * sizeof( ITEMIDLIST ) ) +
    sizeof( DiskEntity );
if ( SUCCEEDED( SHGetMalloc( &pMalloc ) ) )
{
    pidl = reinterpret_cast<LPITEMIDLIST>
```

---

5. This name refers to **SH**ell **ITEM ID**. It is up to you to decide if the name has any derogatory connotations. If nothing else, it does follow the established naming convention for shell functions and structures.

6. Covered in Appendix B.

```
        (pMalloc->Alloc( newPidlSize ));
    // Sets the final ITEMIDLIST.mkid.cb to zero
    ZeroMemory( &pidl, newPidlSize );
    DiskEnity* pEntity = reinterpret_cast<DiskEntity*>
        (&(pidl->mkid.abID[0]));
    // Fill in the entity with your data.
    ...
}
```

At times, we need to provide the full path to an item within our name-space. With our example PIDL, we may need to represent C:\Directory\File.Ext using a string of PIDLs. Using our mechanisms, we would need four ITEMIDLIST structures allocated in contiguous memory. The full chain would be

```
ITEMIDLIST 1
    ITEMIDLIST.mkid.cb = sizeof( ITEMIDLIST ) +
        sizeof( DISKENTITY )
    DiskEntity.m_type = DRIVE
    DiskEntity.m_entityName = "C"

ITEMIDLIST 2
    ITEMIDLIST.mkid.cb = sizeof( ITEMIDLIST ) +
        sizeof( DISKENTITY )
    DiskEntity.m_type = DIRECTORY
    DiskEntity.m_entityName = "Directory"

ITEMIDLIST 3
    ITEMIDLIST.mkid.cb = sizeof( ITEMIDLIST ) +
        sizeof( DISKENTITY )
    DiskEntity.m_type = FILE
    DiskEntity.m_entityName = "File.Ext"

ITEMIDLIST 4
    ITEMIDLIST.mkid.cb = 0
    ITEMIDLIST.abID[0] = 0
```

In each instance except ITEMIDLIST 4, ITEMIDLIST.abID[0] is the first byte of a DiskEntity structure. In Chapter 10, we will develop a class that makes con-catenating and reading the array of PIDLs fairly easy.[7] Your IShellFolder im-plementation will use whatever structure you come up with to generate a meaningful IEnumIDList or turn one of your PIDLs into a string that means something to the user for display in Explorer's title and address bars.

---

7. If you cannot wait to check it out, look for CPidlMgr on the CD or among the files the CD installed on your system.

9.4 Folders and Other Items

Explorer makes very few demands on a namespace extension. Once an extension has registered itself properly, Explorer gets all of information on the folders and their contents via its IShellFolder implementation, which acts as the point of entry for any namespace extension. Explorer expects these folders to be able to do the following:

1. Tell if the folder contains any subfolders *(handled by IShellFolder)*
2. Interpret the display name of any item within the folder *(handled by IShellFolder)*
3. Determine if an item within a folder should be sorted before, after or is equal to another item in the folder *(handled by IShellFolder)*
4. Return icons appropriate for indicating if a folder is opened or closed *(handled by IExtractIcon)*
5. Return a context menu for the namespace extension on Explorer's left-hand side *(handled by IContextMenu)*
6. Display an appropriate view of the contents of a folder in the right-hand Explorer pane *(handled by IShellView)*
7. Return the contents of a folder *(handled by IEnumIDList)*[8]

IShellFolder and its cohorts IPersistFolder, IEnumIDList, and even IExtractIcon are largely independent of their display context. This provides for easy navigation of the system using programs that may or may not have a user interface. Other applications know that if they follow the assumptions of PIDLs they can always get certain information about the items in hand. This means that Microsoft can take advantage of new ideas on how to display this graphical information without hamstringing themselves by not allowing Explorer to grow, evolve, or be replaced. On the other hand, IShellView depends on Explorer, if for no other reason than that it needs an implementation of IShellBrowser so it can do its job.

So, how does this all fit together? For the purposes of our discussion, we will use a non-rooted extension registered under the Desktop named The Example whose CLSID is

```
{04adfa0b-8eab-48c9-89b6-7efbbaf26ced}
```

The interaction begins when Explorer looks under the Desktop key as described in section 9.2.1. Here, it finds our CLSID and uses that information to display the junction point on the screen as shown in Figure 9-2. How did Explorer know what icon, text, and tooltip to display? We provided that infor-

---

8. All these interface are covered in Appendix A.

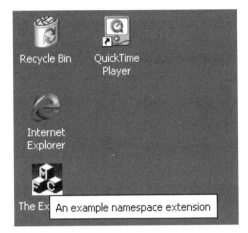

An example namespace extension

Figure 9–2	An infotip for a custom namespace extension.

mation under the HKCR\CLSID section of the registry with this script used to register the IShellFolder implementation:

```
ForceRemove {66805b2a-a5d6-4039-9808-f6bcd54aaaca} =
    s 'The Example'
{
    DefaultIcon = s '%MODULE%,0'
        InprocServer32 = s '%MODULE%'
    {
        val ThreadingModel = s 'Apartment'
    }
    'TypeLib'
        = s '{60fccb97-3e8f-48b7-923f-6bd9878b8ace}'
    ShellFolder
    val InfoTip = s 'An example namespace extension'
}
```

The first line gives the text to display beneath the icon: *The Example.* The next line identifies the icon to display as the one with the resource ID "0" in the DLL implementing the IShellFolder class. Lastly, Explorer retrieved the InfoTip by reading the text under the InfoTip REG_SZ value. Explorer gets all this display information without needing to load our COM object. So, what happens when we go to Open (look at the namespace without the left-hand tree view) or Explore (look at the namespace with the left-hand tree view) the namespace? Assuming that your folder object implements both IPersistFolder and IShell-Folder, you will see the following call-sequence upon opening your extension:

1. **IPersistFolder::Initialize():** Loads up your namespace extension and tells it what the root PIDL is.

2. **IShellFolder::EnumObjects():** Only asks for the folders contained under the root.

3. **IShellFolder::GetDisplayNameOf():** Given a PIDL returned using IEnumIDList implementation returned by IShellFolder::EnumObjects(), Explorer wants to know what text it should use to display the item within the tree view.

4. **IShellFolder::GetAttributesOf():** Given a PIDL returned using IEnumIDList implementation returned by IShellFolder::EnumObjects(), Explorer wants to know how, in general, to handle the PIDL.

5. **IShellFolder::GetUIObjectOf():** Requests the IExtractIcon interface appropriate for the PIDL.

9.5 Displaying All the Contents of the Folder

You may have decided to write a namespace extension because you want to view your data within Explorer. With IShellView, you tell your users how to make sense of some set of data. IShellFolder returns this interface in response to a call to IShellFolder::CreateViewObject(). Theoretically, IShellView should not depend on Explorer having a status bar, toolbar, or menu. In other words, all code should fail gracefully if any of these items cease to be a part of Explorer. Now, for a reality check: most of us will write our views planning on the existence of these items. This goes against Microsoft's recommendations, but it pays attention to the idea that we are better off ignoring artificial limitations and concentrating on overcoming real ones.[9]

Once Explorer asks for the IShellView object, it calls the following functions:

1. **IShellView::GetView():** Asks for the CLSID of the default view.

2. **IShellView::CreateViewWindow() or IShellView2::CreateViewWindow2() (Windows 2000 only):** Passes in information to the view object explaining how and where it should create the view. This function also hands over the controlling IShellBrowser interface. In most cases, this will be Explorer. Third party versions of Explorer do exist. If your extension works with Explorer, you do not need to worry about the other IShellBrowser implementations. If you want to add buttons to the toolbar, do so before returning from this method.

3. **IShellView::GetItemObject():** Used to return various interfaces that Explorer might be able to use. (*See Appendix A for details.*)

4. **IShellView::UIActivate():** The first time this gets called, it lets you know that your view has received the focus. At this point, Explorer expects you to add any menu items to the existing menu structure.

---

9. Any code should fail gracefully if one of these items fails to exist. But how do you test it? Does anyone out there know how to force these items to not show up?

At this point, your view should be visible, have any menus and toolbar buttons installed, and be ready for action. From here on out, you can treat your view like any other window you have ever programmed. The menu and toolbar commands you added will be sent to your window. As long as you create your window the way Explorer wants you to, you should not find any unpleasant surprises lurking. Now, how does Explorer want you to create your view? Create a plain child window and create any controls as children of that window.[10] I did not do that for my first namespace extension and I paid for it, dearly. I had problems with infinite recursion whenever my list control, which was the only window I created, went into *edit label* mode.[11] I put off implementing the rename feature until the end because I could not figure out what was wrong. I tried to tackle this problem on and off for about five weeks. Finally, I was down to implementing the last feature: *rename*. After giving it another fifteen hours of staring at call stacks, implementing my own message loop, and reading everything I could find, I decided to try placing the CListCtrl inside of a CWnd. About thirty minutes after making that decision, I had *rename* working like a charm. Many people have postulated that the difficulty of a problem is inversely proportional to the simplicity of the solution. If this solution were any easier, I would have had to see my doctor for prescription strength Ibuprofen [12]

Through the IShellBrowser interface, you have access to Explorer's toolbar, menu, and status bar. The browser passed in a pointer to the interface when it called your implementation of IShellView::CreateViewWindow() or IShellView2::CreateViewWindow2(). To add menu items, create and initialize an empty HMENU. Pass that HMENU along with a pointer to an OLEMENU-GROUPWIDTHS structure to IShellBrowser::InsertMenusSB(). On return, Explorer will have already reserved space for its menu items. From this point, you can add menu items. Explorer exposes six top-level menus:

1. File
2. Edit
3. View
4. Favorites
5. Tools
6. Help

You can insert extra menus into the structure at will. The MSDN documentation warns you away from adding items to the File, View, and Tools menus.

---

10. This text was intended to be displayed in 36-point bold because of all the pain it caused me. I hope the editors left the formatting alone.

11. In other words, MFC did not know where to send the LVN_BEGINLABELEDIT message, so it kept passing the buck until it ran out of space and blew the call stack.

12. In case you do not get the reference, Ibuprofen is a strong pain reliever. Advil is one of the most popular brands.

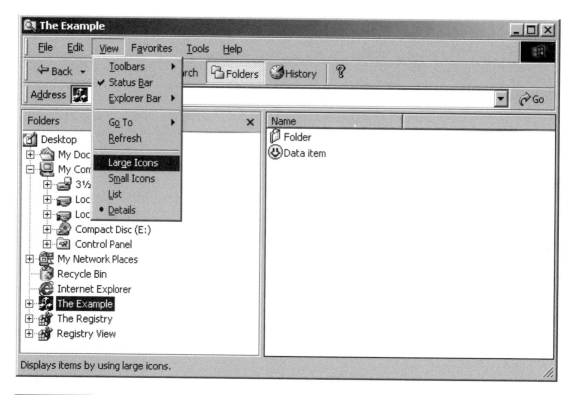

Figure 9-3
This namespace extension has added the bottom four items to the view menu, added the question mark icon in the toolbar, and set the text in the status bar.

The only menu that you should stay away from is the Favorites menu. Explorer ignores any items added to that menu by the namespace extension. When your view gets deactivated, make sure to call IShellBrowser::Remove-MenusSB() with the same HMENU you used to insert your own items.

In order to add items to the toolbar or display text on the status bar, you need to go through IShellBrowser::SendControlMsg(). IShellBrowser does allow you to get the hWnd of these items through IShellBrowser::GetControl-Window(), but Microsoft recommends avoiding this. Besides, using SendControlMsg() is about as difficult as getting the control's HWND and then calling SendMessage() using the HWND. You can see these items in action by looking at Figure 9-3. The example extension added the four items at the bottom of the view menu. It also put the text on the status bar and added the question mark icon, 🦻 (this triggers the display of an About box), on the toolbar.

If you like to use MFC for user interface code as much as I do, you are going to like the tools presented in Chapter 10. In particular, I have a class named CommandHandler that enables you to develop your shell view using MFC. Not only that, but you can design your menus and toolbar using the resource editor. CommandHandler makes short work of merging your menu and toolbar with Explorer's. This class adds a number of features that, in the end, allow you to use ClassWizard to implement any menu command message handlers. For more details, see Section 10.3.

9.6 Testing and Debugging Namespace Extensions

To test a namespace extension, all you need to do is tell DevStudio to use EXPLORER.EXE as the executable for the debug session. A typical Windows installation is set up to launch only one instance of EXPLORER.EXE. That means that the Desktop, taskbar, and Windows Explorer all run in the same address space. That makes things run real fast, but also makes them difficult to debug. If everything runs in the same address space, DevStudio cannot attach to the process unless you kill the Desktop and start it from your debugging session. In order to stop debugging you need to kill the Desktop again, this time using the terminate process command from DevStudio. The fun does not end here. Amazingly, the Desktop will start again so you get to do the kill and restart process all over again.

To kill EXPLORER.EXE, follow these steps:

1. Click the Start button

2. Select Shut Down.

3. Press [CTRL] + [SHIFT] + [ALT] + [Esc] or Press [CTRL] + [SHIFT] + [ALT] and press the Cancel button. The taskbar should disappear at this point.

In the tools directory on the CD, I included an application named ExplorerStarter.EXE. This application Desktop toolbar will stay on your Desktop and allow you to restart EXPLORER.EXE, even when everything else has crashed. If you do not want to run this program, you can press [CTRL] + [SHIFT] + [ESC] to bring up the Task Manager. On the Task Manager menu, select File→New Task (Run) and type in EXPLORER.EXE.

If you do not want to go through this hassle, you have an alternative. Find or create this value (Windows does not create this value—developers do):

```
HKCU\Software\Microsoft\Windows\CurrentVersion\Explorer\
    DesktopProcess
```

DesktopProcess must be a REG_DWORD. Set this to 1 and then shut down the Desktop. When it starts up again, Explorer will run in its own process.

When you perform builds, you will occasionally see problems performing the final link on your DLL. Many times, the DLL will still be sitting in memory. When this happens, you will still need to kill the Desktop, finish your build, and then restart the Desktop. To encourage Explorer to unload the DLL faster, add this key (not value) and set the string to 1:

```
HKLM\Software\Microsoft\Windows\CurrentVersion\Explorer\
    AlwaysUnloadDll
```

Like the previous value, you need to add this the first time you need it because Windows does not create this key by default—only developers do. It may still take a few extra seconds to unload, but this beats waiting minutes for it to happen.

When do you want to run all this in one process? I have had to do it when debugging problems in Opening or Exploring a folder inside of a namespace. Here, you want to see all activity happening in one EXPLORER.EXE process. DevStudio does not attach itself to secondary spawned processes.

Finally, under Windows 2000 you may find that EXPLORER.EXE will continually execute INT 3 (debug break, nothing serious) while loading itself or see SHLWAPI.DLL execute some sort of access violation while EXPLORER.EXE closes. I asked a contact on the shell development team and found out that these are known bugs and are not scheduled to be fixed before Windows 2000 is released. The INT 3 instructions happen whenever you Explorer loads true color icons. If you have NuMega BoundsChecker installed, make sure you have the buttons pressed as shown in Figure 9-4 before beginning your debug session. This magically makes the nasty INT 3 instructions disappear. As for the SHLWAPI.DLL access violation, place a breakpoint just inside the code that unloads your DLL. When DevStudio hits that breakpoint, you should press [Shift] + [F5], Stop Debugging. If you do not do this, DevStudio appears to get unstable and crash after a while. You

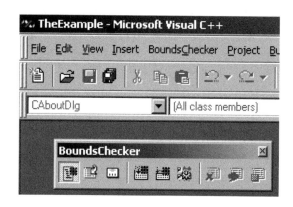

Figure 9–4

If INT 3 begins to annoy you and you own BoundsChecker, make sure you have it set up like this to stop the INT 3 errors from popping up.

should periodically run your namespace extension outside of the debugger just to make sure that when you close Explorer, it does not crash.

9.7 Summary

A namespace extension allows you to add a view of whatever you think is appropriate to Explorer. These namespaces may be a node attached somewhere along the tree rooted at the Desktop or they may be a root in and of themselves. The extension has two major components represented by IShellFolder and IShellView. IShellFolder provides the ability to traverse the extension programmatically. IShellView allows you to display the contents of a folder any way you see fit. The view will usually use a list view to display data but nothing prevents you from using something else—just make sure your option makes things easier, not harder, to understand.

With a namespace extension, you can allow a person or program to view the contents of a file, like in the CabView extension or anything else you can dream up, in any way you see fit. The next two chapters go into detail about one way to implement a namespace extension. Chapter 10 covers a library and wizard that I designed to make construction significantly easier. In Chapter 11, we will go over the design and implementation of a namespace extension that allows you to browse and edit the registry. By now, you should have enough information to construct an extension through trial and error, like I did. Since you bought the book, you might as well keep reading and see what happens. You will not be disappointed.

Tools to Build
a Namespace Extension

*In the process of building a namespace extension, you can ex-
pend a lot of energy on some very small issues. For example, it can
take quite a bit of effort just to insert a popup menu item into Explorer's File menu. There has to be a better way!*

When developing the namespace extension specific classes for the
ShellExtension, library I spent a lot of time thinking about how to make your
job easier. What would it take to accomplish this goal?

- Pre-defined "do nothing" classes that implement the required COM
  interfaces. These classes should either define a common implementation of the method or output a TRACE string and return
  E_NOTIMPL.
- Allow you to design your menu, menu handlers, and toolbars as
  you would for any vanilla MFC application.
- Stick with well-known MFC, ATL, and standard C++ whenever
  possible.
- Create an AppWizard to get most of the "grunt work" done for you.

This work resulted in an enhanced ShellExtension library (introduced in
Chapter 7, "Shell Extensions") and in the creation of the Namespace Extension Wizard. In order for you to use these tools as efficiently as possible, this
chapter will cover the various classes and the wizard by walking you through
a basic project. We will look at the fairly dry *The Example* I showed in Chapter 9, "Namespace Extensions," Figures 9-2 and 9-3.

10.1   The Namespace Extension Wizard Creates a Project

We begin our tool tour by creating a project using the Namespace Extension Wizard. Open up DevStudio and create a new project called *TheExample,* as shown in Figure 10-1. You can place spaces in the name of your project, but you will be responsible for correcting any problems that occur with the MIDL compiler. It does not appear to understand filenames that contain spaces. Once you have the information typed in correctly and the Namespace Extension (ATL/MFC) project type selected you should press OK.

Next, you need to give the project some basic information:

- The text to use at the extension's junction point
- The InfoTip text you want displayed when the mouse hovers over the extension
- Which namespace you want the extension registered under. If you select RemoteComputer, the wizard knows the extra steps needed to

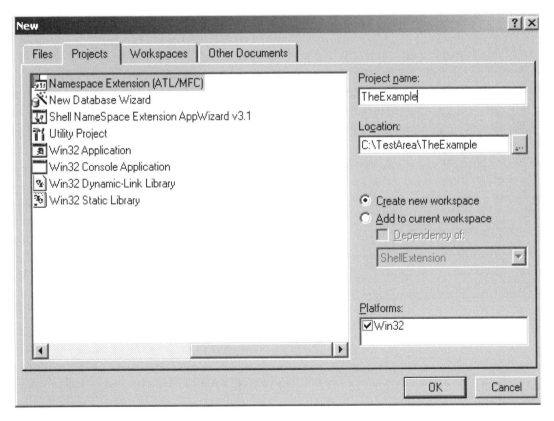

Figure 10–1   *Step 1 for TheExample project.*

make your namespace extension visible under other machines. If none of the options work for you, you will need to edit the IShellFolder class's RGS file. The necessary steps will be covered in Section 10-2.

For this example, fill in the information as shown in Figure 10-2 and press Finish.[1] The next thing you should see is the confirmation dialog in Figure 10-3. From here, press OK and let the wizard build the project.

Once the project has been constructed, build it and force a refresh of your Desktop when the build completes by clicking on the Desktop and pressing [F5]. Your Desktop should now have an icon named *The Example* on

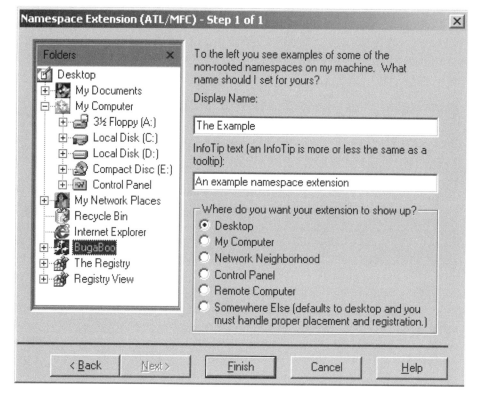

Figure 10–2   *The Namespace Extension wizard. Step 1 of 1 for TheExample project.*

---

1. In case you are wondering why the icons in the figure look a little odd, I run the Desktop Themes package available from www.freethemes.org. From there, you can get many different desktop themes besides the ones that ship with the Plus! packs from Microsoft and from other software that allows you to change your desktop's theme.

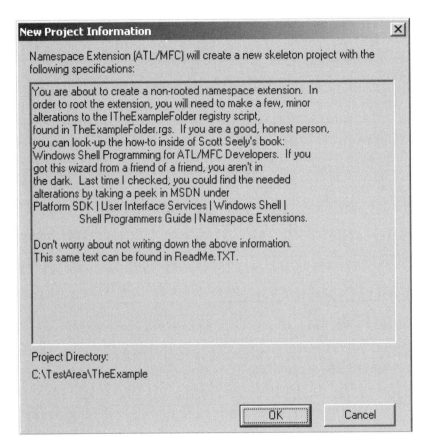

New Project Information

Namespace Extension (ATL/MFC) will create a new skeleton project with the following specifications:

You are about to create a non-rooted namespace extension. In order to root the extension, you will need to make a few, minor alterations to the ITheExampleFolder registry script, found in TheExampleFolder.rgs. If you are a good, honest person, you can look-up the how-to inside of Scott Seely's book: Windows Shell Programming for ATL/MFC Developers. If you got this wizard from a friend of a friend, you aren't in the dark. Last time I checked, you could find the needed alterations by taking a peek in MSDN under
Platform SDK | User Interface Services | Windows Shell |
        Shell Programmers Guide | Namespace Extensions.

Don't worry about not writing down the above information. This same text can be found in ReadMe.TXT.

Project Directory:

C:\TestArea\TheExample

OK   Cancel

Figure 10–3 *The Namespace Extension wizard, project confirmation dialog for TheExample project.*

it, just like in Figure 9-2 in the previous chapter. This display was made possible via the following registry script:

```
HKCR
{
    NoRemove CLSID
    {
        ForceRemove {66805b2a-a5d6-4039-9808-f6bcd54aaaca} =
            s 'The Example'
        {
            DefaultIcon = s '%MODULE%,0'
                InprocServer32 = s '%MODULE%'
            {
                val ThreadingModel = s 'Apartment'
            }
            'TypeLib'
```

```
    = s '{60fccb97-3e8f-48b7-923f-6bd9878b8ace}'
ShellFolder
val InfoTip = s 'An example namespace extension'
      }
    }
  }
}
```

The remainder of the script (found in TheExampleFolder.RGS for those of you playing along at home) registers this as an approved namespace extension that shows up within the Desktop namespace. A few extra lines had to be added to the DllRegisterServer() and DllUnregisterServer() functions so that the namespace extension would be registered as a folder with subfolders. Explorer needs this information to know how to display the root level node of your namespace. You will see the use of a static_cast<LPCTSTR> on the _bstr_t variable, theVal. Do not be alarmed. static_cast<LPCTSTR> will force a call to the _bstr_t conversion operator for const wchar_t* or const char*, depending on whether or not UNICODE is #defined.

```
STDAPI DllRegisterServer(void)
{
    // registers object, typelib and all interfaces
    // in typelib
    HRESULT hr = _Module.RegisterServer(TRUE);
    if ( SUCCEEDED( hr ) )
    {
        // Then we need to add our own binary data
        CString szVal;
        LPOLESTR lpolestr;
        if ( S_OK == StringFromCLSID(
            CLSID_TheExampleFolder, &lpolestr ) )
        {
            _bstr_t theVal = lpolestr;
            szVal.Format( _T("CLSID\\%s\\ShellFolder"),
                static_cast<LPCTSTR>(theVal) );
            DWORD dwData =
                SFGAO_FOLDER | SFGAO_HASSUBFOLDER;
            SHSetValue( HKEY_CLASSES_ROOT, szVal,
                _T("Attributes"), REG_BINARY, &dwData,
                sizeof( dwData ) );
            CoTaskMemFree( lpolestr );
        }
    }
    return hr;
}

STDAPI DllUnregisterServer(void)
{
    //TRUE indicates that typelib is unreg'd
    _Module.UnregisterServer(TRUE);
```

```
// Then we need to add our own binary data
CString szVal;
LPOLESTR lpolestr;
if ( S_OK == StringFromCLSID( CLSID_TheExampleFolder,
    &lpolestr ) )
{
    _bstr_t theVal = lpolestr;
    szVal.Format( _T("CLSID\\%s\\ShellFolder"),
        static_cast<LPCTSTR>(theVal) );
    SHDeleteValue( HKEY_CLASSES_ROOT, szVal,
            _T("Attributes") );
    CoTaskMemFree( lpolestr );
}
return S_OK;
}
```

If you want to implement an extension that opened up a rooted Explorer for a given file type extension, you will want to make some modifications to the RGS script. First, delete these lines from the registry script:

```
NoRemove Explorer
{
    NoRemove Desktop
    {
        NoRemove NameSpace
        {
            '{[Your CLSID]}' =
                s 'The Example'
        }
    }
}
```

To install the extension to activate under your selected file type, you will need to add a couple of additional lines. We will look at two options to make these modifications for the Address Book file type .ABK, introduced in Chapter 6, "File Viewers." The first example involves telling the .ABK extension under CLSID to look at the CLSID key to find out how to handle the file type. This method removes any capabilities added by the shell extensions developed in Chapter 7.

```
HKCR
{
    '.abk' = s 'CLSID\\{66805b2a-a5d6-4039-9808-f6bcd54aaaca}'
    NoRemove CLSID
    {
        'shell'
        {
            'open'
            {
                'command' =
```

```
  s 'Explorer /root,{66805b2a-a5d6-4039-9808-f6bcd54aaaca},%%1'
              }
          }
          ForceRemove {66805b2a-a5d6-4039-9808-f6bcd54aaaca} =
              s 'The Example'
... No changes from this point to the closing brace
}
```

Alternatively, you can incorporate this extension without obliterating the other items related to .ABK, such as the IContextMenu extension.

```
HKCR
{
    'AddressBook.Document'
    {
        'shell'
        {
            'open'
            {
                'command' =
  s 'Explorer /root,{66805b2a-a5d6-4039-9808-f6bcd54aaaca},%%1'
            }
        }
    }
... No changes from this point to the closing brace
}
```

This method removes the ability to open up an AddressBook document using the original editor, but it adds the ability to open, view, and edit that document using Explorer and your namespace extension. Now that we know how the extension tells Windows how to find and use it, let us take a look at the code developed for the IShellFolder implementation.

10.2   The Implementation of IShellFolder (and Its Cohorts)

IShellFolder serves as the main entry point for a namespace extension. The faster you can get this object implemented and working, the sooner you get to work on the interesting parts of the namespace extension. Remember, IShellFolder does all the behind the scenes work and does not worry about user interface issues. The folder class needs to implement IShellFolder and IPersistFolder. IPersistFolder allows Explorer to initialize the folder through IPersistFolder::Initialize() and to retrieve the CLSID through IPersist-Folder::GetClassID().[2] To handle the demands of IPersistFolder, I added the

---

2. Yes, this GetClassID() requirement really shows up because IPersistFolder inherits from IPersist, but you probably knew that already, right?

class CPersistFolderImpl to the ShellExtension library. This class, like most in the library, assumes that the developer chose to use ATL for the COM development.

```
template <class T>
class CPersistFolderImpl : public IPersistFolder
{
public:
    CPersistFolderImpl(){}
    virtual ~CPersistFolderImpl(){}
    STDMETHOD(Initialize)(LPCITEMIDLIST pidl)
    {
        ATLTRACE( _T("CPersistFolderImpl::Initialize")
            _T(" not implemented\n") );
        return E_NOTIMPL;
    }
    STDMETHOD(GetClassID)(CLSID* pClassID)
    {
        // If the pointer is NULL, fail.
        if (pClassID == NULL)
        {
            return E_FAIL;
        }

        // Use the implementation's GetObjectCLSID method.
        // This assumes usage of CComCoClass
        *pClassID = T::GetObjectCLSID();
        return S_OK;
    }
};
```

You might want to take a moment now and quickly peruse the documentation on IShellFolder found in Appendix A. This will help make sense of the header for CTheExampleFolder. The class implements the IShellFolder and IPersistFolder interfaces. It will respond positively to QueryInterface requests for the following interfaces:

- IShellFolder
- IPersistFolder
- IPersist
- IUnknown (but you knew that one, right?)

The class also implements a number of the methods in these interfaces.

```
class ATL_NO_VTABLE CTheExampleFolder :
    public CComObjectRootEx<CComSingleThreadModel>,
    public CComCoClass<CTheExampleFolder,
        &CLSID_TheExampleFolder>,
    public CShellFolderImpl,
    public CPersistFolderImpl<CTheExampleFolder>,
```

```
    public ITheExampleFolder
{
public:
    CTheExampleFolder();

    // CShellFolderImpl overrides
    STDMETHOD(CreateViewObject)( HWND hwndOwner,
        REFIID riid, void **ppv);
    STDMETHOD(EnumObjects)( HWND hwnd, DWORD grfFlags,
        IEnumIDList **ppenumIDList);
    STDMETHOD(GetDisplayNameOf)( LPCITEMIDLIST pidl,
        DWORD uFlags, LPSTRRET lpName);
    STDMETHOD(GetAttributesOf)( UINT cidl,
        LPCITEMIDLIST * apidl, ULONG * rgfInOut);
    STDMETHOD(CompareIDs)( LPARAM lParam,
        LPCITEMIDLIST pidl1, LPCITEMIDLIST pidl2);
    STDMETHOD(GetUIObjectOf)( HWND hwndOwner, UINT cidl,
        LPCITEMIDLIST * apidl, REFIID riid, UINT * prgfInOut,
        void **ppv);
    STDMETHOD(BindToObject)( LPCITEMIDLIST pidl, LPBC pbc,
        REFIID riid, void **ppv);

    // CPersistFolderImpl overrides
    STDMETHOD(Initialize)(LPCITEMIDLIST pidl);

    virtual void FinalRelease();

    DECLARE_REGISTRY_RESOURCEID(IDR_THEEXAMPLEFOLDER)

    DECLARE_PROTECT_FINAL_CONSTRUCT()

BEGIN_COM_MAP(CTheExampleFolder)
    COM_INTERFACE_ENTRY(ITheExampleFolder)
    COM_INTERFACE_ENTRY_IID(IID_IShellFolder, IShellFolder)
    COM_INTERFACE_ENTRY_IID(IID_IPersistFolder,
        IPersistFolder)
    COM_INTERFACE_ENTRY_IID(IID_IPersist, IPersist)
END_COM_MAP()
};
```

CTheExampleFolder inherits from another class in the ShellExtension library, CShellFolderImpl. This class provides an implementation of all the methods in the IShellFolder interface. None of the methods do anything other than output a debug line and return E_NOTIMPL. The class does have two useful member variables: m_pidl and m_pidlMgr. m_pidl is an LPITEMIDLIST. In your code, you will use this member to store your information from when the folder gets initialized. m_pidlMgr is another wonderful little helper. As an instance of the CPidlMgr class, it handles most of the PIDL grunt work for you. It takes a lot of effort to make sure that you can navigate a PIDL effectively. Make one little mistake in PIDL concatenation or navigation and you have a time-consuming debugging btask on your hands. Many of the tutorials on writing namespace extensions use this class for PIDL management. The RegView SDK example uses this class and loads it up with functions specific to the problem at hand. I took the same class, stripped it down, and made it into a fairly generic PIDL management tool. So far, I have been happy with the results.

```
class CPidlMgr
{
public:
    // Constructor/Destructor pair
    CPidlMgr();
    ~CPidlMgr();
public:
    // Delete
    // Uses the IMalloc interface to delete the pidl.
    void           Delete(LPITEMIDLIST pidl);

    // Gets the next node in the ITEMIDLIST
    LPITEMIDLIST   GetNextItem(LPCITEMIDLIST pidl);

    // Allocates and returns a copy of an ITEMIDLIST.
    LPITEMIDLIST   Copy(LPCITEMIDLIST pidl);

    // Returns the size of an entire ITEMIDLIST (not just
    // one node).
    UINT           GetSize(LPCITEMIDLIST pidl);

    // GetLastItem
    // Returns the last node in the ITEMIDLIST— but not
    // the NULL terminator node.
    LPITEMIDLIST   GetLastItem(LPCITEMIDLIST pidl);

    // Concatenate
    // Creates a new ITEMIDLIST with pidl1 first and
    // pidl2 second.
    LPITEMIDLIST   Concatenate(LPCITEMIDLIST pidl1,
        LPCITEMIDLIST pidl2);

    // This is an automatic typecast.  I like this better
    // than the original version distributed with a lot of
    // examples that require a unique implementation
    // just for this typecast.
    template <class T>
    bool GetDataPointer(LPITEMIDLIST pidl, T** ppData)
    {
        AFX_MANAGE_STATE(AfxGetStaticModuleState());
        if (!pidl)
```

```
        {
            return false;
        }
        *ppData = reinterpret_cast<T*>(pidl->mkid.abID);
        return true;
    }

private:
    // Pointer to the shell's IMalloc interface.
    CComPtr<IMalloc> m_pMalloc;
};
```

The generated code and the example application use this class as a convenient wrapper around ITEMIDLIST manipulation routines. If a class uses CPidlMgr in almost all of its functions, you may want to consider making a CPidlMgr member variable. You can also use it as a local variable because it has fairly low initialization costs associated with it. It simply calls SHGetMalloc in its constructor and relies on the CComPtr to release the interface in the destructor. The class also uses a template member function, CPidlMgr::GetDataPointer(), to return whatever is located at pidl→mkid.abID as a pointer to your custom structure. I discarded two alternatives before deciding on the template member function. First, I could have simply used a void* to do the conversion. This is no better than an automatic conversion and makes for some interesting programming when converting between void* and the actual type. Second, I could have had the wizard produce a derived version of this class with a properly customized version of GetDataPointer(). Fortunately, I had read through some examples that use a similar CPidlMgr implementation. When the user has the ability to modify the class within their own project, they treat CPidlMgr as a hammer and everything else as a nail. I did not like the class construction I saw when the user took this path. So, I decided to come halfway between the two ideas: automatic type conversion removes the need to write the extra wizard code and removes the need to do any void* conversions.

CPidlMgr enables navigation using the GetNextItem() and GetLastItem() methods. GetNextItem() helps in navigating between the ITEMIDLIST from start to finish. GetLastItem() comes in handy for getting the display name for a folder or other individual item.[3]

```
LPITEMIDLIST CPidlMgr::GetNextItem(LPCITEMIDLIST pidl)
{
    // Return the next node.
    if (pidl)
    {
```

---

3. More often than not, the last node does contain enough information to generate a simple display string.

```
            // cast pidl to an LPBYTE so that the
            // appropriate pointer arithmetic kicks in.
            return reinterpret_cast<LPITEMIDLIST>(
                ((LPBYTE)pidl) + pidl->mkid.cb);
        }
        return (NULL);
    }


    LPITEMIDLIST CPidlMgr::GetLastItem(LPCITEMIDLIST pidl)
    {
        LPITEMIDLIST   pidlLast = NULL;

        if(pidl)
        {
            // While we haven't hit the last node,
            // keep grabbing.
            while(pidl->mkid.cb)
            {
                pidlLast = const_cast<LPITEMIDLIST>(pidl);
                pidl = GetNextItem(pidl);
            }
        }
        return pidlLast;
    }
```

These methods come in handy for many things. For instance, the generated code will use these methods in CTheExampleFolder::GetDisplayNameOf() to return the display name of the passed pidl argument.

```
STDMETHODIMP CTheExampleFolder::GetDisplayNameOf(
    LPCITEMIDLIST pidl, DWORD uFlags, LPSTRRET lpName)
{
    TheExamplePidl* pData = NULL;
    ATLTRACE( _T("CTheExampleFolder::GetDisplayNameOf\n") );
    HRESULT hr = E_NOTIMPL;
    // We cast away the "const-ness" because we want
    // direct access to the data pointer.  The function
    // signature for this required part of the interface
    // specifies that the PIDL is const.
    if ( m_pidlMgr.GetDataPointer(
        const_cast<LPITEMIDLIST>(pidl), &pData ) )
    {
        IMalloc* pMalloc = NULL;
        LPITEMIDLIST tempPidl = NULL;
        _bstr_t theString;
        if ( SUCCEEDED( SHGetMalloc( &pMalloc ) ) )
        {
            if ( uFlags & SHGDN_INFOLDER )
            {
```

```
        // This is an easy case.
        tempPidl = m_pidlMgr.GetLastItem( pidl );
        m_pidlMgr.GetDataPointer( tempPidl, & pData );
        theString = pData->pDisplayText;
    }
    else if ( ( uFlags & SHGDN_FORADDRESSBAR ) ||
        ( uFlags & SHGDN_FORPARSING ) )
    {
        _bstr_t tempStr;
        LPITEMIDLIST minorPidl = m_pidl;
        tempStr += pData->pDisplayText;

        while ( minorPidl->mkid.cb != 0 )
        {
            // The root of the namespace
            // is usually some unprintable
            // string.  So, skip that part.
            if ( minorPidl->mkid.cb >=
                sizeof( ITEMIDLIST ) +
                sizeof(TheExamplePidl))
            {
                if ( m_pidlMgr.GetDataPointer(
                    minorPidl, &pData ) )
                {
                    if ( theString.length() > 0 )
                    {
                        theString += _T("\\");
                    }
                    theString += pData->pDisplayText;
                }
            }
            minorPidl = m_pidlMgr.GetNextItem(
                minorPidl );
        }

        theString += _T("\\");
        theString += tempStr;
    }
    // You have to return this string as some type.
    // Might as well pick a good one.
    lpName->uType = STRRET_WSTR;
    if ( theString.length() > 0 )
    {
        lpName->pOleStr = reinterpret_cast<LPWSTR>
            (pMalloc->Alloc( (theString.length() + 1)
            * sizeof( wchar_t )));
        wcscpy(lpName->pOleStr, theString);
        hr = S_OK;
    }
```

```
        }
    }
    return hr;
}
```

CPidlMgr also comes in handy for concatenating and copying PIDLs.

```
LPITEMIDLIST CPidlMgr::Copy(LPCITEMIDLIST pidlSrc)
{
    LPITEMIDLIST pidlTarget = NULL;
    UINT cbSrc = 0;

    // This is easy, and fundamentally correct.
    // The copy of NULL is NULL.
    if (NULL == pidlSrc)
    {
        return (NULL);
    }

    // Allocate a properly sized bit of memory.
    cbSrc = GetSize(pidlSrc);
    pidlTarget = reinterpret_cast<LPITEMIDLIST>
        (m_pMalloc->Alloc(cbSrc));
    if (!pidlTarget)
    {
        return (NULL);
    }

    // Create the copy.
    CopyMemory(pidlTarget, pidlSrc, cbSrc);
    return pidlTarget;
}

LPITEMIDLIST CPidlMgr::Concatenate(LPCITEMIDLIST pidl1,
                                   LPCITEMIDLIST pidl2)
{
    LPITEMIDLIST    pidlNew;
    UINT            cb1 = 0,
        cb2 = 0;

    if(!pidl1 && !pidl2)
    {
        return NULL;
    }

    if(!pidl1)
    {
        // NULL + "something" = "something"
        pidlNew = Copy(pidl2);
        return pidlNew;
```

```
    }

    if(!pidl2)
    {
        // "something" + NULL = "something"
        pidlNew = Copy(pidl1);
        return pidlNew;
    }

    // Subtract the size of the NULL terminator
    // to get the amount of memory to allocate.
    cb1 = GetSize(pidl1) - sizeof(ITEMIDLIST);

    cb2 = GetSize(pidl2);

    pidlNew = (LPITEMIDLIST)m_pMalloc->Alloc(cb1 + cb2);

    if(pidlNew)
    {
        CopyMemory(pidlNew, pidl1, cb1);
        CopyMemory(((LPBYTE)pidlNew) + cb1, pidl2, cb2);
    }
    return pidlNew;
}
```

Inside of CTheExampleFolder::GetDisplayNameOf(), you should have noticed a structure named TheExamplePidl. The wizard creates this for you as a starting point for your own structure. At the start it looks like this:

```
enum TheExamplePidlType{
    PIDL_FOLDER,
    PIDL_DATAITEM,
    PIDL_UNKNOWN
};

// TODO: Define your PIDL.
struct TheExamplePidl
{
    int             nVersion;
    TCHAR           pDisplayText[20];
    TheExamplePidlType eType;
};
```

From this point, it is up to you to decide what values should exist in TheExamplePidlType and what they mean. The twenty-character array at TheExamplePidl.pDisplayText does not provide the best way to allocate what might be variable sized data. You would be better off placing this member at the end if the size will vary, and then set the ITEMIDLIST.mkid.cb value when you create the PIDL. Still, I had to start you off somewhere and this seemed like a good bet. These PIDLs usually get instantiated in the

IEnumIDList implementation. Explorer requests a pointer to the example's IEnumIDList by calling CTheExampleFolder::EnumObjects().

```
STDMETHODIMP CTheExampleFolder::EnumObjects( HWND hwnd,
    DWORD grfFlags, IEnumIDList **ppenumIDList)
{
    // Create a new CTheExampleIDList
    CComObject<CTheExampleIDList> *pList =
        new CComObject<CTheExampleIDList>;
    pList->SetType( grfFlags );

    // Set the ppenumIDList pointer
    HRESULT hr = pList->QueryInterface( IID_IEnumIDList,
        (void**)ppenumIDList );

    // Copy the shell folder and PIDL over to the
    // list so that the list knows what to enumerate.
    if ( !pList->SetShellFolder( this, m_pidl ) )
    {
        hr = S_FALSE;
    }
    return hr;
}
```

If you have not guessed yet, the wizard called the generated IEnumIDList CTheExampleIDList. This class is derived from CEnumIDListImpl. Like CShellFolderImpl, it also contains a CPidlMgr and LPITEMIDLIST member. The LPITEMIDLIST pointer stores the value passed to pList→SetShellFolder(). It owns the CPidlMgr value for the same reason CShellFolderImpl does: it uses the class a lot! Otherwise, the class contains nothing special. CTheExampleIDList has this definition:

```
class CTheExampleIDList :
    public CComObjectRootEx<CComSingleThreadModel>,
    public CComCoClass<CTheExampleIDList,
        &CLSID_TheExampleIDLIST>,
    public ITheExampleIDLIST,
    public CEnumIDListImpl
{
public:
    void SetType( DWORD grfFlags );
    CTheExampleIDList();

    DECLARE_REGISTRY_RESOURCEID(IDR_THEEXAMPLEIDLIST)

    DECLARE_PROTECT_FINAL_CONSTRUCT()

BEGIN_COM_MAP(CTheExampleIDList)
    COM_INTERFACE_ENTRY(ITheExampleIDLIST)
    COM_INTERFACE_ENTRY_IID(IID_IEnumIDList, IEnumIDList)
```

```
END_COM_MAP()

    // ITheExampleIDLIST
    bool SetShellFolder(ITheExampleFolder* pFolder,
        LPCITEMIDLIST pItemIDList);
    void FinalRelease();

    // IEnumIDList functions
    STDMETHOD(Clone)( IEnumIDList **ppEnum );
    STDMETHOD(Next)( ULONG celt, LPITEMIDLIST *rgelt,
        ULONG *pceltFetched );
    STDMETHOD(Reset)();
    STDMETHOD(Skip)( ULONG celt );

private:
    DWORD m_grfFlags;
    bool CreateIDList();
    CComPtr<ITheExampleFolder> m_pFolder;
    typedef std::list<LPITEMIDLIST> TheExampleListType;
    TheExampleListType m_vPidl;
    TheExampleListType::iterator m_currentIndex;
};
```

The class creates the ID list when SetShellFolder gets called.

```
bool CTheExampleIDList::SetShellFolder(ITheExampleFolder*
    pFolder, LPCITEMIDLIST pItemIDList)
{
    bool retval = true;

    m_pFolder = pFolder;
    m_pFolderPidl = m_pidlMgr.Copy( pItemIDList );
    retval = CreateIDList();
    m_currentIndex = m_vPidl.begin();
    return retval;
}

bool CTheExampleIDList::CreateIDList()
{
    // TODO: You will probably delete most of this
    // code and start from scratch.  This does
    // get something displaying in the view immediately.
    IMalloc* pMalloc = NULL;
    LPITEMIDLIST pidl = NULL;
    ATLTRACE( _T("CTheExampleIDList::CreateIDList\n") );
    TheExamplePidl* pData = NULL;
    if ( FAILED(SHGetMalloc( &pMalloc ) ) )
    {
        return false;
    }
    USHORT theSize = sizeof(ITEMIDLIST) +
        sizeof(TheExamplePidl);
```

```
    // Include folder items
    if (m_grfFlags & SHCONTF_FOLDERS )
    {
        // The extra ITEMIDLIST is to NULL terminate the
        // list.
        pidl = reinterpret_cast<LPITEMIDLIST>
            (pMalloc->Alloc( theSize + sizeof(ITEMIDLIST) ));
        ZeroMemory( pidl, theSize + sizeof(ITEMIDLIST) );

        if ( m_pidlMgr.GetDataPointer( pidl, &pData ) )
        {
            pData->eType = PIDL_FOLDER;
            _tcscpy( pData->pDisplayText, _T("Folder") );
            pidl->mkid.cb = theSize;
        }
        m_vPidl.insert( m_vPidl.end(), pidl );
    }

    // Include non-folder items
    if ( m_grfFlags & SHCONTF_NONFOLDERS )
    {
        pidl = reinterpret_cast<LPITEMIDLIST>
            (pMalloc->Alloc( theSize + sizeof(ITEMIDLIST) ));
        ZeroMemory( pidl, theSize + sizeof(ITEMIDLIST) );
        pData = NULL;
        if ( m_pidlMgr.GetDataPointer( pidl, &pData ) )
        {
            pData->eType = PIDL_DATAITEM;
            _tcscpy( pData->pDisplayText, _T("Data item") );
            pidl->mkid.cb = theSize;
        }
        m_vPidl.insert( m_vPidl.end(), pidl );
    }
    return true;
}


STDMETHODIMP CTheExampleIDList::Next( ULONG celt,
    LPITEMIDLIST *rgelt, ULONG *pceltFetched )
{
    if ( m_currentIndex == m_vPidl.end() )
    {
        *pceltFetched = 0;
        return S_FALSE;
    }
    for ( int i = 0; (i < celt) &&
        ( m_currentIndex != m_vPidl.end() );
        ++i, ++m_currentIndex )
    {
        rgelt[i] = m_pidlMgr.Copy( *m_currentIndex );
```

```
    }
    *pceltFetched = i;
    return S_OK;
}
```

You have no requirements to load up the entire list of items at this point. Keep in mind that Explorer will ask for every item on your list. You can load the list here if the cost of starting and stopping is greater than the cost of loading everything at once. Explorer will request the entire list because it displays the folder items in ascending order. Explorer loads the list by repeatedly calling IEnumIDList::Next().

The above code, *CTheExampleIDList::Next()*, will return as many items as Explorer has asked for. In practice, Explorer only asks for one item at a time. However, Explorer might not be your only client. Odds are pretty good that your IShellView will also utilize this interface to retrieve all the items in the folder and the number of items depends on you in this case. For example, the wizard generated view loads its data by requesting the IEnumIDList from IShellFolder. Anyhow, once Explorer gets all the items, it returns to IShellFolder to sort the items.

```
STDMETHODIMP CTheExampleFolder::CompareIDs( LPARAM lParam,
    LPCITEMIDLIST pidl1, LPCITEMIDLIST pidl2)
{
    TheExamplePidl* pData1 = NULL;
    TheExamplePidl* pData2 = NULL;
    HRESULT hr = 0;
    if ( !(m_pidlMgr.GetDataPointer(
        const_cast<LPITEMIDLIST>(pidl1), &pData1 ) &&
          m_pidlMgr.GetDataPointer(
        const_cast<LPITEMIDLIST>(pidl2), &pData2 ) ) )
    {
        return 0;
    }

    hr = _tcscmp(pData1->pDisplayText, pData2->pDisplayText);
    return hr;
}
```

CTheExampleFolder::CompareIDs() provides one obvious method of sorting the data. This method works well for use in sorting a list view when the user clicks a column because all your PIDL sorting code will be in one location. The lParam argument can be whatever you want it to be. I have used this fact to pass the column ID I want sorted in my list view and the direction—positive means sort ascending, negative means sort descending. We will see this in use in Chapter 11's WinReg example.

Once Explorer has all the folders and has them sorted properly, it will want to know what properties those folders have. In particular, Explorer will want to know if it should display the folders with *child* indicators. If a node has children, it will usually have a plus sign (+) next to it. You do not have to know this information ahead of time. If you tell Explorer that a given folder has children, and later fail to deliver any child nodes, no harm is done. Explorer will see that the IEnumIDList returns no nodes and will update its display appropriately. You see this behavior when browsing a network share. A directory may appear to have subfolders, but when you go to expand the node in the tree, the little plus sign vanishes if no subdirectories exist. To let Explorer know what to display, you need to implement IShellFolder::GetAttributesOf().

```
STDMETHODIMP CTheExampleFolder::GetAttributesOf( UINT cidl,
    LPCITEMIDLIST * apidl, ULONG * rgfInOut)
{
    TheExamplePidl* pData = NULL;

    // Makes sure only one ITEMIDLIST was sent in.
    // If this starts failing, update the code.
    ASSERT( cidl == 1 );
    if ( m_pidlMgr.GetDataPointer(
        const_cast<LPITEMIDLIST>(*apidl), &pData ) )
    {
        switch ( pData->eType )
        {
        case PIDL_FOLDER:
            // Say that a folder is a folder with
            // children
            *rgfInOut =  SFGAO_HASSUBFOLDER | SFGAO_FOLDER;
            break;
        case PIDL_DATAITEM:
            *rgfInOut = 0;
            break;
        default:
            break;
        }

    }
    return S_OK;
}
```

Explorer needs to know what icon to display for the folders in the tree as well as what context menu should show up when the user presses the right mouse button on a folder within our namespace. It asks for these items through IShellFolder::GetUIObjectOf(). The requested object may be one of the following interfaces:

- IContextMenu
- IContextMenu2
- IContextMenu3
- IDataObject

- IDropTarget
- IExtractIcon
- IQueryInfo

A number of these items depend on how much information you want to present to the user. You should at least return objects for IExtractIcon and IContextMenu. If you choose to add and remove your icons from the system image list, you can avoid implementing IExtractIcon. Instead, just implement the IShellIcon interface on the same object that implements IShellFolder.

```
STDMETHODIMP CTheExampleFolder::GetUIObjectOf( HWND hwndOwner,
    UINT cidl, LPCITEMIDLIST * apidl,
    REFIID riid, UINT * prgfInOut, void **ppv)
{
    if(IsEqualIID(riid, IID_IExtractIcon))
    {
        // The client wants an IExtractIcon object.  Create
        // one, set it up, and send it back to the caller.
        CComObject<CTheExampleIcon> *pei =
            new CComObject<CTheExampleIcon>;
        if ( !pei )
        {
            return E_OUTOFMEMORY;
        }
        LPITEMIDLIST   pidl;

        if ( m_pidl )
        {
            pidl = m_pidlMgr.Concatenate(m_pidl, apidl[0]);
        }
        else
        {
            pidl = const_cast<LPITEMIDLIST>(apidl[0]);
        }
        pei->SetPIDL( pidl );

        // The temp PIDL can be deleted because the new
        // CTheExampleIcon either failed or
        // made its own copy of it.

        m_pidlMgr.Delete(pidl);
        return pei->QueryInterface( riid, ppv );
    }
    else if (IsEqualIID(riid, IID_IContextMenu))
    {
        CComObject<CTheExampleContextMenu> *pcm =
            new CComObject<CTheExampleContextMenu>;
        LPITEMIDLIST pidl = NULL;
        if ( !pcm )
        {
```

```
            return E_OUTOFMEMORY;
        }
        if ( m_pidl )
        {
            pidl = m_pidlMgr.Concatenate( m_pidl, apidl[0] );
        }
        else
        {
            pidl = const_cast<LPITEMIDLIST>(apidl[0]);
        }
        pcm->SetPIDL( pidl, this );
        // The temp PIDL can be deleted because the new
        // CTheExampleContextMenu either failed or
        // made its own copy of it.
        m_pidlMgr.Delete(pidl);
        return pcm->QueryInterface( riid, ppv );
    }
    return E_NOINTERFACE;
}
```

The CTheExampleIcon implementation takes a PIDL and remembers what type of icon it needs to display. It does not store the PIDL itself. Once the CTheExampleIcon knows what type of object it will be representing, it can properly respond to calls for the open and closed versions of the icon so that Explorer can depict the folder's state. It handles this task in the GetIconLocation()/Extract() pair of functions. The IExtractIcon implementation does not differ much from the one presented in Chapter 7, Section 7.3. The only difference here is that we check to see what state the caller wants to reflect.

```
STDMETHODIMP CTheExampleIcon::GetIconLocation(UINT    uFlags,
    LPTSTR szIconFile, UINT cchMax,
    int *piIndex, UINT *pwFlags)
{
    AFX_MANAGE_STATE(AfxGetStaticModuleState());
    // Tell the caller that the icon is
    // allocated on a per-file basis.
    *pwFlags |= GIL_NOTFILENAME ;
    CTheExampleApp* pApp =
        dynamic_cast<CTheExampleApp*>(AfxGetApp());
    switch( m_type )
    {
    case PIDL_FOLDER:
        *piIndex = ( uFlags & GIL_OPENICON ) ?
            pApp->OpenIcon() : pApp->ClosedIcon();
        break;
    case PIDL_DATAITEM:
        *piIndex = IDI_DATA;
        break;
    }
```

```
    return S_OK;
}

STDMETHODIMP CTheExampleIcon::Extract(LPCTSTR pszFile,
    UINT nIconIndex, HICON *phiconLarge,
    HICON *phiconSmall, UINT nIconSize)
{
    AFX_MANAGE_STATE(AfxGetStaticModuleState());
    CTheExamplcApp* pApp =
        dynamic_cast<CTheExampleApp*>(AfxGetApp());

    // Load the large version - Explorer does the proper
    // extraction.
    *phiconLarge = (HICON)nIconIndex;

    // Load the small version - Explorer does the proper
    // extraction.
    *phiconSmall = (HICON)nIconIndex;
    return S_OK;
}
```

Explorer has an odd caching mechanism. If you tell Explorer that it cannot cache the icons in GetIconLocation() by setting the GIL_DONTCACHE flag in pwFlags, you cannot predict when Explorer will display the correct open or closed folder icon, even if your implementation appears to be 100 percent correct. So, we have to let Explorer cache the icons. This presents problem number two. The original version of this library passed an icon ID from GetIconLocation(). The problem came in when I had two or more namespace extensions that were developed using the ShellExtension library and Namespace wizard. When IExtractIcon::Extract() got called, Explorer would display the icon for the first namespace extension that was opened for all namespaces developed with the tools. I could fix this behavior by setting the GIL_DONTCACHE flag, but then Explorer would randomly display the open and closed folder icons. To fix the problem, I went for a workaround. At startup, the application object initializes two member variables with the HICON of the open and closed folder icons.

```
BOOL CTheExampleApp::InitInstance()
{
    AFX_MANAGE_STATE(AfxGetStaticModuleState());
        if (!InitATL())
                return FALSE;

    // Since these haven't been initialized, do it now.
    // This needs to be done here because if we do not
    // load the image list here, we get odd behavior
    // by loading the icons on demand.
    m_iconOpen = (UINT)AfxGetApp()->LoadIcon(IDI_FOLDEROPEN);
```

```
    m_iconClosed = (UINT)AfxGetApp()->LoadIcon(IDI_FOLDER);
      return CWinApp::InitInstance();
}
```

The above operation is very safe. CWinApp::LoadIcon() simply retrieves a pointer to the actual icon within the application/DLL binary. This value will not change throughout the lifetime of the object. This technique avoids the open or closed icon confusion as well as the problem of mysteriously replacing another namespace's icons.

You can see the results of the CTheExampleIcon class in Figure 10-4. The IContextMenu implemented by the wizard does nothing spectacular. The only special thing you need to do is set the PIDL of the creating folder before returning the interface pointer to the caller of IShellFolder:: GetUIObjectOf(). At this point, we have exhausted the code that implements the behind the scenes work for the folder specific part of the user interface. In the next section, we will see what work the library and wizard do to build the view.

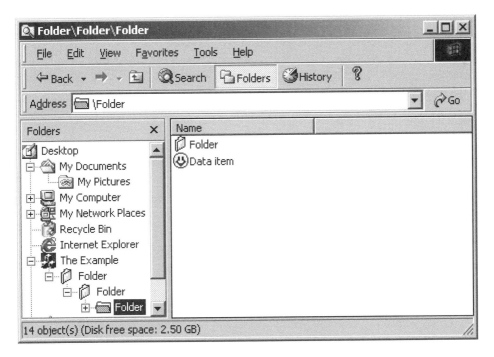

Figure 10–4   *The wizard generated TheExample namespace extension in action.*

10.3 The Implementation of IShellView (and Its Cohorts)

IShellView provides the namespace with the ability to display its contents to the user. Users expect a few things from this view. First of all, they expect that you will show the folder contents as a list. Deviation from this list means you get to do some extra usability testing. Second, the user expects to be able to double-click on a folder item within the list and open up a sub folder. Last, your extension should allow the user to switch between a detail, small icon, large icon, and list view. As a developer, you will want to be able to customize the toolbar and menus to hold items pertinent to your namespace extension.

The wizard and library team up to make accomplishing these tasks easier. Explorer requests your IShellView by calling IShellFolder::CreateViewObject(). Like the IEnumIDList and IExtractIcon implementations, you will need to pass any information your IShellView needs from your IShellFolder in this method.

```
STDMETHODIMP CTheExampleFolder::CreateViewObject(
    HWND hwndOwner, REFIID riid, void **ppv)
{
    AFX_MANAGE_STATE(AfxGetStaticModuleState());

    // If this thing fails, this return value
    // generates the least amount of odd behavior
    // from Explorer.  S_FALSE or E_FAIL don't work
    // as well.
    HRESULT hr = E_NOTIMPL;
    if ( IsEqualIID(IID_IShellView, riid ) )
    {
        CComObject<CTheExampleView> *pView =
            new CComObject<CTheExampleView>;
        *ppv = pView;

        // Manually add the reference.
        pView->AddRef();
        pView->SetFolder( this, m_pidl );
        hr = S_OK;
    }
    return hr;
}
```

The ShellExtension library includes a class named CShellViewImpl to implement the basic parts of IShellView and IShellView2. Recent versions of the shell will ask for IShellView2 before calling for IShellView. You can get started on using this interface by allowing for usage of both interfaces. If nothing else, you can take advantage of the similarities between IShellView::CreateViewWindow() and IShellView2::CreateViewWindow2(). Create-

ViewWindow2() just packages the arguments of CreateViewWindow() into a structure named SV2CVW2_PARAMS. This type of design makes it more difficult to pass in arguments at the wrong location. CShellViewImpl takes advantage of this by packaging the arguments up from CreateViewWindow() and passing them off to CreateViewWindow2(). This way, you only need to maintain one of the two functions for platforms that do and do not know about IShellView2.

```
STDMETHODIMP CShellViewImpl::CreateViewWindow(
    IShellView  *lpPrevView,
    LPCFOLDERSETTINGS lpfs, IShellBrowser  * psb,
    RECT * prcView, HWND  *phWnd)
{
    SV2CVW2_PARAMS params;

    // Pass this on to the better implemented
    // CreateViewWindow2.  It's the same function, only with a
    // nicer parameter list.
    params.cbSize = sizeof( params );
    params.hwndView = *phWnd;
    params.pfs = lpfs;
    params.psbOwner = psb;
    params.prcView = prcView;
    params.psvPrev = lpPrevView;
    HRESULT hr = CreateViewWindow2( &params );
    *phWnd = params.hwndView;
    m_folderFlags = lpfs->fFlags;
    return hr;
}
```

The wizard-generated code next provides the implementation of CreateViewWindow2().

```
STDMETHODIMP CTheExampleView::CreateViewWindow2(
    LPSV2CVW2_PARAMS lpParams)
{
    AFX_MANAGE_STATE(AfxGetStaticModuleState());

    // Defer creation to the list control
    return m_theView.Init( lpParams ) ? S_OK : E_NOTIMPL;
}
```

The wizard code defers the view's activation to m_theView, an instance of the actual view class. This view is a window. Remember my rule: ATL should do COM stuff and MFC should do user interface stuff. Initialization of the view means that the view needs to be created by the time CreateViewWindow2() returns. Anything short of window creation means failure. Before getting into the MFC part of the solution, we might as well quickly wrap up the COM part of the view. It exposes the following interfaces:

- IOleView
- IShellView
- IShellView2
- IOleCommandTarget

```
class ATL_NO_VTABLE CTheExampleView :
    public CComObjectRootEx<CComSingleThreadModel>,
    public CComCoClass<CTheExampleView,
        &CLSID_TheExampleView>,
    public CShellViewImpl,
    public COleCommandTargetImpl,
    public ITheExampleView
{
public:
    CTheExampleView();

    DECLARE_REGISTRY_RESOURCEID(IDR_THEEXAMPLEVIEW)

    DECLARE_PROTECT_FINAL_CONSTRUCT()

BEGIN_COM_MAP(CTheExampleView)
    COM_INTERFACE_ENTRY(ITheExampleView)
    COM_INTERFACE_ENTRY_IID(IID_IShellView, IShellView)
    COM_INTERFACE_ENTRY_IID(IID_IOleWindow, IOleWindow)
    COM_INTERFACE_ENTRY_IID(IID_IShellView2, IShellView2)
    COM_INTERFACE_ENTRY_IID(IID_IOleCommandTarget, IOleCommandTarget)
END_COM_MAP()

        // ITheExampleView
public:
    // From IOleWindow
    STDMETHOD(GetWindow) ( HWND * lphwnd);

    // From IShellView
    STDMETHOD(UIActivate) ( UINT uState);
    STDMETHOD(DestroyViewWindow)();
    STDMETHOD(GetItemObject)( UINT uItem, REFIID riid,
        void **ppv);
    STDMETHOD(Refresh) ();
    STDMETHOD(GetCurrentInfo)( LPFOLDERSETTINGS lpfs);
    STDMETHOD(SaveViewState)();

    // From IShellView2
    STDMETHOD(GetView)( SHELLVIEWID   *pvid, ULONG uView );
    STDMETHOD(CreateViewWindow2)( LPSV2CVW2_PARAMS lpParams);

    // Others
    void SetFolder( IShellFolder* pFolder, LPITEMIDLIST pidl );

private:
```

```
    // Keeps the view close to home.
    CTheExampleListView m_theView;
};
```

The class defers most of its work to CTheExampleListView. Just look at these two functions.

```
STDMETHODIMP CTheExampleView::UIActivate( UINT uState)
{
    HRESULT hr = S_OK;

    // Pass activation to the list control.
    if ( !m_theView.Activate( uState ) )
    {
        hr = E_FAIL;
    }
    return hr;
}


STDMETHODIMP CTheExampleView::DestroyViewWindow()
{
    AFX_MANAGE_STATE(AfxGetStaticModuleState());
    HRESULT hr = S_OK;

    // Get rid of the view.
    if ( !m_theView.DestroyWindow() )
    {
        hr = S_FALSE;
    }
    return hr;
}
```

I mentioned earlier in this section that the view has a number of responsibilities to the user:

- Display the contents of the folder as a list
- Ability to open up a folder using a double-click
- Switch the list view style between detail, small icon, large icon, and list

The library and wizard generated MFC class handle all of these items using both the automatically generated code and a base class named CommandHandler. You will notice that the message map functions look a lot like ones that you would define if you actually owned the menus. You will see handlers to handle ON_UPDATE_COMMAND_UI notifications as well as menu notifications. First, here is the class declaration:

```
class CTheExampleListView : public CommandHandler<CWnd>
{
    // Construction
```

```
public:
    CTheExampleListView();

    // Overrides
    // ClassWizard generated virtual function overrides
    //{{AFX_VIRTUAL(CTheExampleListView)
public:
    virtual BOOL DestroyWindow();
protected:
    //}}AFX_VIRTUAL

    // Implementation
public:
    virtual void Refresh();
    bool Init( LPSV2CVW2_PARAMS lpParams );
    virtual ~CTheExampleListView();
    FOLDERVIEWMODE GetViewMode();

    // Generated message map functions
protected:
    //{{AFX_MSG(CTheExampleListView)
    afx_msg void OnSize(UINT nType, int cx, int cy);
    afx_msg void OnHelpAbout();
    afx_msg void OnUpdateViewDetails(CCmdUI* pCmdUI);
    afx_msg void OnViewDetails();
    afx_msg void OnUpdateViewLargeicons(CCmdUI* pCmdUI);
    afx_msg void OnViewLargeicons();
    afx_msg void OnUpdateViewList(CCmdUI* pCmdUI);
    afx_msg void OnViewList();
    afx_msg void OnUpdateViewSmallicons(CCmdUI* pCmdUI);
    afx_msg void OnViewSmallicons();
    //}}AFX_MSG
    afx_msg void OnDblclk(NMHDR* pNMHDR, LRESULT* pResult);

    DECLARE_MESSAGE_MAP()

private:
    void RemoveCachedPIDLs();
    void SetupReportView();

    // Actually implements the list.
    CListCtrl m_list;

    // Images for use when small icons are needed.
    CImageList m_smallImageList;

    // Images for use when large icons are needed.
    CImageList m_largeImageList;
    static const UINT m_iconIDs[];
};
```

You should notice that the base class is a template class. When designing CommandHandler, I tried a few different designs to get the class to handle the menu and toolbar notifications as well as insert and remove those items from Explorer's user interface. First, I could have forced the user to inherit from CommandHandler and have CommandHandler inherit from CWnd. This works well as long as you want CWnd to be the parent class. If you have some other class that you would like to use as the parent of your view window, this approach fails. For example, you might see more value in your class than in CommandHandler. In this case, you are better off extending your derived class to handle the "namespace stuff." If you do need both classes, you may wind up editing CommandHandler. This makes it difficult to incorporate any future enhancements or bug fixes. Alternatively, you could edit your own class and create a fork in the class's source tree. This causes the same problem as the previous case: difficulty in incorporating changes to the original source.

Also, I could have implemented CommandHandler as a sort of orthogonal base class and extended the MFC-based view through multiple inheritance. This would work, but requires the derived class to implement items such as CWnd::OnCommand() and pass the call on to the parent class. I also was not too sure how the class would interact with the other unknown base class since CommandHandler would be fairly interested in manipulating message maps. For a long time, MFC programmers have known that it is dangerous to multiply inherit from many CObject derived classes. Even if I avoided this path, I still had a good chance of hitting some unknown problems. The safest bet involved some form of single inheritance. But how would I do that, given the problems mentioned with assuming only CWnd→CommandHandler→User's class? Before you move on to the next paragraph, think how *you* would solve that problem.

If you have not learned about the expressiveness and flexibility available from C++ templates, you are missing a large chunk of what makes C++ such a powerful language. You can write very elegant, useful code using templates. Some template functions require certain functions, such as operator <() (for sorting algorithms), to be defined for the class. Other templates assume that an instance has an embedded class named `class::iterator` defined. Through these assumptions, standard C++ has set the stage for templates that require clients to have some set of pre-defined functionality before they can use the template. The CommandHandler class uses a small set of assumptions to do its work. It assumes that the user wants to use CWnd somewhere within the hierarchy and that the user will insert two lines into their message map so that the map has these contents:

```
BEGIN_MESSAGE_MAP(SomeClass, [CWnd or CWnd derived class])
    //{{AFX_MSG_MAP(SomeClass)
    ON_WM_MENUSELECT()
    ON_WM_INITMENUPOPUP()
```

```
        [other message map entries]
        //}}AFX_MSG_MAP
    END_MESSAGE_MAP()
```

The CTheExampleListView has this message map:

```
// Uniquely identifies the list control.
static const int KnListID = 2;

BEGIN_MESSAGE_MAP(CTheExampleListView, CWnd)
    //{{AFX_MSG_MAP(CTheExampleListView)
    ON_WM_SIZE()
    ON_COMMAND(ID_HELP_ABOUT, OnHelpAbout)
    ON_UPDATE_COMMAND_UI(ID_VIEW_THEDETAILS,
        OnUpdateViewDetails)
    ON_COMMAND(ID_VIEW_THEDETAILS, OnViewDetails)
    ON_UPDATE_COMMAND_UI(ID_VIEW_THELARGEICONS,
        OnUpdateViewLargeicons)
    ON_COMMAND(ID_VIEW_THELARGEICONS, OnViewLargeicons)
    ON_UPDATE_COMMAND_UI(ID_VIEW_THELIST, OnUpdateViewList)
    ON_COMMAND(ID_VIEW_THELIST, OnViewList)
    ON_UPDATE_COMMAND_UI(ID_VIEW_THESMALLICONS,
        OnUpdateViewSmallicons)
    ON_COMMAND(ID_VIEW_THESMALLICONS, OnViewSmallicons)
    ON_WM_MENUSELECT()
    ON_WM_INITMENUPOPUP()
    //}}AFX_MSG_MAP
    ON_NOTIFY(NM_DBLCLK, KnListID, OnDblclk)
END_MESSAGE_MAP()
```

Of the possible solutions I evaluated, this one seemed to be the least confusing. As you will see in its comments, CommandHandler also requires the client to be related in some way to an IShellView. That assumption limits the utility of the template but helps it better fulfill its goals. I was not shooting for a completely generic class, just something useful for the task at hand.

```
template <class T>
class CommandHandler : public T
{
public:
    // Constructor/Destructor
    CommandHandler(UINT unToolbarID, UINT unMenuID);
    virtual ~CommandHandler();

    // Init
    // Initializes the window.
    virtual bool Init( LPSV2CVW2_PARAMS lpParams );

    // SetFolder
    // Sets the IShellFolder and pidl that the view represents
```

```
    virtual void SetFolder( IShellFolder* pFolder,
        LPITEMIDLIST pidl );

    // DestroyWindow
    // Performs any cleanup
    virtual BOOL DestroyWindow();

    // Activate
    // Called to handle activation and deactivation of the
    // IShellView.
    virtual bool Activate( UINT unState );

protected:
    // InitMenus
    // Merges your menus with Explorer's
    virtual bool InitMenus();

    // KillMenus
    // Removes your menus from Explorer's
    virtual bool KillMenus();

    // InitToolbar
    // Merges your toolbar with Explorer's
    virtual bool InitToolbar();

    // KillToolbar
    // Removes your toolbar from Explorer's
    virtual bool KillToolbar();

    // OnCommand
    // Interprets toolbar clicks and menu
    // selections to the command the view uses
    // to interpret the messages.
    virtual BOOL OnCommand( WPARAM wparam, LPARAM lparam );

    // OnInitMenuPopup
    // Handle the WM_INITMENUPOPUP message.  Your
    // class needs to add ON_WM_INITMENUPOPUP() to
    // the message map.  You don't need anything else.
    afx_msg void OnInitMenuPopup( CMenu* pPopupMenu,
        UINT nIndex, BOOL bSysMenu );

    // OnMenuSelect
    // Handle the WM_MENUSELECT message.  Your
    // class needs to add ON_WM_MENUSELECT() to
    // the message map.  You don't need anything else.
    afx_msg void OnMenuSelect(UINT nItemID, UINT nFlags,
        HMENU hSysMenu);

    // MergeMenu
    // Merges extension into shell.
```

```
virtual bool MergeMenu( CMenu& shell, CMenu& extension );

// Refresh
// Your derived class should implement this function.
// This version is a no-op, so there is no reason to call
// it.  It exists so that you can build your projects
// a little faster.
virtual void Refresh();

// CreateCommandMap
// Discovers the commands the class can handle.
bool CreateCommandMap();

// InsertSubMenuIntoMap
// Helper function to add a submenu to the command map.
bool InsertSubMenuIntoMap(CMenu& menu);

// GetToolTip
// Returns the tooltip associated with a given command ID.
CString GetToolTip( UINT unID );

// TranslateID
// Translates an ID from the internal representation
// to that used to insert the menu item or toolbar item
// into Explorer.
UINT TranslateID( UINT unID );

// Store the IShellFolder and IShellBrowser
// pointers in COM's version of an auto_ptr.
CComPtr<IShellFolder> m_pFolder;
CComPtr<IShellBrowser> m_psBrowser;

// Typedef to make typing easier.
typedef std::map< UINT, UINT> CommandLookup;

// m_commands
// Used to translate an ID from Explorer's idea
// of what the ID should be to our internal
// representation. (Reverse of what TranslateID does).
CommandLookup m_commands;

// m_unMenuItem
// Stores the ID of the last used Explorer menu
// ID (we generate these separate from our internal
// representations of the numbers).
UINT m_unMenuItem;

// m_menuShared
// The menu that Explorer and the view share.
CMenu m_menuShared;
```

```
// m_nNumButtons
// Stores the number of buttons we are responsible
// for on Explorer's toolbar.
int m_nNumButtons;

// m_pidl
// The PIDL of the folder we represent.
LPITEMIDLIST m_pidl;

// Resource IDs for the toolbar and menu.
// These will be loaded into and removed from
// Explore at the appropriate times.
UINT m_unToolbarID;
UINT m_unMenuID;
};
```

As you can see, the template inherits from whatever CWnd-derived class you specify. It needs to insert itself in between the CWnd-derived class and your view so that it can capture menu activation as well as menu and toolbar WM_COMMAND messages. These Items must map themselves to values FCIDM_SHVIEWFIRST and FCIDM_SHVIEWLAST, [0, 32767]. The resource editor typically starts assigning menu IDs at 32771. To handle these items in your view class using the class wizard, you can either edit the resource IDs by hand to make them fall in the correct range or you can translate the IDs between valid and invalid values. CommandHandler takes the latter approach. It first takes the IDs of the toolbar and menu you want to use as constructor arguments.

```
CTheExampleListView::CTheExampleListView() :
    CommandHandler<CWnd>( IDR_TBEXTENSION,
        IDR_EXTENSION )
{
}
```

We see that the generated view passes in the control IDs of the toolbar and menu to the CommandHandler<CWnd> parent class. CommandHandler simply stores the IDs and waits to act on the information. In our example, we see it first act on this information when CTheExampleView::CreateViewWindow2() calls CTheExampleListView::Init().

```
bool CTheExampleListView::Init(LPSV2CVW2_PARAMS lpParams)
{
[Gratuitous amounts of deleted code that properly set up
the view if it is going to use a list.  If not, you would
get rid of these lines anyhow.]

    // Initialize the toolbar in the command handler
    retval = CommandHandler<CWnd>::Init( lpParams );
    return retval;
}
```

Note

If you look at the generated code, you will see that the previous function eats up a lot of space and contains a number of things that just might belong in a base class somewhere. The need to allow for extra flexibility overrode that decision. If the user does not go with a list control for the main view, most of the code in that function winds up useless. I came up with a number of other reasons to go this route, but the need for flexibility tipped the scales. What kind of flexibility do you get? Here you get full control of the Init function, from head to toe. This follows some of the style seen in the generated CDialog::OnInitDialog, though my code is considerably longer. You should note that most of the code deals with setting up the list control. Remove the list and most of the code disappears.

Once CTheExampleListView::Init() calls CommandHandler<CWnd>::Init(), the toolbar gets installed. The actual CommandHandler<T>::Init() function contains little code.

```cpp
template <class T>
bool CommandHandler<T>::Init( LPSV2CVW2_PARAMS lpParams )
{
    AFX_MANAGE_STATE( AfxGetStaticModuleState() );
    m_psBrowser = lpParams->psbOwner;
    bool retval = true;

    Refresh();
    lpParams->hwndView = GetSafeHwnd();
    retval = CreateCommandMap() && InitToolbar();
    return retval;
}
```

The derived class should implement a Refresh() method to display its data within the view. If it does not, the user will see a line in their debug window stating CommandHandler<T>::Refresh not implemented. Init() captures the IDs on the toolbar and menu by calling the CommandHandler::CreateCommandMap() method.

```cpp
template <class T>
bool CommandHandler<T>::CreateCommandMap()
{
    AFX_MANAGE_STATE( AfxGetStaticModuleState() );
    bool retval = true;
    CMenu menu;

    // Kind of restrictive, but at least it
    // doesn't hook up to a specific number.
    // If this doesn't work, you should
    // have used the wizard that came with the
    // library.
    if ( menu.LoadMenu( m_unMenuID ) )
    {
```

```
        int numItems = menu.GetMenuItemCount();

        // If you asserted here, you were messing
        // with the expected menu structure.  DON'T
        // DO THAT.  Look at fitting your menus within
        // the EXPLORER menu structure.  This class
        // handles submenus like a champ, so you have
        // no excuses.
        ASSERT( numItems == ShellExtension::KnNumMenuItems );
        if ( numItems == ShellExtension::KnNumMenuItems )
        {
            CMenu* pMenu = NULL;
            CMenu* pShellMenu = NULL;
            for ( int i = 0; i < numItems; ++i )
            {
                // Grab the submenu at the
                // named location.
                pMenu = menu.GetSubMenu( i );
                if ( pMenu )
                {
                    // This item has a submenu,
                    // so add it to the list of
                    // menus we know about.
                    retval = InsertSubMenuIntoMap( *pMenu );
                    if ( !retval )
                    {
                        break;
                    }
                }
            }
        }
    }
    menu.DestroyMenu();
    return retval;
}
```

You may have noticed that the toolbar was not evaluated in this step. The above code does not worry about menu items having duplicate IDs, either. Multiple instances of menu items with the same item should not cause any problems. The one menu item should still map to a single WM_COMMAND handler in any case. Once the menu command IDs have been extracted and stored, we load the toolbar.

```
template <class T>
bool CommandHandler<T>::InitToolbar()
{
    AFX_MANAGE_STATE( AfxGetStaticModuleState() );
    bool retval = true;
    HRESULT hr = S_OK;
    CToolBar toolbar;
```

```
// Load the toolbar into memory.
toolbar.CreateEx( this, TBSTYLE_FLAT | CBRS_TOOLTIPS,
    WS_CHILD );
toolbar.LoadToolBar(m_unToolbarID);
CToolBarCtrl& tbCtrl = toolbar.GetToolBarCtrl();

// Get the number of buttons we are about to add.
m_nNumButtons = tbCtrl.GetButtonCount();
TBADDBITMAP tbAddBmp;
long lNewIndex = 0;
long lNewString = 0;

// Allocate an array of buttons equal to the size
// of the toolbar.
TBBUTTON* ptbb = new TBBUTTON[m_nNumButtons];
tbAddBmp.hInst = _Module.GetModuleInstance();
tbAddBmp.nID = m_unToolbarID;

// Add the bitmap to the toolbar.
hr = m_psBrowser->SendControlMsg( FCW_TOOLBAR,
    TB_ADDBITMAP, m_nNumButtons,
    reinterpret_cast<LPARAM>(&tbAddBmp),
    &lNewIndex );

if ( SUCCEEDED( hr ) )
{
    UINT unCommand;
    UINT unItemID;
    CString szLabel;
    int nCount = m_nNumButtons;
    int nCurrentTBB = 0;
    UINT unStyle;
    int nCurrentButton = -1;
    for ( int i = 0; i < nCount; ++i )
    {
        // Extract the command ID and
        // tool tip
        unItemID = toolbar.GetItemID( i );

        // Set the style as needed.
        if ( unItemID == ID_SEPARATOR )
        {
            unStyle = TBSTYLE_SEP;
        }
        else
        {
            unStyle = TBSTYLE_BUTTON;
            ++nCurrentButton;
        }

        // Translate the ID.  If it isn't
```

```
            // found, we must add it to the command list.
            unCommand = TranslateID( unItemID );

            // Commands must be in the range
            // of [0, 0x7FFF].
            if ( unCommand > 0x7FFF )
            {
                // Add the command to the list.
                m_commands[m_commands.size()+1] = unItemID;

                // Just a double check to get the ID
                // using normal procedures.  This wastes
                // a few cycles but validates the
                // procedure.
                unCommand = TranslateID( unItemID );
            }

            // Get the item's tool tip for insertion into
            // the toolbar.
            szLabel = GetToolTip( unItemID );

            // Add the string.
            hr = m_psBrowser->SendControlMsg( FCW_TOOLBAR,
                TB_ADDSTRING, NULL,
                reinterpret_cast<LPARAM>((LPCTSTR)szLabel),
                &lNewString );
            if ( FAILED(hr) )
            {
                break;
            }

            // Insert the remaining data into the
            // TBBUTTON array.
            ZeroMemory( &ptbb[i], sizeof( TBBUTTON ) );
            ptbb[i].iBitmap = lNewIndex + nCurrentButton;
            ptbb[i].idCommand = unCommand;
            ptbb[i].iString = lNewString;
            ptbb[i].fsState = TBSTATE_ENABLED;
            ptbb[i].fsStyle = unStyle;
        }
    }
    if ( SUCCEEDED( hr ) )
    {
        // Finish the job by adding all the toolbar items.
        hr = m_psBrowser->SetToolbarItems(
            ptbb, m_nNumButtons, FCT_MERGE );
    }
    delete[] ptbb;
    return hr == S_OK;
}
```

A little bit later, Explorer will call IShellView::Activate(). In the example code, CTheExampleView::Activate() passes the call on to CTheExampleListView that implements Activate() via CommandHandler. In other words, CTheExampleListView inherits the implementation. When the view receives the focus or gets activated, CommandHandler places the menus into Explorer's menu structure. But how does CommandHandler dispatch these messages back to you?

When a menu first comes up, it dispatches a WM_INITMENUPOPUP message. The wizard added an entry in your message map to handle this and CommandHandler::OnInitMenuPopup() handles the message. It looks at the current menu and checks to see if any of the menu items were placed there by our extension. If an item is found, it tries to call the appropriate ON_UPDATE_COMMAND_UI handler. This is where the payoff in translating the items first kicks in. While building the extension, we were able to add and edit the handlers using Class Wizard without worrying about how Explorer sees things. CommandHandler::OnInitMenuPopup() handles the translation between the two worlds for us.

```
template <class T>
void CommandHandler<T>::OnInitMenuPopup( CMenu* pPopupMenu, UINT nIndex,
BOOL bSysMenu  )
{
    AFX_MANAGE_STATE( AfxGetStaticModuleState() );

    // Get the correct menu
    MENUITEMINFO mii;
    ZeroMemory( &mii, sizeof( mii ) );
    mii.cbSize = sizeof( mii );
    mii.fMask = MIIM_SUBMENU;
    UINT numItems = pPopupMenu->GetMenuItemCount();
    UINT unID;
    CCmdUI cmdUI;
    CommandLookup::iterator it;
    cmdUI.m_pMenu = pPopupMenu;
    cmdUI.m_pSubMenu = NULL;
    cmdUI.m_nIndexMax = numItems + 1;
    for ( UINT i = 0; i < numItems; ++i )
    {
        unID = pPopupMenu->GetMenuItemID( i );
        pPopupMenu->GetMenuItemInfo( i, &mii, TRUE );
        if ( mii.hSubMenu != NULL )
        {
            // The item is a sub menu.  In this case,
            // we will have no need to set the "on update"
            // stuff.  We get another notification when
            // the popup menu pops up.
            continue;
        }
```

```
        if ( unID != ID_SEPARATOR )
        {
            // Update the menu to reflect what we want.
            it = m_commands.find( unID );

            // This may be one of ours— the ID can
            // change based on the source (Explorer or
            // us).
            if ( it != m_commands.end() )
            {
                // Explorer sent this one.
                cmdUI.m_nID = it->second;
            }
            else
            {
                // We are the culprit (message originated
                // in our view).
                cmdUI.m_nID = unID;
            }
            cmdUI.m_nIndex = i;
            OnCmdMsg(cmdUI.m_nID, CN_UPDATE_COMMAND_UI,
                &cmdUI, NULL);
        }
    }
}
```

As the user selects various items in our menus, we would like to see the help text show up on the status bar. Again, we were able to use the DevStudio resource editor and create our strings the "normal" way. The status bar help text comes first, the tooltip second, and the two are separated by a newline ("\n"). See Figure 10-5 for an example. This figure also shows the menus that the wizard gives you. You will need to set the popup style on each menu you add items to. This style will not remain set when the submenu contains no items—sorry. I could have put dummy items in the lists, but this solution was unacceptable to me. The CommandHandler class would have needed workarounds to know not to insert those dummy items. Yuck!

```
template <class T>
void CommandHandler<T>::OnMenuSelect(UINT nItemID,
    UINT nFlags, HMENU hSysMenu)
{
    T::OnMenuSelect(nItemID, nFlags, hSysMenu);

    // Lookup the ID from the class's user perspective
    CommandLookup::iterator it = m_commands.find( nItemID );
    UINT unStringID = -1;
    _bstr_t szValue;
    if ( it != m_commands.end() )
    {
```

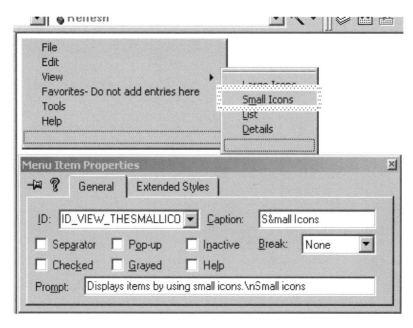

Figure 10–5   *Setting up the wizard generated menus for the status bar text (before the "\n") and tooltip text (after the "n\").*

```
        unStringID = it->second;
    }
    if ( !( ( nFlags & MF_SEPARATOR ) ||
            ( nFlags & MF_POPUP ) )
          && ( unStringID != -1 ) )
    {
        CString szTemp;
        szTemp.LoadString( unStringID );

        int nCRPos = szTemp.Find( _T('\n') );
        if ( nCRPos >= 0 )
        {
            szValue = szTemp.Left( nCRPos  );
        }
        else
        {
            szValue = szTemp;
        }
    }
    m_psBrowser->SetStatusTextSB( szValue );
}
```

CommandHandler lends a hand in two more areas. First, it removes the toolbar buttons and removes the added menu items when Explorer deactivates the view. It just traverses Explorer's toolbar looking for items we own. It then removes those items from the toolbar. Second, whenever a WM_COM-MAND message comes across, CommandHandler checks to see if that message maps back to a toolbar button or menu items. If the relationship exists, CommandHandler translates the message and sends it to the T parent class. T, whatever it is, then processes the message using MFC's message maps and gets the correct function invoked. You probably inserted this method using Class Wizard.

```
template <class T>
BOOL CommandHandler<T>::OnCommand( WPARAM wparam,
    LPARAM lparam )
{
    AFX_MANAGE_STATE( AfxGetStaticModuleState() );
    // Keep in mind, we modify these items
    // to start at 0 and work their way up.
    // We need to translate back to the ID the resource
    // used to that the client of our class can
    // process the message in their own reality.
    CommandLookup::iterator it = m_commands.find( wparam
);
    lparam = reinterpret_cast<LPARAM>(GetSafeHwnd());
    if ( it != m_commands.end() )
    {
        wparam = it->second;
    }
    return T::OnCommand( wparam, lparam );
}
```

Given the constraints I created for this class, I hope you agree that CommandHandler meets the specifications and does the job quite well. The wizard and library tackle a few other minor issues for you. For example, the library creates the ON_UPDATE_COMMAND_UI handlers to indicate the currently selected view style with a radio button on the menu.

10.4 Summary

This chapter presented the namespace extension wizard and some specific portions of the ShellExtension library. It mingled the generated code with the library's code in order to show each piece of work the two collaborate on. These tools allow you to create a namespace extension fairly quickly as long as you do not mind mixing MFC, ATL, and standard C++. I have never worked on a development team that had a problem mixing these technologies, but I have seen Usenet rants claiming that the three should not be mixed the way I do it. I fully expect to get some flaming e-mail on the topic of mixing. I do hope to hear some comments on how the mixtures work for you.

The next chapter presents a full namespace extension. It focuses on the design decisions, navigation issues, and other aspects related to implementing a namespace extension. Chapter 9 went over a number of the ground rules. Chapter 11 walks through an implementation. Like this chapter, it will be more a code review than anything else. I hope you find it educational.

Namespace Extension Example: The Registry

Finally, we get to take a look at a real example built using the namespace extension wizard and the ShellExtension library. This chapter serves a couple of purposes. First and foremost, it demonstrates a useful namespace extension. Second, it discusses the decisions I made while developing the extension so that you might understand why it functions as it does. Last, it provides an explanation of my code.

The chapter details a namespace extension that allows a user to view and edit the registry. This is not the first time this namespace extension example has been used. The Platform SDK has a version of the extension that uses straight SDK programming to browse the registry in Explorer.[1] Various utility bundles have also included tools to browse the registry from the Desktop and Explorer. This example provides you with a better extension than the SDK, but it falls short of the commercial implementations. By the end of the chapter, you should understand the extension well enough to add any features you want. If you should happen to add any features that you are particularly proud of, send them in to me.[2] I want to see how people use the example.

---

1. Not using MFC or ATL is a good idea for examples meant to transcend the various compilers out there.

2. Please send those comments and modifications to scott.seely@technologist.com.

11.1 Requirements for the Registry Namespace Extension

Before writing the namespace extension, we need to evaluate how good this idea is. We plan to create a namespace extension that allows the user to browse and edit the registry. Before moving on we need to answer a few basic questions:

- Do we have hierarchical data?
- Can we easily represent that hierarchical data to our user?
- Who is our intended audience?
- Do we have a good reason for creating the namespace extension?

Without a doubt, we have hierarchical data. We also know that we can present the data to the user fairly easily. This means that the answer to the first to questions is yes. RegEdit provides a template for what we can do to display the contents of the registry.

The next question, "Who is our intended audience?" asks us to think about who will use the extension. It will be used by:

- **Windows developers.** This group (which we are a part of) regularly needs to look up and validate entries in the registry. Often, we need to verify that our code writes values to the correct locations or we need to experiment with setting different values just to see how our application reacts.
- **System administrators.** This group (which some of us may be a part of) needs to view the registry on a regular basis, too. For example, a number of performance enhancements can only be set by manually changing registry values.
- **Students/hobbyists.** At one point or another, all of us belonged to this group. Because of the nature of this group, they will find our tool useful for poking and prodding the settings within the registry.

What about the average user? They should not have a need to edit the registry. It grew from a database of COM objects in the Windows 3.1 days to a system-wide database with the introduction of Windows 95. The registry replaces the need for program specific INI files. The average users, who use word processors, spread sheets, and Web browsers, should stay away from the registry. It is a tool for our applications, not for the users of those applications. We really do not want them playing with the registry unless they are on a "voyage of discovery." Hopefully, the user knows enough to backup the registry before beginning that voyage.

To the last question, "Do we have a good reason for creating the namespace extension?" my answer is yes. When doing COM development, I frequently bring up RegEdit to check and see if the entries are going in as intended. Since I usually have Explorer up and running, it would be nice to check out these things from Explorer. I have another reason besides ease of access. The registry is an integral part of Windows. Placing a registry editor and viewer inside of Explorer allows us to see a more complete view of the computer.

What types of things would we like to see the tool do? We would like to be able to do anything we can in RegEdit. I also would like the ability to change the type of a value. We often create a value in the registry only to immediately see that we created it with the wrong type. Instead of deleting the value, I want to be able to change its type—you know, go from a REG_SZ to a REG_DWORD but keep the name of the value the same. Given the sensitivity of the registry, I do not want to add-drag-and drop capabilities. Can you imagine the harm you could do to your system if you accidentally moved a branch of keys and values? Here is the feature list I came up with:

- View all registry folders in the Explorer tree view.
- View basic data in our custom view.
- Display the date the registry key or its contents were last modified.
- Allow the user to add and edit the following registry types:
  - Keys
  - REG_SZ values
  - REG_DWORD values
  - REG_QWORD values
  - REG_BINARY values
  - REG_MULTISZ values
  - REG_EXPAND_SZ values
- Allow the user to sort items based on name, data, type, and last modified date.
- Display appropriate icons for keys and the value types.

Of course, the tool would have to provide the ability to switch between detail, list, small icon, and large icon views. The namespace extension wizard provides this functionality for us. To get started, we will use the namespace extension wizard to generate our project. The one step in the namespace extension wizard should have the settings displayed in Figure 11-1. We will modify the generated namespace extension throughout the chapter until the extension fulfills the requirements. The extension will not provide two of the features found in RegEdit. It will not provide search capabilities or the ability to save select portions of the registry to REG files. I leave these items as an exercise for the reader.[3]

---

3. An author uses this technique when they do not have the time to complete a feature that is not necessary to understanding the topic at hand. That's what happened here, too.

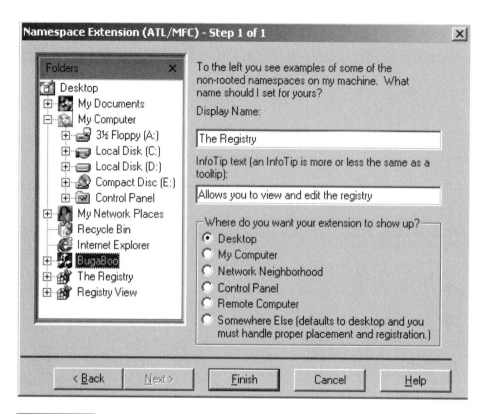

Step 1 of 1 for the registry namespace extension.

11.2 Defining the Registry ITEMIDLIST Structure

What type of information do we want to have readily available with each registry key and value? Knowing the answer to this question will help with designing the behind-the-scenes and visual components of the namespace extension. We want to provide all information related to each and every item in the registry. What do we know about registry entries? We know that any given entry in the registry may be the root of a registry hive, a key, or a value. Explorer should display the root of a hive and any keys as folders. To help store the PIDL type we will change the wizard-generated enumeration.

```
// PT means "P"IDL "T"ype
enum WinRegPidlType{
    PT_ROOT, // Used for the top level of the registry hive
    PT_KEY,  // Used for keys
    PT_VALUE,// Used for straight values
```

```
PT_UNKNOWN // Used when the type is not known.
        // Initialize values of WinRegPidlType to
        // PT_UNKNOWN
};
```

In the cases where we have a registry value, we need some way to store its information that will not use more space than necessary. The RegValueType structure handles this task by storing the various types of data the array might contain. It uses an unnamed union to pack in the various data types we can expect out of the registry.

```
struct RegValueType
{
    DWORD cbSize;

    // Nameless union.  Neat feature of C++.
    // The arrays of [1] are really variable
    // length members.  cbSize indicates how
    // big they really are.
    union {
        BYTE      bData[1];       // REG_BINARY
        DWORD     dwData;         // REG_DWORD
        ULONGLONG qwData;          // REG_QWORD

        TCHAR     pRegSz[1];       // REG_SZ
        TCHAR     pRegExpandSz[1]; // REG_EXPAND_SZ
        TCHAR     *pRegMultiSz[1]; // REG_MULTI_SZ
    };
};
```

Inside you see that the REG_QWORD value type is held by a ULONG-LONG.[4] Many people have never seen this type before. I never had reason to use it before this project for the simple reason that I had no need for 64-bit unsigned numbers before. The registry started handling these numbers with the release of Windows 2000. In order to get access to this registry type, you will need to download the latest Platform SDK from Microsoft. They keep links to it at *msdn.microsoft.com*. The actual location changes every couple of months, but if you start at the MSDN home page, you will be able to find the SDK. As of this writing, they are offering it as a free download.

Last but not least is the structure that holds the information together. When we build our ITEMIDLISTs, we will reference the WinRegPidl at ITEMIDLIST.mkid.abID. This structure contains a lot of information, some of which is specific to registry keys and other pieces that are specific to values. Because the differences account for a fairly small part of the overall structure, I chose to create only one structure. We could employ multiple

---

4. ULONGLONG is a #define for unsigned__int64.

types under the covers if we like. This modification would increase the number of typecasts our code has to perform in order to correctly interpret the PIDL.

11.3 Implementing the IEnumIDList Interface

Now that we have our ITEMIDLIST structure defined, we need to actually create the PIDLs. When Explorer needs to know the contents of a folder, it will ask CWinRegFolder, our IShellFolder implementation, for its IEnumIDList object by calling CWinRegFolder::EnumObjects(). We do not need to change the wizard's version of CWinRegFolder::EnumObjects(). As a result, we can immediately get to work on CWinRegIDList. The folder initializes CWinRegIDList via CWinRegIDList::SetShellFolder() which in turn calls CWinRegIDList::CreateIDList().

The default implementation of CWinRegIDList::CreateIDList() does not do what we need it to do. We have two different types of initialization that we need to do. We first need to create the topmost folders in the registry:

- HKEY_CLASSES_ROOT
- HKEY_CURRENT_USER
- HKEY_LOCAL_MACHINE
- HKEY_USERS
- HKEY_CURRENT_CONFIG
- HKEY_DYN_DATA (if it exists, Win95 only)
- HKEY_PERFORMANCE_DATA (if it exists, WinNT only)

Once the user sees the topmost set of folders, the roots of the registry hives, they will probably open one of those folder. At this point, we actually need to open a key and enumerate its contents. Displaying the hives and enumerating their contents requires different information. CWinRegIDList::CreateIDList() decides which of these two should be displayed.

```
bool CWinRegIDList::CreateIDList()
{
    // Setup everything so that we are ready to get going.
    WinRegPidl* pData = NULL;
    bool retval = false;

    // Iterate over the items until we get to one
    // that looks like it is one of ours.
    LPITEMIDLIST pidl = m_pidlMgr.GetNextItem(m_pFolderPidl);
    while ( ( pidl->mkid.cb < ( sizeof( ITEMIDLIST ) +
        sizeof( WinRegPidl ) ) ) &&
        ( pidl->mkid.cb != 0 ) )
    {
```

```
        pidl = m_pidlMgr.GetNextItem(pidl);
    }

    // If the item appears to be generated by
    // the operating system, then fill in the
    // items found at the root of the namespace.
    if ( pidl->mkid.cb == 0 )
    {
        retval = FillInRootItems();
    }
    // Otherwise, fill in the other key items.
    else if ( m_pidlMgr.GetDataPointer( pidl, &pData ) )
    {
        // This switch on type helps evade a number
        // of potential problems.  If we start
        // seeing things displaying only the Root items,
        // we know a snafu may have happened.
        switch( pData->eType )
        {
            case PT_ROOT:
            case PT_KEY:
                retval = FillInKeyItems();
                break;
            case PT_VALUE:
                break;
            default:
                retval = FillInRootItems();
                break;
        }
    }
    return retval;
}
```

The root items get filled in with this function:

```
bool CWinRegIDList::FillInRootItems()
{
    bool retval = true;

    // Make sure that we are supposed to be retrieving
    // folders.
    if ( (m_grfFlags & SHCONTF_FOLDERS ) == 0 )
    {
        return false;
    }

    // Add the keys we know must exist
    retval = CreateRootPIDL( _T("HKEY_CLASSES_ROOT"),
            HKEY_CLASSES_ROOT ) &&
        CreateRootPIDL( _T("HKEY_CURRENT_USER"),
            HKEY_CURRENT_USER ) &&
```

```
        CreateRootPIDL( _T("HKEY_LOCAL_MACHINE"),
            HKEY_LOCAL_MACHINE )&&
        CreateRootPIDL( _T("HKEY_USERS"), HKEY_USERS ) &&
        CreateRootPIDL( _T("HKEY_CURRENT_CONFIG"),
            HKEY_CURRENT_CONFIG );
    // If we successfully added the root PIDLs, add the
    // ones that may or may not exist, depending on the
    // platform.
    LONG lResult = 0;
    HKEY hKey = NULL;
    if ( retval )
    {
        //open the HKEY_PERFORMANCE_DATA key
        lResult = RegOpenKeyEx( HKEY_PERFORMANCE_DATA, NULL,
            0, KEY_ENUMERATE_SUB_KEYS, &hKey);
        if ( lResult == ERROR_SUCCESS )
        {
            // It exists, add it.
            RegCloseKey(hKey);
            retval =
    CreateRootPIDL( _T("HKEY_PERFORMANCE_DATA"),
                HKEY_PERFORMANCE_DATA );
        }
    }
    if ( retval )
    {
        //open the HKEY_DYN_DATA key
        lResult = RegOpenKeyEx( HKEY_DYN_DATA, NULL,
            0, KEY_ENUMERATE_SUB_KEYS, &hKey);
        if ( lResult == ERROR_SUCCESS )
        {
            // It exists, add it.
            RegCloseKey(hKey);
            retval = CreateRootPIDL( _T("HKEY_DYN_DATA"),
                HKEY_DYN_DATA );
        }
    }

    return retval;
}
```

The function CWinRegIDList::CreateRootPIDL() creates and appends the root level nodes to the list of PIDLs. This method takes a bunch of repetitive code and places it in one place.

```
bool CWinRegIDList::CreateRootPIDL(LPCTSTR itemName,
    HKEY rootName)
{
    IMalloc* pMalloc = NULL;
```

```
LPITEMIDLIST pidl = NULL;
bool retval = true;

// Get the basic IMalloc pointer
if ( FAILED(SHGetMalloc( &pMalloc ) ) )
{
    return false;
}

// Calculate the size of the new PIDL.
USHORT theSize = sizeof(ITEMIDLIST) + sizeof(WinRegPidl);
pidl = reinterpret_cast<LPITEMIDLIST>
    (pMalloc->Alloc( theSize + sizeof(ITEMIDLIST) ));

// Set the whole thing to zeroes.
if ( pidl != NULL )
{
    ZeroMemory( pidl, theSize + sizeof(ITEMIDLIST) );
}
WinRegPidl* pData = NULL;

// Get the data pointer from the recently created
// item.  If it was NULL, then pData points to
// nothing.
if ( m_pidlMgr.GetDataPointer( pidl, &pData ) )
{
    // Set the type to PT_ROOT.
    pData->eType = PT_ROOT;

    // Set the itemName.
    _tcscpy( pData->itemName, itemName );

    // Fill in the remaining items and add it
    // to the end of the list.
    pData->hRoot = rootName;
    pidl->mkid.cb = theSize;
    m_lstPidl.insert( m_lstPidl.end(), pidl );
}
else
{
    retval = false;
}

return retval;
}
```

Most of the time, we will not need to present a list of the root items. Instead, the user will want to see the items contained under those registry hives. To do this, we need to enumerate the contents of each key. This task gets handled in CWinRegIDList::FillInKeyItems(). The first part retrieves information regarding any subkeys; the second half concentrates on retrieving any values. Because the amount of data the values contain varies, we should only allocate enough space to store the WinRegPidl and the data contained by that value. You may find this example handy when creating your own variable length items. Please excuse the length of the method. This is essentially a report writing function, which, in my experience, can get lengthy.

```cpp
bool CWinRegIDList::FillInKeyItems()
{
    HKEY rootHive;
    bool retval = false;
    CString fullKey;
    WinRegPidl* pData = NULL;

    // First, get the first pointer that
    // belongs to the namespace extension.
    LPITEMIDLIST pidl = m_pidlMgr.GetNextItem(m_pFolderPidl);
    if ( !m_pidlMgr.GetDataPointer( pidl, &pData ) )
    {
        return retval;
    }
    rootHive = pData->hRoot;

    // Get the textual name of the current folder.
    fullKey = GetSubKey( m_pFolderPidl, m_pFolder );
    DWORD dwNumSubKeys = 0;
    DWORD dwNumValues = 0;
    DWORD dwMaxSubKeyNameLen = 0;
    DWORD dwMaxValueNameLen = 0;
    DWORD dwMaxValueDataSize = 0;
    FILETIME lastModTime;
    HKEY currentKey = NULL;

    // Open up the key.
    RegOpenKey( rootHive, fullKey, &currentKey );
    if ( currentKey == NULL )
    {
        return retval;
    }

    // Find out the basic enumeration info: how
    // many keys, values, and how big can these things
    // get.
    if ( ERROR_SUCCESS != RegQueryInfoKey( currentKey,
        NULL, NULL, NULL,
        &dwNumSubKeys, &dwMaxSubKeyNameLen, NULL,
        &dwNumValues, &dwMaxValueNameLen,
        &dwMaxValueDataSize, NULL, &lastModTime ) )
```

```cpp
{
    return false;
}

DWORD i = 0;

// Only one string is really needed.
// Allocate one string to get Key names
// and value names.
DWORD dwNameLength = max( dwMaxSubKeyNameLen + 1,
    dwMaxValueNameLen + 1 );
TCHAR *theName = new TCHAR[dwNameLength];
DWORD tempLength = 0;

IMalloc* pMalloc = NULL;
pidl = NULL;

// If we fail to get the malloc pointer, just
// give up and return.
if ( FAILED(SHGetMalloc( &pMalloc ) ) )
{
    RegCloseKey( currentKey );
    return retval;
}

// For folders, the allocation unit size will not change.
USHORT theSize = sizeof(ITEMIDLIST) + sizeof(WinRegPidl);

// Get the folder items.
if ( (m_grfFlags & SHCONTF_FOLDERS ) != 0 )
{
    // For each subkey, ask for the data
    // and get ready for the next key.
    for ( i = 0; i < dwNumSubKeys; ++i )
    {
        tempLength = dwNameLength;

        // Read in the new key and its
        // information.
        RegEnumKeyEx( currentKey, i, theName, &tempLength,
            NULL, NULL, NULL, &lastModTime );

        // Allocate a new ITEMIDLIST.
        pidl = reinterpret_cast<LPITEMIDLIST> (pMalloc->
            Alloc( theSize + sizeof(ITEMIDLIST) ));
        ZeroMemory( pidl, theSize + sizeof(ITEMIDLIST) );
        WinRegPidl* pData = NULL;

        // Get the data pointer and fill in the
        // newly discovered information.
```

```
            if ( m_pidlMgr.GetDataPointer( pidl, &pData ) )
            {
                pData->eType = PT_KEY;
                _tcscpy( pData->itemName, theName );
                pData->hRoot = rootHive;
                pData->lastModTime = lastModTime;
                pidl->mkid.cb = theSize;
                m_lstPidl.insert( m_lstPidl.end(), pidl );
            }
        }
    }

    // Does the user want non-folder information?
    if ( (m_grfFlags & SHCONTF_NONFOLDERS ) != 0 )
    {
        // They want values too.
        DWORD dwType = 0;
        BYTE *byData = new BYTE[dwMaxValueDataSize];
        DWORD tempData = 0;
        for ( i = 0; i < dwNumValues; ++i )
        {
            // Keep theSize separate from a combination of
            // the actual amount of allocated memory.
            // Remember, we pad the allocation with some
            // null data to mark the end of the list.
            theSize = sizeof(ITEMIDLIST) + sizeof(WinRegPidl);
            tempLength = dwNameLength;
            tempData = dwMaxValueDataSize;
            RegEnumValue( currentKey, i, theName, &tempLength,
                NULL, &dwType, byData, &tempData );
            if ( ( dwType == REG_SZ ) ||
                 ( dwType == REG_BINARY ) ||
                 ( dwType == REG_EXPAND_SZ ) ||
                 ( dwType == REG_MULTI_SZ ) )
            {
                theSize += tempData;
            }

            pidl = reinterpret_cast<LPITEMIDLIST>(pMalloc->
                Alloc( theSize + sizeof(ITEMIDLIST) ));
            ZeroMemory( pidl, theSize + sizeof(ITEMIDLIST) );
            WinRegPidl* pData = NULL;
            if ( m_pidlMgr.GetDataPointer( pidl, &pData ) )
            {
                // Add the information to the PIDL.
                pData->uValue.cbSize = tempData;
                pData->eType = PT_VALUE;
                _tcscpy( pData->itemName, theName );
                pData->hRoot = rootHive;
                pidl->mkid.cb = theSize;
```

```
                pData->dwRegType = dwType;
                m_lstPidl.insert( m_lstPidl.end(), pidl );

                // Regardless of the data type, we just
                // need to slam it into the correct
                // spot in memory, which always starts
                // at the beginning of pData->uValue.bData,
                // which happens to easily translate to a
                // pointer.
                memcpy( pData->uValue.bData, byData,
                    tempData );
            }
        }
        delete[] byData;
    }
    delete[] theName;

    // Now that we are done enumerating the key, close it up.
    RegCloseKey( currentKey );
    m_currentIndex = m_lstPidl.begin();
    return retval;
}
```

The above code uses a little utility function called GetSubKey(). This global function parses out an internally meaningful string useful for opening up registry keys and values. You can find it and a friend, ConvertWinReg-PidlToDisplayString(), in the Examples\Chapter 11\WinReg\StdAfx.h and StdAfx.cpp files.

This concludes the construction of the CWinRegIDList class. When you build your own IEnumIDList implementation, take time to make sure your implementation works. You can spend days on this class making sure that everything works just so. The IEnumIDList implementation proved to be one of the hardest classes to get right. When building a namespace extension, I find that most of my bugs show up in this and in the IShellFolder classes. Speaking of IShellFolder, let's move on to it.

11.4   Implementing the IShellFolder Interface

The wizard provides a fairly complete implementation of IShellFolder. In it, only two methods need any substantial modifications. We need to make sure that Explorer will be able to correctly display the folder names within the tree view, the title bar, and the address bar. We also have to implement the PIDL sorting rules.

How do we want Explorer to display the various folder names? For example, do we want to display the full display name of the hive

(HKEY_CLASSES_ROOT) or the abbreviation (HKCR)? How do we want to separate the keys in the name? These are all things that need to be considered. Since most documentation, including this book, separates the key names in the full path using a backslash (\), I stuck with that character. As for the condensed form or the long form of the root name, I went with the long name. I did this because it follows the pattern already established by RegEdit. RegEdit displays the full name of the hive as the first node. The user expects to see the path opened in the tree view accurately reflected in the title bar. Can you imagine opening up HKEY_CURRENT_USER\Environment and seeing HKCR\Environment in the title bar? You could figure out what was going on, but you would not be seeing what you had expected. Whenever Explorer needs the text to display in the address bar, title bar, or in the folder view (the tree control), it calls IShellFolder::GetDisplayNameOf().

```
STDMETHODIMP CWinRegFolder::GetDisplayNameOf(
    LPCITEMIDLIST pidl, DWORD uFlags, LPSTRRET lpName)
{
    WinRegPidl* pData = NULL;
    HRESULT hr = E_NOTIMPL;
    IMalloc* pMalloc = NULL;
    LPITEMIDLIST tempPidl = NULL;
    _bstr_t theString;

    // Get the shell's IMalloc interface so that we
    // can allocate the space for the display name
    // of the pidl.
    if ( SUCCEEDED( SHGetMalloc( &pMalloc ) ) )
    {
        // Check to see what type of name the caller wants
        if ( uFlags & SHGDN_INFOLDER )
        {
            // This is the easy case.
            tempPidl = m_pidlMgr.GetLastItem( pidl );
            m_pidlMgr.GetDataPointer( tempPidl, &pData );
            theString = pData->itemName;
        }
        else if ( ( uFlags & SHGDN_FORADDRESSBAR ) ||
            ( uFlags & SHGDN_FORPARSING ) )
        {
            // The user wants the full name based off of the
            // root.
            _bstr_t tempStr;
            tempPidl = m_pidl;

            // Keep looping until we reach the end of the
            // list/
            while ( tempPidl->mkid.cb != 0 )
            {
                // Make sure that the item is big enough.
```

```
            if ( tempPidl->mkid.cb >=
                sizeof( ITEMIDLIST ) + sizeof(WinRegPidl))
            {
                // If it looks like one of ours,
                // get the data pointer.
                if ( m_pidlMgr.GetDataPointer(
                    tempPidl, &pData ) )
                {
                    if ( theString.length() > 0 )
                    {
                        // If we have already started
                        // adding to the string,
                        // separate items using
                        // a "\"
                        theString += _T("\\");
                    }
                    theString += pData->itemName;
                }
            }

            // Get the next item in the list.
            tempPidl = m_pidlMgr.GetNextItem( tempPidl );
        }

        // Finish building the string.
        LPITEMIDLIST minorPidl =
            const_cast<LPITEMIDLIST>(pidl);

        m_pidlMgr.GetDataPointer( minorPidl, &pData );
        tempStr += pData->itemName;

        if ( !(uFlags & MYSHGDN_SKIPCONCAT) )
        {
            theString += _T("\\");
            theString += tempStr;
        }
    }

    // We get to pick the type.  Might as well
    // use a WSTR.
    lpName->uType = STRRET_WSTR;
    if ( theString.length() > 0 )
    {
        // Copy the name into the passed in
        // STRRET structure.
        lpName->pOleStr = reinterpret_cast<LPWSTR>
            (pMalloc->Alloc( (theString.length() + 1) *
            sizeof( wchar_t )));
        wcscpy(lpName->pOleStr, theString);
        hr = S_OK;
```

```
            }
        }
    return hr;
}
```

Explorer also wants to be able to sort our PIDLs. It will always want to sort the items in ascending order. To perform this task, it calls IShell-Folder::CompareIDs(). Just because Explorer will want to sort things in ascending order does not mean that you can only provide for that situation. You will also need to sort the items in the view if you the display the contents of the folder in a list. The WinReg version of this function has been extended to handle sorting on the column numbers within the shell view.

```
STDMETHODIMP CWinRegFolder::CompareIDs( LPARAM lParam,
    LPCITEMIDLIST cpidl1, LPCITEMIDLIST cpidl2)
{
    // Perform the sort based on the last pidl in the list.
    LPITEMIDLIST pidl1 = m_pidlMgr.GetLastItem( cpidl1 );
    LPITEMIDLIST pidl2 = m_pidlMgr.GetLastItem( cpidl2 );

    // Pointers needed to correctly interpret the PIDLs.
    WinRegPidl* pData1 = NULL;
    WinRegPidl* pData2 = NULL;
    HRESULT hr = 0;

    // The correction determines if the items will be sorted
    // ascending or descending order.
    long lCorrection = ( lParam < 0 ) ? -1 : 1;

    // If we can not extract the data pointers,
    // we might as well give up.
    if ( !(m_pidlMgr.GetDataPointer(
            const_cast<LPITEMIDLIST>(pidl1), &pData1 ) &&
        m_pidlMgr.GetDataPointer(
            const_cast<LPITEMIDLIST>(pidl2), &pData2 ) ) )
    {
        return 0;
    }

    // Always place folders above keys.
    if ( pData1->eType < pData2->eType )
    {
        return -1;
    }
    else if ( pData1->eType > pData2->eType )
    {
        return 1;
    }

    // Sort in ascending order of root type.
```

```
if ( pData1->hRoot < pData2->hRoot)
{
    return -1 * lCorrection;
}
else if ( pData1->hRoot > pData2->hRoot )
{
    return 1 * lCorrection;
}

// Don't worry about losing the sort direction.
// This information was captured by lCorrection.
if ( lParam < 0 )
{
    lParam = -lParam;
}
else if ( lParam == 0 )
{
    // We are comparing items within the tree view.
    // Explorer doesn't fill in LPARAM.
    return _tcscmp( pData1->itemName, pData2->itemName );
}

// The parameter will always be one greater
// than the column name.  Why?  Tell me
// what -0 really is and how I will pass it using
// lParam.
switch ( lParam )
{
    // Sort on Name
case 1:
    {
        CString sz1( pData1->itemName );
        CString sz2( pData2->itemName );

        // Eliminate one test by assuming that
        // they are equal.
        hr = 0;
        if ( sz1 < sz2 )
        {
            hr = -1;
        }
        else if ( sz1 > sz2 )
        {
            hr = 1;
        }
        hr = _tcscmp(pData1->itemName, pData2->itemName);
    }
    break;
case 2:
    // We always sort on type, with keys first and
```

```
        // values second.
        // We do nothing here
        hr = 0;
        break;
    case 3:
        // Sort on data as if it were a string
        {
            long nNumBytes1 = pidl1->mkid.cb -
                (sizeof(ITEMIDLIST) +
                sizeof(WinRegPidl) );
            long nNumBytes2 = pidl2->mkid.cb -
                (sizeof(ITEMIDLIST) +
                sizeof(WinRegPidl) );

            CString pidl1 = ConvertWinRegPidlToDisplayString(
                pData1, nNumBytes1 );
            CString pidl2 = ConvertWinRegPidlToDisplayString(
                pData2, nNumBytes2 );
            // Eliminate one test by assuming that
            // they are equal.
            hr = 0;
            if( pidl1 < pidl2 )
            {
                hr = -1;
            }
            else if ( pidl1 > pidl2 )
            {
                hr = 1;
            }
        }
        break;
    case 4:
        // Sort on date/time
        {
            COleDateTime pidl1( pData1->lastModTime );
            COleDateTime pidl2( pData2->lastModTime );

            if (!((pidl1.GetStatus() == COleDateTime::valid)
                || (pidl2.GetStatus() ==
                    COleDateTime::valid)))
            {
                return 0;
            }
            // Eliminate one test by assuming that
            // they are equal.
            hr = 0;
            if ( pidl1 < pidl2 )
            {
                hr = -1;
            }
```

```
        else if ( pidl1 > pidl2 )
        {
            hr = 1;
        }
    }
}

// Modify the return value by the correction factor.
// This accounts for ascending or descending ordering.
hr = hr * lCorrection;
return hr;
}
```

The remaining functions in CWinRegFolder were more or less left alone because the wizard did a good job of implementing the remaining functionality. CWinRegFolder::GetAttributesOf() required a minor modification: the code extracting the folder type had to check against the new enum values created for WinRegPidl. The rest of the major modifications happened in CWinRegListView and its related classes. Most of this is straight MFC programming.

11.5 Displaying the Contents of the Folder: CWinRegListView

At this point, we need to give some thought to the visual elements of the program. Displaying a tree view to the user does not do anything terribly useful, does it? Right about now we should start to think about what types of visual elements we want to provide. This part of the project may take up the bulk of the code in your namespace extension. Fortunately, this will be the easiest code you write, especially if you already spend a lot of time writing MFC-based user interface code. Even if you do not write a lot of Windows code with MFC, this part of the program should still be fairly easy. With a few exceptions, this section will stay away from presenting any C++. I really do not have a lot to say regarding writing dialog boxes or menu handling code that has not been said before. Many namespace extension articles take some time here to write about inserting menus and toolbar items into Explorer. We skip that because CommandHandler handles that task for us. We just edit the menus as needed, oblivious to any complexity. If we want submenus, we have no need to figure out how to do it. We just do it, knowing that our menu and toolbar will merge with Explorer's. Unlike other namespace extension creators, we are liberated from worrying about how to add the items and remembering to remove them. For us, it just happens.

Some things do not just happen. We need to decide what icons to use and what the report view layout will look like. The view needs to load the registry values. Finally, we have to come up with a way to edit the registry values. For both the icons and the report view, I borrowed from RegEdit.exe. The file contains all the familiar registry related icons. Using DevStudio, I opened the file as a resource and copied the icons from RegEdit.exe to Win-Reg. Then, I went ahead and edited CWinRegListView::SetupReportView() to display the rows I wanted. You can see the end result in Figure 11-2. I took the folder icons from the SDK example—it seemed like a shame to let that artwork go to waste. You should also notice that the folders display the last time the contents of the folder were modified. I did not know that the registry made this information available until I wrote the extension. The last modified time comes in handy when you change a value and want to find it quickly. You navigate to the folder that contains the key that contains your value and then sort based on last modified time. For example, if you modify HKCR\.abk\shellex\somval, navigate to HKCR\.abk and sort on the last modified time column. shellex should pop to the bottom or the top, depending on sort direction. This is where implementing all variations of the sort in CWinRegFolder::CompareIDs() comes in handy. How?

A list sorts items using a function that compares items. The list function, CListCtrl::SortItems(PFNLVCOMPARE pfnCompare, DWORD dwData)

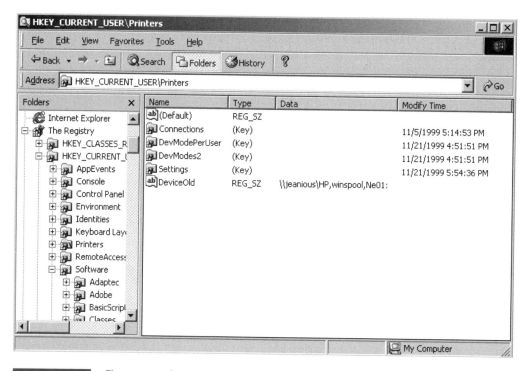

Figure 11-2   *The icons and report view layout for the registry namespace extension.*

takes a pointer to a comparison function and a data value. This data value can be anything we want. To allow the sort to access the folder's compare function, we typecast the IShellFolder pointer to a DWORD and pass that pointer along. Our comparison function then uses the pointer. The sort itself is initiated by CWinRegListView::OnItemClick(), which gets called whenever the user clicks on a column header.

```cpp
void CWinRegListView::OnItemclick(NMHDR* pNMHDR,
    LRESULT* pResult)
{
    // Get the header
        HD_NOTIFY *phdn = (HD_NOTIFY *) pNMHDR;

    // Find the column number.  If it matches the
    // column we sorted on last time, invert
    // the sort order.  m_bSortDir and
    // m_lSortColumn are public, static member
    // variables.  This provides easy access for the
    // sort function.
    if ( (phdn->iItem + 1) == m_lSortColumn )
    {
        m_bSortDir = !m_bSortDir;
    }
    else
    {
        m_lSortColumn = phdn->iItem + 1;
    }

    // Sort the items using the CompareFunc and
    // the raw IShellFolder pointer.
    m_list.SortItems( CompareFunc,
        reinterpret_cast<DWORD>(m_pFolder.p) );
            *pResult = 0;
}
```

Once called, the list will use CompareFunc to sort the items in the list.

```cpp
static int CALLBACK CompareFunc(LPARAM lParam1,
    LPARAM lParam2, LPARAM lParamSort)
{
    // Turn the parameter into the IShellFolder*
    // we know it really is.
    IShellFolder* pFolder =
        reinterpret_cast<IShellFolder*>(lParamSort);

    // If the pointer is NULL, give up and leave.
    if ( !pFolder )
    {
        return 0;
    }
```

```
    // Grab the sort direction.
    LPARAM sortVal = CWinRegListView::m_lSortColumn;

    // If the sort is inverted (sort descending)
    // negate the value.  This allows us to
    // pass column number and sort order to the
    // IShellFolder::CompareIDs() function.
    if ( !CWinRegListView::m_bSortDir )
    {
        sortVal = -sortVal;
    }

    // Let the folder figure it all out.
    return pFolder->CompareIDs( sortVal,
        reinterpret_cast<LPCITEMIDLIST>(lParam1),
        reinterpret_cast<LPCITEMIDLIST>(lParam2) );
}
```

Why is this function declared static? By declaring the function as static, we forbid external linkage. A clever co-worker cannot simply declare

```
extern int CALLBACK CompareFunc(LPARAM lParam1,
    LPARAM lParam2, LPARAM lParamSort);
```

and get access to the sorting function from another module in the COM DLL. Also note that the function does not specifically bind to the CWinRegFolder. This decision means that a future version of the DLL could use an entirely new IShellFolder implementation as long as the new version continued to associate the data in sortVal with the column ID and sort direction. Pretty slick, eh?

The other really neat piece of code lies in CWinRegListView::Refresh(). A number of times, I have mentioned that Explorer will not be the only user of the IEnumIDList implementation. You can have the view use this interface to obtain the PIDLs contained by the folder. The wizard generated version of CWinRegListView::Refresh() does this. We have one problem here—Refresh() needs to learn about WinRegPidl structures and it has to add them to the view.

```
void CWinRegListView::Refresh(
    bool bUpdateFolderList /*=false*/)
{
    // Clear the list
    m_list.DeleteAllItems();
    RemoveCachedPIDLs();

    // Enumerate the items.  We use a safe pointer
    // to handle maintenance.
    CComPtr<IEnumIDList> pEnum = NULL;

    // Note: m_pFolder is an IShellFolder.  It just
    // works using known interfaces.
```

```
m_pFolder->EnumObjects( GetSafeHwnd(),
    SHCONTF_FOLDERS | SHCONTF_NONFOLDERS,
    &pEnum );

// Get the manager.  We'll need this soon.
CPidlMgr pidlMgr;
if ( pEnum )
{
    ULONG numReturned = 0;
    CPidlMgr pidlMgr;
    LPITEMIDLIST pIDList = NULL;
    STRRET strRet;

    // Start up the iteration by getting the
    // first item in the list.
    pEnum->Next( 1, &pIDList, &numReturned );

    // Initialize local variables.
    int i = 0;
    WinRegPidl* pData = NULL;
    UINT iconIndex = 0;
    int newIndex = 0;
    LPTSTR lptstr = NULL;
    long nNumBytes = 0;
    bool bFoundDefault = false;

    // numReturned will be 0 when the last PIDL
    // comes back.
    while ( numReturned > 0 )
    {
        // By placing the variable declaration here, we
        // get clean objects each iteration
        // of the loop.
        CString szData;
        CString szName;
        CString szType;
        CString szDateTime;
        COleDateTime theTime;

        // strRet is a structure, no constructor
        // and no instant cleanliness.  Gotta do
        // the initialization here instead.
        ZeroMemory( &strRet, sizeof(strRet) );

        // Again, use the folder to get the display
        // name of the item.
        m_pFolder->GetDisplayNameOf( pIDList,
            SHGDN_INFOLDER, &strRet );
        StrRetToStr( &strRet, pIDList, &lptstr );
        szName = lptstr;
```

```
// Free the pointer.
CoTaskMemFree( lptstr );
lptstr = NULL;

// Items displayed with the text "Default"
// really are stored as the only value
// with an empty string as their name.
// These are always REG_SZ values.
if ( szName.IsEmpty() )
{
    bFoundDefault = true;
    szName = _T("(Default)");
}

// Get the data pointer.
if ( pidlMgr.GetDataPointer( pIDList, &pData ) )
{
    // Figure out how big the data portion is.
    nNumBytes = pIDList->mkid.cb -
        (sizeof(ITEMIDLIST) +
        sizeof(WinRegPidl) );

    if ( pData->eType == PT_VALUE )
    {
        // Depending on the value type, set the
        // correct icon
        switch (pData->dwRegType)
        {
        case REG_EXPAND_SZ:
        case REG_SZ:
        case REG_MULTI_SZ:
            iconIndex = STRING;
            break;
        case REG_BINARY:
        case REG_DWORD:
        case REG_QWORD:
            iconIndex = BINARY;
            break;
        }

        // New switch to determine
        // what to display as the value
        // type.
        switch( pData->dwRegType )
        {
        case REG_SZ:
            szType = _T("REG_SZ");
            break;
        case REG_EXPAND_SZ:
            szType = _T("REG_EXPAND_SZ");
```

```
                break;
            case REG_MULTI_SZ:
                szType = _T("REG_MULTI_SZ");
                break;
            case REG_BINARY:
                szType = _T("REG_BINARY");
                break;
            case REG_DWORD:
                szType = _T("REG_DWORD");
                break;
            case REG_QWORD:
                szType = _T("REG_QWORD");
                break;
            }

            // Finally, convert the contents of
            // the PIDL to something readable
            // by people.
            szData =
                ConvertWinRegPidlToDisplayString(
                    pData, nNumBytes );
        }
        else
        {
            // Must be a key.
            iconIndex = FOLDER;
            szType = _T("(Key)");
            theTime = pData->lastModTime;
            if ( theTime.GetStatus() !=
                COleDateTime::invalid )
            {
                // We know we have a time on keys.
                // Make it readable.
                szDateTime = theTime.Format(0,
                    LANG_USER_DEFAULT );
            }
        }
    }
}

// Insert a new item into the list.
newIndex = m_list.InsertItem( i, szName,
    iconIndex );

// Set its pointer to the recently retrieved
// PIDL.
m_list.SetItemData( newIndex,
    reinterpret_cast<DWORD>(pIDList) );

// Fill in the remaining columns.
m_list.SetItemText( newIndex, 1, szType );
```

```
        m_list.SetItemText( newIndex, 2, szData );
        m_list.SetItemText( newIndex, 3, szDateTime );
        ++i;

        // Navigate to the next PIDL.
        pEnum->Next( 1, &pIDList, &numReturned );
    }

    // If we need to update the folder list
    // because a new folder was added, tell the browser.
    // Spy++ revealed that the "Refresh" command is
    // 41504.
    if ( bUpdateFolderList )
    {
        HWND hwndBrowser = NULL;
        m_psBrowser->GetWindow( &hwndBrowser );
        ::SendMessage( hwndBrowser, WM_COMMAND,
            41504, 0 );
    }
}
// Sort the folder based on the last sort request.
m_list.SortItems( CompareFunc,
    reinterpret_cast<DWORD>(m_pFolder.p) );
}
```

The view gets refreshed when it is initialized and when the user adds a key or value to the registry using the namespace extension. The only folder that gives a noticeable delay using the function is the HKEY_CLASSES_ROOT folder. That folder also contains over 4000 keys. All other keys provide reasonable, almost instantaneous, refresh times.

The rest of the namespace extension does not provide anything terribly interesting in terms of code. If you are interested in how a given feature was coded, feel free to browse the source on the included CD. Everything you are about to see can be done in regular old MFC applications. Now, let's cover the remaining features of the namespace extension, just to show how far I went with this idea.

First, I added context menus to the view. When one or more items are selected you get the context menu displayed in Figure 11-3. From here, you can delete, rename, or view the properties of the key or value. Additionally, you can change the view type. Figure 11-4 shows what you can do when clicking in the blank part of the list view. This extension allows you to add more than the REG_SZ, REG_DWORD, and REG_BINARY available from RegEdit. You now have the ability to add and edit REG_QWORD, REG_EXPAND_SZ, and REG_MULTI_SZ data types. When you add a new key or value, the extension creates a value named New Key #n or New Value #n. If the n = 1 is taken, the extension will locate the first available number and create the key than way.

To edit a value, simply right-click on the value and select Properties. Depending on the value type, you will get one of the three property pages shown

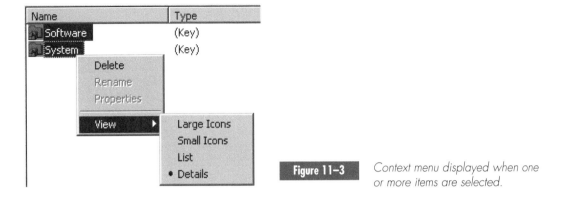

Figure 11-3   *Context menu displayed when one or more items are selected.*

in Figure 11-5, Figure 11-6, and Figure11-7. These pages allow you to edit string data, binary data, and numeric data respectively. The first page, shown in Figure 11-8, provides a button that allows you to change the value's type. Why would anyone want to do this? Sometimes we want to begin using a registry value before we write the code that adds that value to the registry. Maybe that task belongs to someone else responsible for a different feature. So, you quickly add the value and carefully type in the value's name, only to discover you picked the wrong type. The Change Type button allows you to change the type and correct your error. This change will remove any data contained by the value, but it saves you the task of deleting the value and then recreating it with the correct type. Changing the type does not save the data because this change may be between a string and a numeric type. What kind of a conversion should the code perform? `atol` may do a conversion, but will the data be correct? I took the safe route and chose to delete the data. Figure 11-9 shows the dialog that changes the data type.

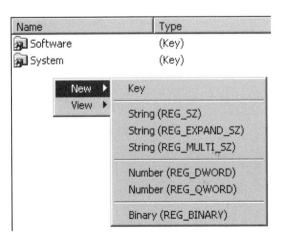

Figure 11-4   *Context menu displayed when no items are selected.*

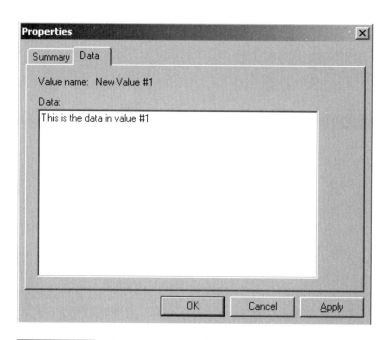

Figure 11-5   *Property page to edit string data.*

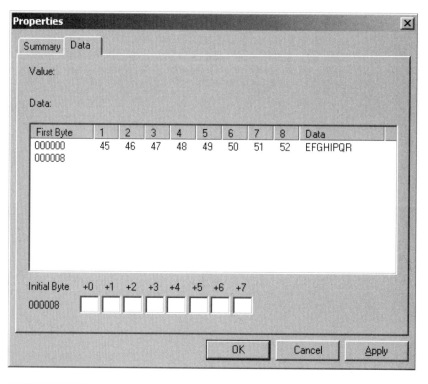

Figure 11-6   *Property page to edit binary data.*

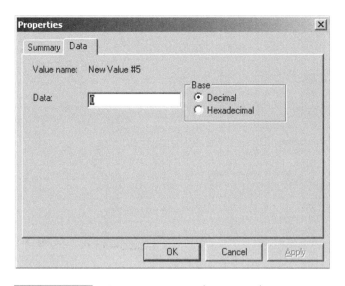

Figure 11–7   *Property page to edit numeric data.*

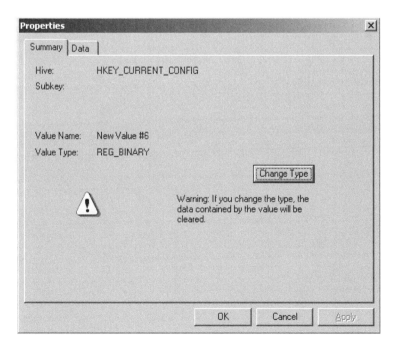

Figure 11–8   *Summary of value property page.*

359

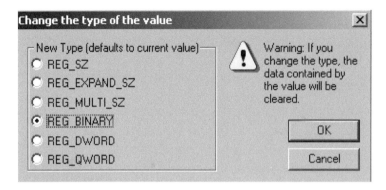

Figure 11–9 *Dialog to change the type of a value.*

If you really need to see how any of this was done, pull up the WinReg example from the CD and take a look. The view uses straight MFC. A lot of work went into getting the view to look nice, but it was the easiest part to get right. Why? Not many of us get paid to write shell extensions day in and day out. Instead, we create dialogs, views, and other CWnd-derived classes for our user interfaces. As a result, we know how to do this kind of thing better.

11.6 Summary

Through the past three chapters, we have taken a look at what namespace extensions are, a library and wizard to implement them, and finally, a useful namespace extension. In this chapter, we saw how easy it is to create a namespace extension if you are provided with the right tools. This extension does not provide for drag-and-drop capabilities. Doing so is no different than for any other application. When the user drags one of your items, make sure that you provide an IDataObject implementation for that object. If you want to allow drops on your view, declare it as a drop target. The task is no different than any other drag-and-drop implementation you have seen before. If you have not ever done this, MSDN contains many examples of how to do it. Chapter 7, "Shell Extensions," Section 7.4 covers data handlers, which are just one implementation of an IDataObject.

The appendices also cover some other aspects of namespace extensions that were not discussed in Chapters 9 through 11. Some extensions may need to use every feature out there, but the complexity of such an example certainly outweighs its usefulness as a teaching tool.

Explorer Bars and Desktop Bands

*At the bottom of your screen as well as in Windows Explorer,[1]
you have these helpful windows that let you do "stuff." In the
taskbar, you have a Quick Launch toolbar that contains links to
frequently used applications. You can add other toolbars, such as
Address, Links, and Desktop, to the taskbar. Explorer allows the
user to add windows to the browser through its View→Explorer
Bars menu. This mechanism allows you to see Search Results, Tip
of the Day, and other windows. These extra items on the taskbar
and Explorer are called band objects. (The name distinguishes
these items from toolbars as a toolbar-like, general purpose, COM-
based window.)*

In Chapter 2, "The Taksbar," I explained how to access and manipulate the
taskbar, and avoided an explanation of how to add toolbars like the Quick
Launch or Links bands to the taskbar. The ability to add bands shipped with
Internet Explorer 4.0 within SHELL32.DLL, version 4.71.

Three types of band objects exist: vertical explorer bars (info bands),
horizontal explorer bars (comm bands), and desk bands. The only difference
between the band types is where they show up in the shell. Info and comm
bands appear in Explorer and allow you to do things such as search the Internet via various search engines or go to your favorite sites. They can also be

---

1. From here on out, I will refer to Internet Explorer and Windows Explorer by the
general term *Explorer*. In Windows 98, Windows 2000, and any version of Windows
that has IE Desktop integration, these two programs are more or less the same.

used as a navigation tool for a Web-based application. For example, an info band could discover all the database servers on your network and let you go to their various HTML-based configuration screens by selecting one of the database servers.

Comm bands should not allow user input if they are used on the bottom of the Explorer window. Instead, they perform functions like displaying a stock ticker, displaying connection information, or other functions involving the display of information. Returning to the database server example, a comm band might go out and find those same servers that you have access to. This time, the comm band displays server statistics: number of concurrent users, processor load, etc. These bands can also be used to add toolbars to Explorer.

12.1   Band Object Basics

A band object must implement a given set of interfaces. At a minimum, it must implement the following interfaces:

- IDeskBand
- IObjectWithSite
- IPersistStream

If the band object wants to accept user input, it must also implement IInputObject. In order to add items to the context menu, it must implement IContextMenu. Because some of these interfaces inherit from other interfaces, you must also implement all functions defined by the class's ancestors as well. See Figure 12-1 for a full picture of what is going on. After seeing all the interfaces that a band object can implement, one has to ask *Why?* One by one, we will cover the interfaces and what they give us. For the sake of this discussion, I assume that you understand IUnknown and what it does. If you need to come up to speed on COM basics, please take some time now to read Crispin Goswell's "The COM Programmer's Cookbook" article, available on MSDN. All the interfaces on Figure 12-1, except for IDeskBand, are covered in Appendix A of this book.

12.1.1   IDeskBand

The IDeskBand interface exists only to make creation of this special docking window easy for the implementer of the interface. IDockingWindow, IDeskBand's parent class, must acquire and release space within the parent window. Additionally, an IDockingWindow object must always keep its parent up to date on how much space the IDockingWindow window occupies. On the surface, this may sound like an easy job. I have a feeling that imple-

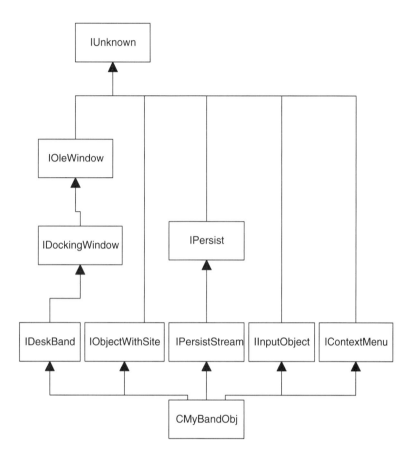

Figure 12–1   *Interfaces inheritance hierarchy for a band object.*

menting this is as difficult as creating and maintaining the space occupied by an application toolbar (Chapter 3, "Application Desktop Toobars"). Given my previous experience, I appreciate the IDeskBand interface. To satisfy the IDeskBand requirements, objects have one method they must implement. That method is GetBandInfo. GetBandInfo has the following signature:

```
HRESULT GetBandInfo(
DWORD dwBandID,
DWOR dwViewMode,
DESKBANDINFO* pdbi)
```

Parameters:

dwBandID: The parent uses this to uniquely identify the band object. The band object can keep this value if it is required.

dwViewMode: The caller uses this to communicate the way that the band object will now be displayed. The view mode may be one of the following values:

- **DBIF_VIEWMODE_NORMAL:** The band object is being displayed in a horizontal band.
- **DBIF_VIEWMODE_VERTICAL:** The band object is being displayed in a vertical band.
- **DBIF_VIEWMODE_FLOATING:** The band object is being displayed in a floating band.
- **DBIF_VIEWMODE_TRANSPARENT:** The band object is being displayed in a transparent band.

pdbi: Address of a DESKBANDINFO structure that the object should populate for the caller. The dwMask member of the structure indicates what information is being requested.

Returns:

Returns NOERROR if successful. Otherwise, returns an OLE-defined error code.

The DESKBANDINFO structure saves you most of the work. The structure defines the basic characteristics about how little or how much room the desk band can occupy. It also relates information regarding what title and background color the container should use for your band object. DESKBANDINFO looks like this:

```
typedef struct {
  DWORD dwMask;
  POINTL ptMinSize;
  POINTL ptMaxSize;
  POINTL ptIntegral;
  POINTL ptActual;
  WCHAR wszTitle[256];
  DWORD dwModeFlags;
  COLORREF crBkgnd;
} DESKBANDINFO;
```

Members:

dwMask: Indicates what members are being requested. More often than not, the requestor asks for everything. dwMask can have any combination of the following values:

- **DBIM_MINSIZE:** The requestor wants the value for ptMinSize.
- **DBIM_MAXSIZE:** The requestor wants the value for ptMaxSize.
- **DBIM_INTEGRAL:** The requestor wants the value for ptIntegral.
- **DBIM_ACTUAL:** The requestor wants the value for ptActual.
- **DBIM_TITLE:** The requestor wants the value for wszTitle.

- **DBIM_MODEFLAGS:** The requestor wants the value for dw-ModeFlags.
- **DBIM_BKCOLOR:** The requestor wants the value for crBkgnd. When GetBandInfo gets called requesting the background color, you can tell the caller *no, you can't have that* by setting this bit to zero (`pdbi->dwMask &= ~DBIM_BKCOLOR`).

ptMinSize: This member communicates the minimum size of the band object. Place the minimum height in the *y* member and the minimum width in the *x* member.

ptMaxSize: This member only tells the caller what the maximum height is. No limits are placed on the width. If there is no limit on the height, set the *y* member to –1.

ptIntegral: This member tells the caller the sizing step of the band object. Like ptMaxSize, only the vertical part, ptIntegral.y, matters. The caller ignores this member if dwModeFlags does not have the DBIMF_VARIABLEHEIGHT flag set.

ptActual: This specifies the ideal height and width of the band object. The band container will try to use these values, but it makes no guarantees. If you are worried about an absolute minimum, set ptMinSize. I always set both the *x* and *y* values of this member to zero.

wszTitle: Holds the title of the band object. This title is used when the band is displayed within Explorer or on the taskbar. The taskbar and Explorer get the menu display values from the registry.

dwModeFlags: These flags specify the mode of operation for the band object. This must be a combination of one or more of these values:

- **DBIMF_NORMAL:** This is a normal, run-of-the-mill band object.
- **DBIMF_VARIABLEHEIGHT:** The height of the band object can only be changed by the integral height specified in ptIntegral.
- **DBIMF_DEBOSSED:** The band object is displayed with a sunken appearance.
- **DBIMF_BKCOLOR:** The band will be displayed with the background color specified in crBkgnd.

crBkgnd: Specifies the background color of the band. If dwModeFlags does not have DBIMF_BKCOLOR set, the caller ignores this member.

Given the information that a band object returns via IDeskBand::GetBandInfo, the container can negotiate the available area itself. As a side benefit, the container never calls IDockingWindow::ResizeBorderDW. A band object should always return E_NOTIMPL from this method. You only need to satisfy the interface requirements to make the compiler happy.

12.1.2   ICatRegister

ICatRegister, an interface implemented by Windows, provides a means to register and unregister component category information, which is stored in the registry. Think of a component category as a family of objects. Each object that claims membership in the category has certain features that they implement. The owner of a category uses ICatRegister to add and remove component categories. The implementer of a category uses ICatRegister to communicate what category or categories it implements. You can see the end result of this collaboration in the OLE/COM Object Viewer, OLEVIEW.EXE, in Figure 12-2. Here, we can see the various Desktop Bands that are installed on my machine.

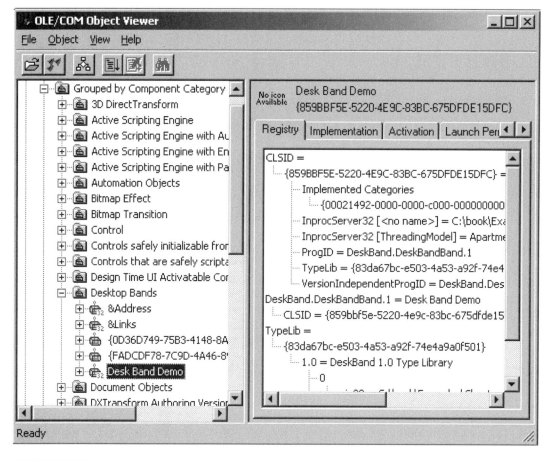

Figure 12–2   *View of the various component categories in use.*

For our purposes, we are only interested in two of ICatRegister's methods: RegisterClassImplCategories and UnRegisterClassImplCategories. An implementer of a category registers the fact that it implements the specified category by calling ICatRegister::RegisterClassImplCategories. A client of a given category discovers the implementers via the ICatInformation interface. The two ICatRegister methods we care about look like this:

```
HRESULT RegisterClassImplCategories(
    REFCLSID rclsid,
    ULONG cCategories,
    CATID* rgcatid
);
```

Parameters:

rclsid: The class ID of the class that implements the category or categories.

cCategories: The number of category CATIDs to associate as category identifiers for the class.

rgcatid: The array of cCategories CATID to associate as category identifiers for the class.

Return Values:
- **S_OK:** The function succeeded.
- **E_INVALIDARG:** One or more arguments are incorrect.

```
HRESULT UnRegisterClassImplCategories(
    REFCLSID rclsid,
    ULONG cCategories,
    CATID* rgcatid
);
```

Parameters:

rclsid: The class ID, i.e., CLSID, of the class that implements the category or categories.

cCategories: The number of category CATIDs to associate as category identifiers for the class.

rgcatid: The array of cCategories CATID to remove as category identifiers for the class. This only removes the associations of the CATIDs specified by the list.

Return Values:
- **S_OK:** The function succeeded.
- **E_INVALIDARG:** One or more arguments are incorrect.

ICatRegister uses the CATID (category ID) to map the CLSID to the CATID. CATID is the name for the GUID that uniquely identifies a category. In your COM component, you register your component as an implementer of the category through ICatRegister in the call to DllRegisterServer. Likewise, you unregister the component with the category in the call to DllUnregisterServer. If your component is implemented by an EXE, then you would look for the /RegServer and /UnregServer command line options to register or unregister the component.[2]

When using ICatRegister, your component will register one of three CATIDs:

- **CATID_DeskBand:** Implements a toolbar for the taskbar. Active Desktop needs to be installed to utilize this type of band object. You do not have to have the Desktop set up to "View as Web Page."
- **CATID_InfoBand:** Implements a vertical toolbar in Explorer, version 4.0 or later. These toolbars typically allow some form of user interaction.
- **CATID_CommBand:** Implements a horizontal toolbar in Explorer, version 4.0 or later. These toolbars typically display information only. The toolbar may exist at the bottom of the window as a comm band or with the toolbars as a toolbar.

12.1.3   Communicating With the Container

Band objects can communicate with their container (the taskbar or Explorer) through the container's IOleCommandTarget interface. You can get a pointer to the interface by calling QueryInterface() on the IInputObjectSite passed to the band through the IDeskBand::SetSite() method. These commands depend on your code storing the band ID passed into the most recent call of IDeskBand::GetBandInfo(). Using the IOleCommandTarget::Exec() method, you can send one of three commands to the container:

- **DBID_BANDINFOCHANGED:** Notifies the container that some of the band's information has changed. This will force a call into IDeskBand::GetBandInfo() from the container. The call will be:

```
_variant_t theVar = static_cast<long>(bandID);
pCmdTgt->Exec( &CGID_DeskBand, DBID_BANDINFOCHANGED,
    OLECMDEXECOPT_DODEFAULT,
    &theVar, NULL );
```

---

2. If you are looking at building an extensible framework like Internet Explorer, you might want to look into using ICatRegister and its companion, ICatInformation, to aid you in the endeavor. An article on how to create extensible applications, "Create Apps That Are Easily Extensible with Our Smart 'Snap-Ins' Methodology," by Steve Zimmerman, appeared in the July, 1997 *Microsoft Systems Journal*.

- **DBID_MAXIMIZEBAND:** Tells the container to set the band to its maximum height/width. The call will be:

```
_variant_t theVar = static_cast<long>(bandID);
pCmdTgt->Exec( &CGID_DeskBand, DBID_MAXIMIZEBAND,
        OLECMDEXECOPT_DODEFAULT,
        &theVar, NULL );
```

- **DBID_SHOWONLY:** Asks the container to hide or show some or all of the bands. To hide all bands but one (identified by pBand) use the following code:

```
CComPtr<IUnknown> pUnknown;
pBand->QueryInterface( IID_IUnknown, (LPVOID*)&pUnknown );
_variant_t theVar = pUnknown;
pCmdTgt->Exec( &CGID_DeskBand, DBID_SHOWONLY,
        OLECMDEXECOPT_DODEFAULT,
        &theVar, NULL );
```

To hide all the bands, set `theVar` equal to `(long)0`. To show all the bands, set `theVar` equal to `(long)1`.

12.2 Creating a Band Object

If you want to create a band object, you have a number of choices. Gauging newsgroup traffic on the *msnews.microsoft.com* server indicates that most people who have done this have taken the SDK sample, BandObjs, and modified it for their own purposes. A few others have taken the SDK sample as a reference for what needs to be done and then implemented it using ATL, MFC, or Visual Basic. Regardless of the approach you take, you must implement the interfaces depicted in Figure 12-1, register your COM module, and register the COM module as an implementer of CATID_DeskBand, CATID_InfoBand, or CATID_CommBand.

I first created a solid, basic implementation of a band object and then analyzed the resulting code. I used a healthy mixture of ATL and MFC to build my first band object. I used ATL to do all the COM related stuff and MFC to handle most of my window related stuff. Then I looked for the things that I believed would be constant from implementation to implementation. I also looked for things that could be customized through user input from a wizard.

To show what code comprises the boilerplate part of creating band objects, I will use the Band Object Wizard (ATL/MFC) that I wrote to generate a vanilla project. When looking at this code, keep in mind that I implemented one of many ways to get the project done right. (The generated code is not included on the CD because Visual C++ will generate this code whenever you use the Band Object Wizard to create a project.)

To create the project, follow these steps:

- Select the *Band Object Wizard (ATL/MFC)* and set the project name to *BoilerPlate*
- Press OK.
- Make sure that Desk Band is selected and that the Display Name is set to Boiler Plate. For an example, see Figure 12-3.
- Click Finish and let the wizard generate the code.

You now have the code that we will begin to examine by looking at the generated code. The tour will progress in the following order:

- Registry entries
- Registration/unregistration code
- Implementation class header file
- Implementation class source file

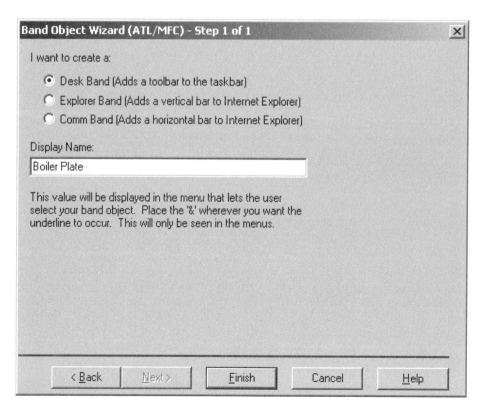

Figure 12–3   *Setting up the BiolerPlate project.*

12.2.1 Registry Entries

The Band Object wizard creates a DLL to house the object. DLLs that use ATL typically register and unregister the various COM objects in the calls to Dll-RegisterServer and DllUnregisterServer, respectively. The object CBoilerPlate-Band has the following declaration in its header file:

```
DECLARE_REGISTRY_RESOURCEID(IDR_BOILERPLATEBAND)
```

This declaration states that the registration information for this object is contained in the resource identified by IDR_BOILERPLATEBAND, which maps to the file BoilerPlateBand.rgs. BoilerPlateBand.rgs contains the registry entries that the CComModule object needs to add or remove. Here are the contents of that file:

```
HKCR
{
    [lines for creation by name removed]
    NoRemove CLSID
    {
        ForceRemove {3c52e6fd-03ba-45c1-89ac-1ec8915dc230} =
            s 'Boiler Plate'
        {
            ProgID = s 'BoilerPlate.BoilerPlateBand.1'
            VersionIndependentProgID =
                s 'BoilerPlate.BoilerPlateBand'
            InprocServer32 = s '%MODULE%'
            {
                val ThreadingModel = s 'Apartment'
            }
            'TypeLib' =
                s '{b4541a9b-f0fc-4419-8957-f1e039ab0e6f}'
            'Implemented Categories'
            {
                '{00021492-0000-0000-c000-000000000046}'
            }
        }
    }
}
HKLM
{
    'SOFTWARE'
    {
        'Microsoft'
        {
            'Windows'
            {
                'CurrentVersion'
                {
                    'Shell Extensions'
```

```
                    {
                      'Approved'
                      {
        val '{3c52e6fd-03ba-45c1-89ac-1ec8915dc230}' =
            s 'BoilerPlate.BoilerPlateBand'
                      }
                  }
              }
          }
      }
  }
```

The first section adds information to the HKEY_CLASSES_ROOT hive. It creates a new key using the CLSID as the name of the key. The text following the key *Boiler Plate* was entered in using the wizard dialog in Figure 12-3. If I had entered an ampersand, it would have appeared within the string, too. Explorer and the taskbar use this string as the display text for the given item. The taskbar displays this string in the Toolbars submenu (see Figure 12-4). Explorer displays available band objects in the View→Explorer Bar submenu (see Figure 12-5).

The InprocServer32 section states that this band object uses the Apartment threading model. (All shell extensions must use the Apartment threading model.) Following the InprocServer32 section, we see the familiar TypeLib identifier. The last piece in HKEY_CLASSES_ROOT is the Implemented Categories section. Here, we declare that this object implements CATID_DeskBand. The conversion from CATID symbol to the GUID version was performed in the wizard with this line:

```
UuidToString( const_cast<GUID*>(&CATID_DeskBand), &catID );
```

Figure 12-4   *The toolbars menu.*

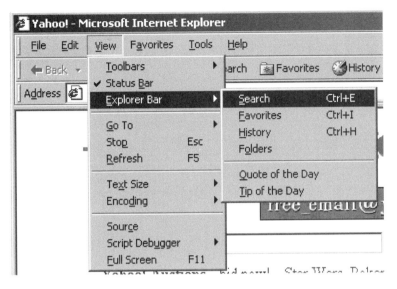

Figure 12–5   *The band objects available from Explorer.*

UuidToString generates a string version of the GUID and populates an unsigned char array with the final value. The generated string was added to the wizard's dictionary and added to the code using the new keyword. You can examine this piece of the magic by looking at the Band Object Wizard project's PPGBandObjectType::OnDismiss() method.

BoilerPlateBand.rgs also adds a value to the HKEY_LOCAL_MACHINE registry hive. This single entry simply states that the shell extension is approved for usage on the machine. Under Windows 2000, if you want to enable the shell extension to be available for use only for the current user, then alter the generated script to put this information under HKEY_CURRENT_USER. This is true for all shell extensions, not just band objects.

12.2.2   Registration/Unregistration Code

During registration and unregistration, the band object DLL needs to inform the shell that your extension exists and what band object category (CATID_DeskBand, CATID_InfoBand, or CATID_CommBand) your class implements. Your DLL performs this magic by registering the category with the ICatRegister object. For this purpose, I borrowed the RegisterComCat function from the SDK BandObjs example and modified it to be able to register and unregister implementers of a category. (The original version only allowed for registering an implementer of a category.) The code to register and unregister the server is fairly simple:

```
STDAPI DllRegisterServer(void)
{
    // registers object, typelib and all interfaces in
    // typelib
    if(!RegisterComCat(CLSID_BoilerPlateBand,
        CATID_DeskBand, true))
    {
        return SELFREG_E_CLASS;
    }
    return _Module.RegisterServer(TRUE);
}


STDAPI DllUnregisterServer(void)
{
    if(!RegisterComCat(CLSID_BoilerPlateBand,
        CATID_DeskBand, false))
    {
        return SELFREG_E_CLASS;
    }
    return _Module.UnregisterServer(TRUE);
}


BOOL RegisterComCat(CLSID clsid, CATID CatID, bool bRegister)
{
    ICatRegister *pcr;
    HRESULT     hr = S_OK ;

    hr = CoCreateInstance( CLSID_StdComponentCategoriesMgr,
        NULL,
        CLSCTX_INPROC_SERVER,
        IID_ICatRegister,
        (LPVOID*)&pcr );
    if(SUCCEEDED(hr))
    {
        if ( bRegister )
        {
            hr = pcr->RegisterClassImplCategories(clsid, 1,
                &CatID);
        }
        else
        {
            hr = pcr->UnRegisterClassImplCategories( clsid,
                1, &CatID );
        }
        pcr->Release();
    }


    return SUCCEEDED(hr);
}
```

As you can see, there is nothing special here. However, you must implement similar code each and every time that you implement a band object. The wizard automatically generates all the code in the CWinApp derived class. The only thing you may need to do to this file is place a call to CWinApp::SetRegistryKey to set up the application to use the registry. RegisterComCat handles the actual conversation between the DLL and ICatRegister.

I modified the original SDK example's version of RegisterComCat by adding the `bool bRegister` parameter. If the caller sets the parameter to true, the code registers the CLSID as implementing the CATID. Otherwise, the code unregisters the CLSID. The other line in DllRegisterServer and DllUnRegisterServer calls the CComModule instance and tells it to register any and all classes in its object map.

12.2.3 Implementation Class Header File

The header file that declares the implementer of the band object (in our case, CBoilerPlateBand) uses ATL and MFC. Because the code does not have the requirement of operating on a Web page, I chose to do the COM parts of the project using ATL and the user interface parts using MFC. In an opinion I have stated many times, a person who really understands MFC can use this library to produce great user interface code. ATL will allow you to create easy to understand COM code, but requires more labor than MFC for user interface code. Likewise, you can create COM code with MFC, but the job gets done quicker using ATL. For these reasons, the generated band is 100 percent MFC for the user interface and 100 percent ATL for the COM interface.

The generated CBoilerPlateBand class, like many ATL classes, uses multiple-inheritance to declare its capabilities. The top part of CBoilerPlateBand's class declaration looks like this:

```
class ATL_NO_VTABLE CBoilerPlateBand :
    public CComObjectRootEx<CComSingleThreadModel>,
    public CComCoClass<CBoilerPlateBand,
        &CLSID_BoilerPlateBand>,
    public IBoilerPlateBand,
    public CDeskBandImpl,
    public IObjectWithSiteImpl<CBoilerPlateBand>,
    public CPersistStreamImpl<CBoilerPlateBand>,
    public CInputObjectImpl
```

The first two classes in the derivation provide for a lot of the basic COM functionality, such as handling IUnknown and getting the object's CLSID. The class relies on the ShellExtension library, introduced in Chapter 7, "Shell Extensions," Section 7.1. CBoilerPlateBand uses the following classes from the library:

- **CDeskBandImpl:** Only declares the required functions. All implementations return E_NOTIMPL and supply a trace statement to the debug window.
- **CPersistStreamImpl:** This class only handles the IsDirty() and GetClassID() functions. You are responsible for maintaining the dirty bit and writing any Load or Save code.
- **CInputObjectImpl:** Only declares the required functions. All implementations return E_NOTIMPL and supply a trace statement to the debug window.

In the body of the class declaration, we see the constructor, destructor, and the functions that the derived class must implement (pure virtual functions). The documentation for the various methods can be found in Appendix A. The documentation for IDeskBand is located in this chapter in Section 12.1.1.

```
CBoilerPlateBand();
~CBoilerPlateBand();

// IDeskBand methods
   STDMETHOD(GetWindow)(HWND* pHwnd);
STDMETHOD(ContextSensitiveHelp)(BOOL);
STDMETHOD(ShowDW)(BOOL fShow);
STDMETHOD(CloseDW)(DWORD dwReserved);
STDMETHOD(GetBandInfo)(DWORD dwBandID,
    DWORD dwViewMode,
    DESKBANDINFO* pdbi);

// IObjectWithSite methods
STDMETHOD(SetSite)(IUnknown* punkSite);

// IInputObject methods
STDMETHOD(UIActivateIO)(BOOL fActivate, LPMSG pMsg);
STDMETHOD(HasFocusIO)();

bool m_bRequiresSave;
```

Following the declarations of the required functions, we see a declaration for the variable m_bRequiresSave. CBoilerPlateBand uses this variable to communicate the need to save the object map to the CPersistStreamImpl base class. The class will store the data in the property map whenever this value is set to true.[3] Section 12.4 contains an example showing how to use the property map.

In the generated band object's private section, we find a pair of helper methods and a few data members:

---

3. This store only gets called for desk bands.

```
DWORD m_dwBandID;    // remembers the band ID (see
                     // IDeskBand::GetBandInfo)
bool m_bFocus;       // Knows if the band has the input
                     // focus
bool CreateTheWindow();
CComPtr<IInputObjectSite> m_pSite; // remembers the site
                     // pointer
HWND m_hwndParent;   // Remembers the parent window
CBoilerPlateWnd m_wndBand; // The band's user interface
void FocusChange(BOOL); // informs the site when focus
                     // changes
```

12.2.4 Implementation Class Source File

I hate to say it, but the actual code does not do much. Odds are fairly good that an average band object will never need to touch the bulk of the code. So, instead of boring you with things you will never touch, let's look at the interesting methods. This discussion will skip over the GetBandInfo method since it was discussed earlier in this chapter. You will modify this method to set minimum widths, menu text, and other items. The Desk Band and Communication Band examples presented in Sections 12.3 and 12.4 show some of the things you may want to do with this method.

The first method you will probably change is CreateTheWindow. In the implementation of SetSite, we can be fairly certain that we have not created our client window yet. When the site gets set, SetSite calls CreateTheWindow.

```
bool CBoilerPlateBand::CreateTheWindow()
{
    AFX_MANAGE_STATE(AfxGetStaticModuleState( ));
    CRect rect;
    CWnd* pWnd = CWnd::FromHandle( m_hwndParent );
    pWnd->GetClientRect( rect );
    bool retval = false;
    retval = m_wndBand.Create( NULL, "BoilerPlateBand",
        WS_CHILD | WS_VISIBLE, rect, pWnd, 100 ) != 0;
    return retval;
}
```

The call to AFX_MANAGE_STATE just makes sure that any information needed by MFC calls has been properly set. The MFC calls need to execute in the context of the DLL, not the container application. In general, if you add a method that uses MFC and then start getting assertion errors when an AfxXXX function gets called, you probably need to add AFX_MANAGE_STATE to the beginning of your method. The code above just creates a new window that occupies the owner's client area. You will want to create any child windows that you need to use in the WM_CREATE handler of the MFC-based window (in our case, CBoilerPlateWnd).

The only other area that I imagine you would need to worry about is handling context menus and making any information persistent across invocations. One word of warning—it appears that Explorer does not invoke any of the IPersistStream functionality. What this means is that you are on your own to come up with a persistence mechanism for comm bands and explorer bands. The taskbar does call into the desk band's IPersistStream interface to load and save the band object. This interface is entirely implemented by CPersistStreamImpl, leaving you to populate the property map. With the explorer bands, I save data as soon as possible. This does mean using files or registry entries that are under my control—not under the control of Explorer. Hence, when listing things to be removed by the uninstall program, be sure to remove any tribbles you create in the course of running your band object.

Creating a context menu is fairly simple. The interface itself is covered fairly well in Appendix A and in Section 7.2 (Context Menu Handlers).[4] I want to cover what I believe is the most non-intuitive thing about implementing this interface: you do not actually create the context menu as would happen in response to a WM_CONTEXTMENU message. Instead, you are adding to an existing menu. This was a bit of a surprise to me the first time I implemented the interface. Here comes the part that really confused me: identifying the commands and executing the correct response to a command. IContextMenu::QueryContextMenu passes in the minimum and maximum values for any of your command IDs. As long as your ID is in that range, everything is cool. When IContextMenu::InvokeCommand or IContextMenu::GetCommandString get called, what value do you process? To answer the question, let's look at how we implement the menu. In the IContextMenu::QueryContextMenu implementation, you insert menu items using code like this:

```
InsertMenu( hMenu,
    indexMenu,
    MF_STRING | MF_BYPOSITION,
    idCmdFirst + FIRST_COMMAND_ID,
    "&Sample Desk Band Command");
```

My intuition told me that any processing would have to be done based on the value of idCmdFirst + FIRST_COMMAND_ID. That is not how things work. Instead, the context menu items are called based on the value of FIRST_COMMAND_ID (or whatever value you provide). As an aside, if you ever implement a mechanism that allows other apps to plug into a menu of any sort, follow this model. It's an official Good Idea™.

The window that implements your band object's user interface starts out life fairly dry. The CBoilerPlateWnd class has the following declaration (unused ClassWizard parts cut out for clarity):

---

4. If you do implement a context menu, make sure that you read Section 7.2. You will find a lot more useful information there.

```
class CBoilerPlateWnd : public CWnd
{
// Construction
public:
      CBoilerPlateWnd();

// Implementation
public:
      // Called to set the view mode from the
      // COM object as passed into IDeskBand::GetBandInfo
        void SetViewMode( DWORD viewMode );
        virtual ~CBoilerPlateWnd();

        // Generated message map functions
protected:
      //{{AFX_MSG(CBoilerPlateWnd)
      afx_msg BOOL OnEraseBkgnd(CDC* pDC);
      //}}AFX_MSG
      DECLARE_MESSAGE_MAP()

private:
      // Stores the view type:
      DWORD m_dwViewType;
};
```

SetViewMode will just copy the value into m_dwViewType. This allows the band to lay itself out properly for horizontal, vertical, or floating layouts. The OnEraseBackground method just displays some text and sets the background. More than anything else, providing the feedback lets you know if the band registered itself and if things are working properly. You get the same type of instant feedback from most AppWizard generated projects and this is no exception.

```
BOOL CBoilerPlateWnd::OnEraseBkgnd(CDC* pDC)
{
    // Get the rectangle area.
    CRect rect;
    GetClientRect( rect );

    // Fill the rect with the dialog background color.
    COLORREF backColor = GetSysColor(COLOR_3DFACE);
    CBrush brush( backColor );
    pDC->FillRect( rect, &brush );
    pDC->SetBkColor( backColor );

    // Display some text to show that things are working.
    pDC->DrawText( _T("TODO: Implement band object."),
        rect, DT_CENTER | DT_VCENTER );
    return TRUE;
}
```

That covers the basics of creating a band object and what the wizard creates for you. The wizard does not do two things that you must do yourself.

- The wizard does not generate the registry code to create a toolbar for Explorer.
- The wizard does not generate the registry code needed to create an HTML based band object.

Handling the first, a toolbar, is easy. Use the wizard to generate a comm band. Once that is done, you will need to open up the band's RGS script and add a few lines. The script will already have the code to navigate to the HKLM\Software\Microsoft folder. When you are done, that part of the script must look like this:

```
... [code to add object under HKCR is here]
}
HKLM
{
    'SOFTWARE'
    {
        'Microsoft'
        {
            'Internet Explorer'
            {
                'Toolbar'
                {
                val '{0d8c64e5-57a5-4582-ad00-39fd32c1a8c0}' =
                    s 'CommRadio.CommRadioBand'
                }
            }
            'Windows'
            {
[script to register object as approved goes here, and will be here if
you used the wizard]
```

The lines between "Internet Explorer" and "Windows"' move your comm band from the bottom of the window to the top. Unlike bottom aligned comm bands or explorer bands, you can have as many "top of the screen" comm bands as you like. This is easy enough. The bare bones band that I created can be seen in Figure 12-6.

What if you want to display HTML based bands? If you came this far to find out how to do this, I apologize. You can forget any C++ that you know because you do not need it. Instead, you can just write the HTML as needed and then create a REG file. I have included the one for this example in the Examples\Chapter 12 directory. First, you need to decide what type of band you will implement.

- **CATID_DeskBand:** {00021492-0000-0000-c000-000000000046}
- **CATID_InfoBand:** {00021493-0000-0000-c000-000000000046}
- **CATID_CommBand:** {00021494-0000-0000-c000-000000000046}

Figure 12–6   *A bare bones tool band.*

Next, you need to decide where the HTML will reside. The easiest thing to do is put it somewhere within one of the folders included in the path. That way, you do not need to specify the exact folder the file lives in. Finally, you need to create a GUID so that the information can be stored in the registry properly. One way to do this is to go to a command prompt and type

```
uuidgen > guid.txt
```

GUID.TXT will contain the generated GUID. For this example, we will use the GUID I generated, 6f1d64ed-40ee-48df-aef2-b93e19c87575. The following script works under Windows 2000. I have used a trailing underscore, "_", to indicate a line continuation. For your own scripts, this trick will not work and all statements must appear on a single line. All comments are in italics and prefaced with a "//". Again, this does not work for real registry files, but does help for illustrative purposes.

```
REGEDIT4

// The following lines create the textual name and set the
// string as it will be displayed within Explorer
 [HKEY_CLASSES_ROOT\CLSID\{6f1d64ed-40ee-48df-aef2- _
   b93e19c87575}]
@="Prentice Hall Example"

// The next two entries setup the type of bar.
[HKEY_CLASSES_ROOT\CLSID\{6f1d64ed-40ee-48df-aef2- _
   b93e19c87575}\Implemented Categories]
```

```
// Part of the "type of bar" entry, change the GUID after
// "Implemented Categories" to get something besides an
// info band.
[HKEY_CLASSES_ROOT\CLSID\{6f1d64ed-40ee-48df-aef2- _
   b93e19c87575}\Implemented Categories\{00021493-0000-0000-_
   c000-000000000046}]


// An HTML band is implemented by Shdocvw.dll, which is why
// we don't have to write any C||!!!
[HKEY_CLASSES_ROOT\CLSID\{6f1d64ed-40ee-48df-aef2- _
   b93e19c87575}\InprocServer32]
@="c:\\winnt\\system32\\Shdocvw.dll"
"ThreadingModel"="Apartment"


// This identifies the IDeskBand object within Shdocvw.dll
[HKEY_CLASSES_ROOT\CLSID\{6f1d64ed-40ee-48df-aef2- _
   b93e19c87575}\Instance]
"CLSID"="{4D5C8C2A-D075-11D0-B416-00C04FB90376}"


// This tells Shdocvw.dll which HTML page should be used with
// the band object.
[HKEY_CLASSES_ROOT\CLSID\{6f1d64ed-40ee-48df-aef2- _
   b93e19c87575}\Instance\InitPropertyBag]
"Url"="c:\\PH.html"
```

This script is located in the Examples\Chapter 12\HTMLBand\-PHBand.REG file. You do not need to register the class with the category manager—SHDocvw.dll has already taken care of this task. You can set the minimum width or height through the following binary registry value:

```
HKCU\Software\Microsoft\Internet Explorer\Explorer Bars\[CLSID of bar]\ BarSize
```

To set the default width to 291 pixels, you would set the value to 23, 01, 00, 00, 00, 00, 00, 00. Do not waste your time setting this value—if the user resizes the band object, that new size becomes the default.

12.3 Debugging Band Objects

Debugging a band object is not all that hard. The problem lies with the fact that the average programmer does not write tons of band objects. To debug a band object you need to know how install it, start it, and trace into it. Fortunately, you already know how to trace into a band object: you have the debugger start up the calling application and you place breakpoints into your code. When the calling application executes your code, the breakpoints fire. To debug a comm band or info band, use Explorer. If you set Internet Explorer as your default Web browser, you can select it as the debug executable by telling Visual Studio to use your default Web browser (see Figure 12-7). To

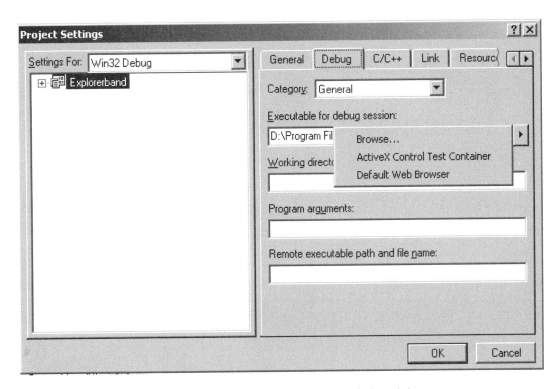

Figure 12–7   *When debugging comm or info bands, use the default Web browser.*

debug a desk band, set the *Executable for debug session* to EXPLORER.EXE. EXPLORER.EXE should be located in the primary Windows directory (usually Windows or WinNT). So, how do you do the hard stuff?

In order to install a band object, something has to run REGSVR32 [dll name] to invoke DllRegisterServer. This can be done from the command line, from an installation program, or by some other means. Typically, Visual Studio will register the object after a successful build. The project will usually have a step indicated on the Custom Build tab of the Project Settings dialog that invokes REGSVR32 as shown in Figure 12-8. Once the band object has been registered, we have to make the taskbar or Explorer see it. We could reboot our machines to do this or we could try something else. To force recognition of the band object we can do the following:

- [This step applies to desk bands only] Run REGEDIT and go to the following entry: **Windows NT and 9x**

HKCR\Component Categories\{00021492-0000-0000-C000-000000000046};
  Windows 2000
HKCU\Software\Microsoft\Windows\CurrentVersion\Explorer\Discardable\

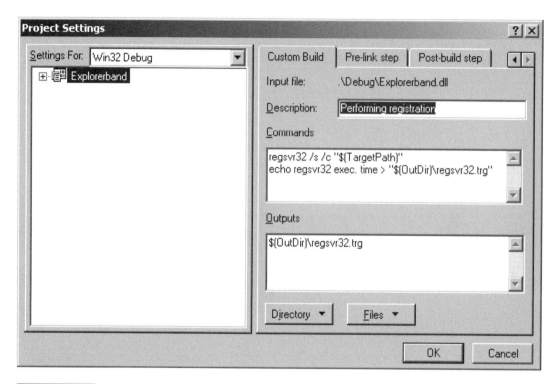

Figure 12–8 *Setting your band object to register itself after a successful compile and link.*

PostSetup\Component Categories\{00021492-0000-0000-C000-000000000046}.
If the category CLSID changes, just make sure that the string value named "400" is set to "Desktop Bands". Delete the "Enum" subkey. Close REGEDIT.

- Close all instances of Internet Explorer and Explorer.
- Shutdown the taskbar. You can either kill the EXPLORER.EXE process or do it the right way. To do it the right way, select Start→Shut Down. When the Shut Down screen comes up, press [SHIFT]+[CTRL]+[ALT]+[ESC]. This kills the taskbar.
- Startup EXPLORER.EXE. The first time Explorer starts up, it updates information about any installed band objects. To start EXPLORER.EXE, I recommend using the Microsoft Office toolbar and having EXPLORER.EXE as one of the buttons. If you do not have Microsoft Office installed, I have included an Application Desktop Toolbar called ExplorerStarter.EXE in the CD's Tools folder. The application took all of three minutes to write—it just calls ShellExecute.

A more pleasant alternative is to use the band object wizard. The wizard generates code in the registry script to delete the correct Enum subkey. For safety, it tries to delete the key from the Windows 9x/Windows NT and Windows 2000 locations. Once this is done, you do not need to stop Explorer—it will refresh the list automatically.

At this point, your band object should be registered. You only need to do the above steps each time you create a new band object. To have modifications made visible, you only need to stop and restart the target. For desk bands, you will need to kill the taskbar as described above. For explorer bands and comm bands, just exit Explorer. All new changes should happen at the DLL level—the registry will already be up to date.

In order to start your band object, you will have to know where to look for it. Desk bands always appear in the Toolbars part of the taskbar's context menu (Figure 12-4). Explorer bands appear in the top part of Explorer's View→Explorer Bar menu (Figure 12-5). Comm bands appear in the bottom of that same menu. By selecting the band, you will now be able to see and debug it—assuming that you started the caller from Visual Studio. Explorer usually remembers what band objects were up last time the program started. As a result, you may not have to select your band object to get it to show up. If you always have to select the band object, then someone set an advanced security setting only available from the Explorer Administrator Kit. At this point in time, I have no idea how to undo this option. I'd appreciate any information you may have about this.[5]

When testing desk bands, make sure you try dragging the desk band off of the taskbar and make sure you like the way it behaves. To drag a desk band, make sure that you are dragging the band object to the Desktop. The Desktop is a drop target for the band object. Most applications will not allow you to drag a desk band and drop it on the application window. To drag the desk band, simply click near the rebar grabber and drag to the Desktop. Then see what happens.

From here on out, you should be able to debug your band object using your normal techniques. If sizing seems to be a problem, go back and read the information in Section 12.1.1 about IDeskBand::GetBandInfo. Odds are pretty good that you have one of the size options off by a bit.[6]

To this point, we have covered the various band objects and their interfaces. We then went over a wizard that creates the bands for you. We are ready to build an actual functioning band object now.

---

5. Send the answer to *scott.seely@technologist.com.*

6. Pun intended.

12.4 Desk Band Example

Of the four band object types (explorer, comm, info, and desk), the desk band is the hardest to create. Desk bands support persistence and have to be able to display horizontally or vertically since the user can dock one on any edge of the screen. This does not make the desk band that much more difficult than the others, but it does give us a chance to go over the various things you might want to do with a band object. Our example will demonstrate how to show and hide desk bands on the taskbar using the taskbar's IOleCommandTarget interface.[7]

      To build the project, start up Visual C++ and create a new project using the Band Object Wizard (ATL/MFC). Call the project *DeskBand* and click on OK. Set up the next screen as shown in Figure 12-9 and click on Finish, then

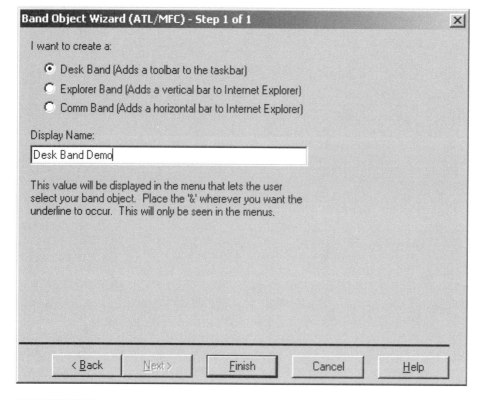

Figure 12–9   *Setting up the example.*

---

7. See Section 12.1.3 for more information on using IOleCommandTarget with band objects.

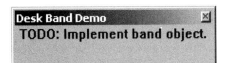

Figure 12–10 *The default desk band in action.*

OK again. At this point, you have a working desk band. Just to test things out, build it and then try to make it appear. (Right-click on the taskbar and select Toolbars→Desk Band Demo.) You should see something similar to Figure 12-10 (shown detached from the taskbar). Next, we have make it do something. The band will have two buttons: one to hide desk bands and one to redisplay them. It will also have a text window that remembers a string between invocations, demonstrating how to use the persistence mechanism. When you implement persistence, you need to understand that the taskbar only stores information on desk bands that are being destroyed as a result of the taskbar shutting down. If you close a desk band, the taskbar will not store any information. This fact comes in handy when you need to remove a bad bunch of data from the IStream presented to your IPersistStream::Load() and Save() methods. To make the data disappear, just close the taskbar and unregister[8] your desk band. Then run the taskbar. When the taskbar fails to load the little troublemaker, its information is removed. You can now re-register your band and continue debugging.

By the time we complete CDeskBandWnd, its class declaration will look like this. (I am jumping the gun a bit, but many of the functions are trivial and it helps to show the big picture now.)

```
class CDeskBandWnd : public CWnd
{
// Construction
public:
   CDeskBandWnd();

// Overrides
   // ClassWizard generated virtual function overrides
   //{{AFX_VIRTUAL(CDeskBandWnd)
   //}}AFX_VIRTUAL

// Implementation
public:
   virtual ~CDeskBandWnd();

   // Returns the smallest rect this window
```

---

8. To unregister, type in regsvr32 –u [dllname] or use the UnRegDLL program included in the Tools directory on the CD.

```
    // is comfortable displaying in.
        CRect GetMinRect();

    // Allows the owner to tell us about itself.
        void SetOwnerBand(CDeskBandBand* pBand );

    // Whenever the band ID changes, we find out.
        void SetBandID( DWORD dwID );

    // Whenever the view mode changes, we find out.
        void SetViewMode( DWORD viewMode );

    // Should only get set once.
    void SetSite( IInputObjectSite* pSite );
        // Generated message map functions
protected:
    //{{AFX_MSG(CDeskBandWnd)
    afx_msg BOOL OnEraseBkgnd(CDC* pDC);
    afx_msg int OnCreate(LPCREATESTRUCT lpCreateStruct);
    afx_msg void OnMove(int x, int y);
    afx_msg void OnDestroy();
    //}}AFX_MSG
    afx_msg void OnHide();
    afx_msg void OnShow();
    afx_msg void OnChangeText();
    DECLARE_MESSAGE_MAP()

private:
    // If bShow is true, we show all hidden bands.
    // Otherwise, we hide everyone but us.
    // (hiding ourselves makes it difficult to use the
    // taskbar).
    void ShowOtherBands( bool bShow );

    // Points to our owner.
    CDeskBandBand* m_pBand;
    DWORD m_bandID;
    DWORD m_dwViewType;

    // Stores the input site.
    CComPtr<IInputObjectSite> m_pSite;

    // Our child windows.
    CButton m_btnHide;
    CButton m_btnShow;
    CEdit   m_txtString;

    // Font data.
    bool m_bFontCreated;
    CFont m_font;
};
```

Our first task is to write the CDeskBandWnd's WM_CREATE handler (a.k.a. OnCreate()). This handler depends on a few constants identifying our control IDs.

```cpp
// Hide button ID
const UINT HIDEID = 10000;
// Show button ID
const UINT SHOWID = 10001;
// Text control ID
const UINT TEXTID = 10002;

// Hide button caption
const CString hideLabel = _T("Hide everyone but me");
// Show button caption
const CString showLabel = _T("Show everyone");

int CDeskBandWnd::OnCreate(LPCREATESTRUCT lpCreateStruct)
{
    AFX_MANAGE_STATE(AfxGetStaticModuleState());
      if (CWnd::OnCreate(lpCreateStruct) == -1)
            return -1;

    // Find out who owns us and what rectangle we
    // occupy now.
    CWnd* pParent = GetParent();
    CRect rect;
    GetClientRect( rect );

    // Hopefully, we are normal.  Figure out where
    // to draw the child windows.
    CRect rectButton;
    rectButton.top = rect.top + 4;
    rectButton.bottom = rectButton.top + 22;
    rectButton.left = rect.left + 2;
    rectButton.right = rectButton.left +
        GetDC()->GetTextExtent( hideLabel ).cx;
    m_btnHide.Create( hideLabel,
        WS_TABSTOP | WS_CHILD | WS_VISIBLE |
        BS_PUSHBUTTON, rectButton, this, HIDEID );

    // Make adjustments and create the remaining windows.
    rectButton.OffsetRect( rectButton.Width() + 3, 0 );
    m_btnShow.Create( showLabel,
        WS_TABSTOP | WS_CHILD | WS_VISIBLE |
        BS_PUSHBUTTON, rectButton, this, SHOWID );

    rectButton.OffsetRect( rectButton.Width() + 3, 0 );
    m_txtString.Create( WS_TABSTOP | WS_CHILD | WS_VISIBLE |
        WS_BORDER, rectButton, this, TEXTID );
    m_txtString.SetWindowText( m_pBand->GetString() );
```

```
            return 0;
}
```

The above code works great if the user has the taskbar docked on one of the horizontal edges. What happens if the taskbar and/or our band object (remember that the user can detach the band at will) are set to float[9] or more to a vertical edge? Well, if our desk band floats, we will do nothing. The current layout is good enough for this situation. When the band switches edges, it needs to lay itself out vertically or horizontally, depending on the edge. We can handle this in OnMove().

```
void CDeskBandWnd::OnMove(int x, int y)
{
    CWnd::OnMove(x, y);
    // Figure out where we are.
    CRect rect;
    GetClientRect( rect );
    CRect rectButton;

    // Adjust the rectangle for what will become
    // the top button.
    rectButton.top = rect.top + 4;
    rectButton.bottom = rectButton.top + 22;
    rectButton.left = rect.left + 2;
    rectButton.right = rectButton.left +
        GetDC()->GetTextExtent( hideLabel ).cx;
    m_btnHide.MoveWindow( rectButton );

    if (DBIF_VIEWMODE_VERTICAL == m_dwViewType)
    {
        // Offset the rectangle based on our
        // new coordinates.
        rectButton.OffsetRect( 0,
            rectButton.Height() + 3 );
        m_btnShow.MoveWindow( rectButton );

        rectButton.OffsetRect( 0,
            rectButton.Height() + 3 );
        m_txtString.MoveWindow( rectButton );
    }
    else
    {
        // Offset the rectangle based on our
        // new coordinates.
        rectButton.OffsetRect( rectButton.Width() + 3, 0 );
        m_btnShow.MoveWindow( rectButton );
```

---

9. The taskbar does not float.

```
        rectButton.OffsetRect( rectButton.Width() + 3, 0 );
        m_txtString.MoveWindow( rectButton );
    }
    if ( m_pSite.p != NULL )
    {

        CComPtr<IOleCommandTarget> pCmdTgt;
        m_pSite->QueryInterface( IID_IOleCommandTarget,
            (LPVOID*)&pCmdTgt );

        if ( pCmdTgt.p != NULL )
        {
            _variant_t theVar = static_cast<long>(m_bandID);

            // Make sure the container updates any
            // assumptions it has made about this band.
            pCmdTgt->Exec( &CGID_DeskBand,
                DBID_BANDINFOCHANGED,
                OLECMDEXECOPT_DODEFAULT,
                &theVar, NULL );
        }
    }
}
```

These bands have a nasty habit of displaying any text using the default, bold system font. To overcome this, you need to set the font for any windows to the thin version of this font. I handle this by creating a CFont object based off my parent's font and then set the thickness of the font to FW_THIN in On-EraseBkgnd(). More likely than not, implementing the functionality in On-EraseBkgnd() is overkill, but the code does not seem to hurt performance and it never fails to work properly.

```
BOOL CDeskBandWnd::OnEraseBkgnd(CDC* pDC)
{
    // Get the rectangle we need to erase.
    CRect rect;
    GetClientRect( rect );

    // Set the color to the dialog
    // background color.
    COLORREF backColor = GetSysColor(COLOR_3DFACE);
    CBrush brush( backColor );
    pDC->FillRect( rect, &brush );

    // See if we created the default font yet.
    if (!m_bFontCreated)
    {
        // Get the parent's font and make sure
        // it shows up normal, not bold.
        CFont* pFont = GetParent()->GetFont();
        LOGFONT lf;
```

```
        pFont->GetLogFont( &lf );
        lf.lfWeight = FW_THIN;

        // Create the font and store whether
        // we were successful or not.
        m_bFontCreated =
            m_font.CreateFontIndirect( &lf ) != 0;
    }

    // Set my font and my child windows' font.
    // No need to force an erase— we're doing that
    // now.
    SetFont( &m_font, false );
    m_btnHide.SetFont( &m_font, false );
    m_btnShow.SetFont( &m_font, false );
    m_txtString.SetFont( &m_font, false );
    return TRUE;
}
```

Next, we need to implement the code to handle button presses. These will either tell the taskbar to hide all taskbars except ours, or to show all hidden taskbars. Normally, you will not want to hide all taskbars (including the one you wrote)— doing so makes it difficult to make the taskbar do anything useful. Two WM_COMMAND handlers handle the buttons:

```
void CDeskBandWnd::OnHide()
{
    ShowOtherBands( false );
}

void CDeskBandWnd::OnShow()
{
    ShowOtherBands( true );
}
```

Both methods call into a common method: ShowOtherBands(). This method extracts the container's IOleCommandTarget interface and executes the appropriate command based on whether it should show or hide the other bands.

```
void CDeskBandWnd::ShowOtherBands(bool bShow)
{
    // Get the interfaces.
    CComPtr<IOleCommandTarget> pCmdTgt;
    CComPtr<IUnknown> pUnknown;
    m_pSite->QueryInterface( IID_IOleCommandTarget,
        (LPVOID*)&pCmdTgt );
    m_pBand->QueryInterface( IID_IUnknown,
        (LPVOID*)&pUnknown );

    // If we failed to get either interface, exit.
```

```
        if ( !pCmdTgt.p || !pUnknown.p )
        {
            return;
        }

        // theVar tells Exec what to do
        _variant_t theVar;
        if ( bShow )
        {
            // Show all currently hidden band objects
            theVar = static_cast<long>(1);
        }
        else
        {
            // hides all band objects except for the one
            // identified by this IUnknown pointer.
            theVar = pUnknown;
        }
        pCmdTgt->Exec( &CGID_DeskBand,
            DBID_SHOWONLY, OLECMDEXECOPT_DODEFAULT,
            &theVar, NULL );
    }
```

Lastly, we will implement the functionality that allows us to store the string displayed in our textbox. Whenever the user changes the text, the textbox will fire an EN_CHANGE message at the parent. CDeskBandWnd captures that message and updates the contents of the CDeskBandBand's m_szText member. CDeskBandBand provides two methods to get and set the string.

```
void CDeskBandBand::SetString(const CString &szVal)
{
    m_szText = szVal;
    // Set the contents as dirty.
    m_bRequiresSave = true;
}

CString CDeskBandBand::GetString()
{
    return m_szText;
}

void CDeskBandWnd::OnChangeText()
{
    CString szVal;
    m_txtString.GetWindowText( szVal );
    m_pBand->SetString( szVal );
}
```

Whenever our desk band starts up, the taskbar will allow us to load our data. Under various circumstances (shutdown and resizing or moving desk bands) we get opportunities to store our data. This is done through three methods: IPersistStream::Load(), IPersistStream::Save(), and IPersistStream:: GetSizeMax().

```
STDMETHODIMP CDeskBandBand::GetSizeMax(
    ULARGE_INTEGER FAR* pcbSize)
{
    // What is the most space we need?
    pcbSize->QuadPart = sizeof( int ) +
        (sizeof(TCHAR) * (m_szText.GetLength() + 1) );
    return S_OK;
}

STDMETHODIMP CDeskBandBand::Save(LPSTREAM pStm,
    BOOL fClearDirty)
{
    if ( fClearDirty )
    {
        // Clear the dirty flag.
        m_bRequiresSave = false;
    }

    // Store the size of the string to make retrieval easier.
    int nStringSize = sizeof(TCHAR) *
        (m_szText.GetLength() + 1);
    HRESULT hr = pStm->Write( &nStringSize,
        sizeof( nStringSize ), NULL );

    // If we successfully wrote the size, write the string.
    if ( SUCCEEDED(hr) )
    {
        TCHAR *pBuff = m_szText.GetBuffer();
        hr = pStm->Write( pBuff, nStringSize, NULL );
        m_szText.ReleaseBuffer();
    }
    return hr;
}

STDMETHODIMP CDeskBandBand::Load(LPSTREAM pStm)
{
    int nStringSize = 0;
    HRESULT hr = S_OK;

    // Check how much we wrote out.
    hr = pStm->Read(&nStringSize, sizeof(nStringSize), NULL);
    if ( SUCCEEDED( hr ) )
    {
        // Make a big enough buffer and read
```

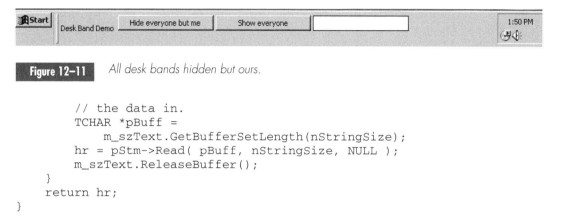

Figure 12-11   *All desk bands hidden but ours.*

```
        // the data in.
        TCHAR *pBuff =
            m_szText.GetBufferSetLength(nStringSize);
        hr = pStm->Read( pBuff, nStringSize, NULL );
        m_szText.ReleaseBuffer();
    }
    return hr;
}
```

You can see the result of the effort in Figure 12-11. When the *Hide everyone but me* button gets hit, you can see just how much stuff gets hidden. You wind up with nothing except for your desk band, the system tray, and the start button. Pretty neat, huh?

Using this information, you should be able to create your own band objects to live in Explorer or the taskbar. If you want to create an HTML based band object you have a lot less work ahead of you—all you need is a REG script and an HTML page.[10]

12.5 Summary

This chapter covered the basics of band object development. With the arrival of Explorer 4.0, Microsoft distributed a new COM interface called IDeskBand. IDeskBand provides an interface to add toolbars to the taskbar and to add band objects, like the search window and tip of the day, to Explorer. We also explored other interfaces, such as ICatRegister and ICatInformation, which help manage component categories. When developing extensible frameworks of your own, these two classes may come in handy. They allow for the implementer of a category (like a band object) to broadcast the fact that it exists and where it exists. For the user of the category (i.e., the application that initially defined the category), these interfaces provide a means to discover and integrate new COM objects after all parties have been built and distributed.

Band objects provide another way to integrate your application with Windows and Explorer. I see a real future for this technology as a way to provide a chunk of the user interface for future distributed applications. The Web server will deliver the primary view and band objects will provide the

---

10. Covered at the end of Section 12.2.

menu, toolbar, and dialog bar functionality. Many views exist that dictate what a proper thin client looks like, and most people agree that the fat client does not work well for distributed applications. Band objects help provide a path towards the *stocky client*[11]—a client that uses the power of the Desktop and recognizes that items like transaction management belong at the server. The stocky client will have some power. It will not require 300MB of storage for installation. On the flip side, it will be platform specific and will have some processing power. Band objects combined with other COM objects provide a way to make distributed applications easier to build. I imagine that groupware applications will benefit from this approach first. For example, the Microsoft Outlook's handy-dandy sidebar could become an Explorer Band. Combine this with what is already possible using DHTML and ActiveX, and we start to see what a stocky client could look like.

---

11. To the best of my knowledge, this term has never been used before. If it becomes popular, tell people you saw it here first.

COM Interfaces Used by the Shell

*T*his appendix describes the various COM interfaces that many of the shell extensions presented in the book implement and use. This section contains all interfaces used in the book. If a chapter covers the interface, this appendix documents the chapter and section where the interface is used. Keep in mind that when an interface gets implemented, not all methods will be implemented. As a result, it is often acceptable for shell extensions to return the OLE-defined error code E_NOTIMPL when you see no use for a given method. Don Box, Microsoft Systems Journal *columnist, author, and respected COM authority, has said that a good COM interface does not need E_NOTIMPL. Seeing the need for this return value shows a lack of thought in the design of the interface. Instead, if certain parts of an interface are optional, then those parts should be designed as extensions to the interface or as separate interfaces. Microsoft made these mistakes in the beginning because they were the first heavy users of COM. Later on, Microsoft figured out what mistakes were made and have done a better job of creating interfaces.*

The interfaces have been listed alphabetically. Each interface documents the following items:

- The purpose of the interface
- The methods of the interface
- The header file defining the interface

- The ID of the interface
- Any example projects that use the interface

A.1 ICatRegister

This interface allows a COM object to declare that it implements a given category. This interface is used by IDeskBand to register itself as an implementer of a desk band, an info band, or a comm band. Chapter 12, "Explorer Bars and Desktop Bands," Section 12.1.2 explains ICatRegister and its use within the shell.

Header:	comcat.h
Example Projects:	Chapter 12\CommBand
	Chapter 12\DeskBand
	Chapter 12\SimpsonBand
Interface ID:	IID_ICatRegister

A.2 IContextMenu

A COM object implements this interface when it needs to add objects to a context menu. A user typically invokes a context menu by pressing the right mouse button. Various shell extensions (context menu handlers, drag-and-drop handlers, desk bands, and others) implement this interface to add more items to a context menu.

Header:	shlobj.h
Example Projects:	Chapter 7\ABKContextMenuHandler
	Chapter 11\WinReg
	Chapter 12\CommBand
	Chapter 12\DeskBand
	Chapter 12\SimpsonBand
Interface ID:	IID_IContextMenu

Objects implementing IContextMenu must implement the following methods:

```
HRESULT GetCommandString(
   UINT idCmd,
   UINT uFlags,
   UINT* pwReserved,
   LPSTR, pszName,
```

```
    UINT cchMax
);
```

Parameters:

idCmd: Menu item identifier offset.

uFlags: Flags specifying the information to retrieve. The flag can be one of the following values:

- **GCS_HELPTEXT:** The function should return the help text for the menu item. Context menu handlers will display this text in the Windows Explorer status bar.
- **GCS_VALIDATE:** The function should validate that the menu item exists.
- **GCS_VERB:** The function should return the language-independent command name for the menu item. If the verb exists, the implementer should fill in pszName. This language-independent command name can be passed to the IContextMenu::InvokeCommand method to activate a command by an application.

pwReserved: Callers must specify NULL for this parameter and implementers must ignore the parameter.

pszName: Address of the buffer to receive the null-terminated string requested by uFlags.

cchMax: Size of the buffer to receive the null-terminated string. Make sure that the buffer is large enough before filling in pszName.

```
HRESULT InvokeCommand(
    LPCMINVOKECOMMANDINFO lpcmi
);
```

Parameters:

lpcmi: Address of a CMINVOKECOMMANDINFO structure containing information about the command. If your application does not use verbs but uses the command id instead, the following code snippet will allow you to decode your message:

```
int value = LOWORD(lpcmi->lpVerb);
```

Inside of QueryContextMenu(), your code inserts a menu item by calling

```
InsertMenu(
    hMenu,
    indexMenu,
    MF_STRING | MF_BYPOSITION,
    idCmdFirst + SomeValue,
    "Display String" );
```

The value you extracted into `value` a few lines ago should be equal to SomeValue.

Return Values:

Returns NOERROR if successful; otherwise, returns an OLE-defined error code.

Remarks:

The shell calls this method when the user chooses a command that the handler added to a context menu. This method may also be called by an application without any user intervention.

```
HRESULT QueryContextMenu(
    HMENU hmenu,
    UINT indexMenu,
    UINT idCmdFirst,
    UINT idCmdLast,
    UINT uFlags
    );
```

Parameters:

hmenu: Handle to the menu. The handler must specify this handle when adding menu items.

indexMenu: Indicates where to insert the first menu item.

idCmdFirst: The minimum value that a menu item identifier can have.

idCmdLast: The maximum value that a menu item identifier can have.

uFlags: Optional flags specifying how the context menu can be changed. This may be set to any combination of the following values:

- **CMF_CANRENAME:** This flag is set if the calling application supports the renaming of items. A context menu extension or drag-and-drop handler should ignore this flag. A namespace extension should add a "Rename" item to the menu if applicable.
- **CMF_DEFAULTONLY:** The caller sets this flag when the user activates the default action, typically by double-clicking. This flag provides a hint for the context menu extension to add nothing if it does not modify the default item in the menu. A context menu extension or drag-and-drop handler should not add any items to the context menu when the caller specifies this flag. Other extensions should add only the default item or nothing.
- **CMF_EXPLORE:** The caller sets this flag when Windows Explorer's tree window is present.

- **CMF_INCLUDESTATIC:** The caller sets this flag when a static menu is being constructed. Only the browser should use this flag. All other extensions should ignore this flag.
- **CMF_NODEFAULT:** This flag is only set when no item in the menu should be the default. When this is set, a namespace extension should not set any of the menu items to the default.
- **CMF_NORMAL:** Indicates normal operation. Any implementer can add all of its "normal" menu items.
- **CMF_NOVERBS:** This flag is set for items displayed in the "Send To:" menu. Context menu handlers should ignore this value.
- **CMF_VERBSONLY:** This flag is set if the context menu is for a shortcut object. Context menu handlers should ignore this value.

Return Values: If successful, this method returns the number of items added to the menu. Return this information using the following snippet:

```
return MAKE_HRESULT(SEVERITY_SUCCESS, 0, <# of items>);
```

Remarks:

The shell calls this method when the user chooses a command that the handler added to a context menu. This method may also be called by an application without any corresponding user action.

A.3 IContextMenu2

IContextMenu2 extends IContextMenu. Implement this interface if your extension needs to handle one of the following messages:

- **WM_INITMENUPOPUP**
- **WM_DRAWITEM**
- **WM_MEASUREITEM**

The operating system will call this interface only when it has confirmed that your application or extension handles this interface.

Header: shlobj.h

Interface ID: IID_IContextMenu2

IContextMenu2 has one method:

```
HRESULT HandleMenuMsg(
    UINT uMsg,
    WPARAM wParam,
```

```
    LPARAM lParam
);
```

Parameters:

> **uMsg:** Specifies the message to process. If the message is WM_INIT-MENUPOPUP, WM_DRAWITEM, or WM_MEASUREITEM, the client object may provide the owner drawn menu items.

> **wParam:** Depends on the uMsg parameter and does not differ from the standard meanings of the message.

> **lParam:** Depends on the uMsg parameter and does not differ from the standard meanings of the message.

Return Values:
- **S_OK:** The object sorted the selected column.
- **Other OLE-Defined value:** Something went wrong.

Remarks: This method gets called whenever a client of the object determines that IContextMenu2 has been implemented by the object.

A.4 IContextMenu3

IContextMenu3 extends IContextMenu2. Implement this interface if your extension needs to handle the WM_MENUCHAR message. The operating system will call this interface only when it has confirmed that your application or extension handles this interface.

Header:	shlobj.h
Interface ID:	IID_IContextMenu3

IContextMenu3 adds one method for the WM_MENUCHAR message:

```
HRESULT HandleMenuMsg2(
    UINT uMsg,
    WPARAM wParam,
    LPARAM lParam,
    LRESULT *plResult
);
```

Parameters:

> **uMsg:** Specifies the message to process. Currently, this method is only called for WM_MENUCHAR.

> **wParam:** Depends on the uMsg parameter and does not differ from the standard meanings of the message.

> **lParam:** Depends on the uMsg parameter and does not differ from the standard meanings of the message.

plResult: Address of an LRESULT value that the owner of the menu will use as the message's return value.

Return Values:
- **S_OK:** The object sorted the selected column.
- **Other OLE-Defined value:** Something went wrong.

Remarks: This method gets called whenever a client of the object determines that the object has implemented IContextMenu3 and it receives a WM_MENUCHAR message.

A.5 ICopyHook

A shell extension can implement this interface in order to find out if a folder object or printer object can be moved, copied, renamed, or deleted. This interface is covered in Chapter 7, "Shell Extensions," Section 7.7.

Header:	shlobj.h
Example Projects:	Chapter 7\ABKCopyHandler
Interface ID:	IID_IShellCopyHook

A.6 IDataObject

IDataObject enables data transfer and notification of changes in data. This object is discussed in Chapter 7, Section 7.4.

Header:	objidl.h
Example Projects:	Chapter 7\ABKDataHandler
	Chapter 7\ABKDropHandler
Interface ID:	IID_IDataObject

A.7 IDeskBand

The IDeskBand interface is used to create toolbars within the taskbar as well as vertical and horizontal explorer bars within Internet Explorer. This object is discussed in detail in Chapter 12, Section 12.1.1.

Header:	shlobj.h
Example Projects:	Chapter 12\CommBand
	Chapter 12\DeskBand
Interface ID:	IID_IDeskBand

A.8   IDockingWindow

Window objects that can be docked within the border space of a Windows Explorer window implement IDockingWindow. The shell browser uses this interface to support docked windows inside the browser frame. The taskbar also uses this interface to support custom toolbars. This interface derives from IOleWindow.

Header:	shlobj.h
Example Projects:	Chapter 12\CommBand
	Chapter 12\DeskBand
Interface ID:	IID_IDockingWindow

Objects implementing IDockingWindow must implement the following methods:

```
HRESULT CloseDW(
    DWORD dwReserved
);
```

Parameters:

dwReserved: This parameter should always be zero.

Return Values: If successful, returns NOERROR; otherwise, returns an OLE-defined error value.

Remarks:

This method gets called before the object gets removed from the frame. The docking window should save any persistent information at this time and close itself.

```
HRESULT ResizeBorderDW(
    LPRECT prcBorder,
    IUnknown* punkToolbarSite,
    BOOL fReserved
);
```

Parameters:

prcBorder: Pointer to a RECT structure that contains the frame's available border space.

punkToolbarSite: Address of the site's IUnknown interface. Using this pointer, the docking window can call QueryInterface requesting IID_IShellToolbarSite. The docking window can then use the IShell-ToolbarSite interface to negotiate its border space. The docking window must release this interface when it is no longer needed. I have no idea if this actually works since none of the header files define the IID_IShellToolbarSite interface ID and this method contains the only mention I know of that pertains to IShellToolbarSite.

fReserved: The parameter is reserved for future use. It should always be zero.

Return Values: If successful, returns NOERROR; otherwise, returns an OLE-defined error value.

Remarks:

Some docking windows do not always implement ResizeBorderDW because other mechanisms exist. For an example, see IDeskBand, discussed in Chapter 12.

```
HRESULT ShowDW(
    BOOL bShow
);
```

Parameters:

bShow: Tells the window that it should show (TRUE) or hide (FALSE) itself. If the docking window is supposed to hide itself, it should return its border space by calling IDockingWindowSite::SetBorderSpaceDW with all zeros. If you didn't implement ResizeBorderDW(), then you do not need to worry about freeing the border space.

Return Values:

- **S_OK:** Success.
- **Other OLE-Defined value:** Something went wrong.

A.9   IDropTarget

This interface allows you to implement drag-and-drop operations. With the shell, this interface makes it possible to give meaning to the act of dropping an object onto a file. This interface and its use with the shell are covered in Chapter 7, Section 7.5.

Header:	oleidl.h
Example Projects:	Chapter 7\ABKDropHandler
Interface ID:	IID_IDroptarget

A.10 IEmptyVolumeCacheCallBack

The disk cleanup manager implements this interface. A disk cleanup handler will use this interface to communicate its progress as it scans for files it can delete and as it deletes those files. It is covered in Chapter 8, "Disk Cleanup Handlers," Section 8.1.

Header:	emptyvc.h
Example Projects:	Chapter 8\DiskCleanup
Interface ID:	IID_IEmptyVolumeCacheCallBack

A.11 IEmptyVolumeCache

This interface implements the actual disk cleanup handler. It allows the disk cleanup manager to ask for information from the handler and to get notified of progress as the handler scans for files to remove and deletes files. It is covered in detail in Chapter 8, Section 8.1.

Header:	emptyvc.h
Example Projects:	Chapter 8\DiskCleanup
Interface ID:	IID_IEmptyVolumeCache

A.12 IEmptyVolumeCache2

This interface extends IEmptyVolumeCache. It provides better localization support than IEmptyVolumeCache through its InitializeEx() method. It is covered in detail in Chapter 8, Section 8.1.

Header:	emptyvc.h
Example Projects:	Chapter 8\DiskCleanup
Interface ID:	IID_IEmptyVolumeCache2

A.13 IEnumIDList

This interface provides a way for an IShellFolder implementation to enumerate the PIDLs of the items in the folder. All IShellFolders must be able to respond to a call to IShellFolder::EnumOjects() by returning an object that implements IEnumIDList.

Header:	shlobj.h
Example Projects:	Chapter 11\WinReg
Interface ID:	IID_IEnumIDList

IEnumIDList exports the normal IEnumXXXX methods:

```
HRESULT Clone(
    IEnumIDList **ppEnum
);
```

Parameters:

> **ppEnum:** On return, this contains a clone of the current IEnumIDList. The caller must free the new enumeration via its Release() method.

Return Values:
- **S_OK:** Success.
- **Other OLE-Defined value:** Something went wrong.

Remarks: Callers use this method so that they can record a particular spot in the enumeration and then return to that point later.

```
HRESULT Next(
    ULONG celt,
    LPITEMIDLIST *rgelt,
    ULONG *pceltFetched
);
```

Parameters:

> **celt:** Number of elements in the rgelt parameter.

> **rgelt:** Address of an array of ITEMIDLIST pointers ready to receive item identifiers. The implementation allocates the item identifiers using the IMalloc interface retrieved by SHGetMalloc(). The caller must free these item identifiers using the same IMalloc interface. The caller will get this interface by also calling SHGetMalloc().

> **pceltFetched:** This parameter is used to return the number of items actually fetched. This value must be less than or equal to celt.

Return Values:
- **S_OK:** Success.
- **S_FALSE:** No more items are available in the enumeration sequence.
- **Other OLE-Defined value:** Something went wrong.

Remarks: If an error occurs part way through filling up the array, an implementation should free any memory allocated for the valid item identifiers before returning. The caller will assume that all the values in the array are garbage and probably will not free the memory. This will result in memory leaks.

```
HRESULT Reset();
```

Return Values:
- **S_OK:** Success.
- **Other OLE-Defined value:** Something went wrong.

Remarks: Returns to the beginning of the enumeration.

```
HRESULT Skip(
    ULONG celt
);
```

Parameters:

celt: Number of item identifiers to skip.

Return Values:
- **S_OK:** Success.
- **Other OLE-Defined value:** Something went wrong.

Remarks: Moves the enumeration forward celt elements.

A.14   IEnumExtraSearch

This interface provides a way for an IShellFolder2 implementation to enumerate the search objects available for the folder. You do not call this interface directly. This interface is requested only through the IShellFolder2::Enum-Searches() method.

Header:	shlobj.h
Interface ID:	IID_IEnumExtraSearch

IEnumExtraSearch exports the normal IEnumXXXX methods:

```
HRESULT Clone(
    IEnumExtraSearch **ppEnum
);
```

Parameters:

ppEnum: On return, this contains a clone of the current IEnumExtraSearch. The caller must free the new enumeration via its Release() method.

Return Values:
- **S_OK:** The object sorted the selected column.
- **Other OLE-Defined value:** Something went wrong.

Remarks: Callers use this method so that they can record a particular spot in the enumeration and then return to that point later.

```
HRESULT Next(
    ULONG celt,
    LPITEMIDLIST *rgelt,
    ULONG *pceltFetched
);
```

Parameters:

celt: Number of elements in the rgelt parameter.

rgelt: Address of an array of EXTRASEARCH structures. On return, they contain information on the enumerated objects.

pceltFetched: This parameter is used to return the number of items actually fetched. This value must be less than or equal to celt.

Return Values:
- **S_OK:** Success.
- **S_FALSE:** No more items are available in the enumeration sequence.
- **Other OLE-Defined value:** Something went wrong.

```
HRESULT Reset();
```

Return Values:
- **S_OK:** Successfully reset.
- **Other OLE-Defined value:** Something went wrong.

Remarks: Returns to the beginning of the enumeration.

```
HRESULT Skip(
    ULONG celt
);
```

Parameters:

celt: Number of item identifiers to skip.

Return Values:
- **S_OK:** Success.
- **Other OLE-Defined value:** Something went wrong.

Remarks: Moves the enumeration forward celt elements.

A.15   IExtractIcon

The shell uses this interface to retrieve the icons for the various objects that it displays. This interface is covered in Chapter 7, Section 7.3.

Header: shlobj.h

Example Projects: Chapter 7\ABKIconHandler

	Chapter 11\WinReg
Interface ID:	IID_IExtractIcon

A.16   IFileViewer

This interface implements a quick viewer. This interface is covered in Chapter 6, "File Viewers," Section 6.2.2.

Header:	shlobj.h
Example Projects:	Chapter 6\AddressBookFV
Interface ID:	IID_IFileViewer

A.17   IFileViewerSite

The shell uses this interface to set and get the pinned window for a quick view implementation. This interface is covered in Chapter 6, Section 6.2.1.

Header:	shlobj.h
Example Projects:	Chapter 6\AddressBookFV
Interface ID:	IID_IFileViewerSite

A.18   IInputObject

The IInputObject interface allows shell objects to handle user input by being able to change UI activation and process accelerators. If your shell object does not handle user input, then you do not need to implement this interface.

Header File:	shlobj.h
Example Projects:	Chapter 12\CommBand
	Chapter 12\DeskBand
Interface ID:	IID_IInputObject

Objects implementing IInputObject must implement the following methods:

```
HRESULT HasFocusIO();
```

Return Values: Returns S_OK if one of the object's windows has the keyboard focus, or S_FALSE otherwise.

```
HRESULT TranslateAcceleratorIO(
    LPMSG lpMsg
);
```

Parameters:

lpMsg: Address of an MSG structure that contains the keyboard message being translated.

Return Values: This returns S_OK if the accelerator was translated, or S_FALSE otherwise.

```
HRESULT UIActivateIO(
    BOOL fActivate,
    LPMSG lpMsg
);
```

Parameters:

fActivate: If this value is FALSE, then the object is being deactivated. Otherwise, it is being activated.

lpMsg: Address of an MSG structure that caused the activation change. The value may be NULL.

Return Values: This returns S_OK if the activation change was successful, or S_FALSE otherwise.

A.19   IInputObjectSite

This interface is used to communicate focus changes to a user input object contained in the shell. As a shell developer, you typically use this interface instead of implementing it. It has one method: OnFocusChangeIS().

Header File:	shlobj.h
Example Projects:	Chapter 12\CommBand
	Chapter 12\DeskBand
Interface ID:	IID_IInputObjectSite

```
HRESULT OnFocusChangeIS(
    IUnknown* punkObj,
    BOOL fSetFocus
);
```

Parameters:

punkObj: Address of the IUnknown interface of the object gaining or losing the focus.

fSetFocus: Indicates if punkObj has gained or lost the focus. TRUE means it just received the focus; FALSE means it lost focus.

Return Values: This returns S_OK if the activation change was successful, or an OLE-defined error code otherwise.

A.20   IObjectWithSite

The IObjectWithSite provides a simple interface between an object and its site in the container. This interface provides a lightweight alternative to IOleObject. Because this is meant as an alternative, do not implement this interface and IOleObject in the same object. IObjectWithSite provides a simple siting mechanism. Using this interface, a container can pass the IUnknown pointer of its site to the object via IObjectWithSite::SetSite(). Callers can retrieve the latest site by calling IObjectWithSite::GetSite(). A third party could also use the GetSite() and SetSite() to intercept calls between the object and its site. An object implements this interface so that the container and object can communicate directly.

Header File:	ocidl.h
Example Projects:	Chapter 12\CommBand
	Chapter 12\DeskBand
	Chapter 12\SimpsonBand
Interface ID:	IID_IObjectWithSite

Objects implementing IObjectWithSite must implement the following methods:

```
HRESULT GetSite(
    REFIID riid,
    void** ppvSite
);
```

Parameters:

riid: The IID of the interface pointer that should be returned in ppvSite.

ppvSite: Address of the pointer variable that receives the interface pointer requested in riid. If the function succeeds, *ppvSite will contain the interface pointer to the site last set in SetSite(). The specific interface returned depends on the riid argument. Essentially, the two arguments behave the same as they do in IUnknown::QueryInterface(). If the appropriate interface pointer is available, the object must call IUknown::AddRef() on the pointer before returning successfully.

If no site is available or if the requested interface is not available, this method sets *ppvSite to NULL and returns a failure code.

Return Values:

This returns S_OK if the requested interface can be found. If the site has not been set, this returns E_FAIL. If the site was set but the interface cannot be found, the method returns E_NOINTERFACE.

```
HRESULT SetSite(
    IUnknown* pUnkSite
);
```

Parameters:

pUnkSite: Points to the IUnknown interface pointer corresponding to the site managing this object. If the object currently has a valid pointer to another site, the object must release that pointer. If pUnkSite is not NULL, the object should store the new pointer.

Return Values: This method always returns S_OK.

Remarks: You must implement this method. If the object does not implement SetSite(), then the IObjectWithSite interface is not necessary.

A.21   IOleCommandTarget

This interface allows a COM object and its container to dispatch messages to each other. Explorer uses this interface with IShellView to pass commands back and forth.

Header:	docobj.h
Example Projects:	Chapter 11\WinReg
Interface ID:	IID_IOleCommandTarget

Objects implementing IOleCommandTarget must implement the following methods:

```
HRESULT Exec(
    const GUID *pguidCmdGroup,
    DWORD nCmdID,
    DWORD nCmdExecOpt,
    VARIANTARG *pvaIn,
    VARIANTARG *pvaOut
);
```

Parameters:

pguidCmdGroup: GUID that uniquely identifies the command group. If this value is NULL, it specifies the standard command group.

nCmdID: The command to be executed. This command must belong to the group specified by pguidCmdGroup.

nCmdExecOpt: Values taken from the OLECMDEXECOPT enumeration, specifying how the object should execute the command.

pvaIn: Points to a VARIANTARG structure containing input arguments. This might be NULL.

pvaOut: Points to a VARIANTARG structure to receive command output. This might be NULL.

Return Values:

- **S_OK**: The command was successfully executed.
- **OLECMDERR_E_UNKNOWNGROUP**: The pguidCmdGroup is not NULL, but specifies an unknown command group.
- **OLECMDERR_E_NOTSUPPORTED:** The nCmdID parameter does not specify a valid command in the command group.
- **OLECMDERR_E_DISABLED:** The command is disabled right now and cannot be executed.
- **OLECMDERR_E_NOHELP:** The caller requested help on the command, but none is available.
- **OLECMDERR_E_CANCELED:** The user cancelled the command.

Remarks: The list of input and output arguments of a command and their packaging is unique to each command. This information should be documented with the specification of the command group. In the absence of any specific information the command is assumed to take no arguments and have no return value.

```
HRESULT QueryStatus(
    const GUID *pguidCmdGroup,
    ULONG cCmds,
    OLECMD *prgCmds,
    OLECMDTEXT *pCmdText
);
```

Parameters:

pguidCmdGroup: GUID that uniquely identifies the command group. If this value is NULL, it specifies the standard command group. All the commands that are passed in the prgCmds array must belong to the group specified by pguidCmdGroup.

cCmds: The number of items in the prgCmds array.

prgCmds: A caller-allocated array of OLECMD structures that indicate the commands the caller wants status information for. This method fills the cmdf member of each structure with values from the OLECMDF enumeration.

pCmdText: Pointer to an OLECMDTEXT structure in which to return name and/or status information of a single command. Set this value to NULL to indicate that the caller does not need this information.

Return Values:
- **S_OK**: The command status and any optional strings were returned successfully.
- **E_POINTER**: The prgCmds argument is NULL.
- **OLECMDERR_E_UNKNOWNGROUP:** The pguidCmdGroup parameter is not NULL, but does not specify a recognized command group.

Remarks: Callers use this to determine which commands the target object supports. For complete information, see the MSDN documentation.

A.22   IOleInPlaceFrame

This interface controls the container's top-level frame window. IOleInPlace-Frame allows the container and server objects to share the menu and status bar, enable or disable modeless text boxes, and translate accelerator keys.

| **Header:** | oleidl.h |
| **Interface ID:** | IID_IOleInPlaceFrame |

Objects implementing IOleInPlaceFrame must implement the following methods:

```
HRESULT EnableModeless(
    BOOL fEnable
);
```

Parameters:

fEnable: TRUE enables modeless dialogs; FALSE disables modeless dialogs.

Return Values:
- **S_OK**: Request completed.
- **Other OLE-Defined value:** Something went wrong.

```
HRESULT InsertMenus(
    HMENU hmenuShared,
    LPOLEMENUGROUPWIDTHS lpMenuWidths
);
```

Parameters:

hmenuShared: Handle to an empty menu.

lpMenuWidths: Pointer to an OLEMENUGROUPWIDTHS structure of six LONG values. Items 0, 2, and 4 reflect the number of menu elements in the File, View, and Window menu groups.

Return Values:
- **S_OK:** Request completed.
- **E_INVALIDARG:** One of the arguments is not correct.
- **E_UNEXPECTED:** Something bad happened.

Remarks: You would normally call this method when an application first activates your object. The container adds its menu items to the menu specified by hmenuShared and sets the group counts in OLEMENUGROUP-WIDTHS. The object application then adds its own menus and counts. An object calls IOleInPlaceFrame::InsertMenus() as many times as it needs to build the composite menus. The container should use the menu handle passed in this function for all menu items in the drop-down menus.

```
HRESULT RemoveMenus(
    HMENU hmenuShared
);
```

Parameters:

hMenuShared: Handle to the composite menu that was constructed by calls to IOleInPlaceFrame::InsertMenus() and the Windows Insert-Menu() function.

Return Values:
- **S_OK**: Request completed.
- **Other OLE-Defined value:** Something went wrong.

Remarks: The object removing the menus should give the container a chance to remove its menu elements from the composite menu before deactivating the shared user interface.

```
HRESULT SetMenu(
    HMENU hmenuShared,
    HOLEMENU hOleMenu,
    HWND hwndActiveObject
);
```

Parameters:

hMenuShared: Handle to the composite menu that was constructed by calls to IOleInPlaceFrame::InsertMenus() and the Windows Insert-Menu() function.

hOleMenu: Handle to the menu descriptor returned by the OleCreateMenuDescriptor() function.

hwndActiveObject: Handle to the window owned by the object. This window receives menu messages, commands, and accelerators.

Return Values:
- **S_OK**: Request completed.
- **Other OLE-Defined value:** Something went wrong.

Remarks: This method asks the container to actually install the composite menu set up by calls to IOleInPlaceFrame::InsertMenus().

```
HRESULT SetStatusText(
    LPCOLESTR pszStatusText
);
```

Parameters:

pszStatusText: A null-terminated string that the object wants the container to display.

Return Values:
- **S_OK:** Request completed.
- **S_TRUNCATED:** Some text was displayed. Due to the length of the text, the string was truncated.
- **Other OLE-Defined value:** Something went wrong.

Remarks: Because the frame owns the status bar, this method provides the only way to display status text in the frame's window. If the container refuses to display the status text, the object can try to get some border space and display its own status window. You must call this function to display information about menu selections. The container does not trap messages meant for the object. As a result, it does not know when it should display status text, enable or disable a menu item, or anything else. It just displays the menu and forwards messages to the object.

```
HRESULT TranslateAccelerator(
    LPMSG lpMsg,
    WORD wID
);
```

Parameters:

lpMsg: Pointer to an MSG structure. This structure contains the keystroke message.

wID: Command identifier corresponding to the accelerator in the container-provided accelerator table. Containers should use this value instead of translating the accelerator again.

Return Values:
- **S_OK:** The keystroke was used.
- **S_FALSE:** The keystroke was not used.
- **Other OLE-Defined value:** Something went wrong.

Remarks: Call this method when the user presses a key-sequence that your object does not recognize.

A.23   IOleWindow

The IOleWindow interface provides methods that allow an application to get the handle to the various windows that participate in in-place activation. Additionally, this interface allows the implementer of the interface to enter and exit context-sensitive help mode. Many other interfaces derive from IOleWindow, including:

- IOleInPlaceObject
- IOleInPlaceActiveObject
- IOleInPlaceUIWindow
- IOleInPlaceFrame
- IOleInPlaceSite
- IOleInPlaceSiteEx
- IOleInPlaceSiteWindowless
- IOleInPlaceObjectWindowless

Header:	oleidl.h
Example Projects:	Chapter 12\CommBand
	Chapter 12\DeskBand
	Chapter 12\SimpsonBand
Interface ID:	IID_IOleWindow

All in-place objects and containers implement the methods specified by the IOleWindow interface. These methods are:

```
HRESULT ContextSensitiveHelp(
    BOOL fEnterMode
);
```

Parameter:

fEnterMode: TRUE if the object should enter help mode; FALSE if the object should exit help mode.

Return Values:
- **S_OK:** Successfully entered help mode.
- **Other OLE-Defined value:** Something went wrong.

Remarks: Context-sensitive help can be invoked when the user presses [SHIFT] +[F1] and clicks a topic or presses [F1] when a menu item is selected. The frame or the active object will receive these keystrokes. If the container's frame receives the keystrokes, it will call the containing document's version of this method, setting fEnterMode to TRUE. The containing document will send this same command to all of its in-place objects so that they have a chance to handle the mouse click or the WM_COMMAND message.

If the active object receives these keystrokes, it will call the container's IOleInPlaceSite::ContextSensitiveHelp() method, setting fEnterMode to TRUE. The container will then recurse through its in-place sites until no more sites can be notified. Finally, the container's document will be called. If an object can handle the help request, it should tell all the other in-place objects to exit context-sensitive help mode. This can be done by calling the IOleInPlaceSite::ContextSensitiveHelp() method and setting fEnterMode to FALSE.

```
HRESULT GetWindow(
    HWND* phwnd
);
```

Parameter:

phwnd: Sets the HWND pointed to by phwnd to the value of the implementer's HWND.

Return Values:
- **S_OK:** Successfully entered help mode.
- **S_FAIL:** Returned by all windowless objects.
- **Other OLE-Defined value:** Something went wrong.

A.24 IQueryInfo

The shell uses IQueryInfo to get flags and info tip information for an item that resides in an IShellFolder. The shell usually uses tooltip controls to display info tips. Callers obtain this interface by passing IID_IQueryInfo as the riid parameter to IShellFolder::GetUIObjectOf(). If the IShellFolder implementation does not support the IQueryInfo interface, the shell will use the standard display text in the info tip.

Header:	objidl.h
Interface ID:	IID_IQueryInfo

IQueryInfo has two methods:

```
HRESULT GetInfoFlags(
    DWORD *pdwFlags
);
```

Parameters:

pdwFlags: This points to the item's information flags on return.

Return Values:
- **S_OK**: Success.
- **Other OLE-Defined value:** Something went wrong.

Remarks: Until the shell uses this method, return E_NOTIMPL and set the DWORD pointed to by pdwFlags to zero. Also, put a debug assertion in this method so that you have a chance of finding out when Microsoft starts calling this method. That's a lot easier than keeping up on the literature. Of course, you will not find out about it until you go in to maintain the namespace extension.

```
HRESULT GetInfoTip(
    DWORD dwFlags,
    ppwszTip:
);
```

Parameters:

dwFlags: This argument is not used right now.

ppwszTip: Points to a null-terminated UNICODE string containing the tip string. Allocate memory for the buffer using the shell's IMalloc interface. You can obtain this interface by calling SHGetMalloc(). The caller assumes responsibility for freeing this memory using the shell's allocator.

Return Values:
- **S_OK**: Success.
- **Other OLE-Defined value:** Something went wrong.

A.25   IPersist

This interface defines a single method, GetClassID(), which supplies the CLSID of an object that can be stored in the system. A call to this method allows the object to state which object to use in the client process. Three commonly used interfaces derive from IPersist: IPersistFile, IPersistStream, and IPersistStorage. The methods of these interfaces allow the object to be serialized to a stream, a file, or an alternative storage mechanism, respectively. These derived interfaces also provide a means for reconstituting the stored object. The taskbar maps active toolbars to the text in the toolbar menu via the object's CLSID.

Header File:	objidl.h
Example Projects:	Chapter 12\CommBand
	Chapter 12\DeskBand
	Chapter 12\SimpsonBand
Interface ID:	IID_IPersist

Objects implementing IPersist must implement the following methods:

```
HRESULT GetClassID(
    CLSID* pClassID
);
```

Parameters:

> **pClassID:** Copy the object's CLSID into the memory block pointed to by pClassID.

> **Return Values:** Returns S_OK if the CLSID was set. If the CLSID could not be set, this method returns E_FAIL.

A.26   IPersistFile

The IPeristFile interface provides a way to load or save an object to a disk file instead of a storage object or a stream. Because the information needed to properly open a file differs from application to application, implementers must also open the disk file in their implementation of IPersistFile::Load(). This interface inherits from IPersist. Any implementation of IPeristFile must also include the methods exposed by IPersist. The shell uses this interface to implement file viewers and various shell extensions, including data handlers, icon handlers, and drop handlers.

Header:	objidl.h
Example Projects:	Chapter 6\AddressBookFV
	Chapter 7\ABKDataHandler
	Chapter 7\ABKDropHandler
	Chapter 7\ABKIconHandler
Interface ID:	IID_IPersistFile

Objects implementing IPersistFile must implement the following methods:

```
HRESULT GetCurFile(
    LPOLESTR *ppszFileName
);
```

Parameters:

> **ppszFileName:** On return, this points to a pointer to a null-terminated string containing the full path and filename of the current file. If no file is open, this returns the default filename prompt (ex. *.txt). If an error occurs, set ppszFileName to NULL.

Return Values:
- **S_OK**: Returned an absolute path.
- **S_FALSE**: Returned the default save prompt.

- **E_OUTOFMEMORY**: The operation failed because of insufficient memory.
- **E_FAIL**: The operation failed for some other reason.

```
HRESULT IsDirty();
```

Return Values:
- **S_OK:** The object has changed since it was last saved.
- **S_FALSE:** The object has not changed since it was last saved.

Remarks: Use this method to determine if an object should be saved before closing it. If your object contains other objects, you must maintain an internal dirty flag that gets set when any of the contained objects change. Hopefully, the contained objects also implement the IDataObject interface. Using the contained object's IDataObject interface, your container would register interest in change notifications by calling IDataObject::DAdvise(). The container would set its internal dirty flag whenever it received an IAdviseSink::OnDataChange() notification.

If the any of the contained objects does not implement IDataObject, you could ask for an IPersistStorage interface instead. Then, iterate over the interfaces, checking IPersistStorage::IsDirty for each of the interfaces.

```
HRESULT Load(
    LPCOLESTR pszFileName,
    DWORD dwMode
);
```

Parameters:

pszFileName: Null-terminated string telling the method the full path of the file to open.

dwMode: Specifies a combination of the values from the STGM enumeration to indicate how to open the file. Your implementation can be more restrictive if needed. If this parameter is zero, you can open the file using whatever default permissions make sense.

Return Values:
- **S_OK**: Loaded the file object.
- **E_OUTOFMEMORY**: The operation failed because of insufficient memory.
- **E_FAIL**: The operation failed for some other reason.

```
HRESULT Save(
    LPCOLESTR pszFileName,
    BOOL fRemember
);
```

Parameters:

> **pszFileName:** Null-terminated string telling the method what full path should be used to save the file. If the parameter is NULL, use the current file if one exists.

> **fRemember:** If this is set to TRUE, pszFileName becomes the current file and the dirty flag should be cleared. If this parameter is FALSE, just save the file and do not clear the dirty flag. If pszFileName is NULL, ignore this flag.

Return Values:
- **S_OK**: Loaded the file object.
- **E_FAIL**: The operation failed for some reason and the file was not saved.

Remarks: While an object is being saved, the object should enter read-only mode. If you have a particularly sophisticated application, you may have to lock writes and then unlock them when the save is complete. If this is the case, look at enlisting the help of IPersistFile::SaveCompleted().

```
HRESULT SaveCompleted(
    LPCOLESTR pszFileName
);
```

Parameters:

> **pszFileName:** Null-terminated string telling where the object was last saved.

Return Values:
- **S_OK**: Always returned.

Remarks: This method notifies an object that it can write to its file. When IPersistFile::Save() gets called, the object should enter read-only mode. Depending on your application, many files may get saved at once. If these files are interdependent, you may lock all writes until the save completes. The controlling application will re-enable writes by calling IPersistFile::SaveCompleted() to indicate that all the files have been saved.

A.27 IPersistFolder

Explorer uses this interface to initialize IShellFolder objects. Its one member function, Initialize(), is used by Explorer to tell it where it is in the shell namespace.

Header:	shlobj.h
Example Projects:	Chapter 11\WinReg
Interface ID:	IID_IPersistFolder

Objects implementing IPersistFolder must implement the following methods:

```
HRESULT Initialize(
    LPCITEMIDLIST pidl
);
```

> **Parameters:**
>
> **pidl:** Address of an ITEMIDLIST specifying the absolute location of the folder.
>
> **Return Values:**
> * **S_OK:** The object was successfully loaded.
> * **Other OLE error code:** Something went wrong.

A.28   IPersistStream

The IPersistStream provides methods for saving and loading objects that can use a serial stream to store data (think CArchive). This interface inherits from the IPersist interface, requiring implementers of IPersistStream to implement GetClassID(). Typically, the user of the object calls these methods. IPersist-Stream gives the user of the object the ability have the object save or restore itself. The user of the object is not under any obligation to actually save your object, even if you implement this interface.

Header:	objidl.h
Example Projects:	Chapter 7\ABKDataHandler
	Chapter 7\ABKDropHandler
	Chapter 7\ABKIconHandler
Interface ID:	IID_IPersistStream

Objects implementing IPersistStream must implement the following methods:

```
HRESULT IsDirty();
```

> **Return Values:**
> * **S_OK:** The object has changed since it was last saved.
> * **S_FALSE:** The object has not changed since it was last saved.
>
> **Remarks:** Callers of this method must assume that the object needs to be saved if this method returns anything other than S_FALSE.

```
HRESULT Load(
    IStream* pStm
);
```

Parameters:

pStm: Identifies the stream that should be used to load the object. The stream pointer is set to the same position it was at during the most recent Save method. This method can seek and read from the stream, but it cannot write to the stream.

Return Values:
- **S_OK:** The object was successfully loaded.
- **E_OUTOFMEMORY:** Operation failed due to a lack of memory.
- **E_FAIL:** All other error conditions.

Remarks: When reading and writing information to the stream, make sure that you leave some clues in the stream that will indicate how much to read or write. This becomes important when reading and writing variable length data. When reading data, the pointer must be at the end of the data written during the last call to Save().

```
HRESULT Save(
    IStream* pStm,
    BOOL fClearDirty
);
```

Parameters:

pStm: Identifies the stream that should be used to save the object.

fClearDirty: Indicates whether to clear the dirty flag after the save is complete. The flag should be cleared if this parameter is set to TRUE. The flag should be left unchanged if this parameter is set to FALSE.

Return Values:
- **S_OK:** The object was successfully saved.
- **STG_E_CANTSAVE:** The operation failed because the object could not save itself to the stream.
- **STG_E_MEDIUM_FULL:** The storage medium ran out of space.

Remarks: When this method is complete, the seek pointer should be positioned immediately past the object data. The position of the pointer is undefined in the case of an error.

A.29 IRemoteComputer

A shell extension can implement this interface on the same object that implements IShellFolder. With it, the namespace extension can be associated with remote computers on the network. This interface is covered in Chapter 9, "Namespace Extensions," Section 9.2.1. The Namespace Extension App-

Wizard will automatically include this interface if you specify that the extension should show up under RemoteComputer in Step 1 of the wizard.

Header:	shlobj.h
Example Projects:	Namespace\ABKCopyHandler
Interface ID:	IID_IShellCopyHook

A.30   ISequentialStream

ISequentialStream provides simplified access to stream objects. Using the Read() and Write() methods, you can read and write to the stream without the worry of where you are in the stream. IStream inherits from this interface and provides some more sophisticated access.

Header:	objidl.h
Interface ID:	IID_ISequentialStream

Objects implementing ISequentialStream must implement the following methods:

```
HRESULT Read(
    void* pv,
    ULONG cb,
    ULONG* pcbRead
);
```

Parameters:

pv: Points to the buffer where the stream data should be read. If an error occurs, this value gets set to NULL.

cb: Specifies the number of bytes to attempt to read from the stream object.

pcbRead: Points to a ULONG that receives the actual number of bytes read from the stream object. If you do not want to know this information, set the parameter to NULL.

Return Values:
- **S_OK:** The stream successfully read the data.
- **S_FALSE:** The data could not be read.
- **E_PENDING:** The stream employs asynchronous storage and part or all of the data to be read is not available.
- **STG_E_ACCESSDENIED:** The caller does not have permission to read the stream.
- **STG_E_INVALIDPOINTER:** The caller passed in an invalid pointer.

- **STG_E_REVERTED:** The object has been invalidated by a revert operation above it in the transaction tree.

Remarks: Implementers may return failure codes if the end of the stream is reached during a read. The caller must decide if the return code indicates a severe failure or if the return code indicates the end of the stream.

```
HRESULT Load(
    IStream* pStm
);
```

Parameters:

pStm: Identifies the stream that should be used to load the object. The stream pointer is set to the same position it was at during the most recent Save() method. This method can seek and read from the stream, but it cannot write to the stream.

Return Values:
- **S_OK:** The object was successfully loaded.
- **E_OUTOFMEMORY:** Operation failed due to a lack of memory.
- **E_FAIL:** All other error conditions.

Remarks: When reading and writing information to the stream, make sure that you leave some clues in the stream that will indicate how much to read or write. This becomes important when reading and writing variable length data. When reading data, the pointer must be at the end of the data written during the last call to Save().

```
HRESULT Write(
    void* pv,
    ULONG cb,
    ULONG* pcbWritten
);
```

Parameters:

pv: Points to the buffer containing the data to be written. The caller must always provide a valid pointer here, even when cb equals zero.

cb: Specifies the number of bytes to attempt to write to the stream object.

pcbWritten: Points to a ULONG that receives the actual number of bytes written to the stream object. If you do not want to know this information, set the parameter to NULL.

Return Values:
- **S_OK:** The stream successfully wrote the data.
- **E_PENDING:** The stream employs asynchronous storage and part or all of the data to be written is not available.

- **STG_E_MEDIUMFULL:** The write operation could not be completed because the storage medium is full.
- **STG_E_ACCESSDENIED:** The caller does not have permission to write to the stream.
- **STG_E_INVALIDPOINTER:** The caller passed in an invalid pointer.
- **STG_E_REVERTED:** The object has been invalidated by a revert operation above it in the transaction tree.
- **STG_E_WRITEFAULT:** The write operation failed due to a disk error. This method also returns this value when attempting to write to a stream opened in simple mode, with the STGM_SIMPLE flag.

A.31 IShellBrowser

Windows Explorer is the best-known implementer of this interface. It provides services for namespace extensions. These namespace extensions implement IShellBrowser's companion, IShellView. IShellBrowser is similar to other site interfaces found in OLE hosting situations like IOleControl and IOleControlSite. This interface allows a namespace extension to communicate with the namespace host by providing menus, status text, and tool bars. This interface also provides a way for an extension to access storage and save its persistent view state.

IShellBrowser derives from the IOleWindow interface. This interface represents the container's top-level window. Through the IShellBrowser interface, a contained view can do the following:

- Insert menus into the composite menu
- Install the composite menu into the appropriate window frame
- Remove the container's menu items from the composite menu

This interface will set and display status text relevant to the IShellView implementation. It also enables or disables the frames modeless dialog boxes and translates accelerator keys for the view.

Header:	shlobj.h
Example Projects:	Chapter 11\WinReg
Interface ID:	IID_IShellBrowser

The IShellBrowser interface provides the following methods:

```
HRESULT BrowseObject(
    LPCITEMIDLIST pidl,
    UINT *wFlags
);
```

Parameters:

pidl: Address of an ITEMIDLIST specifying an object's location. This value depends on the value of the wFlags parameter.

wFlags: These flags specify the folder to be browsed. The flags are divided into four groups that define different aspects of the requested browse behavior.

Group 1: Flags specifying if another window should be created:
- **SBSP_SAMEBROWSER:** Open the new folder in the same Windows Explorer window.
- **SBSP_NEWBROWSER:** Open the new folder in a new Windows Explorer window.
- **SBSP_DEFBROWSER:** Open the new folder using the user settings. In most cases you should be using this flag.

Group 2: Flags specifying the open, explore, or default mode. IShellBrowser ignores these values if SBSP_SAMEBROWSER is set or SBSP_DEFBROWSER is set and the user has selected Browse in Place.
- **SBSP_OPENMODE:** Use a normal folder window.
- **SBSP_EXPLOREMODE:** Use a Windows Explorer window.
- **SBSP_DEFMODE:** Use the current window.

Group 3: Flags specifying the pidl parameter category:
- **SBSP_ABSOLUTE:** The pidl is relative to the Desktop.
- **SBSP_RELATIVE:** The pidl is relative to the current folder.
- **SBSP_PARENT:** Browse the parent folder and ignore the pidl.
- **SBSP_NAVIGATEBACK:** Navigate back and ignore the pidl.
- **SBSP_NAVIGATEFORWARD:** Navigate forward and ignore the pidl.

Group 4: Flags specifying how history is manipulated as a result of navigation:
- **SBSP_WRITENOHISTORY:** Write no history entry.
- **SBSP_NOAUTOSELECT:** Suppress selection in the history pane.

Return Values:
- **S_OK:** Success.
- **Any other value:** Validate against OLE-defined error codes.

```
HRESULT EnableModelessSB(
    BOOL fEnable
);
```

Parameters:

fEnable: Specifies whether modeless dialog boxes are enabled or disabled. TRUE means that modeless dialog boxes should be enabled; FALSE means that modeless dialog boxes should be disabled.

Remarks: This method is similar to IOleInPlaceFrame::EnableMode-less(). You should call this method to enable or disable modeless dialog boxes associated with the Windows Explorer window.

```
HRESULT GetControlWindow(
    UINT id,
    HWND* lphwnd
);
```

Parameters:

id: Identifies which control's window you want. You can get any of these four windows:
- **FCW_TOOLBAR**: Retrieves the browser's toolbar.
- **FCW_STATUS**: Retrieves the browser's status bar.
- **FCW_TREE**: Retrieves the browser's tree view. Only use this flag to determine if the tree is present. Windows Explorer maintains the tree view. Any manipulation of the tree control will result in undefined behavior.
- **FCW_PROGRESS**: Retrieves the browser's progress bar.

lphwnd: Pointer to an HWND. On return, it contains the HWND of the requested Windows Explorer control.

Return Values:
- **NOERROR**: Success.
- **Any other OLE-defined error code**: Failure.

Remarks: Do not send messages directly to the control windows retrieved with this method. You should use IShellBrowser::SendControlMsg() to send messages. Your namespace extension should be prepared for the returned handle to be NULL. Future versions of Windows Explorer may not include any of the controls you can retrieve using IShellBrowser::GetControlWindow().

```
HRESULT GetViewStateStream(
    DWORD grfMode,
    LPSTREAM* ppStrm
);
```

Parameters:

grfMode: Defines what type of IStream you want the IShellBrowser to open. It can be one of the following values:
- **STGM_READ**
- **STGM_WRITE**
- **STGM_READWRITE**

ppStrm: Address that receives the IStream pointer.

Return Values:
- **NOERROR**: Success.
- **Any other OLE-defined error code**: Failure.

Remarks: Use this method to save and restore the persistent state for a view. The state includes things such as icon positions, column widths, and the current scroll position. An IShellView usually calls this method when it creates a view window. IShellView implementations also call this method from IShellView::SaveViewState() to save the persistent state.

```
HRESULT InsertMenusSB(
    HMENU hmenuShared,
    LPOLEMENUGROUPWIDTHS lpMenuWidths
);
```

Parameters:

hMenuShared: Handle to an empty menu.

lpMenuWidths: Points to an OLEMENUGROUPWIDTHS structure. This structure has the following definition:

```
typedef struct tagOleMenuGroupWidths
{
    LONG width[6];
} OLEMENUGROUPWIDTHS, * LPOLEMENUGROUPWIDTHS;
```

Usually, this structure allows an OLE-container and object server to populate a common set of menus. This allows similar interaction, but the menus manipulated are different. With the shell, the container fills elements 0, 2, and 4 to reflect the number of menu elements it provided in the File, View, and Tools submenus. The view will later insert menu items by their identifiers. This is different from typical OLE in-place activation. The command identifiers that the view inserts into the submenus or its own submenus must be between FCIDM_SHVIEWFIRST and FCIDM_SHVIEWLAST.

Return Values:
- **NOERROR**: Success.
- **Any other OLE-defined error code**: Failure.

Remarks: Namespace extensions should call this upon activation to add their menus to the user interface. The extension asks the container to adds it menus first. Then, the extension adds its own menus and counts. The extension calls IOleInPlaceFrame::InsertMenus() as many times as needed to build up the composite menus. The container must use the initial menu handle associated with the composite menu for all items in the drop-down menus.

```
HRESULT OnViewWindowActive(
    IShellView *ppshv
);
```

Parameters:

ppshv: Address of the view object's IShellView pointer.

Return Values:
- **NOERROR**: Success.
- **Any other OLE-defined error code**: Failure.

Remarks: A shell view must call this method when the view window or one of its child windows gets the focus or becomes active. The view must call this method before calling the IShellBrowser::InsertMenusSB() method. This method inserts a different set of menu items, depending on whether the view has focus.

```
HRESULT QueryActiveShellView(
    IShellView **ppshv
);
```

Parameters:

ppshv: Address of an IShellView pointer. On return, this will point to the currently active IShellView.

Return Values:
- **NOERROR**: Success.
- **Any other OLE-defined error code**: Failure.

Remarks: Returns the currently active shell view.

```
HRESULT RemoveMenusSB(
    HMENU hmenuShared
);
```

Parameters:

hmenuShared: Handle to the composite menu constructed by calls to IShellBrowser::InsertMenusSB() and the SDK InsertMenu() function.

Return Values:
- **NOERROR**: Success.
- **Any other OLE-defined error code**: Failure.

Remarks: This method is similar to the IOleInPlaceFrame::Remove-Menus() method. The object should remove its menu elements before it deactivates the shared user interface. Calling this allows the browser to remove its menus.

```
HRESULT SendControlMsg(
    UINT id,
    UINT uMsg,
    WPARAM wParam,
    LPARAM lParam,
    LRESULT *pret
);
```

Parameters:

id: Set to either the toolbar (FCW_TOOLBAR) or the status bar (FCW_STATUS).

uMsg: Message to send to the control.

wParam: Value depends on the uMsg parameter.

lParam: Value depends on the uMsg parameter.

pret: This method calls the SDK function SendMessage(). pret will contain the result of SendMessage() on return.

Return Values:
- **NOERROR**: Success.
- **Any other OLE-defined error code**: Failure.

Remarks: You can send any message to the toolbar or status bar that would be possible if these controls were part of your window. Be prepared for this function to return E_NOTIMPL or some other error. A future version of Windows Explorer may not have a status bar or toolbar.

```
HRESULT SetMenuSB(
    HMENU hmenuShared,
    HOLEMENU holemenuReserved,
    HWND hwndActiveObject
);
```

Parameters:

hmenuShared: Handle to the composite menu constructed by calls to IShellBrowser::InsertMenusSB() and the SDK InsertMenu() function.

holemenuReserved: Reserved for future use.

hwndActiveObject: Handle to the view's window.

Return Values:
- **NOERROR**: Success.
- **Any other OLE-defined error code**: Failure.

Remarks: Call this method to ask the container to install the menu structure set up by calls to IShellBrowser::InsertMenusSB() and the Windows API function, InsertMenu().

```
HRESULT SetStatusTextSB(
    LPCOLESTR lpszStatusText
);
```

Parameters:

lpszStatusText: The null-terminated string to display in the Explorer status bar.

Return Values:
- **NOERROR**: Success.
- **Any other OLE-defined error code**: Failure.

Remarks: You can also send messages directly to the status window using the IShellBrowser::SendControlMsg() method.

```
HRESULT SetToolbarItems(
    LPTBBUTTON lpButtons,
    UINT nButtons,
    UINT uFlags
);
```

Parameters:

lpButtons: Address of an array of TBBUTTON structures.

nButtons: Number of TBBUTTON structures in the lpButtons array.

uFlags: Specifies where the buttons should go. This can be one or more of the following values:
- **FCT_ADDTOEND:** Add at the right side of the toolbar.
- **FCT_CONFIGABLE:** No, this is not a spelling error. At least, not by me. This has not been implemented yet. Maybe we should encourage Microsoft to change the spelling to FCT_CONFIGURABLE.
- **FCT_MERGE:** Merge the toolbar items instead of replacing all of the buttons with those provided by the view. You should usually use this value.

Return Values:
- **NOERROR**: Success.
- **Any other OLE-defined error code**: Failure.

Remarks: Adds toolbar items to the Windows Explorer toolbar.

```
HRESULT TranslateAcceleratorSB(
    LPMSG lpMsg,
    WORD wID
);
```

Parameters:

lpMsg: Pointer to an MSG structure. This structure contains the keystroke message.

wID: Command identifier corresponding to the accelerator in the container-provided accelerator table. Containers should use this value instead of translating the accelerator again.

Return Values:
- **S_OK:** The keystroke was used.

- **S_FALSE:** The keystroke was not used.
- **Other OLE-Defined value:** Something went wrong.

Remarks: Call this method when the user presses a key-sequence that your object does not recognize.

A.32 IShellChangeNotify

This interface allows the shell to notify a namespace extension when the ID of an item has changed. All namespace extensions should implement this interface. The operating system is this interface's only user.

Header:	shlobj.h
Interface ID:	Not listed.

This interface has one method.

```
HRESULT OnChange(
    LONG lEvent,
    LPCITEMIDLIST pidl1,
    LPCITEMIDLIST pidl2
);
```

Parameters:

lEvent: Describes what event occurred. Usually only one event gets specified at a time. If more than one event is specified, then the pidl1 and pidl2 parameters must be the same for all events. See SHChangeNotify() in Appendix B for valid values.

pidl1: First event-dependent item identifier.

pidl2: The other event-dependent item identifier.

Return Values:
- **S_OK:** The keystroke was used.
- **Other OLE-Defined value:** Something went wrong.

Remarks: This method is the companion to SHChangeNotify(). When SHChangeNotify() tells the shell that something changed, this method handles the change.

A.33 IShellDetails

An IShellFolder implementation exposes this interface in order to provide detailed information about the folder's contents. This information gets displayed when Windows Explorer is set to Details. In Windows 2000 and later systems,

IShellFolder2 supersedes this interface. Unless you know that you will not have to support Windows 9x or Windows NT 4.0, you will need to implement and expose both interfaces.

Header: shlobj.h

Interface ID: IID_IShellDetails

```
HRESULT ColumnClick(
    UINT iColumn
);
```

Parameters:

iColumn: The index of the column to rearrange.

Return Values:
- **S_OK:** The object sorted the selected column.
- **S_FALSE:** The caller should sort the selected column. Folder objects typically return S_FALSE.

Remarks: This method gets called when a client of a folder object wants to sort the object based on the contents of one of the Details columns.

```
HRESULT GetDetailsOf(
    LPCITEMIDLIST pidl,
    UINT iColumn,
    LPSHELLDETAILS pDetails
);
```

Parameters:

pidl: The PIDL of the item the call wants information on. If pidl is NULL, return the title of the information field specified by iColumn via the pDetails argument.

iColumn: Zero-based index of the desired information field. This value corresponds to the column number of the information when the Windows Explorer Details view is active.

pDetails: Pointer to a SHELLDETAILS structure.

Return Values:
- **S_OK:** Success.
- **E_FAIL:** iColumn exceeds the number of columns supported by the folder.
- **Other OLE-Defined value:** Something went wrong.

Remarks: This method gets called when a client of a folder object wants to sort the object based on the contents of one of the Details columns.

A.34   IShellExecuteHook

Extends the behavior of the ShellExecute() and ShellExecuteEx() functions. Subsystems that expose "Run-able" objects, or objects that the user can run from the Run command available from the Start menu, usually implement this interface.

Header:	shlobj.h
Interface ID:	IID_IShellExecuteHook

IShellExecuteHook contains one method.

```
HRESULT Execute(
    LPSHELLEXECUTEINFO pei
);
```

Parameters:

pei: Address of a SHELLEXECUTEINFO structure containing information about the object being executed. On return, the implementation must fill in the hInstApp member.

Return Values:

- **S_OK:** The hook processed the execution. ShellExecute() or ShellExecuteEx() (one of these functions caused the interface to be called) should not do anything else. You can also return this value when you want to prevent execution of the object.
- **S_FALSE:** The hook is installed but did not process the execution. ShellExecute() or ShellExecuteEx() should perform the default processing.

Remarks: This method allows an application to hook the execution of an object and to change the default execution. This method can also prevent the execution of an object by returning S_OK. When preventing the execution of a command, set the SHELLEXECUTE.hInstApp member to 32 or higher in order to prevent the shell from generating an error message box.

A.35   IShellExtInit

The shell uses this interface to initialize shell extensions for property sheets, context menus, and drag-and-drop handlers. This interface is covered in Chapter 7, Section 7.1 and used in three examples in the chapter.

Header:	shlobj.h
Example Project:	Chapter 7\ABKContextMenuHandler

	Chapter 7\ABKPropertySheetHandler
	Chapter 7\BSOD
Interface ID:	IID_IShellExtInit

A.36   IShellFolder

This interface manages folders. All shell namespace objects expose this interface. This interface can create a namespace rooted outside of Windows Explorer (where the folder is the root) or rooted within Windows Explorer (where the Desktop is the root).

Header:	shlobj.h
Example Projects:	Chapter 11\WinReg
Interface ID:	IID_IShellFolder

IShellFolder contains the following methods:

```
HRESULT BindToObject(
    LPCITEMIDLIST pidl,
    LPBC pbcReserved,
    REFIID riid,
    LPVOID *ppvOut
);
```

Parameters:

pidl: Address of an ITEMIDLIST. pidl identifies the subfolder relative to its parent folder. This structure must contain exactly one SHITEMID structure followed by a null termination.

pbcReserved: Callers should specify NULL. Implementations can ignore this parameter.

riid: Identifier of the interface the caller wants returned. This must be the IID_IShellFolder interface identifier.

ppvOut: Return NULL if an error occurs. Otherwise, instantiate the IShellFolder object needed for the folder for pidl.

Return Values:
- **S_OK:** Successful.
- **Other OLE-Defined value:** Something went wrong.

Remarks: This method returns the IShellFolder interface of a subfolder.

```
HRESULT BindToStorage(
    LPCITEMIDLIST pidl,
    LPBC pbcReserved,
    REFIID riid,
```

```
    LPVOID* ppvObj
);
```

Return Values:

- **E_NOTIMPL:** Always should return this value.

Remarks: At this point in time, nothing uses this method. I suggest putting a debug assertion in your implementation of this method. That way, if Microsoft suddenly starts calling this method, you will know about it during your own testing.

```
HRESULT CompareIDs(
    LPARAM lParam,
    LPCITEMIDLIST pidl1,
    LPCITEMIDLIST pidl2
);
```

Parameters:

lParam: Specifies the type of comparison to perform. The caller should always specify zero. Zero means that the two items should be sorted by name. Values from 0x00000001 to 0x7FFFFFFF are for folder specific sorting rules. For any values less than 0x80000000, an implementation can assume that it should sort by detail-view column. The system reserves values greater than 0x80000000 for its own uses.

pidl1: Address of an ITEMIDLIST specifying one comparison item. The value is relative to the folder. More than one element may be specified in the ITEMIDLIST structure. One list can be less than, greater than, or equal to the other.

pidl2: Same meaning as pidl1.

Return Values:

- **< 0:** pidl1 < pidl2
- **0:** pidl1 = pidl2
- **>0:** pidl1 > pidl2

```
HRESULT CreateViewObject(
    HWND hwndOwner,
    REFIID riid,
    LPVOID *ppvOut
);
```

Parameters:

hwndOwner: Handle to the window to use as the view object's parent.

riid: Identifies the interface to return. This should be IShellView or IShellView2.

ppvOut: On return, this value will contain a pointer to the view object or NULL if the operation does not succeed.

Return Values:

- **S_OK:** Successful.
- **Other OLE-Defined value:** Something went wrong.

Remarks: This object must be different from the IShellFolder object. The IShellView may get created many times and each IShellView must be independent of the other instantiations. In other words, do not use IShellFolder, IShellView together with multiple inheritance when you are building your namespace extension.

```
HRESULT EnumObjects(
    HWND hwndOwner,
    DWORD grfFlags,
    LPENUMIDLIST *ppenumIDList
);
```

Parameters:

hwndOwner: If the folder requires user input in order to perform the enumeration, use this window handle to take user input. For example, the shell may need a password or need to prompt the user to insert a CD or floppy. If this value is NULL, the enumeration should not display any user interface. If user input happens to be required, the method should fail silently.

grfFlags: Indicates what items to include in the enumeration. See SHCONTF in Appendix B for valid values. grfFlags may contain one or more of the values.

ppenumIDList: On return, this contains a pointer to an IEnumIDList interface for the enumeration object created by the method. If an error occurs, this argument should be set to NULL.

Return Values:

- **S_OK:** Successful.
- **Other OLE-Defined value:** Something went wrong.

Remarks: The caller is responsible for calling Release() on the IEnumIDList object returned by this method.

```
HRESULT GetAttributesOf(
    UINT cidl,
    LPCITEMIDLIST *apidl,
    ULONG *rgfInOut
);
```

Parameters:

cidl: Number of file objects to return the attributes of.

apidl: Address of an array of pointers to ITEMIDLIST structures. Each ITEMIDLIST structure must contain one SHITEMID followed by a null-terminator.

rgfInOut: Points to a ULONG value. On entry, this contains the attributes the caller wants. On exit, this contains the requested attributes common to all of the specified objects. This parameter can have one or more of the following values.

These values specify the file object's capabilites:

- **SFGAO_CANCOPY:** The items in apidl can be copied.
- **SFGAO_CANDELETE:** The items in apidl can be deleted.
- **SFGAO_CANLINK:** The shell can create shortcuts for the items in apidl.
- **SFGAO_CANMONIKER:** Monikers can be created for the items in apidl.
- **SFGAO_CANMOVE:** The items in apidl can be moved.
- **SFGAO_CANRENAME:** The items in apidl can be renamed.
- **SFGAO_CAPABILITYMASK:** Use this flag to mask the capability flags.
- **SFGAO_DROPTARGET:** The items in apidl are drop targets.
- **SFGAO_HASPROPSHEET:** The items in apidl have property sheets.

These values specify the file object's display attributes:

- **SFGAO_DISPLAYATTRMASK:** Use this flag to mask the display attributes flags.
- **SFGAO_GHOSTED:** Display the objects in apidl using a ghosted icon.
- **SFGAO_LINK:** Display the objects in apidl as shortcuts.
- **SFGAO_READONLY:** The items in apidl are read-only.
- **SFGAO_SHARE:** The folders specified in apidl are shared.

These values specify the file object's contents flags:

- **SFGAO_CONTENTSMASK:** Use this flag to mask the contents attributes.
- **SFGAO_HASSUBFOLDER:** The folders specified in apidl have subfolders.

These values specify the file object's miscellaneous attributes:

- **SFGAO_BROWSABLE:** The items in apidl can be browsed in place.
- **SFGAO_COMPRESSED:** The items in apidl are compressed.
- **SFGAO_FILESYSTEM:** The items in apidl are part of the file system, not files, directories, or root directories.
- **SFGAO_FILESYSANCESTOR:** The items in apidl contain one or more file system folders.
- **SFGAO_FOLDER:** The items in apidl are folders.

- **SFGAO_NEWCONTENT:** The items in apidl contain new content.
- **SFGAO_NONENUMERATED:** The items in apidl are nonenumerated.
- **SFGAO_REMOVABLE:** The items in apidl are on removable media.
- **SFGAO_VALIDATE:** Instructs the shell folder to validate cached information. It should check to make sure that all items specified in apidl still exist and will not use cached information when retrieving attributes. If one or more of the items in apidl are gone, the method should return an error code. If the caller passes this flag and sets cidl to zero, the shell will discard all cached information for the shell folder. This is similar to refreshing a folder.

Return Values:

- **S_OK:** Successful.
- **Other OLE-Defined value:** Something went wrong.

Remarks: Do not return unspecified flags unless there is no time penalty for doing so.

```
HRESULT GetDisplayNameOf(
    LPCITEMIDLIST pidl,
    DWORD uFlags,
    LPSTRRET lpName
);
```

Parameters:

pidl: Points to an ITEMIDLIST structure containing exactly one SHITEMID structure followed by a null-terminator. This structure uniquely identifies a file object or subfolder relative to the parent folder.

uFlags: Flags specifying the type of display name to return. This can be any one of the values specified by the SHGNO enumeration.

lpName: Points to a STRRET structure. This structure should contain the display name on return. The type of name may be the requested type. The shell folder may opt to return a different type.

Return Values:

- **S_OK:** Successful.
- **Other OLE-Defined value:** Something went wrong.

Remarks: The easiest way to retrieve the display name from the STRRET structure pointed to by lpName is to use StrRetToBuf() or StrRetToStr(). Both of these functions take a STRRET structure and return the name. You can also examine the STRRET.uType member and perform the interpretation on your own. If you do your own interpretation, you will have some work to do in order to interpret new uType values. Microsoft will probably keep StrRetToBuf() and StrRetToStr() up to date for you.

```
HRESULT GetUIObjectOf(
    HWND hwndOwner,
    UINT cidl,
    LPCITEMIDLIST *apidl,
    REFIID riid,
    UINT *prgfInOut,
    LPVOID *ppvOut
);
```

Parameters:

hwndOwner: Handle to the owner window that the client should use if it needs to display a dialog or message box.

cidl: Number of file objects or subfolders in the apidl array.

apidl: Address of an array of pointers to ITEMIDLIST structures. Each ITEMIDLIST must contain one SHITEMID structure followed by a null-terminator.

riid: Identifier of the COM interface object to return. This can be any valid interface identifier that can be created for an item. The most common interfaces requested are:
- **IContextMenu:** cidl can be greater than or equal to one.
- **IContextMenu2:** cidl can be greater than or equal to one.
- **IContextMenu3:** cidl can be greater than or equal to one.
- **IDataObject:** cidl can be greater than or equal to one.
- **IDropTarget:** cidl can only be one.
- **IExtractIcon:** cidl can only be one.
- **IQueryInfo:** cidl can only be one.

prgfInOut: Reserved.

ppvOut: Pointer to an instance of the requested interface. If an error occurs, this must be NULL.

Return Values:
- **S_OK:** Successful.
- **E_NOINTERFACE:** The interface is not supported.
- **Other OLE-Defined value:** Something went wrong.

Remarks: If cidl is greater than one, an implementation of GetUIObjectOf() should only succeed if one object can be created for all items specified in apidl. If this method cannot do this, the method should fail.

```
HRESULT ParseDisplayName(
    HWND hwndOwner,
```

```
    LPBC pbc,
    LPOLESTR lpwszDisplayName,
    ULONG *pchEaten,
    LPITEMIDLIST *ppidl,
    ULONG *pdwAttributes
);
```

Parameters:

hwndOwner: Handle to the owner window of any dialog or message boxes that the ParseDisplayName() method might need to display. This can be NULL.

pbc: Optional bind context used to control the parsing operation. Callers normally set this parameter to NULL.

lpwszDisplayName: Null-terminated UNICODE string with the display name. Because each shell folder gets to define its own parsing syntax, this string may take different forms. The Desktop folder paths like "C:\SomeDir\SomeFile.txt". It will also accept references to items within the namespace that have an associated GUID. For example, you can retrieve the fully qualified item identifier list for the Control Panel using this path: "*{CLSID for My Computer}\::{CLSID for the Control Panel}*".

pchEaten: Address of a ULONG value. On return, this contains the number of characters that the function parsed.

ppidl: Address of a ITEMIDLIST pointer. On return, this contains the item identifier list for the object relative to the parsing folder. If the object specified by lpwszDisplayName is within the parsing folder, ppidl should contain only one SHITEMID structure. If the object is in a subfolder of the current folder, the item will contain multiple SHITEMID structures. If an error occurs, this value must be set to NULL.

pdwAttributes: See the rgfInOut parameter of IShellFolder::GetAttributesOf() for a list of valid values.

Return Values:
- **S_OK:** Successful.
- **Other OLE-Defined value:** Something went wrong.

Remarks: Use this method to translate a file or folder object's display name into an ITEMIDLIST.

```
HRESULT SetNameOf(
    HWND hwndOwner,
    LPCITEMIDLIST pidl,
    LPCOLESTR lpszName,
    DWORD uFlags,
    LPITEMIDLIST *ppidlOut
);
```

Parameters:

> **hwndOwner:** Handle to the owner window of any dialog or message boxes that the SetNameOf() method might need to display. This can be NULL.

> **pidl:** Address of an ITEMIDLIST structure. The ITEMIDLIST must contain one SHITEMID structure followed by a null-terminator.

> **lpszName:** Address of a null-terminated string specifying the new display name.

> **uFlags:** Specifies the type of name specified by the lpszName parameter. It may be a combination of the values specified by the SHGNO enumeration.

> **ppidlOut:** Points to the new ITEMIDLIST structure. Because some implementations of SetNameOf() may ignore the request, this may not point to a valid ITEMIDLIST on return. If the caller sets this value to NULL, a new ITEMIDLIST should not be returned. This value must be NULL if an error occurs.

Return Values:
- **S_OK:** Successful.
- **Other OLE-Defined value:** Something went wrong.

Remarks: Applications should call the IShellFolder::GetAttributesOf() method before calling IShellFolder::SetNameOf() and check to see if the SFGAO_CANRENAME flag is set. This flag is a hint to namespace clients and does not always imply whether IShellFolder::SetNameOf() will succeed or fail.

A.37 IShellFolder2

This interface extends the capabilities of the IShellFolder interface.

Header:	shlobj.h
Interface ID:	IID_IShellFolder2

IShellFolder2 contains the following methods:

```
HRESULT EnumSearches(
    IEnumExtraSearch **ppEnum
);
```

Parameters:

> **ppEnum:** On return, will contain a pointer to an IEnumExtraSearch interface. The caller can then use this interface to get any available search objects for the folder.

Return Values:
- **S_OK:** Successful.
- **Other OLE-Defined value:** Something went wrong.

```
HRESULT GetItemData(
    LPCITEMIDLIST pidl,
    int nFormat,
    void *pv,
    int cb
);
```

Parameters:

pidl: Points to an ITEMIDLIST structure that identifies the object.

nFormat: Specifies the format of the requested data. It can be one of the following values:
- **SFGID_FINDDATA:** pv points to a UNICODE version of the WIN32_FIND_DATA structure.

- **SFGID_NETRESOURCE:** pv points to a UNICODE version of the NETRESOURCE structure.

- **SFGID_DESCRIPTIONID:** pv points to a UNICODE version of the SHDESCRIPTIONID structure.

pv: Buffer to receive the requested data. nFormat indicates the expected format. When processing a NETRESOURCE structure, only fill in the scope, type, display type, and usage members of the NETRESOURCE structure. Set the remote name, local name, provider, and comment members to NULL.

cb: Size (in bytes) of the buffer pointed to by pv.

Return Values:
- **S_OK:** Successful.
- **Other OLE-Defined value:** Something went wrong.

Remarks: This method is similar to the SHGetDataFromIDList() function.

```
HRESULT GetUIObjectOf2(
    HWND hwndOwner,
    UINT cidl,
    LPCITEMIDLIST *apidl,
    REFIID riid,
    DWORD dwType,
    UINT *prgfInOut,
    LPVOID *ppvOut
);
```

Parameters:

hwndOwner: Handle to the owner window that the client should use if it needs to display a dialog or message box.

cidl: Number of file objects or subfolders in the apidl array.

apidl: Address of an array of pointers to ITEMIDLIST structures. Each ITEMIDLIST must contain one SHITEMID structure followed by a null-terminator.

riid: Identifier of the COM interface object to return. This can be any valid interface identifier that can be created for an item. The most common interfaces requested are:

- **IContextMenu:** cidl can be greater than or equal to one.
- **IContextMenu2:** cidl can be greater than or equal to one.
- **IContextMenu3:** cidl can be greater than or equal to one.
- **IDataObject:** cidl can be greater than or equal to one.
- **IDropTarget:** cidl can only be one.
- **IExtractIcon:** cidl can only be one.
- **IQueryInfo:** cidl can only be one.

dwType: Reserved.

prgfInOut: Reserved.

ppvOut: Pointer to an instance of the requested interface. If an error occurs, this must be NULL.

Return Values:

- **S_OK:** Successful.
- **E_NOINTERFACE:** The interface is not supported.
- **Other OLE-Defined value:** Something went wrong.

Remarks: This function follows the same rules as IShellFolder::GetUI-ObjectOf(). The only difference is the dwType parameter. This parameter will be used to specify how to handle a request for a context menu.

A.38   IShellIcon

This interface retrieves the icon index for an IShellFolder object. A calling application uses IShellIcon to obtain the folder icon and the icon for any object within a folder using one IShellIcon instance. IExtractIcon will allow similar functionality but it requires a separate instance for each object. You should implement this interface whenever you implement IShellFolder to provide quick access to the icon for an object in a folder. If you do not implement IShellIcon with your IShellFolder object, IShellFolder::GetUIObjectOf() will be used to get an icon for all objects.

Header: shlobj.h

Interface ID: IID_IShellIcon

IShellIcon contains one method:

```
HRESULT GetIconOf(
    LPCITEMIDLIST pidl,
    UINT flags,
    LPINT lpIconIndex
);
```

Parameters:

> **pidl:** Address of the ITEMIDLIST structure specifying the relative lo-
> cation of the folder.
>
> **flags:** Specifies which icon the caller wants. It can be zero or one of
> these values.
> - **GIL_FORSHELL:** The icon will be displayed in a shell folder.
> - **GIL_OPENICON:** The shell usually uses this flag for folder ob-
>   jects. If both an open and closed version of the folder exists,
>   return the open version. If this flag is not specified, return the
>   icon for the normal/closed state.
>
> **lpIconIndex:** Points to an integer. On return, this should contain the
> index of the icon within the system image list. The following indexes
> are guaranteed to always correspond to some standard icons:
> - **0:** Document, blank page, unassociated
> - **1:** Document with data on the page
> - **2:** Application (must have an .exe, .com, or .bat extension)
> - **3:** Closed folder
> - **4:** Open folder

Return Values:
- **S_OK:** Able to find the image list index.
- **S_FALSE:** Can find an icon for the object.
- **Other OLE-Defined value:** Something went wrong.

Remarks: It is your responsibility to add the image to the system image
list if it has not been added yet. Do not add images more than once.
Adding the images too many times will cause the image list to grow too
large and will result in permanent memory loss until the system restarts.

A.39   IShellLink

This interface allows you to create, modify, and resolve shell links. It's a very
handy little tool for you to use when looking at links. You do not implement
this interface—Microsoft did.

Header: shlobj.h

Example Project: Chapter 2\StartMenuEditor

Interface ID: IID_IShellLink

IShellLink has the following methods:

```
HRESULT GetArguments(
    LPSTR pszArgs,
    int cchMaxPath
);
```

Parameters:

pszArgs: On return, this buffer will contain the command line arguments for the particular link.

cchMaxPath: Tells IShellLink how large the pszArgs buffer is.

Return Values:
- **S_OK:** Everything worked.
- **Other OLE-Defined value:** Something went wrong.

Remarks: Retrieves the command line arguments for the associated shell link object.

```
HRESULT GetDescription(
    LPSTR pszName,
    int cchMaxName
);
```

Parameters:

pszName: On return, this buffer will contain the description for the particular link.

cchMaxName: Tells IShellLink how large the pszName buffer is.

Return Values:
- **S_OK:** Everything worked.
- **Other OLE-Defined value:** Something went wrong.

Remarks: Retrieves the description for a shell link object.

```
HRESULT GetHotkey(
    WORD *pwHotkey
);
```

Parameters:

pwHotKey: On return, this contains the hot key, if any, for the shell link. The low-order byte contains the virtual key code. The high-order byte contains any modifier flags. The modifier flags can be any of the following values:
- **HOTKEYF_ALT:** ALT key
- **HOTKEYF_CONTROL:** CTRL key

- **HOTKEYF_EXT:** Extended key
- **HOTKEYF_SHIFT:** SHIFT key

Return Values:
- **S_OK:** Everything worked.
- **Other OLE-Defined value:** Something went wrong.

Remarks: Retrieves the hot key for a shell link.

```
HRESULT GetIconLocation(
    LPSTR pszIconPath,
    int cchIconPath,
    int *piIcon
);
```

Parameters:

pszIconPath: On return, this buffer will contain the path of the file that contains the icon.

cchIconPath: Tells IShellLink how large the pszIconPath buffer is.

piIcon: On return, contains the index of the icon within pszIconPath.

Return Values:
- **S_OK:** Everything worked.
- **Other OLE-Defined value:** Something went wrong.

Remarks: Retrieves the path and index of the shell link's icon.

```
HRESULT GetIDList(
    LPITEMIDLIST *ppidl
);
```

Parameters:

ppidl: Pointer to an array of item identifiers. On return, this contains the item identifiers for the shell link.

Return Values:
- **S_OK:** Everything worked. ppidl contains one or more valid PIDLs.
- **S_FALSE:** The function worked but no PIDLs could be retrieved. ppidl should be NULL.
- **Other OLE-Defined value:** Something went wrong.

```
HRESULT GetPath(
    LPSTR pszFile,
    int cchMaxPath,
    WIN32_FIND_DATA *pfd,
    DWORD fFlags
);
```

Parameters:

pszFile: On return, this buffer will contain the shell link's path and filename.

cchMaxPath: Tells IShellLink how large the pszFile buffer is.

pfd: On return, this WIN32_FIND_DATA structure will contain information about the shell link object.

fFlags: Specifies what type of path information to retrieve. It can have any one of the following values:

- **SLGP_SHORTPATH:** Gets the short file name (8.3 format).
- **SLGP_UNCPRIORITY:** Gets the Universal Naming Convention (UNC) filename.
- **SLGP_RAWPATH:** Gets the raw pathname. The raw path might not exist, and it might contain environment variables that you will need to expand.

Return Values:

- **S_OK:** Everything worked.
- **S_FALSE:** Nothing went wrong, but a path could not be returned. For example, the raw path might not exist.
- **Other OLE-Defined value:** Something went wrong.

Remarks: Returns the path and file name of the shell link object, not the object that the shell link points to.

```
HRESULT GetShowCmd(
    int *piShowCmd
);
```

Parameters:

piShowCmd: On return, contains the show command for shell link. The value is confined to a subset of the ShowWindow() values:

- **SW_SHOWNORMAL**
- **SW_SHOWMAXIMIZED**
- **SW_SHOWMINIMIZED**

Return Values:

- **S_OK:** Everything worked.
- **Other OLE-Defined value:** Something went wrong.

```
HRESULT GetWorkingDirectory(
    LPSTR pszDir,
    int cchMaxPath
);
```

Parameters:

pszDir: On return, this buffer will contain the shell link's working directory.

cchMaxPath: Tells IShellLink how large the pszDir buffer is.

Return Values:
- **S_OK:** Everything worked.
- **Other OLE-Defined value:** Something went wrong.

Remarks: Retrieves the shell link's working directory.

```
HRESULT Resolve(
    HWND hwnd,
    DWORD fFlags
);
```

Parameters:

hwnd: The shell will use this window handle as the parent for a dialog box. The shell will use this handle if it needs to ask the user for more information in order to resolve the link.

fFlags: This can be any combination of the following values:
- **SLR_INVOKE_MSI:** Call the Microsoft Software Installer.
- **SLR_NOLINKINFO:** When this flag is not set, IShellLink will use distributed link tracking to track removable media across devices based on the volume name. It will also track file systems on other computers whose drive letters may have changed by using the UNC path. In order to disable link tracking, set this flag.
- **SLR_NO_UI:** If the shell cannot resolve the link, it should not ask the user for help. When you specify this flag, the high order word of fFlags specifies the length of the timeout in milliseconds. The function returns if it cannot resolve the link within the timeout period. If you set the high order word to zero, the timeout period defaults to three seconds.
- **SLR_NOUPDATE:** Do not update the link information.
- **SLR_NOSEARCH:** Do not execute any search heuristics.
- **SLR_NOTRACK:** Do not use distributed link tracking.
- **SLR_UPDATE:** If the link has changed, this will cause the link information to be updated.

Return Values:
- **S_OK:** Everything worked.
- **Other OLE-Defined value:** Something went wrong.

Remarks: After the link has been created, the name or location of the linked item may change. IShellLink::Resolve() first tries to find the file using the path associated with the link. If the item has been moved, IShellLink::Resolve() will try to find it. If you set the SLR_UPDATE flag, this method will update the link if the target has moved.

IShellLink::Resolve() uses two methods to find the target objects. The first requires NTFS 5.0 and the distributed link tracking service.[1] The distributed link tracking service can find an object that was moved from one location to another on the same NTFS 5.0 volume or to another NTFS 5.0 volume on the same machine or a different one.

Distributed link tracking may not be available or it might fail to resolve the link. If it did fail, IShellLink::Resolve() will run its own search heuristics. It will first look in the object's last known location for a file with the same attributes and creation time. It will next look in surrounding directories for a file with the same name or same attributes and creation time. Last, it will apply these rules to the local Desktop and volumes.

If IShellLink::Resolve() has failed, it will ask the user for help unless the user specified the SLR_NO_UI flag.

```
HRESULT SetArguments(
    LPCSTR pszArgs
);
```

Parameters:

pszArgs: Address of a null-terminated string containing the new command line arguments for the link object.

Return Values:
- **S_OK:** Everything worked.
- **Other OLE-Defined value:** Something went wrong.

Remarks: Sets the command line for the shell link object.

```
HRESULT SetDescription(
    LPCSTR pszName
);
```

Parameters:

pszName: Address of a null-terminated string containing the new description for the link object.

Return Values:
- **S_OK:** Everything worked.
- **Other OLE-Defined value:** Something went wrong.

Remarks: Sets the shell link description.

---

1. This is one of the enterprise-class features that have been available for years on other operating systems. I believe I first saw it when I was introduced to OS/2 a few years ago. Most flavors of UNIX have had this feature for even longer.

```
HRESULT SetHotkey(
    WORD wHotkey
);
```

Parameters:

wHotkey: Sets the hot key for the shell link. The low order byte contains the virtual key code and the high-order byte contains the modifier flags. See IShcllLink::GetHotKey() for a list of the valid modifier flags.

Return Values:

- **S_OK:** Everything worked.
- **Other OLE-Defined value:** Something went wrong.

Remarks: Sets the shell links hot key.

```
HRESULT SetIconLocation(
    LPCSTR pszIconPath,
    int iIcon
);
```

Parameters:

pszIconPath: Address of a null-terminated string specifying the name of the file that contains the icon for the link.

iIcon: Index of the icon.

Return Values:

- **S_OK:** Everything worked.
- **Other OLE-Defined value:** Something went wrong.

Remarks: Sets the name of the file that contains the icon and the index of the icon within the file.

```
HRESULT SetIDList(
    LPCITEMIDLIST pidl
);
```

Parameters:

pidl: Address of a list of item identifiers. For best results, make the pidl relative to the Desktop, the root of the namespace.

Return Values:

- **S_OK:** Everything worked.
- **Other OLE-Defined value:** Something went wrong.

Remarks: Sets the path to the shell link using an item identifier list. Use this when the item being linked is not a file, but something else (printer, another computer, etc.).

```
HRESULT SetPath(
    LPCSTR pszFile
);
```

Parameters:

pszFile: Address of a null-terminated string containing the full path of the shell link.

Return Values:
- **S_OK:** Everything worked.
- **Other OLE-Defined value:** Something went wrong.

Remarks: Sets the path and file name of the shell link object.

```
HRESULT SetRelativePath(
    LPCSTR pszPathRel,
    DWORD dwReserved
);
```

Parameters:

pszPathRel: Address of a null-terminated string containing the relative path to the linked item. This must be a file name. Remember: folders are not files.

dwReserved: Must be zero.

Return Values:
- **S_OK:** Everything worked.
- **Other OLE-Defined value:** Something went wrong.

Remarks: You would use this to define a relative link that could be moved with its target. Here's the SDK example of when this might be useful:
- You have a link: c:\MyLink.lnk.
- The link points to c:\MyDocs\MyFile.txt.
- Through code, you want to move the link and c:\MyDocs\My-File.txt to d:\

You would make the following call to help the shell resolve the move:

```
theShellLink.SetRelativePath( "d:\\MyLink.lnk", NULL );
```

and you would make the call after you moved the file. You probably would not use this function much unless your application maintained links and items that can be linked. This method appears to help namespace extensions, not your typical Windows applications.

```
HRESULT SetShowCmd(
    int iShowCmd
);
```

Parameters:

iShowCmd: Sets how the link will display itself when it is activated. It can be one of these three values:

- **SW_SHOWNORMAL**
- **SW_SHOWMAXIMIZED**
- **SW_SHOWMINIMIZED**

Return Values:
- **S_OK:** Everything worked.
- **Other OLE-Defined value:** Something went wrong.

```
HRESULT SetWorkingDirectory(
    LPCSTR pszDir
);
```

Parameters:

pszDir: Address of a null-terminated string containing the working directory of the linked item.

Return Values:
- **S_OK:** Everything worked.
- **Other OLE-Defined value:** Something went wrong.

A.40   IShellPropSheetExt

A property sheet handler must implement this interface. It allows the handler to add or replace pages in the property sheet displayed for a file object and some Control Panel Applets. This interface is covered extensively in Chapter 7, Section 7.6.

Header:	shlobj.h
Example Project:	Chapter 7\ABKPropertySheetHandler
	Chapter 7\BSOD
Interface ID:	IID_IShellPropSheetExt

A.41   IShellView

An IShellView implementation allows a namespace extension to present a view in the Windows Explorer and folder windows. These objects are created by calling IShellFolder::CreateViewObject(). Because IShellFolder:: CreateViewObject() may have to create many instances of the same object for different views, the IShellView cannot be a part of the IShellFolder implementation. Additionally, each IShellView delivered by IShellFolder:: CreateViewObject() must be unique.

The IShellView provides a communication channel between the view object and the Windows Explorer frame window. These two windows translate messages, communicate the state of the frame and document windows, and share the menus and toolbar.

Header:	shlobj.h
Example Project:	Chapter 11\WinReg
Interface ID:	IID_IShellView

IShellView contains the following methods:

```
HRESULT AddPropertySheetPages(
    DWORD dwReserved,
    LPFNADDPROPSHEETPAGE lpfn,
    LPARAM lparam
);
```

Parameters:

dwReserved: Reserved for future use. Set to 0.

lpfn: Address of the callback function to use to add the pages. This function has the following typedef:

```
typedef BOOL (CALLBACK FAR * LPFNADDPROPSHEETPAGE)
    (HPROPSHEETPAGE, LPARAM);
```

lparam: Value to pass to the callback function via the lpfn parameter.

Return Values:
- **S_OK:** Everything worked.
- **Other OLE-Defined value:** Something went wrong.

Remarks: Windows Explorer calls this method when it opens the Options property sheet from the View menu. The view adds pages by creating the pages and then calling the callback function using the page handles. The shell uses this same mechanism for Property Page extensions, which are covered in Chapter 7, Section 7.6.

```
HRESULT CreateViewWindow(
    ISHELLLINK *lpPrevView,
    LPFOLDERSETTINGS lpfs,
    IShellBrowser *psb,
    RECT *prcView,
    HWND *phWnd
);
```

Parameters:

lpPrevView: Address of the view window that is exiting. Views can use this value to communicate with a previous view if the two views share the same implementation. Doing so can help optimize browsing between instances of the same view interface. The pointer may be NULL.

lpfs: Address of a FOLDERSETTINGS structure that the view must use when creating the new view.

psb: Address of the current instance of the IShellBrowser interface. The view is responsible for calling the interface's AddRef() method and for retaining the pointer so that it can communicate with the Windows Explorer Window.

prcView: Dimensions of the new view expressed in client coordinates.

phWnd: Address of the window handle being created.

Return Values:
- **S_OK:** Everything worked.
- **Other OLE-Defined value:** Something went wrong.

Remarks: Implementations should create the view window and restore any persistent state information by calling the IShellBrowser::GetViewStateStream() method.

```
HRESULT DestroyViewWindow();
```

Return Values:
- **S_OK:** Everything worked.
- **Other OLE-Defined value:** Something went wrong.

Remarks: This method is called when a folder window or Windows Explorer is about to be closed. In this method, clean up any states that represent the view, including the window and any resources the view consumes.

```
HRESULT EnableModeless(
    BOOL fEnable
);
```

Parameters:

fEnable: If set to FALSE, this disables modeless dialogs. Any other value enables them.

Return Values:
- **S_OK:** Everything worked.
- **Other OLE-Defined value:** Something went wrong.

Remarks: Right now, this method does not get called. So, what should your view do? I recommend that you play it safe and use modal dialogs only. If you need modeless dialogs, try to make sure that you can create them as modal in case version 6.0 of Internet Explorer or the next Windows release starts calling this method.

```
HRESULT EnableModelessSV(
    BOOL fEnable
);
```

Parameters:

fEnable: Same meaning as IShellView::EnableModeless().

Return Values:

- **E_NOTIMPL:** Because this method has not been specified yet, always return E_NOTIMPL. Place a debug ASSERT in your implementation so that if you do not stay current on what is and is not getting called, you will see the call when you need to maintain or enhance your namespace extension.

Remarks: The only clue to what this method does is hinted at in the SHLOBJ.H header file. Around this method and EnableModeless() is the following, code:

```
#ifdef _FIX_ENABLEMODELESS_CONFLICT
    STDMETHOD(EnableModelessSV) (THIS_ BOOL fEnable) PURE;
#else
    STDMETHOD(EnableModeless) (THIS_ BOOL fEnable) PURE;
#endif
```

You find the same code bracketing the declaration of these methods for IShellView2. I dug through the SHLOBJ.H for some more clues and found these comments:

```
// IShellBrowser::EnableModelessSB(fEnable)
//   Same as the IOleInPlaceFrame::EnableModeless.
```

Just a guess, but I would bet that the object that implements Windows Explorer's frame also implements the file system namespace extension. To avoid conflicts, EnableModelessSB() probably gets called for the file system extension and ignored for any other namespace extension.

```
HRESULT GetCurrentInfo(
    LPFOLDERSETTINGS lpfs
);
```

Parameters:

lpfs: Points to a FOLDERSETTINGS structure. On return, it should contain the settings.

Return Values:

- **S_OK:** Everything worked.
- **Other OLE-Defined value:** Something went wrong.

Remarks: Windows Explorer uses this method to ask the view about standard settings. The implementation should return as many of the settings as apply. This helps maintain the same basic settings (detail view, icon view, view hidden, etc.) when the user browses from one view to another.

```
HRESULT GetItemObject(
    UINT uItem,
    REFIID riid,
    LPVOID *ppv
);
```

Parameters:

uItem: This refers to one aspect of the view. uItem can be one of the following values:

- **SVGIO_BACKGROUND:** Refers to the view's background. This is usually used with IID_IContextMenu to get a context menu for the view background.
- **SVGIO_SELECTION:** Refers to the currently selected items. This is usually used with IID_IDataObject to get a data object that represents the selected items.
- **SVGIO_ALLVIEW:** Same as SVGIO_SELECTION but refers to all items in the view, not just the selected ones.

riid: Identifies the COM interface being requested.

ppv: On return, points to an instance of the requested interface. If an error occurs, the implementation should set this to NULL.

Return Values:
- **S_OK:** Everything worked.
- **Other OLE-Defined value:** Something went wrong.

Remarks: Retrieves an interface that refers to data presented in the view.

```
HRESULT Refresh();
```

Return Values:
- **S_OK:** Everything worked.
- **Other OLE-Defined value:** Something went wrong.

Remarks: Windows Explorer and the folder view call this method to refresh the contents of the view. Implementations should not use cached information. Instead, they should get the information from the storage.

```
HRESULT SaveViewState();
```

Return Values:
- **S_OK:** Everything worked.
- **Other OLE-Defined value:** Something went wrong.

Remarks: Windows Explorer calls this method to save the view state for a particular view. Implementations should make sure that different versions of the implementation could read data from the stream without causing an error. The information is stored in the stream returned by IShellBrowser::GetViewStateStream(). I recommend storing the size of the state in the first 32 bits and always adding new data to the end. This way, you can read all the data from the stream and interpret what the current implementation knows about.

```
HRESULT SelectItem(
    LPCITEMIDLIST pidlItem,
    UINT uFlags
);
```

Parameters:

pidlItem: Points to an ITEMIDLIST.

uFlags: Specifies what type of selection is requested. This can be any one of the following values:
- **SVSI_DESELECT:** Deselect the specified item.
- **SVSI_DESELECTOTHERS:** Deselect everything but the specifieditem. If pidlItem is NULL, you should deselect everything.
- **SVSI_EDIT:** Put pidlItem into edit mode.
- **SVSI_ENSUREVISIBLE:** Make sure that the item specified by pidlItem is visible on the screen.
- **SVSI_FOCUSED:** pidlItem should get the focus.
- **SVSI_SELECT:** Select pidlItem.

Return Values:
- **S_OK:** Everything worked.
- **Other OLE-Defined value:** Something went wrong.

Remarks: This method helps implement the Target command from the File menu of the shell's shortcut property sheet.

```
HRESULT TranslateAccelerator(
    LPMSG lpmsg
);
```

Parameters:

lpMsg: Points to the message to be translated.

Return Values:
- **S_OK:** The view was able to translate the message.
- **S_FALSE:** The view could not translate the message.
- **Other OLE-Defined value:** Something went wrong.

Remarks: Windows Explorer calls this when a key-sequence is keyed in and the view has the focus. The view gets first crack at processing the message. If the view does not have focus, it will get this message after Explorer tried to translate it and failed. By default, you should return S_FALSE and let Windows Explorer do its own accelerator translation and normal menu dispatching. Only return S_OK if you were able to process the message and do not want Explorer to process it further.

```
HRESULT UIActivate(
    UINT uState
);
```

Parameters:

uState: This parameter specifies the window's activation state. It can have one of the following values:
- **SVUIA_ACTIVATE_FOCUS:** Windows Explorer just created the view window and it has the input focus. The shell view should be able to set menu items that are appropriate for the focused state.
- **SVUIA_ACTIVATE_NOFOCUS:** One of two things happened. Either Windows Explorer just created the view window and it does not have the input focus or the view is losing focus. The shell view should be able to set menu items that are appropriate for the non-focused state. No selection-specific menu items should be added.
- **SVUIA_DEACTIVATE:** Window Explorer is about to destroy the shell view window. This view should remove any menu items, toolbars, and other user interface elements.
- **SVUIA_INPLACEACTIVATE:** The shell view is active and does not have the focus. This flag is only valid when the method is exposed through the IShellView2 interface.

Return Values:
- **S_OK:** Everything worked.
- **Other OLE-Defined value:** Something went wrong.

Remarks: Use this method to track the activation state of the view. As needed, change the window behavior based on the flags passed in.

A.42   IShellView2

IShellView2 extends the IShellView interface. This allows things such as new view modes, the ability to get the GUID for the current or default view, adding a rename mechanism, and adding the ability to position an item within a view.

Header:	shlobj.h
Example Project:	Chapter 11\WinReg
Interface ID:	IID_IShellView2

IShellView2 contains the following methods:

```
HRESULT CreateViewWindow2(
    LPSV2CVW2_PARAMS lpParams
);
```

> **Parameters:**
>
> **lpParams:** Points to an SV2CVW2_PARAMS structure. This structure defines the new view window.
>
> **Return Values:**
> * **S_OK:** Everything worked.
> * **Other OLE-Defined value:** Something went wrong.

```
HRESULT GetView(
    SHELLVIEWID     *pvid,
    ULONG uView
);
```

> **Parameters:**
>
> **pvid:** Returns the GUID of the requested view.
>
> **uView:** This value tells the IShellView2 implementation which GUID the caller requested. It can be one of these two values:
> * **SV2GV_CURRENTVIEW:** Return the current shell view.
> * **SV2GV_DEFAULTVIEW:** Return the default shell view.
>
> **Return Values:**
> * **S_OK:** Everything worked.
> * **Other OLE-Defined value:** Something went wrong.

Remarks: Windows Explorer uses this method to request the GUID for the current or the default shell view.

```
HRESULT HandleRename(
    LPCITEMIDLIST pidlNew,
);
```

> **Parameters:**
>
> **pidlNew:** Points to an ITEMIDLIST structure. The current identifier is passed in. On return, this contains the new ITEMIDLIST.
>
> **Return Values:**
> * **S_OK:** Everything worked.
> * **Other OLE-Defined value:** Something went wrong.

Remarks: Used to change an item's identifier.

```
HRESULT SelectAndPositionItem(
    LPCITEMIDLIST pidlItem,
    UINT uFlags,
    LPPOINT point
);
```

Parameters:

> **pidlItem:** This ITEMIDLIST structure uniquely identifies the item to be selected and its position.

> **uFlags:** Specifies the selection type. uFlags can contain one or more of the following values:
> - **SVSI_DESELECT:** Deselects the specified item. You cannot use this flag with SVSI_DESELECTOTHERS.
> - **SVSI_DESELECTOTHERS:** Deselect everything but the specified item. If pidlItem is NULL, you should deselect everything.
> - **SVSI_EDIT:** Put pidlItem into edit mode.
> - **SVSI_ENSUREVISIBLE:** Make sure that the item specified by pidlItem is visible on the screen.
> - **SVSI_FOCUSED:** pidlItem should get the focus.
> - **SVSI_SELECT:** Select pidlItem.
> - **SVSI_TRANSLATEPT:** Convert the point from screen coordinates to client coordinates.

> **point:** Points to the top left corner of the new position.

Return Values:
- **S_OK:** Everything worked.
- **Other OLE-Defined value:** Something went wrong.

A.43   IStream

The IStream interface supports reading and writing data to stream objects. IStream inherits from the ISequentialStream interface. This interface defines methods similar to the MS-DOS FAT file functions. Each stream has its own access rights and a seek pointer. The main difference between an IStream and a DOS file is that the external interface for IStream does not use file handles. Streams can remain open for long periods of time without consuming file systems resources. IStream requires some methods beyond ISequentialStream's Read() and Write() methods.

Header:	objidl.h
Interface ID:	IID_IStream

```
HRESULT Clone(
    IStream** ppstm
);
```

Parameters:

> **ppstm:** If the method is successful, this points to a new IStream pointer. If an error occurs, this parameter points to NULL.

Returns:

- **S_OK:** The stream was successfully cloned.
- **E_PENDING:** The stream employs asynchronous storage and part or all of the data is not available.
- **STG_E_INSUFFICIENT_MEMORY:** The stream could not be cloned because there was not enough memory.
- **STG_E_INVALIDPOINTER:** The caller passed in an invalid pointer.
- **STG_E_REVERTED:** The object has been invalidated by a revert operation above it in the transaction tree.

Remarks: This method creates a new stream object that accesses the same bytes as the current stream. The two streams have separate seek pointers. Changes written to one copy of the stream are immediately seen in the other stream. Range locking is shared between the stream objects. Seek pointers are equal immediately after the clone operation.

```
HRESULT Commit(
    DWORD grfCommitFlags
);
```

Parameters:

grfCommitFlags: Specifies how changes are committed. This could be any one of the following values:

- **STGC_DEFAULT:** This value is used primarily to make the code readable. (Its value is zero.)
- **STGC_OVERWRITE:** The commit operation can overwrite existing data to reduce space requirements. Do not do this unless you are willing to risk losing data. A commit can fail after the old data is overwritten but before the new data has been saved. In this case, no data exists. Use this only when the user can risk losing data or when a previous commit returned STG_E_MEDIUMFULL but an overwrite would provide enough space to commit any changes.
- **STGC_ONLYIFCURRENT:** Prevents multiple users of a storage object from overwriting each other's changes. The commit occurs only if no changes have occurred to the storage object since the last time storage was opened. If another user has changed the object, it returns STG_E_NOTCURRENT.
- **STGC_DANGEROUSLYCOMMITMERELYTODISKCACHE:** Commits the changes to a write-behind disk cache, but does not save the cache to disk. Because the disk write does not happen until after the write operation has already returned, this increases performance. If a problem occurs before the cache is saved, then the data is lost. If you do not specify this value,

then committing changes to root-level storage objects is robust even when caching is used. The two-phase commit process guarantees that data gets written to disk and not just the cache.

- **STGC_CONSOLIDATE: (**Windows 2000 only) This indicates storage should be consolidated after it is committed to create a smaller file on disk. The flag only works if the outermost storage object was opened in transacted mode. This flag can be combined with any of the STGC flags.

Return Values:

- **S_OK:** The stream was committed to the parent level.
- **E_PENDING:** The stream employs asynchronous storage and part or all of the data is not available.
- **STG_E_MEDIUMFULL:** The commit operation failed due to a lack of space on the storage device.
- **STG_E_REVERTED:** The object has been invalidated by a revert operation above it in the transaction tree.

Remarks: This method ensures that an object opened in transacted mode is reflected in the parent storage. Any changes made to the stream since the last save are reflected in the parent object. If the stream was opened in direct mode, any changes are flushed out to the underlying storage object.

```
HRESULT CopyTo(
    IStream* pstm,
    ULARGE_INTEGER cb,
    ULARGE_INTEGER* pcbRead,
    ULARGE_INTEGER* pcbWritten
);
```

Parameters:

pstm: Points to the destination stream. This could be a new stream or a clone of the source stream.

cb: Specifies the number of bytes to copy from the source stream.

pcbRead: Points to the location where this method writes the actual number of bytes read from the source. If you do not want to know this, then set the pointer to NULL.

pcbWritten: Points to the location where this method writes the actual number of bytes written to the destination. Again, if you do not want to know this information, then set the pointer to NULL.

Return Values:

- **S_OK:** The stream was committed to the parent level.
- **E_PENDING:** The stream employs asynchronous storage and part or all of the data is not available.

- **STG_E_INVALIDPOINTER:** One of the pointers passed in is invalid.
- **STG_E_MEDIUMFULL:** The copy operation failed due to a lack of space on the storage device.
- **STG_E_REVERTED:** The object has been invalidated by a revert operation above it in the transaction tree.

Remarks: If this method returns an error, then you can safely assume that the seek pointers are invalid. Additionally, pcbRead and pcbWritten may also be invalid.

```
HRESULT LockRegion(
    ULARGE_INTEGER libOffset,
    ULARGE_INTEGER cb,
    DWORD dwLockType
);
```

Parameters:

libOffset: Specifies the byte offset for the beginning of the range.

cb: Specifies the number of bytes to be restricted.

dwLockType: Specifies the restrictions being requested on accessing the range. This can have any of the following values:

- **LOCK_WRITE:** Only the owner of the lock can write to the locked bytes. Reads are still permitted.
- **LOCK_EXCLUSIVE:** The owner of the lock is the only entity that can access the bytes.
- **LOCK_ONLYONCE:** If the lock is granted, no other LOCK_ONLYONCE locks can be obtained for the range. Typically, implementations use this as an alias for another lock type. Additional behavior may be associated with this lock type.

Return Values:

- **S_OK:** The lock succeeded.
- **E_PENDING:** The stream employs asynchronous storage and part or all of the data is not available.
- **STG_E_INVALIDFUNCTION:** Locking is not supported or the lock type is not supported.
- **STG_E_LOCKVIOLATION:** The requested lock is supported but someone already locked the range.
- **STG_E_REVERTED:** The object has been invalidated by a revert operation above it in the transaction tree.

Remarks: The byte range may extend beyond the end of the stream. Any region locked by LockRegion() must be freed by a corresponding call to UnlockRegion with the same values for libOffset, cb, and dwLockType. Calling Release() will not unlock the region. If two regions happen to be adjacent, they still need two UnlockRegion() calls.

```
HRESULT Revert();
```

> **Returns:**
> - **S_OK:** The stream was successfully reverted to its previous version.
> - **E_PENDING:** The stream employs asynchronous storage and part or all of the data is not available.
>
> **Remarks:** This method discards changes made since the last commit operation.

```
HRESULT Seek(
    LARGE_INTEGER dlibMove,
    DWORD dwOrigin,
    ULARGE_INTEGER* plibNewPosition
);
```

> **Parameters:**
>
> **dlibMove:** Displacement to be added to the location indicated by dwOrigin. If dwOrigin is STREAM_SEEK_SET, the implementer interprets this as an unsigned value rather than a signed value.
>
> **dwOrigin:** Specifies the origin for the displacement specified in dlibMove. It can have any of the following values:
> - **STREAM_SEEK_SET:** The new pointer is an offset from the beginning of the stream.
> - **STREAM_SEEK_CUR:** The new pointer is offset relative to the current position.
> - **STREAM_SEEK_END:** The new seek position is offset relative to the end of the stream.
>
> **plibNewPosition:** Pointer to the location where the method should put the value of the new seek pointer from the beginning of the stream. If you set this to NULL, you will not get the value of the new position.
>
> **Return Values:**
> - **S_OK:** The seek pointer move succeeded.
> - **E_PENDING:** The stream employs asynchronous storage and part or all of the data is not available.
> - **STG_E_INVALIDPOINTER:** plibPosition points to invalid memory.
> - **STG_E_INVALIDFUNCTION:** dwOrigin contains an invalid value or dlibMove contains a bad offset value. For example, the seek may have gone past the beginning of the file.
> - **STG_E_REVERTED:** The object has been invalidated by a revert operation above it in the transaction tree.

Remarks: This method moves the seek pointer so that subsequent reads and writes occur at the new location within the stream object. You can also use this method to discover the current position of the seek pointer by setting dwOrigin to STREAM_SEEK_CUR, dlibMove to 0, and reading the value returned in plibNewPosition.

```
HRESULT SetSize(
    ULARGE_INTEGER libNewSize
);
```

Parameters:

libNewSize: Specifies the new size of the stream as a number of bytes.

Return Values:
- **S_OK:** The stream's size was successfully changed.
- **E_PENDING:** The stream employs asynchronous storage and part or all of the data is not available.
- **STG_E_MEDIUMFULL:** The stream size cannot be changed because the storage device is full.
- **STG_E_INVALIDFUNCTION:** The value of libNewSize is not valid. Because streams cannot exceed 2^{32} bytes in length, the high DWORD of libNewSize must be zero. If it is not, the parameter is invalid.
- **STG_E_REVERTED:** The object has been invalidated by a revert operation above it in the transaction tree.

Remarks: The stream pointer is not affected by changes in stream size. If you are shrinking the stream, you may need to reposition the pointer.

```
HRESULT Stat(
    STATSTG* pstatstg,
    DWORD grfStatFlag
);
```

Parameters:

pstatstg: This is a pointer to a STATSTG struct. If the call to Stat() is succesful, the structure will be populated with information about the stream.

grfStatFlag: Specifies that this method does not return some of the fields in the STATSTG struct. Valid values are:
- **STATFLAG_DEFAULT:** Requests that the pwcsName member of the STATSTG struct be included.
- **STATFLAG_NONAME:** States that the pwcsName member of STATSTG is unimportant. When Stat() can omit the name, there

is no need for the method to allocate and free memory for pwcsName. This allows the call to use less memory.

Return Values:

- **S_OK:** The STATSTG structure was successfully filled in.
- **E_PENDING:** The stream employs asynchronous storage and part or all of the data is not available.
- **STG_E_ACCESSDENIED:** The caller does not have sufficient permissions for accessing statistics for this storage object.
- **STG_E_INSUFFICIENTMEMORY:** The STATSTG structure was not returned due to a lack of memory. Try calling again with STATFLAG_NONAME set.
- **STG_E_INVALIDFLAG:** grfStatFlag has been set incorrectly.
- **STG_E_INVALIDPOINTER:** The pStatStg pointer is invalid.
- **STG_E_REVERTED:** The object has been invalidated by a revert operation above it in the transaction tree.

Remarks: IStream::Stat retrieves a pointer to the STATSTG structure that contains information about this open stream. When this stream is within a structured storage and IStorage::EnumElements is called, it creates an enumerator object with the IEnumSTATSTG interface on it, which can be called to enumerate the storages and streams through the STATSTG structures associated with each of them.

```
HRESULT UnlockRegion(
    ULARGE_INTEGER libOffset,
    ULARGE_INTEGER cb,
    DWORD dwLockType
);
```

Parameters:

libOffset: Specifies the byte offset for the beginning of the range.

cb: Specifies the number of bytes to be restricted.

dwLockType: Specifies the restrictions being requested on accessing the range. See IStream::LockRegion for the values.

Return Values:

- **S_OK:** The range was unlocked.
- **E_PENDING:** The stream employs asynchronous storage and part or all of the data is not available.
- **STG_E_INVALIDFUNCTION:** Locking is not supported or the lock type is not supported.
- **STG_E_LOCKVIOLATION:** The requested unlock cannot be granted.

- **STG_E_REVERTED:** The object has been invalidated by a revert operation above it in the transaction tree.

Remarks: The byte range may extend beyond the end of the stream. Any region locked by LockRegion() must be freed by a corresponding call to UnlockRegion with the same values for libOffset, cb, and dwLockType. Calling Release() will not unlock the region. If two regions happen to be adjacent, they still need two UnlockRegion() calls.

A.44   IUnknown

Every interface derives from IUnknown. IUnknown allows clients to get pointers to other interfaces on a given object through the QueryInterface() method. Additionally, this interface allows the client to manage the object's lifetime through AddRef() and Release(). These three methods comprise the first three entries in the v-table for every interface.

Header:	unknwn.h
Example Projects:	If it uses COM, it uses this interface.
Interface ID:	IID_IUnknown

Objects implementing IUnknown must implement the following methods:

```
ULONG AddRef();
```

Return Values: Returns the value of the new reference count. This information is meant for diagnostic and testing purposes. According to the SDK documentation, certain situations exist where this value may be unstable.

```
ULONG QueryInterface(
    REFIID iid,
    void** ppvObject
);
```

Parameters:

iid: Identifier of the interface being requested.

ppvObject: Address of a pointer that receives the interface pointer requested in iid. Upon a successful return, this has a pointer to the requested object. Otherwise, *ppvObject is set to NULL.

Return Values:

- **S_OK:** Interface is supported and *ppvObject should have a pointer to the requested interface.

- **E_NOINTERFACE:** The object does not support the requested interface. *ppvObject should be NULL.

```
ULONG Release();
```

Return Values: Returns the value of the new reference count. This information is meant for diagnostic and testing purposes. According to the SDK documentation, certain situations exist where this value may be unstable. When the last reference to an object is freed, the object can remove itself from memory.

Shell Functions, Structures, and Enumerations

*M*icrosoft introduced a large number of functions to the Windows API that all begin with the prefix SH. These methods are collectively known as the shell functions. Some of these provide an alternative way to perform a task. For example, to write to a registry value you would:

1. Open the HKEY.
2. Write to a value within the HKEY.
3. Close the HKEY.

This same task could be accomplished using SHSetValue(). The new functions exist to make Windows programming easier. Many of these functions were introduced with Internet Explorer 4.0. As you should know, Microsoft sees a lot of benefits in merging the user interface with the Web browser. Regardless of your stance on the benefits of merging the two, this means that the Windows API grows with Internet Explorer.

The new shell functions add a lot of value for programmers. The only downside to using these functions is that you are relying on version 4.71 of the shell DLLs being installed on the user's machine. (Version 4.71 of these DLLs shipped with Internet Explorer 4.0.) If the user is running Internet Explorer 4.0, Windows 98, Windows 2000,[1] or a later release of Windows (post Windows 98), then the functions within this chapter will be available.

---

1. I included Windows 2000 because of the differences between it and Windows 9x. Remember, Windows 2000 is just the product name of Windows NT 5.0.

The shell contains a number of functions for manipulating *user-specific registry keys*. A user-specific registry key resides in either the HKEY_LOCAL_MACHINE or the HKEY_CURRENT_USER registry hive (or both). If you have not used or seen these functions yet, I recommend taking a look at them so you are at least familiar with the family of functions. The first of these functions in this appendix (listed alphabetically) is SHRegCloseUSKey(). I stumbled onto the family of functions while browsing the MSDN index. Trust me, you will like using these functions better than using Microsoft's first stab at a registry API.

B.1   BrowseCallbackProc

The SHBrowseForFolder() function calls this function to notify the calling application about events.

Header:	shlobj.h
Example Project:	Appendix B\ExSHBrowseForFolder

```
int CALLBACK BrowseCallbackProc(
    HWND hwnd,
    UINT uMsg,
    LPARAM lParam,
    LPARAM lpData
);
```

Parameters:

hwnd: Window handle to the browse dialog box. The window accepts the following messages:

- **BFFM_ENABLEOK:** Enables or disables the dialog box's OK button. Set lParam to TRUE to enable the OK button; set lParam to FALSE to disable the OK button.
- **BFFM_SETSELECTION:** Selects the specified folder. To pass a PIDL, set the message's lParam to the PIDL and wParam to FALSE. To specify the folder's path, set the message's lParam to point to a null-terminated string containing the path, and set wParam to TRUE.
- **BFFM_SETSTATUSTEXT:** Sets the text in the status bar. lParam points to a null-terminated string containing the text to place in the status bar. The status text lives above the tree control and only on the old style browse dialog.

uMsg: Identifies the event that triggered the callback. The event can be one of the following values:

- **BFFM_INITIALIZED:** The browse box has been initialized. lParam should be zero.
- **BFFM_SELCHANGED:** The selection has changed. The lParam parameter points to the item identifier list for the newly selected item.
- **BFFM_VALIDATEFAILED:** Indicates that the user typed an invalid name into the edit box in the browse dialog. You can respond by informing the user that they entered an invalid name. You can also do nothing. Return FALSE to allow the dialog to close or TRUE to keep the dialog open.

lParam: Value depends on the value of the uMsg parameter.

lpData: Application defined value that was specified in BROWSE-INFO.lParam.

B.2 BROWSEINFO

This structure contains parameters for the SHBrowseForFolder() function and receives information about the folder that the user selected.

Header:	shlobj.h
Example Project:	Appendix B\ExSHBrowseForFolder

```
typedef struct _browseinfo {
    HWND hwndOwner;
    LPCITEMIDLIST pidlRoot;
    LPSTR pszDisplayName;
    LPCSTR lpszTitle;
    UINT ulFlags;
    BFFCALLBACK lpfn;
    LPARAM lParam;
    int iImage;
} BROWSEINFO, *PBROWSEINFO, *LPBROWSEINFO;
```

Members:

hwndOwner: Handle to the dialog box's owner window.

pidlRoot: Address of an ITEMIDLIST structure that specifies the location of the root folder to begin browsing. The user will only be able to browse this folder and its subfolders. Pass NULL to use the desktop folder as the root.

pszDisplayName: Points to a buffer to receive the display name of the folder the user selected. This buffer must be set to MAX_PATH bytes.

lpszTitle: Address of a null-terminated string to display above the tree view control in the dialog box. Use this string to give instructions to the user.

ulFlags: Flags to specify the operation of the dialog box. You can specify zero or more of the following values:

- **BIF_BROWSEFORCOMPUTER:** Only return computer names. When the user selects anything other than a computer, the dialog disables the OK button.
- **BIF_BROWSEFORPRINTER:** Only return printer names. When the user selects anything other than a printer, the dialog disables the OK button.
- **BIF_BROWSEINCLUDEFILES:** (Version 4.71): The browse dialog should display files and folders. Normal operation is just folders.
- **BIF_DONTGOBELOWDOMAIN:** Do not include network folders below the domain level in the tree view control.
- **BIF_EDITBOX:** (Version 5.0): The browse dialog includes an edit control for the user to type in the name of an item.
- **BIF_RETURNFSANCESTORS:** Only return file system ancestors. If the user selects anything other than a file system ancestor, the dialog disables the OK button.
- **BIF_RETURNONLYFSDIRS:** Only return file system directories. If the user selects anything other than a file system directory, the dialog disables the OK button.
- **BIF_STATUSTEXT:** Includes a status area in the dialog box. The callback function can set the status text by sending messages to the dialog box.
- **BIF_USENEWUI:** (Version 5.0): Use the new user-interface. This gives the user a larger, resizable dialog box. The new UI has drag-and-drop capability within the dialog box, reordering, context menus, new folders, and delete. You must call CoInitialize(NULL) before calling SHBrowseForFolder() if you specify this flag.
- **BIF_VALIDATE:** (Version 4.71): If the user types an invalid name into the edit box (BIF_EDITBOX was specified), the browse dialog will call the applications BrowseCallbackProc with the BFFM_VALIDATEFAILED message.

lpfn: Pointer to a callback function that follows the rules specified by BrowseCallbackProc. This can be NULL.

lParam: Application defined value that the dialog box will pass to the callback function if a callback function is specified.

iImage: Specifies the image index within the system image list.

B.3 CSIDL_XXXX

This list of values, used with SHGetFolderLocation(), SHGetFolderPath(), SHGetSpecialFolderLocation(), and SHGetSpecialFolderPath(), helps uniquely identify frequently used folders that exist in different places on different systems.

Header:	shlobj.h
Example Project:	Chapter 2\StartMenuEditor

Values:

CSIDL_FLAG_CREATE: (Windows 2000 only) Combines this flag with any of the other flags to force the creation of the specified folder if it does not exist.

CSIDL_ADMINTOOLS: (Windows 2000 only) Stores the administrative tools for an individual user. Microsoft Management Console saves customized consoles to this directory so that they can roam with the user.

CSIDL_ALTSTARTUP: Corresponds to the user's non-localized Startup program group.

CSIDL_APPDATA: Serves as a common repository for application-specific data.

CSIDL_BITBUCKET: The recycle bin.

CSIDL_COMMON_ADMINTOOLS: (Windows 2000 only) Contains administrative tools for all users of the computer.

CSIDL_COMMON_ALTSTARTUP: Non-localized Startup program group for all users. Valid only for Windows NT/2000 systems.

CSIDL_COMMON_APPDATA: (Windows 2000 only) Application data shared by all users.

CSIDL_COMMON_DESKTOPDIRECTORY: Contains the files and folders that appear on the desktops of all the users. Valid only for Windows NT/2000 systems.

CSIDL_COMMON_DOCUMENTS: Contains the documents that are common to all of the users. Valid only for Windows NT/2000 systems.

CSIDL_COMMON_FAVORITES: Common repository of shared *Favorites* items.

CSIDL_COMMON_PROGRAMS: Contains the programs groups that are common to all of the users. Valid only for Windows NT/2000 systems.

CSIDL_COMMON_STARTMENU: Contains the programs and folders that are common to all of the users. Valid only for Windows NT/2000 systems.

CSIDL_COMMON_STARTUP: Contains the programs that appear in the Startup folder for all of the users. Valid only for Windows NT/2000 systems.

CSIDL_COMMON_TEMPLATES: Contains the templates that are common to all of the users. Valid only for Windows NT/2000 systems.

CSIDL_CONTROLS: Contains the icons for the Control Panel applications.

CSIDL_COOKIES: Common repository for Internet cookies.

CSIDL_DESKTOP: The virtual folder that serves as the root of the namespace.

CSIDL_DESKTOPDIRECTORY: Directory used to store the file objects appearing on the desktop.

CSIDL_FAVORITES: Repository for the user's Favorites items. A common path is C:\WinNT\Profiles*username*\Favorites.

CSIDL_FONTS: Contains the fonts installed on the operating system.

CSIDL_HISTORY: Serves as a repository of Internet history items.

CSIDL_INTERNET: Virtual folder used to represent the Internet.

CSIDL_INTERNET_CACHE: Serves as a repository for temporary Internet files.

CSIDL_LOCAL_APPDATA: (Windows 2000 only) Used as an information repository for non-roaming applications.

CSIDL_MYPICTURES: (Windows 2000 only) A place to hold your pictures.

CSIDL_NETHOOD: Contains objects that appear in the Network Neighborhood.

CSIDL_NETWORK: The virtual folder representing the top level of the network hierarchy.

CSIDL_PERSONAL: Used as a repository for documents.

CSIDL_PRINTERS: Virtual folder containing installed printers.

CSIDL_PRINTHOOD: The system directory that contains the system's printer links.

CSIDL_PROFILE: (Windows 2000 only) The user's profile folder.

CSIDL_PROGRAM_FILES: (Windows 2000 only) The Program Files folder.

CSIDL_PROGRAM_FILES_COMMON: (Windows 2000 only) A folder for components that are shared across applications.

CSIDL_PROGRAM_FILES_COMMONX86: (Windows 2000 only) Contains *x*86 programs that are installed on a RISC system. These programs are common to all users of the RISC system.

CSIDL_PROGRAM_FILESX86: (Windows 2000 only) Contains *x*86 programs that are installed on a RISC system. This value corresponds to the %PROGRAMFILES(X86)% environment variable.

CSIDL_PROGRAMS: Contains the user's program groups.

CSIDL_RECENT: Contains the most recently used documents.

CSIDL_SENDTO: Contains the Send To menu items.

CSIDL_STARTMENU: Contains the Start menu items.

CSIDL_STARTUP: Contains the items in the user's Startup program group.

CSIDL_SYSTEM: (Windows 2000 only) The system folder.

CSIDL_SYSTEMX86: (Windows 2000 only) The system folder for *x*86 applications on RISC systems.

CSIDL_TEMPLATES: Serves as a common repository for document templates.

CSIDL_WINDOWS: (Windows 2000 only) The root Windows directory. Corresponds to the %windir% and %SYSTEMROOT% environment variables.

B.4 EXTRASEARCH

IEnumExtraSearch uses this structure to return information on the search objects supported by the IShellFolder object.

Header: shlobj.h

```
typedef struct tagEXTRASEARCH
{
    GUID guidSearch;
    WCHAR wszMenuText[];
    WCHAR wszHelpText[];
    WCHAR wszUrl[2084];
    WCHAR wszIcon[MAX_PATH+10];
    WCHAR wszGreyIcon[MAX_PATH+10];
    WCHAR wszClrIcon[MAX_PATH+10];
}EXTRASEARCH, *LPEXTRASEARCH;
```

Members:

guidSearch: Specifies the search object's GUID.

wszMenuText: Null-terminated string specifying the search object's menu text.

wszHelpText: Null-terminated string specifying the search object's help text.

wszUrl: Null-terminated string specifying the search object's URL.

wszIcon: Specifies the icon to be used in the Search drop down menu. It should be of the same form one would find in the registry:

```
[full path to file], [index of icon within file]
```

wszGreyIcon: Specifies the location of the gray icon for the toolbar. This must be specified using the same form as for wszIcon. The specified icon should have two sizes: 18x16 pixels and 22x20 pixels.

wszClrIcon: Specifies the location of the color icon for the toolbar. This must be specified using the same form as for wszIcon. The specified icon should have two sizes: 18x16 pixels and 22x20 pixels.

B.5 FOLDERFLAGS

This enumeration specifies a folder's view options. These flags are independent and can be used in any combination.

Header: shlobj.h

Values:

- **FWF_AUTOARRANGE:** Implies LVS_AUTOARRANGE is the view implemented by a list view control. In any case, automatically arranges the view's elements.
- **FWF_ABBREVIATEDNAMES:** Names should be abbreviated. The flag is not in use yet.
- **FWF_SNAPTOGRID:** The items should be arranged on a grid. The flag is not in use yet.
- **FWF_OWNERDATA:** This flag is not in use yet.
- **FWF_BESTFITWINDOW:** Tells the view to set the window size so that its contents fit inside the view in the best possible way.
- **FWF_DESKTOP:** Makes the folder behave like the desktop. Typical shell folders do not need to implement this behavior.
- **FWF_SINGLESEL:** Only allow one item at a time to be selected.
- **FWF_NOSUBFOLDERS:** Do not show subfolders.
- **FWF_TRANSPARENT:** This is used by the desktop only. Typical shell folders do not need to implement this behavior.

- **FWF_NOCLIENTEDGE:** This is used by the desktop only. Typical shell folders do not need to implement this behavior.
- **FWF_NOSCROLL:** This is used by the desktop only. Typical shell folders do not need to implement this behavior.
- **FWF_ALIGNLEFT:** If the view is implemented using a list view, this implies that the LVS_ALIGNLEFT style should be used. In any case, the view should be aligned on the left.
- **FWF_NOICONS:** The view should not display icons.
- **FWF_SHOWSELALWAYS:** The view should always show the selection.
- **FWF_SINGLECLICKACTIVATE:** According to the documentation, this flag is not supported, but I think that the documentation is behind. If this flag is set, any single clicks within the view should be interpreted the same way you would interpret a double-click. Single-click activation came with the introduction of Active Desktop and Internet Explorer 4.0.

B.6 FOLDERSETTINGS

Contains folder view information. IShellView uses this structure to communicate display information between IShellView instances.

> **Header:**   shlobj.h

```
typedef struct {
    UINT      ViewMode;
    UINT      fFlags;
}FOLDERSETTINGS; *LPFOLDERSETTINGS;
```

> **Members:**
>
> **ViewMode:** This is the folder view mode. It can be any one of the FOLDERVIEWMODE values.
>
> **fFlags:** Specifies the options for the folder. It can be none or a combination of the FOLDERFLAGS values.

B.7 FOLDERVIEWMODE

This enumeration specifies a folder's view type.

> **Header:**   shlobj.h

Values:
- **FVM_ICON:** The view should display large icons.
- **FVM_SMALLICON:** The view should display small icons.
- **FVM_LIST:** Display the items in a list view.
- **FVM_DETAILS:** Display the items and other information (report view).

B.8 FORMATETC

This structure is used to specify and describe clipboard formats. Data handlers use these to copy information. FORMATETC and its use with data handlers is covered in Chapter 7, "Shell Extenstions," Section 7.4.

Header:	objidl.h
Example Project:	Chapter 7\ABKContextMenuHandler
	Chapter 7\ABKDataHandler
	Chapter 7\ABKDropHandler
	Chapter 7\ABKPropertySheetHandler

B.9 FVSHOWINFO

Contains the information that a file viewer uses to display a file. This structure is covered in Chapter 6, "File Viewers," Section 6.2.3.

Header:	shlobj.h
Example Project:	Chapter 6\AddressBookFV

B.10 CMINVOKECOMMANDINFO

IContextMenu::InvokeCommand() uses this structure. The structure lets the IContextMenu know what command the user picked on a context menu.

Header:	shlobj.h
Example Projects:	Chapter 7\ABKContextMenuHandler
	Chapter 12\CommBand
	Chapter 12\DeskBand

```
typedef struct _CMInvokeCommandInfo{
    DWORD cbSize;
    DWORD fMask;
```

```
    HWND hwnd;
    LPCSTR lpVerb;
    LPCSTR lpParameters;
    LPCSTR lpDirectory;
    int nShow;
    DWORD dwHotKey;
    HANDLE hIcon;
} CMINVOKECOMMANDINFO, *LPCMINVOKECOMMANDINFO;
```

Members:

cbSize: Always set to sizeof(CMINVOKECOMMANDINFO).

fMask: Zero or a combination of the following flags:

- **CMIC_MASK_ASYNCOK:** Wait for the DDE conversation to terminate before returning.
- **CMIC_MASK_FLAG_NO_UI:** Do not display any user interface elements while processing the command. This means no message boxes, dialogs, or anything else.
- **CMIC_MASK_HOTKEY:** dwHotKey is valid.
- **CMIC_MASK_ICON:** hIcon is valid.
- **CMIC_MASK_NO_CONSOLE:** If the handle needs to create a new process, it usually creates a new console. This flag instructs the handler to not create a new console.

hwnd: Handle to the window that owns the context menu. The handler can use this HWND for any windows it might display.

lpVerb: If the high-order work is not zero, this contains the language-independent string that uniquely identifies the command to the IContextMenu. If that high-order word is zero, the low-order word contains the menu identifier offset of the command the IContextMenu should perform. Besides any values you may have, the system provides these command strings:

- **CMDSTR_NEWFOLDER:** String value is NewFolder.
- **CMDSTR_VIEWDETAILS:** String value is ViewDetails.
- **CMDSTR_VIEWLIST:** String value is ViewList.

lpParameters: This string contains parameters that you might want passed to the command. This value is always NULL for menu items inserted by a shell extension.

lpDirectory: This string contains the name of the working directory. This value is always NULL for menu items inserted by a shell extension.

nShow: Zero or more of the values specified for ShowWindow(). Use this value if the command will display a window or start an application.

dwHotKey: Ignore this member if the CMIC_MASK_HOTKEY flag was not set in fMask. This specifies an optional hot key that you can assign to any application activated by the command.

hIcon: Specifies the icon to use for any application activated by the command. If CMIC_MASK_ICON is not specified, ignore this member.

B.11 ITEMIDLIST

Contains a list of item identifiers. Check out SHITEMID for the real interesting information.

> **Header:**   shlobj.h
>
> **Example Project:**   Appendix B\ExSHBrowseForFolder

```
typedef struct _ITEMIDLIST {
    SHITEMID mkid;
} ITEMIDLIST, * LPITEMIDLIST;
```

> **Members:**
>
> **mkid:** List of item identifiers.

B.12 NOTIFYICONDATA

Contains information to process taskbar status area messages. This structure is covered in Chapter 2, "The Taskbar," Section 2.4.

> **Header:**   shellapi.h
>
> **Example Project:**   LibrarySource\Taskbar

B.13 REGSAM

> **Header:**   WINNT.H (REGSAM values)
>
>   WINREG.H (REGSAM typedef)

This data type is used for specifying security access attributes in the registry. A REGSAM value can be a combination of one or more of the following values:

- **KEY_ALL_ACCESS:** Combination of KEY_QUERY_VALUE, KEY_ENUMERATE_SUB_KEYS, KEY_NOTIFY, KEY_CREATE_SUB_KEY, KEY_CREATE_LINE, and KEY_SET_VALUE.

- **KEY_CREATE_LINK:** Permission to create a symbolic link.
- **KEY_CREATE_SUB_KEY:** Permission to create subkeys.
- **KEY_ENUMERATE_SUB_KEYS:** Permission to enumerate subkeys.
- **KEY_EXECUTE:** Read access permission.
- **KEY_NOTIFY:** Permission for change notification.
- **KEY_QUERY_VALUE:** Permission to query subkey values.
- **KEY_READ:** Combination of KEY_QUERY_VALUE, KEY_ENUMER-ATE_SUB_KEYS, and KEY_NOTIFY.
- **KEY_SET_VALUE:** Permission to set values.
- **KEY_WRITE:** Combination of KEY_SET_VALUE and KEY_CRE-ATE_SUB_KEY.

B.14   SHAddToRecentDocs

Adds a document to the shell's list of mostly recently used documents. This function can also clear all documents from the list. This function adds a short-cut to the user's *Recent* directory, identified by CSIDL_RECENT, and the Start menu's *Documents* submenu.

Header:	shlobj.h
Import Library:	shell32.lib
Example Project:	Appendix B\ExSHAddToRecentDocs

```
VOID SHAddToRecentDocs(
    UINT uFlags,
    LPCVOID pv
);
```

Parameters:

uFlags: Indicates the meaning of pv. The flag can have one of the two following values:
- **SHARD_PATH:** The pv parameter points to a null-terminated string. pv must contain the full path for the file.
- **SHARD_PIDL:** The pv parameter points to an ITEMIDLIST structure that identifies the file object. PIDLs that do not iden-tify file objects are not allowed.

pv: Pointer to a null-terminated string or a PIDL. The meaning de-pends on the value of uFlags.

B.15   SHAppBarMessage

Covered in Chapter 2, Section 2.1.

Header:	shlobj.h
Import Library:	shell32.lib
Example Project:	Chapter 2\Step 2\TaskBar

B.16   SHAutoComplete

This is definitely one of the cooler features added to the shell. This function requires version 5.00 and later of SHLWAPI.DLL (Internet Explorer 5.0, Windows 2000). If your user is entering a filename using an edit box, combo box, or ComboBoxEx control, this method attempts to automatically complete the filename or URL that the user is entering. To use this function, the user must have COM initialized. Call CoInitialize(NULL)

Header:	shlwapi.h
Import Library:	shlwapi.lib
Example Project:	Appendix B\ExSHAutoComplete

```
HRESULTHRESULT SHAutoComplete(
    HWND hwndEdit,
    DWORD dwFlags
);
```

Parameters:

hwndEdit: Window handle to the edit box, combo box, or ComboBoxEx control that the user will use to enter in a URL or filename.

dwFlags: Indicates where to get the auto-completion strings from and how the auto-complete text should behave. The first four flags exist to override registry settings. The last five allow you to specify where the auto-complete strings come from.

- **SHACF_AUTOAPPEND_FORCE_OFF:** Force the auto-append feature off. The system will not put the first match into hwndEdit.
- **SHACF_AUTOAPPEND_FORCE_ON:** Force the auto-append feature on. The system will automatically put the first match into hwndEdit.

- **SHACF_AUTOSUGGEST_FORCE_OFF:** Force the auto-suggest feature off. This disables the drop-down list of possible matches.
- **SHACF_AUTOSUGGEST_FORCE_ON:** Force the auto-suggest feature on. This guarantees that the list of matches will show up.
- **SHACF_DEFAULT:** This is the same as specifying SHACF_FILESYSTEM | SHACF_URLALL for dwFlags.
- **SHACF_FILESYSTEM:** Include the file system as well as any virtual folders. Virtual folders include the Desktop and Control Panel.
- **SHACF_URLALL:** This is the same as specifying SHACF_URL-HISTORY | SHACF_URLMRU for dwFlags.
- **SHACF_URLHISTORY:** Include all URLs in the user's history list.
- **SHACF_URLMRU:** Include the URLs in the user's most recently used list.

B.17 SHBindToParent

Header:	shlobj.h
Import Library:	shell32.lib

```
HRESULT SHBindToParent(
    LPCITEMIDLIST pidl,
    REFIID riid,
    VOID **ppv,
    LPCITEMIDLIST *ppidlLast
);
```

Parameters:

pidl: The item's PIDL.

riid: The REFIID of one of the interfaces exposed by the item's parent object.

ppv: A pointer to the interface specified by riid. When you are done with the interface, you must release the object.

ppidlLast: The item's PIDL relative to the parent folder. This PIDL can be used with the many the methods supported by the parent folder's interface(s). If you set ppidlLast to NULL, the relative PIDL will not be returned.

Returns: S_OK on success; some other value otherwise.

B.18   SHBrowseForFolder

Displays a dialog box that enables the user to select a shell folder. You must call CoInitialize(NULL) before calling this function.

Header:	shlobj.h
Import Library:	shell32.lib
Example Project:	Appendix B\ExSHBrowseForFolder

```
LPITEMIDLIST SHBrowseForFolder(
    LPBROWSEINFO lpbi
);
```

Parameters:

lpbi: Pointer to a BROWSEINFO structure.

Return Value: Returns a pointer to an ITEMIDLIST (PIDL) specifying the location of the selected folder. The PIDL is relative to the root of the namespace. When the user presses Cancel, the return value is NULL.

B.19   SHChangeNotify

An application should use this function when it performs an action that may affect the shell.

Header:	shlobj.h
Import Library:	shell32.lib

```
void SHChangeNotify(
    LONG wEventId,
    UINT uFlags,
    LPCVOID dwItem1,
    LPCVOID dwItem2
);
```

Parameters:

wEventID:[2] Describes the event. The caller can specify more than one event at a time. If more than one event is specified, dwItem1 and dwItem2 must be the same for all events. Note: dwItem1 and

---

2. The uFlags statement inserted with the event descriptions will be different with respect to printers. I apologize to the people at Hewlett-Packard, Epson, Canon, and others for the incompleteness here. If anyone can fill in the details, please write to me. I will publish the changes on *www.scottseely.com* and the Prentice Hall Web site, *www.phptr.com*.

dwItem2 do not have to equal each other; they just cannot change for the events specified. This parameter can be one or more of the following values:

- **SHCNE_ALLEVENTS:** All events happened.
- **SHCNE_ASSOCCHANGED:** The application changed a file type association. The uFlags parameter must specify SHCNF_IDLIST. dwItem1 and dwItem2 must be set to NULL.
- **SHCNE_ATTRIBUTES:** The attributes of an item or folder changed. You must specify SHCNF_IDLIST or SHCNF_PATH in uFlags. dwItem1 is the PIDL of the folder that changed. Set dwItem2 to NULL.
- **SHCNE_CREATE:** Reports the creation of a non-folder item. You must specify SHCNF_IDLIST or SHCNF_PATH in uFlags. dwItem1 is the PIDL or name of the new item. Set dwItem2 to NULL.
- **SHCNE_DELETE:** Reports the deletion of a non-folder item. You must specify SHCNF_IDLIST or SHCNF_PATH in uFlags. dwItem1 is the PIDL or name of the deleted item. Set dwItem2 to NULL.
- **SHCNE_DRIVEADD:** Reports the addition of a drive item. You must specify SHCNF_IDLIST or SHCNF_PATH in uFlags. dwItem1 is the PIDL or name of the root of the new drive. Set dwItem2 to NULL.
- **SHCNE_DRIVEADDGUI:** Reports the addition of a new drive and the shell should create a new window for the drive. You must specify SHCNF_IDLIST or SHCNF_PATH in uFlags. dwItem1 is the PIDL or name of the root of the new drive. Set dwItem2 to NULL.
- **SHCNE_DRIVEREMOVED:** Reports the removal of a drive. You must specify SHCNF_IDLIST or SHCNF_PATH in uFlags. dwItem1 is the PIDL or name of the root of the removed drive. Set dwItem2 to NULL.
- **SHCNE_EXTENEDED_EVENT:** Not used, yet.
- **SHCNE_FREESPACE:** The amount of free space on a drive changed. You must specify SHCNF_IDLIST or SHCNF_PATH in uFlags. dwItem1 is the PIDL or name of the drive's root whose free space has changed. Set dwItem2 to NULL.
- **SHCNE_MEDIAINSERTED:** Reports the insertion of a new media into a drive. You must specify SHCNF_IDLIST or SHCNF_PATH in uFlags. dwItem1 is the PIDL or name of the drive's root. Set dwItem2 to NULL.
- **SHCNE_MEDIAREMOVED:** Reports the removal of media from a drive. You must specify SHCNF_IDLIST or SHCNF_PATH in uFlags. dwItem1 is the PIDL or name of the drive's root. Set dwItem2 to NULL.

- **SHCNE_MKDIR:** Reports the removal or creation of a new directory. You must specify SHCNF_IDLIST or SHCNF_PATH in uFlags. dwItem1 is the PIDL or name of the new directory. Set dwItem2 to NULL.
- **SHCNE_NETSHARE:** Reports the sharing of a local folder. You must specify SHCNF_IDLIST or SHCNF_PATH in uFlags. dwItem1 is the PIDL or name of the shared directory. Set dwItem2 to NULL.
- **SHCNE_NETUNSHARE:** Reports the end of sharing of a local folder. You must specify SHCNF_IDLIST or SHCNF_PATH in uFlags. dwItem1 is the PIDL or name of the shared directory. Set dwItem2 to NULL.
- **SHCNE_RENAMEFOLDER:** Reports the renaming of a folder. You must specify SHCNF_IDLIST or SHCNF_PATH in uFlags. dwItem1 is the previous PIDL or name of the folder. Set dwItem2 to the new PIDL or name of the folder.
- **SHCNE_RENAMEITEM:** Reports the renaming of a non-folder item. You must specify SHCNF_IDLIST or SHCNF_PATH in uFlags. dwItem1 is the previous PIDL or name of the item. Set dwItem2 to the new PIDL or name of the item.
- **SHCNE_RMDIR:** Reports the deletion of a folder. You must specify SHCNF_IDLIST or SHCNF_PATH in uFlags. dwItem1 is the PIDL or name of the removed folder. Set dwItem2 to NULL.
- **SHCNE_SERVERDISCONNECT:** Reports disconnection from a server. You must specify SHCNF_IDLIST or SHCNF_PATH in uFlags. dwItem1 is the PIDL or name of the server that was disconnected. Set dwItem2 to NULL.
- **SHCNE_UPDATEDIR:** The contents of an existing folder changed. You must specify SHCNF_IDLIST or SHCNF_PATH in uFlags. dwItem1 is the PIDL or name of the folder that changed. Set dwItem2 to NULL. Do not use this event to indicate that a folder has been created (SHCNE_MKDIR), deleted (SHCNE_RMDIR), or renamed (SHCNE_RENAMEFOLDER).
- **SHCNE_UPDATEIMAGE:** One of the images in the system image list has changed. uFlags must contain SHCNF_DWORD. dwItem1 indicates the index of the changed item. Set dwItem2 to NULL.
- **SHCNE_UPDATEITEM:** A non-folder item has changed. The item still exists and has not been renamed. You must specify SHCNF_IDLIST or SHCNF_PATH in uFlags. dwItem1 is the PIDL or name of the changed item. Set dwItem2 to NULL. Do not use this event to indicate that an item has been created (SHCNE_CREATRE), deleted (SHCNE_DELETE), or renamed (SHCNE_RENAMEITEM).

Still a part of the wEventID parameter, these flags specify combinations of other events:

- **SHCNE_DISKEVENTS:** Specifies a combination of all of the disk event notifiers. SHCNE_RENAMEITEM | SHCNE_CREATE | SHCNE_DELETE | SHCNE_MKDIR | SHCNE_RMDIR | SHCNE_ATTRIBUTES | SHCNE_UPDATEDIR | SHCNE_UP-DATEITEM | SHCNE_RENAMEFOLDER.
- **SHCNE_GLOBALEVENT:** Specifies a combination of all of the global event identifiers. SHCNE_NETSHARE | SHCNE_NETUN-SHARE | SHCNE_DRIVEADD | SHCNE_UPDATEIMAGE | SHCNE_DRIVEADDGUI | SHCNE_FREESPACE | SHCNE_EX-TENDED_EVENT | SHCNE_ASSOCCHANGED.

Still a part of the wEventID parameter, this value modifies others. You cannot use the value by itself:

- **SHCNE_INTERRUPT:** Indicates that the event occurred because of a system interrupt.

uFlags: Specifies the meaning of the dwItem1 and dwItem2 parameters. This must be one of the following values:

- **SHCNF_DWORD:** Interpret the dwItemX parameters as DWORDS.
- **SHCNF_IDLIST:** Interpret the dwItemX parameters as PIDLs.
- **SHCNF_PATH:** Interpret the dwItemX parameters as null-terminated strings. The strings contain the full path names of the items affected by the change.
- **SHCNF_PRINTER:** Interpret the dwItemX parameters as null-terminated strings. The strings contain the "friendly" names of the printers affected by the change.

These two flags modify the above flags. They cannot be used on their own.

- **SHCNF_FLUSH:** The function should deliver the notification to all components before returning.
- **SHCNF_FLUSHNOWAIT:** The function should return as soon as the notification process has begun.

dwItem1: Event-dependent value.

dwItem2: Event-dependent value.

B.20 SHCONTF

Used by IShellFolder::EnumObjects() to determine the type of items included in an enumeration. IShellFolder::EnumObjects() may ask for one or more of the values.

Header:	shlobj.h

Values:

SHCONTF_FOLDERS: Include folders in the enumeration.

SHCONTF_NONFOLDERS: Include non-folders in the enumeration.

SHCONTF_INCLUDEHIDDEN: Include hidden items in the enumeration.

B.21   SHCopyKey

Copies all of the subkeys and values of the source key to the destination key.

Header:	shlwapi.h
Import Library:	shlwapi.lib
Example Project:	Chapter 11\WinReg

(Only available under Windows 2000 or Internet Explorer 5.0.)

```
DWORD SHCopyKey(
    HKEY hkeySrc,
    LPCTSTR szSrcSubKey,
    HKEY hkeyDest,
    DWORD fReserved
);
```

Parameters:

hkeySrc: Pointer to the source key hive (example, HKEY_LOCAL_MACHINE).

szSrcSubKey: Name of the subkey to copy.

hkeyDest: Copy destination.

fReserved: Pass NULL.

Return Value: Returns ERROR_SUCCESS if successful. Otherwise, it returns an error value defined in WINERROR.H. Use FormatMessage() with the FORMAT_MESSAGE_FROM_SYSTEM flag to get the generic description of the error.

B.22   SHCreateShellPalette

The function behaves the same as CreateHalftonePalette() but accommodates the differences between Windows 9x, NT 4.0, and 2000.

Header:	shlwapi.h
Import Library:	shlwapi.lib
Example Project:	Appendix B\IconPro

```
HPALETTE SHCreateShellPalette(
    HDC     hdc
);
```

Parameters:

hdc: Handle to the device context or NULL.

Return Value: If hdc is NULL or the device context is palletized, the function returns a full palette. If the device context is not palletized, then the function returns a default palette.

Remarks: The IconPro example comes straight from the SDK. I modified the code so that it uses SHCreateShellPalette() instead of CreateHalftonePalette(). As a user, I could tell no difference between the two. To invoke the code, open up the IconPro icon for editing. Select the 72x72, 8-bit icon and then go to Edit→Import BMP. Select a 24-bit bitmap. This will cause SHCreateShellPalette() to be invoked and to do nothing spectacular. This function removes any idiosyncrasies between the various Win32 platforms, so any bugs you did have to work around should disappear with this function.

B.23 SHDeleteEmptyKey

This function deletes a key if, and *only* if, the key does not contain any subkeys or values.

| **Header:** | shlwapi.h |
| **Import Library:** | shlwapi.lib |

```
DWORD SHDeleteEmptyKey(
    HKEY     hkey,
    LPCTSTR  pszSubKey
);
```

Parameters:

hkey: Handle to an open key or to one of the predefined HKEY values (HKEY_CLASSES_ROOT, HKEY_CURRENT_CONFIG, etc.).

pszSubKey: Address of a null-terminated string specifying the name of the key to delete.

Return Value: Returns ERROR_SUCCESS if successful. Otherwise, it returns an error value defined in WINERROR.H. Use FormatMessage() with the FORMAT_MESSAGE_FROM_SYSTEM flag to get the generic description of the error.

B.24   SHDeleteKey

This function deletes a key and all of its subkeys and values from the registry.

Header:	shlwapi.h
Import Library:	shlwapi.lib
Example Project:	Chapter 11\WinReg

```
DWORD SHDeleteKey(
    HKEY      hkey,
    LPCTSTR   pszSubKey
);
```

Parameters:

hkey: Handle to an open key or to one of the predefined HKEY values (HKEY_CLASSES_ROOT, HKEY_CURRENT_CONFIG, etc.).

pszSubKey: Address of a null-terminated string specifying the name of the key to delete.

Return Value: Returns ERROR_SUCCESS if successful. Otherwise, it returns an error value defined in WINERROR.H. Use FormatMessage() with the FORMAT_MESSAGE_FROM_SYSTEM flag to get the generic description of the error.

B.25   SHDeleteValue

This function deletes a value from the registry.

Header:	shlwapi.h
Import Library:	shlwapi.lib
Example Project:	Chapter 11\WinReg

```
DWORD SHDeleteValue(
    HKEY      hkey,
    LPCTSTR   pszSubKey,
    LPCTSTR   pszValue
);
```

Parameters:

hkey: Handle to an open key or to one of the predefined HKEY values (HKEY_CLASSES_ROOT, HKEY_CURRENT_CONFIG, etc.).

pszSubKey: Address of a null-terminated string specifying the name of the subkey that contains the value being deleted.

pszValue: Address of the name of the value to be deleted.

Return Value: Returns ERROR_SUCCESS if successful. Otherwise, it returns an error value defined in WINERROR.H. Use FormatMessage() with the FORMAT_MESSAGE_FROM_SYSTEM flag to get the generic description of the error.

B.26 SHDESCRIPTIONID

This structure gets filled in by SHGetDataFromIDList().

Header: shlobj.h

```
typedef struct SHDESCRIPTIONID{
    DWORD    dwDescriptionId;
    CLSID    clsid;
} SHDESCRIPTIONID, *LPSHDESCRIPTIONID;
```

Members:

dwDescriptionId: Used to determine what type the item is. It can be one of the following values:

- **SHDID_ROOT_REGITEM:** The item is registered and on the Desktop.
- **SHDID_FS_FILE:** The item is a file.
- **SHDID_FS_DIRECTORY:** The item is a directory.
- **SHDID_FS_OTHER:** The item is there, but the file system has no clue what it is.
- **SHDID_COMPUTER_DRIVE35:** The item is a 3.5-inch floppy drive.
- **SHDID_COMPUTER_DRIVE525:** The item is a 5.25-inch floppy drive.
- **SHDID_COMPUTER_REMOVABLE:** The item is a removable drive.
- **SHDID_COMPUTER_FIXED:** The item is a fixed drive.
- **SHDID_COMPUTER_NETDRIVE:** The item is a drive mapped to a share on the network.
- **SHDID_COMPUTER_CDROM:** The item is a CD-ROM drive.
- **SHDID_COMPUTER_RAMDISK:** The item is a RAM disk.
- **SHDID_COMPUTER_OTHER:** The item is some type of device, but the function is not sure what type it is.

- **SHDID_NET_DOMAIN:** The item is a network domain.
- **SHDID_NET_SERVER:** The item is a network server.
- **SHDID_NET_SHARE:** The item is a network share.
- **SHDID_NET_RESTOFNET:** This value is not used right now.
- **SHDID_NET_OTHER:** The item is a network resource but the function is not sure what type of network resource it is.

clsid: Receives the CLSID of the object that represents the item.

B.27   Shell_NotifyIcon

Covered in Chapter 2, Section 2.4.

Header:	shlobj.h
Import Library:	shell32.lib
Example Project:	\WorkArea\TaskBar

B.28   ShellAbout

Header:	shellapi.h
Import Library:	shell32.lib
Example Project:	Appendix B\ExSHAddToRecentDocs

```
int ShellAbout (
    HWND hWnd,
    LPCTSTR szApp,
    LPCTSTR szOtherStuff,
    HICON hIcon
);
```

Parameters:

hwnd: Handle to the parent window. This can be NULL.

szApp: Displays text in the title bar of the ShellAbout dialog box and on the first line of the dialog box after *Microsoft*. If the text contains a separator character (#) dividing the name into two parts, the function displays the first part in the title bar and the second part on the first line after the text *Microsoft*.

szOtherStuff: Note the highly descriptive variable name. If you have any stuff that you want displayed as text after the version and copyright information, this is the parameter to fill in.

hIcon: Icon to display in the dialog box. If the parameter is NULL, the function picks the Microsoft Windows or Windows NT icon.

Return Value: Returns TRUE if successful and FALSE if it is a horrible, abysmal failure.[3]

B.29 SHELLDETAILS

Used to return information on an item in a shell folder from IShell-Details::GetDetailsOf().

Header: shlobj.h

```
typedef struct _SHELLDETAILS
{
    int      fmt;
    int      cxChar;
    STRRET   str;
} SHELLDETAILS, *LPSHELLDETAILS;
```

Members:

fmt: Alignment of the column heading and the subitem text in the column. This member can have any one of the following values:
- **LVCMF_CENTER:** Text is centered.
- **LVCMF_COL_HAS_IMAGES:** The header item contains an image in the image list.
- **LVCMF_LEFT:** Text is left justified.
- **LVCMF_RIGHT:** Text is right justified.

cxChar: The number of average-sized characters in the header.

str: A STRRET structure that includes a string with the requested information. To convert the structure to a string, use StrRetToBuf() or StrRetToStr().

B.30 ShellExecute

This function allows you to execute an action on a file. Depending on the file type and the registry contents for that file type, execution may mean different things. Most everything I have read says that you should use ShellExecuteEx

---

3. For a function with a parameter called szOtherStuff, you need to add some humor when documenting it.

instead of ShellExecute. ShellExecute was introduced with NT 3.1. ShellExecuteEx came out with Windows 95 and NT 4.0.

Header:	shellapi.h
Import Library:	shell32.lib
Example Project:	Appendix B\ExSHAddToRecentDocs

```
HINSTANCE ShellExecute(
    HWND hwnd,
    LPCTSTR lpVerb,
    LPCTSTR lpFile,
    LPCTSTR lpParameters,
    LPCTSTR lpDirectory,
    INT nShowCmd
);
```

Parameters:

hwnd: Handle to the parent window. This window will act as the parent of any message boxes produced as a result of calling ShellExecute. This can be NULL.

lpVerb: A string specifying the verb (action) to be performed on lpFile. The set of available verbs depends on the file or folder. Any commands listed in the context menu or registry can be used. Common verbs (i.e., verbs that are usually valid) are:

- **edit:** Opens an editor. If lpFile is not a document type, the function will fail.
- **explore:** Opens Windows Explorer with the folder specified by lpFile as the currently active folder.
- **open:** Opens the file specified by lpFile. The file can be an executable, a document, or a folder.
- **print:** Prints the document specified by lpFile. Anything can be printed if the registry is set up correctly and the correct applications are installed. Having the "right stuff" may mean getting applications from vendors or writing your own code.
- **properties:** Displays the properties of the item specified by lpFile.
- **NULL:** Uses the *open* verb if it is available. If the open verb is not available, then the default verb is used. Windows 2000 will also try to use the first verb listed in the registry if the first two tries fail.

lpFile: Address of a null-terminated string specifying the file on which to perform the verb.

lpParameters: The command line to pass to the file if the file in lpFile is an executable. If lpFile is a document, pass NULL for lpParameters. If yes, use a null-terminated string.

lpDirectory: Specifies the default directory. This can be NULL. Yes, use a null-terminated string.

nShowCmd: Uses any one of the SW_XXXX commands listed with ShowWindow. The flags you will probably use are:
- **SW_SHOWDEFAULT**
- **SW_SHOWMAXIMIZED**
- **SW_SHOWMINIMIZED**
- **SW_SHOWMINNOACTIVE**
- **SW_SHOWNOACTIVATE**
- **SW_SHOWNORMAL**

Return Value: Returns a value greater than 32 if successful. Any values under 32 specify an error. The return value is not a true HINSTANCE. The HINSTANCE return value exists to maintain compatibility with 16-bit Windows applications. If the return value is less than or equal to 32, here are the error values and their meanings:
- **0:** Windows ran out of memory or resources.
- **ERROR_FILE_NOT_FOUND:** Could not find the file specified in lpFile.
- **ERROR_PATH_NOT_FOUND:** Could not find the directory specified in lpDirector.
- **ERROR_BAD_FORMAT:** Windows cannot load the executable. The executable is not a valid Windows or MS-DOS executable or the executable image has an error.
- **SE_ERR_ACCESSDENIED:** The current user does not have access to the file in lpFile.
- **SE_ERR_ASSOCINCOMPLETE:** The file name association is incomplete or invalid.
- **SE_ERR_DDEBUSY:** The DDE[4] transaction could not be completed because another DDE transaction was being processed. I do not think that this error should show up, but it is in the SDK documentation for ShellExecute.
- **SE_ERR_DDEFAIL:** The DDE transaction failed. Again, I am just being complete (but doubtful).
- **SE_ERR_DDETIMEOUT:** The DDE transaction timed out. This is also part of being thorough (and thoroughly doubtful about DDE).

---

4. DDE, or dynamic data exchange, came out of Microsoft around the same time that COM did. From a usage standpoint, DDE is a lot like named-pipes. Today, Microsoft endorses COM for inter-application communication and discourages programmers from using DDE. When DDE and COM (then called OLE) were introduced, OLE was supposed to be there only for embedding files within other files. They built OLE to be adaptable and we all know where that adaptation has gone. ActiveX, DCOM, COM, OLE, DirectX, OLEDB, and others have been created from the original OLE idea. DDE is dead. Unless you support one of the handfuls of applications using DDE (or, God forbid, Net-DDE), do not look at it. Learn COM, instead.

- **SE_ERR_DLLNOTFOUND:** A needed DLL could not be found.
- **SE_ERR_FNF:** Same as ERROR_FILE_NOT_FOUND.
- **SE_ERR_NOASSOC:** No application is associated with the given file name extension. You will also get this value if you try to print a file and no *print* verb exists.
- **SE_ERR_OOM:** Same meaning as 0.
- **SE_ERR_PNF:** Same meaning as ERROR_PATH_NOT_FOUND.
- **SE_ERR_SHARE:** A sharing violation occurred.

B.31   ShellExecuteEx

This function allows you to execute an action on a file. Depending on the file type and the registry contents for that file type, execution may mean different things. Use this function instead of ShellExecute. If you are using multiple monitors and attempting to execute the *properties* verb, the properties window may not appear in the correct position. Microsoft has documented it as a feature, not a bug. I think we all know what it really is.[5]

Header:	shellapi.h
Import Library:	shell32.lib
Example Project:	Appendix B\ExSHAddToRecentDocs

```
BOOL ShellExecuteEx(
    LPSHELLEXECUTEINFO lpExecInfo
);
```

Parameters:

lpExecInfo: Pointer to the SHELLEXECUTEINFO structure. This structure contains all the information needed to execute a file.

Return Value: Returns TRUE on success, FALSE on failure. Call GetLastError() to retrieve the last error. Interpret the error value using the same error values listed under ShellExecute()'s return value.

B.32   SHELLEXECUTEINFO

ShellExecuteEx() uses this structure.

Header:	shellapi.h
Example Project:	Appendix B\ExSHAddToRecentDocs

---

5. If you picked bug, you are correct. Unfortunately, you fail any absolute loyalty tests.

```
typedef struct _SHELLEXECUTEINFO{
    DWORD cbSize;
    ULONG fMask;
    HWND hwnd;
    LPCTSTR lpVerb;
    LPCTSTR lpFile;
    LPCTSTR lpParameters;
    LPCTSTR lpDirectory;
    int nShow;
    HINSTANCE hInstApp;

    // Optional members
    LPVOID lpIDList;
    LPCSTR lpClass;
    HKEY hkeyClass;
    DWORD dwHotKey;
    union {
        HANDLE hIcon;
        HANDLE hMonitor;
    };
    HANDLE hProcess;
} SHELLEXECUTEINFO, FAR *LPSHELLEXECUTEINFO;
```

Members:

cbSize: Always set to sizeof(SHELLEXECUTEINFO).

fMask: Flag that indicates which other structure members are used. This can be a combination of the following values:

- **SEE_MASK_CLASSKEY:** Use the class key in hkeyClass.
- **SEE_MASK_CLASSNAME:** Use the class name in lpClass.
- **SEE_MASK_CONNECTNETDRV:** Validate the share and connect to a drive letter. lpFile is a null-terminated string that contains a UNC path of a file on the network.
- **SEE_MASK_DOENVSUBST:** Expand any environment variable specified in lpDirectory and lpFile.
- **SEE_MASK_FLAG_NO_UI:** Do not display any message boxes if an error occurs.
- **SEE_MASK_HMONITOR:** The hMonitor member is valid.
- **SEE_MASK_HOTKEY:** Use the hot key in the dwHotKey member.
- **SEE_MASK_ICON:** The hIcon member is valid. What does this do for you? If the application does not have an associated icon, then this sets one for it. Otherwise, this flag does nothing.
- **SEE_MASK_IDLIST:** The lpIDList member is valid.
- **SEE_MASK_INVOKEIDLIST:** Use the value in lpIDList to invoke an application. If lpIDList is NULL, the function creates an ID list and invokes the application. This flag overrides SEE_MASK_IDLIST.

- **SEE_MASK_NOCLOSEPROCESS:** The hProcess members receive a process handle. Typically, the caller uses this handle to find out when the process created by ShellExecuteEx() terminates. When execution is handled through a DDE conversation, ShellExecuteEx will not return a handle. The caller must close the handle when the caller no longer needs it.
- **SEE_MASK_NO_CONSOLE:** This one is a little weird. It does not mean that the new process does not get a console. Instead, it tells ShellExecuteEx() to create a new console for the new process. Normally, the new process inherits the caller's console. This is equivalent to setting CREATE_NEW_CONSOLE in a call to CreateProcess().
- **SEE_MASK_UNICODE:** Indicates a Unicode application.
- **SEE_MASK_USERLOGON:** Forces a user logon. The logon dialog box gets displayed. This is only valid for Windows 2000 and later.

hwnd: Handle to the window that the new process should use as a parent when displaying dialogs and message boxes.

lpVerb: Same as lpVerb under ShellExecute().

lpFile: Same as lpFile under ShellExecute().

lpParameters: Same as lpParameters under ShellExecute().

lpDirectory: Same as lpDirectory under ShellExecute().

nShow: Same as nShow under ShellExecute().

hInstApp: If the function succeeds, it sets this member to a value greater than 32. Otherwise, interpret it using the return values listed under ShellExecute().

lpIDList: Address of an ITEMIDLIST structure that uniquely identifies the file to execute.

lpClass: Null-terminated string specifying the file class or GUID to use when executing lpVerb. Read hKeyClass for more information.

hkeyClass: Handle to the registry key for the file class. I suspect that lpClass and hkeyClass should not be used simultaneously. In practice, I do not use these two together. Only use this member or lpClass if you do not want the shell to do the default lookup and usage scenario. For example, you may want to make sure that all .HTML files open up using Internet Explorer, regardless of the default browser. You specify hkeyClass or lpClass to guarantee that the same browser executable opens up the HTML file.

dwHotKey: Hot key to associate with the application. The low-order word is the virtual key code (VK_XXX) and the high-order word is a modifier flag (HOTKEYF_ALT, HOTKEYF_CONTROL, HOTKEYF_EXT,

HOTKEYF_SHIFT). When the user presses the hotkey, Windows will activate the newly created window.

hIcon: Handle to the icon for the file class.

hProcess: Handle to the new application. This member will only be set when SEE_MASK_NOCLOSEPROCESS is set in fMask. If a new process was not launched, this member will still be NULL. For example, if Internet Explorer is running before ShellExecuteEx() got called and the structure called for a URL to be displayed, the running copy Internet Explorer will just load the new URL. No new process got created, so this member will be NULL.

B.33   SHELLFLAGSTATE

SHELLFLAGSTATE contains a set of flags that indicate the current shell settings. SHGetSettings() uses this structure. Instead of forcing the user to decode an integer value, this structure uses bitfields to make the C/C++ programmer's life easy.[6]

Header:	shlobj.h
Example Project:	Appendix B\ExSHGetSettings

```
typedef struct {
    BOOL fShowAllObjects : 1;
    BOOL fShowExtensions : 1;
    BOOL fNoConfirmRecycle : 1;
    BOOL fShowSysFiles : 1;
    BOOL fShowCompColor : 1;
    BOOL fDoubleClickInWebView : 1;
    BOOL fDesktopHTML : 1;
    BOOL fWin95Classic : 1;
    BOOL fDontPrettyPath : 1;
    BOOL fShowAttribCol : 1;
    BOOL fMapNetDrvBtn : 1;
    BOOL fShowInfoTip : 1;
    BOOL fHideIcons : 1;
    UINT fRestFlags : 3;
} SHELLFLAGSTATE, * LPSHELLFLAGSTATE;
```

Members:

fShowAllObjects: Indicates if Show All Files is enabled (TRUE = enabled).

---

6. I am fairly certain that this structure does not do the same for a Visual Basic programmer.

fShowExtensions: Indicates if Windows does show the extensions for Known File Types. If Hide File Extensions is selected, this is FALSE.

fNoConfirmRecycle: I think someone on the Microsoft staff was not getting their sleep quota when this name was invented. TRUE means that the delete file confirmations are not displayed. FALSE means that confirmations are displayed.

fShowSysFiles: If the system IS NOT showing system files, this flag is TRUE. If the system IS showing system files, this flag is FALSE. This is the antithesis of self-documenting code. Perhaps the engineer was working on an entry for the obfuscated C contest?

fShowCompColor: Indicates if Windows Explorer should display compressed files with an alternate color (TRUE = yes).

fDoubleClickInWebView: Indicates if the user must double-click on an item in a Web View in order to activate it (TRUE = yes).

fDesktopHTML: Indicates if Active Desktop→View as Web Page is enabled (TRUE = enabled).

fWin95Classic: Indicates if the Classic Style is enabled (TRUE = enabled).

fDontPrettyPath: Indicates if Allow All Uppercase Names is enabled (TRUE = enabled).

fShowAttribCol: Indicates if the Show File Attributes in Detail View option is enabled (TRUE = enabled).

fMapNetDrvBtn: Indicates if the Show Map Network Drive Button in Toolbar option is enabled (TRUE = enabled).

fShowInfoTip: Indicates if the Show Info Tips for Items in Folders & Desktop option is enabled (TRUE = enabled).

fHideIcons: Not used.

fRestFlags: Not used.

B.34   ShellProc

ShellProc() defines the layout of a callback function used with the SetWindowsHookEx() function. The system calls this function to notify it of shell events. Use the WH_SHELL hook type to install a ShellProc() implementation.

Header:	winuser.h
Example Project:	Appendix B\ExShellProc

```
LRESULT CALLBACK ShellProc(
    int nCode,
```

```
        WPARAM wParam,
        LPARAM lParam
    );
```

Parameters:

> **nCode:** Specifies the hook code. The parameter can be one of the following values:
>
> - **HSHELL_ACCESSIBILITYSTATE:** (Windows 2000 and later) The accessibility state changed. wParam indicates which feature changed: ACCESS_FILTERKEYS, ACCESS_MOUSEKEYS, or ACCESS_STICKYKEYS.
> - **HSHELL_ACTIVATESHELLWINDOW:** The shell should activate its main window.
> - **HSHELL_APPCOMMAND:** (Windows 2000 and later) An application did not handle the WM_APPCOMMAND message generated by a user pressing a command button with the mouse or by a user pressing a command key on the keyboard. wParam indicates the HWND of the window that originally received the WM_APPCOMMAND message. lParam indicates the key press, mouse, and command information. GET_APPCOMMAND_LPARAM(lParam) gets the application command corresponding to the button or key. GET_MOUSEORKEY_LPARAM(lParam) indicates if the command was generated by the mouse (FAPPCOMMAND_MOUSE) or keyboard (FAPPCOMMAND_KEY). GET_KEYSTATE_LPARAM(lParam) indicates which virtual keys were held down: MK_CONTROL, MK_LBUTTON, MK_MBUTTON, MK_RBUTTON, MK_SHIFT, MK_XBUTTON1, MK_XBUTTON2. GET_KEYSTATE_LPARAM() can return any combination of the previous values.
> - **HSHELL_GETMINRECT:** The system needs the coordinates of a minimized rectangle for a window that is being minimized or maximized. wParam holds an HWND for the window in question. lParam holds a pointer to a RECT structure.
> - **HSHELL_LANGUAGE:** Either a new keyboard layout was loaded or the keyboard language changed. wParam holds an HWND for the window using the new keyboard language/layout. lParam holds a handle to the keyboard layout.
> - **HSHELL_REDRAW:** The taskbar has redrawn the title of one of its windows. wParam holds an HWND to the redrawn window. lParam inidicates if the window is flashing (TRUE) or not (FALSE).
> - **HSHELL_TASKMAN:** The user selected the task list. If your shell application provides a task list, return TRUE to prevent Windows from displaying its own tasklist.

- **HSHELL_WINDOWACTIVATED:** The top-level, unowned window has changed. In other words, a different application was (probably) activated. wParam holds the HWND of the activated window. lParam indicates if the HWND is full-screen (TRUE) or not (FALSE).
- **HSHELL_WINDOWCREATED:** A top-level, unowned window has been created. The window already exists when ShellProc() gets called. wParam holds the HWND of the created window.
- **HSHELL_WINDOWDESTROYED:** A top-level, unowned window is about to be destroyed. The window still exists when ShellProc() gets called. wParam holds the HWND of the window to be destroyed.

If nCode is less than zero, your ShellProc() implementation must pass the message to the CallNextHookEx() function without further processing and return the value returned by CallNextHookEx().

wParam: The value of wParam depends on nCode. See nCode for interpretation information. If there is no mention of wParam, it has no meaning for that value of nCode.

lParam: The value of lParam depends on nCode. See nCode for interpretation information. If there is no mention of lParam, it has no meaning for that value of nCode.

Return Value: Should return zero or the value returned by CallNextHookEx().

Remarks: The example only hooks activities within the current application. To hook the operating system, you need to put the hook into a DLL, just like for any other hook.

B.35   SHEmptyRecycleBin

This function allows you to empty the recycle bins on one or more of the drives on your machine.

Header:	shellapi.h
Import Library:	shell32.lib
Example Project:	Appendix B\ExRecycleBin

```
HRESULT SHEmptyRecycleBin(
    HWND hwnd,
    LPCTSTR pszRootPath,
    DWORD dwFlags
);
```

Parameters:

> **hwnd:** Parent window to use for any dialog boxes that might be displayed during the operation. Can be NULL.
>
> **pszRootPath:** This null-terminated string specifies the path of the root drive where the Recycle Bin is located. If you pass NULL, the function will empty all Recycle Bins on the machine.
>
> **dwFlags:** Can be zero or more of these values:
> * **SHERB_NOCONFIRMATION:** Do not display a confirmation dialog.
> * **SHERB_NOPROGRESSUI:** Do not display a progress dialog.
> * **SHERB_NOSOUND:** Do not play any sounds when the operation completes.

Return Values: Returns S_OK when successful; an OLE-defined error otherwise.

B.36 SHEnumKeyEx

Given an open key, SHEnumKeyEx() enumerates its subkeys. Call SHQueryInfoKey() before calling this function to get the number of subkeys. This way, you will know when to stop incrementing dwIndex.

> **Header:**   shlwapi.h
>
> **Import Library:** shlwapi.lib

```
DWORD SHEnumKeyEx(
    HKEY hkey,
    DWORD dwIndex,
    LPTSTR pszName,
    LPDWORD pcchName
);
```

Parameters:

> **hkey:** Handle to an open key or to one of the predefined HKEY_XXX values.
>
> **dwIndex:** Index of the subkey to retrieve. Set this parameter to zero for the first call. Increment the parameter for all subsequent calls.
>
> **pszName:** Buffer to receive the name of the key.
>
> **pcchName:** Address of a DWORD that contains the size of pszName. On return, this contains the number of characters that were copied to pszName.

Return Values: Returns ERROR_SUCCESS if successful. Otherwise, it returns an error value defined in WINERROR.H. Use FormatMessage()

with the FORMAT_MESSAGE_FROM_SYSTEM flag to get the generic description of the error.

B.37 SHEnumValue

Given an open key, enumerates its values. Call SHQueryInfoKey() before calling this function to get the number of values. This way, you will know when to stop incrementing dwIndex.

Header:	shlwapi.h
Import Library:	shlwapi.lib

```
DWORD SHEnumValue(
    HKEY hkey,
    DWORD dwIndex,
    LPTSTR pszValueName,
    LPDWORD pcchValueName,
    LPDWORD pdwType,
    LPVOID pvData,
    LPDWORD pcbData
);
```

Parameters:

hkey: Handle to an open key or to one of the predefined HKEY_XXX values.

dwIndex: Index of the value to retrieve. Set this parameter to zero for the first call. Increment the parameter for all subsequent calls.

pszValueName: Buffer to receive the name of the value.

pcchValueName: Address of a DWORD that contains the size of pszValueName. On return, this contains the number of characters that were copied to pszValueName.

pdwType: Address of a DWORD that receives the value's type (REG_BINARY, REG_DWORD, REG_SZ, etc.).

pvData: Buffer to receive the data contained in the value.

pcbData: Address of a DWORD that contains the size of pvData. On return, this contains the number of bytes that were copied to pvData.

Return Values: Returns ERROR_SUCCESS if successful. Otherwise, it returns an error value defined in WINERROR.H. Use FormatMessage() with the FORMAT_MESSAGE_FROM_SYSTEM flag to get the generic description of the error.

B.38 SHFILEINFO

SHGetFileInfo() uses this structure.

Header: shellapi.h

```
typedef struct _SHFILEINFO{
    HICON hIcon;
    int   iIcon;
    DWORD dwAttributes;
    TCHAR szDisplayName[MAX_PATH];
    TCHAR szTypeName[80];
} SHFILEINFO;
```

Members:

hIcon: Handle to the icon used to represent the file. When you are done with the icon, you must call DestroyIcon().

iIcon: Index of the icon within the system image list.

dwAttributes: Same as those specified under IShellFolder::GetAttributesOf() under the rgfInOut parameter.

szDisplayName: Name of the file as it appears in the Windows shell, or the path and file name of the file that contains the icon used to represent the file.

szTypeName: String used to describe the file.

B.39 SHFileOperation

This function copies, moves, renames, or deletes a file system object. It will place the file in the Recycle Bin on a delete.

Header: shellapi.h

Import Library: shell32.lib

```
int SHFileOperation(
    LPSHFILEOPSTRUCT lpFileOp
);
```

Parameters:

lpFileOp: Pointer to a SHFILEOPSTRUCT that specifies the item to act on and what to do with that item.

Return Values: Returns zero if successful, non-zero if it fails.

B.40 SHFILEOPSTRUCT

Use this structure with SHFileOperation to rename, move, copy, or delete a file or folder.

Header: shellapi.h

```
typedef struct _SHFILEOPSTRUCT{
    HWND hwnd;
    UINT wFunc;
    LPCSTR pFrom;
    LPCSTR pTo;
    FILEOP_FLAGS fFlags;
    BOOL fAnyOperationsAborted;
    LPVOID hNameMappings;
    LPCSTR lpszProgressTitle;
} SHFILEOPSTRUCT, FAR *LPSHFILEOPSTRUCT;
```

Members:

hwnd: Window handle of the dialog box to use to display information about the status of the file operation.

wFunc: Indicates what operation to perform. It can be one of the following values:

- **FO_COPY:** Copy the file in pFrom to the location specified in pTo.
- **FO_DELETE:** Delete the files specified in pFrom.
- **FO_MOVE:** Move the files pFrom to the location specified in pTo.
- **FO_RENAME:** Rename the files specified in pFrom. pFrom must contain the full path name in order to delete the file or folder.

pFrom: Points to a buffer containing one or more source file names. The names are null-delimited. Indicate the end of the list with a double null. You can specify a wildcard path in this member. You should give the full path to each file. Relative pathnames may work, but Windows makes no guarantees.

pTo: Points to a buffer containing the name of the destination file or directory. Copy and Move operations require a pre-existing directory. If fFlags is set to FOF_MULTIDESTFILES and multiple file names are passed, the file names must be null-delimited. Terminate the list with a double null. Use full pathnames. If you use relative pathnames, Windows will store the files in 8.3 format with no way to get back to the long filename.

fFlags: These flags control the file operation. fFlags can have a combination of the following flags:

- **FOF_ALLOWUNDO:** Preserve Undo information if at all possible. If pFrom does not contained full pathnames, the shell ignores this flag.
- **FOF_FILESONLY:** Only operate on files if the wildcard filename is specified.
- **FOF_MULTIDESTFILES:** The pTo member specifies a destination file for each source file instead of a directory for all the source files.
- **FOF_NOCONFIRMATION:** Respond with *Yes to all* to any dialog box the shell displays.
- **FOF_NOCONFIRMMKDIR:** Do not confirm the creation of a new directory if the operation requires a new one.
- **FOF_NO_CONNECTED_ELEMENTS:** Do not move connected files as a group. (Windows 2000 and later only.)
- **FOF_NOCOPYSECURITYATTRIBS:** Do not copy the file's security attributes.
- **FOF_NOERRORUI:** Do not display any windows if an error occurs.
- **FOF_NORECURSION:** Only operate on the local directory. Leave subdirectories alone.
- **FOF_RENAMEONCOLLISION:** If the operation will result in two files with the same name in the same directory, rename the file being acted on.
- **FOF_SILENT:** Do not display a progress dialog.
- **FOF_SIMPLEPROGRESS:** Display a progress dialog but do not display filenames.
- **FOF_WANTMAPPINGHANDLE:** When FOF_RENAMEONCOLLISION is specified, this flag tells the SHFileOperation() function to fill in the hNameMappings member if any files get renamed.
- **FOF_WANTNUKEWARNING:** Send a warning if the operation will destroy a file instead of recycle it. This flag will trigger a user interface even if FOF_NOCONFIRMATION is set. (Windows 2000 only.)

fAnyOperationsAborted: This member is only meaningful after the SHFileOperation() function executes. If the user cancels the operation, this member is TRUE. If the user did not cancel the operation, this member is FALSE.

hNameMappings: Handle to a filename mapping object that contains an array of SHNAMEMAPPING structures. Each structure contains the old and new pathnames for each moved, copied, or renamed file. You must free the handle using the SHFreeNameMappings function.

lpszProgressTitle: Address of the string to use as the title for the progress dialog box.

B.41 SHFreeNameMappings

Frees the name mapping object returned by SHFileOperation().

| **Header:** | shellapi.h |
| **Import Library:** | shell32.lib |

```
VOID SHFreeNameMappings(;
    HANDLE hNameMappings
);
```

Parameters:

hNameMappings: Handle to the name mapping object to free.

B.42 SHGetDataFromIDList

Retrieves property data from a relative identifier list.

| **Header:** | shlobj.h |
| **Import Library:** | shell32.lib |

```
HRESULT SHGetDataFromIDList(
    IShellFolder *psf,
    LPCITEMIDLIST pidl,
    int nFormat,
    PVOID pv,
    int cb
);
```

Parameters:

psf: Pointer to the parent IShellFolder interface. This must be the immediate parent of the ITEMIDLIST pointed to by pidl. If you are trying to get information on c:\SomeDir\SomeFile.txt, IShellFolder must reference c:\SomeDir and pidl must reference SomeFile.txt.

pidl: Pointer to an ITEMIDLIST structure. This structure identifies an object relative to the folder in psf.

nFormat: Tells what type of data is being requested. It can be any of the following values:

- **SHGDFIL_FINDDATA:** Format used for file system objects. pv points to a WIN32_FIND_DATA structure.

- **SHGDFIL_NETRESOURCE:** Format used for network resources. pv points to a NETRESOURCE structure. Do not use
  this structure/value anymore. Instead, use SHGDFIL_DESCRIP-
  TIONID.
- **SHGDFIL_DESCRIPTIONID**: Also used for network resources.
  pv points to a SHDESCRIPTIONID structure.

pv: Points to a buffer to receive the requested data. If nFormat is
SHGDFIL_NETRESOURCE, and the buffer size, specified in cb, is
large enough, the net resource's string information (network name,
local name, provider, and comments) will be placed into the buffer.
Otherwise, only the net resource structure will be placed into the
buffer and the string information pointers will all be NULL.

cb: Size of pv in bytes.

Return Values: Returns S_OK if successful. On failure, returns E_IN-
VALIDARG.

B.43 SHGetDesktopFolder

This function retrieves the IShellFolder interface for the Desktop folder, the
root of the shell's namespace.

Header:	shlobj.h
Import Library:	shell32.lib
Example Project:	Appendix B\ExSHBrowseForFolder

```
HRESULT SHGetDesktopFolder(
    IShellFolder **ppshf
);
```

Parameters:

ppshf: Pointer to a pointer that will be set to the IShellFolder representing the Desktop. The caller must release this pointer when it is
done using it.

Return Values: Returns S_OK if successful, an OLE-defined value otherwise.

B.44 SHGetDiskFreeSpace

Retrieves the size of a volume, the number of bytes available to the caller,
and the number of bytes available on the volume. If the volume uses per-user
quotas, the bytes available to the caller may not equal the bytes available on
the volume.

Header: shellapi.h

Import Library: shell32.lib

```
BOOL SHGetDiskFreeSpace(
    LPCTSTR pszVolume,
    ULARGE_INTEGER *pqwFreeCaller,
    ULARGE_INTEGER *pqwTot,
    ULARGE_INTEGER *pqwFree
);
```

Parameters:

pszVolume: This null-terminated string specifies the volume to look at. This can be a drive letter, UNC name, or a folder path. NULL cannot be used.

pqwFreeCaller: Address of a ULARGE_INTEGER that receives the number of bytes available to the caller on pszVolume.

pqwTot: Address of a ULARGE_INTEGER that receives the size of pszVolume in bytes.

pqwFree: Address of a ULARGE_INTEGER that receives the number of bytes of free space on pszVolume.

Return Values: Returns non-zero if successful; FALSE otherwise.

B.45   SHGetFileInfo

Retrieves information about a file system object such as a file, folder, directory, or drive root.

Header: shellapi.h

Import Library: shell32.lib

```
DWORD_PTR SHGetFileInfo(
    LPCTSTR pszPath,
    DWORD dwFileAttributes,
    SHFILEINFO *psfi,
    UINT cbFileInfo,
    UINT uFlags
);
```

Parameters:

pszPath: Address of a null-terminated string specifying the path and filename. This can be a relative or an absolute path.

dwFileAttributes: Combination of one or more file attribute flags (FILE_ATTRIBUTE_XXX). See WIN32_FIND_DATA for all the flags.

psfi: Address of a SHFILEINFO structure to fill with the file information.

cbFileInfo: Size of the SHFILEINFO structure pointed to by psfi.

uFlags: Tells the function what information it should retrieve. This can be a combination of these values;

- **SHGFI_ATTR_SPECIFIED:** Used in conjunction with SHGFI_ATTRIBUTES. This indicates that the SHFILEINFO structure pointed to by psfi indicates the attributes the caller wants to know about in the dwAttributes member. If this value is not set, SHGetFileInfo() will retrieve all attributes. You cannot specify SHGFI_ATTR_SPECIFIED with SHGFI_ICON.
- **SHGFI_ATTRIBUTES:** Retrieve the item's attributes.
- **SHGFI_DISPLAYNAME:** Get the item's display name.
- **SHGFI_EXETYPE:** You cannot use this flag with any of the other flags. The type of executable is packed into the return value. See *Return Values* for information on interpreting the executable type.
- **SHGFI_ICON:** Retrieve the handle to the icon used to represent the file (psfi->hIcon) and the index (psfi->iIcon) of that icon within the system image list. The return value is a handle to the system image list.
- **SHGFI_ICONLOCATION:** Retrieve the name of the file containing the icon used to represent the file into psfi→szDisplayName.
- **SHGFI_LARGEICON:** If you specify this flag, you must also specify SHGFI_ICON. This causes psfi→hIcon to contain the large icon on return.
- **SHGFI_LINKOVERLAY:** If you specify this flag, you must also specify SHGFI_ICON. This causes psfi→hIcon to contain the link overlay icon on return.
- **SHGFI_OPENICON:** If you specify this flag, you must also specify SHGFI_ICON. This causes psfi→hIcon to contain the file's open icon on return. Typically, this flag only makes sense for folder objects.
- **SHGFI_PIDL:** pszPath is an ITEMIDLIST pointer, not a filename.
- **SHGFI_SELECTED:** If you specify this flag, you must also specify SHGFI_ICON. psfi→hIcon contains the file's icon blended with the system highlight color on return.
- **SHGFI_SHELLICONSIZE:** If you specify this flag, you must also specify SHGFI_ICON. This causes psfi→hIcon to contain a shell-sized icon on return.
- **SHGFI_SMALLICON:** If you specify this flag, you must also specify SHGFI_ICON. This causes psfi→hIcon to contain the small icon on return.

- **SHGFI_SYSICONINDEX:** Retrieves the index of the system image list icon. psfi→iIcon contains the index on return. The return value is a handle to the system image list. Unfortunately, you are only guaranteed validity of the one icon pointed to by iIcon. Attempting to access any other icons in the system image list results in undefined behavior.
- **SHGFI_TYPENAME:** Retrieves the string that describes the file's type and stores it in psfi→szTypeName.
- **SHGFI_USEFILEATTRIBUTES:** Tells the function to pretend that the file in pszPath exists with the file attributes in dwFileAttributes. You would use this feature to get information about a file extension without needing to know the name of a real file with that extension. You cannot use this flag with SHGFI_ATTRIBUTES, SHGFI_EXETYPE, or SHGFI_PIDL.

Return Values:

- If uFlags contains SHGFI_EXETYPE, 0 means the file is not executable. If the LOWORD equals NE or PE and the HIWORD equals 3.0, 3.5, or 4.0, you have a Windows application. If the LOWORD equals MZ, the file is an MS-DOS .EXE, .COM, or .BAT file. If the LOWORD equals PE and the HIWORD is zero, you have a Win32 console application.
- If uFlags contains SHGFI_SYSICONINDEX, the return value is a handle to an image list containing the large icon images. If SHGFI_SMALLICON was used with SHGFI_SYSICONINDEX, you have a handle to an image list containing the small icon images.
- Under all other conditions, zero means success and any other value means failure.

B.46   SHGetFolderLocation

Retrieves the path of a folder specified by a CSIDL value as an ITEMIDLIST. CSIDL values specify the various folders used frequently by applications that often exist in different locations on different systems. Look at CSIDL in this appendix for the CSIDL values. This function is a superset of SHGetSpecialFolderLocation() that was distributed with earlier versions of the shell. Microsoft bundled this function in a redistributable DLL, SHFOLDER.DLL. This DLL simulates many of the new shell folders on Windows 95 and Windows NT 4.0. The DLL tries the current platform's version of the function. If the call fails, SHGetFolderLocation() tries to simulate the correct behavior.

Header:	shlobj.h
Import Library:	shell32.lib

```
HRESULT SHGetFolderLocation(
    HWND hwndOwner,
    int nFolder,
    HANDLE hToken,
    DWORD dwReserved,
    LPITEMIDLIST *ppidl
);
```

Parameters:

hwndOwner: This parameter is usually set to NULL. If a dial-up connection needs to be made to access the folder and this value is not NULL, a UI prompt will appear in this window.

nFolder: A CSIDL value indicating the folder you want to locate. You do not have any guarantees that the folder exists.

hToken: The call will execute as if called by the user identified by this token. If you set hToken to NULL, the current user will be assumed. If the value is non-NULL, the user's registry hive must be mounted.

dwReserved: Set it to zero.

ppidl: Points to an ITEMIDLIST structure relative to the root of the namespace. On failure, this will be returned as NULL. The caller must free this pointer using the shell's IMalloc interface. You can obtain the shell's IMalloc interface with SHGetMalloc().

Return Values: S_OK on success. S_FALSE means that the folder does not exist. E_INVALIDARG means you passed in a bad CSIDL value. You may also get a standard OLE-defined error value.

B.47 SHGetFolderPath

Takes a CSIDL and returns the pathname on the current system. This function is a superset of SHGetSpecialFolderPath() that was distributed with earlier versions of the shell. Microsoft bundled this function in a redistributable DLL, SHFOLDER.DLL. This DLL simulates many of the new shell folders on Windows 95 and Windows NT 4.0. The DLL tries the current platform's version of the function. If the call fails, SHGetFolderPath() tries to simulate the correct behavior.

Header:	shlobj.h
Import Library:	shell32.lib

```
HRESULT SHGetFolderPath(
    HWND hwndOwner,
    int nFolder,
```

```
        HANDLE hToken,
        DWORD dwFlags,
        LPTSTR pszPath
  );
```

Parameters:

hwndOwner: This parameter is usually set to NULL. If a dial-up connection needs to be made to access the folder and this value is not NULL, a UI prompt will appear in this window.

nFolder: A CSIDL value (see CSIDL_XXX in this appendix) indicating the folder you want to locate. You do not have any guarantees that the folder exists.

hToken: The call will execute as if called by the user identified by this token. If you set hToken to NULL, the current user will be assumed. If the value is non-NULL, the user's registry hive must be mounted.

dwFlags: Specifies which path to return. This is used for when the folder associated with the CSIDL might have been moved or renamed by the user.
  • **SHGFP_TYPE_CURRENT:** Returns the folder's current path.
  • **SHGFP_TYPE_DEFAULT:** Returns the folder's default path.

pszPath: Points to a pre-allocated buffer of size MAX_PATH. If an error occurs or the function returns S_FALSE, this string will be empty.

Return Values: S_OK on success. S_FALSE means that the folder does not exist. E_INVALIDARG means you passed in a bad CSIDL value. You may also get a standard OLE-defined error value.

B.48   SHGetInstanceExplorer

Use this to get the address of the Windows Explorer IUnknown interface. This would be used by a shell extension to hold the Windows Explorer open. You would use this when doing work in a background thread or copying files. When done with the interface, make sure you call Release() to decrement the reference count.

Header:	shlobj.h
Import Library:	shell32.lib

```
HRESULT SHGetInstanceExplorer(
    IUnknown **ppunk
);
```

Parameters:

ppunk: Address of an IUnknown interface pointer that will hold Windows Explorer's IUnknown interface on return.

Return Values: S_OK on success, E_FAIL otherwise.

B.49 SHGetMalloc

Use this to get the address of the shell's IMalloc interface. Use this interface to free memory that the shell allocated or to allocate memory that the shell will free. You can also use this interface to allocate and free your own memory.

Header:	shlobj.h
Import Library:	shell32.lib
Example Project:	Chapter 11\WinReg

```
HRESULT SHGetMalloc(
    LPMALLOC  *ppMalloc
);
```

Parameters:

ppMalloc: Address of a pointer that will receive the shell's IMalloc pointer. Call Release() on this pointer when you are done with it.

Return Values: S_OK on success; E_FAIL otherwise.

B.50 SHGetNewLinkInfo

This function does not create a shortcut. It does create the proper name for a new shortcut. The filename returned will end in .PIF if the link is for a DOS application. Otherwise, the new filename will always end in .LNK. Also, if the destination file system only supports 8.3 filenames, the shortcut will be returned in the proper, 8.3 format.

Header:	shellapi.h
Import Library:	shell32.lib

```
BOOL SHGetNewLinkInfo(
    LPCTSTR pszLinkTo,
    LPCTSTR pszDir,
    LPTSTR pszName,
    BOOL *pfMustCopy,
    UINT uFlags
);
```

Parameters:

pszLinkTo: If uFlags contains the SHGNLI_PIDL value, this is a PIDL. Otherwise, this parameter contains a null-terminated string specifying the path and filename of the shortcut's target.

pszDir: Null-terminated string identifying the directory where the shortcut will be created.

pszName: Address of a pre-allocated buffer to receive the path and file name for the shortcut. Allocate MAX_PATH characters for the buffer.

pfMustCopy: Address of a BOOL value that receives a flag indicating if the shortcut will get copied. When the shell creates a shortcut to a shortcut, the shell copies the target shortcut and modifies the copy as needed. Basically, if you are copying a shortcut, this will be TRUE. If you are creating a new shortcut, this will be FALSE.

uFlags: Specifies some options for the function. You can set it to any combination of zero or more of these items:

- **SHGLNI_PIDL:** pszLinkTo is a PIDL, not a null-terminated string.
- **SHGLNI_NOUNIQUE:** Do not create a unique name within the destination folder. When you do not specify this flag, the function generates a name and checks to see if the filename already exists in the destination folder. If the filename exists, the function will generate new filenames until a unique name is found.
- **SHGNLI_PREFIXNAME:** The created name should start with the string *Shortcut to*.

Return Values: TRUE on success; FALSE otherwise.

B.51   SHGetPathFromIDList

Converts an ITEMIDLIST into a file system path. If the item is not a part of the file system, this function will fail.

Header:	shlobj.h
Import Library:	shell32.lib

```
BOOL SHGetPathFromIDList(
    LPCITEMIDLIST pidl,
    LPTSTR pszPath
);
```

Parameters:

pidl: Pointer to the ITEMIDLIST structure. This must specify a file or folder location relative to the root of the namespace.

pszPath: Address of a pre-allocated buffer MAX_PATH characters in size. This buffer will receive the file system path if the function is successful.

Return Values: TRUE on success; FALSE on failure.

B.52   SHGetSettings

Gets the current shell option settings via a SHELLFLAGSTATE structure.

Header:	shlobj.h
Import Library:	shell32.lib
Example Project:	Appendix B\ExSHGetSettings

```
VOID SHGetSettings(
    LPSHELLFLAGSTATE lpsfs,
    DWORD dwMask
);
```

Parameters:

lpsfs: Pointer to the SHELLFLAGSTATE structure. On return, this will contain the shell's option settings.

dwMask: Indicates which SHELLFLAGSTATE members should be filled in. The set of flags does not contain any flag stating *get all of the values*. Being the lazy programmer I am, I tried –1, which usually evaluates to 0xFFFFFFFF... to whatever precision the target variable handles (16, 32, 64 bits). Use –1 when you want to get all the values filled in. If you want only a certain value, use one or more of these flags:

- **SSF_DESKTOPHTML:** Fill in lpsfs→fDesktopHTML.
- **SSF_DONTPRETTYPATH:** Fill in lpsfs→fDontPrettyPath.
- **SSF_DOUBLECLICKINWEBVIEW:** Fill in lpsfs→fDoubleClickInWebView.
- **SSF_HIDEICONS:** Fill in lpsfs→fHideIcons.
- **SSF_MAPNETDRVBUTTON:** Fill in lpsfs→fMapNetDrvBtn.
- **SSF_NOCONFIRMRECYCLE:** Fill in lpsfs→fNoConfirmRecycle.
- **SSF_SHOWALLOBJECTS:** Fill in lpsfs→fShowAllObjects.
- **SSF_SHOWATTRIBCOL:** Fill in lpsfs→fShowAttribCol.
- **SSF_SHOWCOMPCOLOR:** Fill in lpsfs→fShowCompColor.
- **SSF_SHOWEXTENSIONS:** Fill in lpsfs→fShowExtensions.
- **SSF_SHOWINFOTIP:** Fill in lpsfs→fShowInfoTip.
- **SSF_SHOWSYSFILES:** Fill in lpsfs→fShowSysFiles.
- **SSF_WIN95CLASSIC:** Fill in lpsts→fWin95Classic.

B.53   SHGetSpecialFolderLocation

Retrieves the path of a folder specified by a CSIDL value as an ITEMIDLIST. CSIDL values specify the various folders used frequently by applications that often exist in different locations on different systems. Look at CSIDL in this appendix for the CSIDL values. Use SHGetFolderLocation() instead of this function when possible.

  Header: shlobj.h

  Import Library: shell32.lib

```
HRESULT SHGetSpecialFolderLocation(
    HWND hwndOwner,
    int nFolder,
    LPITEMIDLIST *ppidl
);
```

  Parameters:

    hwndOwner: This parameter is usually set to NULL. If a dial-up connection needs to be made to access the folder and this value is not NULL, a UI prompt will appear in this window.

    nFolder: A CSIDL value indicating the folder you want to locate. You do not have any guarantees that the folder exists.

    ppidl: Points to an ITEMIDLIST structure relative to the root of the namespace. On failure, this will be returned as NULL. The caller must free this pointer using the shell's IMalloc interface. You can obtain the shell's IMalloc interface with SHGetMalloc().

  Return Values: S_OK on success. You will get an OLE-defined error value otherwise.

B.54   SHGetSpecialFolderPath

Takes a CSIDL and returns the pathname on the current system. Use SHGetFolderPath() instead of this function when possible.

  Header: shlobj.h

  Import Library: shell32.lib

```
BOOL SHGetSpecialFolderPath(
    HWND hwndOwner,
    LPTSTR pszPath,
    int nFolder,
    BOOL fCreate
);
```

Parameters:

hwndOwner: This parameter is usually set to NULL. If a dial-up connection needs to be made to access the folder and this value is not NULL, a UI prompt will appear using this window as the parent.

pszPath: Points to a pre-allocated buffer of size MAX_PATH. If an error occurs or the function returns S_FALSE, this string will be empty.

nFolder: A CSIDL value (see CSIDL_XXX in this appendix) indicating the folder you want to locate. You do not have any guarantees that the folder exists.

fCreate: If this value is non-zero and the requested folder does not exist, the folder will be created. Otherwise, if the requested folder does not exist, it will not be created.

Return Values: TRUE on success; FALSE on failure.

B.55 SHGetValue

This is another one of those great utility functions. Instead of having to open a registry key, read a value under the key, and close the key, you just read the value located under the named key. A lot of the time, you know exactly where you want to go in the registry. This one function has saved me tons of time in writing code to read a value.

Header:	shlwapi.h
Import Library:	shlwapi.lib
Example Project:	Chapter 11\WinReg

```
DWORD SHGetValue(
    HKEY       hkey,
    LPCTSTR    pszSubKey,
    LPCTSTR    pszValue,
    LPDWORD    pdwType,
    LPVOID     pvData,
    LPDWORD    pcbData
);
```

Parameters:

hkey: Handle to an open key or any of the predefined HKEY_XXX values (HKEY_CLASSES_ROOT, HKEY_CURRENT_USER, etc.).

pszSubKey: Address of a null-terminated string specifying the sub-key containing the desired value.

pszValue: Address of a null-terminated string specifying the value to get.

pdwType: Pointer to a DWORD that will receive the type of value (REG_DWORD, REG_SZ, etc.).

pvData: Pointer to the destination data buffer.

pcbData: Pointer to the size of the destination buffer. Before the call, this value contains the size of the buffer. On return, it contains the number of bytes copied to the buffer. If the function fails, this contains the amount of space required for a successful call.

Return Values: ERROR_SUCCESS if successful. Otherwise, it returns an error value defined in WINERROR.H. Use FormatMessage() with the FORMAT_MESSAGE_FROM_SYSTEM flag to get the generic description of the error.

B.56   SHGNO

This enumeration defines the values used with the IShellFolder::GetDisplay-NameOf() and IShellFolder::SetNameOf() methods.

Header:	shlobj.h
Example Project:	Appendix B\ExSHBrowseForFolder

Values:

The enumeration contains two groups of values. The first group specifies the name's type:

- **SHGDN_NORMAL:** This is a full name, relative to the Desktop.
- **SHGDN_INFOLDER:** The name is relative to the folder processing it.

The second group of values modifies the first group and specifies name retrieval options.

- **SHGDN_FOREDITING:** The name will be used for in-place editing when the user renames the item.
- **SHGDN_FORADDRESSBAR:** The name will be displayed in an address bar combo box.
- **SHGDN_FORPARSING:** The name will be used for parsing. It can be passed to IShellFolder::ParseDisplayName() to recover the object's PIDL.

B.57 SHInvokePrinterCommand

This function executes a command on a printer object.

Header:	shellapi.h
Import Library:	shell32.lib

```
BOOL SHInvokePrinterCommand(
    HWND hwnd,
    UINT uAction,
    LPCTSTR lpBuf1,
    LPCTSTR lpBuf2,
    BOOL fModal
);
```

Parameters:

hwnd: Handle of the window to use as the parent of any windows created during the operation.

uAction: Determines what printer operation will be performed. It can be one of the following values:

- **PRINTACTION_DOCUMENTDEFAULTS:** (Windows NT/2000 only) Displays the default document properties for the printer specified by lpBuf1.
- **PRINTACTION_NETINSTALL:** Installs the network printer specified by lpBuf1.
- **PRINTACTION_NETINSTALLLINK:** Creates a shortcut to the network printer specified by lpBuf1. lpBuf2 specifies the full path to the folder where the shortcut should be created. In order for this to work, the printer must already have been installed on this machine.
- **PRINTACTION_OPEN:** Opens the printer specified by lpBuf1.
- **PRINTACTION_OPENNETPRN:** Opens the network printer specified by lpBuf1.
- **PRINTACTION_PROPERTIES:** Opens the properties specified by the name in lpBuf1.
- **PRINTACTION_SERVERPROPERTIES:** (Windows NT/2000 only) Displays the properties for the server of the printers specified by lpBuf1.
- **PRINTACTION_TESTPAGE:** Prints a test page on the printer specified by lpBuf1.

lpBuf1: Address of a null-terminated string containing extra information for the printer command. The meaning of the string depends on the value of uAction.

lpBuf2: Address of a null-terminated string containing extra information for the printer command. The meaning of the string depends on the value of uAction.

fModal: Determines whether the function should return after initializing the command or wait until the command is completed. TRUE means wait until completed; FALSE means return as soon as the command is initialized.

Return Values: Non-zero if successful; FALSE otherwise.

B.58   SHITEMID

Defines an item identifier. This structure is used by ITEMIDLIST.

> **Header:**   shlobj.h

```
typedef struct _SHITEMID {
    USHORT cb;
    BYTE   abID[1];
} SHITEMID, * LPSHITEMID;
typedef const SHITEMID  * LPCSHITEMID;
```

Members:

cb: Size of the identifier in bytes. This includes cb.

abID: Variable-length item identifier.

B.59   SHLoadInProc

SHLoadInProc() instantiates the specified object within the context of the shell's process.

> **Header:**   shlobj.h
>
> **Import Library:**   shell32.lib

```
HRESULT SHLoadInProc(
    REFCLSID rclsid
);
```

Parameters:

rclsid: CLSID of the object to be created.

Return Values: S_OK if successful; an OLE-defined error result if it fails.

B.60 SHNAMEMAPPING

When you use the SHFileOperation() function, this structure is used to communicate the old and new pathnames of each file that was moved, copied, or renamed. You must specify FOF_WANTMAPPINGHANDLE in the fFlags member of the SHFILEOPSTRUCT you passed to SHFileOperation().

> **Header:**   shellapi.h

```
typedef struct _SHNAMEMAPPING {
    LPTSTR pszOldPath;
    LPTSTR pszNewPath;
    int    cchOldPath;
    int    cchNewPath;
} SHNAMEMAPPING, FAR *LPSHNAMEMAPPING;
```

> **Members:**
>
> **pszOldPath:** Address of a null-terminated buffer containing the old pathname.
>
> **pszNewPath:** Address of a null-terminated buffer containing the new pathname.
>
> **cchOldPath:** The number of characters in pszOldPath.
>
> **cchNewPath:** The number of characters in pszNewPath.

B.61 SHOpenRegStream

This function opens a registry value and returns an IStream interface that you can use to read from or write to the value. This is handy for storing binary data. For example, an application could use this to read and write display information if the user had the Show Data and View Stuff windows open. Combined with that information, you can also store the window position and size. When the user closes the application, you store the data. When the user starts the application, you restore the application to its previous state.

> **Header:**   shlwapi.h
>
> **Import Library:**   shlwapi.lib

```
struct IStream* SHOpenRegStream(
    HKEY hkey,
    LPCTSTR pszSubkey,
    LPCTSTR pszValue,
    DWORD grfMode
);
```

Parameters:

hKey: Handle to an open key or one of the predefined HKEY_XXX (HKEY_LOCAL_MACHINE, HKEY_CURRENT_USER, etc.) values.

pszSubKey: Null-terminated string that specifies the subkey.

pszValue: Null-terminated string specifying the key to open.

grfMode: Type of access for the stream. It can be any one of the following self-explanatory values:

- **STGM_READ**
- **STGM_WRITE**
- **STGM_READWRITE**

Return Values: Pointer to an IStream interface if successful; NULL otherwise. When you are done with the stream, be sure to call the interface's Release() method.

B.62 SHQueryInfoKey

Use this function to retrieve information about a key and its subkey names and values. You would use this function when enumerating a registry key to get the key's values and subkeys. This function reports the size of the buffers needed to receive the largest subkey and value names as well as the number of subkeys and values contained within the key. This function only returns information about the values immediately beneath the named key. This function does not return information about the keys and values contained within a subkey.

Header:	shlwapi.h
Import Library:	shlwapi.lib

```
DWORD SHQueryInfoKey(
    HKEY hkey,
    LPDWORD pcSubKeys,
    LPDWORD pcchMaxSubKeyLen,
    LPDWORD pcValues,
    LPDWORD pcchMaxValueNameLen
);
```

Parameters:

hKey: Handle to an open key or one of the predefined HKEY_XXX (HKEY_LOCAL_MACHINE, HKEY_CURRENT_USER, etc.) values.

pcSubKeys: Address of a DWORD. When the function successfully returns, this value contains the number of subkeys under the specified key.

pcchMaxSubKeyLen: Address of a DWORD. When the function successfully returns, this value contains the number of characters in the name of the subkey that has the longest name.

pcValues: Address of a DWORD. When the function successfully returns, this value contains the number of values under the specified key.

pcchMaxValueNameLen: Address of a DWORD. When the function successfully returns, this value contains the number of characters in the name of the value that has the longest name.

Return Values: ERROR_SUCCESS if successful. Otherwise, it returns an error value defined in WINERROR.H. Use FormatMessage() with the FORMAT_MESSAGE_FROM_SYSTEM flag to get the generic description of the error.

B.63   SHQUERYRBINFO

The SHQueryRecycleBin() function uses this structure to get the number of bytes and items in the recycle bin.

Header:	shellapi.h
Example Project:	Appendix B\ExRecycleBin

```
typedef struct _SHQUERYRBINFO {
    DWORD cbSize;
    __int64 i64Size;
    __int64 i64NumItems;
} SHQUERYRBINFO, FAR *LPSHQUERYRBINFO;
```

Members:

cbSize: Size of the structure in bytes. You should always set this to sizeof(SHQUERYBINFO).

i64Size: Returns the number of bytes in the specified Recycle Bin.

i64NumItems: Returns the number of items in the specified Recycle Bin.

B.64   SHQueryRecycleBin

Using a SHQUERYBINFO structure, this function allows you to find out the number of bytes and items in the recycle bin of a given volume.

Header:	shellapi.h
Import Library:	shell32.lib
Example Project:	Appendix B\ExRecycleBin

```
HRESULT SHQueryRecycleBin(
    LPCTSTR pszRootPath,
    LPSHQUERYRBINFO pSHQueryRBInfo
);
```

Parameters:

pszRootPath: Null-terminated string specifying the root drive for the Recycle Bin in question. The parameter can be something like one of the following:

- `c:\`
- `c:\windows`

If you set pszRootPath to NULL, the function retrieves information for all Recycle Bins on all volumes.

pSHQueryRBInfo: Address of a SHQUERYBINFO structure. Remember to set the cbSize member of the structure before calling SHQueryRecycleBin().

Return Values: S_OK if successful. Otherwise, it returns an OLE-defined error value.

B.65   SHQueryValueEx

Opens a registry key and queries the specific value within that key.

Header:	shlwapi.h
Import Library:	shlwapi.lib

```
DWORD SHQueryValueEx(
    HKEY      hkey,
    LPCTSTR   pszValue,
    LPDWORD   pdwReserved,
    LPDWORD   pdwType,
    LPVOID    pvData,
    LPDWORD   pcbData
);
```

Parameters:

hKey: Handle to an open key or one of the predefined HKEY_XXX values (HKEY_CLASSES_ROOT, HKEY_LOCAL_MACHINE, etc.)

pszValue: Null-terminated string specifying the value to query.

pdwReserved: Set to NULL.

pdwType: Address of a DWORD that will be set to the value's type on return (REG_SZ, REG_DWORD, etc.).

pvData: Pointer to a buffer that will contain the value's data on return. This can be NULL if you do not need to know the data, but instead, only want to know only the value's type and/or the size of the data in the value.

pcbData: When the function is executed, this contains the size of the buffer pointed to by pvData. On return, this contains the number of bytes copied to pvData.

Return Values: ERROR_SUCCESS if successful. Otherwise, it returns an error value defined in WINERROR.H. Use FormatMessage() with the FORMAT_MESSAGE_FROM_SYSTEM flag to get the generic description of the error.

B.66   SHRegCloseUSKey

Closes a handle to a user-specific registry key.

Header:	shlwapi.h
Import Library:	shlwapi.lib
Example Project:	Appendix B\ExSHRegCreateUSKey

```
DWORD SHRegCloseUSKey(
    HUSKEY hUSKey,
);
```

Parameters:

hUSKey: Handle to an open, user-specific key.

Return Values: ERROR_SUCCESS if successful. Otherwise, it returns an error value defined in WINERROR.H. Use FormatMessage() with the FORMAT_MESSAGE_FROM_SYSTEM flag to get the generic description of the error.

B.67   SHRegCreateUSKey

Opens a user-specific key. If the key does not exist, the function creates it.

Header:	shlwapi.h
Import Library:	shlwapi.lib
Example Project:	Appendix B\ExSHRegCreateUSKey

```
LONG SHRegCreateUSKey(
    LPCTSTR    pszPath,
    REGSAM     samDesired,
```

```
    HUSKEY      hRelativeUSKey,
    PHUSKEY     phNewUSKey,
    DWORD       dwFlags
);
```

Parameters:

pszPath: Null-terminated string specifying the path of the registry key to open.

samDesired: Desired security access. See REGSAM for valid values.

hRelativeUSKey: Key to be used as a base for relative paths. If psz-Path is a relative path, it specifies a path relative to hRelativeUSKey. If pszPath specifies an absolute path, set hRelativeUSKey to NULL. The key will then be created or opened under HKLM or HKCU, depending on the value of dwFlags.

phNewUSKey: On return, the parameter contains the handle to the new, user-specific key. Close this key using SHRegCloseUSKey().

dwFlags: Specifies the hive where the key should be opened. These flags are shared by the user-specific functions and have slightly different meanings, depending on the function using the flags. This can be one or more of the following values:

- **SHREGSET_HKCU:** Create or open the key under HKEY_CURRENT_USER.
- **SHREGSET_FORCE_HKCU:** Same meaning as SHREGSET_HKCU.
- **SHREGSET_HKLM:** Create or open the key under HKEY_LOCAL_MACHINE.
- **SHREGSET_FORCE_HKLM:** Same meaning as SHREGSET_HKLM.
- **SHREGSET_DEFAULT:** Contrary to the Microsoft documentation, this does not create the value under the HKLM and HKCU hives. Instead, it just fails.

Return Values: ERROR_SUCCESS if successful. Otherwise, it returns an error value defined in WINERROR.H. Use FormatMessage() with the FORMAT_MESSAGE_FROM_SYSTEM flag to get the generic description of the error.

B.68 SHREGDEL_FLAGS

This enumeration defines a set of values indicating the base key of an item that is about to be deleted.

Header: shlwapi.h

Values:
- **SHREGDEL_DEFAULT:** Delete the specified key under HKCU. If the key cannot be found there, deletes the key from HKLM.
- **SHREGDEL_HKCU:** Deletes from HKCU only.
- **SHREGDEL_HKLM:** Deletes from HKLM only.
- **SHREGDEL_BOTH:** Deletes from both HKCU and HKLM.

B.69 SHRegDeleteEmptyUSKey

Deletes an empty user-specific key. This function will only delete the specified key if the key does not contain any values or subkeys.

Header:	shlwapi.h
Import Library:	shlwapi.lib
Example Project:	Appendix B\ExSHRegCreateUSKey

```
LONG SHRegDeleteEmptyUSKey(
    HUSKEY hUSKey,
    LPCSTR pszValue,
    SHREGDEL_FLAGS delRegFlags
);
```

Parameters:

hUSKey: Handle to an open, user-specific key.

pszValue: Null-terminated string that specifies the empty registry key to delete. If hUSKey points to the actual key, this value may be NULL.

delRegFlags: One of the SHREGDEL_FLAGS specifying the base registry hive to delete the key from.

Return Values: ERROR_SUCCESS if successful. Otherwise, it returns an error value defined in WINERROR.H. Use FormatMessage() with the FORMAT_MESSAGE_FROM_SYSTEM flag to get the generic description of the error.

B.70 SHRegDeleteUSValue

Deletes a value from within the registry

Header:	shlwapi.h
Import Library:	shlwapi.lib

```
LONG SHRegDeleteUSValue(
    HUSKEY          hUSKey,
```

```
    LPCTSTR           pszValue,
    SHREGDEL_FLAGS    delRegFlags
);
```

Parameters:

hUSKey: Handle to an open, user-specific key.

pszValue: Null-terminated string that specifies the value to delete from within hUSKey.

delRegFlags: One of the SHREGDEL_FLAGS specifying the base registry hive to delete the value from.

Return Values: ERROR_SUCCESS if successful. Otherwise, it returns an error value defined in WINERROR.H. Use FormatMessage() with the FORMAT_MESSAGE_FROM_SYSTEM flag to get the generic description of the error.

B.71   SHREGENUM_FLAGS

Defines a set of values used to indicate the base key used for enumerating the registry using the user-specific shell registry functions.

Header: shlwapi.h

Values:

- **SHREGENUM_DEFAULT:** Enumerates under HKCU. If the specified item cannot be found, enumerate under HKLM.
- **SHREGENUM_HKCU:** Enumerates HKCU only.
- **SHREGENUM_HKLM:** Enumerates HKLM only.
- **SHREGENUM_BOTH:** Not used. I wonder if this is a cut-and-paste error that had to be documented because Microsoft felt it was too late to correct the error?

B.72   SHRegEnumUSKey

Enumerates the subkeys contained by a user-specific key. Call SHRegQueryInfoUSKey() before calling this function to get the number of subkeys. This way, you will know when to stop incrementing dwIndex.

Header: shlwapi.h

Import Library: shlwapi.lib

```
DWORD SHRegEnumUSKey(
    HUSKEY hUSKey,
```

```
      DWORD dwIndex,
      LPSTR pszName,
      LPDWORD pcchName,
      SHREGENUM_FLAGS enumRegFlags
);
```

Parameters:

hUSKey: Handle to an open, user-specific key.

dwIndex: Index of the subkey to retrieve. Set this to zero on the first call and increment it for subsequent calls.

pszName: Pointer to a character buffer. On return, this buffer contains the name of the key.

pcchName: Before the call, this contains the size of the pszName buffer. On return, this contains the number of characters copied into pszName.

enumRegFlags: Contains one of the SHREGENUM_FLAGS specifying where the enumeration should take place.

Return Values: ERROR_SUCCESS if successful. Otherwise, it returns an error value defined in WINERROR.H. Use FormatMessage() with the FORMAT_MESSAGE_FROM_SYSTEM flag to get the generic description of the error.

B.73 SHRegEnumUSValue

Enumerates the values contained by a user-specific key. Call SHRegQueryInfoUSKey() before calling this function to get the number of values. This way, you will know when to stop incrementing dwIndex.

Header:	shlwapi.h
Import Library:	shlwapi.lib

```
DWORD SHRegEnumUSValue(
    HUSKEY hUSkey,
    DWORD dwIndex,
    LPTSTR pszValueName,
    LPDWORD pcchValueNameLen,
    LPDWORD pdwType,
    LPVOID pvData,
    LPDWORD pcbData,
    SHREGENUM_FLAGS enumRegFlags
);
```

Parameters:

hUSKey: Handle to an open, user-specific key.

dwIndex: Index of the value to retrieve. Set this to zero on the first call and increment it for subsequent calls.

pszValueName: Pointer to a character buffer. On return, this buffer contains the name of the value.

pcchValueNameLen: Before the call, this contains the size of the pszValueName buffer. On return, this contains the number of characters copied into pszValueName.

pdwType: Address of a DWORD that will contain the data type of the value (REG_SZ, REG_DWORD, etc.).

pvData: Address of a buffer that will receive the data contained by the value entry. This parameter can be NULL if the data is not required.

pcbData: Before the call, this contains the size of the pvData buffer. On return, this contains the number of bytes copied into pvData.

enumRegFlags: Contains one of the SHREGENUM_FLAGS specifying where the enumeration should take place.

Return Values: ERROR_SUCCESS if successful. Otherwise, it returns an error value defined in WINERROR.H. Use FormatMessage() with the FORMAT_MESSAGE_FROM_SYSTEM flag to get the generic description of the error.

B.74   SHRegGetBoolUSValue

Gets a user-specific Boolean value from the registry. This is the only function that gets a specific type from the registry. The shell uses a large number of flags to turn various features on and off and all of these are user-specific. Your shell namespace extensions will also probably have some *on* or *off* features. To help you out, Microsoft published this utility function. The shell probably uses it to respond to the SHGetSettings() function and populate the SHELLFLAGSTATE structure.

Header:	shlwapi.h
Import Library:	shlwapi.lib

```
BOOL SHRegGetBoolUSValue(
    LPCTSTR pszSubKey,
    LPCTSTR pszValue,
    BOOL fIgnoreHKCU,
    BOOL fDefault
);
```

Parameters:

pszSubKey: Null-terminated string containing the name of the key relative to HKLM or HKCU.

pszValue: Null-terminated string containing the name of the value.

fIgnoreHKCU: Looks under HKLM when set to TRUE, HKCU when set to FALSE.

fDefault: Default value to return if the registry value cannot be found. Must be TRUE or FALSE.

Return Values: Returns the value from the registry or fDefault if no value can be found.

B.75 SHRegGetUSValue

Used to retrieve a user-specific value from the registry. This function opens the registry key each time it is used. If you need to get a number of values from the same key, your code will run faster by opening the key with SHRegOpenUSKey() and then using SHRegQueryUSValue() to retrieve the data.

Header:	shlwapi.h
Import Library:	shlwapi.lib
Example Project:	Appendix B\ExSHRegCreateUSKey

```
LONG SHRegGetUSValue(
    LPCTSTR    pszSubKey,
    LPCTSTR    pszValue,
    LPDWORD    pdwType,
    LPVOID     pvData,
    LPDWORD    pcbData,
    BOOL       fIgnoreHKCU,
    LPVOID     pvDefaultData,
    DWORD      dwDefaultDataSize
);
```

Parameters:

pszSubKey: Null-terminated string containing the name of the key relative to HKLM or HKCU.

pszValue: Null-terminated string containing the name of the value.

pdwType: Address of a DWORD that will contain the data type of the value (REG_SZ, REG_DWORD, etc.).

pvData: Address of a buffer that will receive the data contained by the value entry. This parameter can be NULL if the data is not required.

pcbData: Before the call, this contains the size of the pvData buffer. On return, this contains the number of bytes copied into pvData.

fIgnoreHKCU: Looks under HKLM when set to TRUE, HKCU when set to FALSE.

pvDefaultData: Contains the default data. If the value does not exist, pcbData will be set to this value.

dwDefaultDataSize: Number of bytes pointed to by pvDefaultData.

Return Values: ERROR_SUCCESS if successful. Otherwise, it returns an error value defined in WINERROR.H. Use FormatMessage() with the FORMAT_MESSAGE_FROM_SYSTEM flag to get the generic description of the error.

B.76 SHRegOpenUSKey

Opens a user-specific registry key.

Header:	shlwapi.h
Import Library:	shlwapi.lib

```
LONG SHRegOpenUSKey(
    LPCTSTR   pszPath,
    REGSAM    samDesired,
    HUSKEY    hRelativeUSKey,
    PHUSKEY   phNewUSKey,
    BOOL      fIgnoreHKCU
);
```

Parameters:

pszPath: Null-terminated string specifying the path of the registry key to open.

samDesired: Desired security access. See REGSAM for valid values.

hRelativeUSKey: Key to be used as a base for relative paths. If psz-Path is a relative path, it specifies a path relative to hRelativeUSKey. If pszPath specifies an absolute path, set hRelativeUSKey to NULL.

phNewUSKey: On return, the parameter contains the handle to the new, user-specific key. Close this key using SHRegCloseUSKey().

fIgnoreHKCU: Looks under HKLM when set to TRUE, HKCU when set to FALSE.

Return Values: ERROR_SUCCESS if successful. Otherwise, it returns an error value defined in WINERROR.H. Use FormatMessage() with the FORMAT_MESSAGE_FROM_SYSTEM flag to get the generic description of the error.

B.77   SHRegQueryInfoUSKey

This is the user-specific version of SHQueryInfoKey(). Like SHQueryInfoKey(), this function has a lot of value in helping your code allocate properly sized buffers and knowing when to stop an enumeration.

Header:	shlwapi.h
Import Library:	shlwapi.lib

```
DWORD SHRegQueryInfoUSKey(
    HUSKEY hUSKey,
    LPDWORD pcSubKeys,
    LPDWORD pcchMaxSubKeyLen,
    LPDWORD pcValues,
    LPDWORD pcchMaxValueNameLen
);
```

Parameters:

hUSKey: Handle to an open, user-specific key.

pcSubKeys: Address of a DWORD. When the function successfully returns, this value contains the number of subkeys under the specified key.

pcchMaxSubKeyLen: Address of a DWORD. When the function successfully returns, this value contains the number of characters in the name of the subkey that has the longest name.

pcValues: Address of a DWORD. When the function successfully returns, this value contains the number of values under the specified key.

pcchMaxValueNameLen: Address of a DWORD. When the function successfully returns, this value contains the number of characters in the name of the value that has the longest name.

Return Values: ERROR_SUCCESS if successful. Otherwise, it returns an error value defined in WINERROR.H. Use FormatMessage() with the FORMAT_MESSAGE_FROM_SYSTEM flag to get the generic description of the error.

B.78   SHRegQueryUSValue

Used to retrieve a user-specific value from the registry. If you only need to get one value from the registry, you can use SHRegGetUSValue() to open the key and return the value. Use this function when you will read many values from the same key. You open the key using SHRegOpenUSKey() and close it using SHRegCloseUSKey()

Header:	shlwapi.h
Import Library:	shlwapi.lib
Example Project:	Appendix B\ExSHRegCreateUSKey

```
LONG SHRegQueryUSValue(
    HUSKEY    hUSKey,
    LPCTSTR   pszValue,
    LPDWORD   pdwType,
    LPVOID    pvData,
    LPDWORD   pcbData,
    BOOL      fIgnoreHKCU,
    LPVOID    pvDefaultData,
    DWORD     dwDefaultDataSize
);
```

Parameters:

hUSKey: Handle to an open HUSKEY.

pszValue: Null-terminated string containing the name of the value.

pdwType: Address of a DWORD that will contain the data type of the value (REG_SZ, REG_DWORD, etc.).

pvData: Address of a buffer that will receive the data contained by the value entry. This parameter can be NULL if the data is not required.

pcbData: Before the call, this contains the size of the pvData buffer. On return, this contains the number of bytes copied into pvData.

fIgnoreHKCU: Looks under HKLM when set to TRUE, HKCU when set to false.

pvDefaultData: Contains the default data. If the value does not exist, pcbData will be set to this value.

dwDefaultDataSize: Number of bytes pointed to by pvDefaultData.

Return Values: ERROR_SUCCESS if successful. Otherwise, it returns an error value defined in WINERROR.H. Use FormatMessage() with the FORMAT_MESSAGE_FROM_SYSTEM flag to get the generic description of the error.

B.79   SHRegSetUSValue

Opens a user-specific key and writes to a value contained by that key. If you will be writing a series of values, it will be faster to use SHRegOpenUSKey() to open a key and then calling SHRegWriteUSValue() to write out any values to the registry.

Header:	shlwapi.h
Import Library:	shlwapi.lib

```
LONG SHRegSetUSValue(
    LPCTSTR pszSubKey,
    LPCTSTR pszValue,
    DWORD   dwType,
    LPVOID  pvData,
    DWORD   cbData,
    DWORD   dwFlags
);
```

Parameters:

pszSubKey: Null-terminated string specifying the path of the registry key to open.

pszValue: Null-terminated string specifying the value to write to.

dwType: A DWORD that specifies the value's type (REG_BINARY, REG_DWORD, REG_SZ, etc.).

pvData: Buffer that contains the data to write to the registry.

cbData: Number of bytes to write to the registry from the buffer pointed to by pvData.

dwFlags: Specifies the hive where the key should be opened. These flags are shared by the user-specific functions and have slightly different meanings depending on the function using the flags. This can be one or more of the following values:
- **SHREGSET_HKCU:** Write the value to HKCU.
- **SHREGSET_FORCE_HKCU:** Same meaning as SHREGSET_HKCU.
- **SHREGSET_HKLM:** Write the value to HKLM.
- **SHREGSET_FORCE_HKLM:** Same meaning as SHREGSET_HKLM.

Return Values: ERROR_SUCCESS if successful. Otherwise, it returns an error value defined in WINERROR.H. Use FormatMessage() with the FORMAT_MESSAGE_FROM_SYSTEM flag to get the generic description of the error.

B.80   SHRegWriteUSValue

Given an open user-specific key, writes to a value contained by that key. Use SHRegOpenUSKey() to open a key and then calling SHRegWriteUSValue() to write out any values to the registry. If you will only be writing one value to the registry, you can use SHRegSetUSValue(). This function opens the key, writes to the value, and closes the key within the one function call.

Header:	shlwapi.h
Import Library:	shlwapi.lib

```
LONG SHRegWriteUSValue(
    HUSKEY   hUSKey,
    LPCTSTR  pszValue,
    DWORD    dwType,
    LPVOID   pvData,
    DWORD    cbData,
    DWORD    dwFlags
);
```

Parameters:

hUSKey: Handle to an open key that contains the value to write to.

pszValue: Null-terminated string specifying the value to write to.

dwType: A DWORD that specifies the value's type (REG_BINARY, REG_DWORD, REG_SZ, etc.).

pvData: Buffer that contains the data to write to the registry.

cbData: Number of bytes to write to the registry from the buffer pointed to by pvData.

dwFlags: Specifies the hive where the key should be opened. These flags are shared by the user specific functions and have slightly different meanings, depending on the function using the flags. This can be one or more of the following values:

- **SHREGSET_HKCU:** Write the value to HKCU.
- **SHREGSET_FORCE_HKCU:** Same meaning as SHREGSET_HKCU.
- **SHREGSET_HKLM:** Write the value to HKLM.
- **SHREGSET_FORCE_HKLM:** Same meaning as SHREGSET_HKLM.

Return Values: ERROR_SUCCESS if successful. Otherwise, it returns an error value defined in WINERROR.H. Use FormatMessage() with the FORMAT_MESSAGE_FROM_SYSTEM flag to get the generic description of the error.

B.81   SHSetValue

Opens a key and writes to a value contained by that key.

Header:	shlwapi.h
Import Library:	shlwapi.lib

```
DWORD SHSetValue(
    HKEY       hkey,
    LPCTSTR    pszSubKey,
    LPCTSTR    pszValue,
    DWORDvdwType,
    LPCVOID    pvData,
    DWORD      cbData
);
```

Parameters:

hKey: Handle to an open key or to one of the predefined registry keys (HKEY_CURRENT_USER, HKEY_LOCAL_MACHINE, etc.).

pszSubKey: Null-terminated string specifying the name of the subkey relative to the key specified by the hKey parameter.

pszValue: Null-terminated string specifying the value to write to.

dwType: A DWORD that specifies the value's type (REG_BINARY, REG_DWORD, REG_SZ, etc.).

pvData: Buffer that contains the data to write to the registry.

cbData: Number of bytes to write to the registry from the buffer pointed to by pvData.

Return Values: ERROR_SUCCESS if successful. Otherwise, it returns an error value defined in WINERROR.H. Use FormatMessage() with the FORMAT_MESSAGE_FROM_SYSTEM flag to get the generic description of the error.

B.82 SHStrDup

Header:	shlwapi.h
Import Library:	shlwapi.lib

```
HRESULT SHStrDup(
    LPCTSTR pszSource,
    LPWSTR *ppwszTarget
);
```

Parameters:

pszSource: Pointer to the null-terminated string to be copied.

ppwszTarget: Pointer to a Unicode string containing the copied string. This memory was allocated using CoTaskMemAllocate(). You must free the memory with CoTaskMemFree() when you are done with the memory.

Return Values: S_OK if successful. Otherwise, it returns an OLE-defined error value.

B.83   STGMEDIUM

This structure is used to transfer data from an IDataObject implementation to the caller. With respect to the shell, data handlers employ this object to move bytes around.

Header:	objidl.h
Example Project:	Chapter 7\ABKContextMenuHandler
	Chapter 7\ABKDataHandler
	Chapter 7\ABKDropHandler
	Chapter 7\ABKPropertySheetHandler

B.84   STRRET

Header:	shlobj.h
Example Project:	Appendix B\ExSHBrowseForFolder

```
typedef struct _STRRET {
    UINT uType;
    union
    {
        LPWSTR pOleStr;
        LPSTR pStr;
        UINT uOffset;
        char cStr[MAX_PATH];
    } DUMMYUNIONNAME;
} STRRET, *LPSTRRET;
```

Members:

uType: Specifies the format of the string. This member can have one of the following values:
- **STRRET_CSTR:** Return the string in the cStr member.
- **STRRET_OFFSET:** The uOffset member value indicates the number of bytes from the start of the item identifier list to the start of the string.
- **STRRET_WSTR:** The pOleStr member points to the string.

pOleStr: Address of the OLE string. The memory for the string must be allocated using SHGetMalloc. The calling application must free this memory when the calling application is done using the string. Use the IMalloc interface returned by SHGetMalloc to free the memory.

pStr: Not used.

uOffset: Offset into the item identifier list.

cStr: Buffer to receive the display name.

B.85   StrRetToBuf

Header:	shlwapi.h
Import Library:	shlwapi.lib
Example Project:	Appendix B\ExSHBrowseForFolder

Takes a STRRET structure from IShellFolder::GetDisplayNameOf() and converts it to a string.

```
HRESULT StrRetToBuf(
    LPSTRRET pstr,
    LPCITEMIDLIST pidl,
    LPTSTR pszBuf,
    UINT cchBuf
);
```

Parameters:

pstr: Pointer to the STRRET structure to be converted to a string. Upon return, this pointer will not be valid. If the uType member of STRRET is STRRET_WSTR, the pOleStr member of the structure will have been freed on return from this function.

pidl: Pointer to the item's ITEMIDLIST structure (or PIDL).

pszBuf: Buffer to hold the display name. The string will be null-terminated on return. If cchBuf is too small, the name will be truncated to fit.

cchBuf: Tells the function how big pszBuf is.

Return Value: Returns S_OK if successful and OLE error code if it fails.

B.86   StrRetToStr

Header:	shlwapi.h
Import Library:	shlwapi.lib
Example Project:	Appendix B\ExSHBrowseForFolder

```
HRESULT StrRetToStr(
    LPSTRRET pstr,
    LPCITEMIDLIST pidl,
    LPTSTR *ppszName
);
```

Parameters:

pstr: Pointer to the STRRET structure to be converted to a string. Upon return, this pointer will not be valid. If the uType member of STRRET is STRRET_WSTR, the pOleStr member of the structure will have been freed on return from this function.

pidl: Pointer to the item's ITEMIDLIST structure (or PIDL).

ppszName: Pointer to an allocated string containing the result. The memory was allocated with CoTaskMemAllocate(). You must free the string with CoTaskMemFree() when you are done using the string.

Return Value: Returns S_OK if successful and OLE error code if it fails.

B.87   SV2CVW2_PARAMS

Holds the parameters for the IShellView2::CreateViewWindow2 method.

Header:	shlobj.h
Example Project:	Chapter 11\WinReg

```
typedef struct _SV2CVW2_PARAMS
{
    DWORD cbSize;
    IShellView *psvPrev;
    FOLDERSETTINGS const *pfs;
    IShellBrowser *psbOwner;
    RECT *prcView;
    SHELLVIEWID const *pvid;
    HWND hwndView;
} SV2CVW2_PARAMS, *LPSV2CVW2_PARAMS;
```

Members:

cbSize: Size of the structure: sizeof(SV2CVW2_PARAMS).

psvPrev: Points to the previous IShellView interface. If the two views share the same interface, the new view can use this interface to communicate with the old view and to optimize browsing between the views. The parameter might be NULL.

pfs: Points to the FOLDERSETTINGS structure needed to create the new view.

psbOwner: Points to the current IShellBrowser instance. Call Add-Ref() on this pointer and store it for later use.

prcView: RECT defining the view's display region.

pvid: The view mode's GUID.

hwndView: Window handle for the new shell view.

B.88 WIN32_FIND_DATA

Describes a file found by FindFirstFile(), FindFirstFileEx(), FindNextFile(), or SHGetDataFromIDList().

Header: winbase.h

```
typedef struct _WIN32_FIND_DATA { // wfd
    DWORD dwFileAttributes;
    FILETIME ftCreationTime;
    FILETIME ftLastAccessTime;
    FILETIME ftLastWriteTime;
    DWORD    nFileSizeHigh;
    DWORD    nFileSizeLow;
    DWORD    dwReserved0;
    DWORD    dwReserved1;
    TCHAR    cFileName[ MAX_PATH ];
    TCHAR    cAlternateFileName[ 14 ];
} WIN32_FIND_DATA;
```

Members:

dwFileAttributes: Specifies the file attributes. Can be one or more of the following values (descriptions provided for the not-so-obvious attributes):

- **FILE_ATTRIBUTE_ARCHIVE**
- **FILE_ATTRIBUTE_COMPRESSED**
- **FILE_ATTRIBUTE_DIRECTORY**
- **FILE_ATTRIBUTE_ENCRYPTED**
- **FILE_ATTRIBUTE_HIDDEN**
- **FILE_ATTRIBUTE_OFFLINE:** The file data has been moved to offline storage. Remote Storage, the hierarchical storage management software in Windows 2000, uses this attribute. Applications should not change this attribute.
- **FILE_ATTRIBUTE_READONLY**
- **FILE_ATTRIBUTE_REPARSE_POINT:** Used in conjunction with file system filter drivers to enable things like remote storage. Beyond the scope of this text.

- **FILE_ATTRIBUTE_SPARSE_FILE:** Allows the user or administrator to say that certain ranges of bytes within the file are zero. If data in that range is accessed, the file system returns zero. Beyond the scope of this text.
- **FILE_ATTRIBUTE_SYSTEM:** File is part of the operating system or only used by the operating system.
- **FILE_ATTRIBUTE_TEMPORARY**

ftCreationTime: Specifies the time the file was created.

ftLastAccessTime: Specifies the time the file was last accessed.

ftLastWriteTime: Specifies the time the file was last written to.

nFileSizeHigh: Specifies a high-order DWORD value of the file size in bytes. When the file size is less than MAXDWORD, this value is zero. When this value gets set, file size is calculated like so: (nFileSizeHigh * (MAXDWORD + 1)) + nFileSizeLow.

nFileSizeLow: The low-order DWORD value of the file size, in bytes.

dwReserved0: If FILE_ATTRIBUTE_REPARSE_POINT is set, this member specifies the reparse tag. Otherwise, do not use this member.

dwReserved1: Not used.

cFileName: Null-terminated string specifying the name of the file.

cAlternateFileName: 8.3 version of the filename if cFileName, or NULL if cFileName already is in 8.3 format.

INDEX

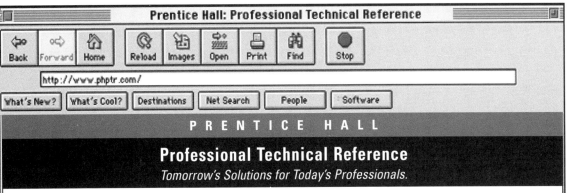

LICENSE AGREEMENT AND LIMITED WARRANTY

READ THE FOLLOWING TERMS AND CONDITIONS CAREFULLY BEFORE OPENING THIS SOFTWARE MEDIA PACKAGE. THIS LEGAL DOCUMENT IS AN AGREEMENT BETWEEN YOU AND PRENTICE-HALL, INC. (THE "COMPANY"). BY OPENING THIS SEALED SOFTWARE MEDIA PACKAGE, YOU ARE AGREEING TO BE BOUND BY THESE TERMS AND CONDITIONS. IF YOU DO NOT AGREE WITH THESE TERMS AND CONDITIONS, DO NOT OPEN THE SOFTWARE MEDIA PACKAGE. PROMPTLY RETURN THE UNOPENED SOFTWARE MEDIA PACKAGE AND ALL ACCOMPANYING ITEMS TO THE PLACE YOU OBTAINED THEM FOR A FULL REFUND OF ANY SUMS YOU HAVE PAID.

1. **GRANT OF LICENSE:** In consideration of your payment of the license fee, which is part of the price you paid for this product, and your agreement to abide by the terms and conditions of this Agreement, the Company grants to you a nonexclusive right to use and display the copy of the enclosed software program (hereinafter the "SOFTWARE") on a single computer (i.e., with a single CPU) at a single location so long as you comply with the terms of this Agreement. The Company reserves all rights not expressly granted to you under this Agreement.

2. **OWNERSHIP OF SOFTWARE:** You own only the magnetic or physical media (the enclosed software media) on which the SOFTWARE is recorded or fixed, but the Company retains all the rights, title, and ownership to the SOFTWARE recorded on the original software media copy(ies) and all subsequent copies of the SOFTWARE, regardless of the form or media on which the original or other copies may exist. This license is not a sale of the original SOFTWARE or any copy to you.

3. **COPY RESTRICTIONS:** This SOFTWARE and the accompanying printed materials and user manual (the "Documentation") are the subject of copyright. You may not copy the Documentation or the SOFTWARE, except that you may make a single copy of the SOFTWARE for backup or archival purposes only. You may be held legally responsible for any copying or copyright infringement which is caused or encouraged by your failure to abide by the terms of this restriction.

4. **USE RESTRICTIONS:** You may not network the SOFTWARE or otherwise use it on more than one computer or computer terminal at the same time. You may physically transfer the SOFTWARE from one computer to another provided that the SOFTWARE is used on only one computer at a time. You may not distribute copies of the SOFTWARE or Documentation to others. You may not reverse engineer, disassemble, decompile, modify, adapt, translate, or create derivative works based on the SOFTWARE or the Documentation without the prior written consent of the Company.

5. **TRANSFER RESTRICTIONS:** The enclosed SOFTWARE is licensed only to you and may not be transferred to any one else without the prior written consent of the Company. Any unauthorized transfer of the SOFTWARE shall result in the immediate termination of this Agreement.

6. **TERMINATION:** This license is effective until terminated. This license will terminate automatically without notice from the Company and become null and void if you fail to comply with any provisions or limitations of this license. Upon termination, you shall destroy the Documentation and all copies of the SOFTWARE. All provisions of this Agreement as to warranties, limitation of liability, remedies or damages, and our ownership rights shall survive termination.

7. **MISCELLANEOUS:** This Agreement shall be construed in accordance with the laws of the United States of America and the State of New York and shall benefit the Company, its affiliates, and assignees.

8. **LIMITED WARRANTY AND DISCLAIMER OF WARRANTY:** The Company warrants that the SOFTWARE, when properly used in accordance with the Documentation, will operate in substantial conformity with the description of the SOFTWARE set forth in the Documentation. The Company does not

warrant that the SOFTWARE will meet your requirements or that the operation of the SOFTWARE will be uninterrupted or error-free. The Company warrants that the media on which the SOFTWARE is delivered shall be free from defects in materials and workmanship under normal use for a period of thirty (30) days from the date of your purchase. Your only remedy and the Company's only obligation under these limited warranties is, at the Company's option, return of the warranted item for a refund of any amounts paid by you or replacement of the item. Any replacement of SOFTWARE or media under the warranties shall not extend the original warranty period. The limited warranty set forth above shall not apply to any SOFTWARE which the Company determines in good faith has been subject to misuse, neglect, improper installation, repair, alteration, or damage by you. EXCEPT FOR THE EXPRESSED WARRANTIES SET FORTH ABOVE, THE COMPANY DISCLAIMS ALL WARRANTIES, EXPRESS OR IMPLIED, INCLUDING WITHOUT LIMITATION, THE IMPLIED WARRANTIES OF MERCHANTABILITY AND FITNESS FOR A PARTICULAR PURPOSE. EXCEPT FOR THE EXPRESS WARRANTY SET FORTH ABOVE, THE COMPANY DOES NOT WARRANT, GUARANTEE, OR MAKE ANY REPRESENTATION REGARDING THE USE OR THE RESULTS OF THE USE OF THE SOFTWARE IN TERMS OF ITS CORRECTNESS, ACCURACY, RELIABILITY, CURRENTNESS, OR OTHERWISE.

IN NO EVENT, SHALL THE COMPANY OR ITS EMPLOYEES, AGENTS, SUPPLIERS, OR CONTRACTORS BE LIABLE FOR ANY INCIDENTAL, INDIRECT, SPECIAL, OR CONSEQUENTIAL DAMAGES ARISING OUT OF OR IN CONNECTION WITH THE LICENSE GRANTED UNDER THIS AGREEMENT, OR FOR LOSS OF USE, LOSS OF DATA, LOSS OF INCOME OR PROFIT, OR OTHER LOSSES, SUSTAINED AS A RESULT OF INJURY TO ANY PERSON, OR LOSS OF OR DAMAGE TO PROPERTY, OR CLAIMS OF THIRD PARTIES, EVEN IF THE COMPANY OR AN AUTHORIZED REPRESENTATIVE OF THE COMPANY HAS BEEN ADVISED OF THE POSSIBILITY OF SUCH DAMAGES. IN NO EVENT SHALL LIABILITY OF THE COMPANY FOR DAMAGES WITH RESPECT TO THE SOFTWARE EXCEED THE AMOUNTS ACTUALLY PAID BY YOU, IF ANY, FOR THE SOFTWARE.

SOME JURISDICTIONS DO NOT ALLOW THE LIMITATION OF IMPLIED WARRANTIES OR LIABILITY FOR INCIDENTAL, INDIRECT, SPECIAL, OR CONSEQUENTIAL DAMAGES, SO THE ABOVE LIMITATIONS MAY NOT ALWAYS APPLY. THE WARRANTIES IN THIS AGREEMENT GIVE YOU SPECIFIC LEGAL RIGHTS AND YOU MAY ALSO HAVE OTHER RIGHTS WHICH VARY IN ACCORDANCE WITH LOCAL LAW.

ACKNOWLEDGMENT

YOU ACKNOWLEDGE THAT YOU HAVE READ THIS AGREEMENT, UNDERSTAND IT, AND AGREE TO BE BOUND BY ITS TERMS AND CONDITIONS. YOU ALSO AGREE THAT THIS AGREEMENT IS THE COMPLETE AND EXCLUSIVE STATEMENT OF THE AGREEMENT BETWEEN YOU AND THE COMPANY AND SUPERSEDES ALL PROPOSALS OR PRIOR AGREEMENTS, ORAL, OR WRITTEN, AND ANY OTHER COMMUNICATIONS BETWEEN YOU AND THE COMPANY OR ANY REPRESENTATIVE OF THE COMPANY RELATING TO THE SUBJECT MATTER OF THIS AGREEMENT.

Should you have any questions concerning this Agreement or if you wish to contact the Company for any reason, please contact in writing at the address below.

Robin Short
Prentice Hall PTR
One Lake Street
Upper Saddle River, New Jersey 07458

ABOUT THE CD

The CD-ROM contains all the wizards and libraries described in the book. You should be able to create applications that use the Windows shell quickly and easily using these tools. Full details are contained in README.txt on the CD.

All of the software was developed and tested using Visual C++ 6.0, SP3 and the January 2000 Platform SDK. Your computer must have Visual C++ 6.0 installed in order to use the material on this CD-ROM effectively. Source code is also included on the CD-ROM. Running SETUP.EXE from the CD-ROM will copy the libraries, wizards, and header files to your machine. It will also make the appropriate changes to Visual C++ 6.0 so that the new directories are visible to the development environment.

The CD-ROM directories are laid out as follows:

- \Examples\[chapter]: Contains any sample code for a given chapter
- \Include: Contains all include files. This gets copied to your computer when you run SETUP.EXE.
- \Lib: Contains all the compiled library files. This gets copied to your computer when you run SETUP.EXE.
- \Library and Wizard Source: Contains the source code to the libraries and wizards.
- \Tools: I developed two tools for the book. The source code and a pre-built version of the tools are included here.
- \Wizards: Pre-built copies of the Visual C++ Wizards. This gets copied to your computer when you run SETUP.EXE.

TECHNICAL SUPPORT

Prentice Hall does not offer technical support for this CD-ROM. However, if there is a problem with the media, you may obtain a replacement copy by emailing us with your problem at:

disc_exchange@prenhall.com